Lecture Notes in Computer Science

Edited by G. Goos and J. Hartmanis

435

G. Brassard (Ed.)

Advances in Cryptology –
CRYPTO '89

Proceedings

Springer-Verlag

New York Berlin Heidelberg London Paris Tokyo Hong Kong

Editor
Gilles Brassard
Département IRO, Université de Montréal
C.P. 6128, Succursale "A"
Montréal (Québec), Canada H3C 3J7

CRYPTO '89

A conference on the Theory and Applications of Cryptology

held at the University of California, Santa Barbara,
through the cooperation of the
Computer Science Department

August 20 – 24, 1989

sponsored by:

The International Association for Cryptologic Research

in cooperation with

*The IEEE Computer Society Technical Committee
on Security and Privacy*

Organizers

General Chairman: Kevin McCURLEY
(IBM Almaden – Sandia National Laboratories

Program Committee: Josh BENALOH,   University of Toronto
Russell L. BRAND,   Lawrence Livermore Laboratory,
Special Session Chairperson
Gilles BRASSARD,   Université de Montréal,
Program Committee Chairperson
Claude CRÉPEAU,   Massachusetts Institute of Technology
Whitfield DIFFIE,   Bell Northern Research
Joan FEIGENBAUM,   AT&T Bell Laboratories
James L. MASSEY,   ETH Zentrum, Zurich
Jim OMURA,   Cylink Corporation
Gustavus J. SIMMONS,   Sandia National Laboratories
Scott VANSTONE,   University of Waterloo

Preface

Pour Alice
Qui est venue au monde
Trois semaines avant l'avalanche

CRYPTO is a conference devoted to all aspects of cryptologic research. It has been held each year on the campus of the University of California at Santa Barbara since 1981, when it was first organized by Alan Gersho. Annual meetings also take place in Europe under the name of EUROCRYPT. Both CRYPTO and EUROCRYPT conferences are now sponsored by the *International Association for Cryptologic Research* (IACR), which was founded in the wake of CRYPTO '82. You are now holding the proceedings of the ninth CRYPTO meeting: CRYPTO '89. Recent previous proceedings of CRYPTO and EUROCRYPT can be cited as [2, 3, 4, 5, 6]. For citations of yet earlier proceedings, please consult the preface of EUROCRYPT '87 [2].

This year's conference took place on August 20–24, 1989. It attracted 263 participants coming from 23 countries, showing a steady increase in size, and requiring a change to a larger lecture room. This growth is better appreciated if one goes back to the preface of CRYPTO '82, which claims that "[it] was the largest conference of its kind [... it] attracted over 100 participants" [1]! Approximately 40% of the attendees were from the industry, 40% from universities, and 20% from governments. The great success of this year's conference was largely due to the enthusiasm and wonderful work done by Kevin McCurley, who was holding the general chair. We all owe him a debt of gratitude for his total commitment to making CRYPTO '89 a memorable event. For a more elaborate report on CRYPTO '89, please read the report that Kevin has written with my collaboration in the *IACR Newsletter* [8]. Details on the new policies that I enforced as program chairperson can be found in [7].

The call for papers resulted in 93 submissions coming from 18 countries. Out of those, 6 were not considered because they arrived after the deadline, 1 was withdrawn, 45 were accepted, and 2 pairs were asked to merge. The accepted papers were selected by the program committee, sometimes on the basis of a rather short abstract. As an experiment for the CRYPTO conference, I enforced a blind refereeing process by which the name of the authors were not revealed to the other members of the program committee. The final papers were not refereed at all, and the authors retain full responsibility for their contents. Several of the papers are preliminary reports of continuing research. It is anticipated that many of these papers will appear in more polished form in various technical journals, including IACR's *Journal of Cryptology*. There will be a special issue of the *Journal of Cryptology* devoted to some of the best papers of the conference this year. These papers will be refereed by the usual process, and Joan Feigenbaum will serve as the special editor for the issue.

In addition to the contributed papers, I scheduled three invited talks: "Keying the German navy's Enigma" by David Kahn, "Digital signatures: The evolution of a fundamental primitive" by Silvio Micali, and "A survey of hardware implementations of RSA" by Ernest F. Brickell. Moreover, in order to encourage a balance between practical and theoretical topics at the conferences, this year's program featured an invited special session on practical aspects of cryptology, which was organized and chaired by Russell L. Brand. Thus, 53 regular papers were presented at the conference. Furthermore, 26 additional papers were submitted on the first day of the conference for the traditional "rump session" of impromptu talks organized as always by Whitfield Diffie. Of those, 17 were accepted for short presentation on Tuesday evening, as selected by Whitfield and me.

These proceedings contain papers for all the contributed and all but one of the invited talks given at the conference. The exception is the invited talk of Silvio Micali. Short papers (I imposed a strict limit of four pages) are also included for 8 of the 17 impromptu talks. Reflecting the structure of the conference, the proceedings are arranged in 13 sections (followed by an author index). Each section corresponds to one session of the conference. The first 12 sections contain the contributed and invited papers in the order in which they were presented. The last section is devoted to the rump session. The sections are organized according to the following themes: opening session, why is cryptography harder than it looks?, pseudo-randomness and sequences, cryptanalysis and implementation, signature and authentication I and II, threshold schemes and key management, key distribution and network security, fast computation, odds and ends, zero-knowledge and oblivious transfer, multiparty computation, and the rump session.

Two papers in this collection are of historical significance. The proceedings open with a short paper by David Kahn on the Enigma. You will also find an antique paper by Ralph Merkle, describing "A certified digital signature", which was accepted a decade ago for publication in the *Communications of the ACM*, but which has never seen the light of day. I trust you will agree that despite its old age, this paper has lost none of its interest. Because I wanted Merkle's paper to appear exactly as it was written ten years ago, I allowed the author one page above the otherwise very strict page limit imposed on all other authors. (Please don't throw bricks at me!)

It is my great pleasure to acknowledge the efforts of those who contributed to making the conference and its proceedings possible. First of all, I wish to thank the program committee, without whom my task would have been hopeless. Most of them read and made detailed comments on at least 29 submissions. Besides myself, the committee consisted of Josh Benaloh (University of Toronto), Russell L. Brand (Special session chairperson, Lawrence Livermore National Laboratory), Claude Crépeau (Massachusetts Institute of Technology), Whitfield Diffie (Bell Northern Research), Joan Feigenbaum (AT&T Bell Laboratories), James L. Massey (ETH Zentrum, Zurich), Jim Omura (Cylink Corporation), Gustavus J. Simmons (Sandia National Laboratories), and Scott Vanstone (University of Waterloo). Moreover, many colleagues outside the program committee offered their occasional help. Among them, Manuel Blum, Ernest F. Brickell, Jeff Lagarias, Michael Merritt, Larry Ozarow, Carl Pomerance, Jim Reeds, and Moti Yung.

Of course, the most important contribution was that of the authors (including those whose submissions could not be accepted because of the large number of very high quality submissions to the conference this year). I wish to thank the authors for taking so seriously into account my deadline for submission of the final papers. The timeliness of these proceedings is their doing, together with heavy use of electronic mail. More than 300 messages were exchanged by electronic mail between me and the authors, totalizing over half a megabyte of information. Compared to that, I had to make only about 25 long distance phone calls, and 8 FAX's were exchanged.

I also wish to thank the session chairpersons. In addition to program committee members, sessions were chaired by Bob Blakley, Joan Boyar, Ernest F. Brickell, and Kevin McCurley. James L. Massey was scheduled to chair session 10, but he was unfortunately unable to attend the conference because of an accident on the way to the airport. Bob Blakley was kind enough to chair his session on short notice.

Many other people deserve thanks for the organization of the conference. Chief among them, of course, is Kevin McCurley, the general chairperson. I wish to thank also everyone else who took part in the organization of the meeting, IACR officers and directors, and all attendees. I am also grateful to three students who helped me greatly with my task: André Berthiaume, Philippe Hébrais and Sophie Laplante. Lynn Montz and Suzanne Anthony were instrumental at Springer-Verlag in helping me put the proceedings together.

Last but not least, I wish to express my deepest gratitude to my wife Isabelle and newborn daughter Alice for putting up with me while I was working overtime on the program in the spring and on the proceedings in the fall.

Montréal, December 1989   *Gilles Brassard*

References

[1] *Advances in Cryptology: Proceedings of Crypto 82*, David CHAUM, Ronald L. RIVEST, and Alan L. SHERMAN, Eds., Plenum Press, 1983.

[2] *Advances in Cryptology — EUROCRYPT '87 Proceedings*, David CHAUM and Wyn L. PRICE, Eds., Lecture Notes in Computer Science, Vol. 304, Springer-Verlag, 1988.

[3] *Advances in Cryptology — CRYPTO '87 Proceedings*, Carl POMERANCE, Ed., Lecture Notes in Computer Science, Vol. 293, Springer-Verlag, 1988.

[4] *Advances in Cryptology — EUROCRYPT '88 Proceedings*, Christoph G. GÜNTHER, Ed., Lecture Notes in Computer Science, Vol. 330, Springer-Verlag, 1988.

[5] *Advances in Cryptology — CRYPTO '88 Proceedings*, Shafi GOLDWASSER, Ed., Lecture Notes in Computer Science, Springer-Verlag, to appear.

[6] *Advances in Cryptology — EUROCRYPT '89 Proceedings*, Jean-Jacques QUISQUATER, Ed., Lecture Notes in Computer Science, Springer-Verlag, to appear.

[7] BRASSARD, Gilles, "Cryptology — Column 1", *SIGACT News*, Vol. 20, no. 3 (Whole Number 72), pp. 15–19, 1989.

[8] BRASSARD, Gilles and Kevin MCCURLEY, "Crypto '89 conference report", *IACR Newsletter*, Vol. 7, No. 1, pp. 9–11, 1990.

Contents

Session 1: Opening session

Session 2: Why is cryptography harder than it looks?

Session 3: Pseudo-randomness and Sequences

Session 4: Cryptanalysis and Implementation

Session 5: Signature and Authentication I

Session 6: Signature and Authentication II

Session 7: Threshold schemes and Key management

Session 8: Key distribution and Network security

Session 9: Fast computation

Session 10: Odds and ends

Session 11: Zero-knowledge and Oblivious transfer

Session 12: Multiparty computation

Rump session: Impromptu talks

Session 1:

Opening session

Chair: GILLES BRASSARD

KEYING THE GERMAN NAVY'S ENIGMA

By David Kahn

The German navy prepared keys for the Enigma cipher machine that was the Wehrmacht's standard cryptographic system in a manner different from the army and the air force. They permitted the encipherers to select "random" starting positions of the rotors. The navy, on the other hand, prescribed these positions in keys when, in 1926, it adopted the Enigma. The motive for this is not known, but it proved superior to the other method, which was often compromised by the encipherers' using as settings three-letter sequences from the typewriter keyboard (QWE and RFV, for example) or from girlfriends' names or from obscene words. The consequence was that while Luftwaffe cryptograms in particular were read by the enemy early on, the Kriegsmarine Enigma defended its messages far better. Only when the British captured important keying documents could they begin to crack German naval messages.

Readying the machine for use began with an officer. Only officers could prepare the so-called "inner settings" of the machine: selecting the three rotors to be inserted into the machine, inserting them in the proper left-to-right order, and setting to its proper position the alphabet ring that rode the rotor like a tire on a wheel. The inner setting remained in use for two days, so before every other midnight — later in the war, before every other noon — the radio officer set the new inner key. After he was finished, the enlisted radiomen arranged the outer settings: turning the rotors to their proper starting positions and inserting the jacks of the two-ended cables into their proper sockets on their plugboard. These settings changed every day. Then, to encipher each message, the radioman handling it had to establish the intricate message key. Only then could he do the easy part: press the letters on the Enigma keyboard to put the plaintext into cipher.

To ready the machine, the officer and the radioman would:

    a) Select the three rotors out of the eight furnished that the machine-setting list specified for that day.

    b) On each, turn the alphabet ring to the position prescribed in the machine-setting list and lock it in place with the pin.

    c) Assemble the rotors on their shaft so that they would be in the order prescribed by the machine-setting list and insert them into the machine.

    d) Rotate the rotors until the three letters specified in the machine-setting list appeared in the lid windows.

    e) Insert plugs into the plugboard to connect the pairs of letters prescribed by the machine-setting list.

With the machine thus prepared, the radioman moved to the message key. He would:

    1) Determine the key net on which the message would be sent.

    2) In the indicators book, find the section for that key net and pick out at random a three-letter key-net indicator.

    3) Write this key-net indicator in the last three cells of the first line of the

encipherment form in the book-group column (perhaps so-called because for some years the German original was encoded in the *Allgemeines Funkspruch-buch* before being enciphered in Enigma).

4) Make up a letter at random (a null) and write it in the first cell.

5) Determine from the message whether it is to be sent as a general-, officer-, or staff-grade message.

6) In the indicators book, turn to the section for that grade and pick out at random a three-letter message-grade indicator.

7) Write it in the first three cells of the second line of the encipherment form's book-group column.

8) Make up a letter at random and write it in the last cell of that line.

9) Combine the letters of the first cells in the two lines into a vertical pair.

10) Look it up in the bigram table in force and replace it with its cipher pair.

11) Write the two letters of this cipher pair horizontally into the first two cells of the first line of the radio-group column.

12) Repeat this process with the three remaining vertical pairs in the book-group column, writing them horizontally into the first two lines of the radio-group column.

13) Press, on the Enigma keyboard, the three letters of the original, unenci-phered message-grade indicator and write down at the top of the message form the letters that light up on the illuminable panel. This is the message key.

14) Turn the rotors until the letters of the message key show in the lid windows.

The cipher clerk then wrote the plaintext into the book-group columns of the cipher form without word breaks but with an *x* to separate sentences and with *q* replacing the invariant letter pair *ch*. Ready at last for the actual encipherment, he summoned a colleague. As he pressed on the typewriter keyboard the succes-sive letters of the plaintext, his co-worker wrote down in the radio-group col-umns of the form the letters that lit up on the illumination panel — the letters of the cryptogram. The cipher clerk crossed out the book-group column to avoid its being transmitted by mistake.

In the U-boat arm, at least, ciphertext was not immediately sent. It was given to another radioman, who, using only the indicators that it carried, determined the message key and deciphered the cryptogram as would be done by a U-boat at sea. If he could not do so, the error was sought and corrected. Only when the cryptogram had been properly deciphered was it transmitted.

— 120 Wooleys Lane, Great Neck, New York 11023

[This is adapted from a book on the British World War II solution of the German naval Enigma, tentatively entitled The Atlantic Enigma, *to be published by Houghton Mifflin in 1991.]*

	131	**132**	**133**	**134**	**135**	**136**	**137**	**138**	**139**
1	BWİ	LPF	TDA	MZZ	PWZ	WAR	İAN	ACQ	ZDD
2	VPP	ETT	CRR	BOE	RAK	QQL	DQG	KMK	VYY
3	YJH	UEN	FZO	İMX	GVV	FME	NLF	ENN	MVO
4	MKA	PDP	OWH	DJE	AYA	PTD	SSL	UQZ	QRD
5	GNN	ZVB	LVG	WWM	EMİ	TJJ	YMQ	HLH	BKA
6	TZM	SHE	YİY	RNJ	KZL	MYY	VTE	ODD	İBT
7	NBQ	İND	JHN	UXU	ZKM	HWH	GEX	RXC	DPZ
8	RYK	BBH	QOF	PCA	NNG	APN	LYO	CTL	SOW
9	ZFO	XKZ	HUU	FYO	WHC	DVG	BDM	XUW	NQK
10	KEF	GFK	VGD	XFR	CİN	JFH	ZXV	SJM	YGB
11	EAL	NYZ	BXZ	QTN	İQD	RUW	PUA	LAJ	HSR
12	AOW	YOG	KCİ	LHC	SRY	YXA	EJD	ZYA	CCV
13	PHB	RSİ	UJM	HBX	MXJ	OZZ	XWJ	FHP	PXX
14	WTT	DGR	ZTC	OLT	DSF	GAQ	CHH	JBF	WEF
15	SCR	JCO	MLL	YPL	QFS	BSY	OPK	TVV	LLS
16	FUU	ASC	EKB	TKB	VBX	KNV	UZP	WİT	FGL
17	OQE	HQS	XQE	NİP	FDQ	ZBM	AGU	MOİ	XTG
18	CGS	VRQ	SAQ	JDK	OCE	UOT	KJE	QRU	TTC
19	İRY	TLL	NDK	VEİ	JGT	ECF	RKW	İWY	GWU
20	XXC	FİY	WBX	KSS	BLO	NKO	JOZ	PZO	AAN

Portion of indicators book

Erster Buchstabe des Buchstabenpaares / ...ster Buchstabe des Buchstabenpaares

j	yp	py	mm	bb	vr	nr	xe	hv	gŭ	ys	ve	hi	kr	**j**
k	ab	pc	rx	ic	sq	gr	ch	vy	pg	fd	of	zr	dm	**k**
l	ye	sv	fy	nm	cŭ	zs	jg	ds	ŭc	at	nn	fz	ns	**l**
m	fi	rq	ax	sf	iw	la	rc	jy	wn	rs	tn	ld	bo	**m**
n	cb	ss	wm	fl	hf	üt	zŭ	gm	el	tf	kk	zm	ok	**n**
o	xq	ky	kc	ep	pz	bt	cq	il	yl	gv	wf	fr	sr	**o**
p	ks	ŭn	cc	hŭ	oj	zt	jd	ph	hq	qs	af	vw	hb	**p**
q	fc	ny	ji	rw	fn	jx	zk	bn	jr	zl	yb	nj	lm	**q**
r	dw	ps	sj	gd	aj	tg	cd	qk	gt	sp	kl	tm	df	**r**
s	th	mŭ	ez	ŭm	ik	zv	ha	jt	yq	em	fe	rj	qg	**s**
t	sg	eg	cj	wd	om	me	ŭŭ	vf	zp	mf	ya	fp	ol	**t**

Portion of a bigram table

Uhrzeitgruppe 1053		Spruchschlüssel: s p l
Gruppenzahl 35		**gültig für 3. 8.**

		Buchgruppen	Bedeutung
Anfangs-kenngruppen	1	b 1 m o 2 g x h y u	Schlüsselkenngruppe
	2	p 3 y u 4 d v f n w	Verfahrenkenngruppe
Verschlüsselt mit Schlüssel M	3	f j i a v e s j	Wespe
	4	t z w r e l e	
	5	l h s c p z i g	Leipzig
	6	q f d x a n a n	an
	7	n o a p f l o t	Flotte
	8	a s w l e y k o	
	9	r p g i l n x s	Köln
	10	e m k n t n d	Standort
	11	w a k k o t n	
	12	y z r z o d e	Norderney
	13	e v i b r y	
	14	c m k e l c r	Leuchtturm
	15	s k e a m i n e	in
	16	l q u d i n s s	1
	17	y f v x e o s n	6
	18	p m b o u l g r	0
	19	o m g l a d r	Grab
	20	q s o h e i m	3 sm
	21	y r h q a g	ab
	22	r q d e e m i	gehe mit
	23	h j f u t t t	T
	24	n c x m e n s	1
	25	d p k l f u n f	5
	26	a b i j d r e i	3
	27	g x t g n a c	nach □
	28	f u c n u n e u	9
	29	p h z t f u	5
	30	t o w v f u	5
	31	u d j b e i n	1
	32	v c y b l i n	links
	33	j i n g k o b n	oben
End-kenngruppen	34	b m o g — — — —	
	35	p y u d — — — —	

A naval Enigma encipherment (from a manual)

Translations: *Uhrzeitgruppe* = time group. *Gruppenzahl* = number of groups. *Spruchschlüssel* = message key. *gültig fur 3.8.* = valid for 3rd August. (Invisible under oblong tint:) *Funkgruppen* = radio groups. *Buchgruppen* = book groups. *Bedeutung* = meaning. *Anfangskenngruppen* = beginning indicator groups. *Schlüsselkenngruppe* = key-net indicator. *Verfahrenkenngruppe* = message-grade indicator. *Verschlüsselt mit Schlüssel M* = enciphered by Enigma. *Endkenngruppen* = final indicator groups.

Making Conditionally Secure Cryptosystems Unconditionally Abuse-Free in a General Context

(Extended Abstract)

Yvo G. Desmedt

Dept. EE & CS, Univ. of Wisconsin – Milwaukee
P.O. Box 784, WI 53201 Milwaukee, U.S.A.

Abstract. *[Sim84] introduced the concept of subliminal channel in the context of signature systems. [Des88b] presented a solution against subliminal channels and extended in [Des88a] the solution to abuse-free coin-flipping, abuse-free generation of public keys, and abuse-free zero-knowledge. In this paper we demonstrate that a whole family of systems (generalized Arthur-Merlin games) can be made abuse-free, avoiding the exhaustive approach of [Des88a]. We will hereto formalize the concept of abuse.*

1 Introduction

[Sim84] found that a secret message can be hidden in a subliminal way through the authentication process. Simmons called the hidden channel the *subliminal channel* Simmons illustrated it, by comparing it with two prisoners who are communicating authenticated messages in full view of a warden. The warden is able to read the messages. The subliminal consists in hiding a message through the authentication scheme such that the warden cannot detect its use nor read the hidden part (for other subliminal channels see [JS86,Sim85,Sim86]).

[Des88b] demonstrated that subliminal-free authentication and signature systems can be made by introducing the concept of active warden (a warden who modifies the authenticator). [Des88a] studied subliminal channels in different contexts (which was then called abuses). [Des88a]'s solutions against abuses are exhaustive, discussing particular solutions to particular problems. The *goal of this paper* is to prove, in a *constructive way*, that *all* cryptosystems can be made abuse-free using a compiler which will transform a given cryptosystem into an abuse-free version (similarly as [GMW86, p. 185], but keeping the solution practical). However, our solution could ruin the security specifications, in other words, it could be that the abuse-free version is no longer a secure cryptosystem. Therefore, we can only prove our theorem for a family of cryptosystems.

2 Formal model for abuses and abuse-freeness

We assume that the reader is familiar with terminology of [GMR89] (will be briefly overviewed in final paper) and notations in [CEvdGP87]. We now introduce a formal description of an active and a passive warden, covering them together to avoid long-windedness. The model has similarities with the one in [BOGKW88].

Definition 1 Let $A_1, \ldots, A_m, A_{m+1}$ be probabilistic Turing machines. If all machines A_i have a shared common read-only tape C and in addition:

- all A_i $(1 \leq i \leq m + 1)$ have their own work-tape and own random tape,

- each A_i $(1 \leq i \leq m + 1)$ has a private read-only tape H_i and the content of these tapes has been written before the machines run,

- for all i such that $1 \leq i \leq m$, A_i has $m - 1$ write-only communication tapes $T_{i,j}$ $(1 \leq j \leq m$ and $i \neq j)$ and A_{m+1} has $m(m-1)$ read only communication tapes $R'_{i,j}$ such that $R'_{i,j} = T_{i,j}$ (for all i and j such that $i \neq j$ and $1 \leq i \leq m$ and $1 \leq j \leq m$),

- for all i such that $1 \leq i \leq m$, A_i has $m - 1$ read-only communication tapes $R_{i,j}$ $(1 \leq j \leq m$ and $i \neq j)$ and A_{m+1} has $m(m-1)$ write only-communication tapes $T'_{i,j}$ such that $T'_{i,j} = R_{i,j}$ (for all i and j such that $i \neq j$ and $1 \leq i \leq m$ and $1 \leq j \leq m$),

- the order in which these machines write on the tapes is fixed (*e.g.*, A_1 starts),

then we call $\mathbf{A} = (A_1, \ldots, A_m, A_{m+1})$ an *m-participant system with warden, A_{m+1}*, or for short *m-participant system*. We will denote A_{m+1} mostly as W. If m could be an indeterminate, we call $\mathbf{A}$ a *multi-participant system* with warden, W. If the warden, W, does not read the common tape C, his random tape, his private read-only tape H_{m+1}; but only writes on tape $T'_{i,j}$ the same symbol which he reads from tape $R'_{j,i}$ (for all i and j, $i \neq j$), *then* we say that the warden is *passive*. In all other cases we say that the warden, W, is *active*.

We remark that the case that the actual communication links don't exist corresponds with machines that don't write on these tapes. Adapting the above model could be useful in other contexts. The private read-only tape H_i can be used *e.g.*, to store *secret keys*. We assume mostly that the length of H_i is polynomial in x, where x is the common input. Simplification of notations is possible by giving each A_i $(1 \leq i \leq m)$ only one tape T_i and one tape R_i. However, in our model in the case that the warden is passive the network corresponds with a complete directed graph. It depends on the context which power the probabilistic Turing machines $A_1, \ldots, A_m$ and W have.

Definition 2 Let $S(x, \mathbf{A})$ be a predicate, (specifications of the security), where $\mathbf{A}$ is a k-participant system and $x \in \{0,1\}^*$. If for a multi-participant system, $\mathbf{B}$ holds that $S(x, \mathbf{B}) = 1$ for all sufficiently long (large) $x \in L$, where $L \subset \{0,1\}^*$, then we call $\mathbf{B}$ an *$S(L)$-system with* (active or passive) *warden, W,* or shorter an *S-system* if there is no ambiguity. We will also say that the m-participant system $\mathbf{B}$ is *S-secure*.

Definition 2 allows us to speak about authentication-systems, signature-systems and so on. For our purposes, we now adapt notations introduced in [GMR89]. For a run of $\mathbf{A}$, an m-participant system, with x on the shared common tape (C) and with h_l on A_l's private read-only tape, *the l-participant's view* corresponds with all that can be seen from his random tape and from the read-only communication tapes $R_{l,j}$ (for all $j \in \{1, \ldots, l-1, l+1, \ldots, m+1\}$). Let $\mathrm{Pview}_{\mathbf{A},l}(x, h_l)$ be the random variable whose value is the l-participant's view. If the warden, W, is an *active* one, we define *the warden's view* to be everything that can be seen from W's random tape and from *all* read only communication tapes $R'_{i,j}$, for $i \neq j$. If the warden is *passive*, and x is on the shared common tape (C), we define *the warden's view* to be everything that can be seen from *all* read only communication tapes, $R'_{i,j}$ ($i \neq j$). $\mathrm{Wview}_{\mathbf{A}}(x)$ is the random variable whose value is the warden's view. To simplify notations, we did not specify the input h_{m+1} in the expression $\mathrm{Wview}_{\mathbf{A}}(x)$.

Definition 3 Let $\mathbf{A} = (A_1, \ldots, A_m, W)$ be an $S(L)$-system, with warden W. Let $\mathbf{A}' = (A'_1, \ldots, A'_m, W)$ be an m-participant system. $\mathbf{A}'$ is a *perfect (statistical) (computational) abuse* of the $S(L)$-system $\mathbf{A}$ if:

1. **Warden-indistinguishable:** $\{\mathrm{Wview}_{\mathbf{A}}(x)\}$ and $\{\mathrm{Wview}_{\mathbf{A}'}(x)\}$ (families of random variables) are *equal (statistically indistinguishable) (computational indistinguishable)* on L', where $L' = L$ if the warden is passive, else $L' = \{(x, h_{m+1}) \mid x \in L$ and $|h_{m+1}| = |x|^c\}$.

2. **k-Participant-distinguishable:** $\exists k, h_k$ $(1 \leq k \leq m)$: the families of random variables $\{\mathrm{Pview}_{\mathbf{A}''_k, k}(x, h_k)\}$ and $\{\mathrm{Pview}_{\mathbf{A}', k}(x, h_k)\}$ are *not* computationally indistinguishable on L'', where $\mathbf{A}''_k = (A''_1, \ldots, A''_m, W)$ is an m-participant system such that $A''_i = A_i$ for all $i \neq k$ and $A''_k = A'_k$ and $L'' = \{(x, h_k) \mid x \in L$ and $|h_k| = |x|^c\}$.

We denote $\mathbf{A}''_k$ as: $\mathbf{A} \star A'_k$ ($\star$ is non-commutative). The aforementioned participant k is called the *subliminal receiver*. *If there exists an m-participant system $\mathbf{A}'$, which is an abuse of the m-participant system $\mathbf{A}$, we say that $\mathbf{A}$ can be abused.*

Definition 4 Let $\mathbf{A} = (A_1, \ldots, A_m, W)$ be an $S(L)$-system, with warden W. We call $\mathbf{A}$ an *abuse-free $S(L)$-system* if for all m-participant systems $\mathbf{A}' = (A'_1, \ldots, A'_m, W)$, $\mathbf{A}'$ is *not* an abuse of the $S(L)$-system $\mathbf{A}$. We call $\mathbf{A}$ a *strong (weak) abuse-free $S(L)$-system* if for all m-participant systems $\mathbf{A}' = (A'_1, \ldots, A'_m, W)$ holds $\forall k, h_k$ $(1 \leq k \leq m)$: *if the families of random variables $\{\mathrm{Wview}_{\mathbf{A}}(x)\}$ and $\{\mathrm{Wview}_{\mathbf{A}'}(x)\}$ are computationally indistinguishable on L', then $\{\mathrm{Pview}_{\mathbf{A} \star A'_k, k}(x, h_k)\}$ and $\{\mathrm{Pview}_{\mathbf{A}', k}(x, h_k)\}$*

are statistically (computationally) indistinguishable on L'', where L' and L'' were defined in Definition 3.

Informal interpretation

In an abuse, the passive warden, W, is listening to all communications going on during the run of the system. However, the passive warden, W, has no access to the tapes H_i. The subliminal receiver k is waiting to receive hidden information and is therefore running his special program A'_k instead of running the normal one, namely A_k.

Abuse-freeness means that one does not exclude that a different system is used than the one intended, but the warden will detect it (almost always). Strong abuse-freeness means that a polynomial-bounded warden will (almost always) detect an abuse even if the other participants have all infinite computer power.

3 A general solution

3.1 A BUILDING BLOCK

Let us first discuss a slightly modified version of [Des88a] abuse-free generation of public keys (the main difference is that W will always publish the public key). In the final paper we will formally define what a public-key generation system is also considering [GMR88, pp. 290–291]'s definition.

Lemma 1 *If $G(\cdot)$ forms a group and r is chosen out of G according to a uniform probability distribution, (the probability to select a given r is $p(r) = 1/|G|$), then: $\forall x \in G : p(x \cdot r) = 1/|G|$ and $p(r \cdot x) = 1/|G|$, or $x \cdot r$ and $r \cdot x$, with x fixed, have uniform distributions.*

Proof.   Trivial: based on group theory and [Sha49].   □

Theorem 1 *If a polynomial-time operation $\oplus$ is defined on G such that $G(\oplus)$ forms a group and f is hard to invert, then the protocol of Figure 1 is a strong abuse-free public-key generation system. The abuse-freeness is unconditional. (If the zero-knowledge protocol used is non-interactive, the length of the input $|x|$ has an upperbound similar as in [BFM88].)*

Proof.   (Sketch)   First observe that such a zero-knowledge protocol exists, because what has to be proven is an **NP** problem [GMW86]. (The fact that the zero-knowledge aspect in [GMW86] is based on unproven assumptions does *not* influence our proof, because its soundness is unconditional.)

Let us call the public-key generation system, which is presented in Figure 1, $\mathbf{A} = (A, B_2, \ldots, B_m, W)$. It is sufficient to prove that for all 2-participant systems $\mathbf{A}'$ holds that: *if* $\{\text{Wview}_{\mathbf{A}}(x)\}$ and $\{\text{Wview}_{\mathbf{A}'}(x)\}$ are computationally indistinguishable on L' then $\left\{\text{Pview}_{\mathbf{A}*A'_2,2}(x, h_2)\right\}$ and $\{\text{Pview}_{\mathbf{A}',2}(x, h_2)\}$ are statistically indistinguishable

Participant A **Warden** W

$r \in_{(R)} G$ and $k \in_{(R)} K$ and
$m := c(r, k)$

$\xrightarrow{\quad m \quad}$

$\xleftarrow{\quad r' \quad}$ $r' \in_R G$

$s := r \oplus r', n := f(s)$ $\xrightarrow{\quad n \quad}$

A proves to W that
$\exists r \in G, k \in K :$ If proof is interactive W asks
$m = c(r, k) \quad \wedge \quad n = f(r \oplus r')$,   questions and proof is
using zero-knowledge. $\xrightarrow{\text{proof}}$ repeated.

                                                                 W verifies A's proof. W
                                                                 publishes A's public key n.

FIGURE 1. Abuse-free generation of public key

on L'', where x specifies a description of G (as its size and so on), and where L' and L'' are similar as in Definition 3. Because the warden doesn't use his private read-only tape H_{m+1}, we replace L' by L without problems. We denote $\mathbf{A}$ as $\mathbf{A} = (A, B, W)$. Observe that $\{\mathrm{Pview}_{\mathbf{A}*A'_2,2}(x, h_2)\} = \{\mathrm{Pview}_{\mathbf{A},2}(x, h_2)\}$ because B is not sending and thus not influencing. We will prove more than required; which is that there exists a poly-size family of circuits C such that *if* $\{\mathrm{Wview}_{\mathbf{A}}(x)\}$ and $\{\mathrm{Wview}_{\mathbf{A}'}(x)\}$ are C-computationally indistinguishable then, $\{\mathrm{Pview}_{\mathbf{A},2}(x, h_2)\}$ and $\{\mathrm{Pview}_{\mathbf{A}',2}(x, h_2)\}$ are statistically indistinguishable on L''.

Consider the circuit which the warden will use to check the zero-knowledge proof. Let the circuit return a 1 if the warden accepts the proof and a 0 otherwise. For this particular circuit, saying that $\{\mathrm{Wview}_{\mathbf{A}}(x)\}$ and $\{\mathrm{Wview}_{\mathbf{A}'}(x)\}$ are C-computational indistinguishable means that for all constants $e > 0$ and all sufficiently long strings $x \in L$: $|p(\text{warden rejects}) - p'(\text{warden rejects})| < |x|^{-e}$, where $p'(\text{warden rejects})$ and $p'(\text{warden rejects})$ denote respectively the probability that the warden will reject (the proof) when A and A' is executed. (A correct proof is not necessarily accepted with probability one, due to the definition of completeness, which is important for non-interactive proofs.)

$\mathrm{Pview}_{\mathbf{A}',2}(x, h_2)$ is nothing else than n sent by W and the probability that a specific n_i is sent is denoted as $p'(n = n_i)$. Similarly $p(n = n_i)$ corresponds to the probability that B receives n_i when A is executed.

Using our reformulations, it is sufficient to prove that *if* (1) holds for all $e > 0$ and all sufficiently long $x \in L$, *then* (2) holds for all $d > 0$ and all sufficiently long $x \in L$.

$$p'(\text{warden rejects}) \quad < \quad |x|^{-e} \tag{1}$$

$$\sum_{n_i} |p(n = n_i) - p'(n = n_i)| \quad < \quad |x|^{-d} \tag{2}$$

We first describe how n is made. First A' makes a string m, not necessarily as specified. So there is a probability that A' returns a specific $m \in \{0,1\}^*$. Then W gives a $r' \in G$. Given this r' and his previous information, A' will make an n. n does not necessarily correspond with $f(s)$. Similarly, A' will make a proof, but nothing guarantees that this proof is correct. We will denote the string (A''s random, r', σ) as α, where σ is the string of W's questions in the zero-knowledge protocol when it is interactive, and when the zero-knowledge proof system is non-interactive, σ corresponds with the shared common random string [BFM88]. The string(s) that A' sends during the zero-knowledge proof is(are) denoted as γ. So:

$$p'(n = n_i) \quad = \quad \sum_{m_j} \sum_{\gamma_l} \sum_{\alpha_z} p'(n = n_i, m = m_j, \gamma = \gamma_l | \alpha = \alpha_z) \cdot p(\alpha = \alpha_z). \quad (3)$$

Remark that $p(\alpha = \alpha_z)$ remains the same independently if A or A' is executed (and independent of h_2).

Let us denote $p'(\lambda = 1)$ the probability that machine A' will return at one or another stage of the protocol something different than it should have returned when it would have followed the protocol. We then prove that:

$$\sum_{n_i} |p(n = n_i) - p'(n = n_i)| \quad \leq \quad 2p'(\lambda = 1).$$

Let us denote $p'(\text{warden rejects})$ as $p'(\rho = 1)$. The problem remaining now is to relate $p'(\lambda = 1)$ with $p'(\rho = 1)$ and then to finally prove the theorem.

We prove that:

$$p'(\lambda = 1) \quad = \quad 1 + \frac{p'(\rho = 1) + p'(\rho = 0|\lambda = 1) - 1}{(p'(\rho = 0|\lambda = 0) - p'(\rho = 0|\lambda = 1))} \quad (4)$$

Assuming (1), this means $p'(\rho = 1) < |x|^{-e}$ for all $e > 0$ and x large enough, and using the definition of completeness and soundness we obtain that for all $t > 0$ and sufficiently large x: $p'(\lambda = 1) < |x|^{-t}$. Then follows that if (1) holds for all $e > 0$ and all sufficiently long $x \in L$, then (2) holds for all $d > 0$ and all sufficiently long $x \in L$. □

We have used the symbol $\oplus$ for a visualization aid in case $G = GF(2^n)$, but the group G does not have to be Abelian.

3.2 OUR SOLUTION

Let us first introduce a special case of a sequential multi-participant system. (What we describe can be run in parallel under some circumstances, but our definition of a multi-participant system requires an order in which the machines write on their communication tapes.)

Definition 5 Let **A** be a sequential m-participant system with *passive* warden W. Let us call x the input of the common input tape, h_i and $q_{i,j}^s$ the content of respectively the private tape H_i and the read-only communication tape $R_{i,j}$ at stage s. The binary string r_i contains the string read by A_i during the protocol from the random tape. We assume that the length of h_i, $q_{i,j}^s$ and r_i and the number of stages (this last requirement could be relaxed) are polynomial in function of the length of x. $q_{i,j}^s$ could be empty. During stage s, $A_{\pi(s)}$ writes n_s on tape $T_{\pi(s),\phi(s)}$. If $\pi(s) \neq l$ (l fixed), then $n_s \in_R G_{x,s}$ or $n_s = f_s(x, q_{\pi(s),1}^1, q_{\pi(s),2}^1, \ldots, q_{\pi(s),m}^1, \ldots, q_{\pi(s),1}^{s-1}, q_{\pi(s),2}^{s-1}, \ldots, q_{\pi(s),m}^{s-1})$, such that:

- the form of n_s is known beforehand in a deterministic way,

- $\forall x, s : G_{x,s}(+)$ forms a group, such that in polynomial-time (in function of the length of x) one can: execute the operations $+$, check if $x \in G_{x,s}$, and select a random element of $G_{x,s}$,

- the functions f_s are executable in polynomial time.

If $\pi(s) = l$, then $n_s = f_s(x, r_l, h_l, q_{l,1}^1, q_{l,2}^1, \ldots, q_{l,m}^1, \ldots, q_{l,1}^{s-1}, q_{l,2}^{s-1}, \ldots, q_{l,m}^{s-1})$, and the predicate $B_s(h_l) = 1$ is satisfied, such that:

- checking if an input exists such that $f_s(\text{input}) = \text{output}$ is an **NP** problem,

- the length of r_l, g, is fixed for a given x.

If **A** satisfies all the described properties here; we call **A** a *generalized Arthur-Merlin game*, with A_l being Merlin [Bab85].

Observe that if A_s is not Merlin *its output is either truly random or a deterministic function of its inputs*, so in the last case the random tape is not used. We would like to prove now that all $S(L)$-systems which are generalized Arthur-Merlin games can be made abuse-free. However, our solution could ruin its (security) specifications; therefore we can only prove a restricted form of it, which is based on a repetitive use of Theorem 1. We claim that most practical, conditionally secure cryptosystems can be made abuse-free if one allows interaction with the warden. Giving a proof of this claim is impossible due to a lack of an adequate formal description of all possible cryptosystems.

Corollary 1 *If* **A** *is a generalized Arthur-Merlin game and an $S(L)$-system, then there exists a multi-participant system* **A'** *(with active warden), such that either:*

- **A'** *is an unconditionally strong abuse-free $S(L)$-system, or*

- **A'** *isn't an $S(L)$-system.*

Proof. Our proof will be constructive by describing the multi-participant system **A'**. A generalized Arthur-Merlin game can be considered to be a system which is mainly publishing public keys, random numbers and/or deterministic calculations. In an initial stage, A_l' sends W a commitment ($m_l = c(r_l, k_l)$) for the bit string r_l.

Then the warden sends his random choice of his bit string r_l' (with length g). Let us now describe what is executed in $\mathbf{A}'$ instead of the execution of stage s in $\mathbf{A}$. We distinguish three different cases. If $\pi(s) \neq l$ and n_s has the form $f_s(x, q^1_{\pi(s),1}, q^1_{\pi(s),2}, \ldots, q^1_{\pi(s),m}, \ldots, q^{s-1}_{\pi(s),1}, q^{s-1}_{\pi(s),2}, \ldots, q^{s-1}_{\pi(s),m})$, then $\mathbf{A}'$ sends the warden n_s and the warden verifies if n_s is correct (if it is not, the warden calculates n_s himself) and sends n_s (writes $q^s_{\phi(s),\pi(s)} = n_s$ on the tape $T'_{\phi(s),\pi(s)}$). If $\pi(s) \neq l$, and n_s had to be chosen randomly from $G_{x,s}$, then the following steps are executed:

1. $A'_{\pi(s)}$ chooses $n_s \in_{(R)} G_{x,s}$ and sends W a commitment $(m_{\pi(s)} = c(n_s, k_{\pi(s)}))$,

2. the warden sends $A'_{\pi(s)}$: $n'_s \in_R G_{x,s}$,

3. $A'_{\pi(s)}$ sends the warden: n_s and $k_{\pi(s)}$.

4. the warden verifies the commitment. If correct, then the warden writes $q^s_{\phi(s),\pi(s)} = n_s + n'_s$, else sends a random $q^s_{\phi(s),\pi(s)} \in_R G_{x,s}$.

If $\pi(s) = l$, then A'_l sends $n_s = f_s(x, r_l \oplus r'_l, h_l, q^1_{l,1}, q^1_{l,2}, \ldots, q^1_{l,m}, \ldots, q^{s-1}_{l,1}, q^{s-1}_{l,2}, \ldots, q^{s-1}_{l,m})$ (where $\oplus$ is the bit-by-bit exclusive-or) and gives a zero-knowledge proof to W that:

$$\exists k_l \in K, r_l \in \{0,1\}^g, h_l: \quad m_l = c(r_l, k_l) \quad \wedge \quad B_s(h_l) = 1$$
$$\wedge \quad n_s = f_s(x, r_l \oplus r'_l, h_l, q^1_{l,1}, q^1_{l,2}, \ldots, q^1_{l,m}, \ldots, q^{s-1}_{l,1}, q^{s-1}_{l,2}, \ldots, q^{s-1}_{l,m}).$$

The warden verifies then A'_l's proof and writes $q^s_{\phi(s),l} = n_s$.

Let us now prove that $\mathbf{A}'$ is abuse-free. It holds that $\forall \mathbf{A}''$: $\{\text{Pview}_{\mathbf{A}' \star \mathbf{A}''_l, i}(x, h_i)\}$ and $\{\text{Pview}_{\mathbf{A}', i}(x, h_i)\}$ are equal, when $i \neq l$; due to the independency of the warden's random choices. Also $\forall \mathbf{A}''$: $\{\text{Pview}_{\mathbf{A}' \star \mathbf{A}''_l, l}(x, h_l)\}$ and $\{\text{Pview}_{\mathbf{A}'', l}(x, h_l)\}$ are equal. This implies that the rest of the proof follows easily from the proof of Theorem 1 (because the remark made after (3) is still valid).

Let us discuss some improvements. Sometimes, it is sufficient for the warden to check once and for all (or at the beginning of the protocol) that h_l satisfies the appropriate predicates. Instead of r_l being modified at the beginning of the protocol, it could be done during the different stages of the protocol. It is then necessary to guarantee independency of randomness when appropriate and to treat earlier altered random as deterministic variables instead of random ones. If a function f_s is deterministic, it means r_l is not used, then there is no need for interaction if A'_l's zero-knowledge proof is non-interactive. $\qquad\square$

We make the important observation that *all* the unconditionally abuse-free cryptosystems discussed in [Des88a,Des88b] are generalized Arthur-Merlin games and therefore special cases of ours and that therefore the *proof of their abuse-freeness has not to be given for each separately.*

Let us discuss the consequences of Corollary 1 by analyzing which cryptosystems can be made abuse-free. One first has to realize that, so far, most cryptosystems have been defined without taking a (passive) warden into consideration. So first, one has to convert them into a definition in which the warden's role and privileges are defined. Mostly, one considers such a warden as an opponent. In particular the above corollary also implies (after a careful redefinition, as mentioned) that *abuse-free interactive proof systems and zero-knowledge systems for* **NP** *languages exist,* using Goldreich–Micali–Wigderson [GMW86] proof for 3-colourability and Corollary 1, *however the verifier's soundness collapses to a conditional soundness, instead of an unconditional one.* It is possible to make abuse-free zero-knowledge proofs for all languages in **NP** such that the soundness of the verifier remains unconditional, as was recently demonstrated [BD89]. This solution is however not based on the above compiler. The protocol described in [Des88a] to make zero-knowledge proof systems for **NP** languages abuse-free is only conditionally abuse-free, while the one here is unconditional.

4 Conclusions and open problems

Our approach to abuse-freeness allows one to make all (generalized Arthur-Merlin games) cryptosystems abuse-free. It is an open problem of whether Corollary 1 can be generalized to more general multi-participant systems (excluding the obvious generalizations). If so, a different proof technique will be necessary.

Trying to apply Corollary 1 on unconditionally secure authentication systems as *e.g.,* [GMS74], ruins the unconditionality of the authentication. The question whether it can be solved in one or another way is an open problem, even if the abuse-freeness would only be weak abuse-freeness (as defined). A similar remark was made related to soundness of zero-knowledge schemes, there also the unconitionality of the soundness was ruined by using above compiler. For zero-knowledge, the same problem could be solved [BD89], but the solution is not based on the above compiler.

The approach followed in this paper is constructive as well as general. It avoids the exhaustive character followed in [Des88a] but gives a global solution to the problem, useful for many situations. One of the advantages of this approach is the reduction of proofs required to demonstrate the abuse-freeness of different cryptosystems to mainly one proof.

5 REFERENCES

[Bab85]   L. Babai. Trading group theory for randomness. In *Proceedings of the seventeenth ACM Symp. Theory of Computing, STOC*, pp. 421–429, May 6-8, 1985.

[BD89]   M. V. D. Burmester and Y. G. Desmedt, June 1989. Text in preparation.

[BFM88]   M. Blum, P. Feldman, and S. Micali. Non-interactive zero-knowledge and its applications. In *Proceedings of the twentieth ACM Symp. Theory of Computing, STOC*, pp. 103–112, May 2–4, 1988.

[BOGKW88] M. Ben-Or, S. Goldwasser, J. Kilian, and A. Wigderson. Multi-prover interactive proofs: How to remove intractability assumptions. In *Proceedings of the twentieth ACM Symp. Theory of Computing, STOC*, pp. 113–131, May 2–4, 1988.

[CEvdGP87] D. Chaum, J.-H. Evertse, J. van de Graaf, and R. Peralta. Demonstrating possession of a discrete logarithm without revealing it. In A. Odlyzko, editor, *Advances in Cryptology. Proc. Crypto'86 (Lecture Notes in Computer Science 263)*, pp. 200–212. Springer-Verlag, 1987. Santa Barbara, California, U.S.A., August 11–15.

[Des88a]   Y. Desmedt. Abuses in cryptography and how to fight them. Presented at Crypto'88, Santa Barbara, California, U.S.A., to appear in: Advances in Cryptology. Proc. of Crypto'88 (Lecture Notes in Computer Science), Springer-Verlag, August 1988.

[Des88b]   Y. Desmedt. Subliminal-free authentication and signature. In C. G. Günther, editor, *Advances in Cryptology, Proc. of Eurocrypt'88 (Lecture Notes in Computer Science 330)*, pp. 23–33. Springer-Verlag, May 1988. Davos, Switzerland.

[GMR88]   S. Goldwasser, S. Micali, and R. Rivest. A digital signature scheme secure against adaptive chosen-message attacks. *Siam J. Comput.*, 17(2), pp. 281–308, April 1988.

[GMR89]   S. Goldwasser, S. Micali, and C. Rackoff. The knowledge complexity of interactive proof systems. *Siam J. Comput.*, 18(1), pp. 186–208, February 1989.

[GMS74]   E. Gilbert, F. MacWilliams, and N. Sloane. Codes which detect deception. *The BELL System Technical Journal*, 53(3), pp. 405–424, March 1974.

[GMW86] O. Goldreich, S. Micali, and A. Wigderson. Proofs that yield nothing but their validity and a methodology of cryptographic protocol design. In *The Computer Society of IEEE, 27th Annual Symp. on Foundations of Computer Science (FOCS)*, pp. 174–187. IEEE Computer Society Press, 1986. Toronto, Ontario, Canada, October 27–29, 1986.

[JS86] T. C. Jones and J. Seberry. Authentication without secrecy. *ARS Combinatoria*, 21(A), pp. 115–121, May 1986.

[Sha49] C. E. Shannon. Communication theory of secrecy systems. *Bell System Techn. Jour.*, 28, pp. 656–715, October 1949.

[Sim84] G. J. Simmons. The prisoners' problem and the subliminal channel. In D. Chaum, editor, *Advances in Cryptology. Proc. of Crypto 83*, pp. 51–67. Plenum Press N.Y., 1984. Santa Barbara, California, August 1983.

[Sim85] G. J. Simmons. The subliminal channel and digital signatures. In T. Beth, N. Cot, and I. Ingemarsson, editors, *Advances in Cryptology. Proc. of Eurocrypt 84 (Lecture Notes in Computer Science 209)*, pp. 364–378. Springer-Verlag, Berlin, 1985. Paris, France, April 9–11, 1984.

[Sim86] G. J. Simmons. The secure subliminal channel (?). In H. C. Williams, editor, *Advances in Cryptology. Proc. of Crypto 85 (Lecture Notes in Computer Science 218)*, pp. 33–41. Springer-Verlag, 1986. Santa Barbara, California, August 18–22, 1985.

On the Existence of Bit Commitment Schemes and Zero-Knowledge Proofs

Ivan Bjerre Damgård[1]

Abstract

It has been proved earlier that the existence of bit commitment schemes (blobs) implies the existence of zero-knowledge proofs of information possession, which are MA-protocols (i.e. the verifier sends only independent random bits) [BrChCr], [GoMiWi].

In this paper we prove the converse result in a slightly modified form: We define a concept called *weakly zero-knowledge*, which is like ordinary zero-knowledge, except that we only require that an *honest* verifier learns nothing from the protocol. We then show that if, using an MA-protocol, P can prove to V in weakly zero-knowledge that he possesses a solution to some hard problem, then this implies the existence of a bit commitment scheme. If the original protocol is (almost) perfect zero-knowledge, then the resulting commitments are secure against an infinitely powerful receiver.

Finally, we also show a similar result for a restricted class of non-MA protocols.

1 Introduction and Related Work.

A bit commitment scheme (blob) is a method that allows protocol participant A to choose a bit b, some random input r and compute from this a *commitment* to b, $BC(b, r)$. To be useful, the bit commitment scheme must satisfy:

- It is hard to predict b from $BC(b, r)$ essentially better than at random.

- A can later *open* the commitment, to convince anybody else about her original choice of b. This is usually done just by revealing r.

- A cannot change her mind about her choice, i.e. she cannot find r, r' such that $BC(1, r) = BC(0, r')$.

This very loose and informal description should be enough to understand the basic ideas in this paper. More formal treatments can be found in [Da] or [BrChCr]. Note also that establishing a commitment may sometimes involve interaction between sender and receiver.

One easy example of a commitment scheme is the case where A is given a large integer n which is the product of 2 prime factors congruent to 3 modulo 4. A can

---

[1] The author is with Mathematical Institute, Aarhus University, Ny Munkegade, DK 8000 Aarhus C, Denmark.

now compute a commitment as $BC(b,r) = r^2 \bmod n$, where r is a randomly chosen residue with Jacobi symbol -1^b. In this case, commitments to 1 have exactly the same distribution as commitments to 0, but knowledge of two square roots of a number modulo n with different Jacobi symbols clearly suffices to factor n. Hence, even with infinite computing power, b cannot be found from $BC(b,r)$, but A could cheat if he had computing power enough to factor n before it was "too late", i.e. before the whole protocol is completed.

Commitment schemes are extremely useful in the construction of cryptographic protocols. The general zero-knowledge proof of [GoMiWi] and [BrChCr] as well as the multiparty computation protocols of [ChDaGr] and [GoMiWi2] are based entirely on commitment schemes.

The existence of bit commitments is implied by the existence of one-way functions, as shown by Naor [Na]. The converse, however, is not necessarily true, even if we exclude from the discussion commmitments that are not binary encodable, like quantum blobs [Br] for example: In the present paper, we base commitments on problems for which one can select hard instances at random. This, however, does not necessarily imply that the problem is in any sense "hard on the average". This adds to the interest of studying bit commitments in general and their connection to zero-knowledge protocols.

Another difference to the work of Naor is that our construction has the potential of producing commitments secure against an infinitely powerful receiver (which implies that the sender can cheat if he has enough computing power). The commitments from [Na] has the dual property: the sender cannot cheat at all, while the receiver must be restricted.

The protocols we will be concerned with here are protocols for proving possession of information (rather than proving language membership as in the original zero-knowledge paper [GoMiRa]). In this setup, a prover P (Peggy) possesses a solution to some problem, and tries to convince a verifier V (Vic) that indeed she knows this solution, while giving Vic absolutely no clue as to what the solution is. A little more formally: suppose a relation R on sets U and V, and an element $y \in V$ are given. Then Peggy is trying to convince Vic that she knows how to compute $x \in U$ such that $(x,y) \in R$ holds.

Following [FiFiSh] and [ToWo], we will let both the prover and the verifier be probabilistic polynomial time Turing machines.

In this model, it was proved in [BrChCr] that the existence of a bit commitment scheme implies the existence of a zero-knowledge proof of information possession (as defined in [ToWo]) for any problem in MA, i.e. for any problem, Peggy can prove to Vic in zero-knowledge that she knows a solution, as long as this solution can be verified by a BPP-algorithm. Furthermore, Vic only has to send independently chosen random bits, i.e. the protocol is an MA-protocol.

Our result can be seen a sort of converse to the above: if a (weakly) zero-knowledge proof of knowledge exists for some hard problem, and the protocol has a structure similar to that of [BrChCr], then a bit commitment scheme exists.

In independent work, Fiege and Shamir [FiSh] found a result similar to ours for the special case where the verifier sends only 1 bit per round. This was used to design two-round zero-knowledge proofs of knowledge for any NP-problem. The key observation there was that commitments constructed by our method are always "chameleon", i.e. the bit contained in a commitment can always be changed if extra information is known. One can then simulate parallelized protocols by making this information available to the simulator.

We would like to point out two interesting facts about our result:

- It adds a theoretical basis to the intuitive belief shared by many researchers, that bit commitment schemes are very fundamental objects ideed, and if they do not exist, zero-knowledge proofs of knowledge - at least interesting ones - are probably, to use an expression of Brassard, a fancy way of talking about the empty set [2].

  Put another way: it shows that zero-knowledge proofs of knowledge based on bit commitments are "as invulnerable as possible" against collapse of cryptographic assumptions: if the assumption falls, no interesting objects exist of the kind we are trying to construct.

- It shows that existence of an MA zero-knowledge proof of knowledge for one hard problem is a sufficient condition for the existence of such proofs for anything in MA (by [BrChCr]), even if the problem we start with is not NP-complete.

The restriction to MA-protocols does not seem to be a severe limitation of the result: the most powerful zero-knowledge proof known ([BrChCr], [GoMiWi]) are MA. Furthermore the result is not limited to MA-protocols, as shown by Section 3.

2   Main Result

In this extended abstract, we will only give informal definitions and proofs. For a rigorous definition of zero-knowledge proofs of information possession, and a detailed description of communicating Turing machines, the reader is referred to [ToWo].

We now describe a proof system of information possession for a relation R on sets X and Y: It consists of a pair of communicating probabilistic polynomial time Turing machines (P, V). Common input to P and V is $y \in Y$. P also gets as input $x \in X$. At the end of the conversation, V outputs "accept" or "reject", and the proof system (P, V) is said to accept or reject accordingly. Let m denote the length in bits of y.

We will restrict our attention in this section to the case of MA-protocols, i.e. the prover speaks first, and the verifier sends only uniformly and independently chosen bits.

Thus, we assume that the conversation between P and V has the following form:

- P sends a message m_1.

---

[2] Zero-knowledge proofs of knowledge do exist for some problems independently of computational assumptions, examples are discrete log, graph isomorphism, and factoring. However if bit commitments did not exist, all these problems would be easy, and their interactive proofs therefore uninteresting.

- V sends bits $b_1, ..., b_k$ to P.

- P sends a message m_2.

- V decides, based on m_1, m_2, $b_1, ..., b_k$ whether to accept or not.

We assume for simplicity that k is constant as a function of m. For generalizations of this, see the remarks after Theorem 1.

We require about (P, V) that:

- For the verifier's protocol V, there exists a *simulator* (a probabilistic polynomial time Turing machine), M_V, which (with the help of V) simulates the conversation between P and V, such that the output of M_V is polynomially (in m) indistinguishable from the real conversation between P and V. Loosely speaking, this means that a polynomial time algorithm cannot guess essentially better than at random whether a given conversation was produced by M_V or by (P, V). Thus we only require that an *honest* verifier learns nothing from the protocol.

- If $(x, y) \in R$, then (P, V) always accepts.

- For any prover's protocol P^*, there exists an *interrogator* (a probabilistic polynomial time Turing machine), M_{P^*}, which (with the help of P^*) tries to compute $x \in X$ such that $(x, y) \in R$. We require that there is a constant $\epsilon < 1$ such that

$$Prob((P^*, V) \text{ accepts AND } M_{P^*} \text{ fails}) \leq \epsilon,$$

for all sufficiently large m. This is the definition proposed in [ToWo]. A very similar - but technically slightly different - definition appeared in [FiFiSh].

If these 3 conditions are satisfied, (P, V) is called a *weakly zero-knowledge proof system of information possession*.

ϵ is called the *error probability* of (P, V).

We can now state the main result:

Theorem 1

Suppose there exists a binary relation R with the following properties:

- It is easy to select y such that an x with $(x, y) \in R$ exists, but such that computing one is a hard problem. Further, given x and y, it is easy to check, whether (x, y) is in R.

- R admits a weakly zero-knowledge proof system of knowledge with error probability ϵ, where the conversation is of the form described above.

Then there exists a bit commitment scheme with the properties described in Section 1. If the proof system is perfect zero-knowledge, then the commitment scheme constructed is secure against an infinitely powerful receiver, i.e. commitments to 0 have the same distribution as commitments to 1.

Remarks

Note that the proof system would be uninteresting, if the first condition above was not satisfied: it does not make much sense for P to try to keep her solution to the problem secret, if V could just compute a solution himself! Also in this case, the existence of an interrogator becomes trivial: M_{P^*} can just compute the solution by itself, without ever talking to P^*.

The assumption about selectability of y is closely related to the notion of *invulnerable generators*. [AABFH] contains the first study of the theory behind this notion, and the results are improved in [FLM].

As mentioned, we assume that k, the number of challenge bits pr. round, is constant as a function of m. The Theorem could be proved in much the same way if $k = O(log(m))$ and we assume that $\epsilon = O(m^{-1})$. With this extension, the result covers all known MA zero-knowledge proofs of information possession.

Proof

We first describe loosely the basic idea of the proof: We will have two players, A who will create commitments, and B who receives them. The idea is that A will create and send to B the start of a conversation between P and V. To open a commitment, A sends the rest of the conversation. B accepts this, if V would have accepted, based on the conversation given.

If A does not know a solution to the problem instance in question, this implies to some extend a commitment: by the properties of (P, V), A is unable to complete the conversation with respect to *all* possible values of the challenge bits $b_1, ..., b_k$. He is therefore "committed" to the set of values for $b_1, ..., b_k$ for which he *can* complete the conversation. The rest of the proof consists of technical lemmas and tricks that amplify this into a regular commitment scheme.

Let t be the smallest integer, such that $\epsilon^t < 1/2$. By Lemmas 2 and 3 in [ToWo], the proof system that consists of t iterations of (P, V) is weakly zero-knowledge and has error probability ϵ^t. Let (P', V') denote this proof system. We let

$$m_1^i, b_1^i, ..., b_k^i, m_2^i$$

denote the conversation produced by the i'th iteration of (P, V). Let $\mathbf{b} = (b_j^i)_{j=1...k, i=1...t}$, and let $\mathcal{B}$ be the set of all possible values of $\mathbf{b}$.

We can now describe how A can create and open what we will call a *quasi bit commitment QBC*:

1. The receiver of the commitments, B, chooses some $y \in Y$ according to the first condition in Theorem 1, and gives it to A.

2. A commits to a bit b by running the simulator $M_{V'}$ to produce a conversation of the form descibed above. He sends $(m_1^1, ..., m_1^t)$ to B.

3. B partitions $\mathcal{B}$ randomly in two subsets C_0, C_1 such that $|C_0| = |C_1|$, and sends them to A.

4. Let v be chosen such that the value for b produced by $M_{V'}$ above is in C_v. A then sends to B $c = b \oplus v$. This concludes the creation of the commitment, we set $QBC(b, r) = (m_1^1, ..., m_1^t, c)$, where r is the random string consumed by the simulator during the process.

5. To open the commitment, A releases the entire conversation produced in step 2, and B checks that V would have accepted, had it been given this conversation. He then determines v as in step 4, and determines the bit A was committed to as $b = v \oplus c$.

We can now prove the following about quasi bit commitments:

- If A follows the protocol, B cannot predict b from $QBC(b, r)$ essentially better than at random.

- With nonnegligible probability, A is committed after completion of steps 2-4, i.e. A can convince B about at most 1 value for b.

First, suppose by contradiction that B could predict b essentially better than at random based on $QBC(b, r)$. Let p be the success probability of B. Then B could be used to distinguish simulated conversations from real ones as follows: given a conversation $(m_1^i, b_1^i, ..., b_k^i, m_2^i), i = 1...t$, feed $m_1^1, ..., m_1^t$ to B, and accept from B a partitioning C_0, C_1. Now choose a bit b and feed $c = b \oplus v$ to B, where v is determined from the conversation as in step 4 above. Now output 1 if B's guess mathces b, and 0 otherwise.

On input a real conversation, this produces output 1 with probability 1/2, since in this case there is no correlation between the m_1^i-values and b. On the other hand, the output is 1 with probability p if the input is simulated. By assumption $p - 1/2$ is non-negligible, contradicting the assumption that M_V is a good simulator.

Clearly, if (P, V) is perfect zero-knowledge, $p = 1/2$, and $QBC(b, r)$ contains no information about b.

Secondly, suppose by contradiction that given y, with non-negligible probability q, A can produce a set of conversations such that all m_1^i-values are constant for a fixed i, and the set of b-values constitute a fraction $\delta > 1/2$ of $\mathcal{B}$. This is what A needs to avoid any chance of committing himself, for if the set of b-values constituted at most half of $\mathcal{B}$, then this set might be contained in C_0 or C_1, which would mean that A would be committed.

We adopt the standard complexity theoretic definition of "non-negligible" and assume that $q \geq 1/Q(m)$ for some polynomial Q and all sufficiently large m.

Consider now the prover P^* with the following strategy: before sending its first message, it runs $mQ(m)$ times whatever method A has for producing sets of conversations as above. If at least one try was successful, it uses the m_1^i produced by this try in the i'th iteration of (P, V). Otherwise, it sends randomly chosen messages. Clearly,

$$Prob((P^*, V') \; accepts) \; > \; (1 - (1 - q)^{mQ(m)}) \cdot \delta$$

Since the first factor is exponentially close to 1 for large m, the acceptance probability larger than 1/2 for all sufficiently large m. Further, since we assume that finding a solution x to $(x, y) \in R$ is a hard problem, and P^* only gets y as input, we may assume that any interrogator M_{P^*} fails to find x with probability essentially 1. Hence,

$$Prob(M_{P^*} \; fails \; AND \; (P^*, V') \; accepts) \simeq Prob((P^*, V') \; accepts) > 1/2,$$

for all sufficiently large m, contradicting the assumption that $\epsilon^t < 1/2$.

Thus we may assume that for each quasi commitment A creates, he will be committed with probability at least

$$p := \frac{(|\mathcal{B}|/2)!^2}{|\mathcal{B}|!},$$

which is a constant, since k and t are constants.

The rest of the proof is concerned with a protocol construction that uses quasi bit commitments to build ordinary ones:

1. The receiver of the commitment B chooses some $y \in Y$ according to the first condition in Theorem 1, and sends it to A.

2. To commit to a bit b, A creates m quasi commitments to b, $QBC(b, r_1), ..., QBC(b, r_m)$.

3. To open the commitment, A reveals b and opens all the quasi commitments. B accepts this if and only if A opens all the quasi commitments correctly.

To prove that this constitutes a bit commitment scheme, we must first argue that B cannot predict b from $QBC(b, r_1), ..., QBC(b, r_m)$ essentially better than at random. This follows from the fact that b cannot be guessed from 1 quasi commitment to b. The argument is completely similar to a corresponding one for probabilistic encryptions (see [GoMi]), and we will not repeat it here (of course, the argument becomes trivial if (P, V) is perfect zero-knowledge).

Secondly, we must prove that A is committed with large probability. Since 1 quasi commitment commits A with probability at least p, m quasi commitments will commit A with probability at least $1 - (1 - p)^m$, which converges exponentially to 1 as a function of m $\square$

Corollary

Suppose the binary relation R satisfies the assumptions of Theorem 1. Then there exists a zero-knowledge proof of information possession for any binary relation S for which $(x, y) \in S$ can be verified efficiently.

Proof

Use R and Theorem 1 to construct a bit-commitment scheme. Represent the verification procedure for S as a (polynomial size) Boolean circuit, and use the protocol from [BrChCr] with the bit-commitment scheme just constructed$\square$

As an example of a protocol satisfying our conditions, consider the following protocol for proving possession of a discrete log, first found by [ChGr]:

We are given a prime p, a generator g of Z_p^*, and $y \in Z_p^*$. The prover claims to know x, such that $g^x = y \bmod p$. She convinces V as follows:

1. P chooses z at random, and sends $c = g^z$ to V.

2. V chooses a bit b, and sends it to P.

3. If $b = 1$, P sends z to V, otherwise he sends $x + z \bmod (p-1)$

4. IF $b = 1$, V checks that $c = g^z$, otherwise he checks that $cy = g^{x+z}$.

It is well-known that this constitutes a zero-knowledge proof system of information possession with $\epsilon =$ any constant larger than $1/2$.

The resulting bit commitment scheme is the following: A is given y, but not its discrete log. Commitments are computed as follows:

$$BC(1,r) = g^r \bmod p, \quad BC(0,r) = yg^r \bmod p$$

This commitment scheme is well known, and was introduced in [ChDaGr], and independently in [BoKrKu]. [ToWo] give similar protocols for any random self-reducible relation, which shows that any random self-reducible relation representing a hard problem can be used as basis for a bit-commitment scheme.

3 Non MA-protocols

It is an open question whether our result can be proved for *any* zero-knowledge proof of information possession. But as shown by the following, there is a subclass of non-MA protocols for which our result does hold.

Consider proof systems where the conversation has the following form:

- V does some computation and sends a message m_1 to P.

- P sends a message m_2.

- V decides whether to accept or not

Theorem 2

Suppose the binary relation R satisfies

- It is easy to select y such that an x with $(x,y) \in R$ exists, but such that computing one is a hard problem.

- R admits a weakly zero-knowledge proof system of knowledge.

- The conversation has the form given above, and there is a one-one correspondence between initial messages m_1 and messages m_2 that will make V accept.

- As a function of m, the error probability vanishes faster than any polynomial fraction.

Then there exists a bit commitment scheme as defined in Section 1.

proof

Suppose m_1 and m_2 are in sets M_1 and M_2, respectively. Then the verifier's decision procedure defines a function $f : M_2 \rightarrow M_1$, such that $f(m_2) = m_1$ precisely if V accepts. Since the error probability is negligible, f is hard to invert almost everywhere, but since the protocol is simulatable, it is feasible to produce m_1, m_2 such that $f(m_2) = m_1$ (note that this is not necessarily the same as saying that $f(m_1)$ is easy to compute given m_1).

Using Yao's Xor-Theorem (see for example [Kr]), one can then from f construct a function f' with similar properties, but such that f' has "a hard bit", i.e. given $f'(x)$, there is a particular bit of x which cannot be guessed essentially better than at random by a polynomial time algorithm. From this, it is straightforward to construct a bit commitment scheme□

Remark: We have assumed the 1-1 correspondence between m_1's and m_2's mainly for simplicity. For our purposes, it would actually suffice if f mapped a constant number of elements to 1. Also, we could of course tolerate a non vanishing error probability by iterating the proof system many times. Note also that the recent work by [GoLe] may make it possible to generalize the result even further.

An example of a protocol of this kind: suppose $n = pq$, where p and q are primes congruent to 3 modulo 4. P knows the factorization of n, and so he can compute square roots modulo n. We then do the following:

1. V chooses x at random and sends $x^4 \ mod \ n$ to P

2. P computes and sends to V $c = x^2 \ mod \ n$ - note that although x^4 has 4 square roots modulo n, exactly one of them is itself a square, by the properties of p and q.

3. V accepts, iff $c^2 = x^4 \ mod \ n$.

We leave it to the reader to show that this protocol satisfies all the conditions given in this section, assuming that factoring is hard.

Note that the protocol is weakly zero-knowledge, but not ordinary zero-knowledge: a cheating verifier can factor n after 1 interaction with P by sending a square for which he knows a square root of Jacobi symbol -1.

The function constructed from the protocol is of course $f(x) = x^2 \ mod \ n$, which is a permutation of the quadratic residues modulo n, and is hard to invert, if factoring n is hard. In this case, Yao's Xor Theorem is not necessary to obtain a bit commitment scheme - it is known that guessing the least significant bit of x from $f(x)$ is polynomially equivalent to factoring n [ACGS].

References

[**AABFH**] Abadi, Allender, Broder, Feigenbaum and Hemachandra: "On Generating Solved Instances of Computational Problems", Proc. of CRYPTO 88, Springer.

[**ACGS**] Alexi, Chor, Goldreich, Schnorr: "RSA and Rabin Functions: Certain Parts are as Hard as the Whole", Siam J. Compt., vol.17, no.2, 1988, pp.194-209.

[**BoKrKu**] Boyar, Krentel and Kurtz: "A Discrete Logarithm Implementation of Zero-knowledge Blobs", Tech. Report, Dept. of Computer Science, University of Chicago, 1987.

[**Br**] Brassard: Modern Cryptology, Lecture Notes in Computer Science, vol.325, Springer-Verlag, 1988.

[**BrChCr**] Brassard, Chaum, Crépeau: "Minimum Disclosure Proofs of Knowledge", JCSS, vol.37, no.2, Oct. 1988, pp.156-189.

[**ChDaGr**] Chaum, Damgård, van de Graaf: "Multiparty Computations Ensuring Privacy of Each Party's Input and Correctness of the Result", Proc. of Crypto 87.

[**ChGr**] Chaum, van de Graaf: "An Improved Protocol for Demonstrating possession of a Discrete Log", Proc. of EuroCrypt 87.

[**Da**] Damgård: "The Application of Claw Free Functions in Cryptography", PhD-Thesis, Aarhus University, Denmark, May 1988.

[**FiSh**] Fiege and Shamir: "Zero-Knowledge Proofs of Knowledge in Two Rounds", these proceedings.

[**FiFiSh**] Fiat, Fiege, Shamir: "Zero-Knowledge Proof of Identity", Proc. of STOC 87.

[**FLM**] Feigenbaum, Lipton and Mahaney: "A Completeness Theorem for Almost-Everywhere Invulnerable Generators", manuscript, AT& T Bell Labs. Tech. Memo, Febr. 89.

[**GoLe**] Goldreich nd Levin: "A Hard-Core Predicate for all One-Way Functions", Proc. of STOC 89, pp.25-32.

[**GoMiRa**] Goldwasser, Micali: "Probabilistic Encryption", JCSS, vol 28, no 2, 1984, pp 270-299.

[**GoMiRa**] Goldwasser, Micali, Rackoff: "The Knowledge Complexity of Interactive Proof Systems", Proc. of STOC 85, pp.291-304.

[GoMiWi] Goldreich, Micali, Wigderson: "Proof that Yield Nothing but the Validity of the Assertion, and the Methodology of Cryptographic Protocol Design", Proc. of FOCS 86.

[GoMiWi2] Goldreich, Micali and Wigderson: "How to Play any Mental Game", Proc. of FOCS 87.

[Kr] Kranakis: Primality and Cryptography, Wiley-Teubner Series in Computer Science, 1986.

[Na] Naor: "Bit Commitment using Pseudo-Randomness", these proceedings.

[ToWo] Tompa, Woll: "Random Self-Reducibility and Zero-Knowledge Proofs of Information Possession", Proc. of FOCS 87.

Session 2:

Why is cryptography harder than it looks?

Chair: RUSSELL L. BRAND

Problems with the Normal Use of Cryptography for Providing Security on Unclassified Networks

Russell L. Brand
Lawrence Livermore National Labs
Livermore, California

Abstract

The normal use of cryptography in unclassified computing systems often fails to provide the level of protection that the system designers and users would expect. This is partially caused by confusion of cryptographic keys and user passwords, and by underestimations of the power of known plaintext attacks. The situation is worsenned by performance constraints and occasionally by the system builder's gross misunderstandings of the cryptographic algorithm and protocol.

1 Introduction

For the past five years, my colleagues and I have been studying unauthorized intrusions (attacks) on unclassified computers owned by government agencies and universities. While some of these attacks were made possible by problem in the computer operating system or the software utilities present on the machine, most of the attack we aided by poor password practices. Some of these practices are caused by users and system designers thinking of a user password as if it were a cryptographic key at some points in their analysis and not treating it as cryptographic key at other points.

Often the use of encryption is incomplete. This leads to "partially signed" message, easily forgable signatures, and simplified ease dropping. In most cases, the design errors are at the level of cryptographic protocol rather encipherment algorithm.

After discussing the typical problems that we have found in practice, we will describe what seems to be needed by the unclassified community by cryptography.

2 A Password is Not a Key

While passwords bear some superficial similarities to cryptographic keys, they are not really keys. They are not quite treated as keys either.

2.1 Passwords are often shorter than the look

Where cryptographic keys tend to be "long" and "random", passwords tend to short and not random. A cryptographic key that is N bits in length is expected to have N bits of randomness (or under certain circumstances where the key is an N bit prime number, there may only be $\log N$ bits of randomness) and N is measured in the hundreds or thousands or bits. Passwords, in contrast tend to be no larger than 64 bits. Of these about 36 of the bits are significant (the others being just padding of one form or another) and these 36 bits tend to contain at most 12 bits of randomness since the password is often a collection of names or proper words. [2]

2.2 Re-used Passwords Lead to Difficulties

While an individual would have a different cryptographic key for each distinct (mutually suspicious) entity he would interact with, it is common practice for a user to have a single password that he uses on computers run by different computer centers in different (potentially competing) firms. While a cryptanalyst would demand proof that none of these agencies can exploit the use of a "key in common", common practice with passwords is to do this with no precautions taken and obvious means of exploitation possible.

2.3 Broadcast of Clear Text "Keys" is Poor Practice

Another difference between a cryptographic key and a password is in their respective handling. It is common practice to broadcast passwords over known insecure channels. This would of course never be done with a cryptographic key. Even after many documented cases of "wire tapping" (which is both effortless and undetectable in a traditionally configured network) the transmission of passwords in clear text remains standard operating procedure. Only recently have serious alternatives begun to be considered [4,6]

There in fact ways to make this even worse. In one system passwords were "usually" sent encrypted. Each password was always encrypted in the same way and hence one could gain full access by just having seen the encrypted password which was both broadcast over insecure channels and stored in public areas. Further, the method for updating a password entailed sending the old password enciphered and the new password in clear text. In this manner the user could pay the extra computational cost of encryption on his slow local machine on each access where a naive attacker would not have to pay any encryption or decryption costs.

3 Known Plaintext Attacks are not Foiled by Salt

The most common use of encryption in unclassified computing is for authentication. In particular many systems keep and encrypted, hashed or "trapped doored" version of the users password in a table. For each access, the user provides his password to the machine which encrypts, hashes, or applies a trap door function as appropriate and then compares the result with the value stored in the table.

There are two good features to this method. First if the encipherment of of the password in the table is effectively uninvertable then compromise of this table will not allow an attacker to impersonate the real user. Second a variety of standard mistakes that can be made in comparing clear text passwords are not possible here.

In common versions of "unix" operating system, the encrypted password table is made publically readable. In many cases this table is stored in such a fashion as to allow copies of it to be read even by people who have no other access to the system. It has become increasingly popular for copies of these tables to be "stolen" by an attacker who then breaks the passwords and later impersonates legitimate users.

While inverting the encipherment is very hard, it is very easy to make a guess at password and then check to see if it is correct. On a small personal computer hundreds of guesses can be made per second and with only 12 bits of randomness, it doesn't take long to guess successfully. Since this testing is done on a separate computer than the one that the password tables were stolen from, it is undetectable.

In the unix system a technique called "salting" is used to make it more difficult to precompute guesses. It does not prevent this "guess and test strategy" and is more fulled discussed in [3]

4 Unauthenticated Authentication Servers lead to Problems

Even when the details of what should be sent encrypted, what should be sent in place plaintext and who should be trusted to make the comparisons are correctly handled, errors in the handling of encrypted passwords can still be made. In some cases there is no authentication of the password servers themselves; any machine can announce that it is itself the password server that all other machines should listen to. Similarly the authentications servers will often provide the crypted passwords to any machine that ask make requests. The authentications server trusts that these machine will prevent unauthorized users from making such requests.

5 Tampering of Signed Packets is often Possible

To prevent the problems of machines claiming to be authentication servers for each other or successfully impersonating each other in other transactions, a variety of crypto-graphically based "secure" transaction mechanism exist. In some cases each request (or packet) contains a the encrypted version of a sequence number. The system designers had confidence in this since an attempt to repeat use of a sequence number could be detected.

Unfortunately it is easy to make sure that a packet never arrives. One can "collide" with the request packet to assure that it is not delivered, steal the encrypted sequence number and put that "signature" into a different packet hence impersonating the legitimate machine. The computational costs of using cryptographic checksums or other more complete digital signature methods were deemed unacceptably high and hence this vulnerability was never fixed.

6 Difficult Factoring Effect the Security of Discrete Logs

One of the secure transaction protocols was based on a discrete log key system. For performance reasons the composite base number that was chosen was much too small. This is not surprising or unusual. Nor is it surprising that the number was factored and the hence the system broken [5]. What is counter-intuitive was the part of team charged maintaining the system seemed to not understand the the underlying cryptosystem and hence improperly choose a non-generator number and did not know that advances in factoring techniques had any impact on a discrete log based system. Further the system designers had posted a "challenge" number and felt secure since noone had solved their challenge. The details of announcing the challenge were such that the cryptographers working on related problems were unaware that a challenge had been posted.

7 Bad Information Leads to Bad Decisions

Designing the security aspects of a computer system is very difficult. It is made harder by a both lack of good information and the prevalence of disinformation. Computations requirements and performance estimates made for the cryptographic sections of system I have been involved with been off by more than 4 orders of magnitude in each direction. There is a general confusion (at the very least) about the legalities, strengths, and speeds of DES and of RSA. Beyond this, there seems to be little consensus on the feasibility of any of the non-DES non factoring based cryptographic methods.

8 User Errors are Compromise otherwise Good Systems

In practice, we often find cryptographic keys and passwords left in publically readable cleartext on otherwise safe machines. Often programs have options for reading passwords and keying information from file encouraging these errors.

Clear text version of encrypted files are often left in system buffers, temporary files or ordinary files. In several cases the unencrypted password has is written to publically readable areas of memory or disk before the encryption itself is done or program break leaving the passwords, keying information and/or clear text data available with other debugging information.

These are traditionally not the problems of the cryptographer but rather the problem of the system designer. Very often these issues are not successfully solved. As a result the attackers we have dealt with in the unsensitive unclassified world haven't had to learn to exploit any weaknesses in the cryptographic system or protocol.

In a similar vein, the unix crypt facility, a modified (one rotor) version of Enigma is still widely used despite the publication of an automated facility for breaking this cypher [1]. I do not claim to understand all of the social factors that encourage this type of inertia. Perhaps misinformation about the security and speed of DES play a major roll in it.

9 Authentication for the Academic World

To make it easier for computer systems designers to create systems with some degree of security, perhaps rather than trying to piece together system from what we find in the literature, we should be making an explicit request. In the hopes that such a request will encourage some of you in the Cryptographic Community to invent, adapt or simply more visibly announce tools that we can use, these requests follow.

1. A method of authentication whereby a user types a short password (about 12 bits) onto a computer and in doing so proves to another using only an insecure broadcast between the two computers that he is indeed that person. It should be the case the watching a large number of these broadcast transaction an attacker can't appreciably improve his chances of guessing the password or otherwise impersonating the user even with $1,000,000$ the computing power of the normal authentication.

2. A method where one computer can prove to another computer on a broadcast network of $5,000,000$ machines that it a given computer such that

   - Adding a new node is easy;

- Disabling the password of a compromised node is easy;
- Watching milions of transactions doesn't allow inpersonation;
- Keys do need to be changed more often then once per billion authentications per node;
- Private channels are very expensive and require human intervention;
- Each authentication can be done in a few million 32 bit instructions.

3. A fast method to tell that small file (less than 1000 bytes) has been signed by a given entity. Preferably using only a few hundred thousand 32 bit operations.

4. A true zero knowledge authentication analogous to the graph homomorphism method than can give a confidence level of one in 2^{20} with a few hundred thousand bytes of traffic and a few million 32 bit operations.

Anyone with practical answers to these requests, is encouraged to contact the author.

10 Conclusion

While social attacks of stolen keys and bribery may continue to offer the greatest threat to the high security environments, academic and other unclassified computing could be greatly simplified by better implementations of security systems. Better use and understanding of cryptosystems can form an important part of these computer systems.

It is hoped that by reviewing the current problems with the cryptographic parts of security systems that future designers can avoid these mistakes and that cryptosystem designer can better warn potential users of their system about the potential hazards and misuses.

References

[1] Robert Baldwin *Rule Based Analysis of Computer Security*. LCS Technical Report 401, Massachusetts Institute of Technology, 1987.

[2] Russell L. Brand *A Computer Security Tutorial*. 1987.

[3] David C. Feldmeier and Philip R. Karn *UNIX Password Security - Ten Years Later* (In this Volume) 1989.

[4] S. P. Miller, B. C. Neuman, J. I. Schiller, and J. H. Slatzer, *Kerberos Authentication and Authorization System*. Project Athena Technical Plan. Project Athena, Massachusetts Institute of Technology. 1987.

[5] Andrew Odlyzko (In preperation).

[6] J. G. Steiner, B. C. Neuman, and J. I. Schiller, *Kerberos: An Authentication Service for Open Network Systems*. IUSENIX Conference Proceedings, Winter 1988, pp. 191-202, USENIX Association, February 1988.

The use of Encryption in Kerberos for Network Authentication

John T. Kohl
Digital Equipment Corporation
MIT Project Athena
Cambridge, Massachusetts

Abstract

In a workstation environment, the user often has complete control over the workstation. Workstation operating systems therefore cannot be trusted to accurately identify their users. Some other method of authentication is needed, and this motivated the design and implementation of the Kerberos authentication service.

Kerberos is based on the Needham and Schroeder trusted third-party authentication model, using private-key encryption. Each user and network server has a key (like a password) known only to it and the Kerberos database. A database server uses this knowledge to authenticate network entities to one another.

The encryption used to achieve this authentication, the protocols currently in use and the protocols proposed for future use are described.

1 Introduction

This paper gives a brief overview of Kerberos, an authentication system developed at Project Athena at M.I.T., and describes the rationale behind and uses of encryption in Kerberos to achieve its goals. More complete descriptions can be found in [8, 4], and in a forthcoming Request For Comments.

It begins with a quick overview of the message scheme used to achieve authentication, then describes the use of encryption in the current protocols (including its flaws), and finishes by describing modifications proposed for the next version of the Kerberos protocols.

2 Terminology

Throughout this paper, we use certain terms relating to Kerberos which may be unfamiliar to the reader. Below is a definition of such terms.

principal An entity which shares a private key with some Key Distribution Center (KDC), and therefore can participate in authentication exchanges. A principal's name is bound to a private encryption key in the KDC's database. The current implementation allows two-part names for principals, consisting of a name field and an instance field. The realm of a principal is determined by the realm name assigned to the KDC with which it shares a private key.

server A principal which provides a Kerberos-mediated service to other principals.

client A principal which desires to use a service.

realm An autonomous unit of authentication authority. All principals in a realm share a key with that realm's KDC. Realms may share keys with each other to allow authentication between principals in different realms.

session key A randomly-generated encryption key contained in a Ticket or in Credentials.

Ticket A data structure cryptographically sealed under a server's private key. The ticket contains information necessary for a principal to verify another's identity based on the trust of the KDC. Tickets can be re-used until they expire.

Credentials A data structure composed of a Ticket and the information needed by a client to use that Ticket.

Authenticator A data structure cryptographically sealed under a temporary key. The authenticator contains information used to aid in replay detection. An authenticator may only be used once.

3 Kerberos overview

Kerberos provides a means for two principals (for example, a workstation user and a network server) to verify each other's identities in the context of an open (i.e. unprotected) network system. This must be accomplished without relying on authentication by the workstation operating system or host addresses, without requiring physical security of all the hosts on the system, and under the assumption that packets traveling along the network can be read and inserted at will. Kerberos performs authentication under these conditions as a trusted third-party authentication service using private key encryption.

Kerberos is based on protocols described by Needham and Schroeder [5], Voydock and Kent [9], Denning and Saco [1], and Watson [10]. A central Key Distribution Center (KDC) maintains a database of principals and private keys (currently only DES keys are supported). When a principal desires to authenticate with some service, it sends a request to the KDC, which responds with a Ticket and other control information encrypted in the principal's private key. The principal decrypts the reply, stores the contents for possible future use, and then forwards the Ticket plus a freshly-constructed Authenticator to the service. The service can verify the identity of the client by examining the Ticket (which itself is encrypted in the service's private key), and verifying its contents with the information contained in the Authenticator.

The current protocols are known as "Version 4" (there were lower-numbered prototype protocols); the protocol revision underway will yield Kerberos protocol "Version 5".

4 Version 4 Protocol

4.1 Encryption

The basic encryption algorithm used in the current version of Kerberos is the U.S. National Institute of Standards and Technology (NIST)[1] Data Encryption Standard (DES) [6]. DES is a block cipher, operating on 64-bit blocks.

The standard mode of encryption under DES is called Electronic Code Book (ECB). ECB mode is not used by Kerberos because it has deficiencies when applied to successive

---

[1]Formerly the National Bureau of Standards.

blocks of data. When block-aligned repetitive data are encrypted using ECB, they can be recognized as identical ciphertext blocks (e.g. an array of zeros larger than several blocks will show up as a set of identical ciphertext blocks). While this does not directly reveal the encrypted data, it does put them at greater risk to discovery through cryptographic analysis.

FIPS 81 [7] defines the Cipher Block Chaining (CBC) mode of DES to alleviate this problem. The ciphertext of the previous block is bitwise exclusively or'ed (XOR'ed) with the cleartext before encryption, so that block-aligned data are masked (see Figure 1). For the first block, the encryption key is used as the Initialization Vector (IV), which is treated as the previous ciphertext block and XOR'ed into the first block before encryption. However, CBC does not provide any integrity assurance (which Kerberos desires). If a ciphertext block is modified, the error induced after decryption spans only the block modified and the following block. An integrity check can be added by computing a checksum on the cleartext before encryption, and encrypting it as part of the cleartext.

But the Kerberos designers wanted to do the encryption and integrity check in a single pass. A first pass to compute a checksum followed by a separate pass to perform the encryption was deemed too expensive for performance reasons [3]. Their design criteria specifically did not expect hardware DES encryption assist, and so they rely on software implementations of the encryption algorithms [4]. As as result, they were not constrained to the officially defined standard modes of operation (which they would have been limited to, had they assumed hardware assist). So they devised what they called "Plaintext Cipher Block Chaining" mode (PCBC) in which the cleartext of the previous block as well as the ciphertext of the previous block are XOR'ed into the current block before encryption (see Figure 2). The result of PCBC is that errors in the decrypted cleartext would propagate themselves to all successive blocks of the cleartext. This property allowed the use of PCBC without a separate integrity check (the encrypted messages contained enough predictable contents at the end of the cleartex to make detection of a modified block highly likely).

However, PCBC has a different deficiency: swapping two ciphertext blocks will foul the cleartext of the corresponding blocks (and all blocks between) upon decryption, but due to the nature of the XOR method with the cleartext and ciphertexts, the errors cancel out, and succeeding blocks are properly decrypted. So if the integrity checks look at the last few blocks to verify message integrity (as the current implementation does), the checks can be fooled into accepting a partially garbled message.

4.2 Cryptographic checksums

In addition to the use of encryption to seal and protect messages, a quadratic checksum algorithm is available in an optional application protocol to achieve a lower-cost assurance of integrity (without assurance of privacy). The algorithm is modified from Jueneman [2] (The modifications have not been analyzed with respect to cryptographic security.). The checksum is computed with the session key used as a seed. However, in the current protocol the checksum is not encrypted when transmitted, leaving the session key exposed to possible attack by inversion of the algorithm. If the checksum were encrypted, an attacker would have to discover the session key through cryptanalysis on the seeded checksum.

Figure 1: The Cipher Block Chaining (CBC) mode of DES

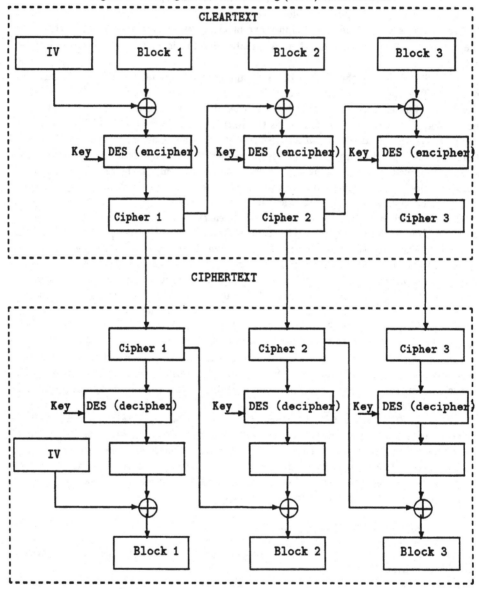

Figure 2: The Plaintext Cipher Block Chaining (PCBC) mode of DES (non-standard)

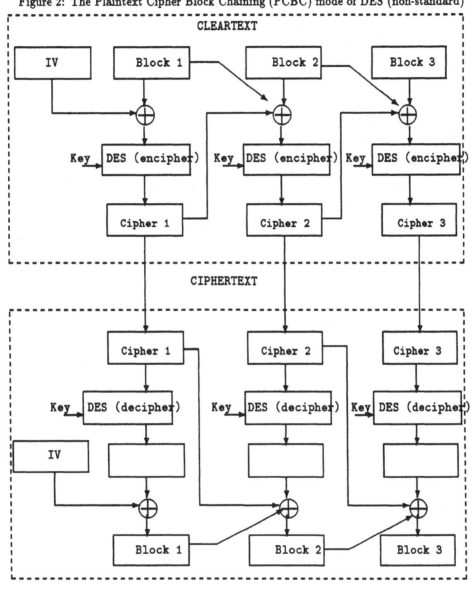

4.3 Cryptanalysis

The Kerberos protocols and their current implementation were designed with the assumption that the cryptosystem was secure. Very little analysis of cryptographic attacks was performed.

4.4 Application protocols

4.4.1 Authentication Service

In order to obtain a Ticket to present to a service, the client sends a cleartext message to the KDC, containing its name, instance, and realm, the client host's time of day, a requested lifetime for the Ticket, and the service name and instance for the desired Ticket.

The KDC retrieves the records for both the client and server, constructs a Ticket and associated credentials information, encrypts the Ticket under the server's key, encrypts the credentials and encrypted Ticket under the client's key, and returns the encrypted data along with some cleartext control information to the client.

The Ticket contains the client's name, the client's host's network address, a session key, a lifetime, the time at which the Ticket was issued, and the server's name, instance, and realm.

The credentials information contains a copy of the session key contained in the Ticket, the server's name, instance, and realm, the lifetime of the Ticket, the key version number of the server's private key used to create the Ticket, the length of the Ticket, the Ticket itself, and the KDC's time of day.

It should be noted that the Ticket itself need not be encrypted along with the rest of the credentials in the response. The Ticket is usually passed over the network from the client to the server, and since the Ticket is encrypted in a secret key, the session key contained therein is safe from release.

4.4.2 Client to Server

After obtaining a Ticket and associated Credentials, the client constructs an Authenticator (which contains the client's name, host network address, and timestamp, to be used as anti-replay information, all encrypted in the session key) and sends the Ticket, Authenticator, and (possibly) other application-protocol information to the application server.

The server decrypts and verifies the Ticket using its private key. If successfully verified, it uses the enclosed session key to decrypt the Authenticator and verifies the anti-replay information.

This achieves authentication of the client to the server; if the client requires the server to authenticate in return, the server can use the session key to generate a reply proving that it has access to the session key. This serves to authenticate the server to the client, since we assume only the correct server knows the private key and could decrypt the Ticket and obtain the session key.

4.4.3 Ticket-Granting Service

There is a special service provided on the KDC which acts like most Kerberos-mediated services, but has access to the KDC database. This service, dubbed the "Ticket-granting service" (TGS) can issue new Tickets without requiring the client to have its private key available (which typically would require a client workstation to store or repeatedly request the user's password).

When a user logs in, the workstation software requests a Ticket for this TGS, using the normal Authentication Service protocol. The user types his password (during the login process), and it is used to decrypt the response. The Ticket and associated Credentials are cached on the workstation. The lifetime of this Ticket is usually short (about 8 hours at MIT Project Athena), so that the exposure of leaving the Ticket and session key stored on the workstation and subject to theft and malicious or unauthorized use is limited to a short time span. If the user's password were stored, a thief could impersonate the user for a potentially much longer time (until the user changed his password).

When Tickets are required for additional service, the client workstation uses the standard client-to-server protocol to send its TGS ticket and an Authenticator, along with a client timestamp, requested lifetime, and the name of the service for which tickets are needed to the TGS. The TGS uses its private key (which it can fetch from the database) to decrypt the ticket, verify the Authenticator, and fulfill the request by constructing a new Ticket and associated Credentials. As in the Authentication Service protocol, the Credentials and ticket are encrypted (but in the session key from the TGS ticket, rather than the client's private key) and returned to the client, which then decrypts and caches the Ticket and Credentials.

4.4.4 Integrity-protected messages

The "KRB_SAFE" protocol message is used when a client and server want to verify the integrity of a message without requiring privacy or degrading performance by utilizing encryption.

The message contains user data, some control information, the sender's network address, and the sender's host's time of day, along with a quadratic "cryptographic" checksum (described above) of the entire message seeded with the shared session key. An incorrect checksum (as verified by the receiver) or incorrect control information indicates a modified or unauthentic message.

4.4.5 Privacy-protected messages

The "KRB_PRIV" protocol message is used when a client and server want to verify the integrity and protect the privacy of a message.

The message contains user data, some control information, the sender's network address, and the sender's host's time of day, encrypted (using PCBC mode of DES) under the session key. Upon decryption, a garbled message or incorrect control information indicates a modified or unauthentic message.

5 Planned version 5 changes

Project Athena plans to be able to support different encryption types in the version 5 protocol messages. We expect to implement only a DES-based version. We hope that other implementors will provide different encryption types.

Due to the above discussed problems with PCBC, we have decided to use the CBC mode of DES combined with a data checksum to provide integrity and privacy. The choice of a checksum algorithm to use is still under discussion; we are seeking an algorithm that won't negatively interact with DES.

We also are seeking a better cryptographic checksum than the quadratic checksum (which doesn't have much analytical proof). The DES CBC checksum mode has better-studied properties, but is computationally much more expensive than the quadratic checksum. We would ideally like a computationally "cheap" checksum which is also reasonably secure.

We expect to fix the "KRB_SAFE" protocol by allowing user selection of a cryptographic checksum algorithm.

6   Conclusion

This paper has discussed the encryption used in the Kerberos protocol and the rationale and design decisions underlying some of the uses of encryption. It has noted deficiencies in the current implementation and protocols, and suggests changes to alleviate those problems in the next version of the protocol.

Kerberos has succeeded in its goal of using software encryption by limiting the amount data required to be encrypted for the base authentication protocols, and allows applications to choose appropriate levels of cryptographic integrity and privacy.

7   Acknowledgments

The author would like to thank Jon Rochlis and Steve Miller for their comments on drafts of this paper.

References

[1] Dorothy E. Denning and Giovanni Maria Sacco. Timestamps in Key Distribution Protocols. *Communications of the ACM*, 24(8):533–536, August 1981.

[2] R. R. Jueneman et al. Message Authentication. *IEEE Communications*, 23(9):29–40, September 1985.

[3] Steven P. Miller. Private communication.

[4] Steven P. Miller, B. Clifford Neuman, Jeffrey I. Schiller, and Jerome H. Saltzer. Section E.2.1: Kerberos Authentication and Authorization System. *Project Athena Technical Plan*, December 1987.

[5] Roger M. Needham and M. D. Schroeder. Using Encryption for Authentication in Large Networks of Computers. *Communications of the ACM*, 21(12):993–999, Dec 78.

[6] National Bureau of Standards. Data Encryption Standard. *Federal Information Processing Standards Publication*, 46, 1977.

[7] National Bureau of Standards. DES Modes of Operation. *Federal Information Processing Standards Publication*, 81, 1980.

[8] Jennifer G. Steiner, B. Clifford Neuman, and Jeffrey I. Schiller. Kerberos: An Authentication Service for Open Network Systems. *Usenix Conference Proceedings*, pages 183–190, February 1988.

[9] Victor L. Voydock and Stephen T. Kent. Security mechanisms in high-level network protocols. *Computing Surveys*, 15(2):135–171, June 1983.

[10] R. W. Watson. Timer-Based Mechanisms in Reliable Transport Protocol Connection Management. *Computer Networks*, 5, 1981.

UNIX Password Security - Ten Years Later*

David C. Feldmeier and Philip R. Karn
Bellcore
445 South Street
Morristown, NJ 07960

Abstract

Passwords in the UNIX operating system are encrypted with the *crypt* algorithm and kept in the publicly-readable file /etc/passwd. This paper examines the vulnerability of UNIX to attacks on its password system. Over the past 10 years, improvements in hardware and software have increased the crypts/second/dollar ratio by five orders of magnitude. We reexamine the UNIX password system in light of these advances and point out possible solutions to the problem of easily found passwords. The paper discusses how the authors built some high-speed tools for password cracking and what elements were necessary for their success. These elements are examined to determine if any of them can be removed from the hands of a possible system infiltrator, and thus increase the security of the system. We conclude that the single most important step that can be taken to improve password security is to increase password entropy.

1 Introduction

Ten years ago, Robert Morris and Ken Thompson wrote the standard paper on UNIX password security [9]. It described a new one-way function to encrypt UNIX passwords for storage in the publicly-readable file /etc/passwd. This *crypt* function, based on the NBS Data Encryption Standard (DES) algorithm, remains the standard in almost every version of UNIX.

Crypt uses the resistance of DES to known plain text attack to make it computationally infeasible to determine the original password that produced a given encrypted password by exhaustive search. The only publicly-known technique that may reveal certain passwords is password guessing: passing large word lists through the crypt function to see if any match the encrypted password entries in an /etc/passwd file. Our experience is that this type of attack is successful unless explicit steps have been taken to thwart it. Generally we find over 30% of the passwords on previously unsecured systems.

Recent well-publicized intrusions into UNIX systems prompted another look at the security of the UNIX password algorithm. In certain cases, intruders are using password-guessing attacks much like those described by Morris and Thompson. One such attack was contained in the ARPA Internet Worm of November 1988[12].

Experiments by the authors demonstrate that the rapid improvements in computer price/performance ratios over the past decade call into question the adequacy of the present UNIX password algorithm. By careful optimization and the liberal use of space/time trade-offs, one of us (Feldmeier) has developed a version of the present standard UNIX crypt

---

*The title refers to the paper by Morris and Thompson printed in Communications of the ACM in 1979[9]

function that executes in 0.92 ms on the latest generation of RISC workstations. The old Version 6 UNIX crypt function (based on the M-209 rotor cipher) executed in 1.25 ms on the PDP-11/70s that were current in the late 1970s when the crypt algorithm was changed. It is interesting to note that the main reason given by Morris and Thompson for abandoning the Version 6 algorithm was that it executed too quickly.

This paper discusses how passwords in the UNIX operating system can be found using high-speed versions of the UNIX crypt algorithm and pre-encrypting large dictionaries. Given that such tools are available to crack passwords, the elements necessary to allow such cracking are examined to determine how some of these necessary elements can be eliminated to improve security.

2   Fast Crypt Implementations

The crypt implementation that is included with UNIX distributions (such as BSD 4.2) is not optimized for speed because it already allows logins in a reasonable amount of time. Several techniques can be used to speed up an implementation. One technique is to alter the crypt algorithm so that it is easier to compute but still produces the same results. Another technique is to take advantage of the architectural features of the computer that runs the algorithm. Space-time tradeoffs are used to minimize the number of table lookups at the expense of table size and carefully designed data structures minimize the manipulation of individual bits.

The result of applying these methods to increase the performance of the crypt implementation leads to a 102.9 times speedup over the crypt implementation in 4.2 Berkeley UNIX on a Sun 3/50 and a top speed of 1092.8 crypts per second on a Sun SPARCStation. A more complete description of these techniques may be found in the appendix.

Using the speeds of several fast crypt implementations[1] and the prices of several computers (adjusted for inflation to 1989 dollars) produces the graph in figure 1 that shows the increase in crypts/second/dollar over the last 15 years. The graph shows both increases in hardware speed ($\square$) and the best combinations of hardware and software speeds ($\times$). At the left side of the graph is the speed of the Version 6 crypt ($\bullet$). Crypts/second/dollar is the correct metric because password cracking is an easily segmented problem. The speedup is nearly linear with the number of machines, so the best performance overall is obtained by using machines with the best price/performance ratio. The computers shown are the DEC PDP 11/70 (1975), the DEC VAX 11/780 (1978), the Sun 3/50 (1986), the Sun 4/280 (1987), the DEC 3100 (1989) and the Sun SPARCStation (1989).

Table 1 shows how much CPU time on the DEC 3100 is required for exhaustive search of various password spaces. Note that these numbers are for a single DEC 3100, but exhaustive searches are easy to parallelize and many workstations could be used at night and on weekends when they are otherwise idle. Given 20 machines and the numbers above, it is probably reasonable to do an exhaustive search of passwords of length 7-8 lower-case letters, 7 lower-case letters and numbers, 6 alpha-numeric characters, 5-6 printable character or 5 ASCII characters. The moral is keep your passwords 8 characters long or use lots of unusual characters, but in no circumstance use less than 6 characters. Of course, if the crypt/second/dollar ratio increases by another five orders of magnitude in the next decade, only eight-character passwords that utilize the entire ASCII character set will be immune from brute-force cracking!

---

[1]See table 6 in the appendix.

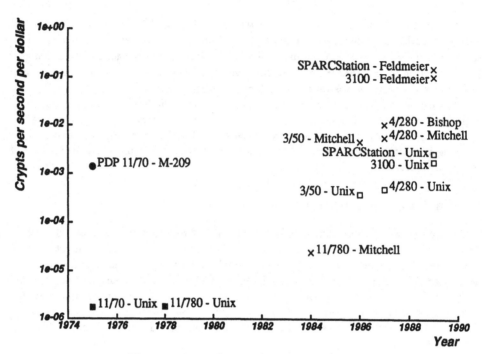

Figure 1: Crypts/Second/Dollar versus Time

n	26 lower-case letters	36 lower-case letters & digits	62 alpha-numeric characters	95 printable characters	128 ASCII characters
4	419 sec	25.7 min	226 min	20.8 hours	68.4 hours
5	182 min	15.4 hours	234 hours	82.2 days	365 days
6	78.8 hours	23.1 days	603 days	21.4 years	128 years
7	85.3 days	832 days	102 years	2.03 kyears	16.4 kyears
8	6.07 years	82.1 years	6.35 kyears	193 kyears	2.03 myears

Table 1: Brute Force Cracking Times of Speed-Crypt on the DEC 3100

Exhaustive search in hardware is possible[5]. One of the aims of including the salt in the crypt algorithm was to remove the threat of using DES hardware to find passwords. However, it would not be too expensive to build VLSI chips that compute the crypt function and run 1000 times faster than these software implementations, not to mention the possible gain due to parallelism and pipelining.

The ultimate size of the key space allowed by the UNIX crypt program is very large: 2^{56} or about 7.2×10^{16} possible keys. Even with only 95 printable characters on a keyboard, there are still 95^8 or about 6.6×10^{15} possible keys. This is large enough to resist brute-force attacks in software, yet most of the passwords selected by users are in a very small part of this total space. It is impossible to use exhaustive search over the large space, but it is possible over the smaller space. What is needed is a list of words that have a high probability of being chosen as a password. Such a list can be derived from dictionaries, telephone directories, etc.

3   Precomputed Encrypted Dictionaries

A fast way of cracking large batches of passwords on a routine basis is to first encrypt a list of likely passwords and then compare each new batch of encrypted passwords against this pre-encrypted list.

Salting was specifically designed to hinder this approach. Because the specific salt values are not known in advance, the pre-encrypted dictionary must encrypt each trial password with all possible salts, increasing storage requirements considerably. However, bulk storage is now far cheaper than it was ten years ago. In 1979, the densest form of bulk storage on the market was 6250 bpi magnetic tape and the corresponding tape drives were expensive. The consumer video cassette recorder boom of the 1980s has produced a spinoff in the form of inexpensive digital cassette drives that can store about 2 gigabytes on a standard 8mm video cassette. These cassettes are about the same size as audio cassettes, yet they can hold the equivalent of fifteen 2400' reels of 6250 bpi tape.

Using a collection of Sun-3 and Sun-4 processors, the authors built a pre-encrypted dictionary from a list of about 107,000 trial passwords. Encrypting each trial password 4,096 times (once for each possible salt value) took several CPU-weeks on these machines; the results fit onto two 8mm cassettes. (Recomputing the dictionary would now take less time, since the fast crypt algorithm was still being tuned while we were generating the dictionary.)

Each encrypted password is stored as an 8-byte value; the plain text is not stored on the tape. Not only does this reduce the amount of tape necessary, but the tapes alone are enough to determine whether an encrypted password is in the password list without revealing the plain text password. This is ideal for improving system security without the possibility of the tapes being used to infiltrate other systems.

The cassettes can be replayed repeatedly and checked against lines from the /etc/passwd file. At a tape transfer rate of 250 kilobytes/second, the CPU can keep up easily with the comparisons; thus the system checks about 30,000 trial passwords/second, faster than the fast crypt code runs in real time. The tapes also can be supplemented with tapes produced from new passwords and with the fast crypt program to check words of local interest, such as names of employees or projects.

The precomputed dictionary approach is therefore 28.6 times faster than real time encryption on a DEC 3100. Twelve tapes containing the encrypted versions of about 732,000 trial passwords would take a day to read on one drive; the crypt implementation running on a single DEC 3100 would take a month, assuming that the password file contains at least one entry for each possible salt. Even so, as long as users change their password less often than once a month, many passwords still can be found. The precomputed dictionary is helpful but not essential for password cracking.

4 Improving Password Security

Since this paper discusses the security of password systems, other possible human-to-machine authentication systems (such as retinal scans or fingerprints) are not considered here. The purpose of this section is to examine the necessary elements for successful password cracking and to suggest which elements might be changed to increase the difficulty of cracking passwords. The elements required to crack passwords as discussed in this paper are:

- High performance/price ratio computers
- Large on-line word lists (dictionaries, etc.)
- A known password encryption algorithm
- A constraint on the acceptable running times for the login program
- A publicly-readable password file
- Passwords with a significant probability of being in the word list

The existence of high performance/price ratio computers and on-line word lists cannot be controlled, so if the difficulty of cracking passwords is to be increased, then one of the remaining four conditions must be changed.

4.1 Known Encryption Algorithm

We consider it a given, as did Morris and Thompson, that the encryption algorithm used for the one-way password crypt function must be published and subjected to public scrutiny. As in cryptography, it is neither practical nor necessary to base the security of a password algorithm on its secrecy. The storm of protest in response to the NSA's recent attempt to replace DES with a secret cipher of its own design indicates the importance of this principle. Furthermore, the enormous success of the UNIX operating system is based largely on the openness of its design and the availability of its algorithms and source code. Assuming that the basic algorithm has not been compromised, there is no real reason to change it.

4.2 Acceptable Running Times

Software de-facto standards, such as the UNIX password algorithm, tend to outlive their original underlying hardware. UNIX now runs on a wide range of processors, from IBM PC/XTs to Cray IIs. A crypt function that is slow enough to thwart password attacks on a Cray II would be intolerably slow to a user logging into an IBM PC, and of course what is slow but tolerable on today's machines will become unacceptably fast on tomorrow's. It is ironic that current fast crypt implementations on 1989 hardware run faster than the old (and "unacceptably fast") Version 6 crypt ran on 1979 hardware.

Also, a crypt routine written specifically for password cracking runs orders of magnitude faster than a version built into a login command. Many of the performance enhancements (e.g., precomputation and the factoring of permutations) are meaningful only for a large scale password cracker that is trying many more keys than encrypted passwords. Also, the amount of memory required for the large tables in fast crypt implementations is not acceptable for a utility program that is to be a standard part of the system. The adversary can afford to dedicate an entire system to password cracking; the "good guy" is unlikely to be willing to dedicate his entire system to the login program.

Morris and Thompson purposely slowed the execution speed of the UNIX crypt implementation in an attempt to hinder password cracking. Adjusting crypt's speed so that the slowest processor running UNIX still has an acceptable login delay thwarts attack only slightly; the fundamental problems with current passwords are not addressed. Other approaches are more likely to be successful. We believe the solution to the password cracking problem lies *not* in penalizing both the good guy and the adversary by deliberately slowing the algorithm. A better approach lies instead in "driving a wedge" between them by increasing the entropy of user passwords. This forces the adversary to search such a large key space as to be impracticable even with a fast algorithm running on the fastest available computer for the foreseeable future.

4.3 Encrypted Password Availability

A resource available to the adversary that is removable is the existence of a publicly-readable encrypted password file (/etc/passwd). For the purposes of this paper, it is assumed that physical access to the machine alone is enough to subvert it and it is assumed that the machine itself is physically secured according to the desired level of security. Many machines can be rebooted into privileged mode with physical access, so that physical access implies that a password-based attack is really unnecessary for system access.

One method of restricting availability of the encrypted passwords is the *shadow password* file. A shadow password file is a file that contains the encrypted passwords and is not publicly accessible. This prevents the average user from accessing the password file. One problem with this approach is that a system administrator has access to the file. This is not a problem while the person remains an administrator, since presumably he has access to everything anyway. The problem is when a system administrator leaves. He may have copied encrypted passwords while he was an administrator and can now use these passwords to infiltrate the system. Also, if an error in access permission is made, the encrypted password file may become available to all users of a system. Shadow password files cannot hurt, but it seems unwise to count on them alone for system security.

A more promising, if more complex, method is to provide each user with a *smart card* that is used to authenticate the user to the system. A smart card in this case is a small computer with a keypad and a general purpose processor. The smart card should be able to communicate directly with the login system (e.g., by electrical or infrared link) rather than require manual I/O. The smart card is more than a physical key; the human authenticates himself to the smart card using a password, so the card alone is worthless. Note that the encrypted password resides in the card and cannot be obtained without possession of the card. Once the human authenticates himself to the card, the card authenticates itself to the computer by some other method not discussed here. Some possibilities include zero-knowledge proofs and public key systems. The main problem would seem to be the rather limited processing capacity of a smart card. However, there are ways of utilizing computing power in untrusted machines to execute complicated secret computations efficiently[7].

4.4 Decreasing Password Guessability

The main weakness in any password system is that users often choose easily guessable passwords: English words, names, trivial extensions to English words, etc., because they are easy to remember. It is important that passwords be difficult to guess. One way to decrease password guessability is to eliminate common passwords from /etc/passwd. At Bellcore, we are using our high-speed password cracking system and a large dictionary to find easily-guessed passwords on systems. Since we have a faster crypt and more CPU cycles than potential intruders, this allows us to use a larger dictionary; thus any passwords that survive our scrutiny are unlikely to be found by an intruder.

Another possibility is to restrict the passwords accepted from the user with a system that filters out easily guessed passwords. Different schemes of filtering are possible and one such method was described by Morris and Thompson[9]. This system acts as a password advisor that indicates insecure passwords, but it does not force the user to accept its recommendation. In some Applied Research laboratories in Bellcore, passwords must have certain characteristics before they are accepted by the system when the user changes his password. In addition, all existing passwords are periodically checked against a large dictionary and anyone whose password is found is forced to change it.

The most drastic solution is to have the system assign an arbitrary password. The problem is that such a password is hard to remember, so the temptation to write it down is strong. A written password is like a physical key, and can be used by anyone who obtains it. A slightly friendlier version of this system assigns a password, but allows the user to rearrange it to make it easier to remember. Then the new password is checked; if it is still acceptable, it becomes the user's new password.

A fundamental problem is that passwords typed by the user are truncated to 8 characters in length. Easily remembered passwords that are this short almost inevitably have much less than the 56 bits of entropy allowed by the crypt algorithm, making them easier to find by exhaustive search. All of the techniques just described attempt to increase entropy in the users' passwords, but they do it in a way that ignores human factors considerations. Almost anyone can remember 56 bits of arbitrary information, but he must be allowed to do it in a way that is suited to human, not computer, memory. The way to do this is by extending the present algorithm to allow *pass phrases*[10]. A pass phrase is simply a longer version of a password that includes several words. According to Shannon [11], English text has a lower bound of 1-2 bits of entropy per character. Therefore an ordinary English phrase of 5-10 words (assuming 5-6 characters/word and no unusual punctuation or capitalization) has sufficient entropy as a pass phrase.

To accommodate this in the UNIX crypt algorithm, a hash function is needed to fold the typed pass phrase into 56 bits, with each input character affecting the result. This function should be backward compatible with the existing UNIX password algorithm for pass phrases of 8 characters or less. One possibility is to treat the first 8 characters as before, exclusive-ORing into it each successive 8-character block from the pass phrase (if the phrase is not a multiple of 8 characters, it is null-padded on the right).

Users might still object to pass phrases if they were required to type them too frequently (e.g., when they must repeatedly log into a several different systems, each for short intervals). A solution to this problem lies in the use of an distributed authentication system such as Kerberos, in which the user need type his password only once to obtain a set of "tickets" that can be used to access other systems repeatedly without having to retype the pass phrase each time[13].

Not only is the entropy of the password important, but also the amount of time available to the cracker to find it. The more infrequently that a user changes his password, the more vulnerable it is to a cracker. Thus it is important that the user occasionally change his password. On System V UNIX, this is accomplished by including an *aging field* for each line of the /etc/passwd file. When a password is sufficiently old, then the user is prompted for a new one. Of course, the system should check that the new password is different from previous ones.

4.5 Other Approaches

Two suggested solutions to the problem of easily cracked passwords are to increase the size of the salt or to change the constant that is encrypted by crypt. Neither of these seems to be particularly helpful.

Increasing the size of the salt does not help prevent attack on an individual password, but it does help defeat checking multiple passwords simultaneously and pre-encrypted wordlist attacks by increasing the time and space required, respectively. The current salt is large enough that few of the lines in a typical /etc/passwd file share the same salt. The only remaining reason to increase the size of the salt is to reduce the number of pre-encrypted passwords that can fit onto a fixed amount of tape. But as shown above, pre-encryption decreases the cracking time by a factor of 30, so this is the maximum penalty that could be exacted by even a large increase in the salt size.

Making the starting constant used by crypt a system configuration variable instead of all zeros was mentioned by Morris and Thompson[9]. This has the advantage of making it harder to use the pre-encrypted wordlist, but unless the constant is kept secret it is still possible to attack individual passwords with a fast crypt. Depending on the implementation, a user might be able to learn the constant by decompiling the login program. If a password/encrypted password pair is known, then the starting constant can be determined simply by reversing the internal crypt operations. The encrypted passwords are known if the /etc/passwd file is publicly readable; a plain text password that matches an encrypted password is available to any user (his own password) and some passwords (such as for UUCP) may be widely known. An adversary with access to the /etc/passwd file alone but no knowledge of the constant could take advantage of the fact that many passwords are in the dictionary. As before, crypt can be run backwards for a dictionary of words on several passwords and the corresponding input constants checked for a match. Once a matching pair of constants is found (there are 2^{64} or about 1.8×10^{19} possibilities for the constant, so a match is unlikely unless both are the hidden constant), the number can be verified simply by using one of the plain text keys that produced the match to attempt to log in. If the attempt is successful, the hidden constant is known and cracking continues as usual. The only cost above the usual cracking technique is the maintenance of the list of constants until a match is found. Table 2 shows the probability of finding the unknown constant after checking n encrypted passwords, for 10%, 20%, and 30% probabilities of finding a password in the dictionary.

Once chosen, the constant could not be changed easily (e.g., in event of compromise) without having every user re-enter his or her password. Another disadvantage of the system-configurable constant is that /etc/password files would no longer be portable across systems with different encryption constants, although it might be argued that such portability de-

Number of Passwords	Success Probability (10%)	Success Probability (20%)	Success Probability (30%)
5	8%	26%	47%
10	26%	62%	85%
15	45%	83%	96%
20	61%	93%	99%

Table 2: Probability of Cracking Two or More Passwords

creases system security by allowing arbitrary (and perhaps easily guessed) passwords to be put in the /etc/password file.

To keep the constant secret, it is necessary to couple the secret constant technique with shadow password files. Since this technique must be implemented in conjunction with shadow password files, has no advantages over that of shadow passwords alone, and has several disadvantages, it is better to implement password file shadowing only.

5 Conclusion

The current UNIX password system is not always sufficient to prevent unauthorized entry because it is fairly easy to crack passwords. An important point is that although the crypt algorithm is a good one, the password system as a whole is weak. Six factors contribute to the ease of cracking passwords: high performance/price ratio computers, large on-line word lists, a known password encryption algorithm, a maximum acceptable running time for the login program, a publicly readable password file, and easily guessable passwords.

Nothing can be done about large on-line dictionaries or high performance/price ratio computers. In fact, the password system should take the exponential speed increase of computers into account. It is argued that the password encryption algorithm must be known to be trusted and that there is a range of acceptable running times for the algorithm which sets an upper limit on the amount of computation that the password encryption algorithm may use. Unfortunately, the computation limit is small enough to allow faster machines to use a dictionary-based attack. It is also argued that Morris and Thompson's assertion that slowing down the implementation of the crypt function improves security does not address the large range of processors that run UNIX.

Two of the main problems with the current system are that users choose easily guessable passwords and that the encrypted password file is publicly readable. A dual approach is suggested. One part is to make passwords less predictable by allowing pass phrases and restricting passwords accepted by the system. This effectively increases the entropy of a password, making wordlist attacks less successful. The other approach is to make the encrypted password file less accessible. How exactly this is done depends on the desired level of security and includes shadow password files and smart cards.

References

[1] Robert W. Baldwin. MIT fdes 5 (crypt) source code.

[2] Matt Bishop. An application of a fast data encryption standard implementation. *Computing Systems*, 1(3):221–254, Summer 1988.

[3] Marc Davio, Yvo Desmedt, Marc Fosseprez, Rene Govaerts, Jan Hulsbosch, Patrik Neutjens, Philippe Piret, Jean-Jacques Quisquater, Joos Vandewalle, and Pascal Wouters. Analytical characteristics of the DES. In *Proceedings of Crypto '83*, pages 171–202, August 1983.

[4] Marc Davio, Yvo Desmedt, Jo Goubert, Frank Hoornaert, and Jean-Jacques Quisquater. Efficient hardware and software implementations for the DES. In *Proceedings of Crypto '84*, pages 144–146, August 1984.

[5] W. Diffie and M. E. Hellman. Exhaustive cryptanalysis of the NBS data encryption standard. *Computer*, 10(6):74–84, June 1977.

[6] Alan G. Konheim. *Cryptography: A Primer*. John Wiley & Sons, 1981.

[7] T. Matsumoto, K. Kato, and H. Imai. Speeding up secret computations with insecure auxiliary devices. In *Proceedings of Crypto '88*, August 1988.

[8] Donald Mitchell. AT&T Questor (crypt) source code.

[9] Robert Morris and Ken Thompson. Password security: A case history. *Communications of the ACM*, 22(11):594–597, November 1979.

[10] Charles P. Pfleeger. *Security in Computing*. Prentice Hall, 1989.

[11] Claude Shannon. Prediction and entropy of printed english. *Bell System Technical Journal*, 30(1):50–64, January 1951.

[12] Eugene H. Spafford. The internet worm program: An analysis. *Computer Communication Review*, 19(1):17–57, January 1989.

[13] J.G. Steiner, C. Neuman, and J.I. Schiller. Kerberos: An authentication service for open network systems. In *USENIX Conference Proceedings*, pages 191–202, Dallas, Texas, February 1988.

A A High-Speed Crypt Implementation

This appendix[2] describes a high-speed software implementation of the UNIX crypt algorithm. This new crypt is 102.9 times faster than the crypt in 4.2 Berkeley UNIX on a Sun 3/50. Many of the results are also applicable to software *Data Encryption Standard* (DES) and other product cipher implementations.

Several techniques are used to increase the program speed. One technique is to alter the crypt algorithm so that it is easier to compute but still produces the same results. Another technique is to take advantage of the architectural features of the computer that will run

---

[2]This appendix was originally a paper entitled *A High-Speed Crypt Implementation* by David C. Feldmeier.

the algorithm. It also is important for high performance to minimize the manipulation of individual bits. A data representation is described that allows the E expansion of DES to be accomplished by a simple register copy and yet allows a fast implementation of the S function of DES without bit manipulation. This appendix assumes that the reader is familiar with the DES [6].

A.1   Overview of Crypt

Crypt is a program used by the UNIX operating system to encrypt user passwords and is based on the DES encryption algorithm. Crypt is designed to be a one-way function; given an input, it is easy to compute the output, but given an output, it is impossible to determine the corresponding input except by guessing. DES can be used to realize a one-way function, so it is a good choice to use for crypt. In particular DES is resistant to a known plain text attack, which means given the plain text and the cipher text, the key can be found only by exhaustive search. The crypt algorithm uses 25 successive DES encryptions of a constant (64 zeros) to produce the encrypted password. The key for all of the DES encryptions is derived from the user's password. The first eight characters of the password are used as a 56-bit key (7 bits for each ASCII character, 8 characters). If the password is less than 8 characters, the password is padded with zeros to the full 56-bit length.

Actually, crypt does not use pure DES. To prevent use of off-the-shelf high-speed DES hardware to crack passwords, crypt modifies the DES algorithm slightly. A randomly generated *salt* is included with each entry in the /etc/passwd file. The 12-bit salt ranges from zero to 4095. Think of the salt as a permutation that immediately follows the expansion function E in DES. If bit 1 of the salt is a 1, then the salt permutation swaps bits 1 and 25 of the 48-bit block generated by E. If bit 2 is a 1, then bit 2 and 26 are swapped and so on. Since there are 12 possible swaps and any combination of these swaps may occur, this produces 4096 possible variations of DES (a salt of zero corresponds to pure DES). More details on the UNIX password mechanism are found in a paper by Morris and Thompson[9].

A.2   The Speed-Crypt Implementation

This section describes some of the ideas behind the implementation of the crypt algorithm written by the author (*speed-crypt*) and why it is fast. The implementation is designed for 32-bit machines; it is possible to run it on other size machines with minor modifications. The DES algorithm has 48-bit, 56-bit and 64-bit wide paths. Since even 48 bits is wider than the expected data path, each operation requires two word manipulations; thus the DES data path is broken into high and low pieces of 32 bits each.

A.2.1   Algorithm Modifications

The basic crypt algorithm can be modified in a number of ways that do not change the function computed by the algorithm. Each DES encryption begins with the *initial permutation (IP)* and ends with the *inverse initial permutation (IP^{-1})*. These two permutations are inverses of each other, so when two DES encryptions are concatenated, the IP of the second encryption immediately follows the IP^{-1} of the first encryption. There is no reason to do either of these permutations, since the net result is no permutation at all. Therefore, any IP^{-1}-IP pairs can be factored out of the algorithm and only the first IP and the last IP^{-1} ever need be done. In fact, because of how crypt works, these remaining permutations can be factored out as well.

Inside of DES, the 64-bit input block is broken into two pieces of 32 bits each called *Left* (L) and *Right* (R). Within each DES encryption there are 16 product-transformation/block-transformation pairs. The block transformation is simply the swapping of the R 32 bits with the L 32 bits. To avoid the block transformation at the end of each product-transformation, speed-crypt uses two different product transformations: one works the usual way and the other operates on L as if it were R and vice-versa. Using these two product transformations alternately eliminates the need for a block transformation between product transformations. The only problem with this scheme is that after the last product-transformation, the L and R blocks are swapped. This reversal is incorporated into the final IP^{-1} because a swap and a permutation is just a permutation. Let ϵ represent the E expansion, σ represent the S function and π represent the P permutation. Let K_i be the ith subkey, R_i be the ith value of Right and L_i be the ith value of Left. By definition:

$$L_i \equiv R_{i-1}$$

$$R_i \equiv L_{i-1} \oplus f_i R_{i-1}$$

$$f_i R_{i-1} \equiv \pi\sigma(K_i \oplus \epsilon R_{i-1})$$

where f_i is the product transformation that uses subkey K_i. After two rounds:

$$L_{i+1} = L_{i-1} \oplus f_i R_{i-1}$$

$$R_{i+1} = R_{i-1} \oplus f_{i+1}(L_{i-1} \oplus f_i R_{i-1})$$

Since there are 16 rounds in DES, 8 double-rounds of the following form can be used instead:

$$L_{i+1} \equiv L_{i-1} \oplus f_i R_{i-1}$$

$$R_{i+1} \equiv R_{i-1} \oplus f_{i+1} L_{i+1}$$

Notice that no intermediate values of R_i and L_i need be retained. After one double-round:

$$L_{i+1} = L_{i-1} \oplus f_i R_{i-1}$$

$$R_{i+1} = R_{i-1} \oplus f_{i+1}(L_{i-1} \oplus f_i R_{i-1})$$

which is the same as before. In effect, the swap has been built into the iteration.

Because the crypt program begins by encrypting all zeros, the first IP permutation and the first E expansion can be factored out because any permutation or expansion of zero is still zero. The first salting operation can be factored out for the same reason.

Another method of increasing speed depends upon the assumption that there are fewer encrypted passwords to be checked than words to be tried. Under these circumstances, it makes sense to do as many operations as possible on the encrypted passwords if operations can be avoided on the words. The encrypted passwords should be operated on to allow their comparison with the results of the crypt program as early as possible, since a single backward step on the password saves as many forward steps as there are words. The final IP^{-1} can be skipped if you are checking to see whether a password is in a wordlist. Instead of doing the IP^{-1} permutation for each word that is being tested as the password, a better way to do this is to take the encrypted password from the passwd file and permute it with IP. The comparison is now done between the output of the last DES round and the permuted encrypted password.

A.2.2 Subkey Generation

Subkey generation means taking a 64-bit password key K and generating 16 48-bit DES subkeys K_i. The generation of subkeys involves taking a 64-bit plain text password and applying the reduction/permutation Permuted Choice 1. Permuted Choice 1 reduces the password from 64 bits to 56 bits by eliminating the parity bits and then permutes the result. The 56-bit result is then divided into low and high 28-bit halves and each half is left-circular shifted by an amount that depends on the particular subkey being generated. The two 28-bit halves are joined and the permutation/reduction Permuted Choice 2 is applied. Permuted Choice 2 permutes the 56-bit result of the rotation and then selects 48 of these bits for the subkey. The combination of the permutations and reductions for each subkey is combined into a single permutation/reduction, for a total of 16 subkey generation functions. Let α represent Permuted Choice 1, β represent Permuted Choice 2, and ρ_i represent the rotations for the ith subkey. Let K_i be the ith subkey and K be the key that the subkey is generated from. Then:

$$K_i \equiv \kappa_i K$$

$$\kappa_i \equiv \beta \rho_i \alpha$$

where κ_i is the permutation/reduction that generates the ith subkey from the original password. To limit the table size, subkey lookups take seven key bits at a time (each ASCII password character is represented by 7 bits). The lookup could take any number of bits at a time because all are independent, but doing lookups a character at a time is convenient and two characters at a time makes the tables too large.

For each character in the password, the partial subkey is found and logical-ORed with the partial subkeys for the other characters in the password. After 16 passes (each requiring two lookups) for each character in the password (a maximum of 128 passes), all 16 subkeys have been generated. At most 256 table lookups are needed to generate all subkeys. A nice side-effect is that the time required for this method of subkey generation is proportional to the password length. Since passwords of less than eight characters are padded with zeros and permutations of zero are also zero, the subkeys will not be changed by these additional zeros, so there is no need to bother with them. The total table size is 2^3 character positions in each password, 2^7 possible characters in each position, 2^4 subkeys per password and 2^3 bytes to hold each subkey for a total table size of 2^{17} or 131,072 bytes.

A.2.3 Table Lookup

The program gets a lot of its speed from a space-for-time tradeoff - almost everything in the program is done by table lookup. Ideally, a table lookup would take the entire input (up to 64 bits) and return the entire output (up to 64 bits). Of course, the maximum size of the input and output of a table are limited by the virtual memory size and the bus width. Thus, on a 32-bit bus, a table with a 64-bit output requires that two lookups be done, one for the low 32 bits and one for the high 32 bits. As for the input to the table, even a 32-bit input would be completely impractical because it is desirable to keep all of the tables in main memory for fast access time and to prevent paging.

To replicate the effect of a single large lookup table with several small lookup tables presents a problem. The problem is that groups of input bits may exist such that all the bits must be read simultaneously to produce a result. An example of this is the S boxes in DES. Each S box takes a 6-bit input and produces a 4-bit output. Because all 6 bits are simultaneously necessary (because the S box is non-affine), all S box lookups must be done in multiples of 6 bits.

However, if groups are independent, then the table lookup can be broken into manageable pieces (ideally of equal size to minimize the total table size), each of which can be manipulated independently. The results can then be logical-ORed together to produce the appropriate output. Because the physical memory available to an application in most workstations is only a few megabytes, this limits the size of the tables.

Changing one lookup to two produces a substantial change in total table size. The ratio is $2^{(n/2)+1}/2^n$ or $2^{1-(n/2)}$, where n is the number of bits used for the table index. The fewer the table lookups, the higher the speed, but also the more memory that is used. The crypt implementations should use as few table lookups as possible given the memory constraints.

The IP^{-1} table takes the 64-bit input a byte at a time and produces two 32-bit outputs that are ORed together in the usual way. The IP table is used only for permuting encrypted passwords that are being searched for to avoid computing the IP^{-1} for each word in the dictionary (remember that IP and IP^{-1} are inverse permutations). Since IP is used on password entries, the password entries must be converted from ASCII form to a 64-bit form. Speed-crypt uses a special version of IP that converts directly from the 11 ASCII character format of the /etc/passwd file to the 64-bit format after the IP permutation. IP does lookups a character at a time and produces two 32-bit outputs that are ORed together.

The S boxes and the P permutation are combined into a single lookup table. The expansion function E is done with a simple register copy. The details of the E expansion will be explained later. Table 3 shows the table sizes for speed-crypt.

Table	Bytes
SP	65,536
key	131,072
IP^{-1}	16,384
total	212,992

Table 3: Table Size in Speed-Crypt

A.2.4 Data Representation

A representation is devised that does not require a table lookup for the expansion function E, allows the S/P function to be implemented as 4 table lookups without the manipulation of individual bits, and allows fast salting. Such a representation is possible, but requires a strange bit order.

Consider the mapping from R (32 bits) to ϵR (48 bits) as shown in table 4. The first thing to notice is that the table is presented in groups of 6. The reason for this is that the eight S boxes each use six bits for their lookup. Because the S boxes are non-affine, the groups of six cannot be broken up. Therefore, they define the granularity of the table lookups (multiples of six bits along the boundaries shown).

An important aspect of the E expansion is that no input bit of R ever becomes more than two output bits in ϵR. This suggests that simply copying R into a second register will give all 48 bits necessary for the expansion E in two 32-bit words. Designate the two copies of R as A and B.

ϵR (48 bit)	1	2	3	4	5	6
R (32 bit)	32	1	2	3	4	5
ϵR (48 bit)	7	8	9	10	11	12
R (32 bit)	4	5	6	7	8	9
ϵR (48 bit)	13	14	15	16	17	18
R (32 bit)	8	9	10	11	12	13
ϵR (48 bit)	19	20	21	22	23	24
R (32 bit)	12	13	14	15	16	17
ϵR (48 bit)	25	26	27	28	29	30
R (32 bit)	16	17	18	19	20	21
ϵR (48 bit)	31	32	33	34	35	36
R (32 bit)	20	21	22	23	24	25
ϵR (48 bit)	37	38	39	40	41	42
R (32 bit)	24	25	26	27	28	29
ϵR (48 bit)	43	44	45	46	47	48
R (32 bit)	28	29	30	31	32	1

Table 4: Expansion Function E (mapping from R to ϵR)

Since as little manipulation as possible of the 32-bit quantities before the SP lookup is desired, the bit order of the 32-bit R (and symmetrically L) is critical. The aim is to do four lookups, two S boxes at a time. Notice that there is a circular structure to the E expansion and that bits from R that occur on line n also occur on lines $(n+1)$ and $(n-1)$ mod 8. This means that the lookup of all odd lines must occur in one copy of R (say A) and the lookup of even lines must occur in the other (B) so that overlapping bits of R may be salted differently. Salting constrains the data representation in yet another way. Because salt exchanges bits between lines 1 & 5, and lines 2 & 6, lines 1 & 5 must be read in a single lookup, as must lines 2 & 6. This also implies that lines 3 & 7 must be a single lookup, as must lines 4 & 8.

To minimize table size, lines 1 & 5, 2 & 6, 3 & 7, and 4 & 8 must be organized as blocks of 12 bits with no intervening bits. In addition, the circular structure of the E expansion requires that the bits for lines 8 and 2 be adjacent to those for line 1, lines 1 and 3 be adjacent to those for line 2, etc. One way to achieve this is to interleave the bits of the pairs of lines. Thus lines 1 & 5 are interleaved, lines 2 & 6 are interleaved, etc. Of course, interleaved lines 1 & 5 are adjacent to interleaved lines 4 & 8 and 2 & 6. Interleaving not only allows the correct adjacencies but also makes salting easy, since aligning the bits for comparison takes only a single shift.

Assume that the bits of a word are numbered such that 0 is the least significant bit and 31 is the most significant bit. The data representation for R starts with the first bit of line 1 in bit 2, the first bit of line 5 in bit 3 and so on, thus interleaving lines 1 and 5. This continues with lines 2 and 6. Notice that bit 10 represents not only the fifth bit of line 1 but also the first bit of line 2, and bit 11 represents the fifth bit of line 5 as well as the first bit of line 6. This pattern continues for lines 3 & 7 and 4 & 8. Notice that lines 4 & 8 wrap around the end of the word, and thus the fourth bit of line 4 is represented by bit 0. This is the 32-bit representation of R:

30	14	29	13	28	12	27	11	26	10	25	09	24	08	23	07	22	06	21	05	20	04	19	03	18	02	17	01	16	32	31	15

To get the 32-bit representation of L (which is not expanded), add 32 to each of the above numbers. Notice that lines 1 & 5 do not start immediately at the least significant bit; there are two extra bits in the least significant byte. This is because when doing pointer arithmetic, normally the value to be found in a table on a machine with a 32-bit (4 byte) word size would have to be multiplied by 4 before addition. In effect, the data representation above "premultiplies" by 4, thus saving an operation in a critical section of the code.

Now apply the mapping from R to ϵR for 1 & 5 and 3 & 7 (which have no overlapping bits in R) to obtain the representation of the 24 of the 48 bits in A (x denotes an unused position):

xx	xx	42	18	41	17	40	16	39	15	38	14	37	13	xx	xx	xx	xx	30	06	29	05	28	04	27	03	26	02	25	01	xx	xx

Now apply the mapping from R to ϵR for 2 & 6 and 4 & 8 (which have no overlapping bits in R) to obtain the representation of the 24 of the 48 bits in B:

45	21	44	20	43	19	xx	xx	xx	xx	36	12	35	11	34	10	33	09	32	08	31	07	xx	xx	xx	xx	24	48	23	47	46	22

A.2.5   Salting

Unlike other functions in crypt, such as E, S and P, the salt permutation is determined at runtime. Salting takes place in the 48-bit data path after the expansion function E and before the subkey is exclusive-ORed with the expanded R. The salt acts as an additional permutation after the E expansion, which can be either done separately or combined with other permutations. Because of the nature of the E expansion, complete salting cannot be done before E (although partial salting can). Let τ represent the salt permutation; then:

$$f_i R_{i-1} \equiv \pi\sigma(K_i \oplus \tau\epsilon R_{i-1})$$

If salting is done separately, then after the E expansion the appropriate bits are swapped according to the salt. For many keys to be encrypted with the same salt, *presalting* may be faster. Presalting involves combining the salt permutation with one or more of the table lookups at runtime before any encryption is done and then using these modified tables for encryption. Since in-line encryption uses one salt operation for each DES round, 400 salt operations are performed on each word. With enough encryptions, it is cheaper to use the salt to adjust each entry of the lookup tables appropriately.

The salting function is relatively fast. Because the salting operation is so regular, it is faster to compute it than to do a table lookup. Speed-crypt has a data representation such that the relative offsets of bits 1-12 is the same as that of bits 25-36, i.e. the distance between 1 and 2 is the same as the distance between 25 and 26, etc. This means that bits 1-12 can be aligned with bits 25-36 in a single operation.

The only bits that need be swapped are those that differ and this *delta bitmap* is computed by exclusive-ORing bits 1-12 with 25-36. Then the delta bitmap is logical-ANDed with the salt mask. The salt mask has a 1 in the positions where bits are to be salted and 0s elsewhere. This leaves a bitmap of those bits that differ and are supposed to be switched in the delta bitmap. This delta bitmap is then exclusive-ORed with bits 1-12 and 25-36, thus completing the salting operation.

Presalting is used exclusively for speed-crypt, since the crossover point for presalting versus in-line salting is only 10 words. Presalting involves altering lookup tables to eliminate the need to exchange bits after the E expansion. The only table lookup in speed-crypt is the SP table, which produces a 32-bit result. Sometimes bits that both can be salted after E appear as a single element in the 32-bit representation of R. This is a problem as the 32-bit element can salt the single bit one way, and perhaps have bits be swapped incorrectly for one of the two lookups. The solution is to reorder the entries of the SP table according to salt. By definition:

$$R_i \equiv L_{i-1} \oplus \pi\sigma(\kappa_i K \oplus \tau\epsilon R_{i-1})$$

Using the fact that $\tau\tau^{-1}$ is the identity permutation:

$$R_i = L_{i-1} \oplus \pi\sigma\tau\tau^{-1}(\kappa_i K \oplus \tau\epsilon R_{i-1})$$

Now distribute τ^{-1} across $\oplus$:

$$R_i = L_{i-1} \oplus \pi\sigma\tau(\tau^{-1}\kappa_i K \oplus \tau^{-1}\tau\epsilon R_{i-1})$$

Canceling $\tau^{-1}\tau$:

$$R_i = L_{i-1} \oplus \pi\sigma\tau(\tau^{-1}\kappa_i K \oplus \epsilon R_{i-1})$$

Because τ is its own inverse:

$$R_i = L_{i-1} \oplus \pi\sigma\tau(\tau\kappa_i K \oplus \epsilon R_{i-1})$$

The table entries have to be permuted or reordered, depending on whether the incorporated permutation is before or after the table.

$$\kappa_i(j) \leftarrow \tau(\kappa_i(j))$$

$$\pi\sigma_i \leftarrow \pi\sigma_{\tau(i)}$$

Thus all of the key table entries are salted with the usual salt function. SP table entries must be exchanged and this can be done quickly. If two bits to be salted are the same (when $i = \tau(i)$), then no exchange is necessary. Since $\tau = \tau^{-1}$, table entry $\pi\sigma_i$ can be swapped with entry $\pi\sigma_{\tau(i)}$ and no temporary storage is needed.

A.2.6 System Issues

Crypt runs DES 25 times and the basic round within DES is run 16 times for a total of 400 rounds. Anything that can be done to speed up this basic round will be multiplied by 400, so it is important that the rounds run efficiently.

In general it is best to keep the number of variables used by the crypt program small so that most of them can be kept in registers. On a fast processor, particularly those with caches, memory fetches slow down the system.

It is best to avoid instructions whenever possible. For example, with the SP table lookup, rather than logical-ORing the table entries together and then exclusive-ORing the result into the L register, it is faster to exclusive-OR the intermediate results into the L register directly, saving one instruction per round (400 instructions total).

For processors with a cache, the main DES rounds should be executed within a loop that is small enough to fit into a processor cache. The execution speedup achieved by the cache more than compensates for the running time of the extra loop instructions. Without a cache, the loop should be unwound so that the loop overhead is avoided. Speed-crypt has a compile-time option to structure the program appropriately depending on whether there is a cache.

Another important point is to take advantage of the processor instruction set, specifically whether the machine is a *Reduced Instruction Set Computer* (RISC) or a *Complex Instruction Set Computer* (CISC). Examples of RISC machines are the Sun 4 (SPARC processor) and the DEC 3100 (MIPS R2000 processor). Examples of CISC machines are the Sun 3 (68020 processor) and the VAX.

A useful feature of CISC processors is auto-increment mode. If possible, it is best to step through tables one element at a time so that auto-increment mode can be used. This is particularly useful for accessing the subkeys. The high and low words of the subkeys alternate and they are extracted one at a time with auto-increment mode. On a RISC machine, a separate addition must be done for each increment, so it does not matter what the step size is. Sometimes a different step size can lead to more efficient operation. Another feature of CISC processors are instructions specifically designed for efficient loops. In particular, it is faster to count down to zero with a single instruction that does the compare-decrement-branch function.

RISC machines generally contain a large number of registers and performance is enhanced if often-used constants are kept in registers. Large constants take two instructions to load into the processor rather than one (this is because the fixed-length RISC instructions can include only small constants).

Speed-crypt is written in C and should be portable with little trouble, although for some machines there are special cases inserted into the code. In particular, sometimes a compiler cannot be convinced to generate efficient assembly code for some portion of C code. An example of poorly generated code is the loop instructions. Compilers sometimes generate non-optimal loops, particularly for CISC processors, which often have good instructions for loops. One case where the compiler is not at fault is the lack of a bit rotation operator in C. Many processors have a bit rotation instruction, but the equivalent in C produces 3 assembly language instructions. In both of these cases there are compile time options to replace some portions of the C code directly with assemble language instructions for specific processors. Another possibility is to edit the assembly language that the compiler produces. Because the VAX compiler is reluctant to use all of the processor registers, speed-crypt on the VAX uses a SED (UNIX Stream EDitor) script that replaces certain memory references with register references in the assembly code.

A.3 Implementation Alternatives

Fast crypt implementations by Baldwin[1], Bishop[2] and Mitchell[8] each utilize most of the suggestions above. Fast DES implementations also use similar techniques[4]. Speed-crypt has a technique for the E expansion that can double the speed of an implementation on 32-bit RISC machines.

The *questor* code was written by Donald Mitchell at Bell Labs and is probably the most straight-forward of the fast crypt implementations[8]. Subkey generation uses two table lookups (Permuted Choice 1 and Permuted Choice 2) and two rotations per subkey. The E expansion is done as eight 64-bit table lookups (4 bits of R at a time). The S function and the P permutation are combined and eight 32-bit lookups are done (6 bits at a time). The swap of L and R occurs between DES rounds. The IP^{-1} lookup is also done 4 bits at a time. The version timed below has presalting, but the original version did in-line salting only. However, the code is well written and it runs quickly.

The implementations by both Baldwin and Bishop use a transformation of DES described by Davio[3]. The recurrence equation is rewritten so that the E expansion is combined with the S function and the P permutation; thus, only a single lookup table is needed for the DES rounds. An ϵ^{-1} function is needed at the end of the 25 DES encryptions, but this can be combined with the IP^{-1} table. The problem with this transformation is that the entire data path of the crypt function is 48-bits wide. This is not a problem on a machine that is 48-bits wide or wider, but it is on a machine with a smaller bus. This doubles the number of memory accesses for the SPE table because each 48-bit word requires two 32-bit fetches. The basic SPE table lookup requires 4 basic lookups, each of which has an 8 byte output, which means that each lookup requires two memory fetches on a 32-bit machine. Because memory fetches slow down the crypt program, speed-crypt executes faster because fewer (4) memory references are needed. The E expansion technique used for speed-crypt has little advantage over a combined SPE table for machines that are 64-bits wide or wider. For machines with smaller bus widths, the speed-crypt implementation should run about twice as fast.

Bob Baldwin wrote the *fdes* code at MIT[1]. The subkeys are computed in the standard way and he avoids the swap between DES rounds. His SPE lookups are done 6 bits at a time. Baldwin has other optimizations that are specific to his design and cannot be implemented in speed-crypt. The fdes program is designed to run well on a VAX. It runs very well on the VAX, but not as well on other machines.

Matt Bishop wrote his *deszip* code at Dartmouth College and the Research Institute for Advanced Computer Science[2]. The code has a variety of options to allow various speed/size tradeoffs. Keys can be computed either the standard way or with a permutation per subkey as speed-crypt does. The SPE lookups can be done 6 or 12 bits at a time. It is also sophisticated about taking advantage of the machine architecture to improve its speed.

A.4 Speed Measurements

Machine	User Time (Seconds)	System Time (Seconds)	Total Time (Seconds)	Crypts per Second	Milliseconds per Crypt
DEC 3100	96.5	1.4	97.9	1089.5	0.92
Sun 3/50	395.2	3.6	398.8	267.5	3.74
Sun 3/60	276.9	7.5	284.4	375.0	2.67
Sun 3/75	343.3	1.1	344.4	309.7	3.23
Sun 3/160	345.1	7.3	352.4	302.7	3.30
Sun 3/200	229.6	1.9	231.5	460.7	2.17
Sun 4/280	101.4	0.8	102.2	1043.6	0.96
VAX 8650	273.2	2.4	275.6	387.0	2.58

Table 5: Speed-Crypt Speeds on Various Machines

Person	Version	Year	DEC 3100	Sun 3/50	Sun 4/280	VAX 11/780
UNIX	bsd 4.2	?	18.8	2.6	16.7	1.4
Baldwin	fdes 5	?	176.9	23.8	123.0	38.2
Mitchell	questor	1984	238.5	31.3	190.3	19.1
Bishop	deszip	1987		71.5		23.9
Feldmeier	speed	1989	1089.5	267.5	1043.6	58.8

Table 6: Crypt Times of Various Implementations

The timings of the speed-crypt implementation are shown in table 5; the length of the test dictionary is 106,661 words. Table 6 shows the speed of the various crypt implementations on a variety of machines. The reason that implementations by others do not speed up as well when they are moved to a RISC machine is that they do many table lookups. The speed-crypt program is larger, but the number of table lookups is smaller, thus allowing it to run faster on a RISC machine. Also, Baldwin's fdes program is optimized for the VAX, not the Sun, so it may not have ported well. Notice that fdes runs 3.2 times faster on the Sun 4 than on the VAX 11/780, while speed-crypt runs 17.7 times faster.

A.5   Conclusion

This appendix describes the implementation of a high-speed crypt program written in C. It discusses how the crypt algorithm works and how it can be modified for higher speed. Implementation decisions and programming tricks for high speed are also discussed. It is worth pointing out that no real breakthroughs were required for the results obtained. What was required is a good understanding of the algorithm and of the computer systems on which it is implemented. The most unique part of the implementation is the unique bit order used in the 48-bit wide product transformation that allows fast E expansion, fast SP table lookup and salting without manipulation of individual bits. Of course, many of the ideas presented in this paper are applicable to software implementations of DES and other product ciphers.

The fastest crypt implementation is 102.9 times faster than the crypt in 4.2 Berkeley UNIX on a Sun 3/50. In absolute speed, the fastest crypt does 1089.5 crypt per second on a DEC 3100.

Practical Problems with a Cryptographic Protection Scheme

Jonathan M. Smith

Distributed Systems Laboratory
Department of Computer and Information Science
University of Pennsylvania
Philadelphia, PA 19104-6389

ABSTRACT

Z is a software system designed to provide media-transparent network services on a collection of UNIX® machines. These services are comprised of file transfer and command execution; Z preserves file ownership on remote transfer, and more significantly, owner and group identity when executing commands remotely. In order to secure known vulnerabilities in the system, enhancements were made. In particular, a cryptographically-derived checksum was added to the messages. After the initial implementation of the checksumming scheme, several iterations of performance improvement occurred. The result was unsatisfactory to the user community, so the checksum was removed. Instead, vulnerabilities were reduced by improved monitoring and maintenance procedures.

1. Introduction

1.1. History

Z was initially implemented *circa* 1978 in order to cope with an ever-increasing number of UNIX systems at a large industrial computation center. The environment was becoming unmanageable; unmanageable in the sense that it was difficult to administer the systems in a controlled and consistent manner. It was clear that some mechanism which allowed a user to operate in a true multi-system environment was necessary. However, there was no consistent network organization. There were a variety of subnetworks of various reliabilities and bandwidths, these included bus-to-bus, channel-to-channel, and synchronous remote job entry (RJE) links. RJE served as a fully-connected network (albeit a slow one) as all systems were connected to some mainframe system for various services, e.g., bulk printing. The Network Systems Corporation HYPERChannel™ bus is a very high speed (*circa* 50Mbits/sec) device that allows machines to be interconnected in a local area network. In late 1981, an NSC HYPERchannel began to connect all the systems, and due to its bandwidth, became the primary media for **Z** communication. **Z** provided an easy to use and uniform interface to the network; the physical media used in the transport is transparent to the user. Use of the media was optimized by a statically-calculated bandwidth-weighted best-path selection scheme coupled with dynamically-calculated reliability data.

1.2. Architecture

Z is viewed by a large segment of its user population as a UNIX command with which they accomplish various tasks across several computing systems. In actuality, **Z** is a large collection of both loosely and tightly coupled cooperating software modules, distributed across all machines on the network. The command invocation is the first link in a long chain of events.

The **Z** command line syntax specifies file transfer or remote execution. The standard input of the local **Z** execution can be used to provide input for the remote command. The **Z** semantics preserve user ids on the remote system, both for file permissions and command execution. One or more systems can be specified as destinations, and aliasing is available for compact naming of subsets of the available systems.

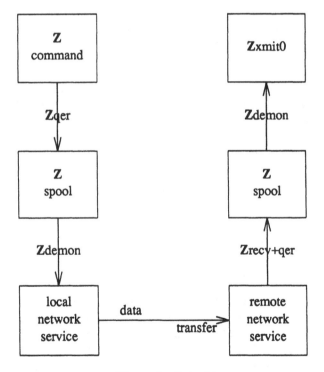

Figure 1: **Z** Architecture

The **Z** system provides facilities for examining queued jobs, retrying jobs when failures occur, removing corrupted files, notifying senders upon error or job completion, and secondary routing on link failure. Various internal machine-to-machine interfaces were devised to mask incompatibilities between heterogeneous processor families.

The basic architecture of the system is illustrated in figure 1.

1.2.1. Local Actions

The **Z** command serves as a gateway to the lower level transport layers of the system. It "packetizes" the data to be transported, storing such information as can only be gathered at invocation time, such as the current directory and identity of the invoking user. If a file name was given as an argument, **Z** ensures that the file is accessible, and saves other information, such as the file's ownership, the access permissions, and the file size in characters. Also on the command line can be a list of one or more destination systems; some validity checking is done on these names. **Z** can also take a command string as an argument.

Based on the arguments and the identity information, **Z** builds a header, which is used by other modules. Any data to be transmitted is then appended to the header. The bound data "packet" is passed to a "gatekeeping" module, **Zqer**. **Zqer** is invoked as the last action of the **Z** command with the *exec()* system call. It takes the formed data packet and enqueues it in a known spool directory, where the transport control module, **Zdemon**, will find it when woken by a signal from **Zqer**. **Zqer** contains knowledge of a spooling directory, spooling and sequencing protocols, and interprocess communication procedures. Since these actions are required both by local invocations of **Z** and by the remote receiving node, good software engineering suggested a common module.

Zdemon is a process which constantly waits for an event to occur: this event is the signal that **Zqer** sends to it, alerting it to the fact that there is work to do. When there are no files to process in its spool directory, it remains in an idle state, waiting on an "event", the "signal" sent to it by the **Zqer** process. When **Zdemon** receives this signal, it scans the known spool directory, looking for the work which should have just appeared. When started by a command line, or when woken by an *alarm* signal or a signal from **Zqer**, **Zdemon** searches the well-known directory where invocations of **Zqer** have placed the packetized data.

Zdemon examines the header information of the enqueued packet to determine its next action. If the packet is to be processed locally, a **Zxmit0** is spawned. The **Zxmit0** carries out the local action; it is given the file as a parameter, and determines how to process it from the enqueued header.

If the packet is to be passed on to another node, the **Zdemon** selects a transmission medium. A transmission route to the destination system is selected, and based on this route, some lower level transport mechanism is used by *fork()* -ing a **Zxmit** sub-process of the appropriate flavor. The **Zxmit** job manages the details of transporting the packet to the remote system and ensures its correct receipt. It uses the underlying transport mechanism both to actually transmit the data and to perform certain actions at the destination. Among these actions is the execution of a copy of the program **Zrecv**.

1.2.2. Remote Actions

All of the transport mechanisms which the Z system uses provide at least a minimal form of remote command execution. When a Z job arrives at a destination UNIX machine, it generates a Zrecv process. Zrecv executes Zqer to let Zdemon know that there is work to be done. Since this is now a "local" job, Zdemon executes Zxmit0 to carry out the specified action. Effectively, Zrecv serves as a "friend" to the traveling process: it appears as if Zrecv is a local-to-local invocation of Z, requested on behalf of the remote (sending) machine. This design is modular and elegant; job-handling is correct with respect to local or remote destinations, while being ignorant, for the most part, of the details.

The details of transmission are handled by Zxmit modules, which prepare a message for transmission over their respective media, and proceed to carry out the transmission. All of these modules must provide some mechanism for invoking the Zrecv module on the remote system once the data/ command packet has arrived.

These modules are perhaps the lowest "layer" of the Z architecture, since unlike the others, they have to concern themselves with details of the communications link, such as file size limitations. In most cases, the Zmit modules merely invoke commands which are provided as part of a link's operational subsystem. If the RJE medium is used, intermediary, non-UNIX system "hops" may have to be made.

So that Z can maintain user id's across systems, several modules must possess super-user (unlimited file access) privileges. While passive interception is potentially dangerous, as it provides *information,* we were rather more concerned with active interlopers; those who intend to *modify* data and/or commands.

1.3. Security Problems

In 1983, we became concerned about the security of Z, and immediately recognized several potential vulnerabilities. These stemmed from several architectural features, as can be gleaned from figure 1. The fact that the system preserves user identity is the major reason for a security threat. First, the ability to execute commands remotely means that a breakin on one system can be extended to others. Second, the complete interconnectivity provided by Z meant that a breakin on one system could be extended to all of the machines. If a Z packet could be modified enroute to its destination, then the user id or any message contents could be set to interesting values. Thus, the points of vulnerability [8] were those which had the potential for message alteration.

First, the spool had to be kept secure, or otherwise files with arbitrary contents could be written. Second, the local network services had to be kept secure. This was more of a problem than it appeared; these systems often spooled jobs internally, and their access-control strategies were not easy to change. To verify the claims we made about the lack of security inherent in the system, we obtained root permissions from an ordinary account. This was done through altering a file spooled by the RJE mechanism. The file resided in the UNIX spool for about 0.5 second, and was enciphered with a simple modification of a Caesar scheme. Unfortunately, the software preserved user ownership of the spooled file, so that a user could modify the file. This was necessary due to the design of the RJE software. Breaking the cipher was trivial, and by repeatedly sending messages and polling, a file was captured, modified, and transmitted to its (unsuspecting!) destination. Simply protecting this spool directory and modifying the RJE software was insufficient; the RJE jobs were spooled on the mainframe as well, where we could not guarantee security.

2. A Server-based solution

After studying the problem, we came to some conclusions:

1. While administrative control was not completely ours (as was the case with intermediate mainframe systems) the system was at risk.

2. We were far less interested in protecting against traffic analysis than in protecting against modification.

3. Sending enciphered messages was undesirable for several reasons, including (1) recovery from errors, (2) use of intermediate nodes needing source and destination data, and (3) system status reporting.

4. In addition, requirements were that the user interface could not change, e.g., by requesting a password.

After examining the literature on data security [2, 5] we decided that the right approach was to use a cryptographic *checksum* in order to detect data modification. The checksum is computed by encrypting the data and then computing a checksum from the encrypted text. Thus, the messages could be sent in cleartext, with a checksum prepended to the header. Modifications could be detected, and modified messages discarded. The improved error-detection was a byproduct. Since changes to either the header (uids) or the message (binaries for system programs) were dangerous, the entire packet had to be involved in the checksum. The initial implementation used a 32-bit checksum.

A variety of encipherment schemes were examined, and experimental implementations were done to evaluate the performance of the schemes. Even after implementation in assembly language, a cryptosystem using large primes consumed unacceptable amounts of CPU time, even for very short strings. DES [4, 5] was examined, but once again the throughput of the implementation was insufficient. While it is clear that DES is intended to be implemented in hardware, the chips available at the time were expensive and slow. In addition, we had three architectures to contend with, and kernel changes would have been necessary. We sped up the UNIX library implementation of DES by a factor of 3 using hand-optimized code and small assembly-language routines. Recent research [1] indicates that speedups up to a factor of 20 or more can be accomplished by applying some mathematical sophistication in the software implementation. Our speedup reduced the CPU time required for encrypting a one megabyte file from about 2340 seconds on an AT&T 3B20S^{TM} (the 3B20S is roughly comparable to a DEC VAX^{TM} 11/780) to about 830 seconds. Execution of a simple command which counts the characters in a file requires about 5 seconds of CPU time, so the contribution of file reading code is low. Considerable computation was necessary to convert byte-oriented files to bitstreams of one bit per character. Use of techniques such as cipher-block chaining would slow an implementation down further.

Bishop's factor of 20 speedup should reduce this time to about 120 seconds of CPU time. Unfortunately, **Z** was often used for transfer of files which were up to a megabyte in size, and response times (comprised of CPU times and delays caused by scheduling, processor sharing, and I/O) measured in minutes were unacceptable. We finally decided that a modification of the UNIX *crypt* command would be the best solution. Even though *crypt* has recently been shown to be insecure, the rotor ciphers, once set up, allow extremely rapid encipherment to take place. While our work preceded Reeds and Weinberger's [7], we seem to have anticipated some of the elements of their approach; we varied the rotor-shifting steps in a password- dependent way in order to frustrate analysis of blocks of text for which one of the rotors remains fixed.

Since we were convinced that encryption technology would improve, we wanted to add the encipherment to the system in such a way that new solutions, e.g., DES chips, could be incorporated easily.

2.1. Encryption Server

The change in the architecture is illustrated in figure 2.

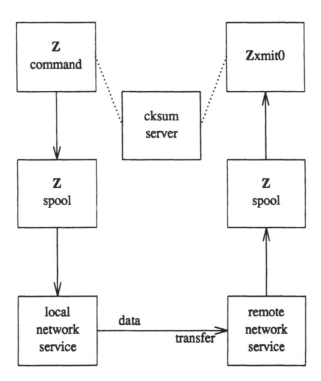

Figure 2: **Z** Architecture with checksum server

The server was passed a filename argument using a secure FIFO queue. The filename was for the packet which **Z** had just gathered. Insertion in the queue by a process woke the server, which enciphered the file, computed the checksum, and passed back the result to the calling process. The passwords were per-system, stored in a secure file, which the server checked frequently for modification. The passwords were encrypted using DES [6], and served as seeds to the rotor generation for the Enigma-clone. If the file hadn't changed, the encryption was cached, for performance reasons. It's clear that a public-key system would have been more effective for this task, but the available systems performed too poorly.

The idea of the server architecture was to emulate the semantics of a remote procedure call. In this way, the server process could be transparently replaced by another server process with the same functionality which used hardware encryption or other tricks to get better response times.

2.2. Problems

The basic design of the server was well thought out, and in another systems environment, may still be the right way to go, because the advantages in terms of software engineering are manifold, e.g. modularity, information-hiding, et cetera. Unfortunately, encryption is a CPU-intensive activity; hence, the UNIX system scheduler assigns the server process lower and lower priority as time goes on, and it becomes "slower" with respect to response time. Improved scheduling technology could remedy this problem, but it was neither available nor administratively desirable, except for our application's use.

Since the process (**Z**) waiting for a reply (the checksum) cannot assume that the server is up, it can time out on the write to the server's request queue, using the *alarm()* facility. While it can retry, if the server is sufficiently slow the request may not be serviced "in time". If this occurs, the packetizing software will assume server failure and therefore fail to packetize the request. On the other hand, if timeouts are not facilitated, the software may appear to be so slow that users will find alternate means of data transport. For large files and a busy server, the response times were measured in minutes.

In addition, the server proved to be an administrative nightmare: it was hard to understand without a great deal of expertise in encipherment, systems programming, and network software; it created "mysterious" files when it wasn't keeping up with the request queueing rate; and it was dependent on the sanity of several files. Consequently, a re-design was done which preserved most of the positive features of the server design, while improving response time and reducing administrative effort.

3. Re-design, no server

The major goal of the redesign effort was (initially) to increase the reliability of the server process, and hence reduce the administrative effort. After a painstaking analysis of the alternatives, it was decided that the server module should be removed and the encryption services be provided by in-line code rather than interprocess communication. While on the one hand, the burden of performing a DES encryption on the cleartext password could not be shared between users of a server, the following were true:

- A small data transfer would not be penalized in real-time response for following a large data transfer in the request queue. (The large transfer would cause an external server to accumulate a large amount of CPU time, thus penalizing it in the scheduling discipline.)

- The DES encryption is not necessary, provided that any cleartext password is encrypted before being put into a secured file.

- Per system passwords were eliminated, as this proved to be of little use in practice. One password is used for all systems on a Z network; eliminating a system would then require changing the password on all machines except the one to be cut off.

- While re-engineered to be robust, the interprocess communication was complex, and slow in response time. Putting the code in-line permitted several optimizations, which led to significant performance improvements, a factor of 3 to 5.

The necessary code to perform checksumming and encrypting of file contents was moved inline. The *Pack()* and *UnPack()* calls were designed so that callers would be ignorant of their methodology; this proved to be true in practice, as not one line of the calling modules had to be re-coded to reflect the fact that the server had been eliminated. The interprocess communication code was eliminated and the *CheckSum()* call made directly. The encryption algorithm was modified to remove a reflecting rotor from the encipherment process, thus removing a memory access and two arithmetic operations from the process of encrypting a byte. This was done without reducing the cryptographic strength of the algorithm, as the reflecting rotor mainly aids decipherment. The checksumming routine was also re-coded for greater efficiency; the net result was that Z required about 20 seconds of CPU time to queue a 1 megabyte file on an AT&T 3B-20S. A command line (no file access) requires a little more than a second of CPU on the same machine. The additional CPU overhead in each invocation is therefore directly proportional to the resource utilization of the request: this seemed fair. Unfortunately, much Z use is administrative, and a traffic analysis showed that the average packet size was about 100K bytes, implying about 2 seconds of response time penalty for using encryption. We felt that this was acceptable, but extensive testing with the user community raised vocal complaints. Thinking these spurious, we surveyed the user community, and concluded that the encryption feature, weakened as it was through:

1. Lack of public key technology,

2. Use of a cipher system known to be breakable, and

3. Increasing dependence on protected files,

was no longer viable.

4. Conclusions

There were several benefits which accrued from our work. The rewriting of the software resulted in a more robust, readable, and elegant system. Various dangling pointer errors were corrected, and buffer size checks were added; this serves to remove other obscure security problems. The desire for end-to-end encryption, or something close, led to a complete, and better redesign for the packet header; it was re-encoded entirely in ASCII. This resulted in better portability in a heterogeneous machine environment. The calls to the encryption routines were commented out of the source code, a total of 4 lines of "C"; no other modifications were necessary. Several utility programs had either been inappropriately placed in the directory hierarchy or gave inappropriate levels of privilege to users. These were changed.

Administrative rigor was applied to reduce the security threat. Vulnerable directories were checked carefully for permissions; they are now monitored on a regular basis. As newer networking technologies are phased in, the old methods, such as RJE, which used potentially unsafe intermediary nodes, are being phased out. Careful administration is used [3] at present to prevent surprises.

Our application points out some of the serious problems with applying cryptographic technology in practice. First, while a cryptographic checksum is the obvious solution, it was clearly an afterthought, and had to be added to an existing architecture. Second, the uses of the system can put severe performance constraints on an otherwise workable system. Our problem was the relatively frequent transfer of large data files, and the demands of timesharing users for good response times. We tried to cure this by weakening the cryptographic checksum scheme, but the results were unacceptable, so security is maintained primarily by administrative vigilance.

However, when the networking technologies such as Ethernet^{TM} are broadcast media, "promiscuous-listeners", and more seriously, "modifiers", start to resurface as an issue. Thus, the increased computational cost of creating a system with a higher cryptographic "work factor" begins to seem more reasonable. The economics of cost/performance might justify special-purpose hardware, e.g., for DES encipherment. The tradeoffs between security and response-time should be examined carefully, and frequently.

In particular, a useful and productive area of research would be one which resulted in a set of curves which related cryptographic strength to some useful performance metric. One such metric, alluded to in this paper, is the number of arithmetic operations required per byte of a large file. The analysis represented by the performance curve allows a system designer to compare systems and select an appropriate system for the application. Without such analysis, most cryptographic work is likely to remain of interest mainly to mathematicians; practical work requires getting the details right.

5. Notes

® UNIX is a Registered Trademark of AT&T Bell Laboratories.

3B20 is a trademark of AT&T.

VAX is a trademark of Digital Equipment Corporation.

HYPERChannel is a trademark of Network Systems Corporation.

Ethernet is a trademark of Xerox Corporation.

6. References

[1] Matt Bishop, "An Application of a Fast Data Encryption Standard Implementation," *Computing Systems* **1**(3), pp. 221-254 (1988).

[2] D.R. Denning, *Cryptography and Data Security,* Addison-Wesley (1982).

[3] F. T. Grampp and R. H. Morris, "UNIX Operating System Security," *AT&T Bell Laboratories Technical Journal* **63**(8, Part 2), pp. 1649-1672 (October 1984).

[4] A. G. Konheim, *Cryptography: A Primer,* Wiley-Interscience, New York (1981).

[5] C. Meyer and S. Matyas, *Cryptography: A New Dimension in Computer Data Security,* Wiley-Interscience (1982).

[6] R. Morris and K. Thompson, "UNIX Password Security," *Communications of the ACM* **22**, pp. 594-597 (November 1979).

[7] J. A. Reeds and P. J. Weinberger, "File Security and the UNIX System Crypt command," *AT&T Bell Laboratories Technical Journal* **63**(8, Part 2), pp. 1673-1684 (October 1984).

[8] D. M. Ritchie, "On the Security of UNIX," in *UNIX Programmer's Manual, Section 2* (1983). AT&T Bell Laboratories

THE SMART DISKETTE
A UNIVERSAL USER TOKEN AND PERSONAL CRYPTO-ENGINE
- Paul Barrett and Raymund Eisele -

1. Security and Personal Computers

It is becoming increasingly common for large, distributed systems to utilise personal computers (PC's) for the purpose of user access, and hence the security arrangements for such an access point have become a focus of attention in systems security design. Generally speaking the functional requirements of a PC security sub-system are as follows:-

(i)   Identity verification of the user, for controlling access both to resources within the local PC workstation and to remote teleprocessing services on other machines.

(ii)   File encryption at the PC for secure storage.

(iii)   Message encryption and message authentication for secure communications.

(iv)   Digital signatures for proof of origin of communications and for data and software certification.

2. A Token-based Solution

In general the solution to this set of requirements must include a user token of some description [1] to provide a method for verifying the personal identity of the user. For identity verification the user must be in possession of the token and be able to supply the password which is verified on the token. There are several good examples of how this has been achieved on stand-alone tokens [2] [3]. To prevent "Trojan Horse" software on the PC from capturing passwords, the token should have its own keypad and display for direct password entry.

Once the token has authenticated its user it may then act as
the agent of that user, performing encryption, decryption and
key management as required to achieve file security, message
security and digital signatures [4].   In this case it
therefore needs a machine-readable interface with the PC,
preferably one which is widely available as a standard feature
without the addition of expensive, extra equipment.

The ideal token must also be user-friendly, highly reliable,
portable and secure, as well as being a low-cost component
that can easily be supplied to each user on a personal basis.
This implies a small size, a method for self-powering,
programmability for multiple applications, fast RSA [5] [6]
processing to implement digital signatures and crypto-key
management, tamper-resistance [7] to protect stored
cryptographic keys and high-performance in its data-transfer
and processing to provide acceptable response times.

These requirements are to some extent met by the "super smart
card" [8], i.e. a smart card with an added keypad and display;
although the size restrictions imposed by copying the form of
the ISO standard magnetic card cause problems with processing
power, reliability and user friendliness. The "intelligent
token" developed by the National Physical Laboratory (NPL) in
the UK comes closer to meeting the ideal specification but
falls short in two critical areas, namely connectivity and
data throughput.

In fact, with all tokens currently available there exist
serious deficiences in respect of a low-cost, universally
available, machine-readable interface, and in respect of a
self-powered device with the sort of processing power that can
deliver a 512-bit RSA decryption in less than one second. If
the solution does not at present exist among the multitude of
smart cards available on the market, what might it look like?
The answer is - a SMART DISKETTE!

3. The Smart Diskette Solution

Consider the following:-

(i)   The smart diskette is identical in size to the industry standard 3.5 inch diskette. Hence it plugs directly into all PC's that have a diskette drive of that size.

(ii)   It isn't really a diskette at all, but a solid state device with a set of coils and magnets which emulate the magnetic field of a rotating diskette. Hence the reading and writing of data is carried out by the PC exactly as if it were a normal diskette.

(iii)   The smart diskette is physically large enough to embed a considerable number of powerful IC's, thus overcoming the memory and processing restrictions imposed by conventional smart card packages. Also there is plenty of space for a usable key-pad and display. Furthermore, reliability issues are considerably easier to resolve within a diskette sized package than with a smart card sized one.

(iv)   As well as fulfilling the role of an identity verification token which can be carried in a shirt pocket, the smart diskette is powerful enough to provide all of the encryption functions normally put into a PC on an add-on circuit board, including the provision of high-performance RSA public key cryptography.

(v)   Self-powering is a combination of back-up batteries and an on-board generator driven by the disk-drive rotor. Furthermore the size of the unit allows for the power dissipation required with present-day technologies to support the performance of this device.

(vi)   Any PC with a 3.5 inch drive can be "secured" by plugging in an appropriate version of the smart

77

diskette. Since software can be loaded through the
diskette drive for execution on the PC, full control
over the PC can be taken by the smart diskette. It
has an enormous potential for those who wish to
distribute software which is truly copy-protected.

4. Implementing the Smart Diskette

The diagram below shows the schematic block diagram for the
circuitry of the smart diskette:

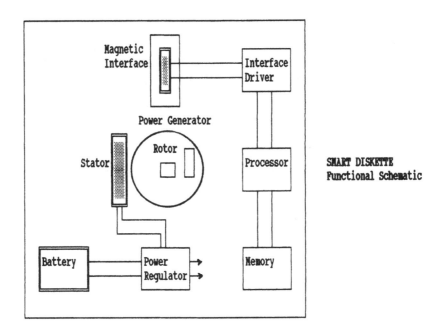

At first sight it may seem that the main area of difficulty
in the development of a smart diskette device would be the
magnetic interface since most of the other components exist
already at least in a form similar to that required.   (For
example, the processor, memory and other logic components
could be produced using standard silicon with hybrid or VLSI
manufacturing techniques).   However, even the magnetic

interface is nothing more complicated than a disk-drive read/write head albeit in a different shaped and sized form. Likewise, the logic to drive the interface will be very similar, if not identical, to that found in a standard disc-drive controller chip.

On reflection, we may conclude that the biggest challenge facing the implementors of the diskette is the design and development of a device which is suitable for high-volume, low-cost, mass production to meet a quality standard which ensures maximum reliability.

In emphasising the hardware aspects of the device, one is not overlooking the software development requirements. Considerable effort will need to go into the design of a general purpose operating system which includes the basic security functionality. However, with the high level of performance available from the hardware, the software should not present as demanding a challenge as that presented by the present alternative of smart-card, reader and/or PC-crypto-board combination.

5. Conclusions

The original smart card concept was an extension of the ISO mag-stripe banking card; the size was an important consideration when integrating the new device into an existing network of card-readers on cash-machines and point-of-sale terminals and, more importantly, into consumers' wallets. Once we consider a token that is for wide applicability in an existing population of PC's, it is sensible to reconsider the issues of compatibility and integration. Putting smart cards onto PCs is an expensive and awkward business, which fails to give the level of performance that is really needed. The logical solution is the one which we have shown meets a very broad spectrum of requirements - the smart diskette.

References:

[1] Sherwood J. R. and Gallo V. A., "The application of smart cards for RSA digital signatures in a network comprising both interactive and store-and-forward facilities", Proc. of Crypto 88, Springer-Verlag, 1988.

[2] Wong R., Berson T. and Feiertag R., "Polonius: An identity authentication system", Proc. of IEEE symposium on secrecy and privacy, 1985.

[3] Eisele R., "Host access security", presented at Interact 86, Orlando, Florida, 1986.

[4] Sherwood J. R., "Digital signature schemes using smart cards", Proc. of Smart Card 88, London, 1988.

[5] Rivest R., Shamir A. and Adleman L., "A method of obtaining digital signatures and public key cryptosystems", Comm. of ACM, Vol 21, No.2 Feb 1978.

[6] Barrett P. D., "Implementing the RSA public key encryption scheme on a digital signal processor", Proc. of Crypto 86, Springer-Verlag, 1986.

[7] Clark A. J., "Physical protection of cryptographic devices", Eurocrypt 87, Amsterdam, 1987.

[8] Chorley, G.J., & Price W.L. "An intelligent token for secure transactions", Pro IFIP/Sec '86, Monte Carlo December 1986 pp 442-450.

On the Quadratic Spans of Periodic Sequences[1]

Agnes Hui Chan[2]
Richard A. Games
The MITRE Corporation, Bedford MA 01730

1. Introduction

Random binary sequences are required in many applications of modern communication systems and in designing reliable circuits. However, truly random sequences are often associated with extremely high costs, and are therefore infeasible to use. Deterministically generated sequences that pass certain statistical tests suggested by random sequences are often used instead and are referred to as *pseudorandom* sequences. In applications involving, for instance, secure or spread spectrum communications, it is essential that these pseudorandom sequences be unpredictable. This paper addresses the problem of predicting the terms of a pseudorandom sequence from some initial portion of the sequence. A good introduction to the issues involved in this area can be found in [7].

Sequences that are generated deterministically by a finite-state machine must ultimately be periodic, and as such, can be generated by a simple feedback shift register (FSR) whose length is long enough to contain the terms of the sequence up to the point where they start to repeat. This pure cycling FSR has a single tap at the point corresponding to the initial point of the periodic part of the sequence, which will be the first stage of the shift register only if there is no initial acyclic part.

If the period is extremely long, this pure cycling FSR is impractical, but there will usually be much shorter FSRs that can be used to generate the sequence. These shorter FSRs will have more general feedback functions, Boolean functions defined on the states of the register. The length of a shortest FSR that generates the sequence is called the *span* of the sequence. Determining the span and an associated Boolean feedback function is difficult because of the nonlinearities involved.

Because of its tractability, most attention has been focused on determining the *linear span* of a sequence—the length of the shortest linear FSR that generates the sequence. If the linear span of a sequence is small, then the feedback function that defines the linear FSR can be determined easily using the Berlekamp-Massey algorithm [6]. Once the feedback function is determined, the remainder of the sequence can be easily generated.

A sequence with very large linear span may be generated by a much shorter FSR if nonlinear terms are allowed in the feedback function. The case of additional quadratic terms $s_i s_{i+j}$ is considered in this paper, since it is the most computationally tractable nonlinear case. The *quadratic span* of a periodic sequence is defined to be the length of the shortest length quadratic FSR that generates the sequence. For example, the periodic sequence $s = \overline{000101101011110001011101}\ldots$ of period 15 has linear span 14, but this sequence is generated by a quadratic FSR of length 4, and in this case, the span and the quadratic span both equal 4.

---

[1]This work was supported by the United States Air Force's Electronic Systems Division under Contract F19628-86-C-0001 and the MITRE-Sponsored Research Program.

[2]A. H. Chan is also with the College of Computer Science, Northeastern University, Boston, MA 02115.

The complexity of binary sequences formed using nonlinear functions has been studied previously in [3], [5], [7], and [8]. These authors have considered sequences obtained by applying nonlinear feedforward functions to the contents of one or more linear FSR's. Their results concern only the linear spans of these nonlinear feedforward sequences. The quadratic spans of this class of sequences have not been analyzed.

The quadratic span of a sequence can be determined by solving certain structured systems of linear equations. Determining the linear span of a sequence also involves solving certain structured systems of linear equations. The Berlekamp-Massey algorithm reduces the complexity of solving the systems involved in the linear case. Updating procedures similar to those used in the Berlekamp-Massey algorithm can only sometimes be applied to the quadratic case. We present an algorithm based on Gaussian elimination for calculating the quadratic span. It is still an open problem whether the special structure of the matrix in the quadratic case can be used to decrease the complexity of this algorithm. We do present a useful result concerning the increase in the quadratic span when an existing linear FSR fails to generate a particular term in a sequence. This is a partial generalization to the quadratic case of theorem 1 of [6].

In addition to obtaining a more efficient algorithm, another important result would be to assess further the predictability of a particular class of sequences by determining their quadratic spans. In this paper, we focus on de Bruijn sequences. The de Bruijn sequences of span n are the sequences of maximum period 2^n generated by nonlinear FSR's of length n. There have been a number of new algorithms proposed for generating large numbers of de Bruijn sequences of span n. The problem of determining the quadratic spans of de Bruijn sequences of span n was introduced in [2]. The linear span of a de Bruijn sequence of span n is greater than half of its period [1], and it has been observed empirically (through $n = 6$) that the vast majority of de Bruijn sequences have linear spans nearly equal to the upper bound of one less than the period.

For the case of quadratic spans of de Bruijn sequences, the situation appears to be quite different. In this paper, we determine a new upper bound on the quadratic span of de Bruijn sequences of span n. We show that the quadratic spans of de Bruijn sequences of span n are bounded above by $2^n - 1 - \binom{n}{2}$, and show that this bound is achieved by de Bruijn sequences obtained from adding the 0 state to maximum-period linear sequences of period $2^n - 1$. It is easy to see that a lower bound for this case is $n + 1$, but we conjecture that a lower bound for $n > 3$ is in fact $n + 2$.

The distributions of quadratic spans for the de Bruijn sequences through span 6 are calculated by computer, correcting and extending the results of [2]. The situation for $n = 6$ is displayed graphically in figure 1, where the linear span distribution may be seen to be concentrated near the linear span upper bound of 63, while the quadratic span distribution is concentrated around 11. The problem of determining the quadratic span distribution of de Bruijn sequences remains open.

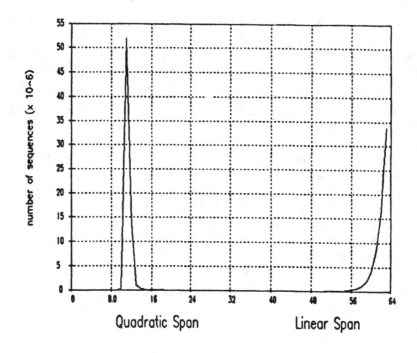

**Figure 1. Linear and Quadratic Span Distribution for
de Bruijn Sequences of Span 6**

2. Definitions and Main Results

In this section, we state without proof the main results of this paper. We first give the necessary definitions. All the sequences we consider have terms in GF(2). Most of the equations and expressions discussed will be over GF(2) unless otherwise stated.

An n-stage FSR with feedback function $f\colon \text{GF}(2)^n \to \text{GF}(2)$ generates a sequence $s = (s_0, s_1, \ldots, s_i, \ldots)$ where $s_0, s_1, \ldots, s_{n-1}$ corresponds to the initial loading and

$$s_{i+n} = f(s_i, s_{i+1}, \ldots, s_{i+n-1}), \quad i \geq 0 \tag{1}$$

The function f in (1) is *linear* if there exist $a_0, a_1, \ldots, a_{n-1}$ in GF(2) such that for all $(x_0, x_1, \ldots, x_{n-1}) \in \text{GF}(2)^n$,

$$f(x_0, x_1, \ldots, x_{n-1}) = \sum_{j=0}^{n-1} a_j x_j.$$

The function f is *quadratic* if there exists $a_{j,k}$, $0 \leq j \leq k \leq n-1$ in GF(2) such that for all $(x_0, x_1, \ldots, x_{n-1}) \in$ GF$(2)^n$,

$$f(x_0, x_1, \ldots, x_{n-1}) = \sum_{j=0}^{n-1} \sum_{k=j}^{n-1} a_{j,k} x_j x_k. \tag{2}$$

Note that $x_j x_j = x_j$ in GF(2); for simplicity we sometimes denote $a_{j,j}$ by a_j. Note this definition implies that $f(0) = 0$. A more general quadratic feedback function could include a constant term. As in [2], we consider the case of no constant term. The generalized results for the constant term case will be reported in the full paper. Higher-order feedback functions are defined in a similar fashion.

A sequence generated by an n-stage FSR, but not an $(n-1)$-stage FSR, is said to have *span n*. *Linear span* and *quadratic span* are defined similarly for FSR's with linear and quadratic feedback functions. The span, quadratic span, and linear span of a sequence **s** will be denoted respectively by $sp(\mathbf{s})$, $q(\mathbf{s})$, and $l(\mathbf{s})$. By definition,

$$sp(\mathbf{s}) \leq q(\mathbf{s}) \leq l(\mathbf{s}).$$

The above notions of span apply to finite sequences as well. Given a sequence $\mathbf{s} = (s_0, s_1, \ldots, s_i, \ldots)$, we denote any finite subsequence of length N starting at s_i by $\mathbf{s}_i^N$, that is,

$$\mathbf{s}_i^N = (s_i, s_{i+1}, \ldots, s_{i+N-1}).$$

We write $\mathbf{s}^N$ for $\mathbf{s}_0^N$. A FSR generates $\mathbf{s}^N$ if (1) is satisfied for $0 \leq i \leq N - n - 1$, i.e. if the terms through s_{N-1} can be successfully generated. Note that any FSR with N or more stages generates $\mathbf{s}^N$, since the entire sequence can be loaded in the N initial stages of the register.

Let E denote the sequence shift operator; that is, $E\mathbf{s}$ denotes the sequence with the i-th term $(E\mathbf{s})_i = s_{i+1}$. We define $(E^j \circ E^k)\mathbf{s}$ to be the sequence with i-th term given by $s_{i+j} s_{i+k}$. For a quadratic feedback function (2), equation (1) can be expressed in terms of the shift operator as

$$(E^n + \sum_{j=0}^{n-1} \sum_{k=j}^{n-1} a_{j,k} E^j \circ E^k)\mathbf{s} = 0.$$

To compute a quadratic feedback function (2) of an n-stage FSR from a given sequence of N terms, a system of linear equations in the unknowns $a_{j,k}$, $0 \leq j \leq k \leq n - 1$, can be formed:

$$
\begin{aligned}
f(s_0, s_1, \ldots, s_{n-1}) &= s_n \\
f(s_1, s_2, \ldots, s_n) &= s_{n+1} \\
&\vdots \\
f(s_{N-n-1}, s_{N-n}, \ldots, s_{N-2}) &= s_{N-1}.
\end{aligned}
\tag{3}
$$

If (3) has a solution, then $q(s^N) \leq n$; otherwise $q(s^N) > n$.

We define the matrix $M(N, n)$ as the coefficient matrix associated with the system of linear equations in (3). This matrix has $N - n$ rows and $n(n+1)/2$ columns indexed by the variables $a_{j,k}$. Actually, the column associated with $a_{j,k}$ is given by $((E^j \circ E^k)s)^{N-n}$. We use a particular ordering of the variables $a_{j,k}$ that simplifies the notation when the number of stages n is increased. For example, when $N = 8$ and $n = 3$, we write (3) as

$$\begin{pmatrix} s_0 & s_1 & s_0 s_1 & s_2 & s_0 s_2 & s_1 s_2 \\ s_1 & s_2 & s_1 s_2 & s_3 & s_1 s_3 & s_2 s_3 \\ s_2 & s_3 & s_2 s_3 & s_4 & s_2 s_4 & s_3 s_4 \\ s_3 & s_4 & s_3 s_4 & s_5 & s_3 s_5 & s_4 s_5 \\ s_4 & s_5 & s_4 s_5 & s_6 & s_4 s_6 & s_5 s_6 \end{pmatrix} \begin{pmatrix} a_0 \\ a_1 \\ a_{0,1} \\ a_2 \\ a_{0,2} \\ a_{1,2} \end{pmatrix} = \begin{pmatrix} s_3 \\ s_4 \\ s_5 \\ s_6 \\ s_7 \end{pmatrix}.$$

Our analysis of quadratic spans involves examining the properties of $M(N, n)$, including its rank. A similar point of view for the linear span case can be found in [4].

Given a sequence s, if an FSR generates s^N, but does not generate s^{N+1}, then we say a *discrepancy* occurs at s_N. The first proposition states when the occurrence of a discrepancy results in an increase in the quadratic span. It uses standard results from linear algebra and forms the basis of an algorithm, which uses Gaussian elimination to solve the system (3), for computing the quadratic span.

PROPOSITION 1. *If a quadratic FSR of length n generates s^N but not s^{N+1}, then no quadratic FSR of length n generates s^{N+1} if and only if $\operatorname{rank}(M(N + 1, n)) = \operatorname{rank}(M(N, n))$.*

An important issue is predicting the increment in the quadratic span when proposition 1 implies there has to be some increase. In the case of linear span, this increment is determined by theorem 1 of [6]. The precise increment for the quadratic case is an open question. However, the increment can be determined in terms of the rank of the matrix $M(N, L)$ if the quadratic FSR that generates s^N is in fact a linear FSR of length L. The following theorem gives the increment for this situation and can be viewed as a partial generalization to the quadratic case of theorem 1 in [6].

THEOREM 2. *If some linear FSR of length L generates the sequence $s^N = (s_0, s_1, \ldots, s_{N-1})$, but no quadratic FSR of length L generates the sequence $s^{N+1} = (s_0, s_1, \ldots, s_N)$, then any quadratic FSR that generates the latter sequence has length Q satisfying*

$$Q \geq N + 1 - \operatorname{rank}(M(N, L)).$$

Sequences with period 2^n generated by a nonlinear FSR of length n are called *de Bruijn sequences* of span n. We derive upper and lower bounds on the quadratic spans of de Bruijn sequences of span n. In these results, we consider matrices $M(2^n + q, q)$, which have 2^n rows, so that each column contains a period of the sequence. It then follows that the quadratic span of a de Bruijn sequence s is given by the smallest number q with the property that $(E^q s)^{2^n}$ is a linear combination of the columns of $M(2^n + q, q)$. The next proposition follows from the observation that the matrix $M(2^n + q, q)$ has rank at most 2^n and $\operatorname{rank}(M(2^n + n, n)) = \binom{n}{2} + n$.

PROPOSITION 3. *If* s *is a de Bruijn sequence of span* n, *then*

$$q(\mathbf{s}) \leq 2^n - \binom{n}{2}.$$

To improve the upper bound to $2^n - \binom{n}{2} - 1$ requires quite a bit of work. The idea is to show that $M(2^n + q, q)$ contains at least one more linearly independent column. We do this by proving the following lemma.

LEMMA 4. *Let* s *be a de Bruijn sequence of span* n, $n \geq 3$. *The column* $((E^0 \circ E^n)\mathbf{s})^{2^n}$ *in the matrix* $M(2^n + n + 1, n + 1)$ *is linearly independent of all the columns in* $M(2^n + n, n)$ *and the column* $(E^n \mathbf{s})^{2^n}$.

Lemma 4 is used to establish the improved upper bound stated below.

THEOREM 5. *If* s *is a de Bruijn sequence of span* $n, n \geq 3$, *then*

$$q(\mathbf{s}) \leq 2^n - \binom{n}{2} - 1.$$

We show that the upper bound given in theorem 5 is best possible by showing it is attained by the class of de Bruijn sequences formed by adding a zero term to the *m-sequences* — maximum-period sequences of period $2^n - 1$ generated by linear FSR's of length n. The proof uses theorem 2 to establish the increase in quadratic span when the discrepancy due to the added term is encountered.

THEOREM 6. *Let* s *be a de Bruijn sequence of span* n *obtained from an m-sequence of span* n *by adding the zero* n-*tuple. Then*

$$q(\mathbf{s}) = 2^n - \binom{n}{2} - 1.$$

For example, 000111101011001 is one period of an m-sequence of span 4. Then 0001111010110010 is a de Bruijn sequence of span 4 with maximum quadratic span 9.

It is easy to see that a lower bound on the quadratic span of a de Bruijn sequence of span n is $n + 1$. From our experimental results, we conjecture the following:

CONJECTURE. *The quadratic span of a de Bruijn sequence of span* n *is at least* $n + 2$, *for* $n > 3$.

Finally, we report the results of computer runs that determined the quadratic spans of the de Bruijn sequences of span n, $n = 3, 4, 5,$ and 6. Our results for $n = 4$ and 5 correct the previously published results [2] for these cases. In each case, the $2^{2^n - n}$ de Bruijn sequences of span n were generated by considering all possible feedback functions. Each time a de Bruijn sequence was found, its linear and quadratic spans were determined and the results tallied. The linear spans were computed and compared with the results of [1] as a check.

The case $n=6$, with its 2^{26} de Bruijn sequences, presented the only real computational burden. In this case, we used several SUN workstations running in parallel, both at the MITRE Corporation and at Northeastern University to complete the run. The quadratic span distributions are listed in figure 2.

N = 3	
Quadratic Span	Number of Sequences
4	2

N = 4	
Quadratic Span	Number of Sequences
6	4
7	8
8	2
9	2

N = 5	
Quadratic Span	Number of Sequences
7	28
8	753
9	877
10	263
11	86
12	11
13	4
14	2
15	0
16	0
17	8
18	0
19	4
20	6
21	6

N = 6	
Quadratic Span	Number of Sequences
8	7
9	356
10	137869
11	5190500
12	1373661
13	962534
14	228087
15	75812
16	31376
17	12362
18	8919
19	5248
20	2220
21	960
22	529
23	223
24	223
25	100
26	72
27	36
28	26
29	44
30	72
31	22
32	6
33	6
34	12
35	8
36	6
37	4
38	2
39	6
40	2
41	2
42	0
43	0
44	8
45	0
46	12
47	6
48	6

LIST OF REFERENCES

1. A. H. Chan, R. A. Games and E. L. Key, "On the Complexity of de Bruijn Sequences," *J. Comb. Theory (A)* **33-3** (1982), 233–246.

2. H. Fredricksen, "A Survey of Full Length Nonlinear Shift Register Cycle Algorithms," *SIAM Review* **24** (1982), 195–221.

3. E. J. Groth, "Generation of Binary Sequences with Controllable Complexity," *IEEE Trans. on Inform. Theory* **IT-17** (1971), 288–296.

4. K. Imamura and W. Yoshida, "A Simple Derivation of the Berlekamp-Massey Algorithm and some Applications," *IEEE Trans. on Inform. Theory* **IT-33** (1987), 146–150.

5. E. L. Key, "An Analysis of the Structure and Complexity of Nonlinear Binary Sequence Generators," *IEEE Trans. on Inform. Theory* **IT-22** (1976), 732–736.

6. J. L. Massey, "Shift-Register Synthesis and BCH Decoding," *IEEE Trans. on Inform. Theory* **IT-15** (1969), 122–127.

7. R. A. Rueppel, *New Approaches to Stream Ciphers*, Swiss Federal Institute of Technology, Zurich, Switzerland: Ph.D. Thesis, 1984.

8. R. A. Rueppel and Staffelbach, "Linear Recurring Sequences With Maximum Complexity," *IEEE Trans. on Inform. Theory* **IT-33** (1987), 126–131.

The Shortest Feedback Shift Register That Can Generate A Given Sequence

CEES J.A. JANSEN

Philips USFA B.V.

P.O. Box 218

5600 MD Eindhoven

The Netherlands

DICK E. BOEKEE

Technical University of Delft

P.O. Box 5031

2600 GA Delft

The Netherlands

Abstract

In this paper the problem of finding the absolutely shortest (possibly nonlinear) feedback shift register, which can generate a given sequence with characters from some arbitrary finite alphabet, is considered. To this end, a new complexity measure is defined, called the maximum order complexity. A new theory of the nonlinear feedback shift register is developed, concerning elementary complexity properties of transposed and reciprocal sequences, and feedback functions of the maximum order feedback shift register equivalent. Moreover, Blumer's algorithm is identified as a powerful tool for determining the maximum order complexity profile of sequences, as well as their period, in linear time and memory. The typical behaviour of the maximum order complexity profile is shown and the consequences for the analysis of given sequences and the synthesis of feedback shift registers are discussed.

1   Introduction

The vast majority of implemented cipher systems consists of streamcipher systems. In a streamcipher system each plaintext block is enciphered with a varying encipherment transformation, where the variation is on a block sequence base such as time or storage location. Therefore, identical plaintext blocks usually do not result in identical ciphertext blocks. In streamciphers the variation of the encipherment transformation inherently implies the presence of memory, whose internal state changes with every subsequent block according to some rule. Examples of streamciphers are the DES in any of its feedback modes [12,3], the *running key generator* (RKG) [8] and the *one-time pad* or *Vernam* cipher [3].

The running key generator is usually depicted as an autonomous finite state device that generates a sequence which is ultimately periodic. This sequence is then added to the stream of plaintext characters. It was the impracticability of the one-time-pad that led to streamciphers based on running key generators. The perfect secrecy of the one-time-pad [15] is approached by not using a random keystream, but rather a keystream generated by some finite state device, acting on a finite length, secret, randomly chosen key. This keystream, produced by a running key generator, should resemble a random keystream as much as possible. In particular, the unpredictability of successive keystream characters should be maintained as long as possible. It turns out that perfect statistical properties and unpredictability are not equivalent, the best example being sequences generated by linear feedback shift registers.

Many people have studied this, seemingly difficult, controversy. Well-known in this respect are Golomb's randomness postulates [5], which measure the randomness of a periodic binary sequence, viz. the disparity between ones and zeroes within one period, the run-length distribution and the number of values assumed by the periodic autocorrelation. Lempel and Ziv [9] introduced a complexity measure for finite sequences, based on the recursive copying of parts of a sequence. Rueppel [14] considered as a measure of randomness the so-called linear complexity profile, denoting the length of the shortest linear feedback shift register which generates that part of the sequence which has already been considered.

Elaborating on Rueppel's work we propose a complexity measure in this paper, called *maximum order complexity*, which denotes in a similar fashion the length of the shortest feedback shift register to generate a given (part of a) sequence, where the feedback function may be any function, mapping states onto characters. The name maximum order complexity was chosen because, unlike with linear (or first order) complexity, quadratic (or second order) complexity, etc., there is no restriction on the nonlinear order of the feedback function.

The import of maximum order complexity is that it tells exactly how many keystream characters have to be observed at least, in order to be able to generate the entire sequence by means of a feedback shift register of that length. Also maximum order complexity can be viewed as an additional figure of merit to judge the randomness of sequences.

2 Theory

In this section we present a summary of the theory of maximum order complexity. Proofs are omitted for the sake of brevity, but can be found in [6]. Section 2.1 introduces maximum order complexity and its elementary properties. In Section 2.2 an algorithm to determine the maximum order complexity profile is discussed. The typical behaviour of the maximum order complexity profile is shown in Section 2.3. Finally, Section 2.4 takes up the problem of the analysis of pseudo-random sequences and the resynthesis with feedback shift registers.

2.1 Maximum Order Complexity

Consider the following problem. Given a sequence $\underline{s} = (\alpha_0, \alpha_1, \ldots, \alpha_{l-1})$ of length l, with characters $\alpha_i \in \mathcal{A}$, where the alphabet $\mathcal{A}$ is some finite set. How many sections (i.e. memory cells) should a feedback shift register at least have in order to generate the sequence $\underline{s}$? So regardless of what the (memoryless) feedback function would have to be, linear or nonlinear. To this end, the following complexity measure is defined:

Definition 1 *The maximum order complexity $c(\underline{s})$ of a sequence $\underline{s} = (\alpha_0, \alpha_1, \ldots, \alpha_{l-1})$ with characters $\alpha_i \in \mathcal{A}$, where the alphabet $\mathcal{A}$ is some finite set, is defined to be the length L of the shortest feedback shift register for which there exists a memoryless feedback mapping, such that the FSR can generate the sequence $\underline{s}$.*

Maximum order complexity is expressed as being L characters. By this it is implicitly assumed that the memory cells can only contain characters from the alphabet $\mathcal{A}$.

Associated with any feedback function F is a substitution table or truth table, which can be seen as a list of argument values with the corresponding function values. The memory cells of the FSR provide for the argument values and hence the truth table is determined by the sequence $\underline{s}$. In general it is possible that a truth table is not specified completely by the sequence it generates, in which case there are no function values specified for one or more argument values.

Maximum order complexity has a number of basic properties, viz.:

Proposition 1

1. *For a sequence $\underline{s}$ consisting of two or more possibly repeated different characters, the complexity $c(\underline{s})$ is equal to the length-plus-one of the longest subsequence that occurs at least twice with different successor characters.*

2. *The complexity of a sequence is 0 iff this sequence consists of one possibly repeated character.*

3. *The maximum value of the complexity of a sequence of length l is $l - 1$. A sequence of length l has a complexity of $l - 1$ iff the sequence consists of $l - 1$ consecutive copies of some character, followed by an unidentical character.*

Periodic sequences of period p are denoted by $\underline{s} = (\alpha_0, \alpha_1, \ldots, \alpha_{p-1})^\infty$. With the period we mean the least integer p, such that $\forall_{i \geq 0} [\alpha_{i+p} = \alpha_i]$. For periodic sequences we have the following property:

Proposition 2

1. *The minimum complexity of a periodic sequence of period p is $\lceil \log_a p \rceil$, where $a = |\mathcal{A}|$, the cardinality of the character alphabet.*

2. *The maximum complexity of a periodic sequence of period p is $p - 1$.*

It seems natural for a FSR to also consider the complexity or degree of difficulty of the feedback function itself. One could consider for example the number of terms and highest degree in some representation of the function like the *Disjunctive Normal Form* (DNF, see e.g. [10, pg. 370]) or the *Algebraic Normal Form* (ANF, see e.g. [14, pg. 54]). As is the case with many complexity measures, the relation between high or low complexity and cryptographically good or bad sequences is not straightforward. Just as with linear complexity high maximum order complexity sequences are not necessarily cryptographically good, as demonstrated by the sequence $(00\cdots01)$ of length l and complexity $l-1$. Clearly, one has to find out the typical complexity values of good sequences or better even the typical complexity profile as done by Rueppel in [14, Ch. 4] for linear complexity.

From our definition of complexity it can be seen that in case the feedback function turns out to be linear, maximum order complexity is equal to linear complexity. This situation occurs with the so-called pseudo-noise or PN-sequences (sometimes called maximum-length or ML-sequences) of period 2^c-1, see e.g. [5].

Example 1 Consider the following sequence of length 25, obtained with an unbiased dice: $\underline{s}_D = (6544552566433434162531433)$. It has a complexity of 3 characters, as all the subsequences of length 3 are distinct, but subsequence (43) has two different successors.

Consider again a sequence $\underline{s} = (\alpha_0, \alpha_1, \ldots, \alpha_{l-1})$, with $\alpha_i \in \mathcal{A}$. The transposed sequence $\underline{t} = T\underline{s} = (\beta_0, \beta_1, \ldots, \beta_{l-1})$, with $\beta_i \in \mathcal{B} = T_{\mathcal{A}}$ is defined to be the sequence which is obtained by substituting each character α_i of $\underline{s}$ by a character β_i from the alphabet $\mathcal{B}$, where the transposition operator T induces a one-to-one correspondence between the α_i and the β_i for all i, $0 \leq i \leq l-1$. For these transposed sequences we have the following result:

Proposition 3 *For all sequences $\underline{s}$ the maximum order complexity of $\underline{s}$ and that of its transpose $T\underline{s}$ have the same value.*

As a consequence, in the binary case the complementary sequence is generated by a feedback function which has inclusion and multiplication interchanged in the DNF representation.

Next we restrict ourselves to periodic sequences of period p. For this type of sequences we have the following result:

Proposition 4 *A periodic sequence $\underline{s} = (\alpha_0, \alpha_1, \ldots, \alpha_{p-1})^{\infty}$ and its reciprocal $\underline{s}^* = (\alpha_{p-1}, \ldots, \alpha_1, \alpha_0)^{\infty}$ have the same complexity.*

It can easily be seen that Proposition 4 does not hold for non-periodic sequences in general. For example the sequence $(aa\cdots ab)$ of length l has complexity $l-1$, its reciprocal $(ba\cdots aa)$ has complexity 1.

Feedback Functions of the Maximum Order FSR Equivalent

The maximum order feedback shift register equivalent of a sequence $\underline{s}$ is defined as the FSR of length $c(\underline{s})$ and a feedback function such that the FSR can generate the sequence $\underline{s}$. We now restrict ourselves to sequences of characters which are elements from some finite field $GF(q)$. For finite field sequences it is customary to use the truth table to derive an analytical expression for the feedback function. In general the truth table of a sequence will not be specified for all q^c possible entries, if c is the maximum order complexity of the sequence. This is due to the fact that not necessarily all q^c possible FSR states occur in a particular sequence. The consequence is that there exists an entire class $\Phi_{\underline{s}}$ of feedback functions which all give rise to the same sequence $\underline{s}$. For this class of feedback functions the following result is obtained:

Proposition 5 *Let $\Phi_{\underline{s}}$ denote the class of feedback functions of the maximum order feedback shift register equivalent of the periodic sequence $\underline{s}$ over $GF(q)$, where $\underline{s}$ has complexity c and period p. The number $|\Phi_{\underline{s}}|$ of functions in the class $\Phi_{\underline{s}}$ satisfies:*

$$|\Phi_{\underline{s}}| = q^{q^c - p}.$$

So, unlike with linear complexity where the feedback function is unique for periodic sequences, $\Phi_{\underline{s}}$ in general contains more than one function and one is able to search for functions exhibiting certain properties such as non-singularity, the least order product function or the function with the least number of terms.

2.2 The Maximum Order Complexity Profile

In [2] Blumer et al. describe a linear-time and -memory algorithm to build a *Directed Acyclic Word Graph* (DAWG) from a given string of letters, using a mechanism of suffixpointers as described in [13]. This DAWG is then used to recognize all substrings (or words) in the string.

The DAWG consists of at most $2l$ nodes connected by at most $3l$ edges, where l is the length of the string. The nodes represent equivalence classes of substrings and the edges are labeled with string letters. An edge points from one node to another if and only if the first equivalence class contains a substring, which extended with the edge's letter belongs to the other equivalence class. The suffix pointer is an edge which points from a node to the node representing the equivalence class with the longest common suffix of all strings of the first node's equivalence class. Two substrings are defined to be equivalent if and only if their endpoint sets are equal. An endpoint set of a given substring is defined as the set containing all positions within a string where the given substring ends. The edges of a DAWG are divided into primary and secondary edges. An edge is called primary if and only if it belongs to the primary path, which is the longest path from the source to a node. With the length of a path the number of edges in that path is meant. The depth $d(\vartheta)$ of a node ϑ is the length of the primary path from the source to that node. The maximum depth $\hat{d}(\underline{s})$ of a sequence $\underline{s}$ is defined as the maximum of the depths of all the nodes with more than one outgoing edges (denoted by the set of branchnodes $BN(\underline{s})$) of the DAWG of $\underline{s}$.

The following proposition relates the complexity of a sequence to its maximum depth in the DAWG.

Proposition 6 *The complexity $c(\underline{s})$ of a sequence $\underline{s}$ with characters from some finite alphabet A satisfies:*

$$c(\underline{s}) = \begin{cases} 0; & BN(\underline{s}) = \emptyset, \\ \hat{d}(\underline{s}) + 1; & else. \end{cases}$$

It appears that the DAWG is an efficient tool to determine the maximum order complexity profile of a given sequence.

Proposition 7 *Blumer's algorithm can be used to determine the complexity profile of a sequence $\underline{s}$ with characters from some finite alphabet A in linear time and memory.*

As Blumer et al. did in their paper, it should be noted that the linearity of their algorithm is with regard to the <u>total</u> processing time related to the length of the sequence.

Blumer's algorithm can be used for a variety of other purposes by postprocessing the DAWG. Examples are: determing the period of a periodic sequence, finding a subsequence in a given sequence (linear in the subsequence length), generating a given sequence based on the least number of observed characters, etc.

The algorithm introduced by Karlin et al. [7] cannot be compared with Blumer's algorithm as it seems to be a two-pass algorithm. This fact renders Karlin's algorithm as unsuitable for the purpose of determining the complexity profile of a given sequence.

2.3 The Typical Complexity Profile

In this section the behaviour of the maximum order complexity profile is viewed at. Let $\underline{s} = (\alpha_0, \alpha_1, \ldots, \alpha_{l-1})$ be a sequence of length l and complexity $c(\underline{s})$ with characters $\alpha_i \in A$, where the character alphabet A is some finite set. In the sequel we will use c_l to denote the complexity $c(\alpha_0, \alpha_1, \ldots, \alpha_{l-1})$.

As with linear complexity, the value $l/2$ forms a boundary value, which determines whether the complexity profile jumps to a higher value or remains the same.

Proposition 8 *If the sequence $\underline{s}$ of length l, mentioned above, has complexity c_l, then the value of the complexity c_{l+1} of the sequence, extended with α_l, is given by:*

$$\begin{aligned} c_{l+1} &= c_l, & c_l \geq l/2 \\ &\leq l - c_l, & c_l < l/2 \\ &\geq c_l + 1, & 2c_l < l < c_l + a^{c_l} \\ &\geq l + 1 - a^{c_l}, & l \geq c_l + a^{c_l}, \end{aligned}$$

where $a = |\mathcal{A}|$ is the cardinality of the character alphabet.

Proposition 8 shows exactly how the complexity profile jumps from one value to some other value if a sequence is extended with some character α_l, a phenomenon illustrated by Figure 1. Another way to look at the jump behaviour of the com-

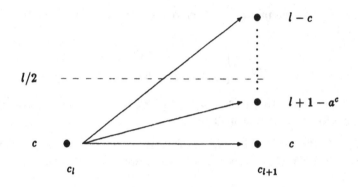

Figure 1: Jumps in the complexity profile.

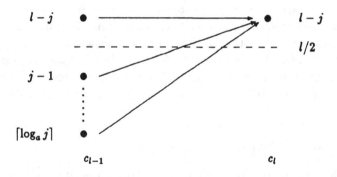

Figure 2: Backwards relationship of complexity values.

plexity profile is the following. Assume that $c_l = l - j$ and $c_{l-1} = j - n$, for positive n. What are the possible values of j and l for certain values of n, i.e. what are the possible values of c_{l-1}? The answer to this question is given by the following proposition.

Proposition 9 *Let $c_l = l - j$ and $c_{l-1} = j - n$, with $1 \le n \le j < l$ then n is additionally restricted by the inequality $n \le j - \log_a j$ and hence $c_{l-1} \ge \log_a j$*

Figure 2 illustrates this backwards relationship between successive complexity values.

2.4 Sequence Analysis and FSR Synthesis

Using various statistical models to describe the behaviour of maximum order complexity with increasing sequence length, in [6] it is demonstrated that the expected maximum order complexity $\bar{c}_l$ of a random sequence of length l with characters from a finite alphabet $\mathcal{A}$ with cardinality a is given by

$$\mathcal{E}(c_l) \approx 2 \log_a l.$$

In fact this turns out to be an upperbound, whereas the lowerbound is proven to be $\log_a l$. This result itself was already known for some time, see e.g. [7] and [1]. Consequently, the maximum order complexity profile of random sequences follows the $2 \log_a l$ curve. This fact in itself can be used to judge the randomness of given sequences. For example, DeBruijn sequences of order n (see e.g. [4]) have a maximum order complexity of n and are therefore clearly qualified as non-random.

In order to construct the shortest feedback shift register which generates a given sequence of length l one first determines its maximum order complexity and then one determines its feedback function. The first operation has order proportional to l and is expected to yield a complexity value of $2 \log l$. The second operation, which can be performed with standard techniques (see [6]), has order $c2^c$ for the binary case. Hence, the expected order of the FSR synthesis procedure is $2l^2 \log l$ (as opposed to $l \log l$ for DeBruijn sequences). This expected order clearly limits the feasibility of general FSR resynthesis to moderate length sequences.

3 Conclusions

Our research has highlighted the problem of finding the shortest feedback shift register which generates a given sequence with characters from some finite alphabet. We have focussed here on the absolutely shortest FSR, regardless of its feedback function, which could be highly nonlinear. To this end, a new complexity measure has been introduced, called the maximum order complexity, as opposed to the first order, or linear complexity, the second order, or quadratic complexity, etc. The basic properties of maximum order complexity have been shown and, in fact, it has been demonstrated that the maximum order complexity is strongly connected with nonlinear feedback shift registers. We believe that our results provide a new contribution to the theory of nonlinear feedback shift registers and a better understanding of their functioning.

The practical import of maximum order complexity has been enhanced by the identification of an efficient algorithm for obtaining the maximum order complexity profile of arbitrary sequences. It has been shown that the maximum order complexity profile can be determined in linear time and memory, using Blumer's algorithm.

By considering the complexity of random sequences, the typical behaviour of the maximum order complexity profile has been clarified.

The consequences for the analysis of pseudo-random sequences and the resynthesis with feedback shift registers have been shown, viz. the total effort to determine the shortest FSR equivalent is of the order $2l^2 \log_2 l$ for the binary case.

Concluding, we can say that the maximum order complexity profile is a useful new tool for judging the randomness of sequences. For example, it declares DeBruijn sequences as non-random, whereas these sequences are considered highly complex according to Lempel and Ziv and some of these sequences are also considered complex according to Rueppel's linear complexity profile.

References

[1] R. Arratia, L. Gordon and M. S. Waterman. "An Extreme Value Theory for Sequence Matching", *The Annals of Statistics*, vol. 14, no. 3, pp. 971–993, 1986.

[2] A. Blumer, J. Blumer, A. Ehrenfeucht, D. Haussler and R. McConnell. "Linear Size Finite Automata for the Set of all Subwords of a Word: An Outline of Results", *Bul. Eur. Assoc. Theor. Comp. Sci.*, no. 21, pp. 12–20, 1983.

[3] D. W. Davies and W. L. Price. *Security for Computer Networks*, John Wiley & Sons, Inc., Chichester, 1984.

[4] H. Fredricksen. "A survey of full-length nonlinear shift register cycle algorithms", *SIAM Rev.*, vol. 24, pp. 195–221, April 1982.

[5] S. W. Golomb. *Shift Register Sequences*, Holden–Day Inc., San Francisco, 1967.

[6] C. J. A. Jansen. *Investigations On Nonlinear Streamcipher Systems: Construction and Evaluation Methods*, PhD. Thesis, Technical University of Delft, Delft, 1989.

[7] S. Karlin, G. Ghandour, F. Ost, S. Tavare and L. J. Korn. "New Approaches for Computer Analysis of Nucleic Acid Sequences", *Proc. Natl. Acad. Sci. USA*, vol. 80, pp. 5660–5664, September 1983.

[8] A. G. Konheim. *Cryptography*, John Wiley & Sons, Inc., New York, 1981.

[9] A. Lempel and J. Ziv. "On the Complexity of Finite Sequences", *IEEE Trans. on Info. Theory*, vol. IT–22, no. 1, pp. 75–81, January 1976.

[10] F. J. MacWilliams and N. J. A. Sloane. *The Theory of Error Correcting Codes*, Amsterdam, North-Holland, 1978.

[11] J. L. Massey. "Shift-Register Synthesis and BCH Decoding", *IEEE Trans. on Info. Theory*, vol. IT–15, January 1969.

[12] C. H. Meyer and S. M. Matyas. *Cryptography: A New Dimension in Computer Data Security*, John Wiley & Sons, New York, 1982.

[13] E. M. McCreight. "A space-economical suffix tree construction algorithm", *JACM*, vol. 23, no. 2, pp. 262–272, April 1976.

[14] R. A. Rueppel. *New Approaches to Stream Ciphers*, PhD. Thesis, Swiss Federal Institute of Technology, Zurich, 1984.

[15] C. E. Shannon. "Communication Theory of Secrecy Systems", *Bell Systems Technical Journal*, vol. 28, pp. 656–715, October 1949.

Perfect Local Randomness in Pseudo-random Sequences

Ueli M. Maurer   and   James L. Massey

Institute for Signal and Information Processing
Swiss Federal Institute of Technology
CH-8092 Zürich, Switzerland

Abstract. The concept of provable cryptographic security for pseudo-random number generators that was introduced by Schnorr is investigated and extended. The cryptanalyst is assumed to have infinite computational resources and hence the security of the generators does not rely on any unproved hypothesis about the difficulty of solving a certain problem, but rather relies on the assumption that the number of bits of the generated sequence the enemy can access is limited. The concept of perfect local randomness of a sequence generator is introduced and investigated using some results from coding theory. The theoretical and practical cryptographic implications of this concept are discussed. Possible extensions of the concept of local randomness as well as some applications are proposed.

1. Introduction

It is well-known that beyond its unicity distance every cipher can be broken in principle, e.g., by an exhaustive key search, which is infeasible except for very simple ciphers. The aim of the designer of a cryptosystem is to make it secure against every attack that is practically feasible. Usually feasibility is specified by computation time, but it is conceivable that an attacker is limited by other restrictions, for instance, by his available storage capacity, by the number of ciphertext bits that he can obtain in a ciphertext-only attack (which is exactly the restriction considered by Ozarow and Wyner [15] in their recent treatment of the wire-tap channel), or by the number of bits of plaintext that he can obtain for a known-plaintext attack. The results of Section 2 show that provably-secure ciphers can be constructed under the restriction that the number of plaintext bits obtainable by the enemy is smaller than the length of the key, divided by the logarithm of the plaintext length. This restriction, to whose formulation we were led by the work of Schnorr [18], is inappropriate for most practical applications and is much stronger than a suitable restriction on computation time. However, inasmuch as no provably-secure practical cipher has yet been devised for a computation-time restriction, the construction of provably-secure stream ciphers for the limited-plaintext restriction appears to be of interest.

At Eurocrypt 88, Schnorr [18] presented a pseudo-random number generator whose security does not rest on any unproven (albeit plausible) assumptions, in contrast to most other proposed pseudo-random number generators [2,3,14]. Schnorr's generator stretches a random seed of length $k = m2^m$ to a pseudo-random sequence of length $n = 2m2^{2m}$, which cannot be distinguished from a random sequence by any statistical test that examines at most $e = 2^{m/3-(\log_2 m)^2}$ bits, even using infinite computational resources. [By a "random binary sequence" of length k we shall always mean a sequence of k binary random variables that takes on all 2^k possible values, each with probability 2^{-k}.] The length of the seed is roughly squared in this expansion, i.e., $n \approx k^2$, and the number $e + 1$ of bits that must be examined by a distinguishing statistical test is roughly the third root of the seed length, i.e., $e \approx \sqrt[3]{k}$, which is very small from a cryptanalytic point of view. The generators constructed in this paper are superior to Schnorr's in two respects: the parameter e is on the order of $k/\log_2 n$ rather than only $\sqrt[3]{k}$ and the generated sequences are truly locally random rather than only (according to Schnorr's definition) locally indistinguishable from a random sequence.

In Section 2, we introduce the concept of a perfect local randomizer, i.e., of a sequence generator that stretches a (binary) random sequence of length k to a pseudo-random sequence of length n such that every subset of e or less bits of the generated sequence is a set of independent random bits. The concept of a perfect local randomizer corresponds to what is known in combinatorics as an orthogonal array. We use many results from coding theory to obtain explicit constructions of perfect local randomizers and to prove bounds on the achievable degree of perfect local randomization. We show that, for any choice of k, n and e satisfying $e \le k/\log_2 n$, there exist perfect local randomizers. A topic closely related to perfect local randomization is the generation of so-called k-wise independent random variables, which was originally introduced in [8] and later also treated in [1] and [11]. The special case of pairwise independence is treated in [4], [7] and [10]. Recent theoretical interest in these schemes was motivated by their application in the con-

struction of deterministic polynomial time algorithms from probabilistic ones for
certain problems.

In the complexity-theoretic approach to pseudo-random number generation, a
pseudo-random number generator is defined to be a family of sequence generators
indexed by the security parameter k ($k = 1, 2, \ldots$) that stretch a sequence of k
random input bits into a pseudo-random sequence of length $n(k)$ where $n(k)$ is
a polynomial in k. In Section 3, we show that, for every integer t, every function $n(k)$ with $n(k) \leq k^t$ for all but finitely many k, and every $\epsilon > 0$, there exist
pseudo-random number generators that stretch k-bit seeds into $n(k)$-bit sequences
with the property that no statistical test (regardless of its computation time) examining not more than $e(k) = \lfloor (1 - \epsilon)k \rfloor$ bits can distinguish them from random
sequences. We also show that $e(k) > k$ is not achievable, thereby giving tight lower
and upper bounds on the achievable $e(k)$. However, we are unable to show that the
stretching function of any of these generators is computable in time polynomial in
k, but the linear sequence generators considered in Section 2 are easily extended
to polynomial-time-computable pseudo-random number generators that achieve a
local randomization of $e(k) = \lfloor k / \log_2 n(k) \rfloor$ bits rather than $e(k) = \lfloor (1 - \epsilon)k \rfloor$ bits.

The restriction that Schnorr [18] puts on statistical tests, namely, that they can
operate on at most a certain number of bits of the generated sequence, appears
to be more information-theoretic than complexity-theoretic. This fact suggests
generalizing the restriction in the following way: assume the enemy is allowed to
obtain e arbitrary bits of information about the generated sequence, i.e., he is not
restricted to acquiring information by examining binary digits but can, for example,
obtain the value of an arbitrary random variable that does not give more than e bits
of information about the sequence. Somewhat surprisingly, it turns out that under
this looser restriction on the enemy's obtainable information, even for arbitrarily
small e, "local" randomization cannot be achieved, as is shown in Section 4. The
quotation marks here emphasize the fact that the accessed information may in this
model very well be global, but its amount is limited. Similarly, if the enemy is able
to obtain e arbitrary parity checks (modulo-two sums) on the sequence bits, perfect
"local" randomization is shown to be impossible. The results of this paper (as well
as Schnorr's result) strongly rely on the assumption that the enemy's information
about the sequence consists of knowing some subset of the digits in the sequence.

In Section 5, we suggest two possible applications of the proposed sequence generators. They might be excellent building blocks within practical ciphers for spreading
local (pseudo-) randomness when used together with compressing transformations
that guarantee confusion, and they are certainly of use wherever a secret key must
be expanded (for example, in key scheduling within block ciphers).

2. Generators Achieving Perfect Local Randomness

Unlike in the literature based on, or motivated by, complexity theory, including [18], we consider in this section individual sequence generators of specific size, rather than infinite families of generators. The asymptotic case is treated in Section 3. Let I_n denote the set of binary sequences of length n, i.e., $I_n = \{0,1\}^n$. A random variable which takes on two values, both with probability 1/2, will be called a cointossing random variable, abbreviated CTRV. Throughout the whole paper, $\log x$ denotes the logarithm to the base 2 of x.

Definition 1: A (k, n) sequence generator G is a function $G : I_k \longrightarrow I_n : \underline{z}^k \mapsto \underline{s}^n = G(\underline{z}^k)$.

Note that a (k, n) sequence generator can be interpreted as the encoder of a binary block code with 2^k codewords of length n, where we think of the randomly-selected key bits as forming the k information bits.

Definition 2: A (k, n) sequence generator G is a (k, n, e) perfect local randomizer (PLR) if, when the input is a sequence of k independent CTRV's, then every subset of e of the n binary output random variables is a set of e independent CTRV's. The degree of perfect local randomness of a (k, n) sequence generator G is $\max\{e : G \text{ is a } (k, n, e) \text{ PLR}\}$.

It is obvious that there exists no (k, n, e) PLR for $e > k$. For $e = k$ and $n > k$, the only PLR's are the two trivial ones where $k = 1$ (example: repeat the input bit n times) or where $k = n - 1$ (example: the first $n - 1$ bits are the input bits and the last bit is their modulo-two sum).

Definition 3: A (k, n) sequence generator is linear if and only if, for all $\underline{z}_1^k, \underline{z}_2^k \in I_k$, $G(\underline{z}_1^k \oplus \underline{z}_2^k) = G(\underline{z}_1^k) \oplus G(\underline{z}_2^k)$, where $\oplus$ denotes bitwise addition modulo 2.

A linear (k, n) sequence generator can be interpreted as an encoder for a linear binary code and can be specified by the binary $k \times n$ matrix $\mathcal{G}$ such that

$$\underline{s}^n = \underline{z}^k \mathcal{G}.$$

The matrix $\mathcal{G}$ is usually called the generator matrix in coding theory. The following Lemma restates a well-known result in coding theory (viz., the condition for the digits in some selected e positions to be choosable as a subset of the k information digits) in terms of PLR's. The proof is omitted.

Lemma: A linear (k, n) sequence generator G is a (k, n, e) perfect local randomizer if and only if every subset of e columns of $\mathcal{G}$ are linearly independent.

The following theorem gives lower and upper bounds on the achievable degree of local randomness for (k, n) sequence generators.

Theorem 1: *There exist linear (k, n, e) perfect local randomizers if*

$$e \leq \frac{k}{\log n} \, ,$$

or if $h[(e - 1)/(n - 1)] < k/(n - 1)$ and $e \leq (n + 1)/2$. There exists no (k, n, e) linear or nonlinear PLR if $h[(e - 1)/2n] \geq (k + 1.5)/n$, which is satisfied when

$$e > \frac{2k + 3 \log n + 2}{\log n - \log(k/2)} \, ,$$

where $h(x) = -x \log x - (1 - x) \log(1 - x)$ is the binary entropy function.

Proof: A well-known fact about linear codes (see [12], Chapter 1, Theorem 10) is that, given any parity-check matrix for the code, the minimum distance equals the minimum positive integer d such that there exists a set of d columns in the parity-check matrix of the code that are linearly dependent or, equivalently, the maximum d such that every subset of $d - 1$ columns are linearly independent. By definition, a parity-check matrix for a linear code is the encoding matrix of the dual code. From the above lemma, we conclude that the degree e of perfect local randomness of a linear (k, n) sequence generator is one less than the minimum distance d of the dual code to the code encoded by this generator. This dual code is a linear code with dimension $n - k$, i.e., a $[n, n - k, d]$ linear code with 2^{n-k} codewords (see [12], p. 9). In other words, a linear (k, n, e) PLR is an encoder of the dual of a linear $[n, n - k, e + 1]$ code and every encoder of the dual of a linear $[n, n - k, d]$ code is a $(k, n, d - 1)$ PLR. We can thus apply the Gilbert-Varshamov existence bound for linear codes (see [12], Ch. 1, Theorem 12) which states that given n and k there exists a binary linear $[n, n - k, d]$ code (and hence a linear (k, n, e) PLR with $e = d - 1$) if

$$\sum_{i=0}^{d-2} \binom{n - 1}{i} = \sum_{i=0}^{e-1} \binom{n - 1}{i} < 2^k.$$

The existence of (k, n, e) PLR's for $e \leq k / \log n$ now follows immediately from the fact that $\sum_{i=0}^{e-1} \binom{n-1}{i} < n^e$ (for $n > 1$). In the following we will make use of the inequalities (see [21], inequalities A.24 and A.30)

$$\frac{1}{\sqrt{2n}} 2^{nh(t/n)} \leq \binom{n}{t} \leq \sum_{i=0}^{t} \binom{n}{i} \leq 2^{nh(t/n)}, \tag{1}$$

where the last inequality holds for $t \leq n/2$. Letting $t = e - 1$ and replacing n by $n - 1$ in the last inequality proves the existence of linear (k, n, e) PLR's if $(n - 1)h[(e - 1)/(n - 1)] < k$ and $(e - 1)/(n - 1) \leq 1/2$, which completes the proof of the first part of Theorem 1.

In order to prove the non-existence claim of Theorem 1 for linear (k, n, e) PLR's, we consider the number Q of all linear combinations of $\lfloor e/2 \rfloor$ or fewer columns of $\mathcal{G}$. If

$$Q = \sum_{i=1}^{\lfloor e/2 \rfloor} \binom{n}{i} \geq 2^k, \tag{2}$$

then either there exists a linear combination of $\lfloor e/2 \rfloor$ or fewer columns that equals the all-zero column or there exist at least two different linear combinations of $\lfloor e/2 \rfloor$ or fewer columns that are equal, and hence there exists a linear combination of e or fewer columns that equals the all-zero column. Thus, satisfaction of inequality (2) implies that there exists no linear (k, n, e) PLR. That (2) also implies the nonexistence of nonlinear (k, n, e) PLR's is equivalent to a result proved in [5] and called the uniform projection lemma. From (1), it follows that inequality (2) is satisfied if

$$\frac{1}{\sqrt{2n}} 2^{nh(\lfloor e/2 \rfloor/n)} > 2^k$$

and thus also if

$$h\left(\frac{e-1}{2n}\right) > \frac{k + \log n + 1/2}{n}, \tag{3}$$

as can easily be verified. To complete the proof of Theorem 1, we note that for $0 < x < 1$, $h(x) \geq -x \log x$. Since $-\log[(e-1)/2n] > -\log(k/2n) = \log n - \log(k/2)$, inequality (3) is satisfied if $(e-1)(\log n - \log(k/2)) > 2k + 2\log n + 1$ and thus also if $e(\log n - \log(k/2)) \geq 2k + 3\log n + 1 - \log(k/2)$. Because $k \geq 1$ and thus $\log(k/2) \geq -1$, the non-existence of (k, n, e) PLR's is established when the last inequality of Theorem 1 is satisfied. $\qquad \square$

Remarks: Note that the lower and upper bounds on the achievable degree e of perfect local randomness given in Theorem 1 differ by a factor of approximately 2. We have shown in the above proof that the problem of determining the maximal achievable degree of perfect local randomness of any linear (k, n) sequence generator is equivalent to the problem of determining the maximal achievable minimum distance d of a linear binary $[n, n-k, d]$ code. Hence every bound on the minimum distance of linear $[n, n-k, d]$ codes can directly be transformed into a bound on the degree of perfect local randomness of linear (k, n) sequence generators. The best table of achievable minimum distances of linear codes known to the authors is that of [20]. The corresponding two problems for nonlinear PLR's and codes, however, are distinct and much less is known about the first of them. It is therefore somewhat surprising that the Hamming bound, a well-known upper bound on the achievable minimum distance of a code (linear or nonlinear) with $n - k$ information bits and codeword length n, is correspondingly valid for the maximal degree e of perfect local randomness of any (k, n, e) PLR. The Hamming (or sphere packing) bound (see [12], Ch. 1, Theorem 6), which follows from the fact that all spheres of radius $(d-1)/2$ (the number of errors guaranteed to be correctable by the code) must be disjoint, states that there exists no binary code with 2^{n-k} codewords of length n and minimum distance d if

$$\sum_{i=0}^{\lfloor (d-1)/2 \rfloor} \binom{n}{i} > 2^k .$$

Because $e = d - 1$, this bound is equivalent to the bound (2) on the maximal degree of perfect local randomness of a (k, n, e) PLR, although the latter was obtained in a different way that applies only for linear PLR's. It is an open problem whether upper bounds on the achievable degree of perfect local randomness corresponding to the McEliece-Rodemich-Rumsey-Welch upper bound [13] on the achievable minimum distance of a code, which is significantly better than the Hamming bound, can be derived. Clearly any upper bound on the minimum distance d gives an upper bound on the degree of perfect local randomness e that can be achieved by linear PLR's, the question is whether the same bound applies to nonlinear PLR's as well.

Theorem 1 gives an existence bound for good linear PLR's. Although the proof of the Gilbert-Varshamov bound is in principle constructive, its application for finding good PLR's for general k and n requires computation time exponential in k and n. The following theorem exhibits an infinite polynomial-time constructable class of linear (k, n, e) PLR's for which $e > k / \log n$, i.e., whose degree of perfect local randomness is approximately equal to the value guaranteed by the Gilbert-Varshamov lower bound.

Theorem 2: *The encoder of an extended Reed-Solomon code over $GF(2^m)$ with e information symbols, codeword length 2^m and design distance $2^m - e + 1$ is a linear $(me, m2^m, e)$ perfect local randomizer when the symbols are appropriately represented by m binary digits.*

Proof: Extended Reed-Solomon codes over $GF(2^m)$ (see [12]) are maximum distance separable, i.e., every subset of e codeword digits may be chosen as the e information digits. By appropriately representing every digit of $GF(2^m)$ as a binary m-tuple, the Reed-Solomon code becomes a binary linear code with $k = me$ information bits and codeword length $n = m2^m$ such that, for random information bits, every subset of e m-bit blocks of the codeword is random. Thus certainly every subset of e bits is random. $\square$

Remark: The maximum-distance-separable property of Reed-Solomon codes derives from the fact that any $k \times n$ generator matrix $\mathcal{G}$ is such that every k columns of $\mathcal{G}$ form a Vandermonde matrix. Other authors have noted the usefulness of the properties of Vandermonde matrices [4,8] or of BCH codes [1] in connection with k-wise independence of random variables.

The PLR's of Theorem 2 can be compared fairly with the pseudo-random number generator suggested by Schnorr [18] since the parameters k and n can be chosen to coincide. Schnorr's generator is a family of $(m2^m, 2m2^{2m})$ sequence generators

(m is the security parameter) such that no test examining at most $2^{m/3-(\log m)^2}$ bits can distinguish the output sequence from a random sequence. An extended Reed-Solomon code over $GF(2^{2m})$ with 2^{m-1} information symbols corresponds to a $(m2^m, 2m2^{2m}, 2^{m-1})$ PLR that not only achieves true local randomness instead of only indistinguishability from randomness but also gives a degree of perfect local randomness greater than the third power of that guaranteed by Schnorr. The smallest value of m for which Schnorr's lower bound is nontrivial is $m = 162$ where the number of bits that must be examined by a distinguishing statistical test is $e = 2$ (out of approximately 10^{100} bits), compared to $e = 2^{161}$ for the Reed-Solomon code. (This example illustrates that the practical significance of asymptotic results in cryptology must always be carefully evaluated.)

In the following, we discuss nonlinear perfect local randomizers. A (k, n, e) PLR (linear or not) is the encoder of a binary block code with 2^k codewords such that for every subset of e positions, every e-bit pattern occurs exactly 2^{n-e} times. Such a configuration is also known as an orthogonal array [17] of size 2^k, n constraints, 2 levels, strength e and index 2^{n-e}. As mentioned earlier, the problems of designing linear codes with large minimum distance and of designing linear PLR's with large degree of perfect local randomness are equivalent. For the nonlinear case, however, the two problems are distinct, and much less is known about the latter. Nevertheless, some results from coding theory can be applied. MacWilliams ([12], Chapter 5) introduced a transform for the distance distribution of a code that yields, for linear codes, the distance (or, equivalently, the weight) distribution of the dual code. The significance of the transform of the distance distribution of a nonlinear code is not obvious since there exists no dual code for a nonlinear code. However, surprisingly enough, if one defines the dual distance d' of a code as the minimum distance value for which the transformed distance distribution is not zero, then one obtains precisely what we are looking for: the degree of perfect local randomness of an encoder for the code considered as a sequence generator is $e = d' - 1$. This remarkable result is due to Delsarte [6].

The question whether for large k and n there exist nonlinear (k, n) sequence generators whose degree of perfect local randomness is greater than that of every linear (k, n) sequence generator is open. However, there do exist some nonlinear PLR's superior to the best linear PLR's. The so-called Kerdock codes $\mathcal{K}(m)$ are $(2^m, 2^{2m}, 2^{m-1} - 2^{(m-1)/2})$ nonlinear codes for all even $m \geq 4$ that yield $(2m, 2^m, 5)$ nonlinear PLR's as shown by determining the dual distance d' of these nonlinear codes (see [12], Ch. 15, Theorem 24 and Corollary 29). The so-called punctured Preparata codes $\mathcal{P}(m)^*$ similarly yield $(2^m - 2m, 2^m - 1, 2^{m-1} - 2^{m/2-1})$ nonlinear PLR's for all even $m \geq 4$ (see [12], Ch. 15, Theorem 32). The Delsarte-Goethals codes $\mathcal{DG}(m, d)$ with $d = (m-2)/2$ yield $(3m-1, 2^m, 7)$ nonlinear PLR's for all even $m \geq 4$ (see [12], pp. 476-477). Thus, $\mathcal{K}(4), \mathcal{K}(6), \mathcal{K}(8), \mathcal{P}(6)^*, \mathcal{P}(8)^*, \mathcal{DG}(4,1) \mathcal{DG}(6,2)$ and $\mathcal{DG}(8,3)$ are $(8, 16, 5), (12, 64, 5), (16, 256, 5), (52, 63, 27), (240, 255, 119), (11, 16, 7),$

$(17, 64, 7)$ and $(23, 256, 7)$ nonlinear PLR's, respectively. From the table in [20], we conclude that the best linear $(8, 16, e)$, $(12, 64, e)$, $(52, 63, e)$, $(11, 16, e)$ and $(17, 64, e)$ PLR's satisfy $e = 4$, $4 \leq e \leq 5$, $25 \leq e \leq 26$, $e = 7$ and $5 \leq e \leq 7$, respectively. The $(8, 16, 5)$ PLR (also known as the Nordström-Robinson code) and the $(52, 63, 27)$ PLR thus beat the best linear PLR's with the same k and n. It is unknown to the authors whether $\mathcal{K}(m)$, $\mathcal{P}(m)^*$ and $\mathcal{DG}(m, (m-2)/2)$ are superior to the best linear PLR's for infinitely many m, or for all $m \geq 2$, $m \geq 2$, and $m \geq 3$, respectively.

3. Locally-Randomized Pseudo-random Number Generators

Section 2 was devoted to sequence generators that stretch, for fixed k and n, a k-bit secret random key to an n-bit sequence. Since the framework of complexity theory is based on the analysis of asymptotic behavior, a pseudo-random number generator G is often defined [3,18] as an infinite class $G = \{G_k : k \geq 1\}$ of $(k, n(k))$ sequence generators G_k, where n is a polynomial function of the index k and where the computation time of each sequence generator is upper bounded by a polynomial function of k. Similarly, a statistical test $S^G = \{S_k^G : k \geq 1\}$ for the pseudo-random number generator G [23] is an infinite class of probabilistic algorithms S_k^G which take as input a binary sequence of length $n(k)$ and emit a binary output. G is said to pass the statistical test S^G if and only if, for all polynomials P and for all but a finite number of integers k,

$$\left| p_k^{S^G, G} - p_k^{S^G, R} \right| < \frac{1}{P(k)},$$

where $p_k^{S^G, G}$ denotes the probability that S_k^G emits a 1 if the input is the sequence generated by G_k for a random k-bit input, and where $p_k^{S^G, R}$ denotes the probability that S_k^G emits a 1 if the input is a random sequence of length $n(k)$.

Definition 4: *Let $e(k)$ be any positive integer-valued function. We shall call a pseudo-random number generator G degree $e(k)$ locally-randomized if G passes every (not necessarily time-bounded) statistical test that examines not more than $e(k)$ of the $n(k)$ bits.*

The following corollary is an immediate consequence of Theorem 1 and the fact that a k-bit row vector can be multiplied by a binary $k \times n(k)$ matrix in time polynomial in k.

Corollary to Theorem 1: *Let t be any positive integer. For any function $n(k)$ satisfying $n(k) \leq k^t$ for all but finitely many k, there exist degree $e(k) = \lfloor k/(t \log k) \rfloor$ locally-randomized pseudo-random number generators.*

The next theorem follows essentially from the fact that the information-theoretic entropy of the output of a sequence generator cannot be greater than the entropy of its input.

Theorem 3: *There exist no degree $e(k)$ locally-randomized pseudo-random number generators if $e(k) > k$ for infinitely many k.*

The following theorem shows that the degree of perfect local randomness can be arbitrarily close to the upper bound k. However, the existence proof is nonconstructive since it is based on a random coding argument, and therefore the polynomial-time computability of the generator cannot be guaranteed. The proof is omitted.

Theorem 4: *Let t be any positive integer. For every $\epsilon > 0$ and for any function $n(k)$ satisfying $n(k) \le k^t$ for all but finitely many k, there exist degree $e(k) = \lfloor (1-\epsilon)k \rfloor$ locally-randomized, not necessarily polynomial-time computable, pseudo-random number generators.*

It is an open problem whether polynomial-time-computable degree $e(k)$ locally-randomized pseudo-random number generators exist for which $\lim_{k \to \infty} e(k) \log k / k > 0$, for instance, with $\lim_{k \to \infty} e(k)/k > C$ for some constant C with $0 < C \le 1$. We conjecture that the answer is yes. Piveteau [16] has recently considered locally-randomized pseudo-random number generators in a setting where all computations are polynomially bounded and proved that there exist locally-randomized pseudo-random number generators if and only if there exist pseudo-random number generators.

4. Extensions of the Concept of Local Randomization

So far we have considered statistical tests that are limited in the total number of bits of the pseudo-random sequence that are examined during the execution. This corresponds to a known-plaintext attack with a limited amount of plaintext data available when the pseudo-random sequence is the "running key" in an additive stream cipher. In general, however, the nature of the enemy's a priori and/or obtainable information about the plaintext is global rather than structured in binary digits. For example, he might know that the plaintext satisfies certain parity checks (e.g., reduced ASCII code). It would therefore be desirable to extend the results of Sections 2 and 3 to purely information-theoretic results by allowing the statistical test to obtain the value of any random variable not giving more than e bits of information about the pseudo-random sequence (or, equivalently, about the plaintext sequence in the additive stream cipher described above). The following theorem, stated here without proof, shows that unfortunately such an extension is not possible.

Theorem 5: *For every (k,n) sequence generator G, there exists a function f^G using only one bit of information about the generated sequence, whose distinguishing probability $|p^{f^G,G} - p^{f^G,R}|$ is lower bounded by $1 - 2^{k-n}$.*

This theorem shows not only that the amount of information that the enemy is allowed to obtain about the generated sequence but also the way in which the enemy can access information must be restricted appropriately if statements similar to theorems 1 and 4 should be proved. A possible relaxation of the restriction that the enemy obtains information about the pseudo-random sequence by observing only bits could, for example, be that he is allowed to obtain at most e parity checks, i.e., linear combinations, on the sequence bits. But even for this model, perfect "local" randomness cannot be achieved because n binary CTRV's are jointly independent if and only if every non-trivial linear combination of these CTRV's is a CTRV (see [22], or the XOR-Lemma in [5]). On the other hand, if the enemy is not allowed to obtain arbitrary bits of the sequence but only subblocks of a certain length, i.e., if the basic alphabet is the set of binary m-tuples rather than the binary alphabet, then (k,n) sequence generators achieving the information-theoretically maximal degree of perfect local randomness equal to k can sometimes be achieved. In coding theory, schemes having this property (e.g., Reed-Solomon codes) are called maximum distance separable, cf. [12]. The problem of determining the minimal alphabet size such that there exists a (k,n,k) PLR for given k and n is open.

Two other ways of generalizing the concept of a (k,n,e) perfect local randomizer would be either to drop perfectness, i.e., to allow slight deviations from the uniform distribution, or to require perfect local randomness only "almost everywhere", i.e., only for all but a small fraction of the subsets of e bits.

5. Applications and Conclusions

We are by no means suggesting that the sequence generators presented in Section 2 be used as practical pseudo-random sequence generators. The two main reasons for this reticence are first that one cannot often validly assume that an enemy is restricted to obtaining only a few bits of the sequence and second that most of our proposed schemes are linear and therefore easily unmasked by a simple appropriate parity check involving $e + 1$ bits. The latter weakness could be obviated by application of an invertible nonlinear transformation on the sequence space, but the first problem is intrinsic. Nevertheless, there are two potential practical cryptographic applications of the proposed perfect local randomizers. We first note that they are expanding transformations providing, in a certain sense, ideal "diffusion".

If combined with appropriate compressing transformations providing "confusion", they might be excellent building blocks for practical ciphers. The second possible application is their use in key scheduling schemes (e.g., within block ciphers) where a small secret key must be stretched to a long key.

In this paper we have explored the concept of local randomization which leads to provable security, but only for an unfortunately weak notion of security. We not also that, once more in cryptologic research, results borrowed from the theory of error-correcting codes have turned out to be useful.

Many proofs have been omitted in this paper. A more detailed version containing all proofs has been submitted to the CRYPTO'89 special issue of the Journal of Cryptology and can be obtained from the authors now upon request.

Acknowledgement

We would like to thank Moni Naor for drawing our attention to references [1] and [4] and Andi Loeliger for helpful comments.

References

[1] N. Alon, L. Babai and A. Itai, *A fast and simple randomized parallel algorithm for the maximal independent set problem*, Journal of Algorithms, Vol. 7, pp. 567-583, 1986.

[2] L. Blum, M. Blum and M. Shub, *A simple unpredictable pseudo-random number generator*, SIAM J. on Computing, Vol. 15, pp. 364-383, 1986.

[3] M. Blum and S. Micali, *How to generate cryptographically strong sequences of pseudo-random bits*, SIAM J. on Computing, Vol. 13, pp. 850-864, 1984.

[4] B. Chor and O. Goldreich, *On the power of two-point based sampling*, Journal of Complexity, Vol. 5, No. 1, pp. 96-106, 1989.

[5] B. Chor, O. Goldreich, J. Hastad, J. Freidmann, S. Rudich and R. Smolensky, *The bit extraction problem or t-resilient functions*, Proc. 26th ann. Symp. on Foundations of Computer Science, pp. 396-407, 1985.

[6] P. Delsarte, *An algebraic approach to the association schemes of coding theory*, Philips Research Reports Supplements, No. 10, 1973.

[7] A. Joffe, *On a sequence of almost deterministic pairwise independent random variables*, Proc. Amer. Math. Soc., Vol. 29, No. 2, pp. 381-382, July 1971.

[8] A. Joffe, *On a set of almost deterministic k-independent random variables*, The Annals of Probability, Vol. 2, No. 1, pp. 161-162, 1974.

[9] E. Kranakis, *Primality and cryptography*, Stuttgart and New York: Wiley-Teubner Series in Computer Science, 1986.

[10] H.O. Lancaster, *Pairwise statistical independence*, Ann. Math. Statist., Vol. 36, pp. 1313-1317, 1965.

[11] M. Luby, *A simple parallel algorithm for the maximal independent set problem*, SIAM J. on Computing, Vol. 15, No. 4, pp. 1036-1053, Nov. 1986.

[12] F.J. MacWilliams and N.J.A. Sloane, *The theory of error-correcting codes*, Amsterdam, New York, Oxford: North-Holland Publishing Company, Fifth Printing, 1986.

[13] R.J. McEliece, E.R. Rodemich, H.C. Rumsey and L.R. Welch, *New upper bounds on the rate of a code via the Delsarte-MacWilliams inequalities*, IEEE Trans. Info. Th., Vol. IT-23, pp. 157-166, 1977.

[14] S. Micali and C.P. Schnorr, *Efficient, perfect random number generators*, Preprint MIT, Universität Frankfurt, Nov. 1988.

[15] L.H. Ozarow and A. D. Wyner, *Wire-tap channel II*, AT&T Bell Lab. Tech. J., Vol. 63, No. 10, pp. 2135-2157, Dec. 1984.

[16] J.-M. Piveteau, *Local pseudorandom generators*, Preprint, ETH Zürich, 1989.

[17] D. Raghavarao, *Constructions and combinatorial problems in Design of Experiments*, New York: Wiley, 1971.

[18] C.P. Schnorr, *On the construction of random number generators and random function generators*, Proc. EUROCRYPT'88, Lecture Notes in Computer Science, Vol. 330, Springer Verlag, pp. 225-232, 1988.

[19] C.E. Shannon, *A mathematical theory of communication*, Bell Syst. Tech. J., Vol. 27, pp. 379-423 and 623-656, 1948.

[20] T. Verhoeff, *An updated table of minimum-distance bounds for binary linear codes*, IEEE Trans. Info. Th., Vol. IT-33, pp. 665-680, 1987.

[21] J.M. Wozencraft and B. Reiffen, *Sequential Decoding*, MIT Press, Cambridge, MA, 1961.

[22] G.Z. Xiao and J.L. Massey, *A spectral characterization of correlation-immune combining functions*, IEEE Trans. Inform. Theory, Vol. 34, pp. 569-571, 1988.

[23] A.C. Yao, *Theory and applications of trapdoor functions*, Proc. 23rd IEEE Symposium on Foundations of Computer Science, pp. 80-91, 1982.

Sparse Pseudorandom Distributions

(Extended Abstract)

Oded Goldreich
Hugo Krawczyk

Computer Science Dept.
Technion
Haifa, Israel

Abstract. Pseudorandom distributions on n-bit strings are ones which cannot be efficiently distinguished from the uniform distribution on strings of the same length. Namely, the expected behavior of any polynomial-time algorithm on a pseudorandom input is (almost) the same as on a random (i.e. uniformly chosen) input. Clearly, the uniform distribution is a pseudorandom one. But do such trivial cases exhaust the notion of pseudorandomness? Under certain intractability assumptions the existence of pseudorandom generators was proven, which in turn implies the existence of non-trivial pseudorandom distributions. In this paper we investigate the existence of pseudorandom distributions, using no unproven assumptions.

We show that *sparse* pseudorandom distributions do exist. A probability distribution is called *sparse* if it is concentrated on a negligible fraction of the set of all strings (of the same length). It is shown that sparse pseudorandom distributions can be generated by probabilistic (non-polynomial time) algorithms, and some of them are not statistically close to any distribution induced by probabilistic polynomial-time algorithms.

Finally, we show the existence of probabilistic algorithms which induce pseudorandom distributions with *polynomial-time evasive* support. Any polynomial-time algorithm trying to find a string in their support will succeed with negligible probability. A consequence of this result is a proof that the original definition of zero-knowledge is not robust under sequential composition. (This was claimed before, leading to the introduction of more robust formulations of zero-knowledge.)

First author was supported by grant No. 86-00301 from the United States - Israel Binational Science Foundation (BSF), Jerusalem, Israel.

1. INTRODUCTION

In recent years, randomness has became a central notion in diverse fields of computer science. Randomness is used in the design of algorithms in fields as computational number theory, computational geometry, parallel and distributed computing, and is of course crucial to cryptography. Since in most cases the interest is in the behavior of efficient algorithms (modeled by polynomial-time computations), the fundamental notion of pseudorandomness arises. Pseudorandom distributions are those distributions which cannot be efficiently distinguished from the uniform distribution on strings of the same length.

The importance of pseudorandomness is in the fact that any efficient probabilistic algorithm performs essentially as well when substituting its source of unbiased coins by a pseudorandom sequence. Algorithms can therefore be analyzed assuming they use unbiased coin tosses, and later implemented using pseudorandom sequences. Such approach is practically beneficial if pseudorandom sequences can be generated more easily than "truly random" ones. This gave rise to the notion of a pseudorandom generator - an efficient deterministic algorithm which expands random seeds into longer pseudorandom sequences.

Most of the previous work on pseudorandomness has in fact focused on pseudorandom generators. Blum and Micali [BM] and Yao [Y] suggested the basic definitions and showed that pseudorandom generators can be constructed under certain intractability assumptions [1]. Several works [GGM, LR, L1, L2, GKL, ILL] further developed this direction. An important aspect of pseudorandom generation, namely its utility for deterministic simulation of randomized complexity classes, is further studied in [NW].

In our paper we investigate the notion of pseudorandomness when decoupled from the notion of efficient generation. The investigation will be carried out using no unproven assumptions. The first question we address is the existence of non-trivial pseudorandom distributions. That is, pseudorandom distributions that are neither the uniform distribution nor statistically close to it [2]. Yao [Y] presents a particular example of such a distribution. Further properties of such distributions are developed here.

We prove the existence of *sparse* pseudorandom distributions. A distribution is called sparse if it is concentrated on a negligible part of the set of all strings of the same length. For example, given a positive constant $\delta < 1$ we construct a probability distribution concentrated on $2^{\delta k}$ of the strings of length k which cannot be distinguished from the uniform distribution on the set of all k-bit strings (and hence is pseudorandom).

---

[1] Intractability assumptions in this approach are inavoidable as long as we cannot prove the existence of one-way functions and, in particular, that $P \neq NP$.

[2] The statistical distance between two probability distributions is defined as the sum (over all strings) of the absolute difference between the probabilities they assign to each string.

Sparse pseudorandom distributions can even be uniformly generated by probabilistic algorithms (that run in non-polynomial time). These generating algorithms use less random coins than the number of pseudorandom bits they produce. Viewing these algorithms as generators which expand randomly selected short strings into much longer pseudorandom sequences, we can exhibit generators achieving subexponential expansion rate. This expansion is optimal since no generator expanding strings into exponential longer ones can induce a pseudorandom distribution (which passes non-uniform tests). On the other hand, one can use the subexponential expansion property in order to construct non-uniform generators of size slightly super-polynomial. (We stress that the existence of non-uniform polynomial-size generators would separate non-uniform-P from non-uniform-NP, which would be a major breakthrough in Complexity Theory).

We also show the existence of sparse pseudorandom distributions that cannot be generated or even approximated by efficient algorithms. Namely, there exist pseudorandom distributions that are statistically far from any distribution which is induced by any probabilistic polynomial-time algorithm. In other words, even if efficient pseudorandom generators exist, they do not exhaust (nor even in an approximative sense) all the pseudorandom distributions.

A stronger notion is that of evasive probability distributions. These probability distributions have the property that any efficient algorithm will fail to find strings in their support [3] (except with a negligible probability). Certainly, evasive probability distributions are sparse, and even cannot be efficiently approximated by probabilistic algorithms. We show the existence of evasive pseudorandom distributions.

Finally, we present an interesting application of these results to the field of zero-knowledge interactive proofs. It has been claimed [F] that the original definition of zero-knowledge (which appeared in [GMR1]) is not robust under sequential composition (and thus more robust variants were introduced [O,GMR2,TW,F]). However, no rigorous proof of this claim has been given to date. Using evasive pseudorandom distributions we construct a zero-knowledge protocol which reveals significant information when executed twice in a sequence.

2. DEFINITIONS

The formal definition of pseudorandomness (given bellow) is stated in asymptotical terms, so we shall not discuss single distributions but collections of probability distributions, called probability ensembles.

---

[3] The support of a probability distribution is the set of elements that it assigns non-zero probability.

Definition: A *probability ensemble* Π is a collection of probability distributions $\{\pi_k\}_{k \in K}$, such that K is an infinite set of indices (nonnegative integers) and for every $k \in K$, π_k is a probability distribution on the set of (binary) strings of length k.

In particular, an ensemble $\{\pi_k\}_{k \in K}$ in which π_k is a uniform distribution on $\{0,1\}^k$ is called a *uniform ensemble*.

Next, we give a formal definition of a pseudorandom ensemble. This is done in terms of polynomial indistinguishability between ensembles.

Definition: Let $\Pi = \{\pi_k\}$ and $\Pi' = \{\pi_k'\}$ be two probability ensembles. Let T be a probabilistic polynomial time algorithm outputting 0 or 1 (T is called a *statistical test*). Denote by $p_T(k)$ the probability that T outputs 1 when fed with an input selected according to the distribution π_k. Similarly, $p_T'(k)$ is defined with respect to π_k'. The test T *distinguishes* between Π and Π' if and only if there exists a constant $c > 0$ and infinitely many k's such that $|p_T(k) - p_T'(k)| > k^{-c}$. The ensembles Π and Π' are called *polynomially indistinguishable* if there exists no polynomial-time statistical test that distinguish between them.

Definition: A probabilistic ensemble is called *pseudorandom* if it is polynomially indistinguishable from a uniform ensemble.

Remark: Some authors define pseudorandomness by requiring that pseudorandom ensembles be indistinguishable from uniform distributions even by *non-uniform* (polynomial) tests. We stress that the results (and proofs) in this paper also hold for these stronger definitions.

In this work we are interested in the question of whether non-trivial pseudorandom ensembles can be effectively sampled by means of probabilistic algorithms. The following definition capture the notion of 'samplability'.

Definition: A *sampling algorithm* is a probabilistic algorithm A that on input a string of the form 1^n, outputs a string of length n. The *probabilistic ensemble Π^A induced by a sampling algorithm A* is defined as $\{\pi_n^A\}_n$, where π_n^A is the probabilistic distribution such that for any $y \in \{0,1\}^n$, $\pi_n^A(y) = Prob(A(1^n) = y)$, where the probability is taken over the coin tosses of algorithm A. A *samplable* ensemble is a probabilistic ensemble induced by a sampling algorithm. If the sampling algorithm uses, on input 1^n, less than n random bits then we call the ensemble *strongly-samplable*.

Traditionally, pseudorandom generators are defined as *deterministic* algorithms expanding short seeds into longer bit strings. With the above definitions one can define them as strong-sampling algorithms (the seed is viewed as the random coins for the sampling algorithm).

We consider as trivial, pseudorandom ensembles that are close to a uniform ensemble. The meaning of "close" is formalized in the next definition.

Definition: Two probabilistic ensembles Π and Π' are *statistically close* if for any positive c and any sufficiently large n, $\sum_{x \in \{0,1\}^n} |\pi_n(x) - \pi_n'(x)| < n^{-c}$.

A special case of non-trivial pseudorandom ensembles are those ensembles we call "sparse".

Definition: A probabilistic ensemble is called *sparse* if (for sufficiently large n's) the support of π_n is a set of *negligible* size relative to the set $\{0,1\}^n$ (i.e for every $c > 0$ and sufficiently large n, $|support(\pi_n)| < n^{-c} 2^n$).

Clearly, a sparse pseudorandom ensemble cannot be statistically close to a uniform ensemble.

Notation: I_k will denote the set $\{0,1\}^k$.

3. THE EXISTENCE OF SPARSE PSEUDORANDOM ENSEMBLES

The main result in this section is the following Theorem.

Theorem 1: There exist strongly-samplable sparse pseudorandom ensembles.

In order to prove this theorem we present an ensemble of sparse distributions which are pseudorandom even against non-uniform distinguishers. These distributions assign equal probability to the elements in their support. We use the following definition.

Definition: A set $S \subseteq I_k$ is called $(\tau(k), \varepsilon(k))$-*pseudorandom* if for any (probabilistic) circuit C of size $\tau(k)$ with k inputs and a single output

$$| p_C(S) - p_C(I_k) | \leq \varepsilon(k)$$

where $p_C(S)$ (resp. $p_C(I_k)$) denotes the probability that C outputs 1 when given elements of S (resp. I_k), chosen with uniform probability.

If for a circuit C and a set $S \subseteq I_k$ the above inequality does not hold then we say that the the set S is $\varepsilon(k)$–*distinguished* by the circuit C.

Note that a collection of uniform distributions on a sequence of sets $S_1, S_2, \dots$ where each S_k is a $(\tau(k), \varepsilon(k))$-pseudorandom set, constitutes a pseudorandom ensemble, provided that both functions $\tau(k)$ and $\varepsilon^{-1}(k)$ are super-polynomial, i.e. grow faster than any polynomial. Our goal is to prove the existence of such a collection in which the ratio $|S_k|/2^k$ is negligibly small.

Remark: In the following we consider only deterministic circuits (tests). The ability to toss coins does not add power to non-uniform tests. Using a standard averaging argument one can show that whatever a probabilistic non-uniform distinguisher C can do, may be achieved by a deterministic circuit in which the "best coins" of C are incorporated.

The next Lemma measures the number of sets which are $\varepsilon(k)$-distinguished by a given circuit. Notice that this result does not depend on the circuit size.

Lemma 2: For any k-input Boolean circuit C, the probability that a random set $S \subseteq I_k$ of size N is $\varepsilon(k)$-distinguished by C is at most $2 \exp\left[-2N\varepsilon^2(k)\right]$. (The function $\exp(\cdot)$

denotes exponentiation to natural base).

Proof: Let $L_C(k)$ be the set $\{x \in I_k : C(x) = 1\}$. Thus, $p_C(I_k) = \dfrac{|L_C(k)|}{2^k}$ and $p_C(S) = \dfrac{|S \cap L_C(k)|}{|S|}$.

Consider the set of strings of length k as a urn containing 2^k balls. Let those balls in $L_C(k)$ be painted white and the others black. The proportion of white balls in the urn is clearly $p_C(I_k)$, and the proportion of white balls in a sample S of N balls from the urn is $p_C(S)$. (We consider here a sample *without* replacement, i.e. sampled balls are not replaced in the urn).

Lemma 2 follows by using the Chernoff-type inequality due to W. Hoeffding [H] (see Appendix)

$$Prob\left[\ |p_C(S) - p_C(I_k)| \geq \varepsilon(k)\ \right]\ <\ 2\exp\left[-2N\varepsilon^2(k)\right]$$

where the probability is taken over all the subsets $S \subseteq I_k$ of size N, with uniform probability. ∎

The following Lemma states the existence of pseudorandom ensembles composed of uniform distributions with very sparse support.

Lemma 3: Let $k(n)$ be any subexponential function of n (i.e. $k(n) = \exp(o(n))$)[4]. There exist super-polynomial functions $\tau(\cdot)$ and $\varepsilon^{-1}(\cdot)$, and a sequence of sets $S_1, S_2, ...$, such that S_n is a $(\tau(k(n)), \varepsilon(k(n)))$-pseudorandom subset of $I_{k(n)}$ and $|S_n| = 2^n$.

Proof: Fix n and let $k = k(n)$. We show the existence of a set $S \subseteq I_k$ of size 2^n which is $(\tau(k), \varepsilon(k))$-pseudorandom, where $\tau(\cdot)$ and $\varepsilon^{-1}(\cdot)$ are suitable chosen super-polynomial functions.

The number of Boolean circuits of size $\tau(k)$ is at most $2^{\tau^2(k)}$. Thus, to show the existence of a set S that is not $\varepsilon(k)$-distinguished by any of these circuits it is sufficient to show that each circuit $\varepsilon(k)$-distinguishes at most $2^{-\tau^2(k)}$ of the sets of size 2^n. Using Lemma 2, this holds provided that

$$2^n \varepsilon^2(k) > \tau^2(k) \tag{1}$$

It is easy to see that for any subexponential function $k(n)$ we can find super-polynomial functions $\varepsilon^{-1}(\cdot)$ and $\tau(\cdot)$ such that inequality (1) holds for each value of n. ∎

The following Lemma states that the sparse pseudorandom ensembles presented above are strongly-samplable. This proves Theorem 1.

Lemma 4: Let $k(n)$ be any subexponential function of n. There exist (non-polynomial) generators which expand random strings of length n into pseudorandom strings of length

---

[4] $o(n)$ denotes any function $f(n)$ such that $\lim_{n \to \infty} f(n)/n = 0$

$k(n)$.

Proof: Let $\tau(\cdot)$ and $\varepsilon(\cdot)$ be as in Lemma 3. We construct a generator which on input a seed of length n finds the $(\tau(k(n)), \varepsilon(k(n)))$-pseudorandom set $S_n \subseteq I_{k(n)}$ whose existence is guaranteed by Lemma 3, and uses the n input bits in order to choose a random element from S_n. Clearly, the output of the generator is pseudorandom.

To see that the set S_n can be effectively found, note that it is effectively testable whether a given set S of size 2^n is $(\tau(k), \varepsilon(k))$-pseudorandom. This can be done by enumerating all the circuits of size $\tau(k)$ and computing for each circuit C the quantities $p_C(S)$ and $p_C(I_k)$. Thus, our generator will test all the possible sets $S \subseteq I_k$ of size 2^n until S_n is found. ∎

Remark 1: Inequality (1) defines a trade-off between the expansion function $k(n)$ and the size of the tests (circuits) resisted by the generated ensemble. The pseudorandom ensembles we construct may be "very" sparse, in the sense that the expansion function $k(n)$ can be chosen to be very large (e.g. $2^{\sqrt{n}}$). On the other hand if we consider "moderate" expansion functions such as $k(n) = 2n$, we can resist rather powerful tests, e.g. circuits of size $2^{n/4}$.

Remark 2: The subexponential expansion, as allowed by our construction, is optimal since no generator exists which expands strings of length n into strings of length $k(n) = \exp(O(n))$. To see this, consider a circuit of size $k(n)^{O(1)}$ which incorporates the (at most) 2^n output strings of the generator. Clearly, this circuit constitutes a (non-uniform) test distinguishing the output of this generator from the uniform distribution on $I_{k(n)}$.

Remark 3: The subexponential expansion implies that the supports of the resultant pseudorandom distributions are very sparse. More precisely, our construction implies the existence of generators which induce on strings of length k a support of size *slightly* super-polynomial (i.e. of size $k^{u(k)}$ for an arbitrary non-decreasing unbounded function $u(k)$). Thus, by wiring this support into a Boolean circuit, we are able to construct *non-uniform* generators of size slightly super-polynomial. (On input a seed s the circuit (generator) outputs the s-th element in this "pseudorandom" support). Let us point out that an improvement of this result, i.e. a proof of the existence of non-uniform pseudorandom generators of polynomial size, will imply that non-uniform-P $\neq$ non-uniform-NP !. This follows by considering the language $\{x \in I_k : x$ *is in the image of* $G\}$, where G is a pseudorandom generator in non-uniform-P. Clearly, this language is in non-uniform-NP, but not in non-uniform-P, otherwise a deciding procedure for it can be transformed into a test distinguishing the output of G from the uniform distribution on I_k.

Remark 4: The (uniform) complexity of the generators constructed in Lemma 4 is slightly super-exponential, i.e. $2^{k^{u(k)}}$, for unbounded $u(\cdot)$. (The complexity is, up to a polynomial factor, $2^{\tau^2(k)} \cdot (2^n + 2^k) \cdot \binom{2^k}{2^n}$, and 2^n is, as in Remark 3, slightly super-polynomial in k). We stress that the existence of pseudorandom generators running in exponential time, and with arbitrary polynomial expansion function, would have interesting consequences in Complexity Theory as $\text{BPP} \subseteq \bigcap_{\varepsilon > 0} \text{DTIME}(2^{n^\varepsilon})$ [Y, NW].

4. THE COMPLEXITY OF APPROXIMATING PSEUDORANDOM ENSEMBLES

In the previous section we have shown sparse pseudorandom ensembles which can be sampled by probabilistic algorithms running super-exponential time. Whether is it possible to sample pseudorandom ensembles by polynomial-time algorithms or even exponential ones, cannot be proven today without using complexity assumptions. On the other hand, do such assumptions guarantee that each samplable pseudorandom ensemble can be sampled by polynomial, or even exponential means? We give here a negative answer to this question, proving that for any complexity function $\phi(\cdot)$ there exists a samplable pseudorandom ensemble which cannot be sampled nor even "approximated" by algorithms in RTIME(ϕ). The notion of approximation is defined next.

Definition: A probabilistic ensemble Π is *approximated* by a sampling algorithm A if the ensemble Π^A induced by A is statistically close to Π.

The main result of this section is stated in the following Theorem.

Theorem 5: For any complexity (constructive) function $\phi(\cdot)$, there is a strongly samplable pseudorandom ensemble that cannot be approximated by any algorithm whose running time is bounded by ϕ.

Proof: We say that two probability distributions π and π' on a set X are *½–close* if

$$\sum_{x \in X} |\pi(x) - \pi'(x)| < \tfrac{1}{2}.$$

We say that a sampling algorithm M ½-approximates a set $S \subseteq I_k$ if the probability distribution π_k^M induced by M on I_k and the uniform distribution U_S on S are ½-close.

We show that for any sampling algorithm M most subsets of I_k of size 2^n are not ½-approximated by M (for k sufficiently large with respect to n). This follows from the next Lemma.

Lemma 6: Let π be a probability distribution on I_k. The probability that π and U_S are ½-close, for S randomly chosen over the subsets of I_k of size 2^n, is less than $(1/2)^{k-n-1}$.

Proof: Notice that if two different sets S and T are ½-close to π, then the two sets are close themselves. More precisely, we have that $\sum_{x \in I_k} |U_S(x) - \pi(x)| < \dfrac{1}{2}$ and $\sum_{x \in I_k} |U_T(x) - \pi(x)| < \dfrac{1}{2}$. Using the triangle inequality we conclude that $\sum_{x \in I_k} |U_S(x) - U_T(x)| < 1$. Denoting the last sum by σ and the symmetric difference of S and T by D, we have that $|D| \cdot \dfrac{1}{2^n} < \sigma < 1$ (this follows from the fact that U_S and U_T

assign uniform probability to the 2^n elements of S and T, respectively). But this implies that $|D| < 2^n$, and then (using $|S| + |T| = |D| + 2 \cdot |S \cap T|$) we get $|S \cap T| > 2^n / 2$.

Let T be a particular subset of I_k of size 2^n which is ½-close to π. From the above argument it follows that the collection of subsets of size 2^n which are ½-close to π is included in the collection $\{S \subseteq I_k : |S| = 2^n, |S \cap T| > 2^n / 2\}$. Thus, we are able to bound the probability that π is ½-close to a random set S of size 2^n, by the probability of the following experiment. Fix a set $T \subseteq I_k$ of size 2^n, and take at random a set S of 2^n elements among all the strings in I_k. We are interested in the probability that $|S \cap T| > 2^n / 2$. Clearly, the expectation of $|S \cap T|$ is $\dfrac{|S| \cdot |T|}{2^k}$. Using Markov inequality for nonnegative random variables we have

$$Prob \left[|S \cap T| > \frac{2^n}{2} \right] \cdot \frac{2^n}{2} < \frac{|S| \cdot |T|}{2^k}$$

and then

$$Prob \ (|S \cap T| > 2^n / 2) < 2 / 2^{k-n} \qquad (2)$$

The lemma follows. $\square$

We now extend the pseudorandom generator constructed in Lemma 4, in order to obtain a generator for a pseudorandom ensemble which is not approximated by any ϕ-time sampling algorithm. On input a string of length n, the generator proceeds as in Lemma 4. Once a $(\tau(k(n)), \varepsilon(k(n)))$-pseudorandom subset S_n is found, the generator checks whether S_n is ½-approximated by some of the first n Turing machines, in some canonical enumeration, by running each of them as a sampling algorithm for $\phi(k(n))$ steps. Clearly, it is effectively testable whether a given machine M ½-approximates a given set S. If the set S_n is ½-approximated by some of these machines, it is discarded and the next $S \subseteq I_k$, $|S| = 2^n$ is checked (first for pseudorandomness and then for approximation).

In section 3 we have actually shown that the probability that a set S is $(\tau(k(n)), \varepsilon(k(n)))$-pseudorandom is almost 1. On the other hand, the probability that a set S is ½-approximated by n sampling machines is, using Lemma 6, less than $n / 2^{k(n)-n-1}$. For suitable $k(\cdot)$, e.g. $k(n) \geq 2n$, this probability is negligible. Thus, we are guaranteed to find a set S_n which is $(\tau(k(n)), \varepsilon(k(n)))$-pseudorandom as well as not ½-approximated by the first n sampling algorithms running ϕ-time. The resultant ensemble is as stated in the theorem. ∎

Remark: The result in Theorem 5 clearly relies on the fact that the sampling algorithms we have run are uniform ones. Nevertheless, if we use Hoeffding inequality to bound the left side in (2), we get a much better bound, which implies that for any constant $\alpha < 1$, there existe strongly-samplable pseudorandom ensembles that cannot be approximated by Boolean circuits of size $2^{\alpha n}$.

5. POLYNOMIAL-TIME EVASIVE PSEUDORANDOM ENSEMBLES

In this section we prove the existence of pseudorandom ensembles which have the property that no polynomial-time sampling algorithm will output an element in their support, except for a negligible probability.

Definition: A probability ensemble $\Pi = \{\pi_k\}_{k \in K}$ is called *polynomial-time evasive* if for any polynomial-time sampling algorithm A, any constant c and sufficiently large k,

$$Prob\left[A(1^k) \in support(\pi_k) \right] < k^{-c}$$

($support(\pi_k)$ denotes the set $\{x \in I_k : \pi_k(x) > 0\}$).

Notice that evasiveness does not imply pseudorandomness. For example, any evasive ensemble remains evasive if we add to each string in the support a leading '0', while the resultant distributions are obviously not pseudorandom. On the other hand, an evasive pseudorandom ensemble is clearly sparse.

Following is the main result of this section. An interesting application of this result appears in section 6.

Theorem 7: There exist (strongly-samplable) polynomial-time evasive pseudorandom ensembles.

Proof: The proof outline is similar to the proof of Theorem 5. We again extend the generator of Lemma 4 by testing whether the $(\tau(k(n)), \varepsilon(k(n)))$-pseudorandom set S_n, found by that generator on input of length n, evades the first n Turing machines (run as polynomial-time sampling algorithms). We have to show that for each sampling algorithm M there is a small number of sets $S \subseteq I_k$ of size 2^n for which machine M outputs an element of S with significant probability. Throughout this proof we shall consider as "significant" a probability that is greater than $2^{3n}/2^k$. (This choice is motivated by a later application of this Theorem. Any negligible portion suffices here. Thus, we are assuming $k \geq 4n$). We need the following technical Lemma.

Lemma 8: Let π be a fixed probability distribution on a set U of size K. For any $S \subseteq U$ denote $\pi(S) = \sum_{s \in S} \pi(s)$. Then

$$Prob\left[\pi(S) > \varepsilon \right] < \frac{N}{\varepsilon K}$$

where the probability is taken over all the sets $S \subseteq U$ of size N with uniform probability.

Proof: Consider a random sample of N *distinct* elements from the set U. Let X_i, $1 \leq i \leq N$, be random variables so that X_i assumes the value $\pi(u)$ if the i-th element chosen in the sample is u. Define the random variable X to be the sum of the X_i's (i.e. $X = \sum_{i=1}^{N} X_i$).

Clearly, each X_i has expectation $1/K$ and then the expectation of X is N/K. Using Markov inequality for nonnegative random variables we get

$$Prob(X > \varepsilon) < \frac{E(X)}{\varepsilon} = \frac{N}{\varepsilon K}$$

proving the Lemma. $\square$

Let π_k^M be the probability distribution induced by the sampling algorithm M on I_k. Consider a randomly chosen $S \subseteq I_k$ of size 2^n. Lemma 8 states that

$$Prob\left[\pi_k^M(S) > \frac{2^{3n}}{2^k} \right] < \frac{1}{2^{2n}} \tag{3}$$

Thus, we get that only $1/2^{2n}$ of the subsets S fail the evasivity test for a single machine. Running n such tests the portion of failing sets is at most $n/2^{2n}$. Therefore, there exists a set passing all the distinguishing and evasivity tests. (Actually, most of the sets of size 2^n pass these tests). This completes the proof of the Theorem. ∎

Remark 1: Actually, we have proven that for any uniform time-complexity class **C**, there exist pseudorandom ensembles which evades any sampling algorithm of the class **C**. Notice that no restriction on the running time of the sampling machines is required. It is interesting to note that we cannot find ensembles evading the output of non-uniform circuits of polynomial-size, since for each set S there exists a circuit which outputs an element of S with probability 1. Thus, the results in this sections imply the results of section 4 on unapproximability by uniform algorithms, but not the unapproximability by non-uniform circuits (see remark after the proof of Theorem 5).

Remark 2: For the results in section 6, we need a slightly stronger result than the one stated in Theorem 3. This application requires a pseudorandom ensemble that evades not only sampling algorithm receiving 1^k as the only input, but also algorithms having an additional input of length n (the parameters k and n are as defined above). The proof of Theorem 3 remains valid also in this case. This follows by observing that each such algorithm defines 2^n distributions, one for each possible input of length n. Thus, the n algorithms we run in the above proof contribute $n \cdot 2^n$ distributions. Using the above bound (3) we can guarantee the existence of sets S that evade any of these distributions.

6. ON THE SEQUENTIAL COMPOSITION OF ZERO-KNOWLEDGE PROTOCOLS

In this section we apply the results of section 5 in order to demonstrate a weakness in the *original* definition of zero-knowledge interactive proofs. Before presenting this result we shall give an informal outline of the notions of interactive-proofs and zero-knowledge. For formal and complete definitions, as well as the basic results concerning these concepts, the reader is referred to [GMR1, GMW].

An *interactive proof* for a language L is a two-sided protocol in which a computationally powerful *Prover* convinces a probabilistic polynomial-time *Verifier* that their common input x belongs to the language L. If the assertion is true, i.e. $x \in L$, then the verifier will be convinced of its validity with very high probability. If the assertion is false then the probability to convince the verifier of the contrary is negligibly small, no matter how the prover behaves during the execution of the protocol.

An interactive proof is called *zero-knowledge* if no polynomial-time verifier (even one that arbitrarily deviates from the predetermined program) gains no information from the execution of the protocol except the knowledge whether x belongs to L. That is, any polynomial-time computation based on the conversations with the prover, on input $x \in L$, can be simulated by a probabilistic polynomial-time machine ("the simulator") that gets x as its only input. More precisely, let $[P, V^*](x)$ denote the probability distribution generated by the interactive machine (verifier) V^* which interacts with the prover P on input $x \in L$. We say that an interactive proof is *zero-knowledge* if for all probabilistic polynomial-time machines V^*, there exists a probabilistic polynomial-time algorithm M_{V^*} (called a *simulator*) that on input $x \in L$ produces a probability distribution $M_{V^*}(x)$ that is polynomially indistinguishable from the distribution $[P, V^*](x)$.
(This notion of zero-knowledge is also called *computational zero-knowledge*. The results in this section concern only this notion [5]).

A natural requirement from the notion of zero-knowledge proofs is that the information obtained by the verifier during the execution of a zero-knowledge protocol will not enable him to extract any additional knowledge from subsequent executions of the same protocol. That is, it would be desirable that the *sequential composition* of zero-knowledge protocols would yield a protocol which is itself zero-knowledge. Such a property is crucial for applications of zero-knowledge protocols in cryptography. See [O] for a formal definition of "sequential composition", and further motivation of its need.

In this section we prove that the original definition of (computational) zero-knowledge introduced by Goldwasser, Micali and Rackoff in [GMR1] (as we have sketched above) *is not closed* under sequential composition. Several authors have previously observed that this definition *probably* does not guarantee its robustness under sequential composition, and hence have introduced more robust formulations of zero-knowledge [GMR2, O, TW, F].

Feige [F] proposed a protocol that appears to be zero-knowledge when executed once but reveals significant information during a second execution. Using the underlying idea of this protocol and the results of the previous section we prove the following

Theorem 9: Computational Zero-Knowledge ([GMR1] formulation) is not closed under sequential composition.

---

[5] Other definitions were proposed in which it is required that the distribution generated by the simulator is *identical* to the distribution of conversations between the verifier and the prover (*perfect* zero-knowledge), or at least statistically close (*statistical* zero-knowledge). See [Fo,GMR2] for further details.

Proof: Let G be a generator as constructed in Theorem 7, i.e. its output induces a pseudorandom and polynomial-time evasive ensemble. Let G expand strings of length n into strings of length $k = 4n$, and let $S_n \subseteq I_{4n}$ be the set of images of G on strings of length n. Also, let K be a hard Boolean function, in the sense that the language $L_K = \{x : K(x) = 1\}$ is not in BPP.

We define the following interactive-proof protocol $<P,V>$ for the language $L = \{0,1\}^*$. (Obviously, this language has a trivial zero-knowledge proof in which the verifier accepts every input, without carrying out any interaction. We intentionally modify this protocol in order to demonstrate a zero-knowledge protocol which fails sequential composition).

Let x be the common input for P and V, and let n denote the length of x. The verifier V begins by sending to the prover a randomly chosen string s of length $4n$. The prover P checks whether $s \in S_n$. If this is the case then P sends to V the value of $K(x)$. Otherwise ($s \notin S_n$), P sends to V a string s_0 randomly selected from S_n. In any case the verifier accepts the input x (as belonging to L).

We stress that the same generator G is used in all the executions of the protocol. Thus, the sets S_n do not depend on the specific input to the protocol, but only on its length. Therefore, the string s_0, obtained by the verifier in the first execution of the protocol, enables him to deviate from the protocol during a second execution in order to obtain the value of $K(x')$, for any x' of length n. Indeed, consider a second execution of the protocol, this time on input x'. A "cheating" verifier which sends the string $s = s_0$ instead of chosing it at random, will get the value of $K(x')$ from the prover. Observe that this cheating verifier obtain information that cannot be computed by itself. There is no way to simulate in probabilistic polynomial-time the interaction in which the prover sends the value of $K(x')$. Otherwise the language L_K is in BPP.

Thus, it is clear that the protocol is not zero-knowledge when composed twice. On the other hand, the protocol is zero-knowledge (when executed the first time). To show that, we present for any verifier V^*, a polynomial-time simulator M_{V^*} that can simulate the conversations between V^* and the prover P. There is only one message sent by the prover during the protocol. It sends the value of $K(x)$, in case that the string s sent by the verifier belongs to the set S_n, and a randomly selected element of S_n, otherwise. By the evasivity condition of the set S_n, there is only a negligible probability that the first case holds. Indeed, no probabilistic polynomial-time machine (in our case, the verifier) can find such a string $s \in S_n$, except with insignificant probability (no matter the input x to the protocol is; see Remark 2 following the proof of Theorem 7). Thus, the simulator can succeed by always simulating the second possibility, i.e. the sending of a random element s_0 from S_n. This step is simulated by randomly choosing s_0 from I_{4n} rather than from S_n. The indistinguishability of this choice from the original one follows from the fact that each S_n is a pseudorandom subset of I_{4n}, and that s_0 is chosen at random from S_n. ∎

Remark: For any language L having a zero-knowledge interactive proof, one can present a zero-knowledge protocol which fails sequential composition. Simply, modify the original protocol for L as done in the above proof. (There, we have arbitrarily chosen $L = \{0,1\}^*$).

ACKNOWLEDGEMENTS

We would like to thank Micha Hofri for referring us to Hoeffding inequality, and to Benny Chor and Eyal Kushilevitz for helpful comments.

REFERENCES

[BM]   Blum, M., and Micali, S., "How to Generate Cryptographically Strong Sequences of Pseudo-Random Bits", *SIAM Jour. on Computing*, Vol. 13, 1984, pp. 850-864.

[C]   Chernoff, H., "A measure of asymptotic efficiency for tests of a hypothesis based on the sum of observations", *Annals of Mathematical Statistics*, Vol. 23, 1952, pp. 493-507.

[F]   Feige, U., M.Sc. Thesis, Weizmann Institute, 1987.

[Fo]   Fortnow, L., "The Complexity of Perfect Zero-Knowledge", *Proc. of 19th STOC*, 1987, pp. 204-209.

[GGM]   Goldreich, O., S. Goldwasser, and S. Micali, "How to Construct Random Functions", *Jour. of ACM*, Vol. 33, No. 4, 1986, pp. 792-807.

[GKL]   Goldreich, O., Krawczyk, H. and Luby, M., "On the Existence of Pseudorandom Generators", *Proc. of the 29th IEEE Symp. on Foundation of Computer Science*, 1988, pp. 12-24.

[GMW]   Goldreich, O., S. Micali, and A. Wigderson, "Proofs that Yield Nothing But their Validity and a Methodology of Cryptographic Protocol Design", *Proc. 27th FOCS*, 1986, pp. 174-187.

[GMR1]   Goldwasser, S., S. Micali, and C. Rackoff, "Knowledge Complexity of Interactive Proofs", *Proc. 17th STOC*, 1985, pp. 291-304.

[GMR2]   Goldwasser, S., S. Micali, and C. Rackoff, "Knowledge Complexity of Interactive Proofs", *SIAM Jour. on Computing*, Vol. 18, 1989, pp. 186-208.

[H]   Hoeffding W., "Probability Inequalities for Sums of Bounded Random Variables", *Journal of the American Statistical Association*, Vol. 58, 1963, pp. 13-30.

[ILL]   Impagliazzo, R., L.A., Levin and M.G. Luby, "Pseudo-Random Generation from One-Way Functions", *Proc. 21st STOC*, 1989, pp. 12-24.

[L1]   L.A. Levin, "One-Way Function and Pseudorandom Generators", *Combinatorica*, Vol. 7, No. 4, 1987, pp. 357-363.

[L2]   L.A. Levin, "Homogeneous Measures and Polynomial Time Invariants", *Proc. of the 29th IEEE Symp. on Foundation of Computer Science*, 1988, pp. 36-41.

[LR]   M. Luby and C. Rackoff, "How to Construct Pseudorandom Permutations From Pseudorandom Functions", *SIAM Jour. on Computing*, Vol. 17, 1988, pp. 373-386.

[NW]   Nissan, N. and Wigderson, A., "Hardness vs. Randomness", *Proc. of the 29th IEEE Symp. on Foundation of Computer Science*, 1988, pp. 2-11.

[O]   Oren, Y., "On the Cunning Power of Cheating Verifiers: Some Observations About Zero-Knowledge Proofs", *Proc. of the 28th IEEE Symp. on Foundation of Computer Science*, 1987, pp. 462-471.

[TW]   Tompa, M., and H. Woll, "Random Self-Reducibility and Zero-Knowledge Interactive Proofs of Possession of Information", *Proc. of the 28th IEEE Symp. on Foundation of Computer Science*, 1987, pp. 472-482.

[Y]   Yao, A.C., "Theory and Applications of Trapdoor Functions", *Proc. of the 23rd IEEE Symp. on Foundation of Computer Science*, 1982, pp. 80-91.

APPENDIX: HOEFFDING INEQUALITY [H]

Suppose a urn contains u balls of which w are white and $u-w$ are black. Consider a random sample of s balls from the urn (without replacing any balls in the urn at any stage).

Hoeffding inequality states that the proportion of white balls in the sample is close, with high probability, to its expected value, i.e. to the proportion of white balls in the urn. More precisely, let x be a random variable assuming the number of white balls in a random sample of size s. Then, for any $\varepsilon, 0 \leq \varepsilon \leq 1$

$$Prob\left[\; | \; \frac{x}{s} - \frac{w}{u} \; | \; \geq \varepsilon \right] < 2 \, e^{-2s\varepsilon^2}$$

This bound is oftenly used for the case of binomial distributions (i.e when drawn balls are replaced in the urn). The inequality for that case is due to H. Chernoff [C]. More general inequalities appear in Hoeffding's paper [H], as well as a proof that these bounds apply also for the case of samples without replacement.

Bit Commitment Using Pseudo-Randomness *

(Extended Abstract)

Moni Naor

IBM Almaden Research Center

650 Harry Road

San-Jose CA 95120

Abstract

We show how a pseudo-random generator can provide a bit commitment protocol. We also analyze the number of bits communicated when parties commit to many bits simultaneously, and show that the assumption of the existence of pseudo-random generators suffices to assure amortized $O(1)$ bits of communication per bit commitment.

1 Introduction

A bit commitment protocol is a basic component of many cryptographic protocols. One party, Alice, commits to the other party, Bob, to a bit b, in such a way that Bob has no idea what b is. At a later stage Alice can reveal the bit b and Bob can verify that this is indeed the value to which Alice committed. A good way to think about it is as if Alice writes the bit and puts it in a locked box to which only she has the key. She gives the box to Bob (the commit stage) and when the time is ripe, she opens it and Bob knows that the contents were not tampered since the box was at his possession.

Bit commitment has been used for zero knowledge protocols [GMW1], [BCC], identification schemes [FS], Multi party protocols [GMW2], [CDG], and can implement Blum's coin flipping over the phone [B].

A current research program in cryptography is to base the security on as general assumptions as possible. Past successes of the program had been in establishing various

---

*Part of this work done while author was at UC Berkeley. Research supported by NSF grant CCR 88 - 13632

primitives on the existence of one-way functions or permutations or on the existence of trapdoor functions. The most general (computational complexity) assumption under which bit commitment was known to be possible is that one way permutations exist [GMW1]. In this paper we show that given any pseudo-random generator, a bit commitment protocol can be constructed. This is a weaker condition, since Yao [Yao] has shown that pseudo-random generators can be based on one-way permutations. A pseudo-random generator is a function that maps a string (the seed) to a longer one, such that if the seed is chosen at random, then the output is indistinguishable from a truly random distribution for all polynomial time machines. Very recently Impagliazzo, Levin and Luby [ILL] have shown that given any one way function (not necessary a permutation), a pseudo-random generator can be constructed. On the other hand, Impagliazzo and Luby [IL] have argued that the existence of one-way functions is a prerequisite for any protocol that must rely on computational complexity. Thus we can conclude that if any computational complexity based cryptography is possible, then bit commitment protocols exist, and so do the protocols that rely on bit commitment, such as zero-knowledge proofs and identification schemes.

What is the communication complexity of a bit commitment protocol (i.e. how many bits must be transferred during the execution of the protocol)? It cannot be the case that only a fixed number of bits will be exchanged during the execution of the protocol, otherwise after the commit stage Bob can guess with non negligible probability what Alice would send in the revealing stage, and can verify that the guess is consistent with what she sent so far and deduce the value of the bit. However, in many applications Alice wants to commit to a collection of bits $b_1, b_2, \ldots b_m$ and they are to be revealed at the same time. These applications include coin flipping over the phone and zero-knowledge protocols such as Impagliazzo and Yung [IY]. Furthermore, Kilian, Micali and Ostrovsky [KMO] have shown that many of the known protocols for zero knowledge can be converted to ones that have this property. Therefore it is desirable to amortize the communication complexity of bit commitment. We show that if m is large enough, at least linear in the security parameter n, then Alice can commit to $b_1, b_2, \ldots b_m$ while exchanging only $O(1)$ bits per bit commitment. The total computational complexity of the protocol is the same as the complexity of the protocol for committing to one bit.

In the next section we give formal definitions of the problem and the assumptions. In Section 3 we show how the commit can be implemented using a pseudo-random generator. Section 4 shows how to get the amortized communication complexity down to $O(1)$ per bit.

2 Definitions

A *bit commitment* protocol consists of two stages:

- The *commit* stage: Alice has a bit b to which she wishes to commit to Bob. She and Bob exchange messages. At the end of the stage Bob has some information that represents b.

- The *revealing stage*: at the end of which Bob knows b.

The protocol must obey the following: For all polynomials p and for large enough security parameter n

1. After the commit stage Bob cannot guess b with probability greater than $\frac{1}{2} + \frac{1}{p(n)}$.

2. Alice can reveal only one possible value. If she tries to reveal a different value she is caught with probability at least $1 - \frac{1}{p(n)}$.

In defining the properties that a bit commitment protocol must obey we have assumed a scenario where Bob cannot guess b with probability greater than $\frac{1}{2}$ prior to the execution of the commit protocol. In the more general case, Bob has some auxiliary input that might allow him to guess b with probability $q > \frac{1}{2}$. The definition for this case is that as a result the commit stage the advantage that Bob gains in guessing b is less than $\frac{1}{p(n)}$. All the results of this paper hold for the general case.

Pseudo-Random Generators

Let $m(n)$ be some function such that $m(n) > n$.

$G : \{0,1\}^n \mapsto \{0,1\}^{m(n)}$ is a a *pseudo-random generator* if for all polynomials p and all polynomial time algorithms A that attempt to distinguish between outputs of the generator and truly random sequences, except for finitely many n's:

$$|Pr[A(y) = 1] - Pr[A(G(s)) = 1]| < \frac{1}{p(n)}$$

where the probabilities are taken over $y \in \{0,1\}^{m(n)}$ and $s \in \{0,1\}^n$ chosen uniformly at random.

Remark: We could have defined pseudo-random generators relative to polynomial sized circuits. The results in this paper would be the same in this case.

It is known that if pseudo-random generators exist for any $m(n) > n$, then they exists for all m polynomial in n [GGM]. We can treat the pseudo-random generator as outputting a sequence of unspecified length, of which we can examine only a fixed prefix (whose length is polynomial in n, the seed length).

In the rest of the paper we will assume some pseudo-random generator G. Let n be a security parameter which is assumed to have been chosen so that no feasible machine can break the pseudo-random generator for seeds of length n. We will use $G_l(s)$ to denote the first l bits of the pseudo-random sequence on seed $s \in \{0,1\}^n$. $B_i(s)$ will be used to denote the ith bit of the pseudo-random sequence on seed s.

3 The Bit Commitment

A property of pseudo-random sequences that is natural to apply in order to achieve bit commitment is the unpredictability of the next bit: it is known that given the first m bits of a pseudo-random sequence, any polynomial time algorithm that tries to predict the next bit in the sequence has probability smaller than $\frac{1}{2} + \frac{1}{p(n)}$ to succeed for any polynomial $p(n)$. (In fact, Blum and Micali [BM] used this property to define pseudo-randomness and Yao [Yao] gas shown that the two definitions are equivalent.)

As a first attempt, consider the following protocol:

- Commit stage - Alice selects seed $s \in \{0,1\}^n$ and sends $G_m(s)$ and $B_{m+1}(s) \oplus b$. (b is the bit Alice is committed to.)

- Reveal stage - Alice sends s, Bob verifies that $G_m(s)$ is what Alice sent him before and computes $b = B_{m+1}(s) \oplus (B_{m+1}(s) \oplus b)$

This protocol has the property that Bob cannot guess the bit that Alice commits to before the revealing stage, except with probability smaller than $\frac{1}{2} + \frac{1}{/poly}$, because he does not have the power to predict the pseudo-random sequence. On the other hand, Alice might be able to cheat: if she finds two seeds s_1 and s_2 such that $G_m(s_1) = G_m(s_2)$, but $B_{m+1}(s_1) \neq B_{m+1}(s_2)$, then she can reveal any bit she wishes (by sending s_1 or s_2). There is nothing in the definition of pseudo-random generators that forbids the existence of such pairs. Furthermore, given any pseudo-random generator G, one can construct another pseudo-random generator G' that has such pairs.

There is no way to force Alice to stick to one seed, since there may be two seeds that yield the same sequence. However, what the following protocol does is to force Alice to stick to the same *sequence*, or she will be caught with high probability.

Bit Commitment Protocol

- Commit stage -

    1. Bob selects a random vector $\vec{R} = (r_1, r_2, \ldots r_{3n})$ where $r_i \in \{0,1\}$ for $1 \leq i \leq 3n$ and sends it to Alice.

2. Alice selects a seed $s \in \{0,1\}^n$ and sends to Bob the vector $\vec{D} = (d_1, d_2, \ldots d_{3n})$ where

$$d_i = \begin{cases} B_i(s) & \text{if } r_i = 0 \\ B_i(s) \oplus b & \text{if } r_i = 1 \end{cases}$$

- Reveal stage - Alice sends s and Bob verifies that for all $1 \le i \le 3n$, if $r_i = 0$ then $d_i = B_i(s)$, and if $r_i = 1$ then $c_i = B_i(s) \oplus b$.

This protocol maintains the property that Bob learns nothing about the bit b, otherwise we claim that Bob has the power to distinguish between outputs of the pseudo-random generator and truly random strings: if Alice had chosen a truly random sequence instead of a pseudo-random sequence, then Bob would not have learned anything about b, since all vectors $\vec{D}$ are equally likely, no matter what b is. If there exists a polynomial time Bob (call him Bob') that can learn something about b when Alice uses a pseudo-random sequence, then Bob' can be used to construct a distinguisher between outputs of G and truly random sequences. Given a sequence x, run the commit stage of the protocol with Alice and Bob', where Alice commits to a random b and instead of a creating a pseudo-random sequence uses x. Let Bob' guess b. If he guesses correctly decide that x is pseudo-random, otherwise decide that x is truly random. The difference in the probability of deciding that the sequence is pseudo-random between a random sequence and a pseudo-random sequence is equal to the advantage Bob' has of guessing b in case x is a pseudo-random sequence.

How can Alice cheat? Her only chance to cheat is if there exist two seeds s_1 and s_2 such that $G_{3n}(s_1)$ and $G_{3n}(s_2)$ agree in all positions i where $r_i = 0$, and totally disagree in all positions i where $r_i = 1$. We say that such a pair fools $\vec{R}$.

Claim 3.1 *The Probability that there exists a pair of seeds s_1 and s_2 that fools $\vec{R}$ is at most 2^{-n}, where the probability is taken over the choices of $\vec{R}$.*

Proof: If a pair s_1, s_2 fools $\vec{R}$, then we know that $r_i = B_i(s_1) \oplus B_i(s_2)$. Therefore, a pair s_1 and s_2 fools exactly one $\vec{R}$. There are 2^{2n} pairs of seeds and 2^{3n} vectors $\vec{R}$. Hence the probability that there exists a pair that can fool the $\vec{R}$ that Bob chose is at most $\frac{2^{2n}}{2^{3n}} = 2^{-n}$.

We can summarize by

Theorem 3.1 *If G is a pseudo-random generator, then the bit commitment protocol presented obeys the following: For all polynomials p and for large enough security parameter n*

1. *After the commit stage Bob cannot guess b with probability greater than $\frac{1}{2} + \frac{1}{p(n)}$*

2. *Alice can reveal only one possible bit, except with probability less than $\frac{1}{p(n)}$*

4   Efficient Commit to Many Bits

The protocol given in the previous section has communication cost of $O(n)$ bits. If Alice wants to commit to many bits $b_1, b_2, \ldots b_m$ which she will reveal simultaneously, then she can do better.

The idea is to use many bits to force Alice to stick to one sequence and use that sequence to commit to many bits.

Suppose we implement a protocol similar to the one in the previous section, but for the part of the pseudo-random sequence that Bob request to see its Xor with b we give its bit-wise Xor with $b_1, b_2, \ldots b_m$. Alice might be able to alter one of the b_i's, since it is enough that there exists a pair of seeds that agree on all the bits but one.

We will prevent this from happening by using error correcting codes with large distance between code words. Let $C \subset \{0,1\}^q$ be a code of 2^m words such that the hamming distance between any $c_1, c_2 \in C$ is at least $\epsilon \cdot q$. We will also require that there will be an efficiently computable function $E : \{0,1\}^m \mapsto \{0,1\}^q$ for mapping words in $\{0,1\}^m$ to C.

What are the requirement from the code? As we shall see, $\log \frac{1}{1-\epsilon} \cdot q$ must be at least $3n$, and we want q/m to be a fixed constant. Such codes exist, and specifically the Justesen code is a constructive example [Ju] . For the amortization to work it sufficient that m be linear in n.

For a vector $\vec{R} = (r_1, r_2, \ldots r_k)$ with $r_i \in \{0,1\}$ and with exactly q indices i such that $r_i = 1$ let $G_{\vec{R}}(s)$ denote the vector $\vec{A} = (a_1, a_2, \ldots a_q)$ where $a_i = B_{j(i)}(s)$ and $j(i)$ is the index of the ith 1 in $\vec{R}$. If $e_1, e_2 \in \{0,1\}^q$, then $e_1 \oplus e_2$ denotes the bitwise Xor of e_1 and e_2.

Commit to Many Bits Protocol
Alice commits to $b_1, b_2, \ldots b_m$.

- Commit stage -

    1. Bob selects a random vector $\vec{R} = (r_1, r_2, \ldots r_{2q})$ where $r_i \in \{0,1\}$ for $1 \le i \le 2q$ and exactly q of the r_i's are 1 and sends it to Alice

    2. Alice computes $c = E(b_1, b_2, \ldots b_m)$. Alice select a seed $s \in \{0,1\}^n$ and sends to Bob $e = c \oplus G_{\vec{R}}(s)$ (the bitwise Xor of $G_{\vec{R}}(s)$ and c), and for each $1 \le i \le 2q$ such that $r_i = 0$ she sends $B_i(s)$.

- Reveal stage - Alice sends s and $b_1, b_2, \ldots b_m$. Bob verifies that for all $1 \le i \le 2q$ such that $r_i = 0$ Alice had sent the correct $B_i(s)$ and computes $c = E(b_1, b_2, \ldots b_m)$ by computing $G_{\vec{R}}(s)$ and verifies that $e = c \oplus G_{\vec{R}}(s)$

As in the previous section, Bob can learn nothing about any of the b_i's. When can Alice cheat? She can cheat if there exists a pair of seeds s_1 and s_2 that agree on all the indices that $\vec{R}$ has a 0, and there exist two different sequences $b_1, b_2, \ldots b_m$ and $b'_1, b'_2, \ldots b'_m$ such that $G_{\vec{R}}(s_1) \oplus E(b_1, b_2, \ldots b_m) = G_{\vec{R}}(s_2) \oplus E(b'_1, b'_2, \ldots b'_m)$. We will say that s_1 and s_2 fool $\vec{R}$ in this case.

Claim 4.1 *For any pair of seeds s_1 and s_2, the Probability that it fools $\vec{R}$ is at most $(1 - \frac{\epsilon}{2})^q$, where the probability is taken over the choices of $\vec{R}$.*

Proof: If s_1 and s_2 can fool any $\vec{R}$, then the hamming distance between $G_{2q}(s_1)$ and $G_{2q}(s_2)$ must be at least ϵq, since $G_{\vec{R}}(s_1) \oplus e = c_1$ and $G_{\vec{R}}(s_2) \oplus e = c_2$ for two different code words c_1 and c_2 whose distance is at least ϵq. Therefore, the probability that the indices i for which $r_i = 0$ will hit only the indices where $G_{2q}(s_1)$ and $G_{2q}(s_2)$ agree is at most $(\frac{2q - \epsilon q}{2q})^q = (1 - \frac{\epsilon}{2})^q$. $\square$

If $\log \frac{1}{1-\epsilon} \cdot q > 3n$, then for at most 2^{-n} of the vectors $\vec{R} \in \{0,1\}^{2q}$ there is a pair of seeds s_1 and s_2 that fool $\vec{R}$. Therefore, Alice's chances of being able to alter any bit are at most 2^{-n}.

The number of bits exchanged in the protocol is $O(q)$, and when amortized over m bits it is $O(q/m)$ which is $O(1)$, since C is a good code. The dominant factor in the computational complexity of the protocol is that of G. Alice has to produce a pseudo-random sequence of length $2q$ which is $O(n)$. This is similar to the requirement in the one bit commitment.

We can summarize by

Theorem 4.1 *If G is a pseudo-random generator, then the many bit commitment protocol presented obeys the following: For all polynomials p and for large enough security parameter n*

1. *After the commit stage Bob cannot guess any b_i with probability greater than $\frac{1}{2} + \frac{1}{p(n)}$, even when told $b_1, b_2, \ldots, b_{i-1}, b_{i+1}, \ldots b_n$*

2. *For all $1 \leq i \leq m$, Alice can reveal only one possible value for b_i, except with probability less than $\frac{1}{p(n)}$*

$\square$

Kilian has suggested a different method for amortizing the communication complexity: commit to a seed s by committing to each of its bits separately and then commit to $b_1, b_2 \ldots b_m$ by providing its Xor with the pseudo-random sequence generated by s. However, in this method the amortization starts only when m is at least n^2.

5 Conclusions

We have shown how to construct bit commitment protocols from pseudo-random generators and have shown how bit commitment to many bits can be implemented very efficiently. Thus, various Zero-Knowledge protocols can be implemented with low complexity.

In both protocols we have presented, Bob selects a random $\vec{R}$, and we have argued that almost all the $\vec{R}$'s are good. Therefore if there is a trusted party at some point in time (say the protocol designer), it can choose $\vec{R}$ and the same $\vec{R}$ will be used in all executions of the protocol.

References

[B]   M. Blum, *Coin Flipping by Telephone*, Proc. 24th IEEE Compcon, 1982, pp. 133-137.

[BM]   M. Blum, S. Micali *How to Generate Cryptographically Strong Sequences of Pseudo-Random Bits*, Siam J. on Computing, vol 13, 1984, pp 850-864.

[BCC]   G. Brassard, D. Chaum, C. Crépeau, *Minimum Disclosure Proofs of Knowledge*, Journal of Computer and System Sciences 37 (1988), pp. 156-189.

[CDG]   D. Chaum, I. Damgård and J. van de Graaf, *Multiparty Computations Ensuring Secrecy of each Party's Input and Correctness of the Output*, Proc. of Crypto 87.

[FS]   A. Fiat and A. Shamir, *How to prove yourself*, Proc. of Crypto 86, pp. 641-654.

[GGM]   O. Goldreich, S. Goldwasser and M. Micali, *How to construct random functions*, Journal of the ACM, vol 33, 1986, pp. 792-807.

[GMW1] O. Goldreich, M. Micali, A. Wigderson, *Proofs that yield nothing but their validity and a methodology of cryptographic protocol design*, Proc. 27th Symposium on Foundations of Computer Science, 1986, pp 174-187.

[GMW2] O. Goldreich, M. Micali, A. Wigderson, *How to play any mental game*, Proc. 19th Symposium on Theory of Computing, 1987, pp. 218-229.

[IL]   I. Impagliazzo and M. Luby, *One-way functions are essential to computational based cryptography*, Proc. 21st Symposium on Theory of Computing, 1989.

[ILL]   I. Impagliazzo, L. Levin and M. Luby, *Pseudo-random generation from one-way functions*, Proc. 21st Symposium on Theory of Computing, 1989.

[IY]   R. Impagliazzo and M. Yung, *Direct Zero-Knowledge Protocols*, Crypto 87.

[Ju]   J. Justesen, *A class of constructive asymptotically good algebraic codes*, IEEE trans. on Information theory 18 (1972) 652-656.

[KMO]   J. Kilian, S. Micali and R. Ostrovsky, *Simple non-interactive zero-knowledge proofs*, Crypto 89.

[Yao]   A. C. Yao, *Theory and Applications of Trapdoor Functions*, Proc. 23rd Symposium on Foundations of Computer Science, 1982, pp 80-91.

Session 4:

Cryptanalysis and Implementation

Chair: JIM OMURA

How to Predict Congruential Generators

Hugo Krawczyk
Computer Science Dept.
Technion
Haifa, Israel

Abstract. *In this paper we show how to predict a large class of pseudorandom number generators. We consider congruential generators which output a sequence of integers $s_0, s_1,...$ where s_i is computed by the recurrence $s_i \equiv \sum_{j=1}^{k} \alpha_j \Phi_j(s_0, s_1,...,s_{i-1}) \pmod{m}$ for integers m and α_j, and integer functions Φ_j, $j=1,...,k$. Our predictors are efficient, provided that the functions Φ_j are computable (over the integers) in polynomial time. These predictors have access to the elements of the sequence prior to the element being predicted, but they do not know the modulus m or the coefficients α_j the generator actually works with. This extends previous results about the predictability of such generators. In particular, we prove that multivariate polynomial generators, i.e. generators where $s_i \equiv P(s_{i-n}, ..., s_{i-1}) \pmod{m}$, for a polynomial P of fixed degree in n variables, are efficiently predictable.*

1. INTRODUCTION

A *number generator* is a deterministic algorithm that given a sequence of initial values, outputs an (infinite) sequence of numbers. Some generators, called *pseudorandom number generators* are intended to output sequences of numbers having some properties encountered in truly random sequences. Such generators appear in diverse applications as Probabilistic Algorithms, Monte Carlo Simulations, Cryptography, etc. For cryptographic applications a crucial property for the sequences generated is their *unpredictability*. That is, the next element generated should not be efficiently predictable, even given the entire past sequence. Efficiency is measured both by the number of prediction mistakes and the time taken to compute each prediction. (A formal definition of an *efficient predictor* is given in section 2).

This research was supported by grant No. 86-00301 from the United States - Israel Binational Science Foundation (BSF), Jerusalem, Israel.

A pseudorandom number generator that has received much attention is the so called *linear congruential generator*, an algorithm that on input integers a, b, m, s_0 outputs a sequence $s_1, s_2, \cdots$ where

$$s_i \equiv a \, s_{i-1} + b \ (mod \ m) \, .$$

Knuth [13] extensively studied some statistical properties of these generators.

Boyar [16] proved that linear congruential generators are efficiently predictable even when the coefficients and the modulus are unknown to the predictor. Later, Boyar [3] extended her method, proving the predictability of a large family of generators. She considered *general congruential generators* where the element s_i is computed as

$$s_i \equiv \sum_{j=1}^{k} \alpha_j \, \Phi_j(s_0, s_1, \cdots, s_{i-1}) \, (mod \ m) \tag{1}$$

for integers m and α_j, and computable integer functions Φ_j, $j=1,...,k$. She showed that these sequences can be predicted, for some class of functions Φ_j, by a predictor knowing these functions and able to compute them, but not given the coefficients α_j or the modulus m. Boyar's method requires that the functions Φ_j have the *unique extrapolation property*. The functions $\Phi_1, \Phi_2, \cdots, \Phi_k$ have the *unique extrapolation property with length r*, if for every pair of generators working with the above set of functions, the same modulus m and the same initial values, if both generators coincide in the first r values generated, then they output the same infinite sequence. Note that these generators need not be identical (i.e. they may have different coefficients).

The number of mistakes made by Boyar's predictors depends on the extrapolation length. Therefore, her method yields efficient predictors provided that the functions Φ_j have a *small* extrapolation length. The linear congruential generator is an example of a generator having the extrapolation property (with length 2). Boyar proved this property also for two extensions of the linear congruential generator. Namely, the generators in which the element s_i satisfies the recurrence

$$s_i \equiv \alpha_1 s_{i-k} + \cdots + \alpha_k s_{i-1} \ (mod \ m)$$

and those for which

$$s_i \equiv \alpha_1 s_{i-1}^2 + \alpha_2 s_{i-1} + \alpha_3 \ (mod \ m)$$

The first case with length $k+1$, the second with length 3. She also conjectured the predictability of generators having a polynomial recurrence:

$$s_i \equiv p(s_{i-1}) \, (mod \ m)$$

for an unknown polynomial p of fixed (and known) degree.

A natural generalization of the above examples is a generator having a *multivariate polynomial recurrence*, that is a generator outputting a sequence $s_0, s_1, ...$ where

$$s_i \equiv P(s_{i-n}, \dots, s_{i-1}) \, (mod \ m)$$

for a polynomial P in n variables. Note that for polynomials P of fixed degree and fixed n, the recurrence is a special case of the general congruential generators. Lagarias and Reeds [15] showed that multivariate polynomial recurrences have the unique extrapolation property. Furthermore, for the case of a one-variable polynomial of degree d, they proved this property with length $d+1$, thus settling Boyar's conjecture concerning the efficient predictability of such generators. However, for the general case they did not give a bound on the length for which these recurrences are extrapolatable (neither a way to compute this length). Thus, unfortunately, Boyar's method does not seem to yield an efficient predicting algorithm for general multivariate polynomial recurrences (since it is not guaranteed to make a *small* number of mistakes but only a *finite* number of them, depending on the length of the extrapolation).

In this paper we show how to predict any general congruential generator, i.e. any generator of the form (1). The only restriction on the functions Φ_j is that they are computable in polynomial time when working over the integers. This condition is necessary to guarantee the efficiency of our method. (The same is required in Boyar's method). Thus, we remove the necessity of the unique extrapolation property, and extend the predictability results to a very large class of generators. In particular, we show that multivariate polynomial recurrence generators *are efficiently predictable.*

Our predicting technique is based on ideas from Boyar's method, but our approach to the prediction problem is somewhat different. Boyar's method tries to simulate the generator by "discovering" its secrets: the modulus m and the coefficients α_j that the generator works with. Instead, our algorithm uses only the knowledge that these coefficients exist, but does not try to find them. Some algebraic techniques introduced by Boyar when computing over the integers, are extended by us to work also when computing over the ring of integers modulo m.

2. DEFINITIONS AND NOTATION

Definition: A *number generator* is an algorithm that given n_0 integer numbers, called the *initial values* and denoted $s_{-n_0}, \cdots, s_{-1}$, outputs an infinite sequence of integers $s_0, s_1, \ldots$ where each element s_i is computed deterministicly from the previous elements, including the initial values.

For example, a generator of the form $s_i \equiv \alpha_1 s_{i-k} + \cdots + \alpha_k s_{i-1} \ (mod\ m)$ requires a set of k initial values to begin computing the first elements $s_0, s_1, \cdots$ of the sequence. Thus, for this example $n_0 = k$.

Definition: A *(general) congruential generator* is a number generator for which the i-th element of the sequence is a $\{0, \ldots, m-1\}$-valued number computed by the congruence

$$s_i \equiv \sum_{j=1}^{k} \alpha_j \, \Phi_j(s_{-n_0}, \cdots, s_{-1}, s_0, \cdots, s_{i-1}) \ (mod\ m)$$

where α_j and m are arbitrary integers and $\Phi_j, 1 \leq j \leq k$, is a computable integer function. For a given set of k functions $\Phi = \{\Phi_1, \Phi_2, \ldots, \Phi_k\}$ a congruential generator working with these functions (and arbitrary coefficients and modulus) will be called a Φ-*generator*.

Example: Consider a generator which outputs a sequence defined by a multivariate polynomial recurrence, i.e. $s_i \equiv P(s_{i-n}, \ldots, s_{i-1}) \,(mod\ m)$, where P is a polynomial in n variables and fixed degree d. Such a generator is a Φ-generator in which each function Φ_j represents a monomial in P and α_j are the corresponding coefficients. In this case we have $k = \binom{n+d}{d}$, and the functions (monomials) Φ_j are applied to the last n elements in the sequence.

Note that in the above general definition, the functions Φ_j work on sequences of elements, so the number of arguments for these functions may be variable. Some matrix notation will be more convenient.

Notation: $s(i)$ will denote the *vector* of elements (including the initial values) until the element s_i, i.e.

$$s(i) = (s_{-n_0}, \cdots, s_{-1}, s_0, \cdots, s_i) \quad i = -1, 0, 1, 2 \cdots$$

Thus, $\Phi_j(s_{-n_0}, \cdots, s_{-1}, s_0, \cdots, s_{i-1})$ will be written as $\Phi_j(s(i-1))$.

Let α denote the vector $(\alpha_1, \alpha_2, \cdots, \alpha_k)$ and $B_i, i \geq 0$, denote the column vector

$$B_i = \begin{bmatrix} \Phi_1(s(i-1)) \\ \Phi_2(s(i-1)) \\ \vdots \\ \Phi_k(s(i-1)) \end{bmatrix}$$

Then we can rewrite the Φ-generator's recurrence as

$$s_i \equiv \alpha \cdot B_i \ (mod\ m) \tag{2}$$

Here, and in the sequel, $\cdot$ denotes matrix multiplication.

Finally, $B(i)$ will denote the matrix

$$B(i) = \begin{bmatrix} B_0 B_1 \cdots B_i \end{bmatrix}$$

For complexity considerations we refer to the size of the prediction problem as given by the size of the modulus m and the number k of coefficients the generator actually works with. (Note that the coefficients as well as the elements output by the generator have size at most $\log m$). We consider as *efficient* generators for which the functions $\Phi_j, 1 \leq j \leq k$, are computable in time polynomial in $\log m$ and k. Also the efficiency of a predictor will be measured in terms of these parameters, which can be seen as measuring the amount of information hidden from the predictor.

We shall be concerned with the complexity of the functions Φ_j when acting on the vectors $s(i)$, but computed over the integers (and not reduced modulo m). This will be referred to as the *non-reduced complexity* of the functions Φ_j. The performance of our predicting algorithm will depend on this complexity.

Definition: Φ-generators having non-reduced time-complexity polynomial in $\log m$ and k are called *non-reduced polynomial-time Φ-generators*.

Next we define the basic concept, throughout this paper, of a *predictor*:

Definition: A *predictor* for a Φ-generator is an algorithm that interacts with the Φ-generator in the following way. The predictor gets as input the initial values that the generator is working with. For $i = 0,1,2,...$ the predictor outputs its prediction for the element s_i and the generator responds with the true value of s_i.

An *efficient predictor* (for a Φ-generator) is a predictor for which there exist polynomials P and Q such that

1) the computation time for every prediction is bounded by $P(k, \log m)$

2) the number of prediction mistakes is bounded by $Q(k, \log m)$

Observe that when computing its prediction for s_i the predictor has seen the entire segment of the sequence before s_i, and the initial values. The only secret information kept by the generator is the coefficients and the modulus. If the generator is not given the initial values then our method cannot be applied to *arbitrary* Φ-generators. However, in typical cases (including the multivariate polynomial recurrence) generators have recurrences depending only on the last n_0 elements, for some constant n_0. In this case the predictor may consider the first n_0 elements generated as initial values, and begin predicting after the generator outputs them.

3. THE PREDICTING ALGORITHM

The predictor tries to infer the element s_i from knowledge of all the previous elements of the sequence, including the initial values. It does not know the modulus m the generator is working with, so it uses different estimates for this m. Its first estimate is $\hat{m} = \infty$, i.e. the predictor begins by computing over the integers. After some portion of the sequence is revealed, and taking advantage of possible prediction mistakes, a new (finite) estimate $\hat{m}_0$ for m is computed. Later on, new values for $\hat{m}$ are computed in such a way that each $\hat{m}$ is a (non-trivial) divisor of the former estimate, and all are multiples of the actual m. Eventually $\hat{m}$ may reach the true value of m. (For degenerate cases, like a generator producing a constant sequence, it may happen that m will never be reached but this will not effect the prediction capabilities of the algorithm).

We shall divide the predicting algorithm into two *stages*. The first stage is when working over the integers, i.e. $\hat{m} = \infty$. The second one is after the first finite estimate $\hat{m}_0$ was computed. The distinction between these two stages is not essential, but some technical reasons make it convenient. In fact, the algorithm is very similar for both stages.

The idea behind the algorithm is to find linear dependencies among the columns of the matrix $B(i)$ and to use these dependencies in making the prediction of the next element s_i. More specificly, we try to find a representation of B_i as a linear combination (modulo the current $\hat{m}$) of the previous B_j's (that are known to the predictor at this time). If such a combination exists, we apply it to the previous elements in the sequence (i.e. previous s_j's) to obtain our *prediction* for s_i. If not correct, we made a mistake but gain information that allows us to refine the modulus $\hat{m}$. A combination as above will not exist if B_i is independent of the previous columns. We show that under a *suitable definition of independence*, the number of possible *independent* B_i's cannot be *too large*. Therefore only a *small* number of mistakes is possible, allowing us to prove the efficiency of the predictor.

The number of mistakes made by the predictor, until it is able to refine the current $\hat{m}$, will be bounded by a polynomial in the size of this $\hat{m}$. Also the total number of distinct moduli $\hat{m}$ computed during the algorithm is bounded by the size of the first (finite) $\hat{m}_0$. Thus, the total number of possible mistakes is polynomial in this size, which in turn is determined by the length of the output of the non-reduced functions Φ_j. This is the reason for which the non-reduced complexity of these functions is required to be polynomial in the size of the true m and k. In this case the total number of mistakes made by the predictor will also be polynomial in these parameters. The same is true for the computation time of every prediction.

The algorithm presented here is closely related to Boyar's [3]. Our first stage is exactly the same as the first stage there. That is, the two algorithms begin by computing a multiple of the modulus m. Once this is accomplished, Boyar's strategy is to find a set of coefficients $\{\alpha_j'\}_{j=1}^{k}$ and a sequence of moduli $\hat{m}$ which are refined during the algorithm until no more mistakes are made. For proving the correctness and efficiency of her predictor, it is required that the generator satisfies the *unique extrapolation property* (mentioned in the Introduction). In our work, we do not try to find the coefficients. Instead, we extend the ideas of the first stage, and apply them also in the second stage. In this way the need for an extrapolation property is avoided, allowing the extensions of the predictability results.

3.1 First Stage

Let us describe how the predictor computes its prediction for s_i. At this point the predictor knows the whole sequence before s_i, i.e. $s(i-1)$, and so far it has failed to compute a finite multiple of the modulus m, so it is still working over the integers. In fact, the predictor is able at this point to compute all the vectors $B_0, B_1, \cdots, B_i$, since they depend only on $s(i-1)$. Moreover, our predictor keeps at this point, a submatrix of $B(i-1)$, denoted by $\overline{B(i-1)}$, of linearly independent (over the rationals) columns. (For every i, when predicting the element s_i, the predictor checks if the column B_i is independent of the previous ones. If this is the case then B_i is added to $\overline{B(i-1)}$ to form

$\overline{B(i)}$). Finally, let us denote by $\overline{s(i-1)}$ the corresponding *subvector* of $s(i-1)$, having the entries indexed with the same indices appearing in $\overline{B(i-1)}$.

Prediction of s_i in the first stage:

The predictor begins by computing the (column) vector B_i. Then, it solves, **over the rationals**, the system of equations

$$\overline{B(i-1)} \cdot x = B_i$$

If no solution exists, B_i is independent of the columns in $\overline{B(i-1)}$ so it sets

$$\overline{B(i)} = \left[\overline{B(i-1)} \ B_i \right]$$

and it fails to predict s_i.

If a solution exists, let c denote the solution (vector) computed by the predictor. The prediction for s_i, denoted $\hat{s}_i$, will be

$$\hat{s}_i = \overline{s(i-1)} \cdot c$$

The predictor, once having received the true value for s_i, checks whether this prediction is correct or not (observe that the prediction $\hat{s}_i$ as computed above may not even be an integer). If correct, it has succeeded and goes on predicting s_{i+1}. If not, i.e. $\hat{s}_i \neq s_i$, the predictor has made a mistake, but now it is able to compute $\hat{m}_0 \neq \infty$, the first multiple of the modulus m, as follows. Let l be the number of columns in matrix $\overline{B(i-1)}$ and let the solution c be

$$c = \begin{bmatrix} c_1/d_1 \\ c_2/d_2 \\ \vdots \\ c_l/d_l \end{bmatrix}$$

Now, let d denote the least common multiple of the dominators in these fractions, i.e. $d = lcm(d_1, \cdots, d_l)$. The value of $\hat{m}_0$ is computed as follows

$$\hat{m}_0 = |\ d\hat{s}_i - ds_i\ |\ .$$

Observe that $\hat{m}_0$ is an integer, even if $\hat{s}_i$ is not. Moreover this integer is a multiple of the true modulus m the generator is working with (see Lemma 1 below).

Once $\hat{m}_0$ is computed, the predictor can begin working modulo this $\hat{m}_0$. So the first stage of the algorithm is terminated and it goes on into the second one.

The main facts concerning the performance of the predicting algorithm during the first stage are summarized in the next Lemma.

Lemma 1:

a)   The number $\hat{m}_0$ computed at the end of the first stage is a nonzero multiple of the modulus m.

b)   The number of mistakes made by the predictor in the first stage is at most $k+1$.

c)   For non-reduced polynomial time Φ-generators, the prediction time for each s_i during the first stage is polynomial in $\log m$ and k.

d)   For non-reduced polynomial time Φ-generators, the size of $\hat{m}_0$ is polynomial in $\log m$ and k. More precisely, let M be an upper bound on the output of each of the functions $\Phi_j, j=1,...,k$, working on $\{0,...,m-1\}$-valued integers. Then, $\hat{m}_0 \le (k+1)k^{k/2}m\,M^k$.

Proof:

a) From the definition of the generator we have the congruence $s_j \equiv \alpha \cdot B_j \pmod{m}$ for all $j \ge 0$, therefore

$$\overline{s(i-1)} \equiv \alpha \cdot \overline{B(i-1)} \pmod{m} \tag{3}$$

Thus,

$$
\begin{aligned}
d\hat{s}_i &= d\,\overline{s(i-1)} \cdot c && \text{(by definition of } \hat{s}_i) \\
&\equiv d\alpha \cdot \overline{B(i-1)} \cdot c \pmod{m} && \text{(by (3))} \\
&= d\alpha \cdot B_i && (c \text{ is a solution to } \overline{B(i-1)} \cdot x = B_i) \\
&\equiv d\,s_i \pmod{m} && \text{(By definition of } s_i \text{ (2))}
\end{aligned}
$$

So we have shown that $d\hat{s}_i \equiv ds_i \pmod{m}$. Observe that it cannot be the case that $d\hat{s}_i = ds_i$, because this implies $\hat{s}_i = s_i$, contradicting the incorrectness of the prediction. Thus, we have proved that $\hat{m}_0 = |\,d\hat{s}_i - ds_i\,|$ is indeed a nonzero multiple of m.

b) The possible mistakes in the first stage are when a rational solution to the system of equations $\overline{B(i-1)} \cdot x = B_i$ does not exist, or when such a solution exists but our prediction is incorrect. The last case will happen only once because after that occurs the predictor goes into the second stage. The first case cannot occur "too much". Observe that the matrices $B(j)$ have k rows, thus the maximal number of independent columns (over the rationals) is at most k. So the maximal number of mistakes made by the predictor in the first stage is $k+1$.

c) The computation time for the prediction of s_i is essentially given by the time spent computing B_i and solving the above equations. The functions Φ_j are computable in time polynomial in $\log m$ and k, so the computation of the vector B_i is also polynomial in $\log m$ and k. The complexity of solving the system of equations, over the rationals, is polynomial in k and in the size of the entries of $\overline{B(i-1)}$ and B_i (see [8], [18, Ch.3]). These entries are determined by the output of the (non-reduced) functions Φ_j, and therefore their size is bounded by a polynomial in $\log m$ and k. Thus, the total complexity of the prediction step is polynomial in $\log m$ and k, as required.

d) As pointed out in the proof of claim c), a solution to the system of equations in the algorithm, can be found in time bounded polynomially in $\log m$ and k. In particular this guarantees that the *size* of the solution will be polynomial in $\log m$ and k. (By size we mean the size of the denominators and numerators in the entries of the solution vector.) Clearly, by the definition of $\hat{m}_0$, the polynomiality of the size of the solution c implies that the size of $\hat{m}_0$ is itself polynomial in $\log m$ and k.

The explicit bound on $\hat{m}_0$ can be derived as follows. Using Cramer's rule we get that the solution c to the system $\overline{B(i-1)} \cdot x = B_i$, can be represented as $c = (c_1/d, \ldots, c_l/d)$ where each c_j and d are determinants of l by l submatrices in the above system of equations. Let D be the maximal possible value of a determinant of such a matrix. We have that $d \hat{s}_i = d \overline{s(i-1)} c \le l\, m\, D$ (here m is a bound on $\overline{s(i-1)}$ entries) and $d s_i \le m D$, then $\hat{m}_0 = |\, d \hat{s}_i - d s_i \,| \le (l+1) m D$. In order to bound D we use Haddamard's inequality which states that each n by n matrix $A = (a_{ij})$ satisfies $det(A) \le \prod_{i=1}^{n} (\sum_{j=1}^{n} a_{ij}^2)^{1/2}$. In our case the matrices are of order l by l, and the entries to the system are bounded by M (the bound on Φ_j output). Thus, $D \le \prod_{i=1}^{l} (\sum_{j=1}^{l} M^2)^{1/2} = (l\, M^2)^{l/2}$, and we get

$$\hat{m}_0 \le (l+1) m D \le (l+1) m (l\, M^2)^{l/2} \le (k+1) k^{k/2} m\, M^k$$

The last inequality follows since $l \le k$. $\square$

3.2 Second Stage

After having computed $\hat{m}_0$, the first multiple of m, we proceed to predict the next elements of the sequence, but now working modulo a finite $\hat{m}$. The prediction step is very similar to the one described for the first stage. The differences are those that arise from the fact that the computations are modulo an integer. In particular the equations to be solved will not be over a field (in the first stage it was over the rationals), but rather over the ring of residues modulo $\hat{m}$. Let us denote the ring of residues modulo n by Z_n. In the following definition we extend the concept of linear dependence to these rings.

Definition: Let $v_1, v_2, \ldots, v_l$ be a sequence of l vectors with k entries from Z_n. We say that this sequence is *weakly linearly dependent mod n* if $v_1 = 0$ or there exists an index $i, 2 \le i \le l$, and elements $c_1, c_2, \ldots, c_{i-1} \in Z_n$, such that $v_i \equiv c_1 v_1 + c_2 v_2 + \cdots + c_{i-1} v_{i-1} \ (mod \ n)$. Otherwise, we say that the sequence is *weakly linearly independent*.

Note that the order here is important. Unlike the case in the traditional definition over a field, in the above definition it is *not* equivalent to say that *some* vector in the set can be written as a linear combination of the *others*. Another important difference is that it is not true in general, that $k+1$ vectors of k components over Z_n must contain a dependent vector. Fortunately, a slightly weaker statement does hold.

Theorem 2: Let $v_1, v_2, \ldots, v_l$ be a sequence of k-dimensional vectors over Z_n. If the sequence is weakly linearly independent mod n, then $l \leq k \log_q n$, where q is the smallest prime dividing n.

Proof: Let $v_1, v_2, \ldots, v_l$ be a sequence of l vectors from Z_n^k, and suppose this sequence is weakly linearly independent mod n. Consider the set

$$V = \{ \sum_{i=1}^{l} c_i v_i \ (mod \ n) : c_i \in \{0, 1, \cdots, q-1\} \}$$

We shall show that this set contains q^l different vectors. Equivalently, we show that no two (different) combinations in V yield the same vector.

Claim: For every $c_i, c_i' \in \{0, 1, \cdots, q-1\}, 1 \leq i \leq l$, if $\sum_{i=1}^{l} c_i v_i \equiv \sum_{i=1}^{l} c_i' v_i \ (mod \ m)$ then $c_i = c_i'$ for $i = 1, 2, \ldots, l$.

Suppose this is not true. Then we have $\sum_{i=1}^{l} (c_i - c_i') v_i \equiv 0 \ (mod \ n)$. Denote $c_i - c_i'$ by d_i. Let t be the maximal index for which $d_t \neq 0$. This number d_t satisfies $-q < d_t < q$, so it has an inverse modulo n (recall that q is the least prime divisor of n), denoted d_t^{-1}. It follows that $v_t \equiv \sum_{i=1}^{t-1} -d_t^{-1} d_i v_i \ (mod \ n)$ contradicting the independence of v_t, and thus proving the claim.

Hence, $|V| = q^l$ and therefore

$$q^l = |V| \leq |Z_n^k| = n^k$$

which implies $l \leq k \log_q n$, proving the Theorem. $\square$

With the above definition of independence in mind, we can define the matrix $\overline{B(i)}$ as a submatrix of $B(i)$, in which the (sequence of) columns are weakly linearly independent *mod* $\hat{m}$. Note that $\hat{m}$ will have distinct values during the algorithm, so when writing $\overline{B(i)}$ we shall refer to its value modulo the current $\hat{m}$.

Prediction of s_i in the second stage:

Let us describe the prediction step for s_i when working modulo $\hat{m}$. In fact, all we need is to point out the differences with the process described for the first stage.

As before, we begin by computing the vector B_i (now reduced modulo $\hat{m}$), and solving the system of equations

$$\overline{B(i-1)} \cdot x \equiv B_i \ (mod \ \hat{m})$$

We stress that this time we are looking for a solution over $Z_{\hat{m}}$. In case a solution does not exist, we fail to predict, exactly as in the previous case. As before, the vector $B_i (mod \ \hat{m})$

is added to $\overline{B(i-1)}$ to form the matrix $\overline{B(i)}$. If a solution does exist, we output our prediction, computed as before, but the result is reduced mod $\hat{m}$. Namely, we set $\hat{s}_i = \overline{s(i-1)} \cdot c \ (mod \ \hat{m})$, where c is a solution to the above system of modular equations. If the prediction is correct, we proceed to predict the next element s_{i+1}. If not, we take advantage of this error to update $\hat{m}$. This is done by computing

$$m' = gcd(\hat{m}, \hat{s}_i - s_i)$$

This m' will be the new $\hat{m}$ we shall work with in the coming predictions.

To see that the prediction algorithm as described here, is indeed an *efficient predictor*, we have to prove the following facts summarized in Lemma 3. (Lemma 3 is analogous to Lemma 1 for the second stage).

Lemma 3: The following claims hold for a predictor predicting a non-reduced polynomial time Φ-generator.

a) The number m' computed above is a nontrivial divisor of $\hat{m}$ and a multiple of the modulus m.

b) Let $\hat{m}_0$ be the modulus computed at the end of the first stage. The total number of mistakes made by the predictor during the second stage is bounded by $(k+1)\log \hat{m}_0$, and then polynomial in $\log m$ and k.

c) The prediction time for each s_i during the second stage is polynomial in $\log m$ and k.

Proof:

a) Recall that $m' = gcd(\hat{m}, \hat{s}_i - s_i)$, so it is a divisor of $\hat{m}$. It is a nontrivial divisor because $\hat{s}_i$ and s_i are reduced mod $\hat{m}$ and m respectively, and then their difference is strictly less than $\hat{m}$. It cannot be zero because $\hat{s}_i \neq s_i$, as follows from the incorrectness of the prediction. The proof that m' is a multiple of m is similar to that of claim a) of Lemma 1. It is sufficient to show that $\hat{s}_i - s_i$ is a multiple of m, since $\hat{m}$ is itself a multiple of m. We show this by proving $\hat{s}_i \equiv s_i \ (mod \ m)$:

$$\hat{s}_i \equiv \overline{s(i-1)} \cdot c \ (mod \ \hat{m}) \qquad \text{(by definition of } \hat{s}_i)$$

$$\equiv \alpha \cdot \overline{B(i-1)} \cdot c \ (mod \ m) \qquad \text{(by (3))}$$

$$\equiv \alpha \cdot B_i \ (mod \ \hat{m}) \qquad (c \text{ is a solution to } \overline{B(i-1)} \cdot x \equiv B_i \ (mod \ \hat{m}))$$

$$\equiv s_i \ (mod \ m) \qquad \text{(By definition of } s_i \ (2))$$

As m divides $\hat{m}$, claim a) follows.

b) The possible mistakes during the second stage are of two types. Mistakes of the first type happen when a solution to the above congruential equations does not exist. This implies the independence modulo the current $\hat{m}$ of the corresponding B_i. In fact, this B_i is also independent *mod* $\hat{m}_0$. This follows from the property that every $\hat{m}$ is a divisor of $\hat{m}_0$. By Theorem 2, we have that the number of weakly linearly independent vectors *mod* $\hat{m}_0$ is at most $k \log \hat{m}_0$. Therefore the number of mistakes by lack of a solution is bounded by this quantity too. The second type of mistake is when a solution exists but the computed prediction is incorrect. Such a mistake can occur only once per $\hat{m}$. After it occurs, a new $\hat{m}$ is computed. Thus, the total number of such mistakes is as the number of different $\hat{m}$'s computed during the algorithm. These $\hat{m}$'s form a decreasing sequence of positive integers in which every element is a divisor of the previous one. The first (i.e. largest) element is $\hat{m}_0$ and then the length of this sequence is at most $\log \hat{m}_0$. Consequently, the total number of mistakes during the second stage is at most $(k+1) \log \hat{m}_0$, and by Lemma 1 claim d) this number is polynomial in $\log m$ and k.

c) By our assumption of the polynomiality of the functions Φ_j when working on the vectors $s(i)$, it is clear that the computation of each $B_i \pmod{\hat{m}}$, takes time that is polynomial in $\log m$ and k. We only need to show that a solution to $\overline{B(i-1)} \cdot x \equiv B_i \pmod{\hat{m}}$ can be computed in time polynomial in $\log m$ and k. A simple method for the solution of a system of linear congruences like the above, is described in [6] (and [3]). This method is based on the computation of the *Smith Normal Form* of the coefficients matrix in the system. This special matrix and the related transformation matrices, can be computed in polynomial time, using an algorithm of [12]. Thus, finding a solution to the above system (or deciding that none exists) can be accomplished in time polynomial in $\log m$ and k. Therefore the whole prediction step is polynomial in these parameters. $\square$

Combining Lemmas 1 and 3 we get

Theorem 4: *For every non-reduced polynomial-time Φ-generator the predicting algorithm described above is an efficient predictor. The number of prediction mistakes is at most $(k+1)(\log \hat{m}_0 + 1) = O(k^2 \log(k\, m\, M))$, where $\hat{m}_0$ is the first finite modulus computed by the algorithm, and M is an upper bound on the output of each of the functions Φ_j, $j=1,...,k$, working over integers in the set $\{0,...,m-1\}$.*

As a special case we get

Corollary: *Every multivariate polynomial recurrence generator is efficiently predictable. The number of prediction mistakes for a polynomial recurrence in n variables and degree d is bounded by $O(k^2 \log(k\, m^d))$, where $k = \binom{n+d}{d}$.*

Proof: A multivariate polynomial recurrence is a special case of a Φ-generator with $M < m^d$, as each monomial is of degree at most d and it is computed on integers less than m. Therefore, by Lemma 1 d) we get $\hat{m}_0 < (k+1) k^{k/2} m^{dk+1}$. The number k of coefficients is as the number of possible monomials in such a polynomial recurrence which is $\binom{n+d}{d}$. The bound on the number of mistakes follows by substituting these parameters in the general bound of Theorem 4. $\square$

Remark: Notice that the number k of coefficients equals the number of possible monomials in the polynomial. For general polynomials in n variables and of degree d, this number is $\binom{n+d}{d}$. Nevertheless, if we consider special recurrences in which not every monomial is possible, e.g. $s_i \equiv \alpha_1 s_{i-n}^2 + \cdots + \alpha_n s_{i-1}^2 \ (mod\ m)$, then the number k may be much smaller, and then a better bound on the number of mistakes for such cases is derived.

4. VECTOR-VALUED RECURRENCES

The most interesting subclass of Φ-generators is the class of multivariate polynomial recurrence generators mentioned in previous sections. Lagarias and Reeds [15] studied a more general case of polynomial recurrences in which a sequence of n-dimensional vectors over Z_m is generated, rather than a sequence of Z_m elements as in our case. These vector-valued polynomial recurrences have the form

$$\bar{s}_i \equiv (P_1(\bar{s}_{i-1,1}, \ldots, \bar{s}_{i-1,n})(mod\ m), \ldots, P_n(\bar{s}_{i-1,1}, \ldots, \bar{s}_{i-1,n})(mod\ m))$$

where each P_l, $1 \le l \le n$, is a polynomial in n variables and of maximal degree d. Clearly, these recurrences extend the single-valued case, since for any multivariate polynomial P which generates a sequence $\{s_i\}_{i=0}^{\infty}$ of Z_m elements, one can consider the sequence of vectors $\bar{s}_i = (s_i, s_{i-1}, \ldots, s_{i-n+1})$ where $\bar{s}_i = (P(s_{i-1}, \ldots, s_{i-n})(mod\ m), s_{i-1}, \ldots, s_{i-n+1})$.

The vector-valued polynomial recurrences can be generalized in terms of Φ-generators as follows. Consider n congruential generators $\Phi^{(1)}, \ldots, \Phi^{(n)}$, where $\Phi^{(l)} = \{\Phi_j^{(l)}\}_{j=1}^k$, and for each $j, l, \Phi_j^{(l)}$ is a function in n variables. For any set $\{\alpha_j^{(l)} : 1 \le j \le k, 1 \le l \le n\}$ of coefficients and modulus m, we define a vector-valued generator which outputs a sequence of vectors $\bar{s}_0, \bar{s}_1, \ldots$, where each $\bar{s}_i = (\bar{s}_{i,1}, \ldots, \bar{s}_{i,n}) \in Z_m^n$ is generated by the recurrence

$$\bar{s}_i \equiv (\sum_{j=1}^k \alpha_j^{(1)} \Phi_j^{(1)}(\bar{s}_{i-1,1}, \ldots, \bar{s}_{i-1,n})(mod\ m), \ldots, \sum_{j=1}^k \alpha_j^{(n)} \Phi_j^{(n)}(\bar{s}_{i-1,1}, \ldots, \bar{s}_{i-1,n})(mod\ m)) \quad (4)$$

It is easy to see that vector-valued recurrences of the form (4) can be predicted in a similar way to the single-valued recurrences studied in the previous section. One can apply the prediction method of Section 3 to each of the "sub-generators" $\Phi_j^{(l)}$, $l = 1, \ldots, n$. Notice that $\bar{s}_i$ is computed by applying the functions $\Phi_j^{(l)}$ to the vector $\bar{s}_{i-1}$, and that this $\bar{s}_{i-1}$ is *known* to the predictor at the time of computing its prediction for $\bar{s}_i$. Thus, each of the sequences $\{s_{i,l}\}_{i=0}^{\infty}$, $l = 1, \ldots, n$ are efficiently predictable and so is the whole vector sequence. The number of possible prediction errors is as the sum of possible errors in each of the sub-generators $\Phi^{(l)}$. That is, at most n times the bound of Theorem 4.

One can take advantage of the fact that the different sub-generators work with the same modulus m in order to accelerate the convergence to the true value of m. At the end of each prediction step, we have n (not necessarily different) estimates $\hat{m}^{(1)}, \ldots, \hat{m}^{(n)}$

computed by the predictors for $\Phi^{(1)}, \ldots, \Phi^{(n)}$, respectively. In the next prediction we put all the predictors to work with the same estimate $\hat{m}$ computed as $\hat{m} = gcd(\hat{m}^{(1)}, \ldots, \hat{m}^{(n)})$. This works since each of the $\hat{m}^{(l)}$ is guaranteed to be a multiple of m (claim (a) in Lemmas 1 and 3). In this way we get that the total number of mistakes is bounded by $(nk+1)(\log \hat{m}_0+1)$. Notice that the dimension of the whole system of equations corresponding to the n $\Phi^{(l)}$-generators is nk (as is the total number of coefficients hidden from the predictor). On the other hand, the bound on $\hat{m}_0$ from Lemma 1 is still valid. It does not depend on the number of sub-generators since we predict each $\Phi^{(l)}$-generator (i.e. solve the corresponding system of equations) separately. Thus, we can restate Theorem 4 for the vector-valued case.

Theorem 5: *Vector-valued recurrences of the form* (4) *are efficiently predictable provided that each* $\Phi^{(l)}$-*generator,* $l = 1, \ldots, n$, *has polynomial-time non-reduced complexity. The number of mistakes made by the above predicting algorithm is* $O(n \, k^2 \log(k \, m \, M))$, *where* M *is an upper bound on the output of each of the functions* $\Phi_j^{(l)}, j = 1, \ldots, k, l = 1, \ldots, n$, *working over integers in the set* $\{0, \ldots, m-1\}$. *In particular, for vector-valued polynomial recurrences in n variables and degree at most d the number of mistakes is* $O(n \, k^2 \log(k \, m^d))$, *where* $k = \binom{n+d}{d}$.

Remark: For simplicity we have restricted ourselves to the case (4) in which the sub-generators $\Phi^{(l)}$ work on the last vector $\bar{s}_{i-1}$. Clearly, our results hold for the more general case in which each of these sub-generators may depend on the whole vector sequence $\bar{s}_{-n_0}, \ldots, \bar{s}_{i-1}$ output so far. In this case the number n of sub-generators does not depend on the number of arguments the sub-generators work on, and the number of arguments does not effect the number of mistakes.

5. CONCLUDING REMARKS

Our prediction results concern number generators outputting all the bits of the generated numbers, and does not apply to generators that output only parts of the numbers generated. Recent works treat the problem of predicting linear congruential generators which output only parts of the numbers generated [9, 14, 19].

A theorem by Yao [21] states that pseudorandom (bit) generators are unpredictable by polynomial-time means if and only if they pass any polynomial time statistical test. That is, predictability is a *universal statistical test* in the sense that if a generator is unpredictable, then it will pass any statistical test. Thus, a generator passing this universal test will be suitable for *any* "polynomially bounded" application. Nevertheless, for specific applications, some weaker generators may suffice. As an example, for their use in some simulation processes, all that is required from the generators is some distribution properties of the numbers generated. In the field of Probabilistic Algorithms the correctness of the algorithm is often analyzed assuming the total randomness of the coin tosses of the algorithm. However, in special cases a more relaxed assumption is possible. For example Bach [2] shows that simple linear congruential generators suffice for guaranteeing the correctness and efficiency of some probabilistic algorithms, even though these generators are clearly predictable. In [7] linear congruential generators are used to "expand randomness". Their method allows the deterministic "expansion" of a truly random string into a sequence of pairwise independent pseudorandom strings.

Provable unpredictable generators exist, assuming the existence of *one-way functions* [4, 21, 10, 11]. In particular, assuming the intractability of factoring, the following pseudorandom bit generator is unpredictable [5, 1, 20]. This generator outputs a bit sequence $b_1, b_2, ...$, where b_i is the least significant bit of s_i, $s_i \equiv s_{i-1}^2$ (*mod m*), and m is the product of two large primes.

ACKNOWLEDGEMENTS

I wish to thank Oded Goldreich for his help and guidance during the writing of this paper, and for many other things I have learned from him. Also, I would like to thank Johan Hastad for suggesting an improvement to my original bound on the number of prediction mistakes.

REFERENCES

[1] Alexi, W., B. Chor, O. Goldreich and C.P. Schnorr, RSA and Rabin Functions: Certain Parts Are As Hard As the Whole, *SIAM J. Comput.*, Vol. 17, 1988, pp. 194-209.

[2] Bach, E., Realistic Analysis of Some Randomized Algorithms, *Proc. 19th ACM Symp. on Theory of Computing*, 1987, pp. 453-461.

[3] Boyar, J. Inferring Sequences Produced by Pseudo-Random Number Generators, *Jour. of ACM*, Vol. 36, No. 1, 1989, pp.129-141.

[4] Blum, M., and Micali, S., How to Generate Cryptographically Strong Sequences of Pseudo-Random Bits, *SIAM J. Comput.*, Vol. 13, 1984, pp. 850-864.

[5] Blum, L., Blum, M., and Shub, M., A Simple Unpredictable Pseudo-Random Number Generator, *SIAM J. Comput.*, Vol. 15, 1986, pp. 364-383.

[6] Butson, A.T., and Stewart, B.M., Systems of Linear Congruences, *Canad. J. Math.*, Vol. 7, 1955, pp. 358-368.

[7] Chor, B., and Goldreich, O., On the Power of Two-Points Based Sampling, *Jour. of Complexity*, Vol. 5, 1989, pp. 96-106.

[8] Edmonds, J., Systems of Distinct Representatives and Linear Algebra, *Journal of Research of the National Bureau of Standards (B)*, Vol. 71B, 1967, pp. 241-245.

[9] Frieze, A.M., Hastad, J., Kannan, R., Lagarias, J.C., and Shamir, A. Reconstructing Truncated Integer Variables Satisfying Linear Congruences *SIAM J. Comput.*, Vol. 17, 1988, pp. 262-280.

[10] Goldreich, O., H. Krawczyk and M. Luby, "On the Existence of Pseudorandom Generators", *Proc. 29th IEEE Symp. on Foundations of Computer Science*, 1988, pp 12-24.

[11] Impagliazzo, R., L.A., Levin and M.G. Luby, "Pseudo-Random Generation from One-Way Functions", *Proc. 21th ACM Symp. on Theory of Computing*, 1989, pp. 12-24.

[12] Kannan, R., and Bachem, A., Polynomial Algorithms for Computing the Smith and Hermite Normal Forms of an Integer Matrix, *SIAM J. Comput.*, Vol. 8, 1979, pp. 499-507.

[13] Knuth, D.E., "The Art of Computer Programming, Vol. 2: Seminumerical Algorithms", Addison-Wesley, Reading, Mass., 1969.

[14] Knuth, D.E., Deciphering a Linear Congruential Encryption, *IEEE Trans. Info. Th.* IT-31, 1985, pp. 49-52.

[15] Lagarias, J.C., and Reeds, J., Unique Extrapolation of Polynomial Recurrences, *SIAM J. Comput.*, Vol. 17, 1988, pp. 342-362.

[16] Plumstead (Boyar), J.B., Inferring a Sequence Generated by a Linear Congruence, *Proc. of the 23rd IEEE Symp. on Foundations of Computer Science*, 1982, pp. 153-159.

[17] Plumstead (Boyar), J.B., Inferring Sequences Produced by Pseudo-Random Number Generators, *Ph.D. Thesis*, University of California, Berkeley, 1983.

[18] Schrijver, A., "Theory of Linear and Integer Programming", Willey, Chichester, 1986.

[19] Stern, J., Secret Linear Congruential Generators Are Not Cryptographically Secure, *Proc. of the 28rd IEEE Symp. on Foundations of Computer Science*, 1987.

[20] Vazirani, U.V., and Vazirani, V.V., Efficient and Secure Pseudo-Random Number Generation, *Proc. of the 25th IEEE Symp. on Foundations of Computer Science*, 1984, pp. 458-463.

[21] Yao, A.C., Theory and Applications of Trapdoor Functions, *Proc. of the 23rd IEEE Symp. on Foundations of Computer Science*, 1982, pp. 80-91.

A Chosen Text Attack on The Modified Cryptographic Checksum Algorithm of Cohen and Huang

Bart Preneel[1], Antoon Bosselaers,
René Govaerts and Joos Vandewalle

ESAT Laboratories, Katholieke Universiteit Leuven

Abstract. *A critical analysis of the modified cryptographic checksum algorithm of Cohen and Huang points out some weaknesses in the scheme. We show how to exploit these weaknesses with a chosen text attack to derive the first bits of the key. This information suffices to manipulate blocks with a negligible chance of detection.*

1. INTRODUCTION

The protection of the integrity of data stored in computers and of messages in a communication network is becoming a problem of paramount importance. Data integrity can only be achieved through adding controlled redundancy under protection of a secret key. Two major approaches can be distinguished [9]. The first solution is a compression of the plaintext with a non-keyed hash function or Manipulation Detection Code (MDC) followed by an encryption of the plaintext and/or the result of the hash function. The other option is the compression of the plaintext under control of a secret key. In this case, the compression function is called a Message Authentication Code (MAC).

The first approach has the advantage that the authentication and encryption can be separated and results in a simplified key management (only one key). Moreover the design of a fast collision free hash function is in general less complicated than the

---

[1]NFWO aspirant navorser, sponsored by the National Science Foundation of Belgium.

design of a good MAC. However, the security of the scheme is completely dependent on the subsequent encryption. More details on the requirements for non-keyed hash functions can be found in [4, 10]. In case when no secrecy of the data is required, a MAC can offer a secure and economical solution. The requirements that are imposed on a MAC are the following:

1. The description of the MAC(.,.) must be *publicly known* and the only secret information lies in the key (extension of Kerckhoff's principle).

2. The data X can be of *arbitrary* length and the MAC has a fixed length n.

3. Given X and K, the computation of MAC(K, X) must be *"easy"*.

4. Given X, it is computationally infeasible to determine MAC(K, X) with a probability of success significantly higher than $1/2^n$. Even when a large set of pairs $\{X_i, MAC(K, X_i)\}$ are known, it is computationally infeasible for an opponent to determine the key K or to compute MAC(K, X') for any $X' \neq X_i$ with a probability of success significantly higher than $1/2^n$.

5. The MAC must be *collision free:* this means that it is computationally infeasible to find two distinct messages which hash to the same result without knowing the secret key K.

However, a good MAC is only a first step in obtaining integrity protection. A secure system should also provide a serial number, time information, a specification of the number of blocks and provide a procedure to deal with plaintexts whose length is not an integer multiple of the blocklength.

2. THE SCHEME OF COHEN AND HUANG

The design of a fast and secure MAC or MDC based on blockciphers can certainly not be considered as a trivial task. One only has to look at the long list of proposals coming from reputed cryptographers that were broken [1, 9, 11, 12]. The scheme proposed in [3] and modified in [8] is based on modular exponentiation (RSA, [13]). The factorization of the modulus is discarded so that the built-in trapdoor cannot be opened.

The plaintext consists of l blocks X_0 through X_{l-1} where X_0 is the filename or the first plaintext block. The logical EXOR operation is denoted with $\oplus$.

Algorithm 1 – A Revised checksum algorithm.

Key	Select an RSA key (K_e, N) and a seed K.
Initialization	Set $Y_0 = \mathbf{RSA}(X_0 \oplus K)$
Main loop	For $i = 1$ to $l - 1$:
	$Y_i = \mathbf{RSA}\left(1 + [(X_i \oplus K) \bmod (Y_{i-1} - 1)]\right)$
Result	The result of the checksum is Y_{l-1}

Here $\mathbf{RSA}(X)$ denotes the RSA encryption of the plaintext X with the key (K_e, N). As indicated in [3], there is no reason to keep the pair (K_e, N) secret, so the actual key of the cryptographic checksum algorithm is the seed K. The use of the RSA algorithm implies that certain parts of the algorithm are cryptographically strong. However, the computation of modular exponentiations is very slow, even with fast dedicated hardware available [2, 7] (17–20 kbit/s for a modulus and an exponent of 512 bits). The performance can be improved by means of a preliminary compression of the plaintext. This can be looked at as a tradeoff between two extremes: in the first case, there is no compression which results in a secure but slow compression algorithm ; on the other hand, the message could be compressed with an MDC and then the result could be encrypted with the RSA algorithm. In the last case, the RSA does not improve directly the cryptographical strength of the MDC. Our attack is worked out under the assumption that there is no preliminary compression such that the scheme takes maximal profit of the strength of the RSA. Because the compression $C(X_i)$ was not specified in [3, 8] we are obliged to omit it. A last remark concerns the length of the result. We believe that there is no reason to keep the full 512 bits of the result. Without decreasing the security level significantly, the result can be reduced to 128 bits by EXORing lower and higher parts.

3. WEAKNESS OF THE MODULO REDUCTION

The coupling of the blocks by a modulo reduction results in specific weaknesses like non-uniform distributions of the intermediate variables. When x and y are independent random integers between 0 and $N - 1$, the probability that $x \bmod y$ equals i is given by[2]:

$$P\left[(x \bmod y) = i\right] = \frac{1}{N^2} \sum_{k=i+1}^{N} \lfloor \frac{N-1+k-i}{k} \rfloor$$

---

[2]we define $x \bmod 0 = x \bmod N = x$.

where $\lfloor z \rfloor$ denotes the largest integer smaller than or equal to z. For $i = N - 1$ this probability equals $\frac{1}{N^2}$ instead of $\frac{1}{N}$ for a uniform distribution. For $i = 0$ the sum can be worked out to [6]

$$\frac{1}{N} \left[\ln(N - 1) + 2\gamma + O(\frac{1}{\sqrt{N}}) \right],$$

where $\gamma = 0.5772156649\ldots$ is Euler's constant.

Because K is a uniform random variable, the same holds for $X_i \oplus K$. The good randomness properties of the RSA cause the result Y_i of the RSA operation also to be random. As a consequence,

$$P\left[X_i \oplus K < Y_{i-1} - 1\right] = \frac{1}{2} - \frac{2}{N}.$$

In that case, Y_i is independent of all previous blocks.

Under the assumption that the plaintext blocks are independent, uniformly distributed random variables, one can easily prove the following theorem.

Theorem 1 *If the first t bits of Y_{l-k} ($2 \le k \le l$) are equal to 1, the probability that Y_{l-1} is independent of Y_{l-k} — and thus of the data blocks X_0 to X_{l-k} — is approximately equal to $1 - 1/2^{k+t-1}$.*

This opens the door to tamper with messages by changing individual blocks and combining blocks of different plaintexts in one new plaintext with a low probability of detection. There is especially a very small dependence of the checksum result on the first plaintext blocks. This clearly violates the imposed requirements. One can wonder how an attacker can obtain the intermediate result, but this is very easy when he can compute the checksum for a shorter version of the plaintext. The error probability of an attack could be significantly lowered when he would know K or at least the first bits of K. In the following paragraph we will show how the first s bits of K can be derived by means of an adaptive chosen plaintext attack.

4. DERIVING THE FIRST s BITS OF THE KEY K

We assume that an attacker can compute the checksum for messages consisting of one block X_0 and of two blocks $[X_0, X_1]$. Later it will be shown that the attack also works for longer messages. The corresponding checksums are given by the following equations:

$$Y_0 = \mathbf{RSA}(X_0 \oplus K)$$
$$Y_1 = \mathbf{RSA}\left(1 + [(X_1 \oplus K) \bmod (Y_0 - 1)]\right)$$

Because the modular exponentiation is bijective, we can extract information on the most significant bits of K by comparing Y_0 and Y_1. For a given X_0, we are looking for a X_1 such that Y_0 equals Y_1.

$$Y_0 = Y_1 \iff X_0 \oplus K = 1 + [(X_1 \oplus K) \bmod (Y_0 - 1)]$$

If $(X_1 \oplus K) < Y_0 - 1$ the modulo operation has no influence and thus

$$X_0 \oplus K = 1 + (X_1 \oplus K).$$

The fact that K is unknown cannot prevent us from solving it for X_1 if $X_1 \oplus K < Y_0 - 1$.

We will denote the components of a vector A with

$$[A(n), A(n-1), \ldots, A(1)].$$

The vector E_i is defined as follows:

$$E_i(j) = \begin{cases} 0 & \text{for } n \geq j \geq i+1 \\ 1 & \text{for } i \geq j \geq 1 \end{cases} \tag{1}$$

Algorithm 2 – Solving for X_1.

$i = 0$
compute Y_0
repeat $i = i + 1$
            $X_1 = X_0 \oplus E_i$
            compute Y_1
            until $(Y_0 = Y_1)$ or $(i \geq j)$

The expected number of trials for this algorithm is 2. It would be possible to try all n possibilities, but in order to speed up the algorithm, we limit the number of trials to j. The error probability equals then $1/2^j$.

We are now able to describe our attack. We will show first how to determine the most significant bit of K and then it will be indicated how the attack can be extended to the higher order bits.

4.1 Deriving the most significant bit of K

results in a special Y_0 and in step 2 we look for a corresponding value of X_1 that results in equality between Y_0 and Y_1.

Step 1
Choose X_0 and compute the corresponding value of $Y_0 = \mathbf{RSA}(X_0 \oplus K)$ until

$$\begin{cases} Y_0(n) & = & 1 \\ Y_0(i) & = & 0, \quad i = n-1, n-2, \ldots, n-k+1 \\ Y_0(1) & = & 0. \end{cases}$$

This will require on the average 2^{k+1} RSA encryptions. In case $Y_0 = 0$ we are very lucky, because this implies $K = X_0$. In the following, we will thus assume that $K \neq X_0$.

Step 2
Use Algorithm 2 to find a X_1 such that $Y_0 = Y_1$. We have to consider two cases:

1. $X_0(n) \oplus K(n) = 0$ (probability $= \frac{1}{2}$).

   The construction of X_1 implies that $(X_1 \oplus K) < Y_0 - 1$ and thus Algorithm 2 will give a solution after on the average 2 RSA encryptions.

2. $X_0(n) \oplus K(n) = 1$ (probability $= \frac{1}{2}$).

   (a) $X_1 \oplus K = Y_0 - 1$ (probability $= \frac{i-1}{2^n}$): in this case we are very lucky again because Y_1 will be 1 and K can be easily computed.

   (b) $X_1 \oplus K < Y_0 - 1$ (probability $\simeq \frac{1}{2^k}$): Algorithm 2 will find a solution as in case 1.

   (c) $X_1 \oplus K > Y_0 - 1$ (probability $\simeq 1 - \frac{1}{2^k}$): because $Y_0(n) = 1$, the modulo operation can be replaced with a subtraction:

   $$1 + [(X_1 \oplus K) \bmod (Y_0 - 1)] = 1 + (X_1 \oplus K) - Y_0 + 1.$$

   Equality of Y_0 and Y_1 can be obtained if

   $$X_0 \oplus K = (X_1 \oplus K) + 2 - Y_0.$$

For the least significant bit, this results in following equation:

$$X_0(1) \oplus K(1) = X_0(1) \oplus E_i(1) \oplus K(1) \oplus Y_0(1).$$

The fact that $E_i(1) = 1$ results in $Y_0(1) = 1$ which contradicts our previous assumption that $Y_0(1) = 0$. However, even when this would not be the case, it is very unlikely that Algorithm 2 would yield a solution.

It is easily seen that the above procedure allows to determine the most significant bit of K: if Algorithm 2 succeeds, we decide that $K(n) = X_0(n)$, else we put $K(n) = \overline{X_0(n)}$. There are two cases in which the algorithm fails. The fact that only j steps are applied in Algorithm 2 implies that it is wrongly decided with a probability of $1/2^j$ that there is no solution, but every additional RSA computation divides this error probability by 2. A more serious problem is that if $K(n) = \overline{X_0(n)}$, Algorithm 2 will succeed with a probability $1/2^k$. A halving of this error probability requires on the average a doubling of the amount of precomputation in step 1. This leads us to the conclusion that these errors will occur more frequently. The results are summarized in the following table.

probability	# RSA calculations	result
$1/2$	$2^{k+1} + 2$	$K(n)$
$1/2^{k+1}$	$2^{k+1} + 2$	$\overline{K(n)}$
$1/2 \left(1 - (1/2^k)\right)$	$2^{k+1} + j$	$K(n)$

4.2 Deriving the s most significant bits of K

The same attack can be extended to derive the first s bits of K. It is not feasible to compute *all* bits of K because the amount of computation doubles for each bit. However, an attacker does not need to know all bits of K to improve his odds significantly. When he knows the first s bits of K, he can force the first s bits of $X_i \oplus K$ to zero, which implies that $X_i \oplus K$ is smaller than Y_{i-1} with a probability of $1 - (1/2^s)$, when Y_{i-1} is uniformly distributed. On the other hand, in case Y_{i-1} is known, it is possible to find a X_i such that $X_i \oplus K < Y_{i-1}$ for $2^n - 2^{n-s}$ values of Y_{i-1}.

The following variation on our attack will compute the sth bit of K under the assumption that the first $s - 1$ bits of K are already known.

Step 1

Choose X_0 and compute the corresponding value of $Y_0 = \mathbf{RSA}(X_0 \oplus K)$ until

$$
\begin{cases}
Y_0(i) \oplus K(i) \oplus X_0(i) &= 0 \quad i = n, n-1, \ldots, n-s+2 \\
Y_0(n-s+1) &= 1 \\
Y_0(i) &= 0, \quad i = n-s, n-s-1, \ldots, n-s-k+2 \\
Y_0(1) &= 0.
\end{cases}
$$

This will require on the average 2^{k+s} RSA encryptions.

Step 2

As for the first bit, use Algorithm 2 to find a X_1 such that $Y_0 = Y_1$.

To derive the first s bits of K, the total number of modular exponentiations can be shown to be approximately

$$
s \cdot \left(1 + \frac{j}{2}\right) + 2^{k+1} \cdot (2^s - 1).
$$

When $j \gg k$, the probability that these s bits are correct equals

$$
\left(1 - \frac{1}{2^{k+1}}\right)^s.
$$

4.3 Further extensions

We assumed for reasons of simplicity that the length of the chosen plaintext was only two blocks. The attack can however be extended to longer plaintexts. It suffices to look for a plaintext that results in a very large checksum Y_{l-1}. We can then add two blocks X_l, X_{l+1} to the text and with a probability $\frac{Y_{l-1}}{N}$ we can write

$$
\begin{aligned}
Y_l &= \mathbf{RSA}\left(1 + [(X_l \oplus K) \bmod (Y_{l-1} - 1)]\right) \\
&= \mathbf{RSA}\left(1 + (X_l \oplus K)\right) \\
Y_{l+1} &= \mathbf{RSA}\left(1 + [(X_{l+1} \oplus K) \bmod (Y_l - 1)]\right)
\end{aligned}
$$

In this case we can repeat the previous attack. The only difference is that the addition of 1 appears also in the first equation and thus Algorithm 2 is no longer necessary. On the other hand, we need a plaintext with a large checksum.

5. SUMMARY

We have shown that the modified version of the cryptographic checksum algorithm proposed by Cohen and Huang is insecure. The result of the checksum is insensitive to changes in the initial part of the plaintext and thus several manipulations are possible. Moreover, an attacker can compute the first bits of the key using an adaptive chosen text attack. Knowledge of these bits reduces significantly the chances on detecting a fraud.

References

[1] S.G. Akl, "On the Security of Compressed Encodings", *Advances in Cryptology, Proc. Crypto 83*, Plenum Press, New York, p. 209–230.

[2] E.F. Brickell, "A Survey of Hardware Implementations of RSA", *Advances in Cryptology, Proc. Crypto '89*.

[3] F. Cohen, "A Cryptographic Checksum for Integrity Protection", *Computers & Security*, Vol. 6, p. 505-510, 1987.

[4] I.B. Damgård, "Design principles for hash functions", *Advances in Cryptology, Proc. Crypto '89*.

[5] M. Girault, "Hash-functions Using Modulo-n Operations", *Advances in Cryptology, Proc. Crypto 86*, Springer Verlag, p. 217–226.

[6] G.H. Hardy and E.M. Wright, *"An introduction to the theory of numbers. 5th edition."*, Oxford University Press, 1979.

[7] F. Hoornaert, M. Decroos, J. Vandewalle and R. Govaerts, "Fast RSA-Hardware: Dream or Reality ?", *Advances in Cryptology, Proc. Eurocrypt 88*, Springer Verlag, p. 257–264.

[8] Y.J. Huang and F. Cohen, "Some Weak Points of One Fast Cryptographic Checksum Algorithm and its Improvement", *Computers & Security*, Vol. 7, p. 503-505, 1988.

[9] R.R. Jueneman, "A High Speed Manipulation Detection Code", *Advances in Cryptology, Proc. Crypto 86*, Springer Verlag, p. 327–347.

[10] R.C. Merkle, "One way hash functions and DES", *Advances in Cryptology, Proc. Crypto '89*.

[11] S.F. Mjølsnes, "A Hash Of Some One–Way Hash functions and Birthdays", preprint.

[12] B. Preneel, R. Govaerts and J. Vandewalle, "Cryptographically Secure Hash Functions: an Overview", *Internal Report, ESAT Laboratories K.U.Leuven*, 1989.

[13] R.L. Rivest, A. Shamir and L. Adleman, "A Method for Obtaining Digital Signatures and Public-Key Cryptosystems", *Comm. ACM*, Vol. 21, No. 2, p. 120–126, 1978.

[14] G.J. Simmons, "A Survey of Information Authentication", *Proc. IEEE*, Vol. 76, No. 5, p. 603–620, 1988.

On the Linear Consistency Test (LCT) in Cryptanalysis
with Applications *

Kencheng Zeng[1], C.H. Yang[2], and T.R.N. Rao[2]

[1]Graduate School of USTC
Academia Sinica
P.O. Box 3908
Beijing
People's Republic of China

[2]The Center for Advanced Computer Studies
University of Southwestern Louisiana
P.O. Box 44330
Lafayette, LA 70504-4330

Abstract. *In this paper, we give at first a precise estimation for the consistency probability of a system of linear algebraic equations $Ax = b$ with random $m \times n$ coefficient matrix A, $m > n$, and fixed non-zero right side b. A new test in cryptanalysis is then formulated on the basis of the estimation and applied to attack the multiplexing generator of Jennings (1980) and the multiple-speed generator of Massey-Rueppel (1984). Some security remarks concerning the perfect linear cipher of the latter authors are also made.*

> Linearity is the curse of the cryptographer
>
> — J. Massey —

I. Introduction

Cryptanalysis is in the last run a matter of searching [1]. In cracking a more or less seriously designed cryptosystem, exhaustive searching at some level is inevitable. The problem is in the range of which objectives to make the searching tests so as to minimize the amount of work needed, and according to which criteria to signalize discovery of the objectives in search so as to maximize the probability of successful key identification.

---

* This research is supported by Board of Regents of Louisiana Grant #86-USL(2)-127-03

If the entire key of secrecy **K** in a system can be revealed by exhaustive searching concentrated on a certain subkey K_1, then this will mean that only the $|K_1|$ key bits in search are responsible for the cryptographic strength of the system, and the remaining $|K| - |K_1|$ bits of key information are redundant. The ratio $\rho = \dfrac{|K| - |K_1|}{|K|}$ can be called the *key information redundancy* rate of the system.

Systems which can be cracked by pure analytic attack, such as those discussed in [2], have key information redundancy rate $\rho = 1$, but similar cases rarely happen in practice.

The problem now is how to discover the redundancy. The rubric of J. Massey quoted above gives us an important hint that in certain cases such redundancy may be found by making use of the linearity latent in the systems under consideration.

Following this idea, we prove in the present paper a theorem on the consistency probability of a system of linear algebraic equations $A x = b$ with random $m \times n$ coefficient matrix A, $m > n$, and fixed non-zero right side vector b. On the basis of this theorem, we set up a new cryptanalytic test, called the linear consistency test (LCT), and apply it to disclose the key information redundancy in several random bit generators published in the open literature.

II. The Consistency Probability of $A x = b$

We start with proving the following two simple algebraic propositions.

Lemma 1. Let $A = \left[a(i,j) \right]$ be an $m \times n$ random binary matrix with entries satisfying, independently from each other, the distribution $Prob\left[a(i,j) = 0 \right] = \dfrac{1}{2}$. Then for any integer r, $0 < r \leqslant n$, the probability for A to have rank r is

$$prob\left[rank(A) = r \right] = C_n^r \, 2^{-m(n-r)} \prod_{i=m-r+1}^{m} (1 - \frac{1}{2^i}) . \tag{1}$$

Proof. Consider the direct product $G = GL(m, F_2) \times S_n$ of the m-dimensional general linear group $GL(m, F_2)$ and the symmetric group S_n of degree n, acting on the object set $\Omega = \{A\}$ of all possible $m \times n$ matrices over F_2, in such a way that for any $A \in \Omega$ and $g = (P, Q)$, $P \in GL(m, F_2)$, $Q \in S_n$, we have $\pi_g(A) = PAQ$. It is well known [5], that the subset of all $m \times n$ matrices of rank r form a G-orbit with representative

$$I_{m,n,r} = \begin{pmatrix} I_r & 0 \\ 0 & 0 \end{pmatrix} .$$

Thus we see the number of all $m \times n$ matrices of rank r over F_2 is equal to

$$N_{m,n,r} = \left| \Omega_{I_{m,n,r}} \right| = \frac{\left| GL(m, F_2) \right| \times \left| S_n \right|}{\left| Stab_G(I_{m,n,r}) \right|}.$$

But we know

$$\left| GL(m, F_2) \right| = 2^{m^2} \prod_{i=1}^{m} (1 - \frac{1}{2^i}), \quad \left| S_n \right| = n!,$$

so for the purpose of computing $N_{m,n,r}$, we need only determine the order of the stabilizer of $I_{m,n,r}$ in G. In doing this, we partition the square matrices P, Q^{-1} into block forms compatible with $I_{m,n,r}$

$$P = \begin{bmatrix} P(1,1) & P(2,1) \\ P(1,2) & P(2,2) \end{bmatrix}, \quad Q^{-1} = \begin{bmatrix} Q(1,1) & Q(2,1) \\ Q(1,2) & Q(2,2) \end{bmatrix}.$$

Then it follows from $PI_{m,n,r} = I_{m,n,r}Q^{-1}$ that

$$P(1,1) = Q(1,1), \quad P(2,1) = 0, \quad Q(1,2) = 0,$$

where

$$P(2,2) \in GL(m-r, F_2), \quad Q(1,1) \in S_r, \quad Q(2,2) \in S_{m-r}.$$

Moreover, we have $Q(2,1) = 0$, since Q^{-1} is a permutation matrix, and $P(1,2)$ can be an arbitrary matrix. Therefore, we have

$$\left| Stab_G(I_{m,n,r}) \right| = r! \, (n-r)! \, 2^{m(m-r)} \prod_{i=1}^{m-r} (1 - \frac{1}{2^i}),$$

and

$$N_{m,n,r} = C_n^r 2^{mr} \prod_{i=m-r+1}^{m} (1 - \frac{1}{2^i}).$$

But $\left| \Omega \right| = 2^{mn}$, so we get (1).

Lemma 2. Let b be any given non-zero vector in the m-dimensional vector space $V_m(F_2)$, and r any non-negative integer not greater than m. If the r-dimensional subspaces of $V_m(F_2)$ can be generated equiprobabilistically, then the probability for a randomly generated r-dimensional subspace W to contain b is

$$Prob\left[b \in W \right] = \frac{2^r - 1}{2^m - 1}. \tag{2}$$

Proof. Every r-dimensional subspace of $V_m(F_2)$ containing b can be spanned by a basis of the form $(b, w_1, w_2, ..., w_{r-1})$. There are altogether

$$B_r = 2^{m(r-1)} \prod_{i=m-r+1}^{m-1} (1 - \frac{1}{2^i})$$

similar vector sets in $V_m(F_2)$, and the vector set $(b, w'_1, w'_2, ..., w'_{r-1})$ will span the same subspace as $(b, w_1, w_2, ..., w_{r-1})$ iff

$$(b, w'_1, w'_2, ..., w'_{r-1}) = (b, w_1, w_2, ..., w_{r-1}) \begin{pmatrix} 1 & c \\ 0 & Q \end{pmatrix},$$

where $Q \in GL(r-1, F_2)$ and c is an arbitrary $(r-1)$-tuple. So we see the number of r-dimensional subspace in $V_m(F_2)$, which contain b, is

$$N_{r,b} = \frac{B_r}{2^{r-1} \left| GL(r-1, F_2) \right|}.$$

On the other hand, the number of arbitrary r-dimensional subspaces of $V_m(F_2)$ can be derived in the same way to be

$$N_r = \frac{2^{mr} \prod_{i=m-r+1}^{m} (1 - \frac{1}{2^i})}{\left| GL(r, F_2) \right|}.$$

So we have

$$Prob\left(b \in W \right) = \frac{N_{r,b}}{N_r} = \frac{2^r - 1}{2^m - 1}.$$

Theorem 1. Let A and b be as described in the lemmas and $m > n$, then the probability for the linear system $A x = b$ to be consistent is

$$Prob\left(A x = b \text{ is consist.} \right) < \frac{1}{2^{m-n}} (1 + \frac{1}{2^{m+1}})^n . \tag{3}$$

Proof. Denote by $L(A)$ the subspace of $V_m(F_2)$ spanned by the n column vectors of A, then the system is consistent iff $b \in L(A)$. Therefore we have

$$Prob\left(A x = b \text{ is consistent} \right) = Prob\left(b \in L(A) \right)$$

$$= \sum_{r=0}^{n} Prob\left(rank\ A = r\right) Prob\left(b \in L(A) \mid dim\ L(A) = r\right)$$

$$= \sum_{r=0}^{n} C_n^r\, 2^{-m(n-r)} \prod_{i=m-r+1}^{m} (1 - \frac{1}{2^i}) \cdot \frac{2^r - 1}{2^m - 1}$$

$$= \frac{1}{2^m} \sum_{r=0}^{n} C_n^r\, 2^{-m(n-r)} \prod_{i=m-r+1}^{m-1} (1 - \frac{1}{2^i}) \cdot (2^r - 1)$$

$$< \frac{1}{2^m} \sum_{r=0}^{n} C_n^r\, 2^{-m(n-r)} \cdot (2^r - 1)$$

$$= \frac{1}{2^m} \sum_{r=0}^{n} C_n^r\, 2^{-m(n-r)} \cdot 2^r - \frac{1}{2^m} \sum_{r=0}^{n} C_n^r\, 2^{-m(n-r)}$$

$$= \frac{1}{2^m} (2 + \frac{1}{2^m})^n - \frac{1}{2^m} (1 + \frac{1}{2^m})^n$$

$$< \frac{1}{2^{m-n}} (1 + \frac{1}{2^{m+1}})^n .$$

III. The Linear Consistency Test (LCT)

In considering a keystream generator, it is sometimes possible to single out a certain subkey K_1 from the entire key of secrecy K and write out a system of linear equations of the form

$$A(K_1)\, x = b , \tag{4}$$

where the coefficient matrix $A(K_1)$ is determined by the bit-generating algorithm and is parametrized by K_1, while b is determined by the captured segment of the output sequence. The solution vector x, in general, can be used to determine the remaining part of K.

If the parameter K_1 coincides with the subkey used in generating the captured segment under consideration, then (4) certainly will be consistent. On the other hand, if the parameter K_1 is not the subkey used, then by theorem 1 the consistency probability of the system will be very small when the captured segment is long enough.

Thus, for the purpose of finding the right subkey K_1, we need only test the consistency of (4) with respect to all possible choices of the parameter K_1, and signalize discovery of the subkey in search whenever the system is found to be consistent. The number of cases to be tested is $2^{|K_1|}$, and the work factor needed for each test is that of the Gauss elimination algorithm applied to the augmented matrix $(A(K_1), b)$.

In order to make the number of false consistency alarms as small as possible, the number of equations in (4) should exceed $|x| + |\mathbf{K}_1|$ significantly. This being the case, another consequence is that the solution x of a consistent system (4) will be, *with probability nearly 1*, unique. In certain situations, for example, in the problems to be considered below, this means no further large scale searches will be needed for revealing the entire key.

The following *pop melody* in stream cipher cryptography is in many cases helpful in forming up the linear system (4) needed in applying the LCT.

Lemma 3. If the linear recursive sequence $c = \{c(t) \mid t \geqslant 0\}$ has a feedback polynomial $f(x)$ of degree n, and

$$x^t = r(x) = r_{t,0} + r_{t,1}x + \cdots + r_{t,n-1}x^{n-1} \quad mod\ f(x)$$

then

$$c(t) = r_{t,0}c(0) + r_{t,1}c(1) + \cdots + r_{t,n-1}c(n-1) . \qquad (5)$$

Proof. Write $x^t = q(x)f(x) + r(x)$, then we have

$$\mathbf{d} \triangleq (x^t + r(x))c = (x^t + r(x))c + q(x)f(x)c = (x^t + q(x)f(x) + r(x))c = 0 ,$$

and (5) follows from examining the expression for the signal $d(0)$.

IV. Cracking the Generators of Jennings and Massey-Rueppel

The generators proposed by Jennings and Massey-Rueppel both use two LFSR sequences with primitive feedback polynomials $f(x)$ and $g(x)$, of degrees l and n respectively, as source sequences, but combine them by different key-controlled algorithms. The LCT will show that both of them suffer from a fairly large key information redundancy.

(A) The Multiplexing Generator of Jennings

According to Chambers [6], similar schemes have been recommended by the European Broadcasting Union as standards for scrambling television broadcasts. The generator produces the output signals $c(t)$, $t \geqslant 0$, in the following way: Fix a positive integer $h \leqslant \min(l, \lfloor \log_2 n \rfloor)$ and a tap pattern $0 \leqslant i_0 < i_1 < \cdots < i_{h-1} \leqslant l-1$ on LFSR-1. For every moment $t \geqslant 0$ form the number

$$u(t) = a(t + i_0) + a(t + i_1)2 + \cdots + a(t + i_{h-1})2^{h-1}$$

and transform it into

$$\theta(u(t)) = s_0(t) + s_1(t)2 + \cdots + s_{k-1}(t)2^{k-1} , \qquad k = \lceil \log_2 n \rceil$$

by an injective mapping $\theta: \{0, 1, ..., 2^b - 1\} \to \{0, 1, ..., n - 1\}$, which together with the initial states of LFSR-1 and LFSR-2 form the key of secrecy of the system. The output signal is $c(t) = b\left[t + \theta(u(t))\right]$.

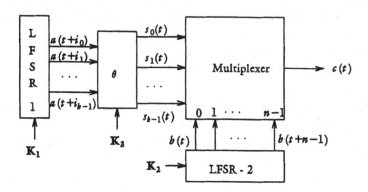

Figure 1. The Jennings Generator

It has been shown [3], that if $(l, n) = 1$, then the output sequence has period $(2^l - 1)(2^n - 1)$ and linear complexity $LC \leqslant n(1 + \sum_{i=1}^{b} C_i^l)$, with equality if the tap positions are spaced at equal intervals. Thus, the strive for the highest linear complexity will greatly limit the choice of the tap patterns. Therefore, without losing any generality of our analysis, we can assume the tap pattern is fixed and known.

Theorem 2. If the feedback polynomials $f(x)$ and $g(x)$ are known to the cryptanalyst, then the Jennings generator can be broken on an output segment of length $N \geqslant l + n 2^b$ by 2^{l+b} linear consistency tests.

Proof. The cracking procedure starts with applying the LCT to determine the initial state $\mathbf{a}_0$ of LFSR-1 corresponding to the captured segment $\mathbf{c}$ of length N.

Step 1. For each $0 \leqslant t \leqslant N-1$, divide x^t by $g(x)$ to obtain the remainder

$$r_t(x) = r_{t,0} + r_{t,1}x + \cdots + r_{t,n-1}x^{n-1}$$

and store the vector $\mathbf{r}(t) = (r_{t,0}, r_{t,1}, ..., r_{t,n-1})$.

Step 2. For every non-zero $\mathbf{a} \in V_l(F_2)$, set LFSR-1 to work with $\mathbf{a}$ as initial state and form 2^b linear systems

$$S_k: A_k x = \mathbf{c}_k, \quad 0 \leqslant k \leqslant 2^b - 1, \tag{6}$$

by putting the equation $(\mathbf{r}(t), x) = \mathbf{c}(t)$ into the system S_k whenever

$u(t) = k$.

For $0 \leqslant k \leqslant 2^b - 1$, test the consistency of S_k. Discard $\mathbf{a}$ whenever inconsistency is alarmed. The vectors $\mathbf{a}$, for which all the systems S_k turn to be consistent, will be reserved as candidates for $\mathbf{a}_0$. The true initial vector $\mathbf{a}_0$ will certainly be reserved and the probability p for an arbitrary $\mathbf{a}$ to be reserved can be estimated in the following way: Let m_k be the number of equations in S_k and assume that $m_k > n$ for $k < q$ and $m_k \leqslant n$ for $k \geqslant q$. By theorem 1, the probability for S_k to be consistent is

$$p_k < \frac{1}{2^{m_k - n}}(1 + \frac{1}{2^{m_k + 1}})^n , \quad 0 \leqslant k \leqslant q - 1 ,$$

so we see

$$p < 2^{qn - \sum\limits_{k=0}^{q-1} m_k} \cdot \prod_{k=0}^{q-1}(1 + \frac{1}{2^{m_k+1}})^n$$

$$\leqslant 2^{2^b n - N} \cdot (1 + \frac{1}{2^{n+2}})^{qn} < 2^{-l}\exp\left(\frac{n^2}{2^{n+2}}\right) .$$

Step 3. Let $\mathbf{a}$ be any candidate vector. Consider any system in (6), for which the coefficient matrix A_k has the largest rank, and denote the set of the solutions as vectors in $V_n(F_2)$ by V. According to lemma 1, we have $|V| = 1$ with probability nearly 1. Choose an arbitrary $v_0 \in V$ and consider the vectors

$$v_{-n+1}, \cdots, v_{-1}, v_0, v_1, \cdots v_{n-1} \tag{7}$$

which can be generated successively by LFSR-2 starting from v_{-n+1}. Check whether there is in (7) a subset of 2^b vectors

$$v_{i_0}, v_{i_1}, \ldots, v_{i_{2^b-1}} , \tag{8}$$

satisfying the following two conditions:

(a) $A_k v_{i_k}{}^T = c_k , \quad 0 \leqslant k \leqslant 2^b - 1 ;$ (b) $\max \{i_k\} - \min\{i_k\} < n .$ (9)

Discard v_0 if such a subset in (7) does not exist. Discard $\mathbf{a}$ if all vectors in V are discarded.

Since the probability for an arbitrary set of 2^b vectors in $V_n(F_2)$ to have the property that LFSR-2, starting from a certain one of them, will generate the remaining vectors within $n - 1$ steps is of the order of magnitude $O\left(2^{-n(2^b-1)}\right)$, all the candidate vectors $\mathbf{a}$, except $\mathbf{a}_0$, will be discarded and $v_0 \in V$ will also be uniquely determined.

Step 4. Write $\quad \sigma \triangleq \min i_k , \quad \tau \triangleq \max i_k , \quad \rho \triangleq n + \sigma - \tau ,$ and suppose LFSR-2, starting from v_σ, arrives at the vector v_{i_k} of (8) in n_k steps, conclude

$$\theta(k) = n_k + \nu , \quad 0 \leqslant k \leqslant 2^b - 1 ,$$

where ν may be any non-negative integer not exceeding ρ, and the corresponding initial state of LFSR-2 will be the vector generated by LFSR-2 after ν steps of work with v_σ as start.

(B) The Multiple Speed Generator and the Perfect Linear Cipher

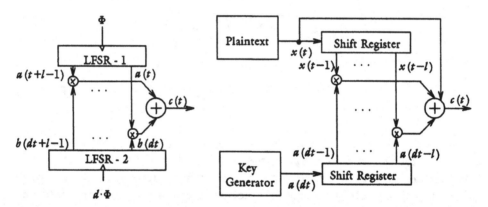

Figure 2. Multiple speed generator   Figure 3. Perfect linear cipher

In the multiple speed generator of Massey-Rueppel, the shift register LFSR-2 is clocked at a speed $d \geqslant 2$ times as fast as the LFSR-1 and the output signal $c(t)$ is produced according to

$$c(t) = \sum_{i=0}^{l-1} a(t + i)b(dt + i) .$$

The speed factor d is variable and is used as a part of the key of secrecy. As a result of various technical limitations, d cannot be too large, and one can estimate an upper bound $d_{\max}$ to it. Therefore, if the feedback polynomials $f(x)$ and $g(x)$ are known, then the cryptanalyst can determine d and the initial state of LFSR-1, and hence break the system by the LCT applied to an output segment of length $N \geqslant l + n + \log_2 d_{\max}$.

More interesting, however, is the perfect linear cipher considered in connection with the problem of introducing automatic authentication into crypto-systems. As pointed out in [7, p.419], in the case of a block cipher, as a result of the existence of the diffusion effect, this can be achieved by applying to the plaintext any error control code, linear or nonlinear, before encrypting. For stream ciphers in general, only non-linear or keyed codes can serve the purpose. In the perfect linear cipher, however, a single error in the plaintext will propagate over a range of length l, so linear codes can be used to realize effective authentication. But the analysis below will show that this will make the system insecure.

Theorem 3. If the key generator in Figure 3 is an LFSR with known primitive feedback polynomial $f(x)$ of degree l, and the plaintext is a string of codewords of a known systematic linear code of information rate $r = k/n$, then the cipher can be broken by a ciphertext-only attack consisting of $n2^l$ LCT applied to a captured segment c of length

$$N \geqslant \frac{2l + \log_2 n}{1 - r} + n .$$ (10)

Proof. Assume the speed factor known and let the generator matrix of the linear code be $\mathbf{G} = [\mathbf{I}_k : (p_{ij})]$. The claimed ciphertext-only attack starts with the observation that if for some $0 \leqslant w \leqslant n - 1$, we assume $x(w)$ to be the first bit of a codeword, then for any $0 \leqslant q < B = \lfloor \frac{N - w}{n} \rfloor$, we shall have $n - k$ linear relations of the form

$$x(w+qn+k+j) = \sum_{i=0}^{k-1} p_{i,j} x(w+qn+i) , \quad 0 \leqslant j \leqslant n - k - 1$$ (11)

to express the parity signals in terms of the information signals. After making these substitutions in the relations

$$c(t) = x(t) + \sum_{i=1}^{l} a(dt - i)x(t - i) , \quad w \leqslant t < w + nB ,$$ (12)

we shall have a set of nB linear equations of the form

$$L_t \left[x(w-l),..,x(w-1);..;x(w+qn),x(w+qn+1),..,x(w+qn+k-1);.. \right] = c(t)$$

(13)

in $l + kB$ unknowns. Thus we can apply the LCT to determine the initial state of the key generator and the number w. Since the consistency probability of (13) is $p < \frac{1}{2^{nB-kB-l}}$, the mathematical expectation of the number of possible consistency alarms will be $E < n2^l p < 1$. False consistency alarms can be effectively discarded by checking the code structure of the recovered plaintext. This proves the theorem.

References

1. Martin E. Hellman, Ehud D. Karnin, Justin Reyneri, *On the Necessity of Cryptanalytic Exhaustive Search*, ACM SIGACT, Vol. 18, No. 2, 1984, pp. 40-44.

2. C.H. Yang, Kencheng Zeng, and T.R.N. Rao, *An Improved Linear Syndrome Algorithm in Cryptanalysis with Applications*, to appear.

3. Sylvia M. Jennings, *A Special Class of Binary Sequences*, University of London, 1980, Ph.D. Thesis.

4. James L. Massey and Rainer A. Rueppel, *Linear Ciphers and Random Sequence Generators with Multiple Clocks*, EUROCRYPT 84, 1984, pp. 74-87.

5. A. Adrian Albert, *Fundamental Concepts of Higher Algebra*, University of Chicago Press, 1956.

6. W.G. Chambers, *Clock-controlled shift registers in binary sequence generators*, Proc. IEE, Pt. E., Jan. 1988, pp. 17-24.

7. Whitfield Diffie, Martin E. Hellman, *Privacy and Authentication: An Introduction to Cryptography*, Proc. IEEE, Mar. 1979, pp. 397-427.

Batch RSA

Amos Fiat[*]
Department of Computer Science
Tel-Aviv University
Tel-Aviv, Israel

Abstract

Number theoretic cryptographic algorithms are all based upon modular multiplication modulo some composite or prime. Some security parameter n is set (the length of the composite or prime). Cryptographic functions such as digital signature or key exchange require $O(n)$ or $O(\sqrt{n})$ modular multiplications ([DH, RSA, R, E, GMR, FS], etc.).

This paper proposes a variant of the RSA scheme which requires only $\operatorname{polylog}(n)$ ($O(\log^2 n)$) modular multiplications per RSA operation. Inherent to the scheme is the idea of batching, *i.e.*, performing several encryption or signature operations simultaneously. In practice, the new variant effectively performs several modular exponentiations at the cost of a single modular exponentiation. This leads to a very fast RSA-like scheme whenever RSA is to be performed at some central site or when pure-RSA encryption (*vs.* hybrid encryption) is to be performed.

An important feature of the new scheme is a practical scheme that isolates the private key from the system, irrespective of the size of the system, the number of sites, or the number of private operations that need be performed.

1 Introduction

Almost all number-theoretic cryptographic schemes in use today involve modular multiplication modulo a composite or prime. Some security parameter n is set, equal to the length of the modulus N. In fact, factoring a composite or solving the discrete log problem can be done in time exponential in $\sqrt{n \log n}$. Thus the *real* security parameter is approximately $\sqrt{n}$. Throughout this paper, N will denote the modulus and $n = \log(N)$.

Irrespective of the scheme, the private operation (decryption, digital signature generation) must depend upon some secret string that is at least as long as the

---

[*]Work performed at UC Berkeley and ARL, Israel

security parameter. If the secret information used during the private operation were shorter than the security parameter then the cryptanalyst could guess the secret and break the scheme.

Various schemes for key-exchange, public key cryptosystems, and digital signature have been proposed ([DH], [RSA], [R], [E], [GMR], [FS], ...). In several schemes the secret is used as an exponent during the private operation and therefore the number of modular multiplications required is at least the security parameter. (In fact, many such schemes above require n modular multiplications per private operation, not $\sqrt{n \log n}$). For example, in the RSA scheme it makes no sense to choose a decryption exponent shorter than the security parameter, $(\Omega(\sqrt{n \log n}))$, otherwise guessing this exponent would break the scheme.

The Fiat-Shamir signature scheme [FS] does not use a secret exponent yet it too requires as many multiplications as the security parameter. This is related to the probability that the the prover cheats in the underlying zero-knowledge proof — essentially, every multiplication cuts down the probability of cheating by a factor of two.

In general, it is not true that the public operation (encryption, digital signature verification) requires poly(n) modular multiplications. Various schemes have a fast public operation, e.g., a small encryption exponent for RSA.

The main result in this paper is to circumvent the "lower bound" above, and obtain fast public and private operations. We achieve polylog(n) multiplications per private operation, in contradiction to the poly(n) "lower bound". We cannot escape using a long secret string, but the work is averaged over several private operations batched together.

In practice, the problem with performance does not seem to be in a distributed setting but rather with centralized applications. Todays microprocessors can perform hundreds of modular multiplications in a few seconds. Large central mainframes are obviously faster, yet much less cost-effective with respect to processing power.

Many applications require a centralized setting. Several suggested applications of digital signatures are almost irrelevant without a large central clearinghouse, and such a clearinghouse may be required to generate digitally signed receipts in response to transactions. Another typical application is a mainframe that has to decrypt many transactions, (financial data, session initiation key exchange, etc.). The scheme presented here is particularly suitable for such centralized applications.

The underlying idea behind our new scheme is to batch transactions. Rather than perform one full-scale modular exponentiation per digital signature as with RSA, the scheme performs one full-size exponentiation and subsequently generates several independent digital signatures.

Our scheme requires $O(\log^2 n)$ multiplications for a batch size of $n/(\log^2 n)$ messages. We also require up to two modular divisions per signature/decryption — this is a low order term and can be ignored.[1] Clearly one must optimize the batch size

---

[1] Modular division is equivalent to multiplication for quadratic algorithms ($O(n^2)$ bit operations — e.g., [K] section 4.5.2 problem 35) and equivalent to $O(\log n)$ multiplications asymptotically (I.e., $O(n \log^2 n \log \log n)$ bit operations — [AHU] section 8.10).

for a specific modulus size, and one can obtain *better* results for smaller batches if the modulus is (relatively) small.

Generally, we have a tradeoff between the batch size b and the number of multiplications per signature. Let cn denote the number of modular multiplications required for an n bit exponentiation ($c \approx 1.5$). Given a batch of b messages, $b < n$, we can generate b digital signatures at a cost of $cn/b + O(\log^2 b)$ multiplications per signature (plus two modular divisions). For a fixed batch size k, the work required to generate *all* k signatures is effectively equal to the work required for *one* RSA signature.

Similarly, rather than perform one full-size exponentiation to decrypt an RSA-encrypted block, the new scheme performs one such exponentiation and subsequently decrypts several RSA-encrypted blocks. This is relevant in the context of mainframe decryption (hybrid scheme or pure) and in the context of pure-RSA decryption generally. With respect to a pure RSA encryption scheme, this simply means that the block size is some multiple of the RSA modulus size. We have a tradeoff between block size and time, for larger blocks we spend less time overall.

Another application of the methods presented here is to generate Shamir's cryptographically secure pseudo-random sequence [S] with the same gain in performance. In this context, the block size penalty mentioned above does not occur. It is noteworthy that Shamir himself considered his scheme in [S] impractical due to the great number of multiplications required.

Even if we completely ignore the issue of performance and use full-sized encryption exponents, one important point concerning Batch RSA is that only one root need be extracted, irrespective of the batch size. This is related to the questions posed in [AFK] on computing with and Oracle. Many private operations can be performed by performing *one* private operation. The preliminary work to merge the batch into one problem involves no secret data, neither does the split-up phase after the root extraction. If the private operations involve decryptions then we can ensure security even if the data flow path passes through insecure devices (multiply with a random value whose appropriate root is known). The communications overhead is minimal, one never needs to transmit more than n bits to the next stage (for both merge and split-up phases). Thus, a multi-site multi-mainframe system could store the private key on one weak processor (at a PC on the CEO's desk?), never transmitting more than n bits to and from a site.

2   Background and Central Observation

An RSA digital signature to a message M is simply the e'th root of M modulo N. The public key is the pair (N, e) whereas the private key is the prime factorization of N, e is chosen to be relatively prime to Euler's totient function ϕ of the public key modulus N.

To generate a digital signature on M one first computes $d = e^{-1} \pmod{\phi(N)}$ and then computes

$$M^d \pmod{N} = M^{1/e} \pmod{N}.$$

Thus, every digital signature consists of one full-sized modular exponentiation. ([QC] suggest the use of the chinese remainder theorem so digital signature generation is slightly faster).

Fundamental to getting polylog(n) multiplications per private operation is the use of (relatively) small encryption exponents for RSA. Using a small encryption exponent means choosing e to be some small constant (say 3), and generating the public key N so that $\phi(N)$ is relatively prime to e. However, choosing a small encryption exponent says nothing about the decryption exponent d. Generally, d will be $\Omega(\phi(N))$. In fact, if d were too small (less than exponential in the security parameter), it would allow the cryptanalyst to attack the scheme. In some sense, we attain the effect of a very small d (length polylog in the security parameter), without compromising security.

Our RSA variant grants some leeway in the value of e. For example, choose two parameters S and R so that S and $R - S$ are small (e.g., $S = n^c$, $R = S + n$.). A public key N is chosen so that $\phi(N)$ is indivisible by all primes in the range $S, \ldots, R$. A valid digital signature is of the form $(s, M^{1/s} \bmod n)$, where s is any prime in the range $S, \ldots, R$.

To motivate this variant consider the following example:

Example 2.1:

Given two messages $0 < M_1, M_2 < N$, we wish to compute the two digital signatures $M_1^{1/3} \pmod{N}$ and $M_2^{1/5} \pmod{N}$.

Let

$$
\begin{aligned}
M &= M_1^5 \cdot M_2^3 \pmod{N}, \\
I &= M^{1/15} \pmod{N}.
\end{aligned}
$$

Now, we can solve for $M_1^{1/3}$, $M_2^{1/5}$ as follows:

$$
\begin{aligned}
\frac{I^6}{M_1^2 \cdot M_2} &= M_2^{1/5} \pmod{N}; \\
\frac{I}{M_2^{1/5}} &= M_1^{1/3} \pmod{N}.
\end{aligned}
$$

Note that we require *one* full-sized exponentiation to compute $I = M^{1/15} \pmod{N}$ and a constant number of modular multiplications/divisions for preprocessing and to extract the two digital signatures. The rest of this paper is devoted to the generalization of example 2.1.

3 Batch RSA

As above, let N be the RSA modulus, $n = \log_2(N)$, and let b be the batch size.

Let $e_1, e_2, \ldots, e_b$ be b different encryption exponents, relatively prime to $\phi(N)$ and to each other. Choosing encryption exponents polynomial in n implies that their product, $E = \prod_{i=1}^{b} e_i$, is $O(b \log n)$ bits long. Choosing the encryption exponents as the first b odd primes gives us $\log(E) = O(b \log b)$.

Given messages $m_1, m_2, \ldots, m_b$, our goal is to generate the b roots (digital signatures/decryptions):

$$m_1^{1/e_1} \pmod{N}, \quad m_2^{1/e_2} \pmod{N}, \ldots, \quad m_b^{1/e_b} \pmod{N}.$$

Let T be a binary tree with leaves labelled $e_1, e_2, \ldots, e_b$. Let d_i denote the depth of the leaf labelled e_i, T should be constructed so that $W = \sum_{i=1}^{b} d_i \log e_i$ is minimized — similar to the Huffman code tree construction. For our main result of $O(\log^2 n)$ multiplications per RSA operation we could simply assume that T is a full binary tree, asymptotically it makes no difference. In practice, there is some advantage in using a tree that minimizes the sum of weight times path length.

Note that $W = O(\log b \log E)$. We will show that the number of multiplications required to compute the b roots above is $O(W + \log N)$.

Our first goal is to generate the product

$$M = m_1^{E/e_1} \cdot m_2^{E/e_2} \cdots m_b^{E/e_b} \pmod{N}.$$

It is not difficult to see that this requires $O(W)$ multiplications.

Use the binary tree T as a guide, working from the leaves to the root. At every internal node, take the recursive result from the left branch (L), raise it to the power E_R where E_R is the product of the labels associated with leaves on the right branch. Similarly, take the result from the right branch (R) and raise it to the power E_L which is the product of the labels on the left branch. Save the intermediate results L^{E_R} and R^{E_L} (required later). The result associated with this node is $L^{E_R} \cdot R^{E_L}$. The product M is simply the result associated with the root. (See figure 1, the ith leaf is labelled with the ith odd prime).

We now extract the Eth root of the product M:

$$M^{1/E} = m_1^{1/e_1} \cdot m_2^{1/e_2} \cdots m_b^{1/e_b} \pmod{N}.$$

This involves $O(\log N)$ modular multiplications — equivalent to one RSA decryption.

The factors of $M^{1/E}$ are the roots we require. Our next goal is to break the product $M^{1/E}$ into two subproducts, the breakup is implied by the structure of the binary tree T used to generate the product M. We repeat this recursively to break up the product into its b factors. (See figure 2).

Let $e_1, e_2, \ldots, e_k$ be the labels associated with the left branch of the root of the binary tree T. We define an exponent X by means of the Chinese remainder theorem:

$$
\begin{aligned}
X &= 0 \pmod{e_1}, \\
X &= 0 \pmod{e_2}, \\
&\vdots \\
X &= 0 \pmod{e_k}, \\
X &= 1 \pmod{e_{k+1}}, \\
X &= 1 \pmod{e_{k+2}}, \\
&\vdots \\
X &= 1 \pmod{e_b}.
\end{aligned}
$$

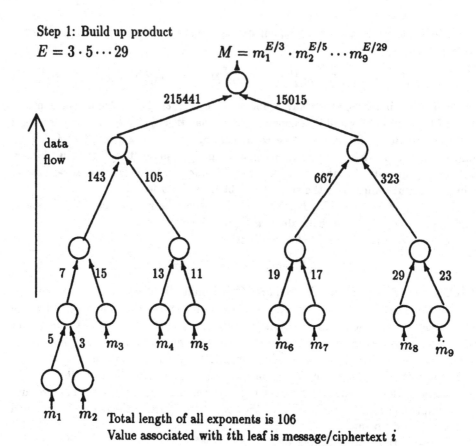

Step 1: Build up product
$E = 3 \cdot 5 \cdots 29$
$M = m_1^{E/3} \cdot m_2^{E/5} \cdots m_9^{E/29}$

data flow

215441   15015

143   105   667   323

7   15   13   11   19   17   29   23

5   3 m_3 m_4 m_5 m_6 m_7 m_8 m_9

m_1 m_2 Total length of all exponents is 106
Value associated with ith leaf is message/ciphertext i

$v_1^{E_R} \cdot v_2^{E_L}$

E_R E_L

v_1 v_2

Step 2: Extract E'th root of product

Figure 1: Build up Product and Extract Root

Step 3: Break up product of roots
$$M^{1/E} = m_1^{1/3} \cdot m_2^{1/5} \cdots m_9^{1/29}$$

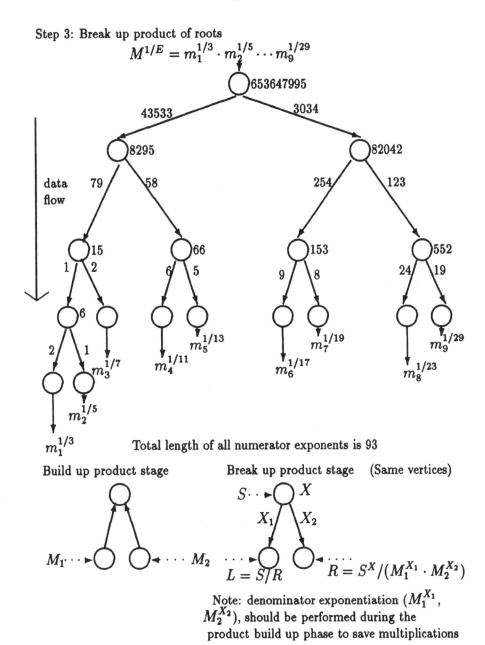

Total length of all numerator exponents is 93

Build up product stage   Break up product stage   (Same vertices)

$$L = S/R \qquad R = S^X/(M_1^{X_1} \cdot M_2^{X_2})$$

Note: denominator exponentiation ($M_1^{X_1}$, $M_2^{X_2}$), should be performed during the product build up phase to save multiplications

Figure 2: Break up Product of Roots

There is a unique solution for X modulo $\prod_{i=1}^{b} e_i = E$.

By definition

$$X = (\prod_{i=1}^{k} e_i) \cdot X_1,$$

$$X - 1 = (\prod_{i=k+1}^{b} e_i) \cdot X_2.$$

Let $P_1 = \prod_{i=1}^{k} e_i$ and $P_2 = \prod_{i=k+1}^{b} e_i$, then $X = P_1 \cdot X_1$ and $X - 1 = P_2 \cdot X_2$. Note that $\log X < \log E$, $\log X_1 + \log P_1 = \log X$, $\log X_2 + \log P_2 = \log X$, $\log E = \log P_1 + \log P_2$, and thus $\log X_1 + \log X_2 < \log X$.

Denote

$$M_1 = m_1^{P_1/e_1} \cdot m_2^{P_1/e_2} \cdots m_k^{P_1/e_k}, \text{ and}$$

$$M_2 = m_{k+1}^{P_2/e_{k+1}} \cdot m_{k+2}^{P_2/e_{k+2}} \cdots m_b^{P_2/e_b}.$$

Note that M_1 and M_2 have already been computed, as the left and right branch values of the root, during the tree based computation of M.

Raise $M^{1/E}$ to the Xth power modulo N:

$$(M^{1/E})^X = (\prod_{i=1}^{b} m_i^{1/e_i})^X$$

$$= (\prod_{i=1}^{k} m_i^{1/e_i})^{P_1 \cdot X_1} \cdot (\prod_{i=k+1}^{b} m_i^{1/e_i})^{P_2 \cdot X_2} \cdot \prod_{i=k+1}^{b} m_i^{1/e_i}$$

$$= M_1^{X_1} \cdot M_2^{X_2} \cdot \prod_{i=k+1}^{b} m_i^{1/e_i}.$$

To solve for $\prod_{i=k+1}^{b} m_i^{1/e_i}$ we raise M_1 to the power X_1, raise M_2 to the power X_2, and divide out. To solve for $\prod_{i=1}^{k} m_i^{1/e_i}$ we divide $M^{1/E}$ by $\prod_{i=k+1}^{b} m_i^{1/e_i}$.

The recursive continuation of this procedure is clear.

Every leaf labelled l contributes $\log l$ bits to the appropriate exponents (X and X_1 or X and X_2) for every level between the leaf and the root. Thus, the overall number of multiplications is $O(W)$. The number of modular divisions required is $O(b)$.

To summarize:

Lemma 1 *Let $e_1, e_2, \ldots, e_b$ be b different encryption exponents, relatively prime to $\phi(N)$ and to each other. Given messages $m_1, m_2, \ldots, m_b$, we can generate the b roots*

$$m_1^{1/e_1} \pmod{N}, \quad m_2^{1/e_2} \pmod{N}, \ldots, \quad m_b^{1/e_b} \pmod{N}$$

in $O(\log b(\sum_{i=1}^{b} \log e_i) + \log N)$ modular multiplications and $O(b)$ modular divisions.

By choosing the e_i exponents to be polynomial in n and choosing the batch size $b = n/\log^2 n$ we get $O(n)$ multiplications overall and $O(\log^2 n)$ multiplications per root.

Remark: We could choose the encryption exponents to be exponential in polylog(n), for any polylog, and still get polylog(n) multiplications for both encryption and decryption operations.

4 Notes on Security

Use of small encryption exponents for RSA was first suggested by Knuth [K]. A problem arises in the use of small exponents for standard RSA *encryption* if the message is numerically small or messages related via some known polynomials are encrypted to several different recipients. (M. Blum [B] for identical messages, Håstad [H] for fixed polynomials).

We have a more serious problem with encryption in that if the same message is encrypted with different (relatively prime) encryption exponents modulo the *same* modulus then the message can be reconstructed.

In both cases, if RSA is used for key exchange then there is no problem, all the cryptanalyst can learn are random values modulo N. Otherwise, it seems that standard cryptographic practices of randomizing cleartext and appropriate feedback mechanisms effectively overcome these attacks.

One variant of our scheme would be to use different encryption exponents for every encryption or digital signature. *E.g.*, the ith prime for the ith operation. As long as there are no more than a polynomial number of transactions then both private and public operations would require polylog(n) multiplications.

Shamir has shown that knowing $m^{1/p_1}, m^{1/p_2}, \ldots, m^{1/p_k}$ cannot give us m^{1/p_0} for pairwise relatively prime p_i [S] (as we could extract m^{1/p_0} using this procedure as a black box).

A possible advantage to this one-to-one message-prime relationship is in that it breaks the multiplicative relationship between different RSA blocks. Standard RSA lets you forge any digital signature for messages that are products of previous messages and their inverses.

As the Batch RSA merger and split-up phases involve no secret information, this lets us use Batch RSA to isolate the private key from the system, irrespective of it's size. All private transactions can be reduced to one root extraction that can be solved on a weak and isolated processor. Every link-encryptor, mainframe, etc., requests one root, these roots can be merged again so the entire system is driven by one root extraction. To ensure security in transit, the root requested can be completely random using the standard Zero-Knowledge trick of multiplying the real value with a random value raised to an appropriate power.

5 Constants and Practical Considerations

We assume that modular exponentiation requires $c \cdot k$ modular multiplications for an exponent of length k, $c = 1.5$. This is true for the standard exponentiation algorithm if the exponent is chosen at random. None of our exponents are really random but this is a reasonable upper bound on the work required.

Generating M as described in the proceeding section requires $c \cdot W$ multiplications. Taking the Eth root requires $c \cdot \log(N)$ multiplications, extracting the factors from $M^{1/E}$ requires $2c \cdot W$ multiplications.

In fact, we can do better — extracting the factors of $M^{1/E}$ can be done in $c \cdot W$

multiplications provided that about $W/4$ additional multiplications are done when computing M. Overall, the number of multiplications required to extract the b roots is therefore $2c \cdot W + W/4 + c \cdot \log N$.

Reducing the number of multiplications to extract the factors of $M^{1/E}$ involves a slight digression: Our goal is to compute $y^{Z_1} \pmod N$ and $y^{Z_2} \pmod N$. If Z_1 and Z_2 are random then it seems that this requires $c \cdot (\log Z_1 + \log Z_2)$ modular multiplications. In fact, we can compute $y^{Z_1 \cap Z_2} \pmod N$ where $Z_1 \cap Z_2$ denotes the bitwise and operation between Z_1 and Z_2, compute $y^{Z_1 \cap \overline{Z}_2}$ and $y^{Z_2 \cap \overline{Z}_1}$ and multiply the appropriate results to get y^{Z_1} and y^{Z_2}. It is not hard to see that computing the three intermediate products can be done in $\log N + 3/4 \cdot \log N$ multiplications given that Z_1 and Z_2 are chosen at random in the range $1 \ldots N$. In addition, this can be done without any significant cost in storage other than the area required to hold the three intermediate results.

We can use the trick described in the last paragraph so as to compute the values $M_1^{X_1}$ and $M_2^{X_2}$ as a byproduct of computing M, at a cost of $1/4(\log X_1 + \log X_2)$ multiplications. Recall that the final stage in computing M involves raising M_1 to some exponent R and M_2 to some exponent L. The same holds for all levels of the recursion.

6   Acknowledgements

I am very grateful to David Chaum for the great deal of time he spent introducing Moni Naor and myself to the world of untraceability in Berkeley coffee shops. This work has its origins in Shamir's cryptographically secure pseudo random sequence [S] and in David Chaum's observation that multiples of different relatively-prime roots are problematic in the context of untraceable electronic cash [CFN] as the roots can be split apart.

I with to thank Noga Alon, Miki Ben-Or, Manuel Blum, Gilles Brassard, Benny Chor, Shafi Goldwasser, Dick Karp, Silvio Micali, Moni Naor, Ron Rivest, Claus Schnorr, Adi Shamir, Ron Shamir and Yossi Tulpan for hearing me out on this work.

References

[AFK]   Abadi, M., Feigenbaum, J., and Kilian, J., On Hiding Information from an Oracle, Proceedings of the 19th Annual ACM Symposium on Theory of Computing.

[AGCS]   Alexi, W., Chor, B., Goldreich, O., and Schnorr, C.P., RSA and Rabin Functions: Certain Parts are as Hard as the Whole, SIAM J. Comput., April, 1988.

[AHU]   Aho, A.V., Hopcroft J.E., and Ullman, J.D., *The Design and Analysis of Computer Algorithms*, Addison-Wesley, 1974.

[B]   Blum, M., Personal communication.

[BM] Blum, M. and Micali, S., How to generate Cryptographically Strong Sequences of Pseudo-Random Bits, SIAM J. Comp., 13, 1984.

[BG] Blum, M. and Goldwasser, S., An Efficient Probabilistic Public Key Encryption Scheme which Hides all Partial Information, Proceedings of Crypto '84.

[CFN] Chaum, D., Fiat, A., and Naor, M., Untraceable Electronic Cash, Proceedings of Crypto '88.

[DH] Diffie, W. and Hellman, M.E., New Directions in Cryptography, IEEE Trans. on Information Theory, Vol IT-22, 1976.

[E] El Gamal, T., A Public Key Cryptosystem and a Signature Scheme Based on Discrete Logarithms, IEEE Transactions on Information Theory, Vol IT-31, 1985.

[FS] Fiat, A., and Shamir, A., How to Prove Yourself: Practical Solutions to Identification and Signature Problems, Proceedings of Crypto '86.

[GMR] Goldwasser, S., S. Micali, and R.L. Rivest, A Secure Digital Signature Scheme, SIAM J. Comput., April, 1988.

[H] Håstad, J., On using RSA with Low Exponent in a Public Key Network, Proceedings of Crypto '85.

[K] Knuth, D., The Art of Computer Programming, vol. 2: Seminumerical Algorithms, 2nd ed., Addison-Wesley, 1981.

[MS] Micali, S., and Schnorr, C.P., Efficient, Perfect Random Number Generators, proceedings of Crypto '88.

[QC] Quisquater, J.–J. and Couvreur, C., Fast decipherment algorithm for RSA public-key cryptosystem, Electronic letters, vol. 18, 1982, pp. 905–907.

[R] Rabin, M.O., Digitalized signatures, in Foundations of Secure Computation, Academic Press, NY, 1978.

[RSA] Rivest, R.L., Shamir, A. and Adleman, L., A Method for Obtaining Digital Signatures and Public Key Cryptosystems, Comm. ACM, Vol. 21, No. 2, 1978.

[S] Shamir, A., On the Generation of Cryptographically Strong Pseudorandom Sequences, ACM Trans. on Computer Systems, Vol. 1, No. 1, 1983.

On the Implementation of Elliptic Curve Cryptosystems

Andreas Bender and Guy Castagnoli
Institute for Signal and Information Processing
Swiss Federal Institute of Technology
ETH Zentrum
CH-8092 Zurich, Switzerland

Abstract

A family of elliptic curves for cryptographic use is proposed for which the determination of the order of the corresponding algebraic group is much easier than in the general case. This makes it easier to meet the cryptographic requirement that this order have a large prime factor. Another advantage of this familiy is that the group operation simplifies slightly. Explicit numerical examples are given that are suitable for practical use.

Introduction

An exponential function and a corresponding discrete logarithm function can be defined in every finite cyclic group [Massey 1983]. There appears to be no reason why the exponential function in the multiplicative group of a finite field should be the hardest one to invert and therefore the best candidate for a one-way function. An attractive alternative is to use a cyclic subgroup of the group of points on an elliptic curve defined over a finite field. There is evidence [Miller 1986] that the discrete logarithm defined for a cyclic subgroup of this group is much more difficult to compute than that in the multiplicative group of a finite field.

Some basic definitions

We describe here briefly how to calculate in a group of points on an elliptic curve. For a more complete treatment of the theory of elliptic curves, see [Koblitz 1987],[Hartshorne 1983].

The group of points on an elliptic curve over an arbitrary field can be defined as the set of solutions (x,y) of a certain third-order algebraic equation, including the "point" at infinity (∞,∞) which is the neutral element of the group, together with an operation on these "points". In a field with characteristic p >3, the general Weierstrass equation can be reduced by means of coordinate transformations to the form $y^2=x^3+ax+b$, whereas for characteristic p =3 it can only be reduced to $y^2=x^3+ax^2+bx+c$, and in the case of characteristic p =2 it can be reduced to $y^2+y=x^3+ax+b$. The condition for nonsingularity is $4a^3+27b^2\neq0$; the group of points of a singular elliptic curve is isomorphic to the multiplicative or additive group of the field over which the curve is defined [Husemoeller 1987, p.78].

We will only deal with the two cases characteristic p = 2 and characteristic p > 3 because these are the cases of greatest practical interest. The group operation for these cases is defined as follows. To an arbitrary pair of points P and Q specified by their coordinates (x_1,y_1) and (x_2,y_2), respectively, the group operation assigns a third point P*Q with the coordinates (x_3,y_3). These coordinates are computed in the following way for characteristic p>3.

$(x_3,y_3) = (\infty,\infty)$ when $P\neq Q$ and $x_1=x_2$.

$x_3=((y_2-y_1)/(x_2-x_1))^2-x_1-x_2$

$y_3=(x_1-x_3)(y_2-y_1)/(x_2-x_1)-y_1$ when $P\neq Q$ and $x_1\neq x_2$

$(x_3,y_3) = (\infty,\infty)$ when P=Q, P=(0,0) and P is an element of the group;

$x_3=((3 x_1^2+a)/(2y_1))^2-2 x_1$

$y_3=(x_1-x_3)(3x_1^2+a)/(2y_1)-y_1$ if P=Q.

In the case of characteristic p=2, the equations become

$(x_3, y_3) = (\infty, \infty)$ when $P \neq Q$ and $x_1 + x_2 = 0$.

$x_3 = ((y_1+y_2)/(x_1+x_2))^2 + x_1 + x_2$

$y_3 = (x_1+x_3)(y_1+y_2)/(x_1+x_2) + y_1 + 1$ when $P \neq Q$ and $x_1 + x_2 \neq 0$.

$(x_3, y_3) = (\infty, \infty)$ when $P=Q$, $P=(0,0)$ and P is an element of the group;

$x_3 = (x_1^2 + a)^2$

$y_3 = (x_1^2 + a)(x_1 + x_3) + y_1 + 1$ if $P=Q$.

The geometric interpretation of the operation * becomes clear if one sketches an elliptic curve in the affine plane over the real numbers. To compute P*Q, one first joins these two points by a straight line. Algebraic considerations show that this line must intersect the curve at a third point. The point P*Q is the point whose x-coordinate is the same as for this third point and whose y-coordinate is the negative of the y-coordinate of this third point.

The order of the group
It is possible to implement the Diffie-Hellman public key-distribution system without knowing the order of the underlying cyclic group. However, the Pohlig-Silver-Hellman algorithm for computing discrete logarithms can be used in an arbitrary cyclic group and runs in time $O(\sqrt{p})$ where p is the largest prime factor of the order of the group. Therefore it is vital to know that the order of the cyclic group is large enough to provide cryptographic security. If we use the multiplicative group of a finite field this problem is trivial: the group order is just equal to $p^n - 1$. However, the computation of the order of the group of points on an elliptic curve over a finite field is difficult in general. Schoof's algorithm to determine this order runs in polynomial time but is not very practical[Schoof 1985].

A Cryptographically Useful Subclass of Elliptic Curves

To avoid cumbersome computation of the group order, we suggest the use of the subclass of elliptic curves having the coefficient a = 0 in their defining equation. These equations then read

$y^2 = x^3 + b$ for characteristic p > 3 and
$y^2 + y = x^3 + b$ for characteristic p = 2.

This specialization has been considered previously in cryptology for random bit generators [Kaliski 1987]. We observe that every nonzero coefficient b satisfies the nonsingularity condition. The following special properties for this specialization are well known.

Property 1: Let p be a prime $\neq 2, 3$. If $p \equiv -1 \pmod 3$ the equation $y^2 = x^3 + b$ has exactly p solutions (x,y) in $GF(p)^2$ (excluding the neutral element) for every b in GF(p)[Kaliski 1987].

Property 2: The integer 3 does not divide $p^f - 1$ if and only if the integer f is odd and $p \equiv -1 \pmod 3$[Grosswald 1984].

Property 3: Let m be an odd positive integer greater than 1. Then $y^2 + y = x^3 + b$ has exactly 2^m solutions (x,y) (excluding the neutral element) in $GF(2^m)^2$[Lidl Niederreiter 1983].

These properties combine to give the following recipe for group orders.

Proposition: The order of the group of the elliptic curve defined by $y^2 = x^3 + b$ over GF(p) with $p \equiv -1 \pmod 3$ is p+1. The order of the group of the elliptic curve defined by $y^2 + y = x^3 + b$ over $GF(2^m)$, where m is odd, is $2^m + 1$.

Choice of the Elliptic Curve and Cyclic Subgroup

1. The case GF(p)

If $p \equiv -1 \pmod 3$, it follows that $p+1$ must be divisible by 3 and, since p is an odd prime, $p+1$ is also divisible by 2. This means that the largest prime factor of the group order $p+1$ will be achived if $p+1$ is of the form $p+1=2.3.p^*$ where p^* is another prime. If $p+1=2.3.p^*$ it is also very easy to find a generating element for the cyclic subgroup of order p^* or greater to use as a base of the discrete logarithm. Since we have the free parameter b in the defining equations of the curves it is no problem to choose an arbitrary element and to compute its sixth power; if the result is not the neutral element, the order of this particular element is a multiple of p^* and so cryptographically useful.

2. The case GF(2^m)

Because 2^m+1 is not divisible by 2, the next smallest possible factor of the order 2^m+1 is 3. Cryptographically, we want $2^m+1=3p^*$ where p^* is a prime. Our computations have shown that this is indeed possible for some interesting m.

Numerical Results

The prime number theorem states that the probability that an integer selected arbitrarily in the interval [1,x] is a prime is $1/\ln(x)$. For $p+1=6p^*$, we are interested in the probability that q and $6q-1$ are both prime when q is randomly selected in the interval [1,x]. For a rough estimate we may assume the two occurrences to be independent, so we have

$$P(\text{x and 6x-1 prime}) \quad \sim \quad 1/(\ln(x)\,\ln(6x-1))$$

If we want to have an x with hundred decimal digits we get

$$P \quad \sim \quad 1/\ln(10^{100})^2 \quad \sim \quad 10^{-4}.$$

This means that with an efficient prime number test (and a reasonably fast computer) it is feasible to search. As numerical results we get

GF(p):

$p*=\{10^{10}+19, 10^{20}+1267, 10^{21}+367, 10^{50}+4209, 10^{100}+42337\}$ and furthermore $p*=28'356'863'910'078'205'288'614'550'619'314'021'777$ for which $p=6p*-1=2^{127}+24933$ is prime. This is the smallest prime greater than 2^{127} for which $(p+1)/6$ is also prime. For this curve which is convenient in computer arithmetic we also give the element (3,5) which lies on the curve defined over GF(p) through $y^2=x^3-2$ and has order p.

The second example of this kind is $p*=1'537'228'672'809'132'109$ for which $p=6p*-1=2^{63}+16845$ is prime. This is the smallest prime greater than 2^{63} for which $(p+1)/6$ is prime. The element (3,5) again lies on the curve $y^2=x^3-2$ and has order p.

GF(2^m):

If we take m=127 there exists the extremely simple irreducible polynomial $g(x)=x^{127}+x+1$ and $p*=(2^{127}+1)/3$ is prime. The element (x,x) has maximal order $2^{127}+1$ on the elliptic curve it generates.

Taking m=61 and generating GF(2^{61}) with the irreducible polynomial $G(x)=x^{61}+x^5+x^2+x+1$, we obtain elliptic curves of order $2^{61}+1=3p*$ whereby $p*=(2^{61}+1)/3$ is prime. The element (x,x) - the components being expressed in GF(2)[x]/(g(x)) - has order $2^{61}+1$ which is maximal on the elliptic curve it generates.

What follows is a list of exponents m for which $(2^m+1)/3$ is prime.

2   - 100: [3,5,7,11,13,17,19,23,31,41,43,47,53,59,61,71,79,83,89]
100 - 200: [101,107,113,127,131,137,149,167,173,179,191,197,199]
200 - 300: [227,233,239,251,257,263,269,281,293]
300 - 400: [311,313,317,341,347,353,359,383,389]
400 - 500: [401,419,431,443,449,461,467,479,491]
500 - 600: [503,509,521,557,563,569,587,593,599]
600 - 700: [617,641,647,653,659,677,683]
700 - 800: [701,719,743,761,773,797]
800 - 900: [809,821,827,839,857,863,881,887]

1500 - 1600: [1511,1523,1553,1559,1571,1583]
>1600 : [1601,1607,1613,1619,1637,...]

Acknowledgement

We thank Ueli Maurer for arising our interest in elliptic curves and Karl Aberer for his help with the computer programming. The first author also expresses his gratitude to Professor James L. Massey for being allowed to do this work as undergraduate research at his institute, for the support concerning the presentation at CRYPTO '89 and for showing him how to formulate a scientific text.

Bibliography

[Grosswald 1984]...............Grosswald, Emil. Topics from the Theory of Numbers. Birkhaeuser Boston 1984.

[Hartshorne 1983]..............Hartshorne, Robin. Algebraic Geometry. Springer New York 1983.

[Husemoeller 1987]..............Husemoeller, Dale. Elliptic Curves. Springer New York 1987.

[Kaliski 1987]......................Kaliski, Burton S. Jr.. "A Pseudo-Random Bit Generator Based on Elliptic Logarithms". Advances in Cryptography: Proceedings of CRYPTO '86. Andrew M. Odlyzko, Ed.. Springer 1987. pp. 84 - 100.

[Koblitz 1987].....................Koblitz, Neal. A Course in Number Theory and Cryptography. Springer New York 1987.

[Lidl Niederreiter 1983].....Lidl, Rudolf; Niederreiter, Harald. Finite Fields. Addison-Wesley Massachusetts 1983.

[Massey 1983].....................Massey, James L.."Logarithms in Finite Cyclic Groups - Cryptographic Issues". Proc. 4th Benelux Symposion on Information Theory, Leuven, Belgium. May 1983, pp.17 - 25.

[Miller 1986]......................Miller, Victor. "Use of Elliptic Curves in Cryptography". Advances in Cryptography: Proceedings of CRYPTO '85. H.C. Williams, Ed.. Springer 1986. pp. 417 - 426.

[Schoof 1985].....................Schoof, Rene. "Elliptic Curves over Finite Fields and the Computation of Square Roots mod p". Mathematics of Computation, vol.44 (1985), pp. 483-494.

Session 5:

Signature and Authentication I

Chair: ERNEST F. BRICKELL

New Paradigms for Digital Signatures and Message Authentication Based on Non-Interactive Zero Knowledge Proofs

Mihir Bellare[*]   Shafi Goldwasser[†]

MIT Laboratory for Computer Science
545 Technology Square
Cambridge, MA 02139

Abstract

Using non-interactive zero knowledge proofs we provide a simple new paradigm for digital signing and message authentication secure against adaptive chosen message attack.

For digital signatures we require that the non-interactive zero knowledge proofs be *publicly verifiable*: they should be checkable by anyone rather than directed at a particular verifier. We accordingly show how to implement non-interactive zero knowledge proofs in a network which have the property that anyone in the network can individually check correctness while the proof is zero knowledge to any sufficiently small coalition. This enables us to implement signatures which are history independent.

1   Introduction

1.1   A NIZK Proof Based Paradigm

We show how to use the random functions of [GGM] and the primitive of non-interactive zero-knowledge proof systems introduced by [BFM] to obtain new paradigms for creating digital signatures secure against adaptive chosen message attack. Namely, any method that yields non-interactive zero-knowledge proof-systems, together with the existence of one-way functions, implies new ways to sign digitally. Our digital signature construction is much simpler than all known constructions which

---

[*] Supported in part by NSF grant CCR-87-19689 and DARPA Contract N00014-89-J-1988

[†] Supported in part by NSF grant CCR-86-57527, DARPA Contract N00014-89-J-1988, and by a US Israel binational grant

are secure against adaptive chosen message attack, putting the burden of the work on non-interactive zero-knowledge proof-systems. Moreover, the signatures produced are independent of previous signatures as long as the non-interactive proofs have this property.

Another application of these ideas is to cryptographic protocols. For example, we show how to implement a memoryless system for distributing and checking secret identification numbers, such as phone calling cards, passwords, etc. By memoryless, we mean that no secret data need be stored to *verify* the correctness of id numbers. The only piece of secret information is kept by the center which *generates* the original secret identification numbers.

1.2 Non-Interactive Zero Knowledge Proof Systems

The paradigms we present in this paper are based on the general ability to provide non-interactive zero knowledge proofs.

Informally, a non-interactive zero knowledge proof of a theorem (NP statement) T is a method by which A can give B a string m such that B, upon examining m, is convinced that the theorem is true, but he obtains zero knowledge about the proof.

We will actually be interested in using non-interactive zero knowledge proofs (henceforth abbreviated NIZK proofs) in a public key network. We will want that

- For any pair of users A and B in the network it is the case that A can send NIZK proofs to B

- The number of theorems that can be proved to B is an arbitrary polynomial in the security parameter.

Such a public key network provides the natural setting for digital signatures.

Non-interactive zero knowledge proofs were introduced in [BFM]. The current literature contains a number of implementations of non-interactive zero knowledge proof systems in models that differ in some of their characteristics. In §3 we give a formal definition of NIZK proof systems suitable for our purposes, and consider the models and implementations available.

For digital signatures we need in addition that the proofs be publicly verifiable. This raises some new issues.

1.3 Publicly Verifiable NIZK Proof Systems

Consider a proof of a theorem T provided by A. There are two possibilities with respect to its verifiability:

(1) The proof is directed at a particular person B and only he can verify it

(2) The proof can be verified by any user in the system.

In the latter case we call the proof *publicly verifiable*. The distinction is important for our applications to digital signatures where the public verifiability of proofs will correspond to signatures which anyone can check.

A new security issue that arises with publicly verifiable proofs is maintaining zero knowledge with respect to a coalition of users: although the proof is by definition zero knowledge to each user, can a group of users combine to extract knowledge from it, and, if so, how large should this group be to do damage?

We implement publicly verifiable NIZK proofs addressing these issues in §6.

We emphasize again, however, that the paradigms we use in our applications do not make reference to any particular implementation of NIZK proofs and rely only on their properties as given in §3 together with public verifiability.

1.4 Random Functions

[GGM] introduced the concept of a *pseudo-random collection of functions*. This is a collection of functions $F_k = \{f_s : |s| = k\}$ such that no probabilistic polynomial time algorithm can distinguish a member f_s of F_k from a truly random function. That is, an algorithm whose only access to a function is through queries of its values at various points will be unable to tell whether he is dealing with a member of f_s or with a truly random function.

Through the work of [GGM] and [ILL] we have

Theorem 1.1 The existence of one-way functions implies the existence of pseudo-random collections of functions.

1.5 Related Results

The ideas we present here have already found other applications.

Micali [M2] has observed that by using interactive proofs rather than non-interactive ones in our signature scheme one can implement *undeniable signatures* [CV] based only on the existence of any one-way function.

Feige and Shamir [F] showed that *witness hiding proofs* [FS] suffice to implement a modified version of our signature scheme; we will discuss their result and its relation to ours further in §6.3.

2 Notation

We use [GMR]'s notation and conventions for probabilistic algorithms.

We emphasize the number of inputs received by an algorithm as follows. If algorithm A receives only one input we write "$A(\cdot)$"; if it receives two we write "$A(\cdot,\cdot)$", and so on. If A is a probabilistic algorithm then, for any input i the notation $A(i)$ refers to the probability space which to the string σ assigns the probability that A, on input i, outputs σ (in the special case that A takes no inputs, A refers to the algorithm itself whereas the notation $A()$ refers to the probability space obtained by running A on no inputs). Sometimes we wish to make the coin tosses explicit; in this case we write for example $A(\sigma; i)$ for the output of A on input i with coins σ.

If S is a probability space we denote by $[S]$ the set of elements to which S assigns positive probability.

If $f(\cdot)$ and $g(\cdot, \cdots)$ are probabilistic algorithms then $f(g(\cdot, \cdots))$ is the probabilistic algorithm obtained by composing f and g (i.e. running f on g's output). For any inputs $x, y, \ldots$ the associated probability space is denoted $f(g(x, y, \cdots))$.

If S is a probability space then $x \leftarrow S$ denotes the algorithm which assigns to x an element randomly selected according to S. If S is a finite set, this denotes the operation of selecting an element of S at random.

For probability spaces $S, T, \ldots$, the notation

$$\boldsymbol{P}(p(x, y, \cdots) \; : \; x \leftarrow S; y \leftarrow T; \cdots)$$

denotes the probability that the predicate $p(x, y, \cdots)$ is true after the (ordered) execution of the algorithms $x \leftarrow S$, $y \leftarrow T$, etc.

A *PPT* algorithm means a probabilistic polynomial time algorithm. We assume that a natural encoding of algorithms as binary strings is used.

If A and B are interactive TMs then $(A \leftrightarrow B)(x)$ denotes the probability space of their outputs (some of these outputs might be common while others are private to one or the other of the parties) on input x. As for algorithms, we write for example $B(\sigma)$ for the interactive TM B running with coins σ.

3 Non-Interactive Zero Knowledge Proof Systems

3.1 Definition

A non-interactive zero knowledge proof system for a language L consists of two stages. The first stage, which could be interactive, establishes some information common to the prover and the verifier as well as (possibly) some private information for each. This pre-processing is performed independently of the theorems to be proved. In a second stage the prover chooses and proves theorems to the verifier in zero knowledge, based on the information from the first stage. This theorem proving stage is non-interactive.

The prover and verifier are regarded accordingly as pairs $P = (P_1, P_2)$ and $V = (V_1, V_2)$. The separation between the stages is total. For example, P_1 and P_2 might be completely distinct: the former a trusted center and the latter a prover in the usual sense who sees only information that the center gives him.

Let k be a security parameter.

Definition 3.1 Suppose P_1, P_2, V_1 are probabilistic interactive TMs and V_2 is a deterministic interactive TM, all polynomial time. The pair $P = (P_1, P_2), V = (V_1, V_2)$ constitute a *non-interactive proof system* for a language L if for all sufficiently large k the requirements of the following two stages are met :

(1) **Pre-Processing Stage:**

P_1 interacting with V_1 yields three outputs p, S_P, S_V of which p is common to P_1 and V_1 while S_P is private to P_1 and S_V is private to V_1. If P_1 does not obey the protocol then with high probability V_1 outputs "cheating".

(2) **Theorem Proving Stage:**

P_2 proves theorems to V_2 without interaction (the communication on any input is a single message from P_2 to V_2).

- *Completeness:* For every $x \in L \cap \{0,1\}^k$
$$P(V_2(1^k, p, S_V, x, \beta) = \text{accept} : (p, S_P, S_V) \leftarrow (P_1 \leftrightarrow V_1)(1^k) ;$$
$$\beta \leftarrow P_2(1^k, p, S_P, x)) \geq 1 - 2^{-2k} .$$

- *Soundness:* For every interactive TM $\hat{P}_2$ and every $x \in \overline{L} \cap \{0,1\}^k$,
$$P(V_2(1^k, p, S_V, x, \beta) = \text{accept} : (p, S_P, S_V) \leftarrow (P_1 \leftrightarrow V_1)(1^k) ;$$
$$\beta \leftarrow \hat{P}_2(1^k, p, S_P, x)) \leq 2^{-2k} .$$

In some cases we will also allow the proof system to have as additional input a history of previous theorems and their proofs.

In order to define zero knowledge we first need the concept of a distinguisher.

Definition 3.2 A *distinguisher* for a language L is a pair (I, ρ) where ρ is a deterministic polynomial time predicate and I is a PPT interactive TM such that $I(1^k, \cdot, \cdot, \cdot) \in L \cap \{0,1\}^k$ for all k.

Notation: For any interactive TM $\hat{V}_1$ we let $(P_1.\hat{V}_1)(1^k)$ denote the probability space consisting of the outputs of the interaction together with the history of the interaction and the coin tosses of $\hat{V}_1$. Coupling the last two into a single entity h we write (p, S_P, S_V, h) for an element of this space.

Notation: Let $P = (P_1, P_2), V = (V_1, V_2)$ be a non-interactive proof system for L. For any PPT interactive TM $\hat{V}_1$ and distinguisher (I, ρ) we let

$$p_k(P, \hat{V}_1, (I, \rho)) = P(\rho(1^k, \sigma, p, S_V, h, x_1 \beta_1 \ldots x_{k^d} \beta_{k^d}) = 1 :$$
$$(p, S_P, S_V, h) \leftarrow (P_1.\hat{V}_1)(1^k) ; \sigma \leftarrow \{0,1\}^{k^e} ;$$
$$x_1 \leftarrow I(\sigma; 1^k, p, S_V, h, \epsilon) ; \beta_1 \leftarrow P_2(1^k, p, S_P, x_1) ; \ldots ;$$
$$x_{k^d} \leftarrow I(\sigma; 1^k, p, S_V, h, x_1 \beta_1 \ldots x_{k^d-1} \beta_{k^d-1}) ; \beta_{k^d} \leftarrow P_2(1^k, p, S_P, x_{k^d})) ,$$

where $d, e > 0$ are constants determined by the running time of I.

Definition 3.3 A pair of sequences $\{p_k\}, \{q_k\}$ of probabilities are *indistinguishable* (written $\{p_k\} \cong \{q_k\}$) if for all $c > 0$ and sufficiently large k it is the case that $|p_k - q_k| < k^{-c}$.

Definition 3.4 A non-interactive proof system $P = (P_1, P_2), V = (V_1, V_2)$ for L is said to be a non-interactive zero knowledge proof system if there is a a pair $M = (M_1, M_2)$ of PPT algorithms such that the following is true: for any PPT interactive TM $\widehat{V}_1$ and any distinguisher (I, ρ) it is the case that $\{p_k(P, \widehat{V}_1, (I, \rho))\} \cong \{q_k(M_1^{\widehat{V}_1}, M_2, (I, \rho))\}$, where

$$
\begin{aligned}
q_k(M_1^{\widehat{V}_1}, M_2, (I, \rho)) \;=\; & P(\, \rho(1^k, \sigma, p, S_V^*, h^*, x_1\beta_1^* \ldots x_{k^d}\beta_{k^d}^*) = 1 : \\
& (p^*, S_V^*, h^*) \leftarrow M_1^{\widehat{V}_1}(1^k)\,;\; \sigma \leftarrow \{0,1\}^{k^e}\,; \\
& x_1 \leftarrow I(\sigma; 1^k, p^*, S_V^*, h^*, \epsilon)\,;\; \beta_1^* \leftarrow M_2(1^k, p^*, S_V^*, x_1)\,;\; \ldots\,; \\
& x_{k^d} \leftarrow I(\sigma; 1^k, p^*, S_V^*, h^*, x_1\beta_1^* \ldots x_{k^d-1}\beta_{k^d-1}^*)\,; \\
& \beta_{k^d}^* \leftarrow M_2(1^k, p^*, S_V^*, x_{k^d})\,)\,.
\end{aligned}
$$

($M_1^{\widehat{V}_1}$ means M_1 with $\widehat{V}_1$ as an oracle). We call $M = (M_1, M_2)$ the *simulator*.

Definition 3.5 A language L is said to have a non-interactive zero knowledge proof (NIZK proof) if there exist $P = (P_1, P_2), V = (V_1, V_2)$ which constitute a non-interactive zero knowledge proof system for it.

3.2 Remarks

General:

We assume that V_2 is deterministic only for simplicity and because it is the case in all current implementations. For greater generality we could allow it coins. Notice that although this would enhance its power in the theorem proving stage the definition of zero knowledge would not have to change: the non-interaction implies that the view of the verifier need not include the coin tosses of V_2.

The Pre-Processing Stage:

Our definition is more general than we need. In the application to signatures there is implicitly a trusted center: since the signer will be proving theorems it is to his advantage to have correct information from the pre-processing stage. In general, however, we must guarantee the privacy and make sure that neither party can cheat.

The Theorem Proving Stage:

The reason for the extremely small error probability of 2^{-2k} in the completeness and soundness conditions is as follows. Since the prover can pick his theorem after seeing the output of the first stage, we would like that for most such outputs, there does not *exist* a false statement that can be proved. Our condition guarantees this. More precisely, if we call $(p, S_P, S_V) \in (P_1 \leftrightarrow V_1)(1^k)$ *good* if $V_2(S_V)$ accepts $P_2(S_P)$'s proof for all $x \in L \cap \{0,1\}^k$ and does not accept any proof for all $x \in \overline{L} \cap \{0,1\}^k$ then

$$
P(\, (p, S_P, S_V) \text{ is good } : (p, S_P, S_V) \leftarrow (P_1 \leftrightarrow V_1)(1^k)\,) \geq 1 - 2^{-k}\,.
$$

The Zero Knowledge:

A distinguisher (I, ρ) models a two stage process. The first is a requesting stage in which I, given (p, S_V, h) from the pre-processing stage, asks the prover to supply zero knowledge proofs, with respect to p, of theorems of its choice. Its requests are adaptive, depending on responses to previous requests. This corresponds to what we will want with digital signatures where the theorems that the signer proves are chosen by an adversary who has seen the public key and responses to previous requests for signatures. In a second stage the predicate ρ is computed on the received information. Our definition of zero knowledge asks that there be a simulator which could interact with this process I in such a way that it would not know that it was not interacting with the real prover; that is, the value of the predicate ρ would be 1 with essentially the same probability in both cases.

Our simulator accordingly simulates the two stages independently. It first creates information (p^*, S_V^*, h^*) pertaining to the pre-processing stage. This is done by M_1 who has blackbox access to a possibly cheating verifier $\hat{V}_1$. In the second stage M_2 is used to supply simulations of zero knowledge proofs that I requests.

A more general definition would be that for every $\hat{V}_1$ there was such an M_1, but to avoid a profusion of quantifiers we stick to the simple case.

Public Verifiability:

The definition as it stands does not address public verifiability. For publicly verifiable proofs the secret information of the the verifier is either void, or there are lots of verifiers each of whom has his own secret. This is considered further in §6.

3.3   A Look at Available Implementations

All the models described in the literature so far do fit our definition. We discuss briefly here these models and implementations.

The first model of NIZK proofs was introduced by Blum, Feldman and Micali [BFM][1]. In this model the prover and the verifier share a common random string with respect to which the prover provides his proofs. In terms of our definition, p is the common random string and there are no private inputs from the first stage (S_P and S_V are both the empty string).

The common string must be random to ensure both the validity of the proofs and their zero-knowledge. For our application to digital signatures we would have the legal signer publish a random string in his public file and give proofs with respect to it. Other users, functioning as verifiers, would read this and check his proofs. Since the signer wishes to avoid forgeries, it is to his interest to pick the string to be truly random, and he will do so. Note that the proofs are indeed publicly verifiable. The drawback of the current implementation however [M1], is that a proof depends on previous proofs resulting in signatures which depend on previous ones.

The model of Kilian, Micali and Ostrovsky [KMO] has an initial interactive pre-processing stage between prover and verifier. This model fits our definition with p being the empty string, S_P the pair of seeds (s_0, s_1) that P oblivious transfers to

---

[1] The implementation described in the original [BFM] paper is not known to have a proof; a correct scheme has been announced by S. Micali [M1]. However we do not know whether this scheme satisfies our more stringent zero knowledge requirements. It does however satisfy the more relaxed requirement stated in Appendix B which, as we indicate there, is really all we need for signatures.

V, and S_V the seed (either s_0 or s_1) that V receives. However the fact that there is an interaction between prover and verifier means that we cannot use it for the applications described in this paper.

Proposed in [BM2] is a public key system under which Kilian-Micali-Ostrovsky type oblivious transfer based proofs can be implemented. In this model a single verifier can receive proofs from many provers and our message authentication between pairs of users (§5.1) can be implemented in this system. Moreover, some of the implementations in [BM2] are quite efficient. In terms of our definition, p would be the verifier's public key and S_V his secret key while S_P would be the empty string.

4   NIZK Proofs and Digital Signatures

Here we show how NIZK proofs together with one-way functions yield digital signatures.

4.1   How to Sign

Let E be a probabilistic public key encryption algorithm [GM] (we implement this via the bit commitment scheme of Naor [N] which is based on any one-way function). Let $F_k = \{f_s : |s| = k\}$ denote a collection of pseudo random functions as defined in [GGM]. Assume we have a publicly verifiable NIZK proof system for some NP complete language. For our purposes the pre-processing stage of this NIZK proof system is best thought of as an algorithm Z which on input a security parameter outputs just some public information p. We denote by $NIZK_p(T)$ a NIZK proof of T with respect to p.

User U's public file is $PK_U = (1^k, E, \alpha, p)$ and his secret file is $SK_U = (r, s)$, where

- k is the security parameter

- $s \in \{0, 1\}^k$ is the randomly chosen index to a pseudo-random function from F_k

- $\alpha = E(r, s)$ is an encryption of s.

- $p \leftarrow Z(1^{k^c})$ is the information needed for the NIZK proofs (c is a constant).

Then, the digital signature of a document D is defined to be

$$\sigma(D) = (D, R, NIZK_p(T_{PK,D,R}))$$

where $R = f_s(D)$ and $T_{PK,D,R}$ is defined to be the NP statement

$$\exists s \exists r \, [\alpha = E(r, s) \text{ and } R = f_s(D)] \ .$$

Since $T_{PK,D,R}$ is an NP statement, there exists a non-interactive zero-knowledge proof $NIZK_p(T_{PK,D,R})$ of it. The public verifiability of the NIZK proof means that this is really a signature: anyone can check the validity of $\sigma(D)$ given the signer's public key PK_U.

4.2 Comparison with Previous Signature Schemes

In all previous signature schemes secure against adaptive chosen message attack [GMR], [BM1], [NY] the signature of the i-th document D_i was a function of all the previous signatures of documents $D_1, \ldots, D_{i-1}$ (we will refer to such schemes as *history dependent*). The sizes of signatures thus quickly become very impractical. Although methods for dealing with this problem and improving the efficiency of these schemes have been suggested (by Levin, with improvements by Goldreich [G]), these methods are complicated and cumbersome. No such problems exist with our scheme where the signature of a document is independent of previous signatures, as long as the underlying NIZK proofs have the property of being independent of previous proofs. Our implementations of NIZK proofs in §6 do have this property.

4.3 Assumptions

In terms of assumptions we have shown that a digital signature scheme secure against adaptive chosen message attack exists if one-way functions and publicly verifiable NIZK proof systems exist. It is known that digital signature schemes secure against adaptive chosen message attack exist if one-way permutations exist [NY], and it is clear that the existence of digital signatures implies the existence of one-way functions. The relation of NIZK proofs to one-way permutations is not known.

4.4 Security

We recall that in an *adaptive chosen message attack* an adversary can request from the true signer the signature of any number of messages of his choice. Moreover, he can ask for these signatures one by one, with his requests depending on the signatures provided in response to previous requests. The scheme is secure against adaptive chosen message attack if, after requesting signatures in this fashion, the adversary remains unable to forge the signature to *any* message whose signature he has not previously seen. This notion of security, which was introduced in [GMR], represents the strongest possible natural notion of security for a digital signature scheme.

Theorem 4.1 The digital signature scheme of §4.1 is secure against adaptive chosen message attack.

A very rough intuition of why this is true is the following. By [GGM] an adversary who can request to see the value of a random function f_s on a polynomial number of strings $D_1, D_2, \ldots$ of his choice cannot compute even one additional pair D, R such that $R = f_s(D)$ and $D \neq D_i$ for all i. The only difference in our scenario is that the adversary sees along with the set of $\{D_i, R_i\}$ where $R_i = f_s(D_i)$ for all i, many $NIZK_p(T_{D_i})$, i.e proofs that in fact R_i is the result of applying f_s to D_i. But, since these are zero-knowledge proofs they convey no extra knowledge and the [GGM] proof applies.

A more complete proof is in Appendix A.

5   Further Applications of the NIZK Paradigm

The NIZK proofs based paradigm of the previous section can also be adapted to message authentication and the memoryless distribution of id numbers.

5.1   Message Authentication between Pairs of Users

Note that the property of public verifiability is not necessary for message authentication between two users. We simply replace the use of publicly verifiable proofs as in §4 by NIZK proofs from A to B.

Efficient implementations of NIZK proofs between pairs of users are known [BM2].

5.2   Memoryless Distribution of Identification Numbers

Consider an application where a central authority like the phone company, or a passport producing facility needs to generate unique unforgeable id numbers for its users. The users should be able to present their identification numbers in numerous distributed local stations, and the local station should have the capability to check the validity of the id.

One previous solution to this problem was presented by [GGM] where they used random functions applied to the user name to create the user id number. The disadvantage of that proposal was that the all the local stations needed to keep secret the index to the random function. Using non-interactive zero-knowledge proofs that disadvantage can now be removed. The idea now is for the center alone to keep secret the single index s to the random function, together with a value r, and for the center to publish in a public file the pair (E, α) where $\alpha = E(r, s)$. When user U needs an id, the center computes $I = f_s(U)$ and gives I to U along with a non-interactive zero-knowledge proof, $NIZK_{center}(T)$ where T is the NP statement

$$\exists s \exists r \left[\alpha = E(r, s) \text{ and } I = f_s(U) \right] .$$

The local center has no knowledge of U or any special information whatsoever. Whenever U needs to authenticate himself, he simply shows the local center I and $NIZK_{center}(T)$ which convinces the local center that the user possesses a legal id number.

6   NIZK Proof Systems with Public Verifiability

We sketch here very briefly some implementations of publicly verifiable NIZK proof systems. In these systems there is a center who publishes some information p that everyone can see, and then gives each user B some secret information S_B. Only the public part p is necessary to prove theorems, and anyone with a secret key can check such a proof.

6.1 A Simple Scheme

We can get a first, simple scheme using methods similar to [BM2]. Let k be the usual security parameter. The center picks at random a number of probabilistic encryption algorithms [GM] with their corresponding decryption keys; let these be

$$\{(E_{i,j}, D_{i,j}) : i = 1, \ldots, k \text{ and } j = 0, 1\} \ .$$

The center now publishes

$$p = ((E_{1,0}, E_{1,1}), (E_{2,0}, E_{2,1}), \ldots, (E_{k,0}, E_{k,1}))$$

as a key visible to all users in the system. To any user B who wishes to be able to verify proofs, the center, having picked $j_1, \ldots, j_k \in \{0, 1\}$ at random, sends[2]

$$S_B = (D_{1,j_1}, D_{2,j_2}, \ldots, D_{k,j_k}) \ .$$

User B makes this his secret key.

The following encoding of proofs was used by Kilian, Micali and Ostrovsky [KMO] (it arises from Blum's ZK proof of Hamiltonian cycle) and will allow us to prove theorems in zero knowledge.

Theorem 6.1 [KMO] Suppose A has a NP theorem T and a proof of it. Then she can compute a sequence

$$s = ((s_{1,0}, s_{1,1}), (s_{2,0}, s_{2,1}), \ldots, (s_{k,0}, s_{k,1}))$$

of pairs of strings which encode a proof of T in the following sense:

(1) if the proof is incorrect then for each $i = 1, \ldots, k$ there is a $j \in \{0, 1\}$ such that seeing $s_{i,j}$ will reveal the incorrectness of the proof

(2) if for each $i = 1, \ldots, k$ one does not see both $s_{i,0}$ and $s_{i,1}$ then the proof is zero knowledge.

A's proof of T is now just

$$NIZK_p(T) = ((r_{1,0}, r_{1,1}), (r_{2,0}, r_{2,1}), \ldots, (r_{k,0}, r_{k,1})) \ ,$$

where $r_{i,j} = E_{i,j}(s_{i,j})$. Each user B can decrypt exactly one of $r_{i,0}$ and $r_{i,1}$ at random for each i. Theorem 6.1 thus guarantees that this is a non-interactive zero knowledge proof system.

In the terminology of [BM2], we have established oblivious transfer channels; however in our case the proof does not depend on any particular verifier but only on p.

Note that in this scheme the proof of a theorem does not depend on the proofs of previous theorems in contrast to [BFM]+[M1].

Also note that A is not special: any user can use the central public key p to provide proofs that all the others can check. All users can thus do digital signatures, publishing in their individual files the necessary information as described in §4 and using the central key for the NIZK proofs.

The drawback of this scheme is that two bad users could combine to break it. If a pair of users put their secret keys together they might know both $D_{i,0}$ and $D_{i,1}$ for

---

[2] If the center is not trusted, oblivious transfer can be used here instead, as described in [BM2].

some i and then the proof would not be zero knowledge to them. They could then forge signatures. The next scheme is more robust in this regard.

6.2 Zero Knowledge to Many Users Simultaneously

Here we show how to provide security against any $O(k)$ users combining. However, the size of the proofs will grow as a function of k. The key to the stronger publicly verifiable NIZK system is the use of a different method, due to Kilian [K], for encoding proofs.

Theorem 6.2 [K] Suppose that A has a theorem T of size n and a proof of it. Then she can construct a *tableau* $\mathcal{T}(T)$ for T. This consists of a sequence $(\mathcal{T}_1, \ldots, \mathcal{T}_{nkp(nk)})$, where each $\mathcal{T}_i$ is a sequence of $p(nk)$ strings (p is some fixed polynomial), such that the following are true:

(1) If $\mathcal{T}(T)$ does not encode a correct proof of T then there is a "check" that reveals this. A check is some predicate that is evaluated on some four positions in the sequence $\mathcal{T}_i$ and there is a total of $p(nk)$ such checks.

(2) If for all i one sees $\leq k - 1$ positions of $\mathcal{T}_i$ then no knowledge about the proof will be revealed.

The strings which constitute the elements of the tableau are of constant length.

For our scheme the center selects at random $nkp(nk)^2$ probabilistic encryption algorithms together with their decryption keys; let these be

$$\{(E_{i,j}, D_{i,j}) : i = 1, \ldots, nkp(nk) \text{ and } j = 1, \ldots, p(nk)\} .$$

The center now publishes

$$p = ((E_{1,1}, \ldots, E_{1,p(nk)}), (E_{2,1}, \ldots, E_{2,p(nk)}), \ldots, (E_{nkp(nk),1}, \ldots, E_{nkp(nk),p(nk)})) .$$

When user B requests a secret key the center picks, for each $i = 1, \ldots, nkp(nk)$, one of the $p(nk)$ checks at random and sends to B

$$S_B = \left\{ (D_{i,j_{i,1}}, D_{i,j_{i,2}}, D_{i,j_{i,3}}, D_{i,j_{i,4}}) : i = 1, \ldots, nkp(nk) \right\}$$

where $1 \leq j_{i,1}, j_{i,2}, j_{i,3}, j_{i,4} \leq p(nk)$ are the four tableau positions which make up the chosen check ($i = 1, \ldots, nkp(nk)$). User B makes this his secret key.

When user A wishes to prove a theorem T she makes a tableau $\mathcal{T}(T) = \mathcal{T}_1, \ldots, \mathcal{T}_{nkp(nk)}$ and encrypts each position with the corresponding encryption algorithm from p. Any user B can see exactly one random check per tableau and hence will detect a false proof with probability

$$\geq 1 - \left(1 - \frac{1}{p(nk)}\right)^{nkp(nk)} \geq 1 - e^{-nk} ,$$

by property 1 of a tableau as given in Theorem 6.2.

Any combination of $\leq \frac{k-1}{4}$ users in the system, pooling their secret keys, see $\leq k - 1$ positions of each $\mathcal{T}_i$. So by property 2 of Theorem 6.2 the proof will be zero knowledge to this coalition.

6.3 History Independent Signatures

Plugging the above implementation into the signature scheme of §4 yields a history independent signature scheme in this model where there is a network of users each possessing certain special public and secret keys enabling NIZK proofs. The question of whether history independent signatures can be achieved without such pre-processing still remains. Feige and Shamir [F] answered this in the affirmative. They modify our scheme so that it uses witness hiding proofs, and then use the [DMP] implementations of one-theorem NIZK to implement the latter. The resulting scheme is based on the specific assumption of quadratic residuosity.

A Appendix: Proof of Security for the Signature Scheme

Here we give a more formal proof of Theorem 4.1.

Suppose $\mathcal{F}$ is a forger who, after an adaptive chosen message attack, succeeds in forgery with probability $\epsilon(k) \geq k^{-e}$, where $e > 0$ is some constant and the probability is over the choice of the public and secret keys and the coin tosses of both the signer and $\mathcal{F}$. We propose to derive a contradiction.

We let $\mathcal{V}$ denote the verification algorithm: $\mathcal{V}$ takes as input a public key $PK = (1^k, E, \alpha, p)$ and a signature (D, R, β) and outputs 1 iff β is a proof of $T_{PK,D,R}$ with respect to p.

The proof below is for a model, like [BFM], in which the verifier has no secret information (a little more care is required in the case of a model like that of §6 where each verifier has a separate secret, and we discuss this in the final paper). For our purposes the pre-processing stage is replaced by the algorithm Z which on input a security parameter outputs simply some public information p for proofs.

We will consider five experiments. Each experiment has the following format:

- *Make Public Key:* Create some value PK which will serve as the public key

- *Sign:* Invoke the forger $\mathcal{F}$ on PK and respond in some manner to his requests

- *Output:* Output either 0 or 1 based on the success of $\mathcal{F}$.

The experiments are as follows.

$E_0(1^k)$: (True signing process)

- *Make Public Key:* Let $s, r \leftarrow \{0,1\}^k$; $\alpha \leftarrow E(r, s)$; $p \leftarrow Z(1^{k^c})$. Let $PK = (1^k, E, \alpha, p)$.

- *Sign:* Invoke the forger $\mathcal{F}$ on input PK. When he requests the signature of a document D give him the signature $(D, f_s(D), NIZK_p(T_{PK,D,f_s(D)}))$.

- *Output:* Output 1 iff the forger outputs a forgery $(\widehat{D}, \widehat{R}, \widehat{\beta})$ such that $\mathcal{V}(PK, (\widehat{D}, \widehat{R}, \widehat{\beta})) = 1$.

$E_1(1^k)$: (Change acceptance criterion)

- *Make Public Key:* Let $s, r \leftarrow \{0,1\}^k$; $\alpha \leftarrow E(r, s)$; $p \leftarrow Z(1^{k^c})$. Let $PK = (1^k, E, \alpha, p)$.

- *Sign:* Invoke the forger $\mathcal{F}$ on input PK. When he requests the signature of a document D give him the signature $(D, f_s(D), NIZK_p(T_{PK,D,f_s(D)}))$.

- *Output:* Output 1 iff the forger outputs a forgery $(\widehat{D}, \widehat{R}, \widehat{\beta})$ such that $\mathcal{V}(PK, (\widehat{D}, \widehat{R}, \widehat{\beta})) = 1$ and, in addition, $f_s(\widehat{D}) = \widehat{R}$.

$E_2(1^k)$: (Use Simulator for Proofs)

- *Make Public Key:* Let $s, r \leftarrow \{0,1\}^k$; $\alpha \leftarrow E(r,s)$; $p^* \leftarrow M_1(1^{k^c})^3$. Let $PK = (1^k, E, \alpha, p^*)$.

- *Sign:* Invoke the forger $\mathcal{F}$ on input PK. When he requests the signature of a document D give him $(D, f_s(D), \beta^*)$ where $\beta^* = M_2(1^{k^c}, p^*, T_{PK,D,f_s(D)})$.

- *Output:* Output 1 iff the forger outputs a forgery $(\widehat{D}, \widehat{R}, \widehat{\beta})$ such that $\mathcal{V}(PK, (\widehat{D}, \widehat{R}, \widehat{\beta})) = 1$ and, in addition, $f_s(\widehat{D}) = \widehat{R}$.

$E_3(1^k)$: (Change the encryption)

- *Make Public Key:* Let $s, s', r \leftarrow \{0,1\}^k$; $\alpha \leftarrow E(r, s')$; $p^* \leftarrow M_1(1^{k^c})$. Let $PK = (1^k, E, \alpha, p^*)$.

- *Sign:* Invoke the forger $\mathcal{F}$ on input PK. When he requests the signature of a document D give him $(D, f_s(D), \beta^*)$ where $\beta^* = M_2(1^{k^c}, p^*, T_{PK,D,f_s(D)})$ is the result of running the simulator on input the (false) statement $T_{PK,D,f_s(D)}$.

- *Output:* Output 1 iff the forger outputs a forgery $(\widehat{D}, \widehat{R}, \widehat{\beta})$ such that $\mathcal{V}(PK, (\widehat{D}, \widehat{R}, \widehat{\beta})) = 1$ and, in addition, $f_s(\widehat{D}) = \widehat{R}$.

$E_4(1^k)$: (Use a random function)

- *Make Public Key:* Let $s', r \leftarrow \{0,1\}^k$; $\alpha \leftarrow E(r, s')$; $p^* \leftarrow M_1(1^{k^c})$. Let $PK = (1^k, E, \alpha, p^*)$.

- *Sign:* Invoke the forger $\mathcal{F}$ on input PK. When he requests the signature of a document D give him (D, R, β^*) where $R \leftarrow \{0,1\}^k$ and $\beta^* = M_2(1^{k^c}, p^*, T_{PK,D,R})$ is the result of running the simulator on input the (false) statement $T_{PK,D,R}$.

- *Output:* Let $R' \leftarrow \{0,1\}^k$. Output 1 iff the forger outputs a forgery $(\widehat{D}, \widehat{R}, \widehat{\beta})$ such that $\mathcal{V}(PK, (\widehat{D}, \widehat{R}, \widehat{\beta})) = 1$ and, in addition, $\widehat{R} = R'$.

For each i let $p_i(k) = P[E_i(1^k) = 1]$.

Fact 1: $p_0(k)$ is by definition the probability $\epsilon(k)$ of successful forgery.

Fact 2: $p_4(k) \leq 2^{-k}$ since the probability that $\widehat{R} = R' = 2^{-k}$.

Now

$$
\begin{aligned}
\frac{\epsilon(k)}{2} &\leq \epsilon(k) - p_4(k) \\
&= p_0(k) - p_4(k) \\
&= \sum_{i=0}^{3} p_i(k) - p_{i+1}(k) \,,
\end{aligned}
$$

We thus have four cases in each of which we derive a contradiction.

Case 1: $p_0(k) - p_1(k) \geq \frac{\epsilon(k)}{8}$

---

[3] With the pre-processing stage represented by Z we do not have a history and coin tosses h in the simulator's output.

This is not possible simply by virtue of having a proof system. With probability $\geq 1 - 2^{-k}$ it is the case that $f_s(\widehat{D}) = \widehat{R}$ iff $\mathcal{V}(PK, (\widehat{D}, \widehat{R}, \widehat{\beta})) = 1$.

Case 2: $p_1(k) - p_2(k) \geq \frac{\epsilon(k)}{8}$.

This would imply an ability to distinguish simulated proofs from real ones. In the final paper we will show how to use the forger to construct a distinguisher (I, ρ) which tells apart real proofs of theorems from simulations of proofs of these theorems.

Case 3: $p_2(k) - p_3(k) \geq \frac{\epsilon(k)}{8}$.

We will distinguish between encryptions of different values.

On input $(1^k, s_0, s_1, \alpha)$ where

$$s_0, s_1 \leftarrow \{0,1\}^k \,;\ b \leftarrow \{0,1\} \,;\ \alpha \leftarrow E(s_b) \,,$$

the following algorithm A predicts b:

- *Make Public Key:* Let $p^* \leftarrow M_1(1^{k^c})$ and set $PK = (1^k, E, \alpha, p^*)$.

- *Sign:* Invoke the forger $\mathcal{F}$ on input PK. When he requests the signature of a document D give him $(D, f_{s_1}(D), \beta^*)$ where $\beta^* = M_2(1^{k^c}, p^*, T_{PK, D, f_{s_1}(D)})$.

- *Output:* Output 1 iff the forger outputs a forgery $(\widehat{D}, \widehat{R}, \widehat{\beta})$ such that $\mathcal{V}(PK, (\widehat{D}, \widehat{R}, \widehat{\beta})) = 1$ and, in addition, $f_{s_1}(\widehat{D}) = \widehat{R}$.

The probability that A correctly predicts b is

$$\begin{aligned}
\boldsymbol{P}[A = b] &= \frac{1}{2}\boldsymbol{P}[A = 1 | b = 1] + \frac{1}{2}\boldsymbol{P}[A = 0 | b = 0] \\
&= \frac{1}{2}p_2(k) + \frac{1}{2}(1 - p_3(k)) \\
&\geq \frac{1}{2} + \frac{\epsilon(k)}{16} \,,
\end{aligned}$$

contradicting the indistinguishability of encryptions.

Case 4: $p_3(k) - p_4(k) \geq \frac{\epsilon(k)}{8}$.

We will distinguish [GGM] functions from random functions.

Given an oracle O_f for a function $f : \{0,1\}^k \to \{0,1\}^k$, the experiment $A^{O_f}(1^k)$ is

- *Make Public Key:* Let $s', r \leftarrow \{0,1\}^k \,;\ \alpha \leftarrow E(r, s') \,;\ p^* \leftarrow M_1(1^{k^c})$. Let $PK = (1^k, E, \alpha, p^*)$.

- *Sign:* Invoke the forger $\mathcal{F}$ on input PK. When he requests the signature of a document D give him (D, R, β^*) where $R = O_f(D)$ and $\beta^* = M_2(1^{k^c}, p^*, T_{PK, D, R})$.

- *Output:* Output 1 iff the forger outputs a forgery $(\widehat{D}, \widehat{R}, \widehat{\beta})$ such that $\mathcal{V}(PK, (\widehat{D}, \widehat{R}, \widehat{\beta})) = 1$ and, in addition, $\widehat{R} = O_f(\widehat{D})$.

Then

$$\begin{aligned}
\boldsymbol{P}[A^{O_f} = 1 | f \leftarrow F_k] &= p_3(k) \\
\boldsymbol{P}[A^{O_f} = 1 | f \leftarrow H_k] &= p_4(k) \,,
\end{aligned}$$

where H_k denotes the set of all functions from $\{0,1\}^k$ to $\{0,1\}^k$. We thus contradict [GGM].

B Appendix: Using a Simpler Zero Knowledge Definition

Is it possible to prove our signature scheme correct with a definition of zero knowledge which is simpler and more like the usual one? We do not know how to do quite that, but we can show something essentially as good: a modified scheme can be proved correct with a simple definition of NIZK.

A simpler definition of the zero knowledge would be of the following form.

Notation: For any constant $c > 0$ let $L_{k^c} = \underbrace{(L \cap \{0,1\}^k) \times \cdots \times (L \cap \{0,1\}^k)}_{k^c}$.

Definition B.1 Let $P = (P_1, P_2), V = (V_1, V_2)$ be a non-interactive proof system for a language L, and let $\widehat{V}_1$ be a PPT interactive TM. Let $c > 0$ be a constant. The *view* of the cheating verifier $\widehat{V} = (\widehat{V}_1, V_2)$ on any input $\vec{x} \in L_{k^c}$ is

$$
\begin{aligned}
View_{\widehat{V}}(1^k, \vec{x}) &= \{ (p, S_V, h, \vec{x}, \vec{\beta}) : (p, S_P, S_V, h) \leftarrow (P_1 . \widehat{V}_1)(1^k) ; \\
&\qquad \beta_1 \leftarrow P_2(1^k, S_P, p, x_1) ; \ldots ; \beta_{k^c} \leftarrow P_2(1^k, S_P, p, x_{k^c}) \}
\end{aligned}
$$

where $\vec{\beta} = (\beta_1, \ldots, \beta_{k^c})$.

Definition B.2 A non-interactive proof system $P = (P_1, P_2), V = (V_1, V_2)$ for L is said to be a non-interactive zero knowledge proof system if for any PPT interactive TM $\widehat{V}_1$ and any constant $c > 0$ there is a PPT algorithm M such that the ensembles $\{M(1^k, \vec{x})\}_{\vec{x} \in L_{k^c}}$ and $\{View_{\widehat{V}}(1^k, \vec{x})\}_{\vec{x} \in L_{k^c}}$ are computationally indistinguishable, where $\widehat{V} = (\widehat{V}_1, V_2)$.

(The indistinguishability is as usual in terms of poly-sized families of circuits).

Crucial to constructing a signature scheme secure against adaptive chosen message attack based on this definition is a theorem of Even, Goldreich and Micali [EGM] which states that any scheme secure against random message attack can be transformed into one secure against adaptive chosen message attack. Moreover, a signature in the transformed scheme is independent of previous signatures if this was true for the original scheme. We are thus done given

Theorem B.1 The digital signature scheme of §4 is secure against random message attack under the above definition of NIZK proofs.

Proof: In the final paper. $\square$

References

[BM1]   Bellare, M., and S. Micali, "How to Sign Given Any Trapdoor Function," STOC 88.

[BM2]   Bellare, M., and S. Micali, "Non-Interactive Oblivious Transfer and Applications," CRYPTO 89.

[BFM]   Blum, M., P. Feldman and S. Micali, "Non-Interactive Zero Knowledge and its Applications," STOC 88.

[CV]   Chaum, D. and H. Van Antwerpen, "Undeniable Signatures," CRYPTO 89.

[DMP]   De Santis, A., G. Persiano and S. Micali, "Non-Interactive Zero Knowledge Proof Systems," CRYPTO 87.

[EGM]   Even, S., O. Goldreich and S. Micali, "On-line/Off-line Digital Signatures," CRYPTO 89.

[F]   Feige, U., personal communication, September 1989.

[FS]   Feige, U. and A. Shamir, "Zero Knowledge Proofs of Knowledge in two Rounds," CRYPTO 89.

[G]   Goldreich, O., "Two Remarks Concerning the GMR Signature Scheme," MIT Laboratory for Computer Science Technical Report 715, (September 1986).

[GM]   Goldwasser, S., and S. Micali, "Probabalistic Encryption," *Journal of Computer and System Sciences* 28 (April 1984), 270-299.

[GGM]   Goldreich, O., S. Goldwasser, and S. Micali, "How To Construct Random Functions," *Journal of the Association for Computing Machinery*, Vol. 33, No. 4 (October 1986), 792-807.

[GMR]   Goldwasser, S., S. Micali and R. Rivest, "A Digital Signature Scheme Secure Against Adaptive Chosen-Message Attacks," *SIAM Journal on Computing*, vol. 17, No. 2, (April 1988), 281-308.

[ILL]   Impagliazzo, R., L. Levin, and M. Luby, "Pseudo-Random Generation from One-Way Functions," STOC 89.

[K]   Kilian, J., "Founding Cryptography on Oblivious Transfer," STOC 88.

[KMO]   Kilian, J., S. Micali and R. Ostrovsky, "Efficient Zero Knowledge Proofs with Bounded Interaction," CRYPTO 89.

[M1]   Micali, S., personal communication, April 1989.

[M2]   Micali, S., personal communication, August 1989.

[N]   Naor, M., "Bit Committment using Pseudo-Randomness," CRYPTO 89.

[NY]   Naor, M., and M. Yung, "Universal One-Way Hash Functions and their Cryptographic Applications," STOC 89.

Undeniable Signatures

David Chaum
Hans van Antwerpen

Centre for Mathematics and Computer Science
Kruislaan 413 1098 SJ Amsterdam

INTRODUCTION & MOTIVATION

Digital signatures [DH]—unlike handwritten signatures and banknote printing—are easily copied exactly. This property can be advantageous for some uses, such as dissemination of announcements and public keys, where the more copies distributed the better. But it is unsuitable for many other applications. Consider electronic replacements for all the written or oral commitments that are to some extent personally or commercially sensitive. In such cases the proliferation of certified copies could facilitate improper uses like blackmail or industrial espionage. The recipient of such a commitment should of course be able to ensure that the issuer cannot later disavow it—but the recipient should also be unable to show the commitment to anyone else without the issuer's consent.

Undeniable signatures are well suited to such applications. An undeniable signature, like a digital signature, is a number issued by a signer that depends on the signer's public key and the message signed. Unlike a digital signature, however, an undeniable signature cannot be verified without the signer's cooperation.

The validity of an undeniable signature can be ascertained by anyone issuing a challenge to the signer and testing the signer's response. If the test is successful, there is an exponentially high probability that the signature is valid. If the test fails, there are two cases: (a) the signature is not valid; or (b) the signer is giving improper responses, presumably in an effort to falsely deny a valid signature. But even if the signer has infinite computing power, the challenger can distinguish case (a) from case (b), with exponentially high certainty, by means of a second challenge.

Quite efficient and practical undeniable signature protocols based on the "discrete log" problem [DH] are presented below. Since all signers can use the same group, signatures created by different signers commute with each other—a useful property [CE] that has not yet been achieved for digital signatures. Furthermore, a new type of "blinding" [C] can be applied in the signing as well as in the challenge and response.

CRYPTOGRAPHIC SETTING

Consider using the group of known prime order p: All values transmitted between the participants are elements of this group, the multiplicatively denoted group operation is easily computed by all participants, and taking the discrete log in the group is assumed to be computationally infeasible.

One potentially suitable representation is the multiplicative group of the field $GF(2^n)$, where $p = 2^n\text{-}1$ is prime. A second is the group of squares modulo prime q, where $q\text{-}1 = 2p$. (Notice that such choices rule out the Pohlig-Hellman attack on discrete log [PH].) An attractive variation on the second approach represents group elements by the integers 1 to p; the group operation is the same, except that all results are normalized by taking the additive inverse exactly when this yields a smaller least positive representative.

PROTOCOL

A suitable group of prime order p and a primitive element g are initially established and made public for use by a set of signers. Consider a particular signer S having a private key x and a corresponding public key g^x. A message m ($\neq 1$) is signed by S to form signature z, which should be equal to m^x. Someone receiving z from S may wish to establish its validity immediately; the challenge/response protocol used to establish this, though, is the same for any later verifier V.

The initial challenge is of the form $z^a(g^x)^b$, where V chooses a and b independently and uniformly from the group elements. The response should be formed by S raising the challenge to the multiplicative inverse of x modulo p. When V computes $m^a g^b$ and finds it equal to the response, then V knows (by Theorem 1 below) that, even if S were to have infinite computing power, the probability of z being unequal m^x (and hence invalid) is at most p^{-1}.

When the value V computes is unequal to the response, the challenge/response protocol should be repeated with independently chosen c and d replacing a and b, respectively. Then V can use the two responses r_1 and r_2 to test whether $(r_1 g^{-b})^c = (r_2 g^{-d})^a$. Equality means that S is answering consistently and z is invalid, with the same high probability as for signature validity; inequality means that S is answering improperly (Theorem 2).

UNDENIABILITY

Two essential points can be proved:

Theorem 1: Even with infinite computing power S cannot with probability exceeding p^{-1} provide a valid response for an invalid signature.

Proof: First notice that each challenge value corresponds to p pairs (a,b), as a simple consequence of the group structure. It is sufficient to show that if the signature is not m^x, then each pair corresponding to a challenge value requires a different response. Suppose $z = m^{x'}$, with $x \neq x'$. If two pairs (a,b) and (a',b') yield the same challenge, then

$$m^{x'a} g^{xb} = m^{x'a'} g^{xb'}$$
$$m^{x'(a-a')} = g^{x(b'-b)}.$$

Assuming, by way of contradiction, that the same response is accepted for both pairs gives

$$m^a g^b = m^{a'} g^{b'}$$
$$m^{(a-a')} = g^{(b'-b)}.$$

But $x \neq x'$. Q.E.D.

Theorem 2: Even with infinite computing power S cannot with probability exceeding p^{-1} avoid detection of inconsistency between two invalid responses to a valid signature.

Proof: It suffices to show that, after a first invalid response, the ability of S to show consistency of the second invalid response contradicts Theorem 1. After the first invalid response, a, b, and m may in the worst case be assumed known to S. The consistency test $(r_1 g^{-b})^c = (r_2 g^{-d})^a$ can be written as $r_2 = (r_1^{1/a} g^{-b/a})^c g^d$. But since $r_1^{1/a} g^{-b/a}$ may be regarded as a known constant at this point, being able to satisfy this test implies an ability to establish the validity of an invalid signature. Q.E.D.

UNFORGEABILITY

Computing the private key from the public key is clearly no more difficult than breaking Diffie-Hellman key exchange. But an open question remains: Can the oracle for inverse roots provided by the signer help a forger? In view of the fact that minimum disclosure versions of these protocols are now known (and will appear in subsequent work), the example shown here is only proposed as a cryptosystem predicated on this open question being answered in the negative.

BLINDING

Of the two blinding techniques appearing in the literature, one of them, called blinding for "unanticipated" signatures [C], can be applied to the present protocols. The blinding party first chooses r independently and uniformly at random, forms the blinding factor g^r, and computes the signature of the blinding factor as $(g^x)^r$. To blind a message before it is signed, the message is multiplied by the blinding factor; unblinding entails multiplying by the multiplicative inverse of the signed form of the blinding factor. The challenge/response protocol requires V to show m to S, but V may blind m in the challenge and use the signed form of m and the blinding factor in verifying the response.

A previously unpublished blinding technique, which may be called "exponential" blinding, can also be used. A message is blinded by raising it to an independently and uniformly chosen random power; unblinding is by raising to the multiplicative inverse of the random power.

CONCLUSION

Undeniable signatures are better suited for many applications and are efficient.

ACKNOWLEDGEMENTS

It is a pleasure to thank Jan-Hendrik Evertse, Bert den Boer, and Gilles Brassard for their interest and comments.

REFERENCES

[BCC] Brassard, G., D. Chaum, and C. Crépeau, "Minimum disclosure proofs of knowledge," *Journal of Computer and System Sciences*, vol. 37, 1988, pp. 156–189.

[C] Chaum, D., "Blinding for unanticipated signatures," Advances in Cryptology—EUROCRYPT '87, D. Chaum & W.L. Price Eds., Springer Verlag, 1987, pp. 227–233.

[CE] Chaum, D. and J.-H. Evertse, "A secure and privacy-protecting protocol for transmitting personal information between organizations," Advances in Cryptology—CRYPTO '86, A.M. Odlyzko Ed., Springer Verlag, 1987, pp. 118–167.

[DH] Diffie, W. and M.E. Hellman, "New directions in cryptography," *IEEE Transactions on Information Theory*, Vol. IT-22, 1976, pp. 644–654.

[EG] ElGamal, T., "A public key cryptosystem and a signature scheme based on discrete logarithm," *IEEE Transactions on Information Theory*, vol. IT-31, 1985, pp. 469–472.

[PH] Pohlig, S. and M.E. Hellman, "An improved algorithm for computing logarithms over GF(p) and its cryptographic significance," *IEEE Transactions on Information Theory*, vol. IT-24, 1978, pp. 106–110.

Session 6:

Signature and Authentication II

Chair: JOAN FEIGENBAUM

A CERTIFIED DIGITAL SIGNATURE

Ralph C. Merkle
Xerox PARC
3333 Coyote Hill Road,
Palo Alto, Ca. 94304
merkle@xerox.com
(Subtitle: That Antique Paper from 1979)

Abstract

A practical digital signature system based on a conventional encryption function which is as secure as the conventional encryption function is described. Since certified conventional systems are available it can be implemented quickly, without the several years delay required for certification of an untested system.

Key Words and Phrases: Public Key Cryptosystem, Digital Signatures, Cryptography, Electronic Signatures, Receipts, Authentication, Electronic Funds Transfer.

CR categories: 3.56, 3.57, 4.9

1. *Introduction*

Digital signatures promise to revolutionize business by phone (or other telecommunication devices)[1] but currently known digital signature methods [5,6,7,8,10,13] either have not been certified, or have other drawbacks. A signature system whose security rested on the security of a conventional cryptographic function would be "pre-certified" to the extent that the underlying encryption function had been certified. The delays and cost of a new certification effort would be avoided. Lamport and Diffie[1][10] suggested such a system, but it has severe performance drawbacks. Lipton and Matyas[4] nonetheless suggested its use as the only near term solution to a pressing problem.

This paper describes a digital signature system which is "pre-certified," generates signatures of about 1 to 3 kilobytes (depending on the exact security requirements), requires a few thousand applications of the underlying encryption function per signature, and only a few kilobytes of

This work was partially supported under contracts F49620-78-C-0086 from the U.S. Air Force Office of Scientific Research and DAAG29-78-C-0036 from the U.S. Army Research Office. Much of this work was done when the author was at Stanford University in the Electrical Engineering Department, and some was done when the author was at BNR in Palo Alto.

memory. If the underlying encryption function takes 10 microseconds to encrypt a block, generating a signature might take 20 milliseconds.

The new signature method is called a "tree signature." The following major points are covered:

1.) A discussion of one way functions.
2.) A description of the Lamport-Diffie one time signature.
3.) An improvement to the Lamport-Diffie one time signature.
4.) The Winternitz one time signature.
5.) A description of tree signatures.

2. *One Way Functions*

One way functions[2,9] are basic to this paper. Intuitively, a one way function F is one which is easy to compute but difficult to invert. If $y = F(x)$, then given x and F, it is easy to compute y, but given y and F it is effectively impossible to compute x.

Readers interested only in getting the gist of this paper are advised to skip this section and continue with section 3.

We will parameterize F, i.e., create a family of one way functions F_1, F_2, F_3 ... F_i ..., to improve security. It is easier to analyze a single function which is used repeatedly than it is to analyze all the different F_i. Often it is desirable for F_i to also compress a large input (e.g. 10,000 bits) into a smaller output (e.g. 100 bits). This will be referred to as a one way hash function and it is required that, for all i:

1.) F_i can be applied to any argument of any size.
2.) F_i always produces a fixed size output, which, for the sake of concreteness, we can assume is 100 bits.
3.) Given x it is easy to compute $F_i(x)$.
4.) It is computationally infeasible to find $x' \neq x$ such that $F_i(x) = F_i(x')$.
5.) Given $F_i(x)$ it is computationally infeasible to determine x.

An important point of notation: when we wish to concatenate two arguments x_1 and x_2, we will write $<x_1,x_2>$. Thus, if x_1 and x_2 are both 100 bits long, $<x_1,x_2>$ will be their 200 bit concatenation.

The major use of one way functions is for authentication. If a value y can be authenticated, we can authenticate x by computing:

$F_i(x) = y$

No other input x' can be found (although they probably exist) which will generate y. A 100 bit y can authenticate an arbitrarily large x. This property is crucial for the convenient authentication of large amounts of information. (Although a 100 bit y is plausible, selection of the size in a real system involves tradeoffs between the reduced cost and improved efficiency of a smaller size, and the improved security of a larger size.)

Functions such as F_i can be defined in terms of conventional cryptographic functions[6]. We therefore assume we have a conventional encryption function C(key,plaintext) which has a 300 bit key size and encrypts 100 bit blocks of plaintext into 100 bit blocks of ciphertext.

In order to prove that F_i is a good one way function, we must make some assumptions about the conventional cryptographic function on which it is based (Rabin has also considered this problem[13]). In particular, we require that it possess certain properties.

A "certified" encryption function C(k,p) = c, in which length(p) = length(c) $\leq$ length(k), must have the following properties:

1.) The average computational effort required to find any four values k, k', p, and c such that C(k,p) = c = C(k',p) and k $\neq$ k' is greater than $2^{length(p)/2}$.

2.) The average computational effort required to find four values k, k', p, and c such that C(k,p) = c = C(k',p) and k $\neq$ k' is $2^{length(p)-1}$ if the following conditions hold:

a.) The plaintext, p, is known and fixed.
b.) The key space is divided into mutually disjoint subsets S_1, S_2, ...
c.) k is an element of the set $\{k_1, k_2, ... \}$
d.) Each k_i is randomly chosen from S_i.
e.) Each S_i must have at least $2^{length(p)}$ elements.
f.) both k and k' must be elements of the same subset S_i.

For the rest of this paper, these will be referred to as "property 1" and "property 2."

Property 1 is rather clear: finding two keys k and k' for the same plaintext-ciphertext pair requires a certain minimum computational effort under all circumstances.

Property 2 requires more explanation. It states that finding two keys k and k' for the same plaintext ciphertext pair requires a full exhaustive search IF certain conditions are satisfied. (Notice that property 1, which applies unconditionally, states that the required effort to find k and k' is proportional to the square root of a simple exhaustive search.)

The most important condition is 2d: k must be randomly chosen. If k is chosen randomly, then c = C(k,p) should also be random. Given a random c, the problem of finding a k' such that C(k',p) = c should require a full exhaustive search.

The additional conditions can be interpreted as meaning that encryption of two plaintexts with two keys from two disjoint key spaces is effectively equivalent to encryption with two unrelated ciphers: knowledge of how to cryptanalyze messages enciphered with keys from one space will be of no help in cryptanalyzing messages enciphered with keys from the other key space. The main reason that F is parameterized is to take advantage of this aspect of property 2. If $i \neq j$, then F_i and F_j are separate one way functions: breaking F_i and breaking F_j are two independent problems. If F were not parameterized, then the many applications of F by many different people to different arguments would constitute a single interrelated problem. The problem of reversing some application of F to one of many possible arguments would be much easier to solve than the problem of reversing a particular application of F to a particular argument. This entire issue can be avoided by parameterization.

Both properties 1 and 2 will be satisfied if C is a "random cipher," a concept described by Shannon [12]. The strength of modern encryption functions is based on their resemblance to random ciphers: to quote Feistel's [11] description of Lucifer, "As the input moves through successive layers the pattern of 1's generated is amplified and results in an unpredictable avalanche. In the end the final output will have, on the average, half 0's and half 1's,..."

Should ciphers that do not satisfy properties 1 and 2 be called "certified?" This is largely a question of the appropriate definition of the term. It seems prudent to demand that a cipher not be considered certified if it fails to satisfy either property 1 or 2: the author would certainly be reluctant to use such a cipher for any purpose.

The reader should note that property 1 is much more robust than property 2: designing systems which depend on property 2 requires special care.

We will define F_i in stages: first we define the one way function $G_{<i,j>}$, which satisfies properties 2, 3, 4, and 5; but whose input is restricted to 200 bits or less. We define

$$G_{<i,j>}(x) = y = C(<x,i,j>, \underline{0})$$

$G_{<i,j>}$ accepts up to a 200 bit input x, 50 bit parameters i and j, and produces a 100 bit output y, as desired. Furthermore, given y the problem of finding an x' such that $G_{<i,j>}(x') = y$ is equivalent to finding a key x' such that $y = C(<x',i,j>, \underline{0})$.

If C satisfies properties 1 and 2 this is computationally infeasible.

We can now define F_i in terms of $G_{<i,j>}$. If the input x to F_i is 100 bits or less, then we can "pad" x by adding 0's until it is exactly 100 bits, and define $F_i(x) = G_{<i,1>}(<\underline{0},x>)$. (Where $\underline{0}$ is 100 bits of 0).

If the input is more than 100 bits, we will break it into 100 bit pieces. Assume that

$$\underline{x} = <x_1, x_2, ... x_n>$$

and that each x_k is 100 bits long. Then F_i is defined in terms of repeated applications of $G_{<i,j>}$. $G_{<i,1>}$ is first applied to x_1 to obtain $y_1 = G_{<i,1>}(<\underline{0},x_1>)$. Then $y_2 = G_{<i,2>}(<y_1,x_2>)$, $y_3 = G_{<i,3>}(<y_2,x_3>)$, $y_4 = G_{<i,4>}(<y_3,x_4>)$, ... $y_j = G_{<i,j>}(<y_{j-1},x_j>)$, ... $y_n = G_{<i,n>}(<y_{n-1},x_n>)$. $F_i(\underline{x})$ is defined to be y_n; the final y in the series.

It is obvious that F_i can accept arbitrarily large values for x. It is less obvious (though true) that it is computationally infeasible to find any vector $\underline{x}'$ not equal to $\underline{x}$ such that $F_i(\underline{x}) = F_i(\underline{x}')$. We shall call finding such an $\underline{x}'$ as "breaking" F_i.

If we assume that C is a certified encryption function, i.e., that property 1 or 2 holds, we can prove inductively that breaking F_i is computationally infeasible. If we utilize assumption 1 we can prove that the average effort required to compute $\underline{x}'$ will be at least $2^{length(p)/2}$; while if we use assumption 2 we can prove that the average effort required to compute $\underline{x}'$ will be at least $2^{length(p)-1}$, although we require that x' be random.

As a basis, when n = 1 the property holds because, by definition, $F_i(\underline{x}) = G_{<i,1>}(<\underline{0},x_1>) = C(<\underline{0},x_1,i,1>,\underline{0})$ and the property holds for C by assumption. To show that the property must hold for n+1 if it holds for n, we need only note that if $F_i(\underline{x}) = F_i(\underline{x}')$, then one of the following two conditions must hold:

A.) $x_k = x'_k$ for all $k \leq n$

B.) $x_k \neq x'_k$ for some $k \leq n$

If (B) holds, then by the induction hypothesis we have already spent the required effort to compute $x_k \neq x'_k$, for some $k \leq n$.

If (A) holds and $\underline{x} \neq \underline{x}'$, then $x_{n+1} \neq x'_{n+1}$. The effort required to compute x'_{n+1} not equal to x_{n+1}, but with $G_{<i,n+1>}(<y_n,x'_{n+1}>)$ equal to $G_{<i,n+1>}(<y_n,x_{n+1}>)$ must be $2^{length(p)/2}$ (if we use property 1), or $2^{length(p)-1}$ (if we use property 2), by definition of $G_{<i,n+1>}$ and properties 1 and 2.

In those cases where the conditions of property 2 do not hold, property 1 will.

It is important in practice to distinguish between those cases where property 2 can be used, and those which can use only property 1. The use of property 2 allows the size of the block cipher to be reduced by a factor of two, while still maintaining the same level of security. This will lead to a factor of two reduction in most storage and transmission costs in the following algorithms.

To clarify further explanations we will omit the subscript from F in the rest of the paper, but the reader should remember that parameterizing F is essential to take advantage of property 2. If property 1 is used, it is still advisable to parameterize F.

3. *The Lamport-Diffie One Time Signature*

The Lamport-Diffie one time signature[1] is based on the concept of a one way function[2,9]. If $y = F(x)$ is the result of applying the one way function F to input x, then the key observation is:

> The person who computed $y = F(x)$ is the only person who knows x. If y is publicly revealed, only the originator of y can know x, and can choose to reveal or conceal x at his whim.

This is best clarified by an example. Suppose a person A has some stock, which he can sell at any time. A might wish to sell the stock on short notice, which means that A would like to tell his broker over the phone. The broker, B, does not wish to sell with only a phone call as authorization. To solve this problem, A computes $y = F(x)$ and gives y to B. They agree that when A wants to sell his stock he will reveal x to B. (This agreement could be formalized as a written contract[4] which includes the value of y and a description of F but not the value of x.) B will then be able to prove that A wanted to sell his stock, because B will be able to exhibit x, and demonstrate that $F(x) = y$.

If A later denies having sold the stock, B can show the contract and x to a judge as proof that A, contrary to his statement, did sell the stock. Both F and y are given in the original (written) contract, so the judge can compute $F(x)$ and verify that it equals y. The only person who could possibly know x would be A, and the only way B could have learned x would be if A had revealed x. Therefore, A must have revealed x: an action which by prior agreement meant that A wanted to sell his stock.

This example illustrates a signature system which "signs" a single bit of information. Either A sold the stock, or he did not. If A wanted to tell his broker to sell 10 shares of stock, then A must be able to sign a several bit message. In the general Lamport-Diffie scheme, if A wanted to sign a message m whose size was s bits, then he would compute $F(x_1) = y_1$, $F(x_2) = y_2$, $F(x_3) = y_3$,... $F(x_s) = y_s$. A and B would agree on the vector $Y = y_1, y_2 ... y_s$. If the jth bit of m was a 1, A would reveal x_j. If the jth bit of m was a 0, A would not reveal x_j. In essence, each bit of m would be individually signed. Arbitrary messages can be signed, one bit at a time.

In practice, long messages (greater than 100 bits) can be be mapped into short messages (100 bits) by a one way function and only the short message signed. It is always possible to use property 2 (described in section 2). F can be parameterized as F_i (also described in section 2), the message can be encrypted with a newly generated random key by the signer before it is signed, and the random key appended to the message. The signed message will therefore be random (assuming that encryption with a random key will effectively randomize the message, a fact that is generally conceded for modern encryption functions [11]). These steps will satisfy the conditions for property 2. We can therefore assume, without loss of generality, that all messages are a fixed length, e.g., 100 bits.

The method as described thus far suffers from the defect that B can alter m by changing bits that are 1's into 0's. B simply denies he ever received x_j, (in spite of the fact he did). However, 0's cannot be changed to 1's. Lamport and Diffie overcame this problem by signing a new message m', which is exactly twice as long as m and is computed by concatenating m with the bitwise complement of m. That is, each bit m_j in the original message is represented by two bits, m_j and the complement of m_j in the new message m'. Clearly, one or the other bit must be a 0. To alter the message, B would have to turn a 0 into a 1, something he cannot do.

It should now be clear why this method is a "one time" signature: Each $Y = y_1, y_2, \ldots y_{2*s}$ can only be used to sign one message. If more than one message is to be signed, then new values $Y_1, Y_2, Y_3, \ldots$ are needed, a new Y_i for each message.

One time signatures are practical between a single pair of users who are willing to exchange the large amount of data necessary but they are not practical for most applications without further refinements. (Rabin [13] has described a different one time signature method).

Between two people, A and his broker B for example, a signature system for n possible messages might be designed as follows. A would compute

$$
\begin{aligned}
Y_1 &= y_{1,1}, y_{1,2} \ldots y_{1,2*s} \\
Y_2 &= y_{2,1}, y_{2,2} \ldots y_{2,2*s} \\
Y_3 &= y_{3,1}, y_{3,2} \ldots y_{3,2*s} \\
&\quad\vdots \\
Y_n &= y_{n,1}, y_{n,2} \ldots y_{n,2*s}
\end{aligned}
$$

(where $y_{i,j} = F(x_{i,j})$, and the $x_{i,j}$ are chosen randomly). However, prior to using this method, A and B would have to agree that $\underline{Y} = Y_1, Y_2 \ldots Y_n$ was to be used for signatures, and B would have to have a copy of $\underline{Y}$. ($\underline{Y}$ would have to be authenticated in some fashion so it could be shown to a judge in the event of a dispute, and proven to be the $\underline{Y}$ that both A and B agreed on.) If each $y_{i,j}$ is 100 bits long, if s = 100, and if n = 1000 (i.e., 1000 possible messages can be signed, each 100 bits in length) then $\underline{Y}$ will be n * 2 * s * 100 = 1000 * 2 * 100 * 100 = 20,000,000 bits or 2.5 megabytes. While this might not be overly burdensome when only two users, A and B, are involved in the signature system, if B had to keep 2.5 megabytes of data for 1000 other users, B would have to store 2.5 gigabytes of data. While possible, this hardly seems economical. With further increases in the number of users, or in the number of messages each user wants to be able to sign, the system becomes completely unwieldy.

How to eliminate the huge storage requirements is a major subject of this paper.

4. *An Improved One Time Signature*

This section explains how to reduce the size of signed messages in the Lamport-Diffie method by almost a factor of 2. It can be skipped without loss of continuity.

As previously mentioned, the Lamport-Diffie method solves the problem that 1's in the original message can be altered to 0's by doubling the length of the message, and signing each bit and its complement independently. In this way, changing a 1 to a 0 in the new message, m', would result in an incorrectly formatted message, which would be rejected. In essence, this represents a solution to the problem:

> Create a coding scheme in which accidental or intentional conversion of 1's to 0's will produce an illegal codeword.

An alternative coding method which would accomplish the same result would be to append a count of the 0 bits in m before signing. The new message, m', would be only $\log_2 s$ bits longer than the original s bit message, m. If any 1's in m' were changed to 0's, it would produce an illegal codeword by either increasing the number of 0's in m, and thus make the count of 0's too small, or it would alter the count of 0's. If the count of 0's is in standard binary, changing a bit in this count from 1 to 0 must reduce the count, and hence result in an illegal codeword. Notice that while it is possible to reduce the count by changing 1's to 0's in the count field, and while it is possible to increase the number of 0's by changing 1's to 0's in the message, these two "errors" cannot be made to compensate for each other.

A small example is in order. Assume that our messages are 8 bits long, and that our count is $\log_2 8 = 3$ bits long. If our message m is

    m = 11010110

Then m' would be

    m' = 11010110,011

(Where a comma is used to clarify the division of m' into m and its 0 count.)

If the codeword 11010110,011 were changed to 01010110,011 by changing the first 1 to a 0, then the count 011 would have to be changed to 100 because we now have 4 0's, not 3. But this requires changing a 0 to a 1, something we cannot do. If the codeword were changed to 11010110,010 by altering the 0 count then the message would have to be changed so that it had only 2 0's instead of 3. Again, this change is illegal because it requires changing 0's to 1's.

This improved method is easy to implement and cuts the size of the signed message almost in half.

5. *The Winternitz Improvement*

Shortly before publication[e.g., in 1979], Robert Winternitz of the Stanford Mathematics Department suggested a further substantial improvement which reduces the size of the signed message by an additional factor of about 4 to 8. Winternitz's method trades time for space: the reduced size is purchased with an increased computational effort.

In the Lamport-Diffie method, given that $y = F(x)$ and that y is public and x is secret, a user signs a single bit of information by either making x public or keeping it secret.

In the Winternitz method we still use y and x, and make y public and keep x secret, but we compute y from x by applying F repeatedly, for example, $y = F^{16}(x)$. This allows us to sign 4 bits of information (instead of just 1) with the single y value. To sign the 4 bit message 1001 (9 in decimal), the signer makes $F^9(x)$ public. Anyone can check that $F^7(F^9(x)) = y$, thus confirming that $F^9(x)$ was made public, but no one can generate that value.

Because $F^9(x)$ is public, $F^{10}(x)$ can be easily computed by anyone. Someone could then (falsely) claim that the signed four bit message was 1010 (10 in decimal) rather than 1001. Overcoming this problem requires a slight extension of the method described in section 4, and adds only log n additional bits.

6. *Tree Authentication*

A new protocol would eliminate the large storage requirements. If A transmitted Y_i to B just before signing a message, then B would not previously have had to get and keep copies of the Y_i from A. Unfortunately, such a protocol would not work. Anyone could claim to be A, send a false Y_i, and trick B into thinking he had received a properly authorized signature when he had received nothing of the kind. B must somehow be able to confirm that he was sent the correct Y_i and not a forgery.

The problem is to authenticate A's Y_i. The simplest (but unsatisfactory) method is to keep a copy of A's Y_i. In this section, we describe a method called "tree authentication" which can be used to authenticate any Y_i of any user quickly and easily, but which requires minimal storage.

Tree authentication can also be used to solve authentication problems which do not involve digital signatures: that it is being used to generate tree signatures in this paper should not prejudice the reader into thinking that that is its only application.

Problem Definition: Given a vector of data items $\underline{Y} = Y_1, Y_2, \dots Y_n$ design an algorithm which can quickly authenticate a randomly chosen Y_i but which has modest memory requirements, i.e., does not have a table of $Y_1, Y_2, \dots Y_n$.

To authenticate the Y_i we apply the "divide and conquer" technique. Define the function $H(i,j,\underline{Y})$ as follows:

1.) $H(i,i,\underline{Y}) = F(Y_i)$

2.) $H(i,j,\underline{Y}) = F(< H(i,(i+j-1)/2,\underline{Y}), H((i+j+1)/2,j,\underline{Y}) >)$

$H(i,j,\underline{Y})$ is a function of $Y_i, Y_{i+1}, \dots Y_j$. $H(i,j,\underline{Y})$ can be used to authenticate Y_i through Y_j. $H(1,n,\underline{Y})$ can be used to authenticate Y_1 through Y_n. $H(1,n,\underline{Y})$ is only 100 bits, so it can be conveniently stored. This method lets us selectively authenticate any "leaf," Y_i, that we wish. To see this, we use an example where $n = 8$. The sequence of recursive calls required to compute $H(1,8,\underline{Y})$ is illustrated in Figure 1. To authenticate Y_5, we can proceed in the following manner:

1.) $H(1,8,\underline{Y})$ is already known and authenticated.

2.) $H(1,8,\underline{Y}) = F(< H(1,4,\underline{Y}), H(5,8,\underline{Y}) >)$. Send $H(1,4,\underline{Y})$ and $H(5,8,\underline{Y})$ and let the receiver compute $H(1,8,\underline{Y}) = F(< H(1,4,\underline{Y}), H(5,8,\underline{Y}) >)$ and confirm they are correct.

3.) The receiver has authenticated $H(5,8,\underline{Y})$. Send $H(5,6,\underline{Y})$ and $H(7,8,\underline{Y})$ and let the receiver compute $H(5,8,\underline{Y}) = F(< H(5,6,\underline{Y}), H(7,8,\underline{Y}) >)$ and confirm they are correct.

4.) The receiver has authenticated $H(5,6,\underline{Y})$. Send $H(5,5,\underline{Y})$ and $H(6,6,\underline{Y})$ and let the receiver compute $H(5,6,\underline{Y}) = F(< H(5,5,\underline{Y}), H(6,6,\underline{Y}) >)$ and confirm they are correct.

5.) The receiver has authenticated $H(5,5,\underline{Y})$. Send Y_5 and let the receiver compute $H(5,5,\underline{Y}) = F(Y_5)$ and confirm it is correct.

6.) The receiver has authenticated Y_5.

Using this method, only $\log_2 n$ transmissions are required, each of about 200 bits. Close examination of the algorithm will reveal that half the transmissions are redundant. For example, $H(5,6,\underline{Y})$ can be computed from $H(5,5,\underline{Y})$ and $H(6,6,\underline{Y})$, so there is really no need to send $H(5,6,\underline{Y})$. Similarly, $H(5,8,\underline{Y})$ can be computed from $H(5,6,\underline{Y})$ and $H(7,8,\underline{Y})$, so $H(5,8,\underline{Y})$ need never be transmitted, either. (The receiver *must* compute these quantities anyway for proper authentication.) Therefore, to authenticate Y_5 only required that we have previously authenticated $H(1,8,\underline{Y})$, and that we transmit Y_5, $H(6,6,\underline{Y})$, $H(7,8,\underline{Y})$, and $H(1,4,\underline{Y})$. That is, we require $100 * \log_2 n$ bits of information to authenticate an arbitrary Y_i.

The method is called tree authentication because the computation of $H(1,n,\underline{Y})$ forms a binary tree of recursive calls. Authenticating a particular leaf Y_i in the tree requires only those values of $H()$ starting from the leaf and progressing to the root, i.e., from $H(i,i,\underline{Y})$ to $H(1,n,\underline{Y})$. $H(1,n,\underline{Y})$ will be referred to as the root of the authentication tree, or R. The information near the path from R to $H(i,i,\underline{Y})$ required to authenticate Y_i will be called the authentication path for Y_i.

The proof that the authentication path actually authenticates the chosen leaf is similar to the proof in section 2 that F(x) correctly authenticates x, and will not be repeated. It is important to decide whether property 1 or property 2 should be used: if property 1 is used the size of the authentication path must be doubled to preserve the same level of security. This choice depends on whether we trust the person who first computed the authentication tree. If we do, then property 2 can be used. If we don't, then property 1 must be used. This is because property 1 is independent of the method of computation. Property 2 requires random selection, and can be subverted by non-random choices.

The use of tree authentication to create tree signatures is now fairly clear. A transmits Y_i to B. A then transmits the authentication path for Y_i. B knows R, the root of the authentication tree, by prior arrangement. B can then authenticate Y_i, and can accept a signed message from A as genuine.

If the jth user has a distinct authentication tree with root R_j, then tree authentication can be used to authenticate R_j just as easily as it can be used to authenticate Y_i. It is not necessary for each user to remember all the R_j in order to authenticate them. A central clearinghouse could accept the R_j from all u users, and compute $H(1,u,\underline{R})$. This single 1-200 bit quantity could then be distributed and would serve to authenticate all the R_j, which would in turn be used to authenticate the Y_i. In practice, A would remember R_A and the authentication path for R_A and send them to B along with Y_i and the authentication path for Y_i.

Because it is impossible to add new leaves (representing new users) to the "user tree" once it has been computed, it is necessary to compute and issue new user trees periodically. It is precisely this "inflexibility" which makes it unnecessary to trust the central clearinghouse. If it is impossible to add new users, it is impossible to add imposters. On the other hand, any system which allows new users to be added quickly, easily, and conveniently can be subverted by quickly, easily, and conveniently adding an imposter.

A different method of authentication would be for the clearinghouse to digitally sign "letters of reference" for new users of the system using a one time signature. This has the virtue of convenience, but requires that the clearinghouse be trusted not to (secretly) sign false letters of reference. Kohnfelder[3] has suggested this method for use with other public key cryptosystems.

A full discussion of the protocols for using tree authentication, digital signatures and one time signatures is well beyond the scope of this paper.

7. The Path Regeneration Algorithm

A must know the authentication path for Y_i before transmitting it to B. Unfortunately this requires the computation of $H(i,j,\underline{Y})$ for many different values of i and j. In the example, it was necessary to compute $H(6,6,\underline{Y})$, $H(7,8,\underline{Y})$, and $H(1,4,\underline{Y})$ and send them to B along with Y_5. This is simple for the small tree used in our example, but computing $H(4194304,8388608,\underline{Y})$ just prior to sending it would be an intolerable burden. One obvious solution would be to precompute $H(1,n,\underline{Y})$ and to save all the intermediate computations: i.e., precompute all authentication paths. This would certainly allow the quick regeneration of the authentication path for Y_i, but would require a large memory.

A more satisfactory solution is to note that we wish to authenticate Y_1, Y_2, Y_3, Y_4, ... in that order. Most of the computations used in reconstructing the authentication path for Y_i can be used in computing the authentication path for Y_{i+1}. Only the incremental computations need be performed, and these can be made quite modest.

In addition, although the X_i (from which the Y_i are generated) must appear to be random, they can actually be generated (safely) in a pseudo-random fashion from a small truly random seed. It is not necessary to keep the X_i in memory, but only the small truly random seed used to generate them.

The result of these observations is an algorithm which can recompute each Y_i and its authentication path quickly and with modest memory requirements. Before describing it we review the problem:

> Problem Definition: Sequentially generate the authentication paths for Y_1, Y_2, Y_3, ... Y_n with modest time and space bounds.

The simplest way to understand how an algorithm can efficiently generate all authentication paths is to generate all the authentication paths for a small example.

An example of all authentication paths for n = 8 is:

leaf	authentication path			
Y_1	H(1,8,$\underline{Y}$)	H(5,8,$\underline{Y}$)	H(3,4,$\underline{Y}$)	H(2,2,$\underline{Y}$)
Y_2	H(1,8,$\underline{Y}$)	H(5,8,$\underline{Y}$)	H(3,4,$\underline{Y}$)	H(1,1,$\underline{Y}$)
Y_3	H(1,8,$\underline{Y}$)	H(5,8,$\underline{Y}$)	H(1,2,$\underline{Y}$)	H(4,4,$\underline{Y}$)
Y_4	H(1,8,$\underline{Y}$)	H(5,8,$\underline{Y}$)	H(1,2,$\underline{Y}$)	H(3,3,$\underline{Y}$)
Y_5	H(1,8,$\underline{Y}$)	H(1,4,$\underline{Y}$)	H(7,8,$\underline{Y}$)	H(6,6,$\underline{Y}$)
Y_6	H(1,8,$\underline{Y}$)	H(1,4,$\underline{Y}$)	H(7,8,$\underline{Y}$)	H(5,5,$\underline{Y}$)
Y_7	H(1,8,$\underline{Y}$)	H(1,4,$\underline{Y}$)	H(5,6,$\underline{Y}$)	H(8,8,$\underline{Y}$)
Y_8	H(1,8,$\underline{Y}$)	H(1,4,$\underline{Y}$)	H(5,6,$\underline{Y}$)	H(7,7,$\underline{Y}$)

TABLE 1

If we had to separately compute each entry in table 1, then it would be impossible to efficiently generate the authentication paths. Fortunately, there is a great deal of duplication. If we eliminate all duplicate entries, then table 1 becomes table 2:

leaf	authentication path			
Y_1	H(1,8,$\underline{Y}$)	H(5,8,$\underline{Y}$)	H(3,4,$\underline{Y}$)	H(2,2,$\underline{Y}$)
Y_2				H(1,1,$\underline{Y}$)
Y_3			H(1,2,$\underline{Y}$)	H(4,4,$\underline{Y}$)
Y_4				H(3,3,$\underline{Y}$)
Y_5		H(1,4,$\underline{Y}$)	H(7,8,$\underline{Y}$)	H(6,6,$\underline{Y}$)
Y_6				H(5,5,$\underline{Y}$)
Y_7			H(5,6,$\underline{Y}$)	H(8,8,$\underline{Y}$)
Y_8				H(7,7,$\underline{Y}$)

TABLE 2

Clearly we can generate all authentication paths by separately computing each of the 2*n-1 entries in table 2, but is this "efficient?" Before we can answer this question and determine the cost of computing these entries, we must decide on the units to be used in measuring this "cost." Because all computations must eventually be defined in terms of the underlying encryption function C(key,plaintext), it seems appropriate to define computational cost in terms of the number of applications of C. One application of C counts as one "unit" of computation. We shall call this "unit" the "et," (pronounced eetee) which stands for "encryption time."

Computing F requires a number of ets proportional to the length of its input. In particular, if the input is composed of k * 100 bits, then F requires k-1 ets.

First, we must determine the cost of computing the individual entries. The algorithm for $H(i,j,\underline{Y})$ does a tree traversal of the subtree whose leaves are Y_i, Y_{i+1}, Y_{i+2}, ... Y_j. At each non-leaf node in this traversal it does 1 et of computation (one application of F to a 200-bit argument). There are j-i non-leaf nodes, so the computation requires j-i ets, excluding the leaves. The computations required to regenerate a leaf will be fixed and finite. Let r be the (fixed) number of ets required to regenerate a leaf. There are (j-i+1) leaves, so the overall cost of computing $H(i,j,\underline{Y})$ is (j-i) + (j-i+1) * r ets. If r is large, we can approximate this by (j-i+1) * r ets.

We can now approximate the cost of computing each entry in table 2. There are n entries which require about r ets, n/2 entries which require about 2 * r ets, n/4 entries which require about 4 * r ets, and n/8 entries which require about 8 * r ets. This means that the total cost of computing all entries in a single column is about 8 * r ets. There are 4 columns, so the total computational effort is about 4 * 8 * r = 32 * r ets. In general, the computational effort required to compute table 2 will be n * (1 + $\log_2$ n) * r ets. This is because computing all the entries in each column will require n * r ets, and there are 1 + $\log_2$ n columns.

This result implies that an algorithm which sequentially generated the authentication paths would require about

$$\log_2 n * r \qquad (1)$$

ets per path, where r is a constant representing the number of ets required to regenerate a leaf. This is quite reasonable. (The peak computational load is also reasonable, as will be seen in the next two paragraphs).

Although the time required to generate each authentication path is small, we must also insure that the space required is small. We can do this by again looking at table 2. As we sequentially generate the authentication paths, we will sequentially go through the entries in a column. This implies that at any point in time there are only two entries in a column of any interest to us: the entry needed in the current authentication path, and the entry immediately following it. We must know the entry in the current authentication path, for without it, we could not generate that path. At some point, we will need the next entry in the column to generate the next authentication path. Because it might require a great deal of effort to compute the next entry all at once -producing a high peak load- we need to compute it incrementally, and to begin computing it well in advance of the time we will actually require it to generate an authentication path.

As an example, $H(5,8,\underline{Y})$ is required in the authentication paths for Y_1, Y_2, Y_3, and Y_4. $H(1,4,\underline{Y})$ is required in the paths for Y_5, Y_6, Y_7, and Y_8. The values of $\hat{H}()$ for the first authentication path must be precomputed. Once this precomputation is complete, the succeeding values of H() required in succeeding authentication paths must be incrementally computed. As we generate the first 4 authentication paths, we must be continuously and incrementally computing $H(1,4,\underline{Y})$ so that it will be available when we reach Y_5. In addition, we must start computing $H(1,2,\underline{Y})$ when we generate the first authentication path; we must start computing $H(7,8,\underline{Y})$ when we reach Y_3; we must start computing $H(5,6,\underline{Y})$ when we reach Y_5; and so on.

By incrementally computing the H() values required in the authentication paths, we insure that the peak computational effort is low ($O(\log_2 n)$ per authentication path) as well as the average computational effort.

If we assume a convenient block size (of 100 bits) and if we ignore constant factors, then the memory required by this method can be computed. We can first determine the memory required by the computations in each column, and then sum over all $\log_2 n$ columns. We must have one block to store the current entry in the column. We must also have enough memory to compute the next entry in the column. The memory required while computing $H(i,j,\underline{Y})$ is $1 + \log_2 (j-i+1)$ blocks. This assumes a straightforward recursive algorithm whose maximum stack depth will be $1 + \log_2 (j-i+1)$. The memory required to recompute a leaf (to recompute $H(i,i,\underline{Y})$) is ignored because it is small (a few blocks), constant, and the same memory can be shared by all the columns. Representing the memory requirements of H() in a new table in the same format as table 2 gives table 3:

leaf	memory required to compute entries in authentication path (in blocks)			
Y_1	4	3	2	1
Y_2				1
Y_3			2	1
Y_4				1
Y_5		3	2	1
Y_6				1
Y_7			2	1
Y_8				1

TABLE 3

Table 3 shows the memory required to compute each entry in table 2. The memory required for each column will be about the memory required during the computation of the next entry. This means the total memory required will be about: $3 + 2 + 1 = 9$ blocks. (This assumes we do not recompute $H(1,8,\underline{Y})$).

There are $\log_2 n$ columns and each column requires, on an average, $(\log_2 n)/2$ blocks. The total memory required will be about:

$(\log_2 n)^2/2$ blocks

This means that the memory required when $n = 2^{20}$ (1,048,576) is about 20*20/2 = 200 blocks. For 100 bit blocks, this means 20 kilobits, or 2.5 kilobytes. Other overhead might amount to 2 or 3 kilobytes, giving an algorithm which requires 5 or 6 kilobytes of memory, in total.

This algorithm can be described by the following program, written in a Pascal-like language with two multiprocessing primitives added:
1.) While <condition> wait
2.) Fork <statement>
In addition, the function "MakeY(i)" will regenerate the value of Y_i. Note that n must be a power of 2.


```
Declare flag:  array[0..log₂(n)-1] of integer;
        AP:    array[0..log₂(n)-1] of block;
               (* AP -- Authentication Path *)
Procedure Gen(i);
Begin
  For j:= 1 to n step 2^(i+1) Do
   Begin
     Emit(i,H(j+2^i,j+2^(i+1)-1));
     Emit(i,H(j,j+2^i-1));
   End;
End;



Procedure Emit(i,value);
Begin
  While flag[i] ≠ 0 wait;
  AP[i]:= value;
  flag[i]:= 2^i;
End;



Procedure H(a,b);
Begin
  (* Note that in a real implementation F must be
     parameterized as described in section 2  *)
  If a = b Return(F(MakeY(a)))
  Else
  Return( F(< H(a,(a+b-1)/2),H((a+b+1)/2,b) >) );
End;


(* The main program  *)
Begin
```

```
For i := 0 to log₂(n)-1 Do
 Begin
  flag[i]:= 0;
  Fork Gen(i);
 End;
 For j:= 1 to n Do
 Begin
  Print("Authentication Path ", j, " is:");
  For k := 0 to log₂(n)-1 Do
   Begin
    While flag[k] = 0 wait;
    Print(AP[k]);
    flag[k]:= flag[k]-1;
   End;
  End;
End;
```

The general structure of this program is simple: the main routine forks off $\log_2 n$ processes to deal with the $\log_2 n$ columns. Then it prints each authentication path by sequentially printing an output from each process. The major omission in this program is the rate at which each process does its computations. It should be clear, though, that each process has adequate time to compute its next output. This follows from the observation that a single call to "Emit" will generate enough output for 2^i authentication paths, while the time required to compute the next entry is approximately 2^i.

There are three major ways of improving this algorithm. First, each process is completely independent of the other processes. However, separate processes often require the same intermediate values of H(), and could compute these values once and share the result.

Second, values of H() are discarded after use, and must be recomputed later when needed. While saving all values of H() takes too much memory, saving some values can reduce the computation time *and also* reduce memory requirements. The reduction in memory is because of the savings in memory when the saved value is not recomputed. Recomputing a value requires memory for the computation, while saving the value requires only a single block.

Finally, the memory requirements can be reduced by carefully scheduling the processes. While it is true that each process requires about $\log_2 n$ blocks of memory, this is a maximum requirement, not a typical requirement. By speeding up the execution of a process when it is using a lot of memory, and then slowing it down when it is using little memory, the average memory requirement of a process (measured in block-seconds) can be greatly reduced. By scheduling the processes so that the peak memory requirements of one process coincide with the minimum memory requirements of other processes, the total memory required can be reduced.

All three approaches deserve more careful study: the potential savings in time and space might be large.

Before the time requirements of the algorithm can be fully analyzed, a description of MakeY is needed: i.e., we must determine r in equation (1). If we assume that the improved version of the Lamport-Diffie algorithm is used, then MakeY must generate pseudo-random X_i vectors, from which Y_i vectors can then be generated. If the messages are all 100 bits, then the X_i vectors will have $100 + \log_2 100 = 107$ elements. (Longer messages can be mapped into a 100 bit message space using one way functions as described in section 2.)

The X_i vectors can be generated using a conventional cipher, C(key,plaintext). A single 300 bit secret key is required as the "seed" of the pseudo-random process which generates the X_i vectors. The output of C is always 100 bits, and the input must be 100 bits or less. We can now define $x_{i,j}$ as

$$x_{i,j} = C(\text{seedkey}, <i,j>)$$

(Where "seedkey" is the 300 bit secret and truly random key used as the "seed" of this somewhat unconventional pseudo-random number generator.) The subscript i is in the range 1 to n, while the subscript j is in the range 1 to 107. There are n possible messages, each 100 bits in length. Each X_i is a vector $x_{i,1}, x_{i,2}, ... x_{i,107}$.

Determining any $x_{i,j}$ knowing some of the other $x_{i,j}$'s is equivalent to the problem of cryptanalyzing C under a known plaintext attack. If C is a certified encryption function, it will not be possible to determine any of the $x_{i,j}$ without already knowing the key. The secret vectors X_i are therefore safe.

We know that $y_{i,j} = F(x_{i,j})$, and that $H(i,i,\underline{Y}) = F(Y_i) = F(<y_{i,1}, y_{i,2}, y_{i,3}, ... y_{i,107}>)$. The cost of computing $F(Y_i)$ is 106 ets, because Y_i is 107 * 100 bits long. The total effort to compute $H(i,i,\underline{Y})$ is the effort to generate the elements of the X_i vector, plus the effort to compute $F(x_{i,1})$, $F(x_{i,2})$, ... $F(x_{i,n})$, plus the effort to compute $F(Y_i)$. This is 107 ets to compute the X_i vector, 107 ets to compute the Y_i vector, and 106 ets to compute $F(Y_i) = H(i,i,\underline{Y})$. This is a total of 320 ets to regenerate each leaf in the authentication tree.

Using equation (1), we know that the cost per authentication path is $\log_2 n$ * 320 ets. For $n = 2^{20}$, this is 6400 ets. To generate authentication paths at the rate of one per second implies 1 et is about 160 microseconds. While easily done in hardware, this speed is difficult to attain in software on current computers. Reducing the number of ets per authentication path is a worthwhile goal. This can effectively be done by reducing either the cost of computing $H(i,i,\underline{Y})$, or by reducing the number of times that $H(i,i,\underline{Y})$ has to be computed.

As mentioned earlier, keeping previously computed values of H() rather than discarding them and sharing commonly used values of H() among the $\log_2 n$ processes reduces the cost of computing each authentication path. In fact, a reduction from over 6000 ets to about 1300 ets (for $n = 2^{20}$) can be attained (due to the complexity of the improvement, however, it will not be described). (To put this in perspective, MakeY *requires* 320 ets and *must* be executed at least once per authentication path. Therefore, 320 ets is the absolute minimum that can be attained without modifying MakeY.) This means the path regeneration algorithm can run in reasonable time (a few seconds) even when the underlying encryption function, C, is implemented in software.

8. *CONCLUSION*

Digital signature systems not requiring public key cryptosystems are not only possible, they can be easier to certify. Such a system was described which had modest space and time requirements and a signature size of from 1 to 3 kilobytes. The method described can be implemented quickly, without the long delays due to certification.

9. *ACKNOWLEDGEMENTS*

It is a great pleasure for the author to acknowledge the pleasant and informative conversations he had with Dov Andelman, Whitfield Diffie, John Gill, Martin Hellman, Raynold Kahn, Loren Kohnfelder, Leslie Lamport, and Steve Pohlig.

10. *BIBLIOGRAPHY*

1. Diffie, W., and Hellman, M. New directions in cryptography. IEEE Trans. on Inform. IT-22, 6(Nov. 1976), 644-654.

2. Evans A., Kantrowitz, W., and Weiss, E. A user authentication system not requiring secrecy in the computer. Comm. ACM 17, 8(Aug. 1974), 437-442.

3. Kohnfelder, L.M. Using certificates for key distribution in a public-key cryptosystem. Private communication.

4. Lipton, S.M., and Matyas, S.M. Making the digital signature legal--and

safeguarded. Data Communications (Feb. 1978), 41-52.

5. McEliece, R.J. A public-key cryptosystem based on algebraic coding theory. DSN Progress Report, JPL, (Jan. and Feb. 1978), 42-44.

6. Merkle, R. Secure Communications over Insecure Channels. Comm. ACM 21, 4(Apr. 1978), 294-299.

7. Merkle, R., and Hellman, M. Hiding information and signatures in trapdoor knapsacks. IEEE Trans. on Inform. IT-24, 5(Sept. 1978), 525-530.

8. Rivest, R.L., Shamir, A., and Adleman, L. A method for obtaining digital signatures and public-key cryptosystems. Comm. ACM 21, 2(Feb. 1978), 120-126.

9. Wilkes, M.V., *Time-Sharing Computer Systems*. Elsevier, New York, 1972.

10. Lamport, L., Constructing digital signatures from a one way function. SRI Intl. CSL - 98

11. Feistel, H., Cryptography and computer security. Scientific American, 228(May 1973), 15-23.

12. Shannon, C.E., Communication theory of secrecy systems. Bell Sys. Tech. Jour. 28(Oct. 1949) 656-715.

13. Rabin, M.O., Digitalized signatures. In *Foundations of Secure Computation*, R. Lipton and R. DeMillo, Eds., Academic Press, New York, 1978, pp. 155-166.

ADDENDUM

This article was originally submitted to Ron Rivest, then editor of the Communications of the ACM, in 1979. It was accepted subject to revisions, and was revised and resubmitted in November of 1979. Unfortunately, Ron Rivest passed over the editorship to someone else, the author became involved in a startup, and the referees reportedly never responded to the revised draft. The version printed here is the final revised version submitted to CACM in 1979. The only change (besides formatting) is the author's affiliation. Then, he was at BNR in Palo Alto, CA. Now, he is at Xerox PARC in Palo Alto, CA.

EFFICIENT IDENTIFICATION AND SIGNATURES
FOR SMART CARDS [§]

C.P. Schnorr
Universität Frankfurt

1. Introduction

We present an efficient interactive identification scheme and a related signature scheme that are based on discrete logarithms and which are particularly suited for smart cards. Previous cryptoschemes, based on the discrete logarithm, have been proposed by El Gamal (1985), Chaum, Evertse, Graaf (1988), Beth (1988) and Günter (1989). The new scheme comprises the following novel features.

(1) We propose an efficient algorithm to preprocess the exponentiation of random numbers. This preprocessing makes signature generation very fast. It also improves the efficiency of the other discrete log-cryptosystems. The preprocessing algorithm is based on two fundamental principles *local randomization* and *internal randomization*.

(2) We use a prime modulus p such that p-1 has a prime factor q of appropriate size (e.g. 140 bits long) and we use a base α for the discrete logarithm such that $\alpha^q = 1 \pmod p$. All logarithms are calculated modulo q. The length of signatures is about 212 bits, i.e. it is less than half the length of RSA and Fiat-Shamir signatures. The number of communication bits of the identification scheme is less than half that of other schemes.

The new scheme minimizes the work to be done by the smart card for generating a signature or for proving its identity. This is important since the power of current processors for smart cards is rather limited. Previous signature schemes require many modular multiplications for signature generation. In the new scheme signature generation costs about 12 modular multiplications, and these multiplications do not depend on the message/identification, i.e. they can be done in preprocessing mode during the idle time of the processor.

The security of the scheme relies on the one-way property of the exponentiation $y \mapsto \alpha^y \pmod p$, i.e. we assume that discrete logarithms with

[§] european patent application 89103290.6 from 24.2.1989

base α are difficult to compute. The security of the preprocessing is established by information theoretic arguments.

This abstract is organised as follows. We present in section 2 a version of the signature scheme that uses exponentiation of a random integer. In section 3 we propose an efficient algorithm that simulates this exponentiation. We study its security in section 4. The performance of the scheme is exemplified in section 5.

2. The identification and signature scheme

Notation. For $n \in \mathbb{N}$ let $\mathbb{Z}_n$ be the ring of integers modulo n. We identify $\mathbb{Z}_n$ with the set of integers $\{1,...,n\}$.

Initiation of the key authentication center (KAC). The KAC chooses
- primes p and q such that $q \mid p-1$, $q \geq 2^{140}$, $p \geq 2^{512}$,
- $\alpha \in \mathbb{Z}_p$ with order q, i.e. $\alpha^q = 1 \pmod p$, $\alpha \neq 1$,
- a one-way hash function $h : \mathbb{Z}_q \times \mathbb{Z} \rightarrow \{0,...,2^t-1\}$,
- its own private and public key.

The KAC publishes p,q,α,h and its public key.

COMMENTS. The KAC's own keys are used for signing the public keys issued by the KAC. The KAC can use for its own signatures any public key signature scheme, e.g. RSA, Fiat-Shamir, Rabin or the new scheme presented here. The hash function h is only used for signatures and is not needed for identification.

The function h outputs random numbers in $\{0,...,2^t-1\}$; for the choice of the function h see the end of section 2. The *security number* t can depend on the application intended, we consider $t = 72$. The scheme is designed such that forging a signature or an identification requires, with $t = 72$, about 2^{72} steps.

Registration of users. When a user comes to the KAC for registration the KAC verifies its identity, generates an identification string I (containing name, address, ID-number etc.) and signs the pair (I,v) consisting of I and the user's public key v. The user can generate himself his private key s and the corresponding public key v.

The user's private and public key. Every user has a private key s which is a random number in $\{1,2,...,q\}$. The corresponding public key v is the number $v = \alpha^{-s} \pmod p$.

Once the private key s has been chosen one can easily compute the corresponding public key v. The inverse process, to compute s from v, requires to compute the discrete logarithm with base α of v^{-1}, i.e. $s = -\log_\alpha v$.

The following protocol is related to protocol 1 in Chaum, Evertse, Graaf (1988); it condenses this protocol to a single round.

The identification protocol
(Prover A proves its identity to verifier B)

1. *Initiation.* A sends to B its identification string I and its public key v. B checks v by verifying KAC's signature transmitted by A.

2. *Preprocessing.* A picks a random number $r \in \{1,...,q-1\}$, computes $x := \alpha^r$ (mod p), and sends x to B (see section 3 for an efficient simulation of this exponentiation).

3. B sends a random number $e \in \{0,...,2^t-1\}$ to A.

4. A sends to B $y := r + se$ (mod q).

5. *Identification test.* B checks that $x = \alpha^y v^e$ (mod p) and accepts A's proof of identity iff equality holds.

Obviously if A and B follow the protocol then B always accepts A's proof of identity. We next consider the possibilities of cheating for A and B. We call (x,y) the *proof* and e the *exam* of the identification. The proof (x,y) (the exam e, resp.) is called *straight* if A (B, resp.) has followed the protocol, otherwise the proof (exam, resp.) is called *crooked*.

A fraudulent A can cheat by guessing the correct e and sending the crooked proof

$$x := \alpha^r v^e \text{ (mod p)}, \quad y := r .$$

The probability of success for this attack is 2^{-t}. By the following proposition this success rate cannot be increased unless computing $\log_\alpha v$ is easy.

Proposition 2.1 *Suppose there is a probabilistic algorithm AL with time bound $|AL|$ which takes for input a public key v and withstands, with probability $\varepsilon > 2^{-t+2}$, the identification test for a straight exam. Then the discrete logarithm of v can be computed in time $O(|AL|/\varepsilon)$ and constant, positive probability.*

Proof. This is similar to Theorem 5 in Feige, Fiat, Shamir (1987). The following algorithm AL' computes $\log_\alpha v$.

1. Repeat the following steps at most $1/\varepsilon$ times: generate x the same way as does algorithm AL, pick a random e' in $\{0,...,2^t-1\}$ and check whether AL passes the identification test for (x,e'); if AL succeeds then fix x and go to 2.

2. Probe $1/\varepsilon$ random numbers e" in $\{0,...,2^t-1\}$. If algorithm AL passes the identification test for some e" that is distinct from e' then go to 3 and otherwise stop.

3. Choose the numbers y', y" which AL submits to the identification test in response to e', e". (y'-y" is the discrete logarithm of $v^{e"-e'}$ (mod p).)

4. Output (y'-y")/(e"-e') (mod q) .

We bound from below the success probability of this algorithm. The algorithm finds in step 1 a passing pair (x,e') with probability at least $\frac{1}{2}$. With probability at least $\frac{1}{2}$, the x chosen in step 1, has the property that AL withstands the identification test for at least a $\frac{1}{2}$ ε-fraction of all e $\in$ $\{0,...,2^t-1\}$. For such an x step 2 finds a passing number e" that is distinct from e' with probability at least

$$1 - (1-\varepsilon/2)^{1/\varepsilon} > 1 - 2.7^{-1/2} > 0.3 .$$

This shows that the success probability of the algorithm is at least 0.3/4.

$\square$

The verifier B is free to choose the bit string e in step 3 of the identification protocol, thus he can try to choose e in order to obtain useful information from A. The informal (but non rigorous) reason that A reveals no information is that the numbers x and y are random. The random number x reveals no information. Furthermore it is unlikely that the number y reveals any useful information because y is superposed by the discrete logarithm of x, y = $\log_\alpha x + e \cdot s$ (mod q) , and the cryptanalyst cannot infer r = $\log_\alpha x$ from x. The scheme is not zero-knowledge because the tripel (x,y,e) may be a particular solution of the equation x = $\alpha^y v^e$ (mod p) due to the fact that the choice of e may depend on x.

Minimizing the number of communication bits. We can reduce the number of communication bits for identification. For this A sends in step 2 h(x) (instead of x) and B computes in step 5 $\overline{x}$:= $\alpha^y v^e$ (mod p) and checks that h(x) = h($\overline{x}$). It is not necessary that h is a one-way function because x = α^r (mod p) is already the result of a one-way function. We can take for h(x) the t least significant bits of x. The total number of communication bits for h(x),e,y is 2t + 140 which is less than half that of other schemes. The transmission of e is not necessary, e can be fixed to h(x). Then the pair (y,h(x)) is a signature of the empty message with respect to the following signature scheme.

Protocol for signature generation.
To sign message m using the private key s perform the following steps:
1. *Preprocessing* (see section 3). Pick a random number r $\in$ {1,...,q} and

   compute x := α^r(mod p).

2. Compute e := h(x,m) $\in$ {0,...,2^t-1}.
3. Compute y := r + se (mod q) and output the *signature* (e,y).

Protocol for signature verification.
To verify the signature (e,y) for message m and public key v compute $\overline{x}$ = $\alpha^y v^e$ (mod p) and check that e = h($\overline{x}$,m) *(signature test)*.

A signature (e,y) is considered to be *valid* if it withstands the signature test. A signature generated according to the protocol is always valid since

$$x = \alpha^r = \alpha^{r + se} v^e = \alpha^y v^e \pmod{p} .$$

With $t = 72$ and $q \approx 2^{140}$ the signature (e,y) is 212 bits long.

Efficiency. The work for signature generation consists mainly of the preprocessing (see section 3) and the computation of se(mod q) where the numbers s and e are about 140 and $t = 72$ bits long. The latter multiplication is negligible compared with a modular multiplication in the RSA-scheme.

Signature verification consists mainly of the computation of $\overline{x} = \alpha^y v^e$ (mod p) which can be done on the average using $1.5\,l + 0.25\,t$ multiplications modulo p where $l = \lceil \log_2 q \rceil$ is the bit length of q. For this let y and e have the binary representations

$$y = \sum_{i=0}^{l-1} y_i 2^i , \quad e = \sum_{i=0}^{l-1} e_i 2^i \text{ with } y_i, e_i \in \{0,1\} , \quad e_i = 0 \text{ for } i \geq t .$$

We compute αv in advance and we obtain $\overline{x}$ as follows

    1. $i := l$, $z := 1$,

    2. while $i \geq 0$ do $[i := i-1, \ z := z^2 \alpha^{y_i} v^{e_i} \pmod{p}]$,

    3. $\overline{x} := z$.

This computation requires at most $l + t - 1 + \sum_{i=t}^{l} y_i$ modular multiplications. If half of the bits y_i with $i \geq t$ are zero, and $e_i = y_i = 0$ holds for one fourth of the $i < t$, then there are at most $1.5\,l + 0.25\,t$ modular multiplications.

Comparison with ElGamal signatures. An ElGamal signature (y,x) for the message m and keys v,s with $v = \alpha^{-s} \pmod{p}$ satisfies the equation $\alpha^m = v^x x^y$ (mod p) and can be generated from a random number r by setting $x := \alpha^r \pmod{p}$ and by computing y from the equation

$$ry - sx = m \pmod{p-1} \qquad\qquad (1)$$

We replace in equation (1) x by the hash value $e = h(x,m)$. Then we can dispense with the right side m in equation (1) which we make zero. We further simplify (1) in that we replace the product ry by y·r and p-1 by q. This transforms (1) into the new equation $y = r + es \pmod{q}$. The new signatures are much shorter.

The choice of the prime q. The prime q must be at least 140 bits long in order to sustain a security level of 2^{72} steps. This is because $\log_\alpha(x) \in \{1,...,q\}$ can be found in $O(\sqrt{q})$ steps by the baby step giant step method. In order to compute $u,v \leq \lceil \sqrt{q} \rceil$ such that $\log_\alpha(x) = u + \lceil \sqrt{q} \rceil v$ we enumerate the sets $S_1 = \{\alpha^u \pmod{p} \mid 0 \leq u \leq \lceil \sqrt{q} \rceil\}$ and $S_2 = \{x\,\alpha^{-\lceil \sqrt{q} \rceil v} \pmod{p} \mid 0 \leq v \leq \lceil \sqrt{q} \rceil\}$ and we search for a common element $\alpha^u = x\alpha^{-\lceil \sqrt{q} \rceil v} \pmod{p}$.

The choice of the hash function h. We distinguish two types of attacks:

a) Given a message m find a signature for m,

b) *chosen message attack*. Sign an unsigned message by using signatures of messages of your choice.

In order to thwart the attack a) the function $h(x,m)$ must be almost *uniform* with respect to x in the following sense. For every message m, every $e \in \{0,...,2^t-1\}$ and random $x \in \mathbb{Z}_p^*$ the probability $prob_x[h(x,m) = e]$ must be near to 2^{-t}. Otherwise, in case that for fixed m,e the event $h(x,m) = e$ has nonnegligible probability with respect to random x, the cryptanalyst can compute $\overline{x} := \alpha^y r^e \pmod{p}$ for arbitrary y-values until the equality $e = h(\overline{x},m)$ holds. The equality yields a signature (y,e) for message m. If $h(x,m)$ is uniformly distributed with respect to random x then this attack requires about 2^t steps.

In order to thwart the chosen message attack the function $h(x,m)$ must be *one-way* in the argument m. Otherwise the cryptanalyst can choose y,e arbitrarily, he computes $\overline{x} := \alpha^y v^e \pmod{p}$ and solves $e = h(\overline{x},m)$ for m. Then he has found a signature for an arbitrary message m.

It is not necessary that the function $h(x,m)$ is collision-free with respect to m. Suppose the cryptanalyst finds messages m and m' such that $h(x,m) = h(x,m')$ for some $x = \alpha^y \pmod{p}$. If he asks for a signature for m' then this signature is based on a new random number x' and cannot simply be used to sign m. The equality $h(x,m) = h(x,m')$ only helps to sign m if a signature (y,e) for m' is given such that $x = \alpha^y v^e \pmod{p}$. But if $h(x,m)$ is one-way in m then it is difficult to solve $h(x,m) = h(x,m')$ for given x,m'.

3. Preprocessing the random number exponentiation

We describe an efficient method for preprocessing the random numbers r and $x := \alpha^r \pmod{p}$, that are used for signature generation. This preprocessing mode also applies to other discrete log-cryptosystems such as the schemes by ElGamal (1985), Beth (1988) and Günter (1989).

The smart card stores a collection of k independent random pairs (r_i,x_i) for i=1,...,k such that $x_i = \alpha^{r_i} \pmod{p}$ where the numbers r_i are independent random numbers in $\{1,...,q\}$. Initially these pairs can be generated by the KAC. For every signature/identification the card uses a random combination (r,x) of these pairs and subsequently rejuvenates the collection of pairs by combining randomly selected pairs. We use a random combination (r,x) in order to release minimum information on the pairs (r_i,x_i) i = 1,...,k . For each signature generation we randomize the pairs (r_i,x_i) so that no useful information can be collected on the long run. We give an *example* of a preprocessing algorithm that demonstrates the method. It uses a *security parameter* d, for all practical purposes d and k can be fairly small integers, for this paper we assume that $6 \leq d, k$.

Preprocessing algorithm

Initiation Load r_i, x_i for $i=1,...,k$, $\nu := 1$ (ν is the *round number*).

1. Pick random numbers $a(0),...,a(d-3) \in \{1,...,k\}$, $a(d-2) := a(d) := \nu-1 \pmod{k}$, $a(d-1) := \nu$.

2. $$r_\nu := \sum_{i=0}^{d} r_{a(i)} \, 2^i \pmod{q}, \quad x_\nu := \prod_{i=0}^{d} x_{a(i)}^{2^i} \pmod{p},$$

   (Below we give a detailed algorithm for this computation.)

3. Keep for the next signature/identification the pair r, x with

$$r := r_\nu^{old} + 2 \cdot r_{\nu-1} \pmod{q}, \quad x := x_\nu^{old} \cdot x_{\nu-1}^2 \pmod{p}.$$

4. $\nu := \nu+1 \pmod{k}$, go to 1 for the next round.

REMARKS. 1. By the choice of $a(d-1)$ the preprocessing preserves the uniform distribution on $(r_1,...,r_k)$.

2. The setting $a(d) := \nu-1 \pmod{k}$ has the effect that step 2 shifts the binary representation of $r_{\nu-1}$ for d positions to the left and subsequently adds it to r_ν. Theorem 4.2 relies on the choice of $a(d-1)$. Lemma 4.3 relies on the choice $a(d)$, and Theorem 4.4 relies on the choice of $a(d-2)$, $a(d-1)$ and $a(d)$.

3. The preprocessing algorithm must not be public. Each smart card can have its own secret algorithm for preprocessing. There are many variations of the above technique. It is possible to take for $(r_{a(i)}, x_{a(i)})$ with $0 \leq i < d-2$ the key pair $(-s, v)$.

We describe step 2 of the preprocessing algorithm in detail. Step 2 can be done using only 2d multiplications modulo p, d additions modulo q and d shifts.

Step 2 of the preprocessing algorithm.

1. $u := r_{a(d)}$, $z := x_{a(d)}$, $i := d-1$.

2. while $i \geq 0$ do $[u := 2u + r_{a(i)} \pmod{q}$, $z := z^2 x_{a(i)} \pmod{p}$,
   if $i = d-1$ then $(r := u, x := z)$, $i := i-1]$.

3. $r_\nu := u$, $x_\nu := z$.

4. Cryptanalysis of preprocessing

The preprocessing algorithm combines two fundamental principles *local randomization* and *internal randomization*. The pairs (r, x) that are used for signatures are locally random in the sense that every k consecutive pairs are independent, see Theorem 4.2. The random indices $a(0),...,a(d-3)$ perform an internal randomization. The principles of local and of internal randomization are complementary and can also be used for the construction of pseudo-random number generators and hash functions.

Notations. We denote the number a(i) of round ν as $a(i,\nu)$. Let T_ν be the k×k integer matrix that describes the transformation of the numbers $r_1,...,r_k$ in round ν of the preprocessing algorithm, i.e. step 2 of round ν performs $r^T := T_\nu r^T \pmod{q}$ where $r = (r_1,...,r_k)$. For $j \geq 0$ let r_j^* be the number r after j rounds. The sequence of r-values that is used for signatures is $r_1^*, r_2^*,...,r_j^*$.

Lemma 4.1 *If the initial vector $(r_1,...,r_k)$ is uniformly distributed over $\{1,...,q\}^k$ then this distribution is preserved throughout the preprocessing provided that $2^d < q$.*

Proof. T_ν is the identity matrix except for row ν. Row ν is determined by the transformation of r_ν in step 2:

$$r_\nu := r_\nu (\det T_\nu) + \sum_{a(i,\nu)\neq\nu} r_{a(i,\nu)} 2^i \pmod{q}$$

where $\det T_\nu = \sum_{a(i,\nu)=\nu} 2^i$. It follows from $a(d-1,\nu) = \nu$ and $a(d,\nu) \neq \nu$ that det T_ν is a nonzero integer and thus $1 \leq \det T_\nu < 2^d < q$. We see that T_ν is invertible modulo q. Therefore T_ν preserves the uniform distribution on $\{1,...,q\}^k$. □

A similar argument proves the next theorem.

Theorem 4.2 *If the initial vector $(r_1,...,r_k)$ is uniformly distributed over $\{1,...,q\}^k$ then for all $j \geq 0$ and for all numbers $a(i,\nu)$, $0 \leq i \leq d-3$, $\nu \leq k+j$ the vector $(r_{1+j}^*,...,r_{k+j}^*)$ is, for sufficiently large q, uniformly distributed over $\{1,...,q\}^k$.*

It is an open problem whether the vector $(r_{i_1}^*,...,r_{i_k}^*)$ is uniformly distributed for all indices $1 \leq i_1 < i_2 \cdots < i_k$. We believe that this holds for all but a negligible fraction of the instances for $a(i,\nu)$, $1 \leq \nu \leq i_k$.

Because of Theorem 4.2 the cryptanalyst can only attack a sequence of more than k consecutive signatures/identifications. The set of the first k+1 signatures can be attacked by guessing the numbers $a(0),...,a(d-3)$ of the first k rounds. Given these numbers and the first k+1 signatures the cryptanalyst can determine the secret key s and the initial numbers $r_1,...,r_k$ by solving a system of k+1 linear equations modulo q. This attack requires an exhaustive search over $k^{(d-2)k}$ cases.

Let r_ν^{new} be the number r_ν after ν rounds of preprocessing. If q and the numbers $a(0),...,a(d-3)$ for ν rounds are fixed then the number r_ν^{new} is a function of the initial numbers $r_1,...,r_k$ which is linear over $\mathbb{Z}_q$.

Lemma 4.3 *Pairwise distinct instances for the numbers* $a(0),...,a(d-3)$ *of* ν *rounds generate, for sufficiently large q, pairwise distinct linear functions* $r_\nu^{new} = r_\nu^{new}(r_1,...,r_k)$ *depending on the initial numbers* $r_1,...,r_k$ *and q.*

Proof. Let $S_\nu := T_\nu T_{\nu-1} \cdots T_1$ be the product matrix that describes the transformation on r for the first ν rounds of preprocessing. This is an integer matrix that does not depend on q. The dominant row (i.e. the row with the maximal entry) of S_ν is the row $\nu (\text{mod } k)$, call this row vector s_ν. We show how to decipher all numbers $a(i)$ of the first ν rounds from s_ν. To simplify the argument let $a(i,1)$ for $i=0,...,d$ be pairwise distinct. Then the j-largest entry of s_ν is in column $a(d-j+1,1)$ for $j=0,...,d$. (In general we can determine from the relative size of the largest entries of s_ν which of the numbers $a(i,1)$ coincide.) This clearly holds for $\nu = 1$ and the induction step from $\nu - 1$ to ν follows from $a(d,\nu) = \nu-1 \pmod{k}$. This shows how to obtain from s_ν the matrix T_1. Given the matrix T_1 we form the vector $s_\nu T_1^{-1}$ which is the dominant row of the matrix $T_\nu T_{\nu-1} \cdots T_2$ that corresponds to $\nu-1$ rounds starting with round number 2. Thus we can decipher in the same way the numbers $a(i,2)$ for $i=1,...,d$ and the matrix T_2 from $s_\nu T_1^{-1}$. Recursively we obtain from s_ν all numbers $a(i)$ of the first ν rounds. Now the claim follows from the equation

$$r_\nu^{new} = s_\nu r^T \pmod{q}$$

where $r = (r_1,...,r_k)$ is the initial r-vector. $\square$

For random input $(r_1,...,r_k) \in (\mathbb{Z}_q)^k$ two distinct linear functions over $\mathbb{Z}_q$ give the same output with probability $1/q$. Therefore if the number of choices for $a(0),...,a(d-3)$ over ν rounds is about q then the number r_ν^{new} is completely randomised by the numbers $a(0),...,a(d-3)$ of ν rounds, and thus r_ν^{new} is quasi-independent of $r_1,...,r_k$.

Let **a** be the vector $\mathbf{a} = (a(i,\nu) \mid i=0,...,d-3, \nu=1,...,k)$. The number r_{k+1}^* is determined by $r_1,...,r_k$, q and **a**. We know from Theorem 4.2 that the linear transformation $(r_1,...,r_k) \mapsto (r_1^*,...,r_k^*)$ is invertible modulo q. Therefore we have a function $r_{k+1}^* = r_{k+1}^*(r_1^*,...,r_k^*,q,\mathbf{a})$ that is linear in $r_1^*,...,r_k^*$ over $\mathbb{Z}_q$. By the next theorem distinct instances of **a** yield, for sufficiently large q, distinct functions r_{k+1}^* in $r_1^*,...,r_k^*$.

Theorem 4.4 *Pairwise distinct instances for the numbers* $a(0),...,a(d-3)$ *of the first k rounds generate, for sufficiently large q, pairwise distinct linear functions* r_{k+1}^* *depending on* $r_1^*,...,r_k^*$.

Proof. We show that distinct vectors **a** generate, for sufficiently large q, distinct linear functions $r_{k+1}^*(r_1,...,r_k,q,\mathbf{a})$ where the inputs are the initial numbers

$r_1,...,r_k$. Let s^*_{k+1} be the coefficient vector of the linear function $r^*_{k+1}(r_1,...,r_k,q,a)$, i.e. $r^*_{k+1}(r_1,...,r_k,q,a) = s^*_{k+1} r^T \pmod{q}$ with $r = (r_1,...,r_k)$. By the method in the proof of Lemma 4.3 we can decipher from s^*_{k+1} all numbers $a(i)$ of the first k rounds.

Now the claim follows from the choice $a(d-2,\nu) = \nu-1 \pmod{k}$. It follows by an argument that is similar but more involved than the one for the proof of Lemma 4.3. □

The fastest attack to the preprocessing algorithm that we are aware of enumerates the linear functions $r^*_{k+1}(r^*_1,...,r^*_k,q,a)$ that have high probability; the probability space is the set of all vectors a. For the security level 2^{72} it is necessary that the maximal probability for these linear functions is not much larger than 2^{-72}. In order to break the preprocessing it is sufficient to guess two functions $r^*_{k+1}(r^*_1,...,r^*_k,q,a)$ and $r^*_{k+2}(r^*_2,...,r^*_{k+1},q,a)$. Given these two functions we can uncover the secret key s from the first k+2 signatures by solving a system of linear equations.

We finally consider attacks on arbitrarily many signatures from a different point of view. The problem to recover the secret key s and the initial numbers $r_1,...,r_k$ when the first n signatures are given, can be put into the following form.

Given   integers $y_1,...,y_n \in \{1,...,q\}$ and $e_1,...,e_n \in \mathbb{Z}$
Find   integers $s,r_1,...,r_k \in \{1,...,q\}$ such that there exist integers $t_{i,j}$, $0 \le t_{i,j} < 2^{i(d+1)}$, satisfying $y_i = e_i s + \sum_{j=1}^{k} t_{i,j} r_j \pmod{q}$ $i=1,...,n$.   (4.1)

The searched integers $t_{i,j}$ are from the linear transformation $(r_1,...,r_k) \mapsto (r^*_1,...,r^*_n)$, hence $0 \le t_{i,j} \le 2^{i(d+1)}$. If $k^{(d-2)k} > q$ the equation (4.1) is, for almost all $y_1,e_1,...,y_n,e_n,s,r_1,...,r_k$, solvable for $t_{i,j}$ such that $0 \le t_{i,j} < 2^{i(d+1)}$. This makes this attack useless. However if k and d are small the solvability of equation (4.1) with $0 \le t_{i,j} < 2^{i(d+1)}$ may characterize the searched numbers $r_1,...,r_k$. It is interesting to determine the complexity of finding $r_1,...,r_k$ such that (4.1) is solvable with "small" integers $t_{i,j}$. It seems that this problem is more difficult than the knapsack problem since in our case all knapsack items s and $r_1,...,r_k$ are unknown.

Conclusion. There is a trade-off between the parameters k and d. It is sufficient to have $q \ge 2^{140}$, $k = 8$ and $d = 6$, then $k^{(d-2)k} = 2^{96}$. It is possible to further reduce k and d but we must have $k^{(d-2)k} \ge 2^{72}$.

5. The performance of the signature scheme

We wish to achieve a security level of 2^{72} operations, i.e. the best known method for forging a signatures/identification should require at least 2^{72} steps. In order to obtain the security level 2^{72} we choose $q \geq 2^{140}$ and $t = 72$. We choose for the preprocessing algorithm, the parameters $k = 8$, and $d = 6$. For the new scheme the number of multiplication steps and the length of signatures are independent of the bit length of p. Only the length of the public key depends on p. For this we assume that p is 512 bits long. We compare the performance of the new scheme to the Fiat-Shamir scheme (k=8, t=9) the RSA-scheme and the GQ-scheme of Guillou and Quisquater.

# of multiplications	new scheme t=72	Fiat-Shamir k=8 , t=9	RSA	GQ
signature generation (without preprocessing)	0	45*	750*	216*
preprocessing	12*	0	0	0
signature verification	228*	45*	≥ 2	108*

*) can be reduced by optimisation

Fast algorithms for signature verification exist for the RSA-scheme with small exponent and for the Micali-Shamir variant of the Fiat-Shamir scheme. The new scheme is most efficient for signature generation.

# bytes for the new scheme	
system parameters p,q	82.5 (26, resp. see below)
" α	64
public key v	64
private key s	18.5
signature (e,y)	26.5
preprocessing (r_i, x_i) i=1,...,8 (6, resp.)	660 (495, resp. see below)

We can choose particular primes q and p such that

$$|q - 2^{140}| \leq 2^{40} , \quad |p - 2^{512}| \leq 2^{170} .$$

The particular form simplifies the arithmetic modulo q and modulo p, and requires only 26 bytes to store p and q. We are not aware of any disadvantage of this particular form for p and q. In total about 800 (635, resp.) bytes EEPROM are sufficient to store p,q,v,e,y and (r_i, x_i) for i=1,...,8 (6, resp.), α is not needed for signature generation. About 192 bytes RAM are necessary to perform modular multiplications with a 512 bit modulus p. The program for signature generation requires less than 500 bytes ROM.

Optimization. We give a variant of the preprocessing algorithm that uses only k=6 pairs (r_i, x_i) and which require on the average 12.76 modular multiplications per round. First let k=6 and let (r_7, x_7) be the pair $(-s, v)$.

Optimized preprocessing

1. $r := r_{\nu-1} + r_{\nu} \pmod q$, $x := x_{\nu-1} \cdot x_{\nu} \pmod p$,
   keep the pair r, x for the next signature/identification,
   $u := r + r_{\nu-1} \pmod q$, $z := x \cdot x_{\nu-1} \pmod p$

2. for $j = 1,...,4$ do
   [pick with probability 7·3/29, 7/29, 1/29 resp.
   2 , 1 , 0 resp. distinct random numbers $a \in \{1,...,7\}$.
   $u := 2u + \sum_a r_a \pmod q$, $z := z^2 \prod_a x_a \pmod p$].

3. $r_{\nu} := u$, $x_{\nu} := z$, $\nu := \nu+1 \pmod 7$, go to 1 for the next round.

The number of possible transformations per round is about $[7 \cdot 3 + 7 + 1]^4 = 29^4$. The number of possible transformations over 6 rounds is about $29^{4 \cdot 6} \approx 2^{116}$ which is sufficiently large to perform an internal randomization. The average number of modular multiplications is $6 + 4(2 \cdot 7 \cdot 3 + 7) / 29 \approx 12.76$.

We can further reduce either the number of pairs (r_i, x_i) or the number of modular multiplications by inserting write operations into step 2 of the preprocessing. We can at the end of the inner loop of step 2 decide, based on a coin flip, whether to replace some pair (r_a, x_a) by (u,z). This will increase the number of possible transformations per round. However this variant will only be practical if write operations are sufficiently fast.

Acknowledgement I wish to thank J. Hastad for his criticism of the previous version of the preprocessing algrithm.

References

BETH, T.: A Fiat-Shamir-like authentication protocol for the ElGamal scheme. Proceedings of Eurocrypt' 88, Lecture Notes in Computer Science 330, (1988) pp. 77-86.

CHAUM, D., EVERTSE, J.H. and van de GRAAF, J.: An Improved protocol for Demonstration Possession of Discrete Logarithms and some Generalizations. Proceedings of Eurocrypt' 87, Lecture Notes in Computer Science 304, (1988), pp. 127-141.

COPPERSMITH, D., ODLYZKO, A. and SCHROEPPEL, R.: Discrete Logarithms. Algorithmica 1, (1986), pp. 1-15.

ELGAMAL, T.: A Public Key Cryptosystem and a Signature Scheme Based on Discrete Logarithms. IEEE Transactions on Information Theory 31 (1985), pp. 469-472.

FEIGE, U., FIAT, A. and SHAMIR, A.: Zero knowledge proofs of identity Proceedings of STOC 1987, pp. 210-217.

FIAT, A. and SHAMIR, A.: How to Prove Yourself: Practical Solutions of Identification and Signature Problems. Proceedings of Crypto 1986, in Lecture Notes in Computer Science (Ed. A. Odlyzko), Springer Verlag, 263, (1987) pp. 186-194.

GOLDWASSER, S., MICALI, S. and RACKOFF, C.: Knowledge Complexity of Interactive Proof Systems. Proceedings of STOC 1985, pp. 291-304.

GÜNTER, C.G.: Diffie-Hellman and ElGamal protocols with one single authentication key. Abstracts of Eurocrypt' 89, Houthalen (Belgium) April 1989.

MICALI, S. and SHAMIR, A.: An Improvement of the Fiat-Shamir Identification and Signature Scheme. Crypto 1988.

QUISQUATER, J.J. and GUILLOU, L.S.: A practical zero-knowledge protocol fitted to security microprocessor minimizing both transmission and memory. Proceedings Eurocrypt' 88. Springer Verlag, Lecture Notes in Computer Sciences, vol. 330, (1988), pp. 123-128.

RABIN, M.O.: Digital signatures and public-key functions as intractable as factorization. Technical Report MIT/LCS/TR-212 (1978).

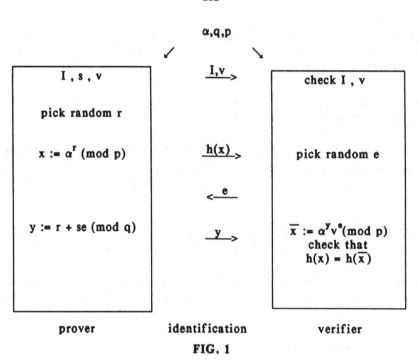

prover   identification   verifier

FIG. 1

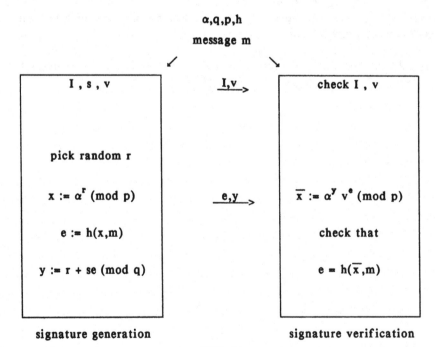

signature generation   signature verification

FIG. 2

A signature with shared verification scheme

Marijke De Soete[(1)], *Jean–Jacques Quisquater*[(2)] and *Klaus Vedder*[(3)]

(1)*MBLE–I.S.G.*, Rue des Deux Gares 82, B–1070 Brussels, Belgium
(2)*PRLB*, Avenue Van Becelaere 2, B–1170 Brussels, Belgium
(3)*GAO*, Euckenstraße 12, D–8000 München 70, Federal Republic of Germany

Abstract This paper presents a signature scheme for a single user or a group of users. The shared verification of such a signature uses the principle of threshold schemes. The constructions are based on a special class of finite incidence structures, so called generalised quadrangles.

1   Introduction

The schemes generate a signature for a single user X, denoted by $sign_x$, or for a group of users G, denoted by $sign_G$. The verification system, knowing the identity of X or G, can check the validity of the signature using the principle of threshold schemes (see Simmons [5]). This means that there exists a group of verifiers and the scheme only needs a certain number of them for the verification of the signature. We will call this a *shared verification scheme*, for which a more formal definition reads as follows:

A t-shared verification scheme consists of $s \geq t$ classes called *verifiers* such that

- any t of the s verifiers can execute the verification

- the verification cannot be done by any $t - 1$ or fewer of the s classes.

The construction of the schemes is based on a special class of geometric incidence structures, so called generalised quadrangles. Generalised quadrangles have been used before to construct threshold schemes (see [3]) which are closely related to the topic of this paper.

A typical environment where these schemes could be employed is described by Simmons in [4]. Here they could serve the purpose of checking the signature on data transmitted by a seismic station. The verification could be done by a central body which also selects, possibly randomly, the required number of verifiers from the group of all verifiers.

Another field of application might be any system where a central institution supervises its member bodies. The signing of a document by one of the member bodies has to be verified by the central institution. This can use therefore a shared verification scheme where the classes of verifiers consist of delegates of the various member bodies.

2   Geometric background

An *incidence structure* is a triple (P, B, I) which consists of two non-empty and disjoint sets P and B and a subset $I \subseteq P \times B$. The elements of P and B are called *points* and *blocks* (or in our context *lines*), respectively. I is called the *incidence relation*. We say that a point x and a line L are incident with each other and write $x I L$ if and only if the pair (x, L) is an element of I.

A (finite) *generalised quadrangle* (GQ) of order σ, $\sigma \geq 1$, is an incidence structure $S=(P, B, I)$ which satisfies the following axioms:

(i) Each point is incident with exactly $\sigma + 1$ lines and two distinct points are incident with at most one line,

(ii) Each line is incident with exactly $\sigma + 1$ points and two distinct lines are incident with at most one point,

(iii) For every point x and every line L which are not incident with each other, there exists a unique line which is incident with both x and a (unique) point on L.

The definition allows us to identify each line with the set of points it is incident with. This and the obvious geometric structure of a GQ are the reasons for expressions such as "x lies on L", "x is contained in L" for $x I L$ and "L and M intersect each other in the point x" for $L I x I M$.

Axiom (iii) is crucial for understanding most of the arguments in this paper. It means that, with the exception of one line, all the remaining σ lines through x do not intersect the line L. So a generalised quadrangle does not contain a "triangle".

We call two not necessarily distinct points x and y collinear and write $x \sim y$, if there exists a line which contains both of them. If there is no such line we say that they are not collinear and write $x \not\sim y$. The set of points collinear with a point x is denoted by $x^\perp$ (note that $x \in x^\perp$).

The proof of the following lemma is left as an easy exercise to the reader.

Lemma *Let (P, B, I) be a generalised quadrangle of order σ, then*

(i) $|P| = |B| = (\sigma + 1)(\sigma^2 + 1)$

(ii) $|x^\perp| = \sigma^2 + \sigma + 1$, for all points $x \in P$.

The *trace* of a pair (x, y) of distinct points is defined to be the set $x^\perp \cap y^\perp$ and is denoted as trace(x, y). Notice that $|\text{trace}(x, y)| = \sigma + 1$. The span of two distinct points x and y, is defined as span$(x, y) = \{u \in P \mid u \in z^\perp, \forall z \in \text{trace}(x, y)\}$. Hence it consists of all points which are collinear with every point in the trace of x and y. More generally, one can define for $A \subset P$, the set $A^\perp = \cap_{x \in A} x^\perp$. In this notation trace$(x, y) = \{x, y\}^\perp$ and span$(x, y) = \{x, y\}^{\perp\perp}$.

If x and y are collinear, then trace$(x, y) = $span$(x, y)$ is the unique line through x and y having $\sigma + 1$ points. If x and y are not collinear, then no two distinct points of trace(x, y) are collinear. We note that x, y are in span(x, y), no two distinct points of span(x, y) are collinear and $|\text{span}(x, y)| \leq \sigma + 1$. The upper bound follows from the fact that the points of span(x, y) are contained in the $\sigma + 1$ lines through any of the points of $x^\perp \cap y^\perp$. Furthermore, two spans intersecting in at least two points define the same trace and hence coincide.

A pair (x, y) is called *regular* if $|\text{span}(x, y)| = \sigma + 1$. The point x is regular if and only if (x, y) is regular, for all $y \neq x$.

An *ovoid* of a generalised quadrangle S is a set θ of points of S such that each line is incident with a unique point of θ. One verifies easily that $|\theta| = \sigma^2 + 1$.

The following property of quadrangles of order σ (see [8] p. 21) is fundamental for the construction of the schemes.

Theorem *Let (x, y) be a regular pair of non-collinear points in a GQ of order σ. Then any ovoid contains exactly two points of trace(x, y) and none of span(x, y) or exactly two points of span(x, y) and none of trace(x, y).*

As an example of a generalised quadrangle satisfying these properties we consider a non-degenerate quadric Q in a finite projective space $PG(4, q)$. The points of Q together with the lines (which are the subspaces of maximal dimension on Q) define a generalised quadrangle $Q(4, q)$ of order σ.

If q is even this quadrangle contains ovoids and all its points are regular. The sheme may be implemented on a computer using the coordinatisation of these quadrangles given by Payne [7]. Note that this coordinatisation is based on a finite field $GF(q)$. For further information on generalised quadrangles we refer to the book by Payne and Thas [8].

3 Signature for a single user

3.1 The scheme

We consider a generalised quadrangle S of order σ containing an ovoid θ and a regular point $y \in \theta$.

The *individual users* correspond to the points of $\theta \setminus \{y\}$ while the *verifiers* correspond to the lines through y. Hence we have at most σ^2 users and up to $\sigma + 1$ verifiers.

The general signature of user X is defined to be the set

$$sign_x = \text{span}(x, y) \setminus \theta.$$

In view of the preceding theorem and the regularity of y, we have $sign_x = \text{span}(x, y) \setminus \{x, y\}$ and therefore $|sign_x| = \sigma - 1$. Since different spans can have at most one point in common (here the point y), it follows that different users have different signatures.

Due to the fact that y is regular, the span (x, y) and thus $sign_x$ are uniquely determined by any two of its points. So we may represent a specific signature of the user X by two distinct points in $sign_x$, say x_1 and x_2, where one of these points could be x depending on the specific implementation.

To check a signature we need at least two verifiers, say V_1 and V_2. Let L_1 and L_2 be their corresponding lines. Verifier V_i constructs the respective unique lines through x, x_1 and x_2 which intersect L_i, $i = 1, 2$. The points x_1 and x_2 are elements of $sign_x$ if and only if the lines constructed by V_1 are concurrent in the same point u_1 on L_1 and those constructed by V_2 are concurrent in the same point u_2 on L_2. Indeed, x_1 and x_2 are in $sign_x = \mathrm{span}(x, y) \setminus \theta$ if and only if they are collinear with the two points u_1 and u_2 of $\mathrm{trace}(x, y)$ on the lines L_1 and L_2, respectively.

3.2 Implementation and security

The security of the scheme will clearly depend on the particular implementation. First of all we have to make the assumption that the computer producing the signature (host) has a high security module for this purpose which also contains y. Anybody knowing y can produce "authentic" verifiers and stands a good chance of totally compromising the system by guessing the correct ovoid through y. Therefore care has to be taken that nobody can compute y from information such as a line L_i or a $\mathrm{span}(x_1, x_2)$. Each user has a personal IC card with his distinguished name and his secret identification number (SIN) which could be the coordinates of x. Having a SIN distinct from x can be of an advantage in certain environments. When a user wants to produce his signature, he enters his IC card and the host reads its information. Clearly, for the welfare of X, its SIN should be kept secret. Hence the SIN should go neither in clear nor encrypted with a constant key over the interface since this could lead to replay attacks. SIN has to be transmitted as a dynamic (time-variant) variable. One way would be that the host supplies the IC card with a true random number which is used to derive the key for the algorithm which encrypts the SIN.

The host checks that the SIN belongs to the distinguished name and derives, if necessary, the point x from SIN by means of a cryptographic algorithm, a coordinate transformation, or just by looking it up in a secret table. This last possibility has the disadvantage that the table need to be updated when a new user joins the system.

The host then produces $sign_x$ and the two points x_1 and x_2.

The verifying system can be laid out in such a way that it checks a signature with respect to a specific signatory or that it just proves that someone has presented a valid signature. The requirements for the individual verifiers are very similar except that in the first case it has to derive x from SIN. In either case a verifier need not know anything about the underlying geometry. It just has to be capable of constructing and intersecting lines. This also means that verifiers can be added to the system without any problem by a trusted third party which has to know y, a list of existing verifiers together with their lines and the means which protect the communication between the entities.

Hence the verifying system can consist of secure boxes. Each verifier V_i receives a box which can make the necessary calculations and contains information about the lines L_i so that when a point is entered, the box can check the collinearity with points on L_i. Depending on the outcome of this process the box gives the message "YES" or "NO" and, if required, the distinguished name of X. So we consider the following two scenarios.

- User X presents his SIN and the two points x_1 and x_2 to the verifying system. Two verifiers enter this information into their secure box. Each box derives x from SIN and checks for collinearity. A box gives the message YES if x, x_1 and x_2 are collinear with the same point on its line. If the two verifiers have received a YES from their respective boxes for the same distinguished name, the signature is accepted. We should point out that it is sufficient for the verification of the signature $sign_x$ to use SIN and one further point x_1, say. This would however give an attacker a better chance to cheat in certain cases as we will see in the next section.

- User X presents two points of his signature x_1 and x_2 to the verifying system. Two verifiers enter this information into their secure box and each box checks that the two points are collinear with the same point on its line. If two verifiers obtain a positive answer, they know that a user X presented a valid signature. Indeed, the collinearity of the two points with the same point on the respective lines means that $y \in \text{span}(x_1, x_2)$. It follows from the theorem that $\text{span}(x_1, x_2)$ contains a second point of the ovoid θ, i.e. a user. However, the verifiers do not know if this point is x. In other words they cannot check that the valid signature is indeed the one corresponding to X.

To conclude this section we summarize the different steps necessary for producing and verifying a signature. It is assumed that all communication between entities is done in a secure way. For an eavesdropper can derive y from two pairs x_1, x_2 and z_1, z_2 belonging to different spans, if he knows the coordinatisation of the underlying geometry.

I. Signature process

Step 1. User X feeds his SIN to the host in a secure way.

Step 2. The host constructs $sign_x$.

Step 3. The host picks two distinct points x_1, x_2 of $sign_x$.

Step 4. The host feeds the two points x_1 and x_2 to the user X.

II. Verification of the signature

Step 1. User X presents his SIN and the two points to the verifying system.

Step 2. At least two verifiers feed the information to their boxes.

Step 3. Each box checks the necessary collinearity with a point on its line.

Step 4. The boxes give the message YES or NO and, possibly, the distinguished name of X.

Step 5. The signature (of X) is accepted if and only if all verifiers obtained a YES (and the distinguished names are the same).

3.3 Attacks

For running a successful attack it is not sufficient to find the correct values for the points. They also have to be accepted by the sytem as such. This means that a potential attacker has also to overcome the secure communication system between the entities. As this is up to a specific implementation we will make our considerations on the assumption that this can be done.

The first case we consider is that the verifying box requires SIN and the attacker knows SIN but not x. Then he has to guess two correct points in $sign_x$. This probability is approximately $1/\sigma^4$. For the probability to find a first correct point is given by

$$\frac{\sigma - 1}{(\sigma^2 + 1)(\sigma + 1)} \approx \frac{1}{\sigma^2}$$

since $sign_x$ contains $\sigma - 1$ points and the quadrangle has $\sigma^3 + \sigma^2 + \sigma + 1$ points in total. The probability to choose a matching second point is given by

$$\frac{\sigma - 2}{\sigma^3} \approx \frac{1}{\sigma^2}$$

for the opponent can rule out all the points collinear with his first one. This gives him a probability of $\approx 1/\sigma^4$ to find two points of a specific signature.

If he also knows x, then he can rule out for his choice of x_1 all $\sigma^2 + \sigma + 1$ points collinear with x. He has therefore a probability to guess a point in $sign_x$ of $(\sigma - 1)/(\sigma^3) \approx 1/\sigma^2$. The second point he can construct by considering $\mathrm{span}(x, x_1)$.

In our second scenario the verifying system just checks that the points entered are in $\mathrm{span}(y, x) \setminus \{y, x\}$ for some point x on the ovoid. In this case the attacker picks an arbitrary point for x_1 not on the ovoid and for x_2 one which is not collinear with x_1. The probability that x_1, x_2 get accepted as a signature is

$$\frac{\sigma^3 + \sigma}{(\sigma^2 + 1) \cdot (\sigma + 1)} \cdot \frac{\sigma - 2}{\sigma^3} \approx \frac{1}{\sigma^2}.$$

The situation is completely different if the attacker knows y. In the second scenario he can produce "valid" signatures with a probability of 1. He picks two lines L_1 and L_2 through y and a 4-gon $u_1 x_1 u_2 x_2$ where u_1 is on L_1, u_2 on L_2 and x_1, x_2 are not on L_i, $i = 1, 2$. The points x_1, x_2 will get accepted as a valid signature.

Next one can ask for the probability to break the whole system by determining the ovoid θ. Suppose an opponent knows two points x_1 and x_2 of a valid signature. Then he has to consider all ovoids intersecting $\mathrm{span}(x_1, x_2)$ in two points. This depends now on the particular generalised quadrangle used and we cannot say anything in the general case. For $Q(4, q)$, q even, it follows from papers due to Bagchi and Sastry (see [1], [2]) who studied the intersection of ovoids in $PG(3, q)$ in detail that there are sufficiently many ovoids through two points to guarantee the security of the system.

Similarly, the probability of two verifiers to construct "genuine" signatures depends on the number of ovoids through the point y their corresponding lines have in common. As a verifier need not know his line, only the verifying box should be in possession of the coordinates of the line to make it more difficult for two verifiers to cooperate.

4   Signature for a group of users

We consider again the same geometric structure as before with an ovoid θ and a regular point y on θ. The *groups of users* are defined to be the sets $G = \mathrm{span}(x,y) \setminus \theta$, $x \in P$, $x \not\sim y$. By the theorem we have $|\mathrm{span}(x,y) \cap \theta| = 2$ (since $y \in \mathrm{span}(x,y) \cap \theta$) and hence $|G| = \sigma - 1$. These spans partition the set of points not collinear with y of the GQ. It follows that we have at most σ^2 groups each consisting of $\sigma - 1$ users. Again we let the *verifiers* correspond to the lines through y, so we have up to $\sigma + 1$ of them.

The signature of a group G is defined to be the unique point of G which lies in the set $\theta \setminus \{y\}$, i.e.

$$sign_G = G \cap (\theta \setminus \{y\}).$$

The uniqueness of this point is guaranteed by the theorem. Different groups have necessarily different signatures since the spans we consider only have the regular point y in common.

To verify the signature of a member X_G of a certain group G, two verifiers are sufficient. If the two points X_G and $sign_G$ are presented to the verifying system, at least two verifiers V_1 and V_2 check if the two given points are collinear with the same point on each of their corresponding lines L_1 and L_2. If and only if this is the case for both, $sign_G$ is accepted.

The implementation can be done by installing a similar system as the one described for a single user. The detailed description of it as well as an overview of the possible attacks in this case are left to the reader.

References

[1] B. Bagchi and N. S. Sastry, *Even order inversive planes, generalised quadrangles and codes*, Geom. Ded. 22 (1987), 137–147.

[2] B. Bagchi and N. S. Sastry, *Intersection pattern of the classical ovoids in symplectic 3-space of even order*, Preprint.

[3] M. De Soete and K. Vedder, *Some new classes of geometric threshold schemes*, Proceedings of Eurocrypt '88, ed. G. Günther, L.N.C.S. 330 (1988), Springer Verlag, 389–401.

[4] G. J. Simmons, *A Natural Taxonomy for Digital Information Authentication Schemes*, Proceedings of Crypto '87, ed. C. Pomerance, L.N.C.S. 293 (1988), Springer Verlag, 269–288.

[5] G. J. Simmons, *How to really share a secret*, Proceedings of Crypto '88, L.N.C.S., Springer Verlag, to appear.

[6] G. J. Simmons, *Shared Secret and / or Shared Control Schemes*, Eurocrypt '89 Houthalen (Belgium), April 10–13, extended abstract.

[7] S. E. Payne, *Generalised quadrangles of even order*, J. Algebra 31 (1974), 367–391.

[8] S. E. Payne and J. A. Thas, *Finite generalised quadrangles*, Research Notes in Math. #110, Pitman Publ. Inc., 1984.

ON-LINE/OFF-LINE DIGITAL SIGNATURES

Shimon Even*
Oded Goldreich**
Silvio Micali***

ABSTRACT

We introduce and exemplify the new concept of ON-LINE/OFF-LINE digital signature schemes. In these schemes the signing of a message is broken into two phases. The first phase is $off-line$. Though it requires a moderate amount of computation, it presents the advantage that it can be performed leisurely, before the message to be signed is even known. The second phase is $on-line$. It starts after the message becomes known, it utilizes the precomputation of the first phase and is much faster.

A general construction which transforms *any* (ordinary) digital signature scheme to an on-line/off-line signature scheme is presented, entailing a small overhead. For each message to be signed, the time required for the off-line phase is essentially the same as in the underlying signature scheme; the time required for the on-line phase is essentially negligible. The time required for the verification is essentially the same as in the underlying signature scheme.

In a practical implementation of our general construction, we use a variant of Rabin's signature scheme (based on factoring) and DES. In the on-line phase, all we use is a moderate amount of DES computation. This implementation is ideally suited for electronic wallets or smart cards.

On-line/Off-line digital schemes may also become useful in case substantial progress is made on, say, factoring. In this case, the length of the composite numbers used in signature schemes may need to be increased and signing may become impractical even for the legitimate user. In our scheme, all costly computations are performed in the off-line stage while the time for the on-line stage remains essentially unchanged.

An additional advantage of our method is that in some cases the transformed signature scheme is invulnerable to chosen message attack even if the underlying (ordinary) digital signature scheme is not. In particular, it allows us to prove that the existence of signature schemes which are unforgeable by *known* message attack is a (necessary and) sufficient condition for the existence of signature schemes which are unforgeable by *chosen* message attack.

* Computer Science Department
Technion - Israel Institute of Technology
Haifa 32000, Israel.
Supported by the Fund for the Promotion of Research at the Technion.
** Computer Science Department
Technion - Israel Institute of Technology
Haifa 32000, Israel.
*** Computer Science Department
MIT - Massachusetts Institute of Technology
545 Technology Square
Cambridge, MA 02139.

1. INTRODUCTION

Informally, in a digital signature scheme, each user U publishes a *public key* while keeping secret a *secret key*. U's signature of a message m is a value σ, depending on m and his secret key, such that U can (quickly) generate σ and anyone can (quickly) verify the validity of σ, using U's public key. However, it is hard to forge U's signatures without knowledge of his secret key.

A signature scheme has the following components:

* A *security parameter* (chosen by the user when he creates his public and secret keys). This parameter determines the length of the keys (and hence the security), the running time of the signing and verification algorithms, and the number of (hashed) messages to be signed.

* A *message space* which is the set of (unhashed) messages to which the signature algorithm may be applied. To simplify our exposition, we assume that all finite binary strings are legitimate messages.

* A probabilistic polynomial time *key generation algorithm G* which can be used by any user U to produce a pair (PK, SK) of matching public and secret keys.

* A probabilistic polynomial time *signing algorithm S* which given a message m and a secret key SK produces a signature of m with respect to the corresponding public key PK. In the sequel we denote by $S_{SK}(m)$ the probability distribution of signatures of message m with secret key SK.

* A polynomial time *verification algorithm V* which given σ, m and PK tests whether σ is a valid signature for the message m with respect to the public key PK.

Many signature schemes are known by now and several have been proved secure even against chosen message attack [GMR84, BM88, NY89]. In all of them signing by the legitimate user, though feasible, is not sufficiently fast for some practical purposes. Let us exemplify why this is so, in detail, for the case of Rabin's scheme [R79]. We choose this scheme as a test case both because of its simplicity and because we will use a variation of it in a concrete illustration of the general construction.

In Rabin's scheme, a user U publishes a composite numbers n_U, product of 2 primes, as his public key, and keeps n_U's prime factorization as his secret key. The signature of a message m (regarded as an element of the multiplicative group mod n_U) is computed by taking a square root modulo n_U of either m or a small perturbation of m. (The perturbation is used to make the element a quadratic residue mod n_U.)

A square root of x modulo n_U is computed by raising x to a large exponent, modulo the factors of n_U (the exponent being a number roughly as large as the factor). In Rabin's scheme, as in all currently known schemes, signing is feasible, though not super-fast. Furthermore, the computation of the signature of a message m can start only after m has been chosen; no significant speed-up can be obtained by relying on a *reasonable* amount of preprocessing performed before m has been chosen.

Another point worthwhile noting is that the above described scheme is totally insecure against an adaptive chosen message attack.

In contrast to the above signature scheme we are interested in signature schemes which are very fast. We observe that in many applications (e.g. electronic wallet [E, EGY83]) signatures have to be produced very fast once the message is presented. However, one can tolerate slower precomputations, provided that they do not have to be performed on-line. This suggests the notion of an *on−line/off−line* signature scheme, in which the signing process can be broken into two phases. The first phase, is performed *off−line*, independent of the particular message to be signed; while the second phase is performed *on−line*, once the message is presented. We will be interested in on-line/off-line signature schemes in which the off-line stage is feasible (though relatively slow) and both on-line signing and verification are fast.

We present a general construction transforming an ordinary, digital signature scheme to an on-line/off-line one. This is done by properly combining three main ingredients:

(1) An (ordinary) signature scheme;

(2) A fast *one−time* signature scheme (i.e., a signature scheme known to be unforgeable, provided it is used to sign a single message);

(3) A fast one-way hashing scheme (i.e., a hashing scheme for which it is infeasible to find two strings which hash to the same value).

The essence of the construction is to use the ordinary signature scheme to sign (off-line) a randomly constructed instance of the information which enables one-time signature, and later to sign (on-line) the message using the one-time signature scheme. The above informal description does not mention the hashing scheme, and in fact there is a version of our scheme which does not use hashing at all. A more practical version uses the one-way hashing scheme to map messages into shorter strings which are then signed, using the one-time signature scheme. In the version which uses the hashing, the message is assumed to be a binary string (of any finite length) and the (one-time) signature is always applied to the hashed message. In the version which does not use hashing, messages are first broken into "linked" binary words of fixed length.

A sufficient condition for the resulting signature scheme to withstand chosen message attack is that both signature schemes used (i.e., (1) and (2)) do withstand such attacks. However, in particular implementations it suffices to require that these underlying schemes withstand known message attack.

In the practical illustration we use a modification of Rabin's signature scheme [R79] in the role of the ordinary signature scheme, and DES to build the one-time signature scheme. The security of this implementation is based on the intractability of factoring large integers and the assumption that DES behaves like a random cipher. The only computations (possibly) required, in the on-line phase of the signature process, are applications of DES. The costly modular computation, of extracting square roots modulo a large (e.g. 512-bit) composite integer with known factorization, is performed off-line. A reasonable choice of parameters allows to sign 100-bit values using only 200 on-line DES computations (which can be performed as fast as one modular multiplication of 512-bit integers). Verification requires the same amount of DES computation and one modular multiplication.

For the theoretical result we use a signature scheme, secure against known message attack, both in the role of the ordinary signature scheme and in order to implement a one-time signature scheme. One-way hashing is not used at all. The resulting scheme is secure against chosen message attack. Hence we get

Theorem:

> Digital signature schemes that are secure against an adaptive chosen message attack exist if and only if signature schemes secure against known plaintext attack exist.

An *adaptive chosen message attack* is an attempt of an adversary to forge a signature of a user after getting from him signatures to messages of the adversary's choice. The adversary's choice may depend on the user's public key and the previous signatures the adversary has received. A *known message attack* is an attempt of an adversary to forge a signature of a user after getting from him signatures to messages which are randomly selected in the message space. (These messages are selected independently of the adversary's actions.) In both (chosen and known) cases, security means the infeasibility of forging a signature to any message for which a signature has not been obtained before (i.e., *existential forgery* in the terminology of [GMR84]).

Notice that, so far, only *sufficient* conditions for the existence of schemes secure against adaptive chosen message attack have been known. We exhibit a *minimal* such condition; that is, a necessary and sufficient one. Moreover, in all known schemes, proven secure against adaptive chosen message attack, the length of the signatures increases (explicitly or implicitly) with the number of signatures produced. An advantage of our scheme is that the length of each signature is fixed.

2. THE GENERAL CONSTRUCTION

Notice that implicit in the definition of a signature scheme is that one can sign securely as many messages as one wants. One may also define schemes with less stringent security properties. Namely,

Definition:

A *one-time signature scheme* is a digital signature scheme which can be used to legitimately sign a single message. A one-time signature scheme is *secure* against known (resp. chosen) message attack if it is secure against attacks which are restricted to a single query.

Notice the analogy with a one-time pad, which allow one to send private messages securely as long as he does not use the secret pad twice. An early version of one-time signature was suggested by Rabin [R78]. It required an exchange of messages between the signer and signee. Schemes which avoid such an exchange were suggested by various authors; see Merkle [M].

We believe that the importance of one-time signature schemes stems from their simplicity. They can be implemented very efficiently. Our construction demonstrates that one-time signatures can play an important role in the design of very powerful and useful signature schemes. As our construction uses both one-time and ordinary signature schemes, we will attach the term "one-time" to terms such as "secret key" and "public key" associated with the one-time signature scheme, to avoid confusion.

Notation:

Let H denote an (agreed upon) one-way hashing function, mapping arbitrarily long messages to n-bit long strings. Let (G,S,V) denote an (agreed upon) ordinary signature scheme (G is the key-generation algorithm, S is the signing algorithm, and V is the verification algorithm). Let (g,s,v) denote an (agreed upon) one-time signature scheme.

Key Generation:

The signer runs G to generate (PK, SK). The public key, PK, is announced. The "signing key", SK, is kept secret.

Off-Line Computation:

Before any message has been chosen, the signer runs algorithm g to randomly select a one-time public key pk and its associated one-time secret key sk. (This pair of one-time keys is unlikely to be used again.) He then computes the signature of pk using the ordinary signature scheme

$$\Sigma = S_{SK}(pk) ,$$

and stores the "precomputed signature", Σ, as well as the pair of one-time keys, (pk, sk).

On-Line Signature:

To sign the message m, the signer retrieves from memory the precomputed signature Σ, and the pair (pk, sk). Using H, he hashes m into a string of length n, denoted by $H(m)$. He then computes a one-time signature

$$\sigma = s_{sk}(H(m)) .$$

The signature of m consists of the concatenation of the strings pk, Σ, and σ.

Verification:

To verify that the triple (pk,Σ,σ) is indeed a signature of m with respect to the public key PK, the verifier acts as follows. First, he uses algorithm V and the public key PK to check that Σ is indeed a signature of pk. Next, he computes $h = H(m)$ and checks, by running v, that σ is indeed a signature of h with respect to the one-time public key pk. Namely, verification amounts to evaluating the following predicate

$$V_{PK}(pk, \Sigma) \qquad v_{pk}(H(m), \sigma) .$$

Security:

The scheme can be proven secure against adaptive chosen message attacks if some conditions are true about the main ingredients. For example, it suffices to assume that both the ordinary and one-time signature schemes are secure against chosen message attack and that the hashing is the identity map. Milder conditions are discusses in Sections 3 and 4. Here we confine ourselves to just give some plausibility arguments concerning the security.

First, notice that a chosen message attack by a forger, attempting to find a new pk (for which he knows a corresponding sk) and a matching Σ, amounts to a known message attack on the ordinary signature scheme, since the previous pk's for which the forger has seen matching Σ's have not been chosen by him. This is the reason why the ordinary signature scheme need not withstand a chosen message attack (as indeed is the case for Rabin's scheme [R79]).

Second, an attempt to use an old pk (for which a matching Σ is known) and forge σ for a new m', amounts to either an attack on the one-time signature scheme (producing a signature for $H(m')$ which is different from all previously hashed values) or finding a new m' such that $H(m) = H(m')$. However, we assume either task to be infeasible.

Efficiency

Notice that the off-line computation essentially coincides with computing the signature of a single string in the ordinary scheme. Since there are extremely fast one-way hashing functions and one-time signature schemes, the effort required in the on-line phase is negligible with respect to that of computing an ordinary signature.

Most ordinary signing algorithms are based on the computational difficulty of integer factorization. Should some moderately faster factoring algorithm come about, then longer ordinary public and secret keys will be necessary. This will cause a slow-down in the off-line stage, but not in the on-line one. Thus, our construction may become even more useful if ordinary signature schemes will become slower due to increasing security requirements.

3. PROOF OF THE THEORETICAL RESULT

Let (G,S,V) be a signature scheme secure against known message attack. We construct the signature scheme (G^*,S^*,V^*) as follows:

G is used twice to produce two pairs of matching public and secret keys, (PK_1, SK_1) and (PK_2, SK_2). To sign a message m of length n the signer randomly selects $2n$ strings of length n each, denoted $r_1,...,r_{2n}$, and signs the string R, obtained by concatenating them. Namely, $\Sigma = S_{SK_1}(R)$. Let $m = b_1 \cdots b_n$. Then, the signer computes $\sigma_i = S_{SK_2}(r_{2i-b_i})$ and sets $\sigma = \sigma_1 \cdots \sigma_n$. The signature of message m consists of R, Σ and σ.

Hence

$$G^*(1^n) \equiv G(1^n) \circ G(1^n),$$

$$S^*_{(SK_1, SK_2)}(b_1 \cdots b_n) \equiv (r_1 \cdots r_{2n}, \Sigma, \sigma_1 \cdots \sigma_n),$$

$$V^*_{(PK_1, PK_2)}(b_1 \cdots b_n, r_1 \cdots r_{2n}, \Sigma, \sigma_1 \cdots \sigma_n) \equiv$$

$$V_{PK_1}(r_1 \cdots r_{2n}, \Sigma) \qquad (1 \le i \le n) \; V_{PK_2}(r_{2i-b_i}, \sigma_i).$$

Note that the scheme (G^*, S^*, V^*) is an on-line/off-line signature scheme, in which no computation is necessary in the on-line phase; one may just retrieve the appropriate precomputed σ_i's.

Proposition:

If (G^*, S^*, V^*) is existentially forgeable via a *chosen* message attack then (G, S, V) is existentially forgeable via a *known* message attack.

Proof's sketch:

Let F^* be a probabilistic polynomial time algorithm which forges signatures of (G^*, S^*, V^*), with success probability $\varepsilon(n) \ge 1/n^{O(1)}$, via a chosen message attack. Such a forged signature either uses a sequence of r_i's which has appeared in a previous signature or uses a sequence of r_i's which has not appeared previously. One of these two cases occurs with probability $\ge \varepsilon(n)/2$.

Case 1:

With probability $\ge \varepsilon(n)/2$, algorithm F^* forms a new signature using a sequence of r_i's used in a previous signature.

We construct an algorithm, F_1, forging signatures of (G, S, V) as follows. On input PK (and access to *known* message attack on S_{SK}), algorithm F_1 uses G to obtain a new pair of corresponding keys (SK', PK'). Algorithm F_1 initiates algorithm F^*, on input (PK', PK), and supplies it with signatures to messages of F^*'s choice. To get a signature for the message $m = b_1 \cdots b_n$, requested by F^*, algorithm F asks for new signatures of n random messages. Suppose that F is given the message-signature pairs

$$(\mu_1, S_{SK}(\mu_1)), \ldots, (\mu_n, S_{SK}(\mu_n)).$$

Algorithm F_1 sets $r_{2i-b_i} \leftarrow \mu_i$ and selects the other n strings r_i at random. It uses its secret key SK' to compute $\Sigma = S_{SK'}(r_1 \cdots r_{2n})$, and gives F^* the triple

$$(r_1 \cdots r_{2n}, \Sigma, S_{SK}(r_{2-b_1}) \cdots S_{SK}(r_{2n-b_n}))$$

as a signature of m. Eventually, with probability $\ge \varepsilon(n)/2$, algorithm F^* yields a signature to a new message in which the r_i-sequence is identical to a r_i-sequence used in a previous message. This signature contains, with very high probability, a signature $S_{SK}(r_j)$ to a string r_j for which a signature has not been seen so far. (It is unlikely that the oracle signing random messages will sign the same message twice since the message space is huge). Outputting this $(r_j, S_{SK}(r_j))$ pair, algorithm F_1 achieves existential forgery, via a known message attack.

Case 2:

With probability $\geq \epsilon(n)/2$, algorithm F^* forms a new signature using a sequence of r_i's not used in previous signatures.

The forging algorithm we construct here, denoted F_2, uses (SK', PK') for the second phase. Namely, F_2 answers the signature requests of F^* by obtaining a S_{SK}-signature to a random message $r_1 \cdots r_{2n})$ and computing $S_{SK'}(r_{2i-b_i})$. If the new signature obtained from F^* contains a S_{SK}-signature of a new sequence of r_i's, F_2 outputs it. This happens with probability $\geq \epsilon(n)/2$, and hence F_2 commits existential forgery, via a known message attack.

$\square$

4. CONCRETE IMPLEMENTATIONS

We now suggest concrete implementations of our general scheme leading to fast on-line computations (both for signer and verifier).

In the role of the ordinary signature scheme we use a modification of Rabin's scheme [R79]. In this modification, we use integers which are the product of two large primes one congruent to 3 modulo 8 and the other congruent to 7 modulo 8. For such an integer N and for every integer $v \in Z_N^*$ (the multiplicative group modulo N) exactly one of the elements in the set $S_v = \{v, -v, 2v, -2v\}$ is a square modulo N (see [W80, GMR84]). Moreover, each square modulo N has exactly 4 distinct square roots mod N. Let us define the *extended* square root of v modulo N, denoted $^{ext}\sqrt{v}$ mod N, to be a distinguished square root modulo N (say, the smallest one) of the appropriate member of S_v. Its computation is feasible if the factorization of N is known, and considered intractable otherwise.

The message space is associated with the elements of the above multiplicative group. Larger messages are first hashed into such an element. It is assumed that the message space satisfies the following condition: If $v \neq u$ then $S_v \cap S_u = \emptyset$. This can be enforced by using only values of the 2nd eighth of Z_N^* (i.e., $\{v \in Z_N^*: N/8 < v < N/4\}$).

Anyone can verify that α is a legitimate signature of m by computing $\alpha^2 \bmod n_A$ and checking that it indeed belongs to the set S_m.

For the one-time signature scheme, we propose to use the DES algorithm as a one-way function $f(x) = DES_x(M)$; that is, the value obtained by encrypting a standard message, M, using DES with key x. Also, the notation $DES_x^i(M)$ means $f^i(x)$; that is, iterating the one-way function i times on input x (using each time, for example, the first 56 bits of the previous value as the next key).

In role of the one-way hashing function we use any standard way of using DES in a hashing mode. (See, for example, [R78].) We recommend that H maps arbitrarily long strings to $n = 128$-bit long strings. For some applications, one may be content with $n = 64$.

For the sake of presentation, let us describe now three versions of the concrete implementation, adding each time a new concept. These concepts have been suggested previously. (See, for example, [M].)

4.1 The Basic Implementation

Off-Line Computation

A chooses randomly 256 keys for DES. Thus, the one-time secret key is

$$sk = K_1 K_2 \cdots K_{256.}$$

Next, A computes the corresponding public key as follows:

$$pk = DES(M, K_1)DES(M, K_2) \cdots DES(M, K_{256}),$$

where M is a standard message, known to all. Next, A one-way hashes and signs pk. A can perform this task with reasonable efficiency, since she knows the two prime factors of n_A. Thus, she has

$$v = H(pk),$$

$$\Sigma = {}^{ext}\sqrt{v} \ (mod \ n_A).$$

She now stores pk, its precomputed signature Σ, and sk.

On-Line Signature

Assume now, that A wants to sign message m. She retrieves from memory the precomputed pk, Σ and the one-time secret key sk and then computes the 128-bit string

$$x = H(m) = b_1 \cdots b_{128}.$$

She then prepares the 7168-bit string

$$\sigma = K_{2-b_1} K_{4-b_2} \cdots K_{256-b_{128}},$$

This completes the signing process. The signature consists of pk, Σ, and σ. Its total length is 24,064 bits (16,384 + 512 + 7168).

Verification

First one computes $v = H(pk)$, and verifies that Σ is an extended square root of v modulo n_A; that is, that $\Sigma^2 \ mod \ n_A$ is one of the four members of S_v.

Second, one computes $x = H(m)$ and, using the blocks of σ, one verifies that for every ($1 \le i \le 128$), $DES(M, K_{2i-b_i})$ is equal to the $(2i-b_i)$'th block of pk.

Security

Assuming that factoring is hard, a forger cannot produce a Σ for a new string pk. Notice again, that a chosen message attack on this part of the new scheme amounts to a known message attack on Rabin's signature.

Assuming that $DES(M, \cdot)$ is a secure one-way function, a forger cannot find any of the 128 keys not revealed to him in σ, and therefore cannot forge a one-time signature to any message which does not hash to the same x. Clearly, the probability that the same key will be generated again (to be part of a new sk) is negligible.

4.2 Shortening the signature

In this version the length of the transmitted signature is shortened while the number of DES computations remains unchanged. The only damage is that the scheme is less suitable for parallel implementations.

Off-Line Computation

A chooses randomly 129 keys for DES. Thus, the one-time secret key is

$$sk = K_1 K_2 \cdots K_{129} .$$

Next, A computes the corresponding public key as follows:

$$pk = DES(M,K_1)DES(M,K_2) \cdots DES(M,K_{128})DES^{128}(M,K_{129}).$$

Next, A one-way hashes and signs pk. Thus, she has

$$v = H(pk),$$
$$\Sigma = \sqrt[ext]{v} \; (mod \; n_A).$$

She now stores pk, its precomputed signature Σ, and sk.

On-Line Signature

Assume now, that A wants to sign message m. She retrieves from memory the precomputed pk, Σ and the one-time secret key sk and computes the 128-bit string

$$x = H(m) = b_1 \cdots b_{128} .$$

Let

$$B = \sum_{i=1}^{i=128} b_i ,$$

and let β_j, $0 \le j \le B$, be the index of the j'th 0 in the vector x. A prepares the $(56 \cdot (128-B) + 64)$-bit string

$$\sigma = K_{\beta_1} K_{\beta_2} \cdots K_{\beta_{128-B}} DES^{128-B}(M, K_{129}) .$$

This completes the signing process. The signature consists of pk, Σ, and σ. Its total length is bounded by 16,000 bits (8,256 + 512 + 7,168 + 64).

Verification

First one computes $v = H(pk)$, and verifies that Σ is an extended square root of v modulo n_A.

Second, one computes $x = H(m)$. B and β_j are defined as above. Using the first $(128-B)$ (56-bit) blocks of σ, one verifies that for every $1 \le j \le (128-B)$, $DES(M, K_{\beta_j})$ is equal to the β_j'th block of pk. Also, using the last (64-bit) block of σ, and extracting from it the (first) 56-bit key K', one verifies that $DES^B(M, K')$ is equal to the 129-th block of pk. Altogether, there are 128 applications of DES.

Security

The argument concerning the security of Σ remain essentially unchanged. For the security of the one-time signature, assume that $DES(M, \cdot)$ is a secure one-way function, and consider the possibility of forging a one-time signature for $m' \neq m$. We assume that $H(m') \neq H(m)$. Let

$$H(m') = b'_1 \cdots b'_n \ .$$

If there exists an i such that $b_i = 1$ but $b'_i = 0$ then the forger is stuck: He cannot provide the corresponding DES key. If no such i exists, then

$$B' \equiv \sum_{i=1}^{i=128} b'_i \ > \ B \ ,$$

and the forger is supposed to produce $DES^{128-B'}(M, K_{129})$, which he cannot, since $128 - B' < 128 - B$ and $DES(M, \cdot)$ is a one-way function.

4.3 Further shortening of the signature

The method described here shortens the signature by a factor of 3.38, but increases the number of DES applications by a factor of 3.75. Yet, running DES 1,000 times takes less than .2 seconds. Thus, this method seems to be suitable for the electronic wallet. **Off-Line Computation**

A uses her spare time to produce the concatenation of 33 DES keys. Each key (56 bit-long) is chosen randomly. Thus,

$$sk = K_1 K_2 \cdots K_{33}$$

is the one-time secret key. A computes now the corresponding public key pk as follows:

$$pk = DES^{15}(M,K_1) \cdots DES^{15}(M,K_{32})DES^{480}(M,K_{33}).$$

Next, A one-way hashes and signs pk.

$$v = H(pk),$$
$$\Sigma = {}^{ext}\sqrt{v} \ (mod \ n_A).$$

She now stores the precomputed signature pk, Σ, and sk.

On-Line Signature

Assume now, that A wants to sign message m. She retrieves from memory the precomputed pk, Σ and the one-time signing key sk and computes the 128-bit string

$$x = H(m) = B_1 \cdots B_{32} \ ,$$

the concatenation of 32 blocks, each 4-bit long (representing an integer between 0 and 15). Thus, the sum of the B_i's is at most $32 \cdot 15 = 480$. She then computes the 2112-bit string ($2112 = 33 \cdot 64$)

$$\sigma = \sigma_1 \cdots \sigma_{32}\sigma_{33} \ ,$$

where

$$\sigma_i = DES^{B_i}(M, K_i)$$

for $i = 1,...,32$ and

$$\sigma_{33} = DES^{480 - (B_1 + \cdots + B_{32})}(M, K_{33}) .$$

This completes the signing process. The signature consists of pk, Σ, and σ. Its total length is 4,736 bits (2112 + 512 + 2112).

Verification

To verify the signature, one computes $v = H(pk)$, and checks that Σ is an extended square root of v module n_A; that is, that $\Sigma^2 \bmod n_A$ is one of the four members of S_v. Next, one computes $x = H(m)$ and divides x into 32 blocks of 4-bits each, $x = B_1...B_{32}$. One then verifies that pk equals

$$DES^{15-B_1}(M, \sigma_1) \cdots DES^{15-B_{32}}(M, \sigma_{32}) DES^{B_1 + \cdots + B_{32}}(M, \sigma_{33}) .$$

Security

The security of Σ is as above. Let us consider the security of the one-time signature.

We need to show that, even after seeing the signature of a legitimately one-time signed string x, an adversary (who does not know the one-time secrete key) cannot find any other string, x', whose one-time signature he is able to forge. Divide x' and x into $k = 32$ blocks of 4 bits each, $B'_1 \cdots B'_k$ and $B_1 \cdots B_k$, respectively. Consider again each block as a number between 0 and 15. If for some i, $B'_i < B_i$ then the adversary is stuck, since $f(s) = DES(M, s)$ is a one-way function and to obtain σ'_i, a valid signature of B'_i, he must invert (i.e. find a counter-image of) f at least once, on input σ_i. Otherwise, we have $B'_i \geq B_i$ for all i. But as we assume that $x' \neq x$,

$$480 - (B'_1 + \cdots + B'_k) < 480 - (B_1 + \cdots + B_k)$$

holds. Thus, the adversary is again stuck since he cannot invert f even once, as he needs to do to derive σ'_{k+1} on input σ_{k+1}.

5. REFERENCES

[BM88]   Bellare, M., and Micali, S., "How to Sign Given Any Trapdoor Function", *STOC 88.* , pp. 32-42.

[DES77] National Bureau of Standards, Federal Information Processing Standards, Publ. 46 (DES 1977).

[E]   Even, S., "Secure Off-Line Electronic Fund Transfer Between Nontrusting Parties", to appear in the Proceedings of Smart Card 2000, a conference held in Laxenburg, Austria, Oct. 1987.

[EGY83]   Even, S., Goldreich, O., and Yacobi, Y., "Electronic Wallet", Advances in Cryptology: Proc. of Crypto 83, D. Chaum (ed), Plenum Press, 1984, pp. 383-386.

[G86]   Goldreich, O., "Two Remarks Concerning the Goldwasser-Micali-Rivest Signature Scheme", *Advances in Cryptology - CRYPTO 86,* , A.M. Odlyzko (ed), Springer-Verlag, 1987, pp. 104-110.

[GMR84]   Goldwasser, S., Micali, S., and Rivest, R.L., "A Digital Signature Scheme Secure Against Adaptive Chosen-Message Attacks", *SIAM J. on Computing,* April 1988, pp. 281-308.

[M]   Merkle, R.C., "A Digital Signature Based on a Conventional Encryption Function", *Advances in Cryptology - CRYPTO '87,* Pomerance (ed), Lecture Notes in Computer Science, Vol. 293, Springer-Verlag, 1987, pp. 369-378.

[NY89]   Naor, M., and Yung, M., "Universal One-Way Hash Functions and their Cryptographic Application", *21st STOC,* 1989, pp. 33-43.

[R78]   Rabin, M.O., "Digital Signatures", in *Foundations of Secure Computation,* R.A. DeMillo, et. al. (eds). Academic Press, 1978, pp. 155-168.

[R79]   Rabin, M.O., "Digitalized Signatures and Public-Key Functions as Intractable as Factorization", Lab. for Computer Science, MIT, Report TR-212, January 1979.

[RSA78]   Rivest, R.L., Shamir, A., and Adleman, L., "A Method for Obtaining Digital Signatures and Public-Key Cryptosystems", *Comm. ACM 21 (2),* 1978, pp. 120-126.

[W80]   Williams, H. C., "A Modification of the RSA Public-Key Encryption Procedure", *IEEE Trans. Inform. Theory* IT-26 (6), 1980, pp. 726-729.

Session 7:

Threshold schemes and Key management

Chair: Josh Benaloh

On the Classification of Ideal Secret Sharing Schemes

(Extended Abstract)

Ernest F. Brickell
Daniel M. Davenport

Sandia National Laboratories *
Albuquerque, NM 87185

Abstract

In a secret sharing scheme, a dealer has a secret key. There is a finite set P of participants and a set Γ of subsets of P. A secret sharing scheme with Γ as the access structure is a method which the dealer can use to distribute shares to each participant so that a subset of participants can determine the key if and only if that subset is in Γ. The share of a participant is the information sent by the dealer in private to the participant. A secret sharing scheme is ideal if any subset of participants who can use their shares to determine any information about the key can in fact actually determine the key, and if the set of possible shares is the same as the set of possible keys. In this paper, we show a relationship between ideal secret sharing schemes and matroids.

1   Introduction

In a secret sharing scheme, a dealer has a key. There is a finite set P of participants and a set Γ of subsets of P. A secret sharing scheme with Γ as the access structure is a method which the dealer can use to distribute shares to each participant so that a subset of participants can determine the key if and only if that subset is in Γ. A secret sharing scheme is said to be *perfect* if any subset of participants who can use their shares to determine any information about the key can in fact actually determine the key. The *share* of a participant is the information sent by the dealer in private to the participant.

In any practical implementation of a secret sharing scheme, it is important to keep the size of the shares as small as possible. The reason for this is obvious. The most

*This work performed at Sandia National Laboratories and supported by the U.S. Department of Energy under contract No. DE–AC04–76DP00789.

secure method for a participant to store a share is in his own memory. However, if his share is too large, he will be inclined to write down information which will help him to remember his share. This, of course, will degrade the security of the scheme. This paper deals with secret sharing shemes in which the shares are as small as possible, i.e. the shares are the same size as the keys.

Let $\mathcal{K}$ be the set of keys and let S be the set of shares used in a secret sharing scheme. The *information rate* for the secret sharing scheme is defined to be $\log_2 |\mathcal{K}| / \log_2 |S|$. A perfect secret sharing scheme is said to be *ideal* if it has information rate 1.

The first constructions of perfect secret sharing schemes were the threshold schemes of Blakley [2] and Shamir [5]. In a threshold scheme, there is a threshold t such that the access structure is $\Gamma = \{A \subseteq P : |A| \geq t\}$.

A set of subsets Γ of a set P is said to be *monotone* if $B \in \Gamma$ and $B \subseteq C$ implies that $C \in \Gamma$ for any $B, C \subseteq P$. Ito, Saito, and Nishisehi [4], and also Benaloh and Leichter [1] showed that for any monotone set of subsets Γ of P, there exists a perfect secret sharing scheme with Γ as the access structure. However, for both the ISN and the BL constructions, the information rate could be exponentially small in $|P|$.

The schemes of Blakley and Shamir can be implemented so that they are ideal secret sharing schemes. Benaloh and Leichter [1], Brickell [3], and Simmons [6] have constructed ideal secret sharing schemes for other access structures.

The main contribution of the current paper is to give a description of ideal secret sharing schemes in terms of classical combinatorial objects by showing a direct relationship between ideal secret sharing schemes and matroids.

In order to make the definitions more precise, we will define a secret sharing scheme to be a finite matrix M in which no two rows are identical. We will identify the columns of M as the set of participants P and will use $M(r, p)$ to denote the entry of M in row r and column p. We will denote the first column as p_0 and will assume that p_0 always receives the key as his share. It is sometimes useful to think of this special participant p_0 as the dealer. For $p \in P$, let $S(p) = \{M(r, p) \mid r$ is a row in $M\}$. That is, $S(p)$ is the set of the elements occurring in column p and $S(p_0) = \mathcal{K}$. The dealer can distribute a key $\alpha \in S(p_0)$ by picking a row r of the matrix in which $M(r, p_0) = \alpha$ and using $M(r, p)$ as the share for participant p for each $p \in P$. We assume that the matrix is public knowledge, but that the dealer's choice of r is private.

Let $A \subseteq P$. Each participant $a \in A$ receives a share, say α_a, from the dealer. If the participants in A pool their information, they will know that the dealer picked a row r in which $M(r, a) = \alpha_a$ for each $a \in A$. It is now easy to define the access structure Γ. A subset $A \subseteq P$ will be in Γ if and only if any two rows r and $\hat{r}$ such that $M(r, a) = M(\hat{r}, a)$ for all $a \in A$ also satisfy $M(r, p_0) = M(\hat{r}, p_0)$.

Given a subset $A \subseteq P$ and a participant $b \in P$ with $b \notin A$, we will say that A has *no information* about the share given to b, denoted $A \not\rightarrow b$, if for all rows r of M and $\beta \in S(b)$ there is a row r' such that $M(r, a) = M(r', a)$ for all $a \in A$, and $M(r', b) = \beta$. Otherwise, we will say that A has *some information* about b, and denote this by $A \rightarrow b$. We will say that A *knows* the share given to b, denoted by $A \Rightarrow b$ if all rows that are identical on the participants in A are also identical on b.

Then $\Gamma = \{A \subseteq P \mid A \Rightarrow p_0\}$ is the collection of access sets.

A secret sharing scheme is *perfect* iff for all subsets $A \subseteq P$, $A \rightarrow p_0$ implies that $A \Rightarrow p_0$. A secret sharing scheme is *ideal* iff it is perfect and $|S(p)| = |S(p_0)|$ for all $p \in P$. Thus if a secret sharing scheme is ideal, we will assume WLOG that $S(p) = S(p_0)$ for all $p \in P$ and we will denote $S(p)$ as simply S.

Let Γ_m denote the set of minimal elements of Γ. If there is a participant $p \in P$ such that p is not contained in any subset in Γ_m, then this participant is not needed since there is never a case in which his share is useful in determining the key. It is not interesting to study secret sharing schemes in which some participants receive useless shares. Therefore, we will say that the secret sharing scheme is *connected* if every participant $p \in P$ is contained in some subset in Γ_m, and for the remainder of this paper, will only consider connected secret sharing schemes.

For M an ideal secret sharing scheme, let $D(M) = \{A \subseteq P \mid$ there exists $y \in A$ such that $A \backslash y \Rightarrow y\}$. Intuitively, a set of participants is in $D(M)$ if there is a dependency among them.

Before we state the main results of this paper, we need to introduce the definitions of matroids and nearfields.

Matroids are well studied combinatorial objects (see for example Welsh [8]). A matroid $\mathcal{T} = (V, \mathcal{I})$ is a finite set V and a collection $\mathcal{I}$ of subsets of V such that (I1) through (I3) are satisfied.

(I1) $\emptyset \in \mathcal{I}$.

(I2) If $X \in \mathcal{I}$ and $Y \subseteq X$ then $Y \in \mathcal{I}$.

(I3) If X, Y are members of $\mathcal{I}$ with $|X| = |Y| + 1$ there exists $x \in X \backslash Y$ such that $Y \cup \{x\} \in \mathcal{I}$.

The elements of V are called the *points* of the matroid and the sets $\mathcal{I}$ are called *independent sets*. A *dependent set* of a matroid is any subset of V that is not independent. The minimal dependent sets are called *circuits*. A matroid is said to be *connected* if for any two elements, there is a circuit containing both of them.

A *right nearfield* is a set R with distinguished elements 0 and 1 and binary operations $+$ and $\cdot$ such that $(R, +)$ is an Abelian group, $(R \backslash 0, \cdot)$ is a group, and $(R, +, \cdot)$ is right distributive (i.e. $(a + b) \cdot c = a \cdot c + b \cdot c$ for all $a, b, c \in R$). If a right nearfield is also left distributive then it is a field. When R is finite its cardinality is always a power of a prime (see [7]). The nearfields we will consider are finite. A right near vector space and its dot product are defined analogously to a vector space only defined over a right nearfield instead of a field. A vector v in a right near vector space V is said to be *dependent* on a set A of vectors iff for every vector $u \in V$, if $u \cdot a = 0$ for all $a \in A$ then $u \cdot v = 0$. In the case that the right nearfield is actually a field, this definition of dependence is equivalent to stating that a vector v is dependent on a set A of vectors iff v is a linear combination of the vectors in A. A set A of vectors is said to be a *dependent set* if there exists $a \in A$ such that a is dependent on $A \backslash a$. A matroid is representable over a right nearfield if there is a dependence preserving injection from the points of the matroid into the set of vectors of a right near vector space.

In this paper, we prove the following two theorems which together almost characterize ideal secret sharing schemes.

Theorem 1 *Let M be a connected ideal secret sharing scheme. Then the sets $D(M)$ are the dependent sets of a connected matroid.*

Theorem 2 *Let $\mathcal{T} = (V, \mathcal{I})$ be a connected matroid representable over a nearfield. Let $v_0 \in V$. Then there exists a connected ideal secret sharing scheme M such that $p_0 = v_0$, $P = V$, and $D(M) = $ the dependent sets of $\mathcal{T}$.*

We say that this almost characterizes ideal secret sharing schemes because there may be connected matroids that are not representable over any nearfield, and for any such matroids, we do not know if there exist corresponding ideal secret sharing schemes.

Another interesting result that can be easily proven from the methods used in proving Theorem 1 is the following.

Theorem 3 *Let M be a connected ideal secret sharing scheme. Let $A \subseteq P$ and $b \in P$. If $A \to b$, then $A \Rightarrow b$.*

This theorem shows that any participant in a connected ideal secret sharing scheme can be thought of as the special participant, p_0.

There is an alternate definition for ideal secret sharing that at first glance appears to be a weaker definition. Let $A \subseteq P$ and $b \in P \backslash A$. We will say that A has *no probabilistic information* about the share given to b, denoted $A \not\leadsto b$, if for all rows r of M, there exists an integer n such that for all $\beta \in S(b)$, there are exactly n distinct rows $r'_1, \cdots, r'_n$ such that for $1 \le i \le n$, $M(r, a) = M(r'_i, a)$ for all $a \in A$ and $M(r'_i, b) = \beta$. Otherwise we will say that A has *probabilistic information* about the share given to b and denote this by $A \leadsto b$.

It would be reasonable to define a perfect secret sharing scheme as one in which $A \leadsto p_0$ implies that $A \Rightarrow p_0$. But the next theorem shows that at least for connected secret sharing schemes with information rate 1, this definition would be equivalent to our original definition.

Theorem 4 *Let M be a connected ideal secret sharing scheme. Then $A \leadsto p_0$ implies that $A \Rightarrow p_0$.*

In the next section, we consider a special case in which we are able to establish necessary and sufficient conditions for the existence of an ideal secret sharing scheme. The proofs of the general case will not be presented in this extended abstract, but will be contained in the final paper. We conclude the extended abstract with some open problems in Section 3.

2 Example: The Rank 2 Case

In this section we will prove Theorems 1 and 2 in a special case that is much easier to prove and more intuitive than the general case. But first we need some lemmas that will hold for the general case as well.

Let M be a connected ideal secret sharing scheme. Let $q = |S|$. For $A \subseteq P$, let $M(r, A)$ be the row r in M restricted to the columns indexed by A and define $s(A) = \{M(r, A) : r \text{ is a row of } M\}$. That is, $s(A)$ is the set of distinct entries in M under A. Let $\sharp A = |s(A)|$.

Lemma 1 *Let $A \subseteq P$ and $p \in P$. If $A \Rightarrow p$, then $\sharp A = \sharp(A \cup p)$.*

Proof: If $\sharp(A \cup p) > \sharp A$, there exists rows r_1 and r_2 such that $M(r_1, a) = M(r_2, a)$ for all $a \in A$ and $M(r_1, p) \neq M(r_2, p)$. But this contradicts $A \Rightarrow p$. $\square$

Lemma 2 *Let $A \subseteq P$ and $p \in P$. Suppose $A \not\Rightarrow p_0$ and $A \cup p \Rightarrow p_0$. Then $A \cup p_0 \Rightarrow p$.*

Proof: Define a function $\phi : S \to S$ by $\phi(\beta) = \gamma$ iff there exists a row r such that $M(r, a) = M(r_1, a)$ for all $a \in A$, and $M(r, p) = \beta$ and $M(r, p_0) = \gamma$. Since $(A \cup p) \Rightarrow p_0$, this function is well defined. Since $A \not\Rightarrow p_0$, ϕ must be onto and hence 1-1. $\square$

For a secret sharing scheme M, let $\hat{P} = \{p \in P \mid p \not\Rightarrow p_0\}$. Let $G(M)$ be a graph with vertices the participants in $\hat{P}$ and with $p_1, p_2 \in \hat{P}$ joined with an edge iff $\{p_1, p_2\} \in \Gamma$.

A connected ideal secret sharing scheme, M, is said to have rank 2 iff (S1) - (S3) are satisfied.

(S1) There exists a set in Γ_m of cardinality 2.

(S2) All sets in Γ_m have cardinality 1 or 2.

(S3) $G(M)$ is connected.

We then have the following Theorem.

Theorem 5 *Let M be a rank 2 connected ideal secret sharing scheme. Let G' be the complementary graph of $G(M)$. Then G' is a disjoint union of cliques.*

Proof: Let $\{p_1, p_2\} \in \Gamma_m$. If there exists α_1, α_2 both in S such that there is no row r of M with $M(r, p_i) = \alpha_i$ for $i = 1, 2$, then $p_1 \to p_2$. Hence, $p_1 \to p_0$ and thus $p_1 \Rightarrow p_0$. Contradiction. Thus, $\sharp\{p_1, p_2\} = q^2$.

Let $A \subseteq P$ be maximal set such that $\sharp A = q^2$ and $\{p_1, p_2\} \subseteq A$. By Lemma 1, $p_0 \in A$ and $P \backslash \hat{P} \subseteq A$. Suppose $P \backslash A \neq \emptyset$. Since $G(M)$ is connected, there exists $b \in P \backslash A$ and $a \in A$ such that $\{a, b\} \in \Gamma$. By Lemma 2, $\{a, p_0\} \Rightarrow b$. Since $\{a, p_0\} \in A$, $\sharp A = \sharp(A \cup b)$. Contradiction. Thus $\sharp P = q^2$.

Suppose $\{a, b\} \subseteq \hat{P}$ and $\{a, b\} \notin \Gamma$. Let r be a row of M. Then for all $\beta \in S$, there exists a row r_β such that $M(r_\beta, a) = M(r, a)$, $M(r_\beta, b) = M(r, b)$ and $M(r_\beta, p_0) = \beta$.

Thus, $q\#\{a,b\} = \#\{a,b,p_0\} \leq q^2$. Since $\#a = q$, $\#\{a,b\} = q$. Since $\#b$ is also q, we must have $a \Rightarrow b$. Suppose now that $\{a,b,c\} \subseteq \hat{P}$ and $\{a,b\} \notin \Gamma$ and $\{b,c\} \notin \Gamma$. Since $a \Rightarrow b$ and $b \Rightarrow c$ implies $a \Rightarrow c$, we also have $\{a,c\} \notin \Gamma$. Theorem 5 now follows. $\square$

The converse to Theorem 5 is also true.

Theorem 6 *Let G' be a graph which is a disjoint union of cliques. Then there exists a rank 2 connected ideal secret sharing scheme M, with $P = V(G') \cup p_0$ such that $G(M) = $ complement of G'.*

Proof: Let C be the set of distinct components of G'. Let n be the number of components of G'. Let $\hat{C} = C \cup p_0$. Let $\hat{S} = (\hat{C}, S, \hat{M})$ be an ideal 2 out of n threshold scheme with $|S| = q$. Using the Shamir construction, such a threshold scheme exists for all prime power q such that $q > n$. Let M be a matrix with the same number of rows as $\hat{M}$ and with columns indexed by the vertices of G'. For a vertex $v \in G'$ contained in component $c \in C$, and r a row of $\hat{M}$, let $M(r,v) = \hat{M}(r,c)$. Let $M(r,p_0) = \hat{M}(r,p_0)$ for all rows r of $\hat{M}$. It is straightforward to check that M is a rank 2 connected ideal secret sharing scheme. $\square$

These two theorems now make it easy to prove Theorems 1 and 2 for this special case.

For M a rank 2 connected ideal secret sharing scheme, let $\mathcal{I}(M) = \{\emptyset\} \cup \{p \mid p \in P\} \cup \{\{p_1,p_2\} \mid p_1 \Rightarrow p_0 \text{ and } p_2 \not\Rightarrow p_0\} \cup \{\{p_1,p_2\} \mid \{p_1,p_2\} \subseteq \Gamma_m\}$.

It is easy to see that $\mathcal{I}(M) = 2^P \backslash D(M)$ (where 2^P is the set of all subsets of P).

Theorem 7 *Let M be a rank 2 connected ideal secret sharing scheme. Then the sets $D(M)$ are the dependent sets of a connected matroid.*

Proof: We need to show that the set $\mathcal{I}(S)$ satisfies (I1) - (I3). Conditions (I1) and (I2) are trivially satisfied. The same applies to (I3) if $X = \emptyset$ or $X \subset Y$. Thus assume that $|X| = 1$ and $X \nsubseteq Y$. Let $X = \{x\}$ and $Y = \{y_1, y_2\}$. WLOG, we may assume that $y_1 \subseteq \hat{P}$. If $x \in P \backslash \hat{P}$, then $\{x, y_1\} \subseteq \mathcal{I}(S)$. If $x \notin P \backslash \hat{P}$ and $y_2 \in P \backslash \hat{P}$, then $\{x, y_2\} \in \mathcal{I}(S)$. So we can assume that $x, y_1, y_2, \in \hat{P}$. Since $(y_1, y_2) \in E(G)$, then by Theorem 5, for $i = 1$ or 2, $(x, y_i) \in E(G)$ and so $\{x, y_i\} \in \mathcal{I}(S)$. $\square$

For a set $X \in V$, the rank of X, $\rho(X)$ is defined as

$$\rho(X) = \max\{|A| \; : \; A \subseteq X, A \in \mathcal{I}\}.$$

Theorem 8 *Let $\mathcal{T} = (V, \mathcal{I})$ be a rank 2 connected matroid. Let $v_0 \in V$. Then there exists a connected ideal secret sharing scheme M such that $p_0 = v_0$, $P = V$, and $D(M) = $ the dependent sets of $\mathcal{T}$.*

Proof: Let $\hat{V} = \{v \in V \mid \{v, v_0\} \in \mathcal{I}\}$. Let G be the graph on $\hat{V}$ such that $\{u,v\}$ is an edge of G iff $\{u,v\} \in \mathcal{I}$. From (I3), it follows that the complement of G is a disjoint union of cliques. By Theorem 5, there exists a rank 2 connected ideal secret sharing scheme $\hat{M}$, with $\hat{P} = \hat{V} \cup p_0$ such that $G(\hat{M}) = G$. Let M be the matrix with columns $P = \hat{P} \cup V \backslash \hat{V}$ and with $M(r,p) = \hat{M}(r,p)$ for all $p \in \hat{P}$

and $M(r,p) = \hat{M}(r,p_0)$ for all $p \in P\backslash\hat{P}$. It is straightforward to check that M is a connected ideal secret sharing scheme and the sets $D(M)$ are exactly the dependent sets of $\mathcal{T}$. □

Thus in the rank 2 case, we did not need the condition used in Theorem 2 that the matroid was representable over a nearfield and therefore we were able to completely characterize the connected ideal secret sharing schemes. One possible reason why we were successful in this case but not in the general case is that all rank 2 matroids are representable over fields.

3   Open Questions

The most obvious open question is to determine if Theorem 2 is still true if the condition of the matroid being representable over a nearfield is removed.

There are several other open questions which could also be addressed.

1. Characterize the perfect secret sharing schemes that have a fixed information rate.

2. Characterize the perfect secret sharing schemes that have an information rate that is at least 1/(polynomial in $|P|$).

3. Find a nontrivial lower bound on the information rate of all perfect secret sharing schemes.

4. Find an algorithm that given a secret sharing scheme, will determine the smallest information rate that could be used to implement that scheme.

Yao [9] has made some progress on problem 2. He has shown that if trap door functions exist, then any set Γ which can be recognized by a polynomial (in $|P|$) size monotone circuit can be the access structure of a secret sharing scheme in which the information rate is at least 1/(polynomial in $|P|$).

4   Acknowledgments

We would like to thank Mike Saks for useful conversations concerning this research and Kevin McCurley for comments on an earlier draft of this paper.

References

[1] J. C. BENALOH AND J. LEICHTER, *Generalized secret sharing and monotone functions.* to appear in Advances in Cryptology - CRYPTO88.

[2] G. R. BLAKLEY, *Safeguarding cryptographic keys*, in Proceedings AFIPS 1979 National Computer Conference, vol. 48, 1979, pp. 313–317.

[3] E. F. BRICKELL, *Some ideal secret sharing schemes.* to appear in the Journal of Combinatorial Mathematics and Combinatorial Computing.

[4] M. ITO, A. SAITO, AND T. NISHIZEKI, *Secret sharing scheme realizing general access structure*, in Proceedings IEEE Globecom'87, Tokyo, Japan, 1987, pp. 99–102.

[5] A. SHAMIR, *How to share a secret*, Communications of the ACM, 22 (1979), pp. 612–613.

[6] G. J. SIMMONS, *Robust shared secret schemes.* to appear in Congressus Numerantium, Vol. 68-69.

[7] S. VAJDA, *Patterns and Configurations in Finite Spaces*, Hafner Publishing, New York, 1967.

[8] D. J. A. WELSH, *Matroid Theory*, Academic Press, London, 1976.

[9] A. YAO. Presentation at the Cryptography conference in Oberwolfach, West Germany, Sep. 1989.

DYNAMIC THRESHOLD SCHEME BASED ON THE DEFINITION OF CROSS-PRODUCT

IN AN N-DIMENSIONAL LINEAR SPACE

CHI-SUNG LAIH[*], LEIN HARN[**], JAU-YIEN LEE[*] and Tzonelih Hwang[***]

[*]   Department of Electrical Engineering
      National Cheng Kung University
      Tainan, Taiwan, Republic of China
[**] Computer Science Program
      University of Missouri-Kansas City
      Kansas City, MO 64110, U.S.A.
[***] Institute of Information Engineering
      National Cheng Kung University
      Tainan, Taiwan, Republic of China

ABSTRACT

This paper investigates the characterizations of threshold /ramp schemes which give rise to the time-dependent threshold schemes. These schemes are called the "dynamic threshold schemes" as compared to the conventional time-independent threshold scheme. In a (d, m, n, T) dynamic threshold scheme, there are n secret shadows and a public shadow, p^j, at time $t=t_j$, $1 \leq t_j \leq T$. After knowing any m shadows, $m \leq n$, and the public shadow, p^j, we can easily recover d master keys, K_1^j, K_2^j, ..., and K_d^j. Furthermore, if the d master keys have to be changed to K_1^{j+1}, K_2^{j+1}, ..., and K_d^{j+1} for some security reasons, only the public shadow, p^j, has to be changed to p^{j+1}. All the n secret shadows issued initially remain unchanged. Compared to the conventional threshold/ramp schemes, at least one of the previous issued n shadows need to be changed whenever the master keys need to be updated for security reasons. A $(1, m, n, T)$ dynamic threshold scheme based on the definition of cross- product in an N-dimensional linear space is proposed to illustrate the characterizations of the dynamic threshold schemes.

This work was sponsored by the National Science Council, Republic of China, under Contract NSC79-0408-E006-02.

I INTRODUCTION

A threshold scheme is used to ensure that the information needed careful protection does not get lost, destroyed, or into wrong hands. As described by Denning [1, pp.179-185], an (m, n) threshold scheme is designed to break the single master key K into n different "shadows" such that:

(1) With knowledge of any m shadows, $m \leq n$, the master key K can be easily derived; and

(2) With knowledge of any m-1 or fewer "shadows", it is impossible to derive the master key K.

The idea of threshold schemes (or sometimes referred as key safeguarding schemes or secret sharing schemes) was introduced independent by Blakley [2] and Shamir [3]. Since then, threshold schemes have been well-studied over the past decade [4-7]. In 1984, the relationships between these schemes and a generalized linear scheme are established by Kothari [8]. However, as shown by Blakley and Meadows [9], although (m, n) linear threshold schemes provide Shannon perfect security up to threshold value, unfortunately they require a very large data expansion. That is, m shadows are needed to reclaim one secret which is very inefficient as a conveyor of information. In order to overcome this drawback, Blakley and Meadows presented the idea of (d, m, n) ramp schemes. In a (d, m, n) linear ramp scheme, it is designed to allow d secrets and m-d other predetermined types of secrets to be combined to produce n "shadows", in such a fashion that these d secrets can be reconstructed from any m shadows. However, there is a predetermined level of uncertainty (also called Shannon relative security) regarding the secrets if only j, j<m, shadows are known. It has been observed by Blakley and Meadows that $1 \leq d \leq m \leq n$. It is obvious that many conventional (m, n) threshold schemes are just the special case of the (1, m, n) ramp scheme.

We observe that the (d, m, n) ramp scheme is just the space expansion (with d times) of the conventional threshold schemes. In this paper, we will consider the time expansion of the threshold/ramp schemes. We will call them the "dynamic threshold schemes" (or, briefly, a (d, m, n, T) dynamic scheme, where T indicates time).

Any threshold/ramp scheme can be referred to as an "m out of secret sharing system." The one or d secrets can be divided into n shadows and securely distributed to n trustees in such a way that any m of them can reconstruct the secrets, but any m-1 of fewer of them cannot learn anything about it. However, it seems that two time-dependent phenomena are not discussed in the previous papers:

(1) When any m out of n trustees recover the secrets, whether the secrets are known by these trustees or not.

If these secrets can be known by m trustees when they are

reconstructed at time t^j, then the threshold/ramp schemes can be used only before time t^j. However, in practice applications, we may assume that these m trustees do not known these secrets. For example, in the access control system, any m trustees may simply insert their magnetic strip cards which contain the shadow information into the card reader and the system calculates these secrets to decide whether the door can be opened or not. In that case, these secrets are not known by m trustees when they get together to reconstruct these secrets, and therefore, the scheme can be used continually. But, conventional threshold/ramp schemes still exist the following disadvantage.

(2) Whenever these secrets under protection by threshold/ramp schemes need to be updated for some security reasons, at least one of the previously issued n shadows need to be changed.

This paper will focus on investigating the characterizations of threshold/ramp schemes which give rise to the time-dependent threshold/ramp schemes. We call the time-dependent threshold/ramp schemes the "dynamic threshold/ramp schemes" (or, more precisely, the (d, m, n, T) threshold /ramp schemes, where d, m, and n are the number of secrets, threshold value of shadows, and number of all shadows, respectively, and T indicates time). A (1, m, n, T) dynamic threshold scheme based on the definition of cross-product in an n-dimensional linear space is used to explain the characteristics of the dynamic threshold scheme.

II THE CHARACTERIZATIONS OF DYNAMIC THRESHOLD/RAMP SCHEMES

The security of a (d, m, n, T) dynamic threshold/ramp scheme is based on the following assumption:

Whenever <u>any</u> <u>m</u> <u>of</u> n trustees <u>are</u> <u>combined</u> <u>to</u> <u>recover</u> <u>d</u> <u>secrets,</u> <u>the</u> <u>secrecy</u> <u>of</u> <u>those</u> <u>shadows</u> <u>held</u> <u>by</u> <u>these</u> <u>m</u> <u>trustees</u> <u>is</u> <u>still</u> <u>maintained.</u>

Under practical implementation, this is a reasonable assumption, since the trustees may simply insert their magnetic strip cards which contain the shadow information into a card reader consecutively and the system calculates these secrets automatically . Therefore, the shadows are still kept secret for each individual trustee. Under this assumption, a dynamic threshold/ramp scheme may achieve the following characteristics:

Whenever these secrets under protection by a threshold/ramp scheme need to be updated for security reasons, all the previously issued n shadows <u>do</u> <u>not</u> need to be changed.

Since these secrets under protection are time-dependent and all previously issued shadows are time-independent, a time-dependent variable which we call the public shadow, P^j, have to be inserted into the system. The model of the dynamic threshold scheme is shown in Fig.(1). A (1, m, n, T) dynamic threshold scheme can be expressed by a function F such that

$$F(W_1, W_2, \ldots, W_m, P^j) = K^j \tag{1}$$

where K^j is the secret under protection at time t^j,

$W_1, W_2, \ldots, W_m \in$ {the set of all n shadows},

P^j is the public shadow at time t_j.

As shown in Eq.(1), knowing any m shadows, and the public shadow, P^j, at time t_j, it is sufficient to recover the secret (or master key) K^j. Whenever the master key, K^j, needs to be changed to K^{j+1} for some security reasons, only the public shadow, P^j, need to be changed to P^{j+1}. All the n secret shadows may remain unchanged.

In the ideal situation, the dynamic threshold/ramp schemes must satisfy the following characteristics:

(1) At the beginning of the time, $t_j=1$, dynamic threshold/ramp

schemes, like conventional threshold/ramp schemes, provide perfect security [9] up to the threshold value. For the

master key K^j, $j=1$, conveyed by the scheme, we have

probability (K^j/given that m-1 (or fewer) shadows and the public

shadow, P^j, are known) = Probability (K^j)

(2) If the previous master keys, K^j, $j=1, 2, \ldots, v-1$, are kept secret, the scheme also provides Shannon perfect security for

the following master keys, K^j, $j \geq v$. More clearly, knowing any

u (even $u \geq m$) public shadows, P^i, $i=1, 2, \ldots, u$, cannot

provide any information to derive any new master keys, K^j, $j \geq v$. That is

Probability (any new master keys K^j, $j \geq v$,/given that any u public

shadows, P^i, $i=1, 2, \ldots, u$, are known) = Probability (any new

master keys K^j, $j \geq v$)

(3) Knowing any v-1 previous master keys K^j, $j=1, 2, \ldots, v-1$, the scheme also provides Shannon perfect security for the

following new master keys K^j, $j \geq v$. That is, knowing all v-1

($\geq$m) previous master keys K^j, j=1, 2, ..., v-1, cannot provide any information to derive the following new master

keys K^j, j$\geq$v, i.e.,

Probability (any new master keys K^j, j$\geq$v/given that all K^j, j<v,

and p^i, i=1, 2, ..., u) = Probability (any new master keys K^j, j$\geq$v)

In general, it is very difficult to design an ideal dynamic threshold/ramp scheme to satisfy the characteristics (1)-(3). Alternatively, we define the "relative dynamic threshold/ramp scheme" which satisfies the above characteristics (1)-(2). That

is, knowing v-1 previous master keys K^j, j=1, 2, ..., v-1, and u

(>v) public shadows p^i, i=1, 2, ..., u, the scheme provides

Shannon <u>relative</u> security for the following master keys K^j, j$\geq$v, (the threshold number of shadows is decreased to m-v from m.) Note that the relative dynamic/ramp scheme is sufficient to the practice applications (e.g. the access control system discussed in the above section.) A dynamic threshold scheme based on the definition of cross-product in an N-dimensional space is proposed to illustrate the characteristics of relative dynamic threshold schemes. We encourage readers to propose any scheme which satisfies the characteristics of ideal threshold/ramp scheme.

III. THE DYNAMIC THRESHOLD SCHEME BASED ON

THE DEFINITION OF CROSS-PRODUCT IN N-DIMENSIONAL SPACE

Our proposed (1, m, n, T) dynamic threshold scheme is based on the following definition.

<u>Definition</u> :   The cross-product of s-1 linearly independent s-dimensional row vectors Z_1, Z_2, ..., Z_{s-1} is defined as :

$$Z_1 \ X \ Z_2 \ X \ ... \ X \ Z_{s-1} =$$

$$\left(\begin{vmatrix} z_2^1, & z_3^1, & ..., & z_s^1 \\ z_2^2, & z_3^2, & ..., & z_s^2 \\ . & . & ... & . \\ . & . & ... & . \\ . & . & ... & . \\ z_2^{s-1}, & z_3^{s-1}, & ..., & z_s^{s-1} \end{vmatrix}, \begin{vmatrix} z_3^1, & z_4^1, & ..., & z_s^1, & z_1^1 \\ z_3^2, & z_4^2, & ..., & z_s^2, & z_1^2 \\ . & . & ... & . & . \\ . & . & ... & . & . \\ . & . & ... & . & . \\ z_3^{s-1}, & z_4^{s-1}, & ..., & z_s^{s-1}, & z_1^{s-1} \end{vmatrix}, ..., \begin{vmatrix} z_1^1, & z_2^1, & ..., & z_{s-1}^1 \\ z_1^2, & z_2^2, & ..., & z_{s-1}^2 \\ . & . & ... & . \\ . & . & ... & . \\ . & . & ... & . \\ z_1^{s-1}, & z_2^{s-1}, & ..., & z_{s-1}^{s-1} \end{vmatrix} \right)$$

with $Z_i = (z_1^i, z_2^i ... z_s^i)$

$$(2)$$

The determinants of $(s-1)*(s-1)$ matrices in Eq. (2) can be computed by using the probabilistic algorithm proposed by Wiedemann [10]. Given a $r*r$ matrix, Wiedemann showed that the probabilistic algorithm for finding the determinant required an expected $O(r(w+r))$ number of field operations, where w is approximately the number of field operations needed to apply the matrix to a test vector. Since Eq. (2) contains s determinants, the complexity of Eq. (2) is about $O(s(s-1)(w+s-1))$ operations.

Now, assume that n is the total number of "shadows" need to be constructed and m is the threshold value which works with the public shadow, P^j, to recover the single master key, K^j. The scheme is described as follows :

Shadows generation:

For $j=1$ to T repeat step 1-3.

Step 1 : The key generation center randomly selects $m+1$ linearly independent $(m+2)$-dimensional row vectors V_1, V_2, ..., V_m and V_{m+1}^j.

Step 2 : The center then evaluates a new vector $U^j=(u_1^j, u_2^j, ..., u_{m+2}^j) = V_1 X V_2 X ... X V_t X V_{m+1}^j$, and system master key, K^j, at the time t_j, $1 \le j \le T$, is obtained from U^j as follows :

$$K^j = \prod_{i=2}^{m+2} abs(u_i^j)$$

where $abs(x)$ means the absolute value of x. The master key, K^j, is kept secret, but the first element, u_1^j, of the vector U^j is made public (system security is not affected by revealing this element). u_1^j will be used for normalizing purposes, as described later as part of the master key computation and it cannot to be zero.

Step 3 : The n "shadows" S_i, $i=1, 2, ..., n$, and the public shadow, P^j, are constructed by randomly selecting an $(n+1)*(m+1)$ matrix A^j and then executing the following operation :

$$
\begin{bmatrix} S_1 \\ S_2 \\ \cdot \\ \cdot \\ \cdot \\ S_n \\ P^j \end{bmatrix} = \begin{bmatrix} a_{11}, & a_{12}, & \ldots, & a_{1m}, & 0 \\ a_{21}, & a_{22}, & \ldots, & a_{2m}, & 0 \\ \cdot & \cdot & \ldots & \cdot & \cdot \\ \cdot & \cdot & \ldots & \cdot & \cdot \\ \cdot & \cdot & \ldots & \cdot & \cdot \\ a_{n1}, & a_{n2}, & \ldots, & a_{nm}, & 0 \\ b_1^j, & b_2^j, & \ldots, & b_m^j, & b_{m+1}^j \end{bmatrix} \begin{bmatrix} v_1 \\ v_2 \\ \cdot \\ \cdot \\ \cdot \\ v_m \\ v_{m+1}^j \end{bmatrix} \tag{3}
$$

where in matrix A^j, any m row vectors (excluding the (m+1)-th column) need to be a full rank square matrix and $b_{m+1}^j \neq 0$.

The key center then secretly distributes these n secret shadows S_i, $1 \leq i \leq n$, one to each trustee publishes the public shadow, P^j.

Master key recomputation:

Knowledge of any m "shadows" W_i, $i=1, 2, \ldots, m$, from S_1, S_2, $\ldots$, S_n, and the public shadow, P^j uniquely determines the master key K^j as follows :
First, evaluate

$$
W_1 \ X \ W_2 \ X \ \ldots \ X \ W_m \ X \ P^j = (w_1^j, \ w_2^j, \ \ldots, \ w_{m+2}^j), \tag{4}
$$

where $W_k \in \{S_i, \ i=1, 2, \ldots, n\}$, $k=1, 2, \ldots, m$.

Then the system master key can be calculated as

$$
K^j = \prod_{i=2}^{m+2} [abs(w_i^j/h^j)], \ \text{with} \ h^j = w_1^j/u_1^j. \tag{5}
$$

From Eq.(3), it can be seen that the n secret shadows, S_i, $1 \leq i \leq n$, can be used for computing different master keys, K^j, $j=1, 2, \ldots, T$.

Example : Let t=2, n=5.

The key generation center randomly selects $V_1=(1, 2, 3, 4)$, $V_2=(5, 6, 7, 8)$ and $V_3^1=(2, 2, 1, 1)$ and evaluates $U^1=V_1 X V_2 X V_3^1=(-4, -4, 4, 4)$. The system master key at t=1 is calculated as $K^1=4*4*4=64$. The first element of the row +vector U^1, which is -4, is made public. Next, the key generation center randomly selects a 6*3 matrix A^1, as for example

$$A^1 = \begin{bmatrix} 1, & 2, & 0 \\ -1, & 1, & 0 \\ 4, & 5, & 0 \\ 2, & 3, & 0 \\ 2, & -3, & 0 \\ 4, & 1, & -2 \end{bmatrix}$$

Then the n shadows and the public shadow P^1 are generated as

$$S_1 = (11, 14, 17, 20),$$
$$S_2 = (4, 4, 4, 4),$$
$$S_3 = (29, 38, 47, 56),$$
$$S_4 = (17, 22, 27, 32),$$
$$K_5 = (-13, -14, -15, -16),$$

and $P^1 = (5, 10, 17, 22).$

Knowing any two "shadows" and the public shadow, P^1, one can reconstruct the master key K^1. For example, $S_1 \times S_5 \times P^1 = (24, 24, -24, -24)$, and $h^1 = 24/(-4) = -6$. Thus $K^1 = (24/6) * (24/6) * (24/6) = 64$.

If the master key needs to be updated at t=2, then the key center randomly selects $V_3^2 = (1, 2, 1, -1)$, b_1^2, b_2^2, and $b_3^2 = (-2, 1,1)$ (as shown in Eq.(3)). It evaluates $U^2 = V_1 \times V_2 \times V_3^2 = (4, 16, 20, 8)$ and $P^2 = (4, 4, 2, -1)$. The new master key is calculated as $K^2 = 16*20*8 = 2560$. Next, the system publishes the first element of the new row vector U^2, which is 4, and the new public shadow P^2. Then knowing any two shadows and P^2 can reconstruct K^2. For example, $S_4 \times S_5 \times P^2 = (-48, 192, -240, -96)$, and $h^2 = 48/4 = 12$. Thus $K^2 = (192/12)*(240/12)*(96/12) = 2560$.

IV SECURITY ANALYSIS AND DISCUSSIONS

The dynamic threshold scheme proposed in the section III is satisfied the requirements of relative dynamic threshold schemes. We will discuss this scheme as follows:

(1) At the beginning time, $t_j = 1$, the scheme provides Shannon perfect security.

It is obvious that the master key K^1, is concealed in the vector U^1, which is perpendicular to the original vectors V^1, V^2, ..., V^m and the time dependent vector V^1_{m+1}. Hence U^1 can be evaluated by at least m+1 independent vectors which are linearly combined by the vectors V_1, V_2, ..., V^1_{m+1}. If only r shadows, r<m, and the public shadow, P^1, are known (as shown in Eq.(3)) then the combination of those r shadows and the public shadow, P^1, cannot evaluate U^1 since they cannot construct m+1 independent vectors which are linearly combined by the vectors V_1, V_2, ..., V_m and V_{m+1}. On the other hand, if only r shadows, r<m, are known, then the cross-product of these r shadows with the public shadow, P^1, is meaningless (i.e., these cannot form m+2 square submatrices as required in the definition). Therefore, the scheme provide Shannon perfect security at the beginning time, $t_j=1$.

(2) If the previous v-1 master keys, K^j, j=1, 2, ...,v-1, are kept secret, then this scheme also provide Shannon perfect security.

Without loss of generality, we assume that m-1 trustees want to use their shadows, W_j, $1 \leq j \leq m-1$, to derive the new master key, K^v, with some of the public shadows, p^1 and p^k. Then these m-1 trustees can compute $W_1 X W_2 X ... X W_{m-1} X P^1 X P^k$ which is a cross-product of vectors within the vectors space spanned by V_1, V_2, concealed by the vector $U^j = V_1 X V_2 X ... X V_m X V^v_{m+1}$, which is a cross-product of vectors within the vector space spanned by V_1, V_2, ..., V_m, and V^v_{m+1} only. Therefore, even v=i or k, the cardinality of $W_1 X W_2 X ... X W_{m-1} X P^1 X P^k$ is larger than the cardinally of the new master key, K^v by at least one. It implies that the scheme provide Shannon perfect security, if all the previous master keys are kept secret.

(3) Knowing any v previous secrets K^j, j=1, 2, ..., V, the scheme provide Shannon relative security. It implies that knowing any v previous master keys, the threshold value is decreased, from m to m-v.

At first, we assume that the previous master key, K^1, is known. If we know m-1 shadows, W^j, j=1, 2, ..., m-1, we can construct the following cross-product form

$$U^1 = W_1 X W_2 X \ldots X W_{M-1} X P^1 X Y = (u_1^1, u_2^1, \ldots, u_{m+2}^1) =$$

$$\left(
\begin{vmatrix}
w_2^1, & w_3^1, & \ldots, & w_{m+2}^1 \\
w_2^2, & w_3^2, & \ldots, & w_{m+2}^2 \\
\cdots & \cdots & \cdots & \cdots \\
w_2^{m-1}, & w_3^{m-1}, & \ldots, & w_{m+2}^{m-1} \\
p_2^1, & p_3^1, & \ldots, & p_{m+2}^1 \\
y_2, & y_3, & \ldots, & y_{m+2}
\end{vmatrix}
\begin{vmatrix}
w_1^1, & w_3^1, & \ldots, & w_{m+2}^1 \\
w_1^2, & w_3^2, & \ldots, & w_{m+2}^2 \\
\cdots & \cdots & \cdots & \cdots \\
w_1^{m-1}, & w_3^{m-1}, & \ldots, & w_{m+2}^{m-1} \\
p_1^1, & p_3^1, & \ldots, & p_{m+2}^1 \\
y_1, & y_3, & \ldots, & y_{m+2}
\end{vmatrix}
\cdots
\begin{vmatrix}
w_1^1, & w_2^1, & \ldots, & w_{m+1}^1 \\
w_1^2, & w_2^2, & \ldots, & w_{m+1}^2 \\
\cdots & \cdots & \cdots & \cdots \\
w_1^{m-1}, & w_2^{m-1}, & \ldots, & w_{m+1}^{m-1} \\
p_1^1, & p_2^1, & \ldots, & p_{m+1}^1 \\
y_1, & y_2, & \ldots, & y_{m+1}
\end{vmatrix}
\right)$$

$$(6)$$

where $Y=(y_1, y_2, \ldots, y_{m+2})$ is an unknown shadow. Eq.(6) can be reformulated to the following $(m+2)$ linear equations:

$$0 + b_{12}y_2 + b_{13}y_3 + \cdots + b_{1,m+2}y_{m+2} = u_1^1$$

$$b_{21}y_1 + 0 + b_{23}y_3 + \cdots + b_{2,m+2}y_{m+2} = u_2^1$$

$$\cdots \qquad \cdot$$
$$\cdots \qquad \cdot$$
$$\cdots \qquad \cdot$$

$$b_{m+2,1}y_1 + b_{m+2,2}y_2 + \cdots + b_{m+1,m+2}y_{m+1} + 0 = u_{m+2}^1 \qquad (7)$$

Since U_1^1 is public and $K^1 = \prod\limits_{j=2}^{m+2} abs(u_j^1)$ is known, it is possible to evaluate u_j^1, for $j=2, 3, \ldots, m+2$. Thus one secret shadow Y can be derived from Eq.(7). Once the secret shadow Y was derived, then knowing other $m-1$ shadows and the following public shadow, p^i, $i \geq 2$, can evaluate any following master key, K^i, $i \geq 2$. The same ideas can be extended to more general cases. In general, knowing any v previous master keys, the threshold value of this dynamic threshold scheme is decreased, from m to $m-v$. If v previous master keys are known, then the level of uncertainly is decreased to zero. It is why the assumption

$$1 \leq T < m \leq n$$

is implicit in the linear dynamic threshold scheme.

V CONCLUSION

In this paper, the model of a time-dependent threshold/ramp scheme is proposed. We call the time-dependent threshold/ramp scheme a "dynamic threshold/ramp scheme", as compared to the conventional threshold/ramp scheme. If the previous master keys are not known by all trustees, the dynamic threshold/ramp scheme is similar to the conventional threshold/ramp scheme at any time $t=t_j$. However, the dynamic threshold/ramp scheme has the major

advantage, that is, whenever the master key, K^j, needs to change

to k^{j+1} for some security reasons, the system needs to change

only the public shadow, p^j, to p^{j+1}. All the n trustees do not need to be notified since all the n secret shadows issued initially do not need to be changed.

We have defined the characterizations of the ideal and relative threshold/ramp scheme. The unique difference between ideal and relative threshold/ramp schemes is that the ideal scheme can provide Shannon <u>perfect</u> security at any time regardless how many previous master keys and public shadows are known. However, the relative scheme just can provide Shannon <u>relative</u> security when some of the previous master keys are known. As shown in the section IV, knowing any v previous master keys, the threshold value of the dynamic threshold/ramp scheme is decreased from m to m-v. Notice that, the conventional threshold/ramp scheme is useless in this assumption, i.e., if the master key can be known by any m trustees when they get together at time t, then anyone of these m trustees do not need to cooperate with other m-1 trustees after the time t.

Since almost all proposed threshold schemes are linear, it seems very difficult to propose an ideal dynamic threshold scheme. Instead, we propose a (1, m, n, T) dynamic threshold scheme based on the definition of cross-product in an N-dimensional dimensional space which satisfies the characterizations of the relative dynamic threshold scheme. The ideal dynamic threshold schemes may or may not exit, we encourage readers to further study and investigate the applications about this field.

REFERENCES

[1] D.E.R. Denning, Cryptography and Data Security, (Addison-Wesley Reading Mass., 1982.

[2] G.R. Blakley, Safeguarding crytographic keys, Proc. NCC, Vol.48, AFIPS Press, Montvale, N.J., 1979, pp. 313-317.

[3] A. Shamir, How to share a secret, Comm. ACM, vol.22, no.11, 1979, pp.612-613.

[4] G.I. Davida, R.A. Demillo and R.J. Liption, "Protecting shared cryptographic keys," Proc. Symp. on security and privacy, IEEE computer society, 1980, pp.100-102.

[5] D.E. Denning and F.B. Schneider, "Master keys for group sharing, " Information Processing Letters, vol.12, no.1, pp.23-25, 1981.

[6] E.D. Karnin, J.W. Greene and M.E. Hellman, "On secret sharing systems, " IEEE Trans. on Inform. Theory, vol.IT-29, no.2, pp.208-210, 9183.

[7] C. Asmuth and J. Bloom, "A modular approach to key safe-guarding," IEEE Trans. on Inform. Theory, vol.IT-29, no2, pp.208-210, 1983.

[8] S.C Kothari, Generalized linear threshold scheme, Proc. of crypto 84, Springer-Verlag, 9185, pp.231-241.

[9] G.R. Blakley and C. Meddows, "Security of Ramp Schemes," Advances in Cryptology: Proceeding of CRYPTO'84, Springer-Verlag.

[10] D.H. Wiedemann, "Solving sparse linear equations over finite fields," IEEE Trans. Information Theory, vol.IT-32, pp.54-62, 1986.

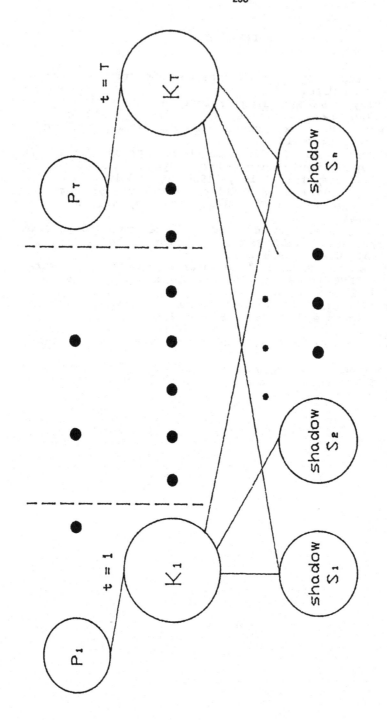

Fig.(1) The model of dynamic threshold/ramp scheme

Secret Sharing Over Infinite Domains*
(extended abstract)

Benny Chor[†]
Eyal Kushilevitz[‡]

Department of Computer Science
Technion, Haifa 32000, Israel

Abstract: A (k, n) secret sharing scheme is a probabilistic mapping of a secret to n shares, such that

- The secret can be reconstructed from any k shares.

- No subset of $k - 1$ shares reveals any partial information about the secret.

Various secret sharing schemes have been proposed, and applications in diverse contexts were found. In all these cases, the set of secrets and the set of shares are finite.

In this paper we study the possibility of secret sharing schemes over *infinite* domains. The major case of interest is when the secrets and the shares are taken from a *countable* set, for example all binary strings. We show that no (k, n) secret sharing scheme over any countable domain exists (for any $2 \leq k \leq n$).

One consequence of this impossibility result is that no *perfect private-key encryption schemes*, over the set of all strings, exist. Stated informally, this means that there is no way to perfectly encrypt all strings without revealing information about their length.

We contrast these results with the case where both the secrets and the shares are real numbers. Simple secret sharing schemes (and perfect private-key encryption schemes) are presented. Thus, infinity alone does not rule out the possibility of secret sharing.

*Supported by Technion V.P.R. fund 120-722 – New York Metropolitan research fund.
[†]benny@techsel.bitnet
[‡]eyalk@techunix.bitnet

1. INTRODUCTION

Let A be an arbitrary set of possible secrets. A *(k,n)-secret-sharing scheme* is a probabilistic mapping $\Pi : A \to B_1 \times B_2 \times \cdots \times B_n$ from the set of secrets to a set of n-tuples (the shares) such that:

1) The secret a can be reconstructed from any k shares. That is, for any subset $T \subseteq \{1,2,...,n\}$ of size $|T| = k$, there exists a function $h_T : B_{i_1} \times \cdots \times B_{i_k} \to A$ such that $h_T(\{s_i\}_{i \in T}) = a$.

2) No subset of less than k shares reveals any partial information about the secret (in the information theoretic sense). Formally, for any subset $T \subseteq \{1,2,...,n\}$ of size $|T| \leq k-1$, for every two secrets $a_1, a_2 \in A$ and for every possible shares $\{s_i\}_{i \in T}$:

$$Pr(\{s_i\}_{i \in T} \mid a_1) = Pr(\{s_i\}_{i \in T} \mid a_2)$$

We remark here that this definition is valid even if no specific probability distribution is associated with the secrets.

Secret-sharing schemes were first introduced by Blakley [Bl] and Shamir [Sh]. Since then, other constructions were given (see [Ko]), the characteristics of these schemes were studied [Bh,SV], and various applications were found (e.g. [Ra , GMW , BGW]).

In all the abovementioned works, the set of secrets and the set of shares are finite. In this paper, we investigate the possibility of secret sharing over infinite domains. The main motivation for studying the question comes from infinite domains where every member has a finite description (over a finite alphabet). Typical examples are the set of all integers and the set of all binary strings. Can we share any secret string using only strings as shares? More generally, can we share a secret from any infinite set, using only elements of this set as shares? It turns out that the possibility (or impossibility) of secret-sharing schemes is not based on infinity alone. One has to examine the cardinality of the domain. In particular we show

1) If the sets of secrets and shares are *countable* (that is, of the same cardinality as the integers) then no (k,n) secret-sharing schemes exist for any $2 \leq k \leq n$.

2) If the sets of secrets and shares has cardinality $\aleph$ (the cardinality of the reals), then (k,n) secret-sharing schemes exist for any $1 \leq k \leq n$.

A *perfect private-key encryption scheme* [Shannon] is an encryption scheme where an eavesdropper gets no partial information about the plaintext by examining the ciphertext. Again, the notions used are not complexity-based but rather information theoretic. The classical example of perfect private-key encryption scheme is Vernam "one time pad". This scheme is perfect provided all messages are of equal length. Otherwise one could distinguish between ciphertexts encrypting different length plaintexts merely by observing the length of the ciphertext. A simple counting argument would show that it is not possible to have a perfect private-key encryption scheme over all strings and still bound the length of all possible ciphertexts of any individual string. Here, we show that even if one removes this restriction, perfect private-key encryption over a countable domain is not possible. This holds even for schemes where a key is used just once, to encrypt a single plaintext. Interestingly, the proof is by a reduction to the problem of secret-sharing. Again, we complement this result by giving a perfect private-key encryption scheme over the reals.

The remaining of this paper is organized as follows: In section 2 we discuss secret-sharing schemes over countable domains. Section 3 deals with perfect private-key encryption schemes over countable domains. Finally, in section 4 we treat the real case.

Note added in proof: The same results have appeared in works of Blakley and Swanson [BS1,BS2]. The main difference between these works and ours is in the proof methods.

2. SECRET SHARING OVER COUNTABLE SETS

In this section we deal with secret-sharing schemes in which both the secrets and the shares are taken from countable sets. We prove that such schemes do not exist.

Clearly, if the set of secrets is infinite then the set of shares must be infinite too. Otherwise, if there are only m possible shares, they can encode at most m^n secrets. Therefore if we are interested in countable sets of secrets (such as the set of all integers or the set of all strings) then the set of shares must be at least countable too. It is also easy to see that no secret-sharing scheme can map every n bit long secret s into shares of length less or equal $f(n)$, for any function $f(n)$ (This observation is used, in a different context, in [AFK, Theorem 4.2]). However, in this section we show that a countable set of shares is not enough even if there is no bound on the length of possible shares.

Lemma 1: Let $2 \le k \le n$. If there exists a (k,n) secret-sharing scheme then there exists a (k,k) secret-sharing scheme.

Proof: The (k,k) scheme will work by generating the n shares as in the (k,n) scheme and then distributing only k of them. The k shares enable the reconstruction of the secret since they enable it in the original scheme. On the other hand any $k-1$ shares do not reveal any information about the secret since they do not reveal such information in the original scheme. Therefore the new scheme is a (k,k) secret-sharing scheme. $\square$

Lemma 2: Let $2 \le k$. If there exists a (k,k) secret-sharing scheme then there exists a $(2,2)$ secret-sharing scheme.

Proof: The $(2,2)$ scheme will work by generating the k shares as in the (k,k) scheme. $k-1$ of the shares will be the first share in the new scheme and the last share will be the second share in the new scheme. The two new shares determine what is the secret since they carry the same information as the k shares have in the original (k,k) scheme. On the other hand each of the two new shares do not reveal any information about the secret since any set of less than k shares does not reveal any information in the original scheme. Therefore the new scheme is a (2,2) secret-sharing scheme $\square$

Theorem 1: Let A be a countable set. For every $2 \leq k \leq n$ there is no secret-sharing scheme distributing secrets taken from A using shares taken from a countable set.

Proof: Using the two lemmas above it is enough to show that a (2,2) secret-sharing scheme does not exist in order to prove that for every $2 \leq k \leq n$ a (k,n) secret-sharing scheme does not exist. Denote by h the function which reconstruct the secret from the two shares $(h : B_1 \times B_2 \to A)$. Recall that a (2,2) secret sharing-scheme on the set A is a probability distribution Π which defines for every secret a and every pair of "shares" (s_1, s_2), the probability $Pr((s_1, s_2) \mid a)$ in a way that:

1) If $h(s_1, s_2) \neq a$ then $Pr((s_1, s_2) \mid a) = 0$.

2) Any two secrets a_1 and a_2, and any share $s_2 \in B_2$ satisfy

$$Pr(s_2 \mid a_1) = \sum_{s_1 \in B_1} Pr((s_1, s_2) \mid a_1) = \sum_{s_1 \in B_1} Pr((s_1, s_2) \mid a_2) = Pr(s_2 \mid a_2)$$

3) Any two secrets a_1 and a_2, and any share $s_1 \in B_1$ satisfy

$$Pr(s_1 \mid a_1) = \sum_{s_2 \in B_2} Pr((s_1, s_2) \mid a_1) = \sum_{s_2 \in B_2} Pr((s_1, s_2) \mid a_2) = Pr(s_1 \mid a_2)$$

Let $a_0 \in A$ be an arbitrary secret. Since B_1 and B_2 are countable (and so is $B_1 \times B_2$) there must be a pair of shares (s_1', s_2') such that $Pr((s_1', s_2') \mid a_0) > 0$ (otherwise the secret a_0 could not be shared). Let $\varepsilon > 0$ denote $Pr(s_1' \mid a_0)$. From (3), for every $a \in A$ we have $Pr(s_1' \mid a) = \varepsilon$. Given any secret $a \in A$, we define

$$B_2^a = \{ s_2 \mid h(s_1', s_2) = a \}.$$

Then

$$\sum_{s_2 \in B_2^a} Pr(s_2 \mid a) = \sum_{s_2 \in B_2^a} \sum_{s_1 \in B_1} Pr((s_1, s_2) \mid a)$$

$$\geq \sum_{s_2 \in B_2^a} Pr((s_1', s_2) \mid a)$$

$$= Pr(s_1' \mid a) \qquad\qquad \text{by } B_2^a \text{ definition}$$

$$= \varepsilon.$$

That is

$$\sum_{s_2 \in B_2^a} Pr(s_2 \mid a) \geq \varepsilon \qquad\qquad (*)$$

Also note that by B_2^a definition the sets $B_2^{a_1}$ and $B_2^{a_2}$ are disjoint for any two secrets

$a_1 \neq a_2$, and furthermore

$$\bigcup_{a \in A} B_2^a = B_2. \qquad (**)$$

Thus

$$1 = \sum_{s_2 \in B_2} Pr(s_2 | a_0)$$

$$= \sum_{a \in A} \sum_{s_2 \in B_2^a} Pr(s_2 | a_0) \qquad \text{by } (**)$$

$$= \sum_{a \in A} \sum_{s_2 \in B_2^a} Pr(s_2 | a) \qquad \text{by } (2)$$

$$\geq \sum_{a \in A} \varepsilon \qquad \text{by } (*)$$

$$= \infty \qquad \text{since } A \text{ is infinite}$$

Contradiction. □

The intuition behind the proof is that over the Cartesian product of two countable domains, it is not possible to assign any probability distribution where countable number of points get non-zero mass and the projection on any single coordinate is uniform.

3. PERFECT ENCRYPTION OVER COUNTABLE SETS

In this section we deal with perfect private-key encryption schemes. We show that there is no such scheme which encrypts an arbitrary string using a string. We start with the formal definitions:

A *private-key encryption scheme* consists of three parts:

1) A way of choosing keys from a set K. This way is expressed by a probability distribution Π over the set K.

2) A private-key encryption function E that takes a plaintext p and a key k and produces a ciphertext c (that is $E(p,k)=c$).

3) A decryption function D that takes a ciphertext c and a key k and produces the original plaintext p (that is $D(E(p,k),k)=p$).

An encryption scheme is called *perfect* if it also satisfies:

4) For every two possible plaintexts p_1 and p_2 and every ciphertext c, an eavesdropper does not learn from the ciphertext any information which of the two is the plaintext which was sent. Formally:

$$Pr(c | p_1) = Pr(c | p_2)$$

We stress again that this definition is valid even if no probability distribution on plaintexts is assumed. In case that such probability distribution exists, then (4) is equivalent to Shannon's definition [Shannon] stating that every plaintext p and every ciphertext c satisfy $Pr(p \mid c) = Pr(p)$. That is, the a-priori probability of the plaintext equals the a-posteriori probability of the plaintext after seeing the ciphertext.

The most famous perfect private-key encryption scheme is the "one time pad" system which enables a user A to send any plaintext (of the same length as the key) to a user B in a way that an eavesdropper cannot get any information about the plaintext. The claim of our theorem is that such a scheme does not exist for encrypting arbitrary strings. We emphasize that this is true even though ciphertexts corresponding to a single plaintext can have unbounded length.

Theorem 2: Let K, P, C be countable sets of possible keys, plaintexts and ciphertexts (respectively). Then there is no perfect private-key encryption scheme encrypting plaintext taken from P using keys from K and ciphertext from C.

Proof: The idea is to show that if a perfect encryption scheme exists then a (2,2) secret-sharing scheme over countable sets of secrets and shares exists. This is done by observing that a perfect private-key encryption scheme is a special case of a (2,2) secret-sharing scheme, in which one of the shares (the key) is chosen before the secret is known.

We assume the existence of perfect encryption scheme and we construct the following (2,2) secret-sharing scheme for distributing a secret p taken from the countable set P: The share of the first participant, P_1, will be a $k \in K$ chosen according to the probability distribution Π, and the share of the second participant, P_2, will be $c = E(p, k)$. Clearly P_1 and P_2 together can reconstruct p, since $D(c, k) = p$. P_1 does not learn anything about p since k is chosen independently from p. P_2 does not learn anything about p since according to condition (4) of perfect encryption schemes $Pr(c \mid p_1) = Pr(c \mid p_2)$. $\square$

4. SECRET SHARING OVER THE REALS

In this section we deal with secret-sharing schemes over the real numbers. Although it has no practical implications, it is interesting to ask the question whether secret-sharing schemes do not exist over every infinite set, or maybe some properties of countable sets are the cause of the results of section 2.

We introduce a simple secret-sharing scheme using real numbers. Since there is a 1–1 and onto transformation from the real numbers to the unit interval [0,1), it is more convenient to use this interval as the set of secrets. We use the same interval as the set of shares, as it allows us to use the uniform probability distribution.

We first have to define what we mean by a secret-sharing scheme over the reals. More specifically, we have to define what we mean by saying that no set of at most $k-1$ shares reveals any information about the secret. The following natural definition is used:

For every two secrets $a_1, a_2 \in A$, for any set of indices T of size $|T| \leq k$ and for any k-tuple of measurable sets $\{C_i\}_{i \in T} \subseteq [0,1)$ the following holds:

$$Pr(\forall i \in T : s_i \in C_i \mid a_1) = Pr(\forall i \in T : s_i \in C_i \mid a_2)$$

We can now present a secret-sharing scheme for every $2 \leq k \leq n$, using ideas that were used in the finite case [Bh,BL]. We first introduce a (k,k) secret-sharing scheme which distributes a secret a taken from the interval $[0,1)$. We use the Lebesgue measure on $[0,1)$.

1) Choose independently, with a uniform distribution, $k-1$ real numbers, $s_1, \cdots, s_{k-1}$ in the interval $[0,1)$.

2) Choose $s_k \in [0,1)$ which satisfies $s_1 + \cdots + s_{k-1} + s_k = a \; (mod \; 1)$.

The proof that this is indeed a secret-sharing scheme is similar to the proof of its analogue in the finite case.

For introducing a (k,n) secret-sharing scheme for every $k \leq n$, we observe that the same technique described in [BL] works here as well.

Corollary: There is a (k,n) secret-sharing scheme for distributing secrets taken from a countable set usings shares which are real numbers.

We can arbitrarily embed the countable set of secrets in the interval $[0,1)$, and distribute the result according to the above scheme. It is easy to see that the result is a secret-sharing scheme. Similarly, it is possible to construct perfect private-key encryption schemes with keys uniformly distributed in $[0,1)$.

The difference between the case of countable sets and the case of the real numbers stems from different properties of the cardinalities $\aleph_0$ and $\aleph$. Our results were generalized to other infinite cardinalities by Shai Ben-David [Be].

ACKNOWLEDGEMENTS

We would like to thank Shai Ben-David, Oded Goldreich and Hugo Krawczyk for helpful discussions on the topics of this paper.

REFERENCES

[AFK]   Abadi, M., J. Feigenbaum, and J. Kilian, "On Hiding Information from an Oracle", *JCSS*, Vol. 39, No. 1, pp. 21-50, 1989.

[Be]   Ben-David, S., Private Communication.

[BGW]   Ben-or M., S. Goldwasser, and A. Wigderson, "Completeness Theorems for Non-Cryptographic Fault-Tolerant Distributed Computation" *Proc. of 20th STOC*, pp. 1-10, 1988.

[Bh]   Benaloh, (Cohen), J.D., "Secret Sharing Homomorphisms: Keeping Shares of a Secret Secret", *Advances in Cryptography - Crypto86 (proceedings)*, A.M. Odlyzko (ed.), Springer-Verlag, Lecture Notes in Computer Science, Vol. 263, pp. 251-260, 1987.

[BL]   Benaloh, J., and J. Leichter, "Generalized Secret Sharing and Monotone Functions", *Advances in Cryptography - Crypto86 (proceedings)*, A.M. Odlyzko (ed.), Springer-Verlag, Lecture Notes in Computer Science, Vol. 263, pp. 213-222, 1987.

[Bl]   Blakley, G.R., "Safeguarding Cryptographic Keys", *Proc. NCC AFIPS 1979*, pp. 313-317, 1979.

[BS1]   Blakley, G.R., and L. Swanson, "Security Proof for Information Protection Systems", *Proc. IEEE Symposium on Security and Privacy*, 1981, pp. 75-88.

[BS2]   Blakley, G.R., and L. Swanson, "Infinite Structures in Information Theory", *Proc. Crypto82*, pp. 39-50.

[GMW]   Goldreich, O., S. Micali, and A. Wigderson, "How to Play Any Mental Game", *Proc. of 19th STOC*, pp. 218-229, 1987.

[Ko]   Kothari, S. C., "Generalized Linear Threshold Scheme", *Advances in Cryptography - Crypto84 (proceedings)*, G.R. Blakely and D. Chaum (ed.), Springer-Verlag, Lecture Notes in Computer Science, Vol. 196, pp. 231-241, 1985.

[Ra]   Rabin M.O., "Randomized Byzantine Generals " *Proc. of 24th FOCS*, pp. 403-409, 1983.

[Sh]   Shamir, A., "How to Share a Secret", *Comm. ACM* , Vol. 22, 1979, pp. 612-613.

[Shannon]   Shannon, C.E., "Communication Theory of Secrecy Systems", *Bell System Technical Jour.*, Vol. 28, 1949, pp. 657-715.

[SV]   Stinson, D. R., and S. A. Vanstone, "A Combinatorial Approach to Threshold Schemes", *SIAM Jour. on Disc. Math.*, Vol. 1, 1988, pp. 230-236.

Threshold cryptosystems

Yvo Desmedt　　　*Yair Frankel*

EE & CS Department
University of Wisconsin-Milwaukee
Milwaukee, WI 53201

Abstract. *In a society oriented cryptography it is better to have a public key for the company (organization) than having one for each individual employee [Des88]. Certainly in emergency situations, power is shared in many organizations. Solutions to this problem were presented [Des88], based on [GMW87], but are completely impractical and interactive. In this paper practical non-interactive public key systems are proposed which allow the reuse of the shared secret key since the key is not revealed either to insiders or to outsiders.*

1 Introduction

When a society oriented cryptosystem is used, an individual should be able to send an encrypted message to an organization without knowing the public key for every person within the receiving company. The destination organization should also be able to set up its own security policy to determine who can read the messages it receives. The cryptosystem must be designed such that the sender cannot circumvent the security policy, and the individual can send the message without knowing the policy [Des88].

Societies are organized in a multi-level structure [Sim88]. Organizations in a group oriented society must consider many issues when determining its security policy. Companies which are organized in a hierarchical structure (*e.g.*, board of directors, supervisors, executives) may require fewer individuals to read the messages if they are at a higher level. The security policy might also require that a specific number of individuals work together in order to be able to read the message.

Certainly when public key systems are used, it is not appropriate to use threshold schemes to determine the key. Otherwise all the individuals who work together can determine the key, or the one who receives all shares (shadows) may keep the key. This would be terrible in a public key system since modifying a public key is more difficult than modifying a secret key in a conventional system.

We propose a method in which every organization has a *single* public key. However for anyone within the company to read the message, they must get "enough" people with the appropriate number of shadows to calculate the message. Some of the earlier solutions [Des88,GMW87] to this problem require an impractical ping-pong protocol. A solution using clerks is discussed in [Fra89]. This method modifies the decryption process of RSA by requiring each of the multiple clerks to do a partial calculation. The use of clerks, however, is not very robust. In our solution, which is practical and non-interactive (see Figure 1 and 2), the receiving company will allow all of its employees to view the ciphertext. Each shareholder will calculate their "partial result" separately and transmit the result to a designated individual. The designated individual will be able to decrypt the message using these partial results.

2 Background

To obtain the above we will adapt the ElGamal [ElG85] public key cryptosystem to meet our needs. This cryptosystem's security is based on the discrete log problem. (For an overview of the security of discrete logarithm, see [BvOV88,IBV85,Odl84]). It will be proven that even $t-1$ shadows are not sufficient for the calculation of the plaintext; and the system will also give no information on what the key is until t individuals act in collusion, both under the assumption that the ElGamal system is secure.

2.1 THRESHOLD SCHEMES

A (t,n) threshold scheme [Bla79,Sha79] does not reveal a secret S unless any t out of n participants, or *shadowholders*, work together. Each participant i will have a unique shadow K_i which he/she must keep secret. When any $t-1$ shadowholders work together, they can *not* receive any information about the secret S. In this way, a secret can be shared by many people. If a share is burned in a fire or someone forgets his/her shadow, there should be enough shareholders to recover the secret. In our system, a *modified shadow* is a result after making certain computations on the shadow. These modified shadows must also be secret. Let us explain the concept of a modified shadow with an example.

A (t,n) threshold scheme (see also [Den82]) based on Lagrange interpolation was developed by Shamir [Sha79]. To implement it, a polynomial f of degree $t-1$ is chosen in a field such that $f(0)$ will equal the secret S. Each of the shadowholders i will be given a secret $K_i = f(i)$. The reconstruction of the polynomial can be done with any subset B of t shadows, $K_{\pi_B(1)}, K_{\pi_B(2)}, \ldots, K_{\pi_B(t)}$ (for a given subset B of t out of n, $\pi_B : B \rightarrow \{1, 2, \cdots, n\}$ and $|B| = t$). Hereto the following is calculated where the field corresponds to $GF(p)$:

$$f(x) = \sum_{s=1}^{t} K_{\pi_B(s)} \prod_{j=1, j \neq s}^{t} \frac{(x - x_{\pi_B(j)})}{(x_{\pi_B(s)} - x_{\pi_B(j)})} \pmod{p},$$

where the x_i are public. The *modified shadows* $a_{\pi_B(i)}$ in our scheme are computed such that $a_{\pi_B(s)} = K_{\pi_B(s)} \prod_{j=1, j \neq s}^{t} \frac{(0 - x_{\pi_B(j)})}{(x_{\pi_B(s)} - x_{\pi_B(j)})} \pmod{p}$. Giving away the modified shadows $a_{\pi_B(s)}$ to others has the same effect as giving away the shadows $K_{\pi_B(s)}$. It

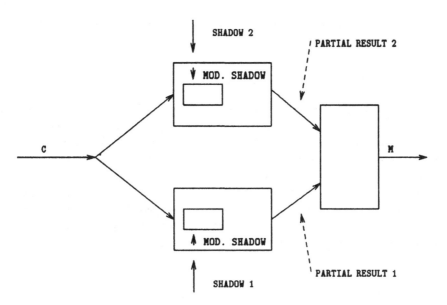

FIGURE 1. Our non-interactive solution

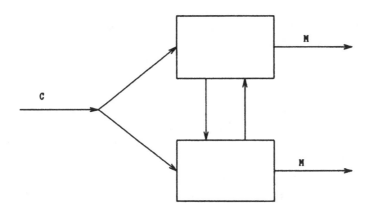

FIGURE 2. The impractical interactive solution

is imperative that each of the participant's modified shadow has the same security protection as the actual shadow.

2.2 ElGamal cryptosystem

The ElGamal cryptosystem is a public key extension of [DH76]. Its security is based on the discrete log problem. To use this cryptosystem, an element g (which should be a generator) is chosen in a finite field F_q. A trusted source will generate a random integer a within the the range $0 < a < q - 1$. Before destroying its copy of a, the trusted source will supply the company with the a as its private key and publish g^a as the public key. To transmit the message M, the sender will create a random integer k and send the tuple $C = (g^k, Mg^{ak})$. To decrypt the message, the receiver needs only raise g^k to the power a. The multiplicative inverse g^{-ak} of this result will be multiplied with the second entry of the tuple, Mg^{ak}, to get the message M.

3 Solutions

Both of the methods, which will be described to solve the problem, are implemented with the ElGamal cryptosystem. Each approach, however, will use a different threshold scheme to calculate a modified shadow for each participant. The modified shadow and the ciphertext will be used to get a *partial result* which is transmitted to a designated individual. This person will receive all the partial results and be able to calculate the message by using multiplication. In one of the approaches, any subset B of t individuals can perform the required operations.

3.1 The basic idea

Lets first modify the set-up phase in the ElGamal scheme. The one who has chosen the secret decryption key will give each shadowholder a shadow of a, where a is the secret decryption key in the ElGamal scheme. Once each shadowholder has his shadow a_i, the center can blow itself up. The encryption phase remains the same as described in 2.2. Let us now explain how decryption is performed.

Unless stated otherwise all the calculations to be performed in this section will be done in F_q. When a message is received, any subset B of t participants $\pi_B(s)$ will calculate their modified shadow $a_{\pi_B(s)}$ using threshold schemes explained in Section 3.2 and 3.3. The sum of these modified shadows will be congruent to the secret $a \mod \phi(q)$ (a as in Section 2.1). Each $\pi_B(s)$ will then raise g^k by $-a_{\pi_B(s)}$ to get $g'_{\pi_B(s)}$ as their *partial result.* These partial results will be transmitted to the designated individual. To get M, the designated individual needs to multiply each of the $g'_{\pi_B(s)}$ together. This result g^{-ak} is multiplied with the second entry of the ciphertext (Mg^{ak}) to get the message M. An example using a $(3, n)$ threshold is given below. Let $\pi_B(1) = 1$, $\pi_B(2) = 2$, and $\pi_B(3) = 3$ such that $a_1 + a_2 + a_3 = a \mod \phi(n)$. Each of the participants will transmit their $g'_{\pi_B(s)}$ to a designated individual. That individual will perform the following calculation:

$$
\begin{aligned}
Mg^{ak} \prod_{i=1}^{3} g'_{\pi B(i)} &= Mg^{ak}g^{k(-a_1-a_2-a_3)} \\
&= Mg^{ak}g^{-ak} \\
&= M.
\end{aligned}
$$

To make this algorithm truly non-interactive, have each individual send $(g^{kK_{\pi_B(i)}}, \pi_B(i))$ to the designated individual. That individual can now exponentiate the first tuple by $\prod_{j=1, j\neq s}^{t} \frac{(0-x_{\pi_B(j)})}{(x_{\pi_B(s)}-x_{\pi_B(j)})}$ to generate $g^{ka_{\pi_B(i)}}$.

3.2 USING LAGRANGE INTERPOLATION FOR MODIFIED SHADOW GENERATION

If q is a prime, then the calculations of the exponents is performed $\bmod \phi(q)$, which isn't a prime (except when $q = 3$ in which case we are not interested). This implies that Lagrange interpolation for calculating the modified shadows will not work. So choosing $q = 2^l$ is a solution *if* $q-1$ is a *Mersenne prime* that is large enough. We, therefore, will perform the ElGamal system in $GF(2^l)$ where "depending on the level of security that is desired, it seems that the fields $GF(2^n)$ to be used ought to have n large, no smaller than 800 and preferably at least 1500"[Odl84, p. 226]$(i.e., l = 1,279$ or 2,203). The Lagrange interpolation will be done in Z_{q-1} where $q-1$ is a prime. The modified shadows $a_{\pi_B(s)}$ will be generated by each person as described in Section 2.1.

3.3 USING A GEOMETRY BASED THRESHOLD

Another (t, n) threshold scheme which can be used in our system is based on geometry. All n individuals in the organization are given a plane $s_{i,1}x_1 + s_{i,2}x_2 + \cdots + s_{i,t}x_t = K_i$ whose slope is public. These planes are created in such a manner that the intersection of t of them is at a secret point $S = [x_1, x_2, \ldots, x_t]$. The secret $a \bmod \phi(q)$ is the sum of the intersection coordinates. Each individual in the company will have their public $1 \times t$ matrix representing slope of their plane. During initialization a trusted center will multiply each $1 \times t$ slope matrix with the $t \times 1$ matrix to obtain each secret threshold K_i. Then the center will distribute each K_i to the correct individual i before destroying itself. To use the system, a subset B of t people generate each a $t \times t$ matrix T_B by putting each of their slope matrices on top of each other. The following relation holds:

$$
\begin{vmatrix} s_{\pi_B(1),1} & \cdots & s_{\pi_B(1),t} \\ & \vdots & \\ s_{\pi_B(t),1} & \cdots & s_{\pi_B(t),t} \end{vmatrix} * \begin{vmatrix} x_1 \\ \vdots \\ x_t \end{vmatrix} = \begin{vmatrix} K_{\pi_B(1)} \\ \vdots \\ K_{\pi_B(t)} \end{vmatrix}.
$$

Once the T_B matrix has been generated, it is inverted. To calculate the intersection one needs only to compute $S = T_B^{-1}K_B$. But this cannot be done in a straight forward manner since the entries in K_B are secret. As in the case of Lagrange interpolation, it is possible to calculate a modified shadow which will be used to determine the partial result. This is done by having the participant who supplied $K_{\pi_B(i)}$ determine his modified shadow $a_{\pi_B(i)} = \sum_{r=1}^{t} K_{\pi_B(i)} s'_{\pi_B(r),\pi_B(i)} \bmod \phi(q)$ where $s'_{\pi_B(r),\pi B(i)}$ are from the T_B^{-1} matrix. For example, the person who supplied the $K_{\pi_B(2)}$ will multiply that value with each element in second column of T_B^{-1} and then add them all up to get his/her modified threshold. It is easy to see the the sum of all the modified thresholds will be congruent to a.

This method will only work if the matrix T_B is in $GL_t(R)$, thus has an inverse. The probability that a randomly chosen matrix is invertible is: $|GL_t(R)| / |M_t(R)|$. If $R = Z_p$ where p is prime, then the above ratio is $(1 - \frac{1}{p})(1 - \frac{1}{p^2}) \cdots (1 - \frac{1}{p^n})$ (See [Kob87]). When the prime is large, this probability is high enough to insure that the matrix will be invertible. This implies that if q is a prime and the n planes are chosen randomly (by the center during initialization), there is a large probability that t users are not able to invert T_B and are unable to perform their job. In some cases, when excluding some collisions is not detrimental, this method is advantageous. If special planes are used, the above can be avoided. These are easy to generate if t and n are small. If ElGamal is used in $GF(2^l)$ with $2^l - 1$ a Mersenne prime, there is no problem.

4 Enhancements

There are two enhancements given which will increase the security and practicality of this scheme.

4.1 Avoiding Galois fields

Peralta has made the following suggestion to us to avoid the use of Galois fields for executing the ElGamal cryptosystem. Since $\phi(n)$ is even, use g^2 rather then g.

In more general terms, if we drop in this text the requirement that g is a generator, then our solution presented in previous paragraphs (using Lagrange) always works when Elgamal is executed in any (finite) *group* as long as the order of g ($\mathrm{ord}(g)$) is a prime.

If ElGamal is done in a group and $\mathrm{ord}(g) = RS$ where S does not contain any factors less than n, it will always work when using g^R instead of g and when Lagrange is done mod S. This is true because $\mathrm{ord}(g^R) = S$ and the only inverses that must be calculated are those of $(x_i - x_j)$, which are between $-n$ and n since $0 < x_i, x_j \leq n$.

4.2 Anonymity

If in an organization the shadowholders are known to each other, the temptation for t of them to collude could be irresistible. As a result, they would find the secret key of the company, which will be continued to be used. To increase security, only pseudonyms of the shadowholders are known to outsiders. The shadowholders are then going to send their partial results in an untraceable way [Cha81,Cha88]. Anonymous threshold is evidently applicable in other situations. Other obvious measures can be used to increase security such as using local organized encryption (using local public key system).

5 Proof of security

To prove its security we will use the concept of zero-knowledge [GMR89]. We only need the simulatability concept and not the interactive proof part. In our system, we have the following participants: a sender, a receiver and t shadowholders. Let us take a subset, V, and call those participants not in this subset P. Given a legitimate pair (message, ciphertext), we will prove that the interaction between the participants in P and the participants in V can be simulated (to be more precise, the probability distribution of the views can be simulated). To illustrate let us take an example in which P corresponds with one of the shadowholders. Because k is known (sender of message is part of V), it is trivial to simulate the interaction between P and V.

Informally, this implies that "no" extra information is leaked about $a_{\pi_B(s)}$ than $g^{ka_{\pi_B(s)}}$. If the discrete logarithm is hard, then the calculation of the modified shadow will also be hard.

6 Failures with RSA

The implementation of the Lagrange threshold scheme was modified and another one presented, in order to allow each person to calculate, on his own, the modified shadows. Other attempts to use the same approach with RSA failed mainly because $\phi(n)$ has to remain secret.

Lagrange interpolation cannot be used since $\phi(n)$ is even and calculations mod $\phi(n)$ does not form a field. Given persons i and j it can happen that $(i - j)$ is even and therefore not invertible. There is no way of selecting the number i in order for each person to get around this difficulty. The Chinese remainder interpolation method [AB80] is not possible since $\phi(n)$ must be revealed. Other methods using projective geometry cannot be used since all t individuals must provide their shadows to a designated person who will do the required calculation. The secret, however, will be known to that person.

7 Conclusion

We have shown a practical non-interactive scheme which allows an organization to use a public key system, yet still require t out of n people work together to read the message. Our scheme uses the ElGamal cryptosystem and modified threshold schemes to solve many of the problems associated with a group oriented society.

Recently we have been able to come up with a threshold signature scheme. This is a signature system where the signature can be verified by anyone knowing the public key of the signing company. To generate a signature requires t out of n individuals and one interaction. The scheme is partially based on [GQ88].

ACKNOWLEDGMENTS

We wish to thank René Peralta for his suggestion given in Section 4.1. We thank Andrew Odlyzko for a discussion about $|GL_t(R)|/|M_t(R)|$ and Jean–Jacques Quisquater for pointing out his paper on signatures, discussed in the conclusion.

8 REFERENCES

[AB80] C. Asmuth and J. Bloom. A modular approach to key safeguarding. Technical report, Math Dept., Texas A & M Univ., College Station, Tx., 1980.

[Bla79] G. R. Blakley. Safeguarding cryptographic keys. In *Proc. Nat. Computer Conf. AFIPS Conf. Proc.*, pages 313–317, 1979. vol.48.

[BvOV88] I. F. Blake, P. C. van Oorschot, and S. Vanstone. Complexity issues for public key cryptography. In J. K. Skwirzynski, editor, *Performance Limits in Communication, Theory and Practice, NATO ASI Series E: Applied Sciences–Vol. 142*, pages 75–97. Kluwer Academic Publishers, 1988. Proceedings of the NATO Advanced Study Institute Il Ciocco, Castelvecchio Pascoli, Tuscany, Italy, July 7–19, 1986.

[Cha81] D. Chaum. Untraceable electronic mail, return addresses, and digital pseudonyms. *Commun. ACM*, 24(2):84–88, February 1981.

[Cha88] D. Chaum. The dining cryptographers problem: unconditional sender and recipient untraceability. *Journal of Cryptology*, 1(1):65–75, 1988.

[Den82] D. E. R. Denning. *Cryptography and Data Security*. Addison – Wesley, Reading, Mass., 1982.

[Des88] Y. Desmedt. Society and group oriented cryptography : a new concept. In C. Pomerance, editor, *Advances in Cryptology, Proc. of Crypto'87 (Lecture Notes in Computer Science 293)*, pages 120–127. Springer–Verlag, 1988. Santa Barbara, California, U.S.A., August 16–20.

[DH76] W. Diffie and M. E. Hellman. New directions in cryptography. *IEEE Trans. Inform. Theory*, IT–22(6):644–654, November 1976.

[ElG85] T. ElGamal. A public key cryptosystem and a signature scheme based on discrete logarithms. *IEEE Trans. Inform. Theory*, 31:469–472, 1985.

[Fra89] Y. Frankel. A practical protocol for large group oriented networks. Presented at Eurocrypt'89, Houthalen, Belgium, to appear in: Advances in Cryptology. Proc. of Eurocrypt'89 (Lecture Notes in Computer Science), Springer–Verlag, April 1989.

[GMR89] S. Goldwasser, S. Micali, and C. Rackoff. The knowledge complexity of interactive proof systems. *Siam J. Comput.*, 18(1):186–208, February 1989.

[GMW87] O. Goldreich, S. Micali, and A. Wigderson. How to play any mental game. In *Proceedings of the Nineteenth ACM Symp. Theory of Computing, STOC*, pages 218 – 229, May 25-27, 1987.

[GQ88] L. C. Guillou and J. J. Qisquater. A "pardoxical" identity–based signature scheme resulting from zero-knowledge. Presented at Crypto'88, Santa Barbara, California, U.S.A., to appear in: Advances in Cryptology. Proc. of Crypto'88 (Lecture Notes in Computer Science), Springer–Verlag, August 1988.

[IBV85] R.C.. Mullin I.F. Blake, R. Fuji-Hara and S.A. Vanstone. Computing logrithms in a finite field of characteristic two. *SIAM J. Alg. Disc. Meth.*, 5:276–285, 1985.

[Kob87] N. Koblitz. *A Course in Number Theory and Cryptology*. Springer–Verlang, 1987.

[Odl84] A. M. Odlyzko. Discrete logs in a finite field and their cryptographic significance. In N. Cot T. Beth and I. Ingemarsson, editors, *Advances in Cryptology, Proc. of Eurocrypt'84 (Lecture Notes in Computer Science 209)*, pages 224–314. Springer–Verlag, 1984. Paris, France April 1984.

[Sha79] A. Shamir. How to share a secret. *Commun. ACM*, 22:612 – 613, November 1979.

[Sim88] G. J. Simmons. How to (really) share a secret. Presented at Crypto'88, Santa Barbara, California, U.S.A., to appear in: Advances in Cryptology. Proc. of Crypto'88 (Lecture Notes in Computer Science), Springer–Verlag, August 1988.

Flexible Access Control with Master Keys

Gerald C. Chick and Stafford E. Tavares
Queen's University at Kingston

Abstract. *We show how to create a master key scheme for controlling access to a set of services. Each master key is a concise representation for a list of service keys, such that only service keys in this list can be computed easily from the master key. Our scheme is more flexible than others, permitting hierarchical organization and expansion of the set of services.*

1. Introduction

In many situations it is necessary to control access to a set of objects or services. If a distinct cryptographic key is used for each service, it becomes necessary to develop a scheme for providing the correct keys to each user at minimal expense. Previous attempts at this problem are either awkward and restrictive, or do not fully solve the problem, or end up providing an excess of information to each user. Some examples are found in [2, 5, 4, 7, 14].

Let $S_1, S_2, \ldots, S_N$ represent a set of N distinct services in a system. These services may be organized by a subordinating relation, $\leq$. If $S_i \leq S_j$ then service S_i is subordinate to S_j and access to S_j confers access to S_i. Each S_i is assigned a key SK_i. The equivalent statement $SK_i \leq SK_j$, indicates that the key of the subordinate service can be derived from that of the superior service.

A *master key* is a compact representation for a subset of the service keys. For any master key MK, $SK_i \leq MK$ for one or more SK_i. The trivial case is $MK = SK_i$. To provide a master key for each of N services, the master key space may contain up to $2^N - 1$ members. Figure 1 is a graphical example of an organized set of services and one possible master key.

In this paper we show how to develop a master key system based on modular exponentiation. A simple computation is used to derive SK_i from MK, if and only if $SK_i \leq MK$.

Our idea is an extension of the work of Akl and others in [2, 1, 9]. They describe a method of creating a rigid hierarchy so that keys lower in the hierarchy can be derived from those at higher levels. We relax the hierarchical requirements to create a system with more flexibility. Only master keys in use are defined. This takes less overhead and allows the system to be expanded to control more services.

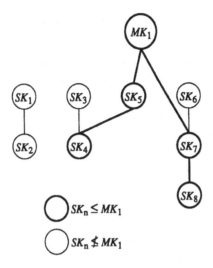

Figure 1:

This diagram represents the organization of a set of 8 services. The arcs connecting nodes show that the lower node is subordinate to the upper node. For example, $SK_2 \leq SK_1$ and $SK_8 \leq SK_6$. MK_1 is a master key, and provides access only to services S_4, S_5, S_7 and S_8.

2. Hierarchical Keying

Akl and Taylor [2] establish a a rigid hierarchy for a set of users partially ordered by the $\leq$ relation. A user U_j can compute the key of user U_i if and only if $U_i \leq U_j$. Arithmetic is performed (mod M) in the ring of integers $(0, M-1)$ defined by $M = P_1 \times P_2$, where P_1 and P_2 are large primes.

A trusted central authority (CA) is designated U_0, and chooses a random key K_0. Each user U_i is assigned a public integer t_i and a key $K_i = K_0^{t_i}$. In principle, user U_j with key K_j can compute

$$K_i = K_j^{t_i/t_j}.$$

However, this computation is feasible only if t_i/t_j is an integer, and the t_i's are assigned such that t_j divides t_i if and only if $U_i \leq U_j$. Then user U_j can generate the key for U_i by

$$K_i = K_0^{t_i} = \left(K_0^{t_j} \right)^{t_i/t_j} = K_j^{t_i/t_j} \quad \text{iff } U_i \leq U_j. \tag{1}$$

To accomplish this, each U_i is assigned a small prime p_i, and t_i is computed as

$$t_i = \prod_{U_n \nleq U_i} p_n.$$

A near-optimal assignment of primes — which produces the smallest values for the t_i's — results from careful application of the following rules [10]:

1. If $U_j \nleq U_i$ and $U_i \nleq U_j$, then $p_i \neq p_j$.
2. If $U_i \leq U_j$, $p_i = p_j$ where this does not conflict with rule 1.
3. p_i is the smallest allowable prime.

This system is too rigid. For a large number of users, the t_i's become very large. The entire system must be predefined by the CA, and there is no way to expand or modify an existing hierarchy.

3. Master Keys

Our master key system is similar to the hierarchical system, but we take a different approach. A small prime p_i is assigned to each service following the same rules, but no primes are assigned to the CA or master keys. Service keys are defined in a like manner; although the result is the same, we use a slightly different notation. Let

$$T = \prod_{n=1}^{N} p_n.$$

For each service a number u_i is computed as

$$u_i = \prod_{S_n \leq S_i} p_n$$

and the service key is defined as $SK_i = K_0^{T/u_i}$.

Defined this way, the service keys behave just like the user keys of Akl's hierarchical system. However, in the hierarchical system all users must be ordered by the $\leq$ relation, whereas here we have organized only the services. By not imposing a structure on the entire system, we are freed to create master keys as required.

We begin by computing

$$v_j = \prod_{SK_n \leq MK_j} p_n$$

where the set $\{SK_i \leq MK_j\}$ is all the keys for services accessible with master key MK_j. The master key is defined as

$$MK_j = K_0^{T/v_j}.$$

The computation of a service key from a master key is much like equation (1),

$$SK_i = (K_0)^{\frac{T}{u_i}} = \left(K_0^{T/v_j}\right)^{v_j/u_i} = (MK_j)^{v_j/u_i} \qquad \text{iff } SK_i \leq MK_j. \qquad (2)$$

We will now proceed to show that our master key system works. We will first show that the condition on equation (2) holds, for the keys as we have defined them. We will also show that it is impossible to use a group of master keys to compromise any of the service keys.

Computation of a service key is feasible if and only if $SK_i \leq MK_j$. If $SK_i \leq MK_j$, then (by definition) u_i divides v_j and $MK_j^{v_j/u_i}$ is easily computed as in (2). Let $u_i = \alpha \cdot p_i$, so that $MK_j^{v_j/u_i} = \left[(MK_j)^{v_j/p_i} \right]^{1/\alpha}$. When $SK_i \nleq MK_j$, p_i does not divide v_j, and the p_i^{th} root of MK_j must be computed. But computing r^{th} roots mod M for $r > 1$ is believed to be as difficult as factoring M [13, 6]. So when p_i does not divide v_j, $MK_j^{v_j/p_i}$ cannot be computed if the factors of the modulus are unknown.

This scheme is secure against illicit cooperation (like attacks described in [12] and [16], where a group of people may have sufficient information to do things none of them are capable of individually). A sufficient condition is that no group of master keys can be used to gain access to additional services. That is, from a group of master keys we cannot create a key MK, such that $SK_i \leq MK$, if none of the keys in the group have access to service S_i. Let $\mathbf{G}$ be a set of master keys, which are integer powers of K_0, $\left\{ MK_1 = K_0^{t_1}, MK_2 = K_0^{t_2}, \ldots, MK_k = K_0^{t_k} \right\}$. A power K_0^t can be feasibly computed from the set $\mathbf{G}$ only if

$$\gcd \left\{ t_i : MK_i \in \mathbf{G} \right\} \mid t.$$

This is proven in the appendix to [2]. Let $K_0^{t_n} = K_0^{T/v_n} = MK_n$, be a master key not in $\mathbf{G}$. Given that there exists some $SK_m \leq MK_n$, assume that MK_n can be computed from the set $\mathbf{G}$. Then

$$\gcd \left\{ t_i : MK_i \in \mathbf{G} \right\} \mid t_n.$$

Now let $SK_m \nleq MK_i \ \forall \ MK_i \in \mathbf{G}$. If we could compute SK_m from $\mathbf{G}$ we would gain access to a service not available to a key in $\mathbf{G}$. However, p_m is a common factor of all the t_i's for keys in $\mathbf{G}$, and

$$p_m \mid \gcd \left\{ t_i : MK_i \in \mathbf{G} \right\}.$$

Therefore, p_m divides t_n. But

$$SK_m \leq MK_n \Rightarrow p_m \mid v_n$$

and thus p_m does not divide t_n. This is contradictory, so the assumption that MK_n can be derived from $\mathbf{G}$ is wrong. It is not possible to use a group of master keys to gain access to a service not already available through one of the keys in the group.

4. Expansion

It is possible to add services to the system, without affecting existing keys, provided that a new addition is not subordinate to any existing service. This is a weak limitation in a system where most services are independent. Yet this constraint inhibits expansion of Akl's hierarchical scheme, since a user added to the hierarchy will often be subordinate to someone.

For any r relatively prime to M, we can calculate an inverse $1/r$ such that

$$r \times 1/r \equiv 1 \pmod{\phi(M)}.$$

When the factors of M are known, this calculation is not difficult.

We choose a new prime p_{N+1}, relatively prime to M and not previously assigned to a service, and compute $1/p_{N+1}$. Let $K_0' = (K_0)^{1/p_{N+1}}$, and $T' = T \cdot p_{N+1}$. We can then write

$$SK_i = (K_0)^{\frac{T}{u_i}} = \left(K_0^{1/p_{N+1}}\right)^{\frac{T \cdot p_{N+1}}{u_i}} = (K_0')^{\frac{T'}{u_i}}.$$

Obviously, the keys are unchanged by the substitution of T' and K_0', and the introduction of p_{N+1}.

The key for the new service is computed in the usual manner,

$$SK_{N+1} = \left(K_0'\right)^{\frac{T'}{u_{N+1}}}, \quad u_{N+1} = \prod_{S_n \leq S_{N+1}} p_n.$$

This new service key cannot be derived from any of the existing master keys. Since $u_{N+1} = \alpha \cdot p_{N+1}$ and p_{N+1} is not a factor of v_j for any of the existing keys, u_{N+1} does not divide v_j. However, new master keys can be distributed by the CA as required.

5. Implementation

A trusted third party is not unusual, and is required in some situations where systems are otherwise not secure (see [3, 11] for examples). One may complain that the central authority is a weakness of the master key system, and that if the CA is compromised the whole keying system becomes useless. This is certainly so, but precautions can be taken to ensure that the CA is difficult to attack.

The CA is responsible for selection of a secure modulus M and its factors, P_1 and P_2. If expansion will not be required, P_1 and P_2 can be discarded. Otherwise the factors of M must be kept secret. The central authority also selects K_0. All other information is non-critical and is published for use by owners of master keys.

The central authority can be protected. A single person or entity is easy to protect physically, but this has its drawbacks. The CA knows K_0 and could be coerced into using this knowledge in a compromising manner. We suggest that the CA be a committee. Critical information is shared among committee members using a threshold scheme (for example, Shamir's polynomial interpolation method [15, 8]). This provides both safety and security; loss of a member of the CA committee is not disastrous, and no single member has enough information to compromise the master key system.

6. Summary

We have described a cryptographic system for regulating access to a set of services through the creation and distribution of master keys. Our system is elegant, simple and general. There are no restrictions on the organization of services or on the master keys which can be used. Since all master keys and service keys are the same size, the master key takes less space than a list of service keys.

By computing integer exponents of a master key, one can derive keys for accessible services. Keys for inaccessible services are non-integer powers of a master key, and cannot be computed from that master key. Furthermore, it is impossible for a group of people with keys to create a master key with access privileges beyond those of the group as a whole.

The scheme can provide access to a large number of services using only a small amount of public storage and a fixed overhead per user. If required, the services can be organized into a multilevel security structure, and the system can be expanded when necessary.

The system suggests many uses, such as access to services or special interest groups (SIGs) in a distributed communication environment. If each group is assigned a separate key, master keys can be distributed for access to any particular combination of SIGs. The system is also well-suited to encryption of information in a database. Records and fields can be enciphered individually with a key determined by their classification and security level.

An obvious application of this scheme is file storage. When many people require shared access to secure data and files, it is convenient to partition the files into several classes and encrypt each class individually. A key management problem can be avoided by providing a master key to permit access to the required classes.

References

[1] S. G. Akl and P. D. Taylor, *Cryptographic solution to a multilevel security problem*, in Advances in Cryptology - Proceedings of Crypto '82, Springer-Verlag, 1983, pp. 237–249.

[2] ——, *Cryptographic solution to a problem of access control in a hierarchy*, ACM Trans. Comput. Syst., 1 (1983), pp. 239–248.

[3] B. L. Chan and H. Meijer, *A multiple trusted nodes security system*, in 13th Biennial Symposium on Communications, Kingston, Canada, 1986, Queen's University.

[4] D. E. Denning, H. Meijer, and F. B. Schneider, *More on master keys for group sharing*, Inf. Process. Lett., 13 (1981), pp. 125–126.

[5] D. E. Denning and F. B. Schneider, *Master keys for group sharing*, Inf. Process. Lett., 12 (1981), pp. 23–25.

[6] W. Diffie, *The first ten years of public key cryptography*, Proceedings of the IEEE, 76 (1988), p. 565.

[7] I. Ingemarsson, D. T. Tang, and C. K. Wong, *A conference key distribution system*, IEEE Trans. Information Theory, IT-28 (1982), pp. 714–720.

[8] E. D. Karnin, J. W. Greene, and M. E. Hellman, *On secret sharing systems*, IEEE Trans. Information Theory, IT-29 (1983), pp. 35–41.

[9] S. J. MacKinnon and S. G. Akl, *New key generation algorithms for multilevel security*, in IEEE Symposium on Security and Privacy, 1983, pp. 72–78.

[10] S. J. MacKinnon, P. D. Taylor, H. Meijer, and S. G. Akl, *An optimal algorithm for assigning cryptographic keys to control access in a hierarchy*, IEEE Trans. Comput., C-34 (1985), pp. 797–802.

[11] H. Meijer, *Cryptology: Complexity and Applications*, PhD thesis, Department of Mathematics and Statistics, Queen's University, Kingston, Canada, 1983.

[12] J. H. Moore, *Protocol failures in cryptosystems*, Proceedings of the IEEE, 76 (1988), pp. 594–602.

[13] R. L. Rivest, A. Shamir, and L. Adelman, *A method for obtaining digital signatures and public-key cryptosystems*, Comm. ACM, 21 (1978), pp. 120–126.

[14] R. S. Sandhu, *Cryptographic implementation of a tree hierarchy for access control*, Inf. Process. Lett., 27 (1988), pp. 95–98.

[15] A. Shamir, *How to share a secret*, Comm. ACM, 22 (1979), pp. 612–613.

[16] G. J. Simmons, *A 'weak' privacy protocol using the RSA cryptoalgorithm*, Cryptologia, 7 (1983), pp. 180–182.

Chair: WHITFIELD DIFFIE

Key Distribution Protocol
for
Digital Mobile Communication Systems

Makoto Tatebayashi [1]

Natsume Matsuzaki

Matsushita Electric Industrial Co. Ltd.

Moriguchi, 570, JAPAN

and

David B. Newman, Jr.

The George Washington University

Washington, DC 20052

ABSTRACT. *A key distribution protocol is proposed for digital mobile communication systems. The protocol can be used with a star-type network. User terminals have a constraint of being hardware-limited.*

Security of the protocol is discussed. A countermeasure is proposed to cope with a possible active attack by a conspiracy of two opponents.

1 Introduction

Proposed digital mobile communication systems potentially offer means for communications security using encryption techniques. For a secure secret key cryptosystem, a key should be changed for each session and shared by both terminals of a communication link. Thus, we have to solve the problem of key distribution.

Mobile communication systems may be regarded as star-type networks. Each user terminal in the network communicates with another user via a network center. Restrictions on hardware and implementation cost of a secure mobile communication system are more strict in user terminals than in a network center.

---

[1] Visiting Research Scholar at The George Washington University, 1988–1990

In this paper we propose a key distribution protocol suitable for digital mobile communication systems. A public key cryptosystem is employed for uplink channels (from a user terminal to a network center); it makes the mobile communication systems free from key management problems. A secret key cryptosystem is employed for downlink channels (from a network center to user terminals); It enables high speed performance at hardware-limited terminals. The security of the key distribution protocol is discussed.

The protocol is shown not to degenerate the level of security of the cryptoalgorithm employed, if an opponent makes a passive attack. The protocol may be unsafe, however, by a conspiracy of two opponents and their active attack. We propose a countermeasure in the protocol to cope with this attack.

2 Previous Key Distribution Schemes

In this section we review previous key distribution schemes and their problems when they are applied to mobile communication systems.

2.1 Centralized Key Distribution Protocol

This protocol [DEN83] assumes that a network has a centralized key distribution facility which distributes a session key to the requesting terminals. The session key is encrypted by the terminal's encryption key.

If a classical key cryptographic method is employed for the key-encryption, then the central facility should manage each user's private key.

If a public key cryptographic method is employed for the key-encryption, then the management problem is reduced. Decryption at a hardware-limited user terminal may, however, take an impractically long time.

2.2 Public Key Distribution Protocol

The public key distribution protocol, invented by Diffie and Hellman [DH76], enables direct key distribution between two user terminals in a system and eliminates the key management problem at a network center. This protocol requires computation in a finite field. For the scheme to be secure, the order of the finite field should be very large, making realization of this scheme impractical without using special hardware or high-speed digital signal processors (DSP's).

3   Proposed Key Distribution Protocol

The objectives of our key distribution protocol for a mobile communication system
are:

(1) to remove the key management at a network center, and

(2) to enable hardware-limited user terminals to obtain a common secret key in a
reasonable time.

When a first user at a first terminal desires to share a common key or secret
message with a second user at a second terminal, the first user generates a random
number r_1 as a first key-encryption-key. The first key-encryption-key signal is passed
to the network center using a public key scheme. Using a public key scheme in this
uplink enables each user terminal to keep only a public key of the network center.
This type of scheme also allows hardware-limited users to perform the encryption in
a reasonable time since a public-key-encryption scheme can be employed in first and
second user terminal which requires only a small computation.

The network center, upon receiving the first key-encryption-key signal, generates a
request signal and transmits the request signal to the second terminal. In response to
receiving the request signal, the second terminal generates a second key-encryption-
key signal r_2. The second key-encryption-key r_2 will become a common key or message
between the first terminal and the second terminal. The second terminal encrypts the
second key-encryption-key signal using a public key scheme. This encrypted signal is
then passed to the network center over the communications channel.

The network center, in response to receiving the first ciphertext signal and the
second ciphertext signal, decodes these as the first key-encryption-key signal and the
second key-encryption-key, respectively, using a public-key-decoding device. Thus the
network center has the first and second key-encryption-key signals r_1 and r_2. The
network center then can encrypt the second key-encryption-key signal r_2 with the
first key-encryption-key signal r_1 using the classical-key-encoding device, employing
any type of classical encryption device. At this point, public key encryption concepts
are not required.

The following are examples of what might be used in the public key schemes. For
example, consider the RSA cryptographic method used as the public key scheme.
The modulus n is a product of p and q, where p and q are prime numbers. The
encryption exponent e is chosen to be 3. The decryption exponent d is a number
satisfying $ed = 1$ (modulo L) where L is the least common multiplier $p-1$ and $q-1$.

Additionally, consider a simple substitution cipher which may be used as a classical key encryption scheme. An example of a simple substitution cipher is the Vernam cipher. The encryption and decryption transformations are as follows:

Encryption: $E(x,k) = x \oplus k$
Decryption: $D(x,k) = x \oplus k$
Where "$\oplus$" denotes addition modulo 2 for each bit.

A second example of a simple substitution cipher is based on addition modulo n:

Encryption: $E(x,k) = x + k \pmod{n}$.
Decryption: $D(x,k) = x - k \pmod{n}$.
Where x and k are any element in the modulo ring.

The protocol for the key distribution, as illustratively shown in Figure 1, can be summarized as follows:

KEY DISTRIBUTION PROTOCOL 1 (KDP1)

1. First terminal, A, generates r_1 as a key-encryption key.

2. A encrypts r_1 with S's public key ($e = 3$) and sends $r_1{}^e \pmod{n}$ to S.

3. S decrypts $r_1{}^e \pmod{n}$ by its secret key d and gets $(r_1{}^e \pmod{n})^d \pmod{n} = r_1$.

4. S calls B.

5. B generates r_2 as a session key between A and B.

6. B encrypts r_2 with S's public key ($e = 3$) and sends $r_2{}^e \pmod{n}$ to S.

7. S decrypts $r_2{}^e \pmod{n}$ by its secret key d and gets $(r_2{}^e \pmod{n})^d \pmod{n} = r_2$.

8. S encrypts r_2 by a key-encryption key r_1 and sends $E(r_2, r_1)$ to A.

9. A decrypts $E(r_2, r_1)$ by its key-encryption key r_1 and gets $D(E(r_2, r_1), r_1) = r_2$ as a session key with B.

Choosing an RSA exponent e of 3 and the Vernam cipher enables the first terminal to be easily implemented.

The following discusses the security of the proposed method with an exponent $e = 3$ and modulo n classical encryption.

One might question whether revealing $r_1 + r_2 \pmod{n}$, as well as $r_1{}^3 \pmod{n}$ and $r_2{}^3 \pmod{n}$, degrades the security of the method. Under the assumption that an opponent has knowledge of only those parameters, we can show that the security of the method is not degraded as follows.

A cryptoanalyst, by knowing the transmitted ciphertexts, obtains the following simultaneous congruencies:

$$r_1{}^3 = a \pmod{n} \tag{1}$$

$$r_2{}^3 = b \pmod{n} \tag{2}$$

$$r_1 + r_2 = c \pmod{n} \tag{3}$$

Where a, b, and c are known constants. From these congruencies one can yield a quadratic congruence of $r_1(r_2)$ in modulo n,

$$r_1{}^2 - c\,r_1 + (1/3c)(c^3 - a - b) = 0 \pmod{n} \tag{4}$$

if $\gcd(3c, n) = 1$ holds.

Rabin [RAB79] showed that solving the quadratic congruence (4), without the knowledge of the factors of n, is as difficult as factorizing $n = pq$. Since the security of the RSA cryptography depends on the difficulty of factorization of n, we can conclude that revealing $r_1 + r_2 \pmod{n}$ in this protocol does not degrade the security of the protocol.

In this discussion we assume that an opponent makes only a passive attack; the cryptoanalyst only uses the knowledge of transmitted ciphertext and does not participate in the protocol.

In the next section, we will discuss the case of an active attack to the key distribution protocol.

4 An Active Attack to the Key Distribution Protocol

It was pointed out by G. J. Simmons [SIM89] that the method provided as KDP1 has a vulnerability. When legitimate first and second terminals communicate with each other to generate a common key signal, a first opponent may conspire with a second opponent to obtain the common key. As discussed herein, the common key is the key-encryption-key signal shared by the first and second terminals. The break-in protocol requires the first opponent to conspire with the second opponent in advance.

The first and second opponents agree that when either receives a request from the network center to establish a session key for communication with the other, that they will use a jointly known key, R.

First, consider the following attack. The first opponent, listening the first terminal's communication with the network center, initiates the KDP1 method to have a session key with the second opponent, sending $r_1{}^3 \pmod{n}$, replaying the first terminal's message to the network center. The second opponent sends a prearranged number, R, to the first opponent. Then the first opponent can apparently obtain r_1 and thus the common key r_2. Thus, the method of KDP1 is vulnerable to a replay attack.

Second, even if the network center has a mechanism for protecting against a replay attack, the following break-in protocol enables the first opponent to obtain a common key r_2, avoiding the protect mechanism against a replay attack.

SIMMON'S BREAK-IN PROTOCOL AGAINST KDP1

1. The first opponent, C, chooses a random number r_3 and calculates $r_3{}^{-1} \pmod{n}$. He also calculates $r_1{}^3 r_3{}^3 \pmod{n}$ and sends it with a request that the network center, S, set up a session key for him with the second opponent, D.

2. S decrypts $r_1{}^3 r_3{}^3 \pmod{n}$ to obtain $r_1 r_3 \pmod{n}$.

3. S calls D.

4. D sends $R^3 \pmod{n}$ to S.

5. S decrypts $R^3 \pmod{n}$ to obtain R and computes $R + r_1 r_3 \pmod{n}$ which it sends to C.

6. C subtracts R and multiplies the result by $r_3{}^{-1}$ to recover r_1.

7. C observed $r_1 + r_2 \pmod{n}$, so he can subtract r_1 from it to recover r_2, that is, the session key being used by the first terminal, A, and the second terminal, B.

Since r_3 is unknown to the center, $r_3{}^3$ becomes a one-time key that the first opponent can use to conceal the fact that $r_1{}^3$ is involved in $r_1{}^3 r_3{}^3$.

The source of weakness is the fact that $r_1{}^3 r_3{}^3 = (r_1 r_3)^3 \pmod{n}$, i.e. that the RSA encryption commutes with modular multiplication.

5   A Countermeasure Against the Active Attack

5.1   A Structure in the Sending Data

A countermeasure against the attack may be obtained by adding structure with the first key-encryption-key signal.

In order to destroy the ability of the first and second opponents to make use of the multiplicative property of the RSA scheme, a certain predetermined structure should be provided in the data to be encrypted. One example of the structure in the data is restricting a random number, r, to be stored in the least significant 256 bit, keeping the significant 256 bit to be zero. The center should have a mechanism to check that the decrypted message is in the predetermined set, $\mathcal{M}$, of the message. If r_1 and r_2 are chosen randomly in $\mathcal{M}$, then the probability that $r_1 r_2 \pmod{n}$ is in $\mathcal{M}$ is negligibly small. Thus if an opponent sends $r_1{}^3 r_2{}^3 \pmod{n}$ to the network center, then the center can, with high probability, recognize that an illegal message is sent.

5.2   A Measure to Prevent a Replay Attack

Another measure to prevent a replay attack is generating a timestamp which can be generated at the first terminal, and concatenating it with the first key-encryption-key. The transmitting data from the first terminal to the center is now

$$(t_a \,\|\, r_1)^3 \pmod{n}$$

where t_a denotes a timestamp, $\|$ denotes a concatenation and r_1 denotes a random number.

The network center should have a mechanism for checking the timeliness of the timestamp. The timestamp may include a transmitted date and time and expiring date.

5.3   User Identity Verification

A mechanism for user identity verification should also be provided in the protocol, since the key distribution protocol KDP1 does not solve the user authentication problem. From our basic standpoint the identity verification should not require the center to manage secret information for each user.

We will describe a possible user verification scheme for the key distribution protocol.

The network center generates each user i's secret s_i from user i's identifier, IDi,

$$s_i = f(IDi)$$

where f is a polyrandom function which the center only knows. The network center distributes s_i to user i in secret, possibly in the form of a smart card.

The first terminal constructs a data signal, which is a concatenation of user i's secret, s_a, a random number, r_1, and other information. The first terminal encrypts the data signal and the network center decrypts the encrypted data signal and gets the user i's secret, s_a'. The network center calculates $f(IDa)$ and checks if it is the same as s_a' which he received. If they coincide, the network center verifies the sender. Otherwise the network center rejects the sender and quits the protocol.

Combining these three mechanisms the key distribution protocol, as illustratively shown in Figure 2, can be summarized as follows:

KEY DISTRIBUTION PROTOCOL 2 (KDP2)

1. The first terminal, A, generates r_1 as a key-encryption key.

2. A sends to the network center, S, IDa and $(t_a \| s_a \| r_1)^3 \pmod{n}$.

3. S decrypts the encrypted data signal and gets $(t_a \| s_a \| r_1)$. S extracts t_a, s_a and r_1 from the decrypted data. S checks the validity of the timestamp t_a. S verifies A.

4. S calls the second terminal, B.

5. B generates r_2 as a session key between A and B.

6. B sends to S, IDb, $(t_b \| s_b \| r_2)^3 \pmod{n}$.

7. S decrypts the encrypted data and gets $(t_b \| s_b \| r_2)$. S extracts t_b, s_b, r_2 from the decrypted data. S checks the validity of the timestamp t_b. S verifies B.

8. S sends A, $r_1 + r_2 \pmod{n}$.

9. A subtracts r_1 and gets r_2 as a session key with B.

In this protocol, a structure in the transmitted data prevents an enemy from utilizing the distribution property of the RSA cryptography. A timestamp mechanism prevents a replay attack. A mechanism for identity verification prevents masquerading.

In the protocol, the second terminal can obtain $(t_a \| s_a \| r_1)^3 \pmod{n}$ and r_1. The second terminal can easily guess a timestamp t_a. If the second terminal can get the first terminal's secret s_a, this cryptosystem is unsafe.

In general this problem is considered to find a plaintext, with a part of which being known to a cryptoanalyst. We do not know any successful attack at present. In order to avoid an exhaustive search for s_a, a field length for user secret should be long. We believe that 200 bits, for example, are sufficiently long.

This protocol may be exposed to a "low exponent protocol failure" [MOO88], since we restricted ourselves to a case where the RSA exponent is a small number. As long as we consider a case where only one network center exists, this protocol is safe. But if we extend our scheme to a case with multiple network centers, we have to be careful about the inherent weakness of the low exponent scheme.

Since the data transmitted from user terminals to a network center have a structure, mathematical analysis of the security is no more possible on the assumption that the opponent only has the information known by himself. But we believe that the previous results on KDP1 give us a lower bound on the security of KDP2 under the same assumption, since the opponent in KDP2 obtains less information than in KDP1.

6   Conclusions

In this paper we proposed a key distribution protocol for mobile communication systems. In the protocol a public key cryptography is employed in uplinks and a secret key cryptography is employed in downlinks. We focused our discussions on a special case using the RSA scheme with encryption key $e = 3$ for uplinks, and of simple substitution ciphers for downlinks. The protocol makes a network center free from key management problems and enables hardware-limited user terminals to operate in a reasonable time to get a common key.

We introduced a structure in the transmitted data and a mechanism checking a replay attack in order to avoid a protocol failure based on the multiplicative property of the RSA cryptography.

Acknowledgements

The authors thank Dr. G. J. Simmons for showing the active attack in Section 4. The authors thank Dr. J. K. Omura for very helpful discussions.

References

[DEN83]   D. E. Denning, "Cryptography and Data Security", Addison–Wesley, 1983.

[DH76]   W. Diffie and M. Hellman, "New Directions in Cryptography", IEEE Trans. on Info. Theory, Vol. IT–22, No. 6, pp. 644–654, 1976.

[JC85]   W. de Jonge and D. Chaum, "Attacks on Some RSA Signatures", Advances in Cryptology: Proceedings of Crypto'85, Springer–Verlag, pp. 12–27, 1986.

[MOO88]   J. H. Moore, "Protocol Failures in Cryptosystems", Proc. of IEEE, Vol. 76, No. 5, pp. 594–602.

[RAB79]   M. O. Rabin, "Digitalized Signatures and Public-Key Functions as Intractable as Factorization", MIT/LCS/TR–212, MIT Lab for Computer Science, Cambridge, Massachusetts, January 1979.

[SIM87]   G. J. Simmons, "An Impersonation-proof Identity Verification Scheme", Advances in Cryptology: Proceedings of Crypto'87, Springer–Verlag, pp. 211–215, 1988.

[SIM89]   G. J. Simmons, private letter, January 1989.

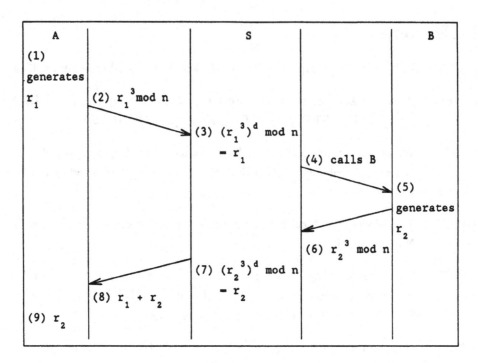

Figure 1. Key Distribution Protocol 1 (KDP1)

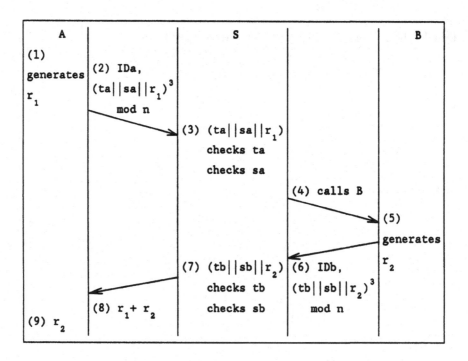

Figure 2. Key Distribution Protocol 2 (KDP2)

A key exchange system based on real quadratic fields
Extended abstract

Johannes A. Buchmann
FB 10–Informatik
Universität des Saarlandes
6600 Saarbrücken
West Germany

Hugh C. Williams
Department of Computer Science
University of Manitoba
Winnipeg, Manitoba
Canada R3T2N2

1   Introduction

In [3] Diffie and Hellman described a novel scheme by which two individuals could exchange a secret cryptographic key over a public channel. This scheme is based on the arithmetic in the multiplicative group $F^\times$ of a finite field F. It is secure because computing discrete logarithms in finite fields is a very hard problem. It has been noted subsequently by several authors (e.g. [1], [5], [6]) that any finite abelian group G may be used to replace $F^\times$ in this scheme as long as the discrete logarithm problem in G is difficult.

In this paper we will for the first time present a Diffie-Hellman key exchange protocol based on a finite subset of an infinite abelian group, which is not a subgroup, namely on the set $\mathcal{R}$ of reduced principal ideals of a real quadratic order. Currently, the best known algorithms for breaking this scheme are exponential in the size of the key. Moreover, the problem of breaking the s cheme is closely related to the very difficult problems of computing class numbers of real quadratic orders and factoring large integers.

2   The idea

Let D be a positive integer which is not a square, $D \equiv 0, 1 \bmod 4$. Let

$$K = \mathcal{Q} + \mathcal{Q}\sqrt{D}$$

be the *real quadratic number field* generated by $\sqrt{D}$. For $\xi = x + y\sqrt{D}$, $x, y \in \mathcal{Q}$, we denote by $\xi' = x - y\sqrt{D}$ its algebraic conjugate. Let

$$\mathcal{O} = \mathcal{Z} + \mathcal{Z}\frac{D + \sqrt{D}}{2}$$

be the *real quadratic order* of discriminant D. A number $\mu \in \mathcal{O}$ is called a *minimum* of $\mathcal{O}$ if $\mu > 0$ and if there is no $\alpha \neq 0$ in $\mathcal{O}$ with $|\alpha| < \mu$ and $|\alpha'| < |\mu'|$. The set of minima in $\mathcal{O}$ is denoted by M. A *principal ideal* of $\mathcal{O}$ is a subset of K of the form $\mathbf{a} = \frac{1}{\alpha}\mathcal{O}$ with $\alpha \in K^{\times}$. Such an ideal is called *reduced* if $\alpha \in M$. Denote the set of principal ideals of $\mathcal{O}$ by $\mathcal{P}$ and the set of reduced principal ideals of $\mathcal{O}$ by $\mathcal{R}$. Each $\mathbf{a} \in \mathcal{R}$ has a presentation

$$\mathbf{a} = \mathcal{Z} + \mathcal{Z}\frac{b + \sqrt{D}}{2a} \tag{1}$$

where $a, b \in \mathcal{Z}$, $0 < a < \sqrt{D}$ and $0 \leq b < 2a$. In our key exchange protocol the communication partners will agree on a reduced ideal which will serve as the secret key. Unfortunately, $\mathcal{R}$ does not carry a group structure and therefore, the ideas of Buchmann/Williams [1] cannot be used in this context. Instead, we will use the infrastructure idea of Shanks [9] which basically tells us that $\mathcal{R}$ is "almost" a group.

It can easily be shown that the set

$$\{\log \mu : \mu \in M\}$$

is discrete on the real line R. Hence, we can arrange the minima of $\mathcal{O}$ in a two sided sequence $(\mu_j)_{j \in \mathcal{Z}}$ which is defined by the two properties

$$\mu_0 = 1 \quad \text{and} \quad (\mu_i < \mu_j \Leftrightarrow i < j).$$

Correspondingly, we put $\mathbf{a}_j = \frac{1}{\mu_j}\mathcal{O}$ for $j \in \mathcal{Z}$. Then we have

$$\mathcal{R} = \{\mathbf{a}_1, \dots, \mathbf{a}_p\}$$

for some $p \in \mathcal{Z}_{\geq 1}$ which is chosen such that $\mathbf{a}_i = \mathbf{a}_j \Leftrightarrow i \equiv j \bmod p$. For any $x \in R$ and for any $\mathbf{a} \in \mathcal{P}$ we define the *distance* $\delta(\mathbf{a}, x)$ of $\mathbf{a}$ and x as follows: let $\alpha \in K_{>0}$ such that $\frac{1}{\alpha}\mathcal{O}r = \mathbf{a}$ and $|x - \log \alpha|$ is minimum. Put $\delta(\mathbf{a}, x) = x - \log \alpha$. We denote by $\hat{\delta}(\mathbf{a}, x)$ the approximation to $\delta(\mathbf{a}, x)$ which is actually computed in our scheme. We say that $\mathbf{a} \in \mathcal{P}$ is *on the left* (*on the right*) of x if $\delta(\mathbf{a}, x) > (<)0$. We say that $\mathbf{a} \in \mathcal{P}$ is *closer* to x than $\mathbf{b} \in \mathcal{P}$ if $|\delta(\mathbf{a}, x)| < |\delta(\mathbf{b}, x)|$. We denote by $\mathbf{a}_+(x)$ the closest reduced principal ideal on the right of x, by $\mathbf{a}_-(x)$ the closest reduced principal ideal on the left of x, and by $\mathbf{a}(x)$ the reduced principal ideal which is closest to x. We write $\delta_1(x) = \delta(\mathbf{a}(x), x)$. The notation $\hat{\mathbf{a}}(x)$ will be used for the ideal computed by our procedure. We also use $\delta_2(x)$ to represent $\delta(\hat{\mathbf{a}}(x), x)$ and $\hat{\delta}_1(x) = \hat{\delta}(\mathbf{a}(x), x)$, $\hat{\delta}_2(x) = \hat{\delta}(\hat{\mathbf{a}}(x), x)$ to denote the approximations we obtain to $\hat{\delta}_1(x)$ (if $\mathbf{a}(x)$ is actually computed in our algorithm) and $\hat{\delta}_2(x)$ respectively.

The protocol can roughly be described as follows: The communication partners are A and B. A secretely chooses $a \in \{1, 2, \dots, \lfloor\sqrt{D}\rfloor\}$ and B secretely chooses $b \in \{1, 2, \dots, \lfloor\sqrt{D}\rfloor\}$. A computes $\hat{\mathbf{a}}(a)$, $\hat{\delta}(a)$ and transmits the result to B. B determines $\hat{\mathbf{a}}(b)$, $\hat{\delta}(b)$ and sends the result to A. From this information both partners are able to calculate $\hat{\mathbf{a}}(ab)$. Although, this ideal is not neccessarily the same for A and B since the computational error might slightly differ with the different computing methods of A and B, a little additional work will allow A and B to agree on a common ideal which is the secret key.

We will denote the roundoff errors by

$$
\begin{aligned}
\epsilon(\mathbf{a}, x) &= |\delta(\mathbf{a}, x) - \hat{\delta}(\mathbf{a}, x)|, \\
\epsilon_i(x) &= |\delta_i(x) - \hat{\delta}_i(x)|.
\end{aligned}
$$

3 Procedures

In the calculations, a basic precision constant δ_0 is used which will be specified later.

In order to calculate the secret key the communication partners use the following procedures which are described in Williams/Wunderlich [12]:

Procedure 1 *1.* **Input**: *$\mathbf{a}, \mathbf{b} \in \mathcal{R}$, $\hat{\delta}(\mathbf{a}, x)$, $\hat{\delta}(\mathbf{b}, y)$ for some $x, y \in R_{>0}$.*

  2. **Output**: *$\mathbf{ab}$, $\hat{\delta}(\mathbf{ab}, x + y) = \hat{\delta}(\mathbf{a}, x) + \hat{\delta}(\mathbf{b}, y)$.*

  3. **Property**: *$\epsilon(\mathbf{ab}, x + y) \leq \epsilon(\mathbf{a}, x) + \epsilon(\mathbf{b}, y)$.*

The error estimate in the previous procedure holds if $\max\{|\delta(\mathbf{a}, x)|, |\delta(\mathbf{b}, y)|\} < R/4$ where R is the regulator of K. This inequality will always be satisfied in our protocol.

Procedure 2 *1.* **Input**: *$\mathbf{a} \in \mathcal{P}$ which is a product of two reduced ideals, $\hat{\delta}(\mathbf{a}, x)$ for some $x \in R_{>0}$.*

  2. **Output**: *$\mathbf{b} \in \mathcal{R}$, $\hat{\delta}(\mathbf{b}, x)$.*

  3. **Property**: *$|\hat{\delta}(\mathbf{b}, x) - \hat{\delta}(\mathbf{a}, x)| \leq \log(2D) + \delta_0$, $\epsilon(\mathbf{b}, x) \leq \epsilon(\mathbf{a}, x) + \delta_0$.*

Procedure 3 *1.* **Input**: *$\mathbf{a} \in \mathcal{R}$, $\hat{\delta}(\mathbf{a}, x)$ for some $x \in R_{>0}$.*

  2. **Output**: *The right neighbor $N_+(\mathbf{a})$ or the left neighbor $N_-(\mathbf{a})$ of $\mathbf{a}$ in the sequence $(\mathbf{a}_j)$ of reduced principal ideals and $\hat{\delta}(N_+(\mathbf{a}), x)$ or $\hat{\delta}(N_-(\mathbf{a}), x)$.*

  3. **Property**: *$\epsilon(N_\pm(\mathbf{a}), x) \leq \epsilon(\mathbf{a}, x) + \delta_0$.*

If δ_0^{-1} and x and y are bounded by polynomials in D then the running time of all those procedures is a polynomial in $\log D$. The procedures are used in

Procedure 4 *1.* **Input**: *$\hat{\mathbf{a}}(x)$, $\hat{\mathbf{a}}(y)$, $\hat{\delta}(x)$, $\hat{\delta}(y)$ for some $x, y \in R_{>0}$.*

  2. **Output**: *$\hat{\mathbf{a}}(x + y)$, the ideal that minimizes $\hat{\delta}(\mathbf{a}, x + y)$ over all $\mathbf{a}$ which are determined in this procedure. The ideal $\mathbf{a}(x + y)$ will be among those ideals although $\hat{\delta}_1(x + y) > \hat{\delta}_2(x + y)$ is possible and therefore $\mathbf{a}(x + y)$ might not be recognized. $\hat{\delta}_2(x + y)$ is also output.*

8. **Property:** *If* $\hat{a}(x) \in \{a_-(x), a_+(x)\}$ *and* $\hat{a}(y) \in \{a_-(y), a_+(y)\}$, *then* $\epsilon(a, x + y) \leq (\epsilon_2(x) + \epsilon_2(y))C_1 + C_2$ *for every* a *determined in the procedure where* $C_1 = (1 + 4\delta_0/\kappa_3)$ *and* $C_2 = \delta_0(20\kappa_2 + 5\kappa_3 + 4\delta_0)/\kappa_3$ *and with* κ_2 *and* κ_3 *from (2) and (3) below.*

In order to describe Procedure 4 and to prove the above property we need the following inequalities which can also proved by using results of Williams [11]:

$$\kappa_1 = \frac{1}{1 + \sqrt{D}} < \delta(N_+(a), a), -\delta(N_-(a), a) < \log\sqrt{D} = \kappa_2, \qquad (2)$$

$$\delta(N_+^2(a), a), -\delta(N_-^2(a), a) > \log 2 = \kappa_3, \qquad (3)$$

for every $a \in \mathcal{R}$. Here we have used the notation $\delta(a, b) = \log\alpha$ for $a, b \in \mathcal{P}$ where $\alpha \in K_{\geq 1}$ is such that $b = \frac{1}{\alpha}a$ and $|\log\alpha|$ is minimal. Analogously, we will write $\hat{\delta}(a, b)$ for the corresponding approximate value.

In Procedure 4 we first apply Procedure 1 to determine $c = \hat{a}(x)\hat{a}(y)$ and $\hat{\delta} = \hat{\delta}(c, x + y) = \hat{\delta}(x) + \hat{\delta}(y)$. Since $\delta(c, x + y) = \delta_2(x) + \delta_2(y)$, we have

$$|\delta(c, x + y) - \hat{\delta}| \leq \epsilon_2(x) + \epsilon_2(y)$$

Next, we apply Procedure 2 to obtain b and $\hat{\delta}(b, x + y)$. We then have

$$|\delta(b, x + y) - \hat{\delta}(b, x + y)| < \epsilon_2(x) + \epsilon_2(y) + \delta_0.$$

In the sequel we assume that

$$\delta_0 \leq \kappa_3/4.$$

This guarantees by (3) that two consecutive applications of N_+ increase $\hat{\delta}$ at least by $\kappa_3/2$ and, analogously, that two consecutive applications of N_- decrease $\hat{\delta}$ at least by $\kappa_3/2$. Apply N_+ or N_- n times to b to obtain b' such that $|\hat{\delta}(b', x + y)|$ is minimal. Put $\hat{a}(x + y) = b'$.

If $\hat{a}(x) \in \{a_-(x), a_+(x)\}$ then

$$|\delta_2(x)| < |\delta_1(x)| + \kappa_2 < 3\kappa_2/2.$$

It follows that

$$|\delta(b, x + y)| < 3\kappa_2 + \log(2D) = 5\kappa_2 + \kappa_3$$

and

$$|\hat{\delta}(b, x + y)| < \epsilon_2(x) + \epsilon_2(y) + 5\kappa_2 + \kappa_3 + \delta_0.$$

Hence no more than $4(\epsilon_2(x) + \epsilon_2(y) + 5\kappa_2 + \kappa_3 + \delta_0)/\kappa_3$ applications of Procedure 3 are required to find $\hat{a}(x + y)$ and $\hat{\delta}(x + y)$. Moreover, the error is bounded as asserted in Procedure 4.

Using Procedure 4 we are able to explain the basic algorithm used in the protocol which is based on the well known fast exponentiation technique.

Procedure 5   *1.* **Input***: $\hat{\mathbf{a}}(x)$, $\hat{\delta}(x)$, for some $x \in \mathcal{R}_{>0}$, $y \in \mathcal{Z}_{>0}$.*

2. **Output***: $\hat{\mathbf{a}}(xy)$, $\hat{\delta}(xy)$.*

3. **Algorithm**

    (a) Determine the binary decomposition

$$y = \sum_{i=0}^{L} b_i 2^{L-i}, \qquad b_i \in \{0,1\}.$$

    Set $z = 1$, $\hat{\mathbf{a}}(z) = \hat{\mathbf{a}}(x)$.

    (b) For $1 \le i \le L$ do:

        i. Compute $\hat{\mathbf{a}}(2z)$, $\hat{\delta}(2z)$ by Procedure 4. Replace $\hat{\mathbf{a}}(z)$, $\hat{\delta}(z)$ by $\hat{\mathbf{a}}(2z)$ and $\hat{\delta}(2z)$ respectively.

        ii. If $b_i = 1$, use Procedure 4 to compute $\hat{\mathbf{a}}(z+x)$, $\hat{\delta}(z+x)$. Replace $\hat{\mathbf{a}}(z)$ by $\hat{\mathbf{a}}(z+x)$ and $\hat{\delta}(z)$ by $\hat{\delta}(z+x)$.

    (c) Set $\hat{\mathbf{a}}(xy) = \hat{\mathbf{a}}(z)$, $\hat{\delta}(xy) = \hat{\delta}(z)$.

4 The protocol

We must now discuss how the communication partners can calculate the common secret key. We first require

Proposition 1 *Let $x, y \in \mathcal{R}_{>0}$. Assume that for the input of Procedure 4 we have $\hat{\mathbf{a}}(x) \in \{\mathbf{a}_-(x), \mathbf{a}_+(x)\}$, $\hat{\mathbf{a}}(y) \in \{\mathbf{a}_-(y), \mathbf{a}_+(y)\}$, and $E = C_1(\epsilon_1(x) + \epsilon_2(x)) + C_2 < \kappa_1/2$. Then the ideal $\hat{\mathbf{a}}(x+y)$, determined by that Procedure, is either $\mathbf{a}_-(x+y)$ or $\mathbf{a}_+(x+y)$.*

Proof: It follows from the assumption and from the property of Procedure 4 that

$$|\hat{\delta}_2(x+y)| - |\hat{\delta}_1(x+y)| \ge |\delta_2(x+y)| - |\delta_1(x+y)| - 2E.$$

If $\hat{\mathbf{a}}(x+y) \notin \{\mathbf{a}_-(x+y), \mathbf{a}_+(x+y)\}$, then by (2) we have

$$|\hat{\delta}_2(x+y)| - |\hat{\delta}_1(x+y)| > \kappa_1 - 2E > 0$$

which contradicts the definition of $\hat{\mathbf{a}}(x+y)$. □

We must now develop a condition under which Procedure 5 will find an ideal $\hat{\mathbf{a}}(xy) \in \{\mathbf{a}_+(xy), \mathbf{a}_-(xy)\}$. We put $E_0 = \epsilon_2(x)$ and define

$$
\begin{aligned}
E'_{i+1} &= 2E_i C_1 + C_2 \\
E_{i+1} &= \begin{cases} E'_{i+1} & \text{when } b_{i+1} = 0 \\ (E'_{i+1} + E_0)C_1 + C_2) & \text{when } b_{i+1} = 1 \end{cases} .
\end{aligned}
$$

If at the ith iteration of Procedure 5 we have $\hat{\mathbf{a}}(z) \in \{\mathbf{a}_-(z), \mathbf{a}_+(z)\}$ then at the $i+1$-st iteration we have $\epsilon_2(z) < E_{i+1}$ and $\hat{\mathbf{a}}(z) \in \{\mathbf{a}_-(z), \mathbf{a}_+(z)\}$ when $E_{i+1} < \kappa_1/2$ by Proposition 1. If we put $M_0 = E_0$ and define

$$M_{i+1} = C_3 M_i + C_4$$

where $C_3 = 2C_1^2$, $C_4 = C_1 C_2 + E_0 C_1 + C_2$, then $E_i \leq M_L$ for $0 \leq i \leq L$. Thus,

$$\hat{\mathbf{a}}(xy) \in \{\mathbf{a}_-(xy), \mathbf{a}_+(xy)\}$$

when $M_L < \kappa_1/2$. Since

$$M_L = C_3^L M_0 + C_4(C_3^L - 1)/(C_3 - 1)$$

and

$$C_3^L < ey$$

for $\delta_0 < \kappa_3/(8L)$, we get

$$M_L < ey(E_0 + C_4).$$

Hence,

$$\epsilon_2(xy) < ey(E_0 + C_4). \tag{4}$$

We now calculate $\hat{\mathbf{a}}(1)$ and $\hat{\delta}_2(1)$ such that $\epsilon_2(1) < \delta_0$. Clearly, such values can be determined by the use of Procedure 3 and they are made public. Procedure 5 can then be used to determine $\hat{\mathbf{a}}(a)$, $\hat{\mathbf{a}}(b)$, $\hat{\delta}(a)$, $\hat{\delta}(b)$ and for the calculation of the value of $\hat{\mathbf{a}}(ab)$.

If δ_0^{-1} is polynomially bounded in D then this computation requires only polynomial time in $\log D$. From the error estimate (4) above, we see that

$$\epsilon_2(ab) = O(\delta_0 D \log D).$$

Thus both communaction partners A and B can compute one of two possible ideals in polynomial time in $\log D$.

Now consider one of the communication partners A or B and denote his ideal $\hat{\mathbf{a}}(ab)$ by $\hat{\mathbf{a}}$, Also write $\hat{\delta} = \hat{\delta}_2(ab)$, $\epsilon = \epsilon_2(ab)$, and $x = ab$. In order to develop a little additional protocol which makes the choice unique we need

Proposition 2 *Let $\epsilon < \kappa_1/8$. If $|\delta_1(x)| > \kappa_1/4$ then both communication partners can find out whether $\hat{\mathbf{a}} = \mathbf{a}_+(x)$ or $\hat{\mathbf{a}} = \mathbf{a}_-(x)$ and they can therefore both find $\mathbf{a}_+(x)$. If $|\delta_1(x)| < \kappa_1/4$ then they can both find $\mathbf{a}(x)$.*

Proof: It can be decided whether $\hat{\mathbf{a}}$ is on the left or on the right of x if $|\hat{\delta}| > \epsilon$. If $|\delta_1(x)| > \kappa_1/4$ then it follows from the minimality of $\delta_1(x)$ and from the choice of ϵ that $|\hat{\delta}| > \kappa_1/4 - \epsilon > \epsilon$.

On the other hand, both communication partners know that $\mathbf{a}(x) \in S = \{N_\pm(\hat{\mathbf{a}}), \hat{\mathbf{a}}\}$. If $|\delta_1(x)| < \kappa_1/4$ then S contains an ideal $\mathbf{b}$ with $|\hat{\delta}(\mathbf{b}, x)| < 3\kappa_1/8$ and thus both partners can deduce that $|\delta(\mathbf{b}, x)| < \kappa_1/2$ which by (2) means that $\mathbf{b} = \mathbf{a}(x)$. $\square$

We can now formally describe the protocol:

Protocol 1 *1. A and B agree publically on D on $\hat{a}(1)$ and on $\hat{\delta}(1)$ with $\epsilon(1) < \delta_0$ where δ_0 is chosen sufficiently small that the errors never exceed $\kappa_1/8$.*

2. A secretely chooses $a \in \{1, \ldots, \lfloor\sqrt{D}\rfloor\}$. A uses Procedure 5 to compute $\hat{a}(a)$ and $\hat{\delta}(a)$. Both are sent to B.

3. B secretely chooses $b \in \{1, \ldots, \lfloor\sqrt{D}\rfloor\}$. B uses Procedure 5 to compute $\hat{a}(b)$ and $\hat{\delta}(b)$. Both are sent to A.

4. From $\hat{a}(a), \hat{\delta}(a)$ and b, B calculates $S_B = \{\hat{a}(ab), N_\pm(\hat{a}(ab))\}$. If possible, B computes $a(ab)$ and sends '0' to A. Otherwise, B determines $a_+(ab)$ and sends '1' to A.

5. From $\hat{a}(b), \hat{\delta}(b)$ and a, A calculates $S_A = \{\hat{a}(ab), N_\pm(\hat{a}(ab))\}$. If A has received '0' from B, then A attempts to calculate $a(x)$ and in case of success he sends '0' back to B. The secret key is $a(x)$. Otherwise, A determines $a_+(x)$ and sends '1' to B. If A has received '1' from B, then A attempts to calculate $a_+(x)$ and in case of success he sends '1' back to B. The secret key is $a_+(x)$. Otherwise, A determines $a(x)$ and sends '1' to A.

6. If B has sent '0' and receives '1' then B determines the secret key $a_+(x)$ which is possible by Proposition 2. If B has sent '1' and receives '0' then B determines the secret key $a(x)$ which is possible by Proposition 2. Otherwise, the ideal determined initially by B is the secret key.

5 Security

In order to guarantee the security of our scheme it is neccessary that the number p of reduced principal ideals of $\mathcal{O}$ be sufficiently large. From Williams [11] we know the following lower bound :

$$p \geq \frac{1}{\log D} R$$

where R is the regulator of $\mathcal{O}$. Moreover, as noted by Shanks [10], it follows from a result of Littlewood (see also Mollin/Williams [7]) that

$$hR >> D^{1/2-\epsilon}$$

for arbitrarily small ϵ where h is the class number of $\mathcal{O}$. To make p large we must therefore find and use real quadratic orders with small class numbers. For certain choices of D the even part of h can easily be bounded, e.g. if D is a prime number, 8 times a prime number, or the product of two prime numbers which are both congruent to 3 mod 4 then h is odd (see Kaplan [4]). On the other hand, it follows from the conjectural statements of Cohen/Lenstra [2] that the probability for the odd part of the class number to be bounded by $\log D$ is $1 - o(1)$ for $D \to \infty$.

We can therefore expect that if we choose the right discriminants then the probability that $p >> D^{1/2-\epsilon}$ is $1 - o(1)$ for arbitrarily small ϵ and $D \to \infty$.

We must now discuss the difficulty of breaking the scheme. We conjecture that being able to break the scheme implies being able to factor. So far we can only prove the following: Consider the *discrete logarithm problem* for reduced ideals of real quadratic orders (DLP): for any given reduced ideal **a** compute $\delta(\mathbf{a}, \mathcal{O})$.

Proposition 3 *If DLP can be solved in polynomial time then the key exchange protocol can be broken in polynomial time.*

Proof: Knowing $\hat{\mathbf{a}}(a)$ and $\hat{\delta}(a)$ the enemy can use the algorithm for solving DLP to come up with $x, y \in R$ such that $\hat{\mathbf{a}}(a) = \hat{\mathbf{a}}(x)$. Knowing $x, \hat{\mathbf{a}}(b), \hat{\delta}(b)$ he can then use Procedure 5 to calculate the secret key. □

Proposition 4 *If there is a polynomial time solution of DLP then one can factor in polynomial time.*

Proof: We show that a polynomial time solution of DLP can be used to determine the regulator R of $\mathcal{O}$ in polynomial time. One can then use the method described in Schoof [8] to factor in polynomial time.

In order to find the regulator, we start with the second reduced ideal $\mathbf{a}_2$. Its distance from $\mathcal{O}$ is by (3) at least $\log 2$. By repeatedly squaring and reducing this ideal we obtain a sequence of reduced ideals whose distances from $\mathcal{O}$ will be first increasing exponentially. Since those distances are bounded by R we find in polynomial time a reduced ideal whose distance is less than the distance of the previous ideal in the sequence. By applying a "divide and conquer" method, the regulator can be found in polynomial time. □

References

[1] J. Buchmann and H.C. Williams, *A key exchange system based on imaginary quadratic fields*, J. Cryptology **1** (1988), 107–118.

[2] H. Cohen and H.W. Lenstra Jr., *Heuristics on class groups of number fields*, Number Theory (Nordwijkerhout, 1983), Lecture Notes in Math. **1068**, 33–62, Springer Verlag Berlin and New York, 1984.

[3] W. Diffie and M. Hellman, *New directions in cryptography*, IEEE Trans. Inform. Theory **22** (1976), 472–492.

[4] P. Kaplan, *Sur le 2-groupe des classes d'idéaux des corps quadratiques*, J. Reine Angew. Math. **283/284** (1976), 313–363.

[5] N. Koblitz, *Elliptic curve cryptosystems*, Math. Comp. **48** (1987), 203–209.

[6] K.S. McCurley, *A key distribution system equivalent to factoring*, J. Cryptology **1** (1988), 95–105.

[7] R.A. Mollin and H.C. Williams, *Computation of the class number of a real quadratic field*, preprint (1988).

[8] R.J. Schoof, *Quadratic fields and factorization* in *Computational methods in number theory*, H.W. Lenstra Jr. and R. Tijdeman, eds. , Math. Centrum Tracts **155**, Part II, Amsterdam (1983), 235–286.

[9] D. Shanks, *The infrastructure of a real quadratic field and its applications*, Proc. 1972 Number Theory Conf., Boulder, Colorado, (1973), 217–224.

[10] D. Shanks, *Systematic examination of Littlewood's bounds on* $L(1, \chi)$, Proc. Sympos. Pure Math. **24**, AMS Providence RI (1973), 267–283.

[11] H.C. Williams, *Continued fractions and number-theoretic computations*, Rocky Mountain J. Math. **15** (1985), 621–655.

[12] H.C. Williams and M.C. Wunderlich, *On the parallel generation of the residues for the continued fraction factoring algorithm*, Math. Comp. **48** (1987), 405–423.

On Key Distribution Systems

Y. Yacobi
Bellcore, 445 South St.
Morristown NJ 07960
yacov@bellcore.com

Z. Shmuely
Computer Science Department
Technion, Haifa 32000, Israel

Zero Knowledge (ZK) theory formed the basis for practical identification and signature cryptosysems (invented by Fiat and Shamir). It also was used to construct a key distribution scheme (invented by Bauspiess and Knobloch); however, it seems that the ZK concept is less appropriate for key distribution systems (KDS), where the main cost is the number of communications. We propose relaxed criteria for the security of KDS, which we assert are sufficient, and present a system which meets most of the criteria. Our system is not ZK (it leaks few bits), but in return it is very simple. It is a Diffie-Hellman variation. Its security is equivalent to RSA, but it runs faster.

Our definition for the security of KDS is based on a new definition of security for one-way functions recently proposed by Goldreich and Levin. For a given system and given cracking-algorithm, I, the cracking rate is roughly the average of the inverse of the running-time over all instances (if on some instance it fails, that inverse is zero). If there exists a function $s : N \rightarrow N$, s.t. for all I, the cracking-rate for security parameter n is $O(1)/s(n)$, then we say that the system has at least security s. We use this concept to define the security of KDS for malicious adversary (the passive adversary is a special case). Our definition of a malicious adversary is relatively restricted, but we assert it is general enough for KDS. This restriction enables the proof of security results for simple and practical systems. We further modify the definition to allow past keys and their protocol messages in the input data to a cracking algorithm. The resulting security function is called the "amortized security" of the system. This is justified by current usage of KDS, where the keys are often used with cryptosystems of moderate strength. We demonstrate the above properties on some Diffie-Hellman KDS variants which also authenticate the parties. In particular, we give evidence that one of the variants has super-polynomial security against any malicious adversary, assuming RSA modulus is hard to factor. We also give evidence that its amortized security is super-polynomial. (The original DH scheme does not authenticate, and the version with public directory has a fixed key, i.e. zero amortized security.)

1. Introduction

Zero Knowledge theory [GMR] formed the basis for some practical identification and signature cryptosystems, most notably the Fiat-Shamir [FS] identification scheme. Recently, a zero-knowledge key distribution system was proposed [BK]. The advantage of a zero knowledge system is that no information leaks from the system; therefore, repeated use of the system does not make it less secure. This is true for the case of a malicious adversary, too.

However, it seems that the ZK concept is less appropriate for key distribution systems (KDS), where the main cost is the number of communications. We argue that by allowing some insignificant leak of information we can achieve simpler systems.

We propose relaxed criteria for the security of KDS, which we assert are sufficient, and present a system which meets most of the criteria. Our system is not ZK (it leaks few bits), but in return it is very simple. It is a Diffie-Hellman variation. Its security is equivalent to RSA, but it runs faster.

Our definition for the security of Key-Distribution Systems is based on a new definition of security for one-way functions recently proposed by Goldreich and Levin [GL]. For a given system and given cracking-algorithm, I, the cracking rate is roughly the average of the inverse of the running-time over all instances (if on some instance it fails, that inverse is zero). If there exists a function $s : N \rightarrow N$, s.t. for all I, the cracking- rate for security parameter n is $O(1)/s(n)$, then we say that the system has at least security s. We use this concept to define the security of KDS for a malicious adversary (the passive adversary is a special case). Our definition of a malicious adversary is relatively restricted (compared to [GMW]), but we assert it is general enough for KDS. This restriction enables the proof of security results for simple and practical systems. We further modify the definition to allow past keys and their protocol messages in the input data to a cracking algorithm (similarly to known-plaintext attack on cryptosystems). The resulting security function is named the "amortized security" of the system. This is justified by current usage of KDS, where the keys are often used with cryptosystems of moderate strength, e.g. DES. Ideally we would like the amortized-security to equal the security, and be super-polynomial.

There is a trivial solution to the problem of achieving key-distribution together with party authentication using public-key cryptosystems. This solution has a disadvantage though, when using RSA or its derivatives. We need a distinct modulus for each user, and this complicates computations. A potential family of KDS which can use a common modulus is the Diffie-Hellman [DH] scheme and its variants. The original Diffie-Hellman scheme does not authenticate, and the version with public directory (see section 3) has a fixed key, i.e. zero amortized security. We propose a simple and practical KDS (two exponentiations and one transmission per party) which authenticates the parties, and we give evidence for its super-polynomial security for any malicious adversary, assuming RSA modulus is hard to factor. We also give evidence that its amortized security is super polynomial.

In section 2 we define our security criteria, in section 3 we present some variants of the Diffie-Hellman KDS, and show their pitfalls, and in section 4 we show a relatively secure Diffie-Hellman variant. In the appendix, we modify the Goldreich-Levin definition of security for cryptosystems, taking into account the long neglected fact that messages of low probability may often be the most important ones (according to information theory they have high information content).

While some encryption schemes offer very good protection to every bit of information [GM], it may happen that the same protection value could be achieved with simpler systems, which concentrate on protecting the most important messages. This is captured by our new definition.

Some other KDS were proposed in [G], [KO], [MTI]and [O], with new features, but with no proofs of security. Bauspiess and Knobloch [BK] published a zero-knowledge KDS, but their system is more complicated than ours. We argue that at the cost of leaking few bits of our secrets we buy simplicity.

2. Proposed Criteria

2.1 General

We first give the Goldreich-Levin [GL] definition of security for one-way functions. We use their notation. Let S be the set of finite and Ω of infinite strings over $\{0,1\}$, and let $S_n \subseteq S$ be the set of strings of length n. Let $N = \{0,1,..\}$. $E_x f(x)$ denotes the expected value of f (for a given distribution function $x = d(r)$). Let $I(\omega,y)$ be a probabilistic algorithm which attempts to invert a function f, i.e. to recover $x \in S$ from $y = f(x)$, using $\omega \in \Omega$. Let $T_I(\omega,y)$ be $I's$ running time. Let $I's$ "success bit" $S_{I,f}(\omega,x) = 1$ if $I(\omega,f(x)) = x$ and 0 otherwise. The inverting rate $R_{I,f,d}(n) = E_{r,\omega}(S_{I,f}(\omega,d(r))/T_I(\omega,f(d(r))))$.

Definition 1 [GL]: A function f is called *one-way* on distribution d with security $s:N \rightarrow N$ if $R_{I,f,d}(n) = O(1)/s(n)^\varepsilon$, for some $\varepsilon > 0$ and all probabilistic algorithms I.

We next define our general KDS, restricting our attention to two-party systems. These (honest) parties try to establish a session-key, to be used later in some crypto-system. Each of the parties has a secret key and a public key. The parties exchange messages according to some protocol. At the end of the protocol they compute the session-key. That is

A 2 *party Key Distribution System (KDS)* is defined by the following i/o relation:

Input: $clear: P = (P_1,P_2), x = (x_1,..x_q); secret: U = (U_1,U_2),$

Output: $secret: K = f_1(P,U_1,x) = f_2(P,U_2,x)$

For security parameter n, each of the variables P_i,U_i,x_i,k is in S_n. P is the set of public keys, U is the set of secret keys, and x is the ordered set of messages exchanged between the parties during the execution of the protocol. Usually q is very small. K is the resulting session-key. f_1 and f_2 are polynomial time functions, mapping binary strings to binary strings.

The distribution of P,U,x is determined by some multidimensional distribution function d with random variable r, $r \in N$, as input.

2.2 Passive Adversary

We give here a variant of Definition 1 which we tailor for KDS (see above). Let $I(\omega,P,x)$ be any probabilistic algorithm trying to compute K. I models an adversary that tries to crack the system. Let $T_I(\omega,P,x)$ be I's running time. Let I's "success bit" $S_{I,f}(\omega,P,S,x) = 1$ if $I(\omega,P,x) = K$ (and 0 otherwise). The *cracking rate* for security parameter n is $R_{I,f,d}(n) = E_{r,\omega}(S_{I,f}(\omega,P,U,x)/T_I(\omega,P,x))$, where P_i,U_i,x_i,k are in S_n.

Definition 2: A KDS has at least *security* $s:N \rightarrow N$ against passive adversaries if $R_{I,f,d}(n) = O(1)/s(n)$ for all probabilistic algorithms I.

Note that we defined a lower bound on the security, not "exact" security. Also, we omited the ε, since we want to distinguish between security functions which are polynomially related (however, this point is not significant).

2.3 Malicious Adversary

Goldreich, Micali and Wigderson [GMW] treat the problem of finding a secure protocol for carrying out any feasible distributed protocol. They define a malicious adversary as a machine that can deviate from its prescribed program in any possible action, and describe a way to transform any protocol into a protocol which is secure against any minority of malicious adversaries.

In KDS protocols we have three players, namely, the two (honest) parties, trying to authenticate each other, and establish a session key, and the adversary, playing in the middle, trying to compute the key, in the the case of a passive adversary, or trying to establish some key with each of the parties, pretending to be his counterpart, in the case of a malicious adversary. So, since the adversary is a minority, by [GMW] we know that a secure polynomial time protocol exists (i.e. such that it overcomes any possible malicious adversary).

Our aim, therefore, is to use the fact that ours is a special case to achieve a very efficient protocol which overcomes any malicious adversary. In section 4 we show a KDS protocol which requires just two exponentiations for each of the parties, and the proof of its security is very simple.

A malicious adversary can interfere in a KDS protocol in various ways, he can initiate a protocol, cut the line of a user and connect himself instead, waiting to receive some initiative, he may initiate a KDS protocol with two sides simultaneously, or interfere between two honest parties trying to run KDS protocol.

Let $(\underline{x}_1,..\underline{x}_q)$ be the ordered set of messages exchanged between a malicious adversary z and an honest party in the course of KDS protocol, and let $\underline{x}^i=(\underline{x}_1,..\underline{x}_i)$, for $i=1,...,q$. If the honest party initiates then $\underline{x}_1=x_1$. If z initiates then $\underline{x}_1=h_1(P,U_z,x_1)$, where x_1 is a legitimate protocol message that the honest party could get when communicating with the party he assumes he communicates with, and h_1 (and later we use h_i) is any probabilistic polynomial time algorithm. h may have any other non-secret input. To simplify denotations we omitted it.

Definition 3: A *malicious adversary* z interferes with KDS protocols in such a way that a legitimate party ends up with protocol messages $\underline{x}=\underline{x}^q$, where for $i=1,2,...,q$, $\underline{x}_i=h_i(P,U_z,\underline{x}^{i-1})$. Accordingly, the legitimate party computes $\underline{K}=f(P,U,\underline{x})$, instead of the key K. The attack is *successful* if z can efficiently compute $\underline{K}$.

The case in which z interferes between two legitimate parties trying to carry out a KDS protocol is called "two-way impersonation attack." See [Y] for an example of such a successful attack. Note that, in this case, the malicious adversary may compute two distinct keys, one with each of the honest parties. He doesn't even have to use the same functions $h_i(.)$ in both directions.

The definition of *security* for malicious adversary is the same as for passive adversary with one modification, namely, the function I is replaced by $\underline{I}(\omega,P,\underline{x})$ trying to compute $\underline{K}$.

Clearly, the passive adversary is a special case of the malicious adversary for which $\underline{x}=x$ and $\underline{K}=K$.

2.4 Amortized Security

The *amortized security* of a KDS is roughly the complexity of its cracking problem given a history of keys and their respective protocol messages x. It is very similar to the definition of a "known cleartext attack" for cryptosystems. The motivation for this definition in the context of KDS stems from current usage of public KDS, where the resulting key is used in conventional cryptosystems, like DES, which are of moderate strength. Ideally we would like the complexity of this problem to be independent of the extra information contained in the old keys and their sessions. We consider amortized security for passive and malicious adversaries. The definitions of security are the same as before, only the algorithm I, which tries to crack the system, is modified to get more information, old keys and their sessions.

3. Some Diffie-Hellman variations

Next, we discuss some Diffie-Hellman (DH) KDS variations, which authenticate the parties, and show that their amortized security is low. In all the DH variations presented in this paper the parties should compute identical keys, if nobody cheated. Authentication is completed by trying to use the resulting key on recognizable messages (e.g., a message appended with 20 zeros).

3.1 The original Diffie-Hellman system

The original DH KDS [DH] has a variation which enables authentication of the parties. In this system there is a public trusted read-only directory in which the name, phone number, and public key of each participant appears. The public-key of participant i is $P_i \equiv \alpha^{x_i} \, mod \, m$, where x_i is randomly chosen by i, and known only to i. In the original scheme m was a prime, and α a generator in $GF(m)$. Let Zm denote the ring of integers modulo m, for any m. Recently some other groups were suggested for this application, where m is a composite, and α generates a large enough fraction of Zm (e.g., a quarter of it). See for example [S] and [M].

When j wants to communicate secretly with i, he computes $K_{j,i} \equiv P_i^{x_j} \, mod \, m$, and tells i in the clear that he wants to secretly communicate with her. Party i computes $K_{i,j}$ likewise, so that $K_{i,j}=K_{j,i}$. Clearly, this system can authenticate and establish a session key, but, since whenever two specific parties i and j establish a key, they end up with the same key, this system has zero amortized security for a passive adversary.

3.2 Time dependent Diffie-Hellman variation

Here we assume that at each moment there is time t known to every participant. When i wants to establish a session key with j she computes $K_{i,j,t} \equiv (K_{i,j})^t \, mod \, m$, where $K_{i,j}$ is as before, tells j in the clear that she, i, wants to communicate with him, and j computes $(K_{j,i})^t$. As before, $K_{i,j,t}=K_{j,i,t}$, if nobody cheated.

Given two keys $K_{i,j,t}$ and $K_{i,j,t+1}$ one can easily compute any key $K_{i,j,t} \equiv (K_{i,j,t+1} \cdot K_{i,j,t}^{-1})^{t'} \mod m$.

If the adversary has $K_{i,j,t+\delta}$, for some small δ, instead of $K_{i,j,t+1}$, then he still can compute every key of the form $K_{i,j,\delta \cdot p}$, for every integer p. Therefore, this system has a negligible amortized security for a passive adversary.

3.3 Randomized Diffie-Hellman variation

Let $K_{i,j}$ be as before. Here the parties randomly choose R_i and R_j, and exchange these values in the clear. They now compute $K'_{i,j} \equiv (K_{i,j})^{R_i + R_j} \mod m$.

A malicious adversary, who knows one key $K'_{i,j}$ and wants to impersonate j as a receiver, can disconnect j, and connect himself instead. Whenever i initiates a call to j, sending her R'_i, the adversary responds with $R'_j = R_i + R_j - R'_i$ (this is not a modular operation, since the adversary doesn't know $\phi(m)$). The result is a "new" key which equals the known one. Therefore, this system has zero amortized complexity for a malicious adversary.

4. A relatively secure Diffie-Hellman variation

In this section we describe another Diffie-Hellman variation which authenticates the parties, and we give evidence that its security is super-polynomial for passive and malicious adversary. We do not know the status of its amortized security, but believe it to be super-polynomial.

4.1 Description

Shmuely [S], and later McCurley [M], gave evidence that the Composite Diffie-Hellman (CDH) scheme (i.e. DH scheme with RSA-like modulus) is hard to break, in the sense that if there was an efficient algorithm which breaks a fixed fraction δ, $0 < \delta < 1$, of the instances, then we could factor the modulus with high probability in time proportional to δ^{-1}. If the system uses an "RSA modulus," believed to be hard to factor "almost everywhere," we conclude that it is probably impossible to break a fixed fraction δ, for any δ, of the instances of CDH. The proof may be extended to any $n^{-O(1)}$ fraction, where n is the problem size in bits. In this case we claim that if there exists an efficient algorithm which cracks $n^{-O(1)}$ of the instances of CDH, then it could be used to efficiently factor the modulus with high probability.

With the proper (now conventional) assumptions about the difficulty of factoring the modulus (RSA modulus), one can show that CDH KDS has a super-polynomial security. We base our system on this CDH system, and inherit this important property for passive and malicious adversaries.

The system

Each user i possesses a *public key* P_i, and a *secret key* S_i, $P_i, S_i \in [0,m)$, where $P_i \equiv \alpha^{S_i} \mod m$, m is an "RSA modulus" and α is a base element which generates a large enough fraction of Zm, the ring of integers modulo m. Suppose that two legitimate users of this system i and j want to establish session key $K_{i,j}$. They follow this protocol:

begin

i selects a random number $R_i \in [0,m)$ and sends the message $X_i = R_i + S_i \in [0, 2m-1)$ to j, who reciprocates likewise computing and sending X_j to i,

i computes $K_{i,j} \equiv (\alpha^{X_j} \cdot P_j^{-1})^{R_i} \equiv \alpha^{R_i R_j} \mod m$ and j reciprocates likewise computing $K_{j,i}$, which equals $K_{i,j}$ if nobody cheated.

end

Note that in this system none of the users needs to know the factorization of the modulus m. However, the central authority, which publishes the public directory, and is responsible for its integrity, must be able to prove that indeed m is a legitimate RSA modulus. Galil, Haber and Yung [GHY] showed a direct, efficient method to prove in zero-knowledge that a given number m is of the form pq, where p and q are primes. In principle all the other properties of our modulus, i.e. that $p-1=2p'$, and that $p-q > b$, for some given b, can be proven in zero-knowledge, since the corresponding decision problems are in NP. However, we know of no direct, efficient proof of these properties. To implement the proofs of [GHY], the central authority must know the factorization of m.

4.2 Distributional problems

A distributional problem is a decision problem with probability of appearance attached to each of the instances. For a detailed explanation the reader is referred to [BCGL] page 206. The notion of distributional problem is crucial to the definition of randomized reductions (which preserve average case complexity). In our system, we assume that R_i and S_i are uniformly distributed in $[0,m)$. This implies that $X_i = R_i + S_i$ has a triangular distribution in $[0,2m-1)$, i.e. $Pr(X_i = x \mid 0 \leq x < m) = x/m^2$, and $Pr(X_i = x \mid m \leq x < 2m-1) = (2m-x)/m^2$.

In [BCGL] there is also a definition of *randomized Turing reduction* of the kind we need. It has to be efficient, valid, and has to have the *domination* property, which roughly means that the "natural" probability of each instance of C (assuming we reduce B to C) must be $\geq$ the probability to get that instance via a reduction from B, given B's distribution of instances.

4.3 Passive adversary

As mentioned before, the passive adversary is a special case of the malicious adversary, therefore it is sufficient to prove for the latter. However, we believe that reading the proof for the passive adversary helps in understanding the malicious adversary case, therefore we do not omit it. We prove that cracking this system passively, i.e., finding the key $K_{i,j}$ given all the data communicated between the parties is equivalent to breaking the CDH KDS believed to be hard.

The CDH cracking problem (denoted B) is defined as follows: (everything here is *modulo m*, except operations in the exponents which are modulo $\phi(m)$, Euler's totient function, so we won't mention it any more.)

Input: α^x, α^y, α, m **find:** $\alpha^{xy} \mod m$

The new cracking problem (denoted C) is:

Input: $X_i = R_i + S_i$, $X_j = R_j + S_j$, α^{S_i}, α^{S_j}, α, m **find:** $\alpha^{R_i R_j} \ mod \ m$.

We first show that a passive adversary can deduce on the average less than 2 bits of information. This is negligible. Given X_i the adversary may learn something about R_i or S_i, which are supposed to be secret. For example, if $X_i = 0$ he can deduce that $S_i = R_i = 0$. Likewise, if $X_i = 2m - 2$ he knows that $R_i = S_i = m - 1$. We would like to compute the average number of bits released to the adversary that way. For simplicity we omit in this discussion the subscript i. So we have $x = s + r$. Following the traditional information-theoretic approach we define *equivocation* of a given variable y given x (denoted $H(y \mid x)$) to be the expected amount of freedom of choice of the value of y given x, measured in bits. If $x \in [0,m)$ then the combined uncertainty of r and s is x (r can have any value between 0 and x, but once it is fixed there is no freedom of choice for s). If $x \in [m, 2m-1)$ then the combined uncertainty of r and s is $2m - x$ (each of r and s is in the range $[x-m, m)$, which is of size $m - (x - m) = 2m - x$). So, we have two triangular functions, which should not be confused. (Here it is the uncertainty function, and previously we discussed the distribution function of X_i). To compute the equivocation we must take the expected value of the logarithm of the uncertainty from 0 to $2m$, but from the symmetry of our uncertainty function and the symmetry of the distribution function of X_i around $x = m$ it follows that it is sufficient to take twice the value from 0 to m. Let $c = log_2 e \approx 1.44$. We approximate the discrete sum by continuous integral, and get

$$H(r, s \mid x) = 2(1/m^2) \int_0^m x \log_2(x) dx = 2c / m^2 (\tfrac{1}{2} x^2 (\ln(x) - \tfrac{1}{2}) \Big|_0^m = \log_2(m) - c/2.$$

Compared to the maximum possible value of $H(r, s \mid x)$, which is $log(2m) = log(m) + 1$ we lost less than 2 bits. This is the average number of bits that leak per a single interception. In later section we analyze the average number of bits leaking when r sessions are intercepted, and show it to be of the order of $log(r)$.

A trivial (worst-case) reduction from B to D can be achieved with $X_i = X_j = 0$, $\alpha^{S_i} \equiv \alpha^{-x} \ mod \ m$, $\alpha^{S_j} \equiv \alpha^{-y} \ mod \ m$, however, we need a reduction with random X_i and X_j to claim super polynomial security for the new system. (In the trivial reduction the domination property does not hold. All of B's instances are reduced to $X_i = X_j = 0$, which is of negligible "natural" probability.)

In problem C, for a given S_i, X_i is uniformly distributed in $[S_i, S_i + m)$. Let D denote the same problem, but we allow X_i to be anywhere in the range $[0, 2m-1)$, with the previously mentioned triangular distribution.

In Lemma 1 we show a randomized reduction from B to D. Lemma 2 explains why this gives evidence for the super polynomial security of problem C.

We assume uniform natural distribution for B. That is, α^x and α^y are uniformly distributed in $[0,m)$. Similarly, we assume for problem D that R_i and S_i are uniformly distributed in $[0,m)$. As mentioned earlier, this implies that $X_i = S_i + R_i$ has triangular distribution in $[0, 2m-1)$.

$Pr(X_i=x \mid 0 \le x < m)=x/m^2$, and $Pr(X_i=x \mid m \le x < 2m)=(2m-x)/m^2$.

Lemma 1: There exists a randomized Turing reduction from B to D.

Proof: Given an instance of B, create an instance of D as follows: pick random X_i and $X_j \in [0, 2m-1)$, with triangular distribution, and set $\alpha^{S_j} \equiv \alpha^{-y} \bmod m$; $\alpha^{S_i} \equiv \alpha^{-x} \bmod m$ (which means $R_i \equiv X_i+x \bmod \phi(m)$; $R_j \equiv X_j+y \bmod \phi(m)$).

Therefore, the oracle outputs $\alpha^{(X_i+x)(X_j+y)} \equiv \alpha^{X_i X_j} \cdot \alpha^{X_i y} \cdot \alpha^{x X_j} \cdot \alpha^{xy} \bmod m$. The first three multiplicands can be calculated easily, therefore we can also compute the fourth, the desired output of B.

Given the uniform distribution of B's variables, this reduction yields distributions for D's variables, which equals their natural distributions, i.e. the domination property holds. Q.E.D.

Lemma 2: On the average, 2/3 of D's input instances in the construction of lemma 1 are legitimate instances of C.

Proof: For each given S_i, the "legitimate" X_i's are in $[S_i, S_i+m)$, and their probability is the area of the triangular distribution in this interval. We must take the expected value of this probability over all $s \in [0,m)$, where the distribution of $S_i=s$ is uniform in that interval. As before, we use continuous integrals to approximate the discrete sum.

$$E_s Pr(s \le X_i < s+m \mid s) = \int_0^m 1/m \left[\int_s^m (x/m^2)dx + \int_m^{s+m} \left(\frac{2m-x}{m^2}\right)dx \right] ds = 2/3. \quad \text{Q.E.D.}$$

The implication of lemma 2 is that in the reduction of lemma 1, if instead of using oracle D we use oracle C, in 2/3 of the cases the oracle will yield a correct answer. So, we can call oracle C a few times, and use majority voting, to get a negligible probability of error.

This together with the results in [S] and [M] on B imply

Theorem 1: If factorization of RSA modulus is a one-way function with super-polynomial security then the new system has super-polynomial security against passive adversaries.

4.4 Malicious adversary

We apply Definition 3 (malicious adversary) to our system. Suppose the adversary uses some probabilistic poly-time algorithm $h(.)$ on input X_j, i.e., he captures X_j, and instead sends $h(X_j)$ to i. (As before, h may have other inputs like P, S_z, etc. We write it this way just to simplify notations.) When communicating with j, he may act likewise. We do not need the assumption that he uses the same algorithm $h(.)$ in both directions. We'll prove just one way, the other way goes likewise. When i receives $h(X_i)$, she follows the protocol, computing $\underline{K}_{i,j} \equiv (\alpha^{h(x_j)} \cdot \alpha^{-s_j})^{R_i} \bmod m$. We prove now that there is no probabilistic poly-time function $h(.)$, for which the malicious adversary can effectively compute $\underline{K}_{i,j}$.

Assume the contrary. We show a polynomial reduction from B (see section 4.2) to the problem of finding $\underline{K}_{i,j}$, given $X_j, X_i, \alpha^{S_j}, \alpha^{S_i}, \alpha, m$. This reduction is parametrized by h, i.e., for every given h we give a reduction. We denote this malicious adversary cracking problem, for a given function $h(.)$, by C_h.

The relations between C_h and D_h are the same as between C and D.

To prove that the new system has a super-polynomial security for malicious adversaries we need a randomized reduction from B to D_h, the way we did for passive adversaries.

Lemma 3: There exists a randomized Turing reduction from B to D_h.

Proof: Given an instance α^x, α^y of problem B, we create the following instance of problem D_h: Randomly choose $X_j, X_i \in [0, 2m-1)$, with triangular distribution, and set $\alpha^{S_i} \equiv \alpha^{-x} \mod m$; $\alpha^{S_j} \equiv \alpha^{-y} \cdot \alpha^{h(X_j)} \mod m$.

The oracle outputs $\underline{K_{i,j}} \equiv (\alpha^{h(X_j)} \cdot \alpha^y \cdot \alpha^{-h(X_j)})^{R_i} \mod m$, but $R_i \equiv X_i - S_i \equiv X_i + x \mod \phi(m)$, hence $\underline{K_{i,j}} \equiv \alpha^{yx} \cdot \alpha^{y \cdot X_i} \mod m$, but $\alpha^{y \cdot X_i}$ is known, hence so is α^{yx}. Q.E.D.

By analysis similar to that of Lemma 2, and the following remarks, we conclude:

Theorem 2: If factorization of RSA modulus is a one-way function with super-polynomial security then the new system has super-polynomial security against any malicious adversary.

4.5 Amortized Security

We believe that the system leaks on the average the order of $log(r)$ bits when r sessions are intercepted. Clearly this isn't a zero-knowledge system, but a leak of just a few bits buys us much simplicity (compared with [BK]).

Suppose r $X's$ transmitted by A are intercepted. Denote the largest of them X_{max}. Clearly, $X_{max} = S + R_{max}$. Since The $R's$ are uniformly distributed in the interval $[0, m)$, from elementary order statistics we know that the expected value of R_{max} is $m - m/(r+1)$, and the variance of R_{max} is m/r^2. So a reasonable guess for the value of S is just $X_{max} - (m - m/(r+1))$, however, this guess of the value of S has the same variance that R_{max} has, so $S's$ uncertainty losses the order of $log(r)$ bits. Using the other mean values of the $X's$ in a similar way will not further reduce the interval in which S is expected to be.

Acknowledgements

We are most grateful to Stuart Haber for countless helpful discussions. Many thanks are due to Gilles Brassard for crucial remarks concerning lemmas 1 and 3, as well as numerous editorial comments, and to Rich Graveman for many helpful comments regarding the amortized security. Debbie Bloom was helpful in the analysis of the information revealed by the new key-distribution protocol. Finally we thank Pil Lee and Jim Katz for their remarks.

5. Appendix: The definition of security for cryptosystems

We define *security* for cryptosystems using the previous formalism, combined with another measure. We not only assign a probability to each message, but also importance. This measure may be, for example, Shannon's information-content, $-log(p)$, where p is the probability of the message. We use this particular measure throughout this appendix. The main idea is that when now defining the *cracking rate* of a cryptosystem we compute an entropy function, instead of simple expected value, thus taking into account the "information content" of each cracked message.

While some encryption schemes offer very good protection to every bit of information [GM], it may happen that the same protection value could be achieved with simpler systems, which concentrate on protecting the most important messages. This is captured by our new definition.

A *cryptosystem* (CS) is defined by the following i/o relation:

Input: *clear*: $P = (P_1, P_2)$, *secret*: $U = (U_1, U_2)$, m,

Output: *clear*: $c := f(P, U, m)$.

As before, P is the set of public keys, U is the set of secret keys. m and c are the message and cryptogram, respectively. f is a probabilistic polynomial time algorithm. For conventional cryptosystems, P is empty, and $U_1 = U_2 = U$. f is some general function which exists, and therefore we can define i/o relations using it. It is not the actual function used by the parties. For Public-Key systems, the actual function uses just one of the public keys and none of the secret keys, while for conventional systems the actual function has U as a key.

Let $I(\omega, P, c)$ be any probabilistic algorithm trying to compute m. Let $T_I(\omega, P, m)$ be I's running time. Let I's success bit $S_{I,f}(\omega, P, U, m) = 1$ *iff* $I(\omega, P, c) = m$ (and 0 otherwise).

Let $g : N \to N$, be any probabilistic function with ω as one of its inputs. Let d be a distribution function on N, and r a random variable (d's input). The *entropy* of g under the distribution function d is $H_d(g) = -\Sigma_{r,\omega} Pr(d(r)) \log(Pr(d(r))) g(\omega, d(r))$. Likewise, d may be a multidimensional distribution function generating P, U, m.

The *Cracking Entropy* for security parameter n is

$$CE_{I,f,d}(n) = H_d(S_{I,f}(\omega, P, U, m) / T_I(\omega, P, m)).$$

Definition 4: A cryptosystem has at least *security* $s : N \to N$ if $CE_{I,f,d}(n) = O(1)/s(n)$, for all probabilistic algorithms I.

6. References

[BCGL] Ben-David, S., Chor, B., Goldreich, O., Luby, M.: "On the Theory of Average Case Complexity", *STOC*, 1989 pp. 204-216.

[BK] Bauspiess, F., Knobloch, H.: "How to Keep Authenticity Alive in a Computer Network", *Eurocrypt'89*.

[DEK] Dolev, D., Even, E., Karp, R.M.: "On the Security of Ping-Pong Protocols", *Information and Control*, Vol. 55, Nos 1-3, Nov. Dec. 1982, pp. 57-68.

[DH] Diffie, W.,, Hellman, M.: "New Directions In Cryptography", *IEEE Trans. on Inf. Theory*, 1976, IT-22, pp. 644-654.

[FS] Fiat, A., Shamir, A.: "How to Prove Yourself: Practical Solutions to Identification and Signature Problems", *Proceedings of Crypto 86*.

[G] Günther, C.G.: "Diffie-Hellman and El-Gamal Protocols With One Single Authentication Key", *Eurocrypt' 89*.

[GHY] Galil, Z., Haber, S., Yung, M.: "Minimum-Knowledge Interactive Proofs for Decision Problems", *SIAM J. on Computers* Vol. 18, No. 4, , Aug. 1989.

[GL] Goldreich, O., Levin, A.L.: "A Hard-Core Predicate for All One-Way Functions", *STOC'89* , pp. 25-32.

[GM] Goldwasser, S., Micali, S.,: "Probabilistic Encryption", *JCSS*, Vol. 28, No. 2 , 1984, pp. 270-279.

[GMR] Goldwasser, S., Micali, S., Rackoff, C.: "The knowledge Complexity of Interactive Proof Systems", *Proc. 17th ACM Symposium on Theory of Computing* 1985, and SIAM 1989.

[GMW] Goldreich, O., Micali, S., Wigderson, A.: "How to Play Any Mental Game", *Proc. STOC* 1987, pp 218-229

[HU] Hopcroft,J.E., Ullman, J.D. : *"Introduction to automata theory, languages, & computation"* Addison-Wesley, 1979

[KO] Koyama,K., Ohta, K.: "Identity Based Conference Key Distribution Systems", *Proc. Crypto'87*.

[M] McCurley, K.S.: "A Key Distribution System Equivalent to Factoring", *J. of Cryptology,* Vol.1, No. 2, 1988, pp. 95-106.

[MTI] Matsumoto, T., Takashima, Y., Imai, H.: "On Seeking Smart Public-Key-Distribution Systems", *Trans. of IECE Japan* Vo. E 69, No. 2, Feb 1986.

[O] Okamoto, E.: "Proposal for Identity-Based Key Distribution Systems", *Electronic Letters* 1986, 22, pp. 1283,1284.

[RSA] Rivest, R.L., Shamir, A., and Adelman, L.: "A Method for Obtaining Digital Signatures and Public-Key Cryptosystems", *Commun. ACM* 1978, 21, pp. 120-126.

[S] Shmuely, Z.:"Composite Diffie-Hellman Public-Key Generating Systems Are Hard to Break", TR #356, *Computer Science Dept. Technion, IIT* , Feb. 1985.

[Y] Yacobi, Y.: "Attack on The Koyama-Ohta Identity Based Key-Distribution System", *Proc. Crypto'87* .

SDNS ARCHITECTURE AND END-TO-END ENCRYPTION

Ruth Nelson and John Heimann
Electronic Defense Communications Division
GTE Government Systems Corporation
100 First Avenue
Waltham, MA 02254

INTRODUCTION

The Secure Data Network System (SDNS) is intended to provide secure data communications to a variety of DoD and commercial users. SDNS services include key management and system management as well as data encryption, authentication and access control. The program is a U. S. Government/Industry effort, with participation by the National Security Agency, National Institute for Standards and Technology, other government agencies and about a dozen government contractors. During the concept definition and prototyping phases, a joint working group defined the set of security services to be provided and developed protocols for key management and for secure communications [1]. The protocols and architecture are compatible with the International Standards Organization (ISO) Reference Model for Open Systems Interconnection (OSI), and the end-to-end encryption (E3) protocols are being proposed as U.S. and international standards. The E3 protocols are publicly released and appropriate for the OSI environment.

SDNS includes security protocols at the Application, Transport, Network and Link layers of the OSI protocol hierarchy [2], as shown in Figure 1. The security services provided at each layer are a subset of those in the Security Addendum to the OSI Reference Model [3]. MSP, an application layer protocol, provides electronic mail security compatible with the CCITT X.400 series recommendations. KMP, a single key management protocol, negotiates keys and security parameters for all of the lower layer encryption services. The transport and network layer E3 protocols, which are the main subject of this paper, provide protection for the user data but allow the forwarding and handling of the data units by the network packet switches. Link encryption protocols are being defined by the working group for a variety of communication links and local networks.

END-TO-END ENCRYPTION

In packet networks and internets, the term *end-to-end encryption* has been used to refer to an encryption scheme that encrypts the user data but provides unencrypted network headers. This allows the data to be routed and delivered by the network communications switches. A number of schemes have been proposed at various layers of the protocol architecture. If the E3 is too high in the protocol hierarchy, then the scheme is sensitive to the higher level protocols and formats used by the communicating parties, and different security protocols may be required for different applications. If it is too low in the hierarchy, then the encryption must be undone at each switch so that the control information can be read. These constraints have meant that most of the E3 schemes are either at the transport or the network protocol layer. Both network layer and transport layer encryption are permitted by the OSI Security Addendum. Each location has its avid proponents, and each has certain advantages and limitations.

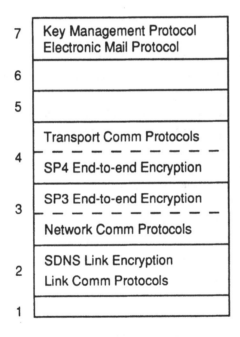

Figure 1. Placement of SDNS Protocols in the OSI Architecture

SECURITY PROTOCOL (SP)

SDNS has defined a security protocol (SP), which logically fits between the network and transport layer of the protocol hierarchy. Since OSI does not permit the addition of extra layers, we have defined this single protocol in two ways: as SP3 at the network layer and as SP4 at the transport layer [4,5]. The two representations share a common format and common basic functionality. Extensions to each protocol provide the extra services that are layer-specific. The common protocol subset is extremely simple: it encapsulates the user data (encryption and/or integrity protection) and identifies the encryption key to the receiver. SP3 and SP4 implementations can interoperate within their common domain. The protocols are independent of key management; they assume that the two parties have a common key and that each knows how to designate that key to the other. For SDNS, a key management protocol has been defined at the application layer, to provide a pairwise key for each secure association. If the key is shared by only two parties, then the protocol supports data origin authentication.

The SP service is negotiated by a separate mechanism before use, and the service is fixed for each key. The basic services are confidentiality (encryption) and connectionless integrity (each encapsulated unit protected from undetectable change). Either or both can be negotiated. The service is "connectionless;" i.e., it is provided on a per-protocol-data-unit basis and does not include sequencing or reliability. This is a major simplification in the security protocol. The needed reliability can be provided by the transport communications protocol functions operating above the security protocol, because the transport control information is encapsulated and protected by SP. SP relies on lower layer protocols for the communications functions (delivery, routing, bit-error detection on the links), and this makes the protocol simpler than some earlier designs.

SP does allow the use of multiple keys between two parties by providing a key identifier with the encrypted data. There is also an SP option (negotiated ahead of time) to carry a security label with each protected data unit. Another option allows the sender of the data to add octets of padding to the data unit.

SP3 and SP4 each have OSI-compliant definitions. SP3 is defined as a subnet-independent-convergence-protocol [6]. It is a separate protocol sublayer which sits on top of the network communications sublayer(s). The resulting network service is a secure version of the connectionless network service delivered by the OSI Connectionless Network Protocol (CLNP), which is functionally equivalent to the DoD Internet Protocol (IP). SP4 is defined as an addendum to OSI Transport Protocol (TP), which, together with TP4, can be used to provide a secure, connection-oriented service. SP3 and SP4 have identical formats. The common format is compatible with TP, so that SP4 can legitimately be an addendum to TP. Figure 2 shows the SP format. The SP data unit includes a clear header, a protected header and protected data. The header and data are protected by an integrity check value (ICV) if integrity is provided, and they are encrypted if confidentiality is provided. The clear header identifies the data as secure (Type SE) and specifies the key for decrypting and/or integrity checking.

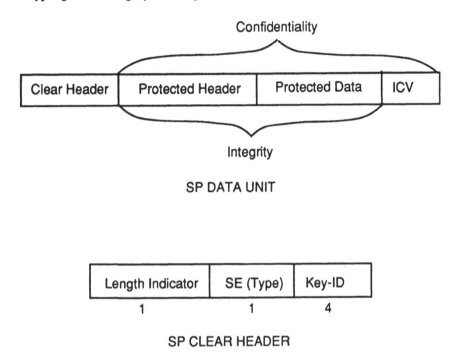

SP DATA UNIT

SP CLEAR HEADER

Figure 2. SP Header Formats

NETWORK LAYER ENCRYPTION (SP3)

OSI restricts transport layer protocols to end-systems, which are the computer systems that originate or terminate user data. At the network layer, however, the protocols can terminate at end-systems or intermediate systems, which are communications switching elements like packet switches or network gateways. It is often convenient to terminate "end-to-end" encryption at an intermediate system, and this requires that the encryption protocol be at the network layer or below. Terminating the encryption makes sense at the entrance to a local area network (LAN), for example, where all of the users are allowed access to all of the traffic or where another protection mechanism is used on the LAN. Terminating the encryption is also necessary if the communicating parties do not share a key and an intermediate system must translate the protection to another security system. Figure 3 shows the interconnection of a protected LAN and two different E3 networks, one using SP3.

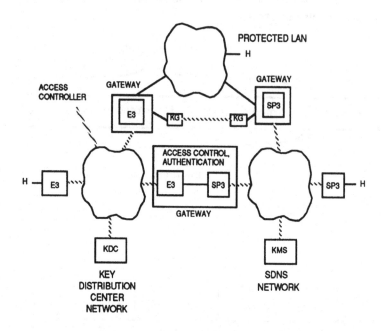

H - Host Computer
KMS - Key Management System
KDC - Key Distribution Center
KG - Key Generation, for link encryption
E^3 - Non-SDNS end-to-end encryption device
SP3 - SDNS SP3 devices

Figure 3. Interconnection of SDNS and Other Security Systems

Figure 4 shows the relationship between SP3, the transport protocol above it and the network protocol below it. The OSI model allows the network service to be provided by protocols that form sublayers of the network layer. An external key management service provides keys and security parameters, which are accessible to SP3 through a management information base. The service request to SP3 specifies a unit of data (Transport Protocol Data Unit) and some control information. The requestor can specify the source and destination addresses and a set of Quality-of-Service parameters. The Quality-of-Service parameters specify confidentiality, integrity, or both and can also request the inclusion of an explicit security label with the data.

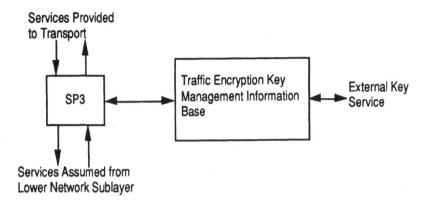

Figure 4. SP3 Interfaces

We have defined extensions to the basic SP protocol to handle the termination of SP3 at an intermediate point. The most basic of these extensions, called SP3A, simply encapsulates the end-system source and destination network addresses in the protected data unit. To completely protect these addresses, SP3A provides integrity protection, even if it was not specifically requested by the service user. The communications protocol below SP3 uses only the network address of the communicating SP3 entity and does not need to have access to the actual end-system address. At the encryption gateway, the encapsulated data is unsealed and the end-system destination address is used for routing and relaying the data unit to the end-system.

Figure 5 shows the protocol relationships in a gateway encryption scheme. In this figure, the E3 terminates at the gateway and is replaced by CLNP. The network protocols below SP3 and CLNP also are terminated at the gateway. Because the protocol on the unencrypted network is CLNP, the translation is very straightforward: the addressing schemes and data units are the same. CLNP can also be the communications protocol on NET B, operating below SP3, but this does not imply the existence of a single network protocol end-to-end. In a situation like this, end-to-end security is not provided by the E3 protocol, and other mechanisms must be used within the gateway and on the non-SP3 network.

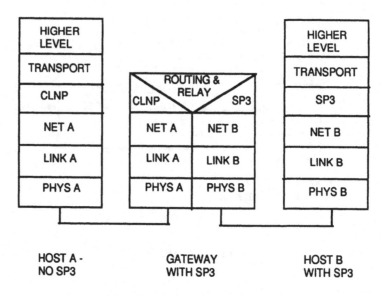

Figure 5. SP3 and CLNP at a Gateway

Additional extensions to SP3, SP3I for CLNP and SP3D for IP, permit the independent encryption and decryption of datagram "fragments," which are allowed by both CLNP and IP. Fragments are portions of a data unit which contain enough control information to be reassembled in order. They can be formed at any intermediate point in the communications path, normally when data unit size constraints require breaking up the data for passage through a particular network. They are normally reassembled only at the destination end-system, although reassembly can take place at an intermediate point if all the fragments arrive at that point. SP3I and SP3D encapsulate entire network data units or fragments, including both the address and the rest of the CLNP or IP header information. When the SP3 data unit is received at a gateway, the encapsulation is removed and normal CLNP or IP processing is done on the communications header. This mode of operation has some additional flexibility, because fragments do not have to be reassembled before encryption, but it is also more complex, because the communications processing takes place on the unencrypted data unit and so must be done securely. Two separate versions of the encryption protocol are needed because the formats of CLNP and IP headers are different. Both SP3I and SP3D provide integrity protection, even if not specifically requested, to protect the addressing and control information in the encapsulated CLNP or IP headers.

Figure 6 illustrates the SP3 addressing options. SP3N is the basic SP protocol and operates only between end-systems.

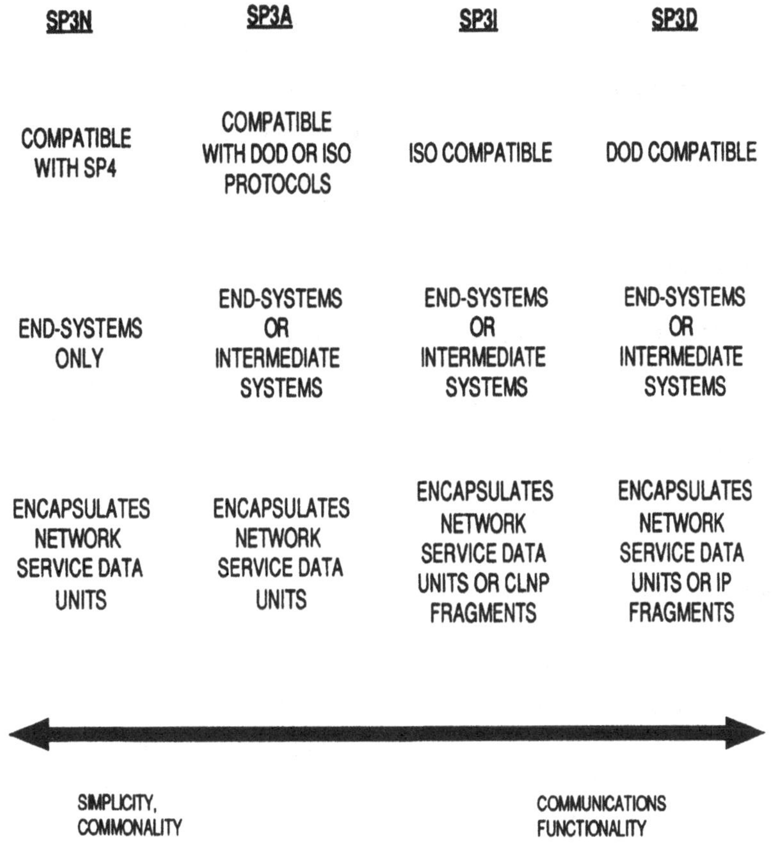

SP3N	SP3A	SP3I	SP3D
COMPATIBLE WITH SP4	COMPATIBLE WITH DOD OR ISO PROTOCOLS	ISO COMPATIBLE	DOD COMPATIBLE
END-SYSTEMS ONLY	END-SYSTEMS OR INTERMEDIATE SYSTEMS	END-SYSTEMS OR INTERMEDIATE SYSTEMS	END-SYSTEMS OR INTERMEDIATE SYSTEMS
ENCAPSULATES NETWORK SERVICE DATA UNITS	ENCAPSULATES NETWORK SERVICE DATA UNITS	ENCAPSULATES NETWORK SERVICE DATA UNITS OR CLNP FRAGMENTS	ENCAPSULATES NETWORK SERVICE DATA UNITS OR IP FRAGMENTS

SIMPLICITY, COMMONALITY ←——————————————————→ COMMUNICATIONS FUNCTIONALITY

Figure 6. SP3 Addressing Options

TRANSPORT LAYER ENCRYPTION (SP4)

SP4 is defined as an addendum to the OSI transport protocols, TP. Because it is integrated with the transport protocol, it has access to all of the TP control information. The simplest form of SP4 acts identically to the simplest SP3. On output to the network, after all of the transport layer communications processing is finished, it encapsulates the Transport Protocol Data Unit (TPDU) by encrypting it, integrity-protecting it or both. This secure PDU is designated as a TPDU-type SE, reserved for SP4, and is then handed to the network layer for processing. On receipt, the security processing is completed to expose a TPDU which is then processed normally. The extensions to SP4 allow provision of a connection-oriented secure service with truncation protection. This service includes use of a separate key for each transport connection, integrity protection on the data and the transport sequence numbers, and transmission of a Final Sequence Number at the close of a connection. SP3 with integrity protection can protect transport sequence numbers for normal TP processing, but it cannot provide the key-per-transport-connection granularity or final sequence numbers. Figure 7 shows the protected header formats used with each of the SP3 and SP4 options.

CONCLUSIONS

The SDNS end-to-end encryption protocols offer a simple, secure solution to the problem of sending sensitive data through a packet network or internet. The common subset, SP, provides a minimal solution suitable for end-system to end-system protection. The SP3 extensions provide added communications flexibility and the SP4 extensions provide added connection-oriented integrity.

ACKNOWLEDGEMENTS

The architecture and protocols described in this paper were developed by the SDNS Protocols and Signalling Working Group during the concept definition and prototyping phases of the program. The members of this group represented ten SDNS terminal contractors, GTE (the key management contractor), Analytics, the National Computer Security Center (NCSC) and various other government groups. Ruth Nelson had the privilege of chairing the group and John Heimann was an active member. Some of the concepts for the SDNS security architecture, and particularly for the end-to-end encryption protocols, were developed by GTE under an NCSC research program on Internet Security Architecture and Protocols, whose participants included GTE, Unisys, NCSC and the Defense Communications Agency.

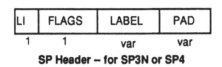

SP Header -- for SP3N or SP4

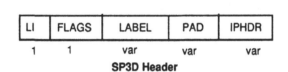

SP3A Header

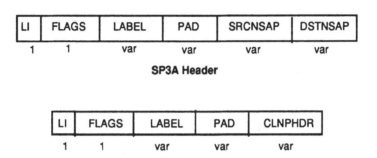

SP3I Header

SP3D Header

SP4 Header with FSN

LI indicates length of protected header in octets
Label and PAD are optional
SRCNSAP and DSTNSAP are network addresses
CLNPHDR and IPHDR are complete network headers
FSN is present only for connection release TPDUs
All variable length fields are given as Type, Length, Value

Figure 7. SP Protected Header Options

REFERENCES

1. Ruth Nelson, SDNS Services and Architecture, National Computer Security Conference, Baltimore, Maryland, October, 1988

2. ISO 7498, Information Processing Systems -- Open Systems Interconnection -- Basic Reference Model

3. ISO 7498/2, Information Processing Systems -- Open Systems Interconnection -- Security Architecture

4. SDNS Program Office, SDN.301, Revision 1.3, Security Protocol 3 (SP3), July 1988

5. SDNS Program Office, SDN.401, Revision 1.2, Security Protocol 4 (SP4), July 1988

6. ISO 8648, Information Processing Systems -- Data Communications -- Internal Organization of the Network Layer

Session 9:

Fast computation

Chair: SCOTT VANSTONE

A Survey of Hardware Implementations of RSA

(Abstract)

Ernest F. Brickell

Sandia National Laboratories *
Albuquerque, NM 87185

Today, a dozen years after the discovery of the RSA encryption algorithm [12], there are many chips available for performing RSA encryption [1] [3] [4] [5] [8] [9] [13] [15]. The purpose of this paper is to briefly describe some of the different computational algorithms that have been used in the chip designs and to provide a list of all of the currently available chips. In this abstract, we will simply mention some of these computational algorithms and give references. The full paper will contain more details of these algorithms and will appear in a book on survey articles in Cryptology which is being edited by Gus Simmons and will be published by IEEE in 1990.

Recall that the RSA encryption function consists of computing $m^e \bmod N$, where $N = pq$ for primes p and q. All of the chips perform the exponentiation as a series of modular multiplications. The modular multiplications are computed either as a standard multiplication followed by a modular reduction, or, more commonly, the computation of the multiplication and the modular reduction is combined. Finally, the multiplications are implemented as a series of additions.

For each of these arithmetic functions, we will mention some choices in how they can be implemented on a chip. By using redundant number systems to avoid carries the addition can be speeded up at a cost of more storage. Multiplication can be speeded up by the techniques of multiple bit scanning. See for instance [6]. There are several techniques that have been developed for implementing modular reduction. The quotient digits can be approximated using only the high order bits of the divisor and the current remainder[3]. Division can be avoided all together by several different methods. The reciprocal of the modulus can be stored, thus replacing division by multiplication. For well chosen values of i, the reduced values of $2^i \bmod N$ can be stored, so that modular reduction can be achieved through multiplication by these values. Peter Montgomery [10] has a method for modular reduction without division which uses a nonstandard technique of identifying the residue classes.

There are also techniques available to save on the number of multiplications needed to perform an exponentiation. Compared with the standard binary method of expo-

---

*This work performed at Sandia National Laboratories and supported by the U.S. Department of Energy under contract No. DE–AC04–76DP00789.

nentiation, addition chains [7] can give a significant savings in the number of multiplications needed at a cost of increasing the storage necessary. For the user who knows the factorization of N, it is possible to speed up the computation by the use of the Chinese Remainder Theorem[7]. Since some of the chip manufacturers give their speeds assuming the use of the Chinese Remainder Theorem while others do not, it is often difficult to compare the performance of the different chips. The following chart contains all of the actual RSA chips that the author is aware of.

	Year	Tech.	# bits per chip	Clock	Baudrate (# bits)	# Clocks per 512 bit encryption
Sandia	1981	3μm	168	4MHz	1.2K (336)	$4.0 * 10^6$
Bus. Sim.	1985	Gate Array	32	5MHz	3.8K (512)	$.67 * 10^6$
AT&T	1987	1.5μm	298	12MHz	7.7K (1024)	$.4 * 10^6$
Cylink	1987	1.5μm	1024	16MHz	3.4K (1024)	$1.2 * 10^6$
Cryptech	1988	Gate Array	120	14MHz	17K (512)	$.4 * 10^6$
CNET	1988	1μm	1024	25MHz	5.3K (512)	$2.3 * 10^6$
Brit. Telecom	1988	2.5μm	256	10MHz	10.2K (256)	$1 * 10^6$
Plessy	1989		512		10.2K (512)	
Sandia	1989	2μm	272	8MHz	10K (512)	$.4 * 10^6$
Philips	1989	1.2μm	512	16MHz	2K (512)	$4.1 * 10^6$

The last column in this table was estimated if the chips could not do a 512 bit encryption or if the timing for a 512 bit encryption was not available. The 12MHz listed for the AT&T chip is for 1024 bit encryption. For a 512 bit encryption, it runs at 15MHz. AT&T has recently come out with an improved version of their chip which has 520 bit slices per chip and is slightly faster. At first glance, the Philips design does not appear competitive with the others. However, this is a design for smart cards and only takes 4mm^2 of silicon. Cylink and Siemanns are also planning smart card implementations.

There are chip designs that promise much greater speeds than current chips [11, 14], but chips based on these designs have not yet been built.

In recent years, digital signal processors (DSP) have become a viable alternative to building a custom chip for RSA encryption. Kochanski [8] was the first to consider this possibility. DSPs have improved since his work and Michael Weiner of BNR has announced an implementation on the Motorola 56000 that achieves a 125 ms encryption on a 512 bit modulus for a throughput of 4K bits per second without using the Chinese Remainder Theorem. Using the Chinese Remainder Theorem, he can achieve a 50 ms encryption.

Another alternative to custom design has been recently proposed by Bertin, Roncin, and Vuillemin [2]. They implemented RSA on a pair of Programmable Active Memory chips. The maximum modulus size that they can accommodate on two chips is 508 bits. Using the Chinese Remainder Theorem, the encryption time is 17 ms for a baudrate of 30K bits per second.

References

[1] AT&T, *T7002/t7003 bit slice multiplier*. Product Announcement, 1987.

[2] P. BERTIN, D. RONCIN, AND J. VUILLEMIN, *Introduction to programmable active memories*. Internal Report, Digital Equipment Corporation, 1989.

[3] E. F. BRICKELL, *A fast modular multiplication algorithm with applications to two key cryptography*, in Advances in Cryptology, Proceedings of Crypto 82, D. Chaum, R. L. Rivest, and A. T. Sherman, eds., New York, 1982, Plenum Press, pp. 51–60.

[4] P. GALLAY AND E. DEPRET, *A cryptography processor*, in 1988 IEEE International Solid-State Circuits Conference Digest of Technical Papers, 1988, pp. 148–149.

[5] F. HOORNAERT, M. DECROOS, J. VANDEWALLE, AND R. GOVAERTS, *Fast RSA-hardware: Dream or reality?*, in Advances in Cryptology-EUROCRYPT'88, C. G. Günther, ed., 1988.

[6] K. HWANG, *Computer Arithmetic*, John Wiley, New York, 1979.

[7] D. KNUTH, *The art of computer programming, Vol. 2 : Seminumerical algorithms*, Addison-Wesley, Reading,MA, 1981.

[8] M. KOCHANSKI, *Developing an RSA chip*, in Advances in Cryptology-CRYPTO'85, H. C. Williams, ed., New York, 1985, Springer-Verlag, pp. 350–357.

[9] S. MIYAGUCHI, *Fast encryption algorithm for the RSA cryptographic system*, in Proceedings of Compcon 82, Los Angeles, 1982, IEEE, pp. 672–678.

[10] P. L. MONTGOMERY, *Modular multiplication without trial division*, Mathematics of Computation, 44 (1985), pp. 519–521.

[11] G. ORTON, M. ROY, P. SCOTT, L. PEPPARD, AND S. TAVARES, *VLSI implementation of public-key encryption algorithms*, in Advances in Cryptology-CRYPTO'86, A.M.Odlyzko, ed., New York, 1986, Springer-Verlag, pp. 277–301.

[12] R. RIVEST, A. SHAMIR, AND L. ADLEMAN, *A method for obtaining digital signatures and public-key cryptosystems*, Communications of the ACM, 21 (1978), pp. 120–126.

[13] R. L. RIVEST, *RSA chips (past/present/future)*, in Advances in Cryptology-EUROCRYPT'84, T.Beth, N.Cot, and I.Ingemarsson, eds., New York, 1984, Springer-Verlag, pp. 159–168.

[14] H. SEDLAK AND U. GOLZE, *An RSA cryptography processor*, Microprocessing and Microprogramming, 18 (1986), pp. 583–590.

[15] A. VANDEMEULEBROECKE, E. VANZIELEGHEM, T. DENAYER, AND P. G. JESPERS, *A single chip 1024 bits RSA processor*. to appear in Advances in Cryptology - EUROCRYPT'89.

Modular Exponentiation Using Recursive Sums of Residues

P.A.Findlay and B.A.Johnson (Hatfield Polytechnic, UK)

1. Summary

This paper describes a method for computing a modular exponentiation, useful in performing the RSA Public Key algorithm, suitable for software or hardware implementation. The method uses conventional multiplication, followed by partial modular reduction based on sums of residues. We show that for a simple recursive system where the output of partial modular reduction is the input for the next multiplication, overflow presents few problems.

2.Rivest, Shamir, and Adleman public key cryptosystem

The Rivest, Shamir, and Adleman (RSA) [6] public key cryptosystem uses exponentiations of the form:

$$y = x^k \bmod m.$$

where y is either ciphertext, or deciphered plaintext, and (k,m) form the enciphering/deciphering key. Note that k is different for enciphering and deciphering. In an encryption system offering a practical level of security, x,k, and m need to be 256 bits or more in length. Exponentiation is performed by repeated squaring operations, along with conditional multiplications by the original x, e.g.

$$x^5 \bmod m = ((x^2 \bmod m)^2 \bmod m).x \bmod m$$

Note that in each case, the previous modulo reduced result is fed back to be multiplied by itself, or by x. Modulo reduction

is associative, so can be carried out at each stage to prevent the intermediate results from growing too large.
Several algorithms for performing this exponentiation already exist . These can be divided into algorithms that are suitable for hardware implementation [1,3,5], and those that are suitable for software implementation [2,7].

3. The Method as implemented in Hardware

The core operation of exponentiation is modulo multiplication, and this can be performed in two ways:

a) Multiplication and reduction can be combined into a single operation. As multiplication partial products are formed, a decision is taken whether or not to perform a reduction on these partial products.

b) Multiplication and reduction are separate tasks, with the output of the multiplier feeding the input of the reduction unit.

For the purposes of this paper, case b) is being considered. Also, for the purposes of the hardware method, multiplication is best performed in a bit-serial form using a multiplier as described in [4,8]. These multipliers take the two arguments in bit-serial form, least significant bit first, and produce the product in bit-serial form, least significant bit first. They have the advantage that they are simple, are of cellular construction, and are easily expandable to larger bit-widths.

3.1 Sums-of-Residues Reduction

Modulo reduction can be performed by division, which is slow, or by trial subtractions incorporated into the multiplication that modify the partial products formed in the multiplication process [1,3]. It is suggested that neither of these is used as a reduction method. If the number, P, to be reduced by the modulus, m, is expressed as a binary vector:

$$P = [p_1, p_2, .. p_n], \quad p_i = \{0, 1\} \text{ for } i = 1 \text{ to } 2n.$$

then the modulo reduction could be expressed as:

$$P \bmod m = (\sum_{i=1}^{i=2n} p_i . 2^{i-1}) \bmod m.$$

The modulus operation is associative, so the above could be expressed as:

$$P \bmod m = (\sum_{i=1}^{i=2n} p_i . (2^{i-1} \bmod m)) \bmod m.$$

Now the reduction is simply a conditional sum of powers of 2 reduced modulo m: "residues", hence the name of sums-of-residues (SOR) reduction. This reduction is simple to calculate, given a table of residue values [5].

The final modulus operation in the above equation is necessary because of the possibility of getting incomplete reductions. For example, 15 mod 13 using the above method is still 15. This may lead to the conclusion that a conventional reduction using division or other techniques is still required. In order to perform an exponentiation, these incomplete reductions could lead to the multiplications in the next exponentiation step overflowing. A limited overflow does occur, but one which is bounded above, and can be taken into account by using extra hardware. A simple derivation of this upper bound is now given.

3.2 Sums-of-Residues Overflow Bound

Let P be the result of a squaring or multiplication step, i, in the exponentiation, i.e.

$$P_i = X_i^2 \quad \text{or} \quad P_i = A.X_i; \text{ where } A < m < 2^n,$$

and X_i is an intermediate result of bit-length L_i.

Clearly, the product will give a maximum bit-length following
a squaring, rather than a multiplication, and hence the maximum
bit-length of P_i is $2L_i$.

$$\text{Let } P = \sum_{j=1}^{j=2L} p_j . 2^{j-1} \text{ define } p_j, \text{ and}$$

$$\text{let } r_k = 2^{k-1} \text{mod } m, \text{ where } m < 2^n.$$

Then the next value of X will be $X_{i+1} = \sum_{j=1}^{j=2L_i} p_j r_j$

Simplifying things slightly, this new X value can be considered
to be the sum of at most $2L_i$ n-bit numbers. Therefore,

$X_{i+1} < 2L_i(2^n-1)$, hence L_{i+1}, the max. bit-length of X_{i+1} is
$$L_{i+1} < \lceil \log_2(2L_i) \rceil + n.$$

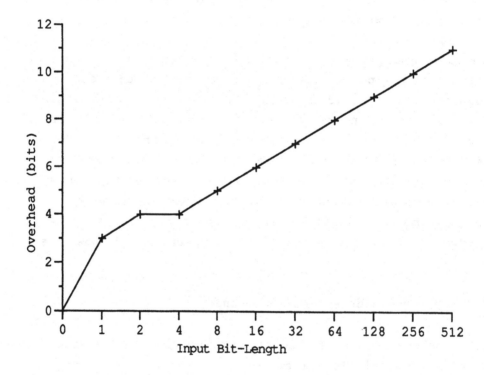

Figure 1: Bit-length overhead versus input bit-length

To find the maximum for L, the above equation is relaxed, starting with an initial L = n. A graph of the bit-length overhead, h (= L-n), is shown in figure 1.

The results show that for a typical input bit-length of 256 bits, the actual hardware is required to handle 266 bit numbers. This represents an overhead of only 4%.

Any final reduction then becomes necessary only at the very output of the exponentiation, and not at the output of each modulo multiplication.

3.3 Residue Calculation

The residues can be stored in a look-up table [5], and used when needed. This uses a modest amount of storage, typically 2n by n-bits. However, the data paths for this storage are very wide, and this is undesirable in silicon. It is easier to calculate the residues, r, as they are needed, and this can be done with a simple recursive formula:

$$r_i = \begin{cases} 2.r_{i-1} & \text{iff } (2.r_{i-1} - m) < 0 \\ 2.r_{i-1} - m & \text{iff } (2.r_{i-1} - m) \geq 0 \end{cases}, \quad i = 2..2n, \quad r_1 = 1.$$

Figure 2 shows a possible architecture for sum-of-residues calculation corresponding to the serial product P, assuming that P appears lsb first. It is also assumed that n-bit encryption is being performed, and that the multiplier is able to handle (n+h) bit numbers.

Two n-bit registers, M and R, hold (-m); the two's complement of the modulus, and r, the current residue. The residue is initially set to 1. As the system is clocked, the residue register is reloaded with either (2r), or with (2r-m), depending on the sign bit of the (2r-m) calculation. An (n+h) bit accumulator sums those residues which are gated into it by the incoming 2(n+h) bits of the serial product P.

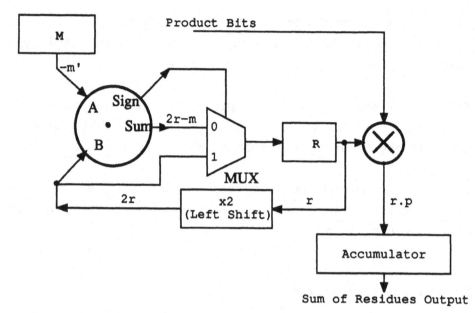

Figure 2: Parallel Sums-of-Residues Calculation

For practical sizes of n, the time taken for the sign bit to appear is prohibitive because of the long carry-propagate path. However, for a given modulus, the sequence of sign bits is always the same. Therefore, they can be precomputed by a host machine each time the modulus is changed, and stored as a sequence of bits in a shift register. (In an RSA system, the modulus changes only when the enciphering or deciphering keys are changed). This allows the carry chain to be pipelined.

In fact, not all of the sign-bit sequence needs to be stored. Suppose m is q bits long, $q \leq n$, then

$$2^{q-1} < m < 2^q, \text{ so for } i = 1 \ldots (q-1), \; r_{i+1} = 2r_i = 2^{i-1}.$$

and hence the sign bits are all the same.

To make the most of this fact, a 'working modulus', m', can be used; being the actual modulus multiplied by an appropriate power of 2 (left shifted) to make an n-bit number, i.e.

$$m' = m.2^{n-q}$$

The sum of residues derived from the working modulus will be congruent to that of the real modulus, and the bit length of the result will still not exceed the upper bound previously described. The first n bits of the product P, may be loaded directly into the accumulator, and the residue register, R, may be preloaded with (-m') in two's complement form; as this is the residue of 2^{n+1} mod m'.†

So far the SOR system has been described as being essentially parallel in operation, using the serial output of the multiplier to gate a parallel accumulation of the residues. This parallel architecture may be transformed into a bit serial array format by 'skewing' the original data paths in both time and space. The modulus and residue registers are now effectively shift registers, and the sign bit register is essentially static. Static storage is also required for the (n+2h) most significant data bits, hence (n+2h) 'cells' are needed if they are all to be identical (essential for expandability). Each cell contains two full adders, a 2:1 multiplexer, nine flip flops, and one AND gate. The functional description of a cell is shown in figure 3.

Each 'T' block in figure 3 represents a commonly-clocked storage element. The SELECT signal is a pulse that is passed from one cell to the next at each clock signal, and the arrival of this signal will cause the current input on the global PRODUCT line to be stored into the P-register. The two's complement of the working modulus (-m') circulates in the shift register formed by the MODULUS, MODULUS(out) chain. ADR1

---

† Note: if the lower n bits of P represent a number, $\geq$ m', then the preloading of the accumulator results in m' being added to the accumulation. However, this still yields a final sum that is congruent to the true residue, and within the maximum bit length defined. It does however mean that the sign bit register is (n+2h) long, as opposed to (n+2h+1).

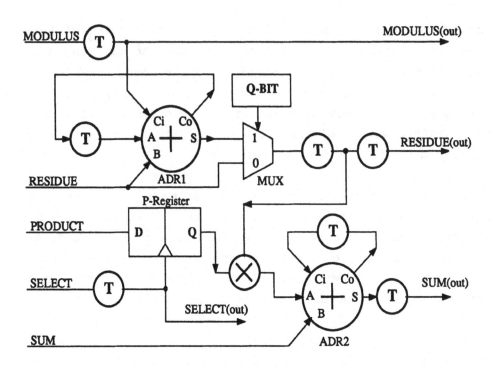

Figure 3: SOR reduction hardware cell

corresponds to the adder required in calculating the (2r-m')
term in the SOR residue calculation. The sign bit (Q-bit) for
the cell is permanently stored, having previously been set up
by the host system, and is used to gate either 2r or 2r-m'
via multiplexer MUX. The result is propagated to the next cell
via double storage elements. This double delay achieves the
doubling of the residue presented to the next cell. The single
delayed ADR1 output is gated by the stored product bit into
the carry-save adder ADR2. Using the single delayed residue
result further pipelines the design, making the critical timing
path within the cell little more than a single adder delay.

The sum of residues is calculated as follows: consider time
step i=1..2(n+h), and cell number j=1..(n+2h).

During time steps i = 1..n, the array stores the least n
bits of the product P.

During time steps $i = n..2(n+h)-1$, cell j calculates the $(i-j-n+2)$th bit of the residue modulo m' of 2^{j+n}

During time steps $i = (n+1)..2(n+h)$, cell j also holds the $(j+n)$th product bit, which gates the accumulation of the $(i-j-n)$th bit of the residue of 2^{j+n}, for all $j \leq (i-n)$.

The accumulator is effectively preloaded by bits $1..n$ of the product. In practice this is achieved by adding bit $(i-n)$ of the product to the accumulating adder ADR2 during time steps $i=(n+1)..2n$. Array operation is illustrated for cells $1,2,3$ at time steps $i=n,n+1,n+2$ in figure 4 below. Note that P is the product to be reduced, and that the carry terms for the accumulator are not shown.

Time Step		Processing Element		
		1	2	3
n	**ADR1 Calculates:**	Bit 1 of 2^{n+1} mod m'		
	ADR2 Accumulates:			
n+1	**ADR1 Calculates:**	Bit 2 of 2^{n+1} mod m'	Bit 1 of 2^{n+2} mod m'	
	ADR2 Accumulates:	Bit 1 of P + Bit 1 of 2^{n+1} mod m'		
n+2	**ADR1 Calculates:**	Bit 3 of 2^{n+1} mod m'	Bit 2 of 2^{n+2} mod m'	Bit 3 of 2^{n+3} mod m'
	ADR2	Bit 2 of P + Bit 2 2^{n+1} mod m'	Bit 1 of 2^{n+2} mod m'	

Figure 4: Array Operation after time step $(n-1)$

This results in the sum-of-residues appearing serially, lsb first, at cell $(n+2h)$. The latency between input of the product msb, and output of the sum-of-residues lsb is just one clock cycle.

FROM MULTIPLIER ARRAY

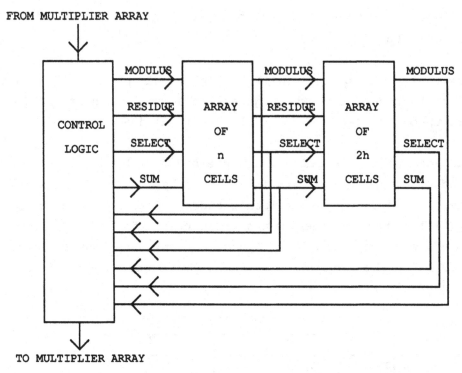

TO MULTIPLIER ARRAY

Figure 5: SOR Array interconnect

A scheme for interconnecting a practical sum-of-residues array is shown in figure 5. This also shows part of the accumulator being used as a shift register to buffer the first n bits of the product P. The feedback paths for the 'shifting' modulus and a circulating 'select' pulse are also included. The function of the select pulse allows the array to be self-sizing, and hence easily expandable.

3.4 Practical Exponentiator Hardware

A practical hardware modulo exponentiation system will therefore consist of a hardware bit serial multiplier, followed by a SOR reduction unit, as shown in figure 6. Extra hardware is required for the exponent and plaintext registers, and to control the flow of reduction unit output into the multiplier.

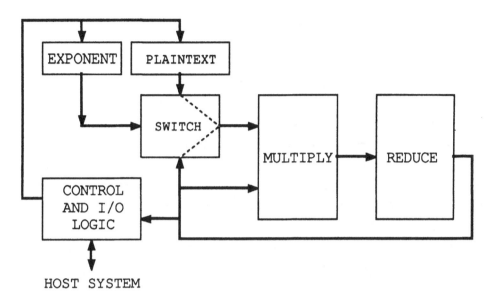

Figure 6: Practical Exponentiator Hardware System

3.5 Advantages and Disadvantages of this Architecture

This implementation of the RSA algorithm requires slightly more hardware than some of the existing systems [1,3]. It requires roughly twice as many clock cycles to perform a modular multiplication, but each clock cycle requires only 8 gate delays, and no broadcast fanout logic – as opposed to the 20-28 or so gate delays plus fanout time required for the two other schemes mentioned. Therefore, a speed improvement of approximately 50% would be expected using similar process technology.

Broadcasting is only required at the interface between the multiplier and the reduction unit, hence an extra clock cycle can be allowed for broadcast propagation with minimal loss of throughput.

The system needs minimal host support for loading the modulus, performing the final reduction, etc. These tasks could be handled by a dedicated single chip microcomputer.

4. Partitioned Sums-of-Residues

We now give a generalisation of the method that can be used with both hardware and software, at the cost of higher overheads, either in hardware or operational complexity.

In a parallel system, treating the multiplier output product, P, one bit at a time is inefficient, as observed in the previous section. However, for the price of introducing greater redundancy in the result, the product can be partitioned into discrete words; each word being multiplied by the residue of the least significant power of two that the word begins with, and the results accumulated. This still gives a result congruent to the true reduced result.

Consider a single multiply and SOR step. Suppose the product is 2n bits long, and is divided up into c-bit long words. This is illustrated in figure 7, where n = 2c.

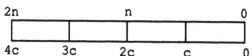

Figure 7: Partitioning the Product into c-bit Segments

A look-up table holds the residues of $2^0, 2^c, 2^{2c}, 2^{3c}$, etc. Each c-bit segment of the product is then multiplied by the appropriate residue, and the results accumulated. For instance, if n=8, and c=4, then 50000 mod 23 (=21) is computed as:

$$(0*2^0 \bmod 23) + (5*2^4 \bmod 23) + (3*2^8 \bmod 23) + (12*2^{12} \bmod 23) = 113$$

which is congruent to the true result.

The overhead incurred during exponentiation using recursive partitioned sums-of-residues (PSOR) must be calculated. Using a simple approach to maximum bit-length calculation, the ith multiplication followed by by PSOR reduction will yield a SOR of bit-length not more than:

$$L_{i+1} = \left(n + c + \left\lceil \log_2 \left\lceil 2 \cdot \frac{L_i}{c} \right\rceil \right\rceil \right).$$

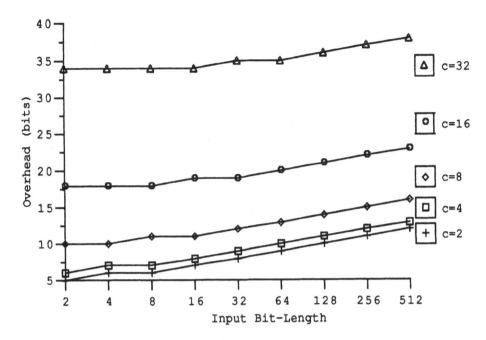

Figure 8: Graph of bit-length overheads for PSOR scheme

Note: this expression is not valid for the case c=1, as multiplying a number by 1 does not increase the bit-length.

To simulate exponentiation, and hence find the maximum bit-length obtained, the above equation is relaxed starting with L=n, until L reaches a maximum. Figure 8 is a graph of maximum bit length overhead, h, versus modulus bit-length n, for various values of c, the partition width.

It is feasible to use the "working modulus" optimisation again, and thereby simply accumulate the first n bits of the non-reduced product. This decreases the size of any look-up table, and the number of multiplies required to perform the PSOR.

The operations used in PSOR could be performed by dedicated hardware multiplier-accumulator chips, or as multiply and add instructions in software. The same hardware or software instructions could be used to generate the non-reduced product.

The total number of fixed-length multiply-accumulate cycles to perform the complete PSOR modulo multiplication is now determined. The multiplication to form the product requires

$$\left(\left\lceil (n+h)\middle/ c \right\rceil\right)^2$$

operations, using a c-bit multiply function. The PSOR reduction would be expected to take

$$\left\lceil (n+2h)\middle/ c \right\rceil * \left\lceil n\middle/ c \right\rceil$$

operations using the same function. In practice, it would make sense to adjust n such that either the left-hand or right-hand term above is an integer. Figure 9 shows total numbers of multiply-accumulate cycles necessary for a complete multiplication and PSOR reduction.

n	c	Mult-Accs.
256	8	2308
256	16	628
256	32	188
283	32	188
474	32	541

Figure 9: Typical numbers of Multiply-Accumulate cycles for PSOR

Finally, the storage requirements for the look-up table for PSOR operation will be considered. Assuming a working modulus is used, a table of

$$\left\lceil (n+2h)\middle/ c \right\rceil$$

n-bit residues will be needed, i.e. a memory requirement of

$$\left\lceil (n+2h)\middle/ c \right\rceil * n \text{ bits}.$$

Figure 10 below shows the residue look-up capacity for the set of "typical" values given in figure 9 above. The memory requirement is also expressed as number of registers, or memory locations, assuming that they are the same bit-width as the multiplier.

n	c	Residue Bits	No.c-bit Registers
256	8	17408	2167
256	16	8960	560
256	32	4864	152
283	32	5120	160
474	32	8192	256

Figure 10: Typical Residue Table sizes for PSOR algorithm

5.Conclusions

An optimised hardware algorithm has been proposed for performing RSA public key encryption. This algorithm lends itself to a high speed efficient VLSI implementation of an encryption system, using serial data and one-dimensional semi-systolic arrays. The system consists of a serial multiplier array coupled with a unique serial sum-of-residues reduction array. Based on this architecture, it is possible to build an easily expandable RSA engine with hardware complexity $O(n)$ and speed proportional to $\frac{1}{n^2}$.

The partitioned sums-of-residues method has significant advantages over the bit-level method as far as operation on standard hardware/software is concerned. It is readily implemented with typical Digital Signal Processing chips, and could be programmed efficiently on any general-purpose machine with a fast integer multiply function, and a large register set (or a data cache). No bit testing or conditional branching need be performed, hence the algorithm would run extremely efficiently on highly pipelined processors, or RISC machines, since no instruction queue flushing would be required.

6.Acknowledgements

The authors would like to thank John Guppy, the British Aerospace (Dynamics) Technology Executive, for the contribution of his mathematical expertise. The original theoretical work behind this paper formed part of B.A.Johnson's PhD programme, which was funded by the UK Science and Engineering Research Council. The work in this paper is the subject of a patent application.

7.References

[1] Baker, P.W.
'Fast computation of A*B mod N'
IEE Electronics Letters, Vol.23, No.15,16 July 1987, pp794.

[2] Blakley, G.R.
'A Computer Algorithm for Calculating the Product AB Mod M'
IEEE Trans. Comp. Vol.C32 No.5 May 1983

[3] Brickell, E.F.
'A Fast Modular Multiplication Algorithm with application to two-key Cryptography'
In "Advances in Cryptology",conf. proc. CRYPTO'82, Plenum Press, 1982.

[4] Ngo-Chen, I., Willoner, R.
'An O(n) Parallel Multiplier having Bit Sequential Input and Output'
IEEE Trans. Comp. Vol.C28 No.10 Oct.1979

[5] Ngo-Chen, I., Willoner, R.
'An Algorithm for Modular Exponentiation'
Proc. 5th Symp. Comp. Arith. IEEE 1981

[6] Rivest, R.L., Shamir, A., and Adleman, L.
'On Digital Signatures and Public Key Cryptosystems',
Comms. ACM, Vol.21, No.2, Feb. 1978 pp120-126

[7] Selby, A., Mitchell, C.
'Algorithms for Software Implementations of RSA'
IEE Proc. May 1989 Vol.136 Part E No.3 p166

[8] Strader,N.R., Rhynne, V.T.
'A Canonical Bit Sequential Multiplier'
IEEE Trans. Comp. Vol.C31 No.8 Aug.1982

A Fast Modular-multiplication Algorithm based on a Higher Radix

Hikaru Morita

NTT Communications and Information Processing Laboratories
3-9-11, Midori-cho, Musashino-shi, Tokyo, 180 Japan

Abstract

This paper presents a new fast compact modular-multiplication algorithm, which will multiply modulo N in $log(N)/log(r)$ clock pulses when the algorithm is based on radix r ($r \geq 4$).

1 Introduction

Modular multiplication is essential for public-key cryptosystems such as the Rivest-Shamir-Adleman scheme (RSA) [1]. To guarantee security, the multiplication-word lengths have to be significantly greater than conventional computer word lengths. Therefore, techniques for speeding-up the modular multiplication are important.

Brickell [2] has shown how to design a compact operation based on radix 2 without frequent data transmission between processors performing modular multiplication and memories storing data in progress.

This paper proposes a new modular multiplication algorithm based on a radix higher than two that is faster than conventional algorithms based on radix 2. This new algorithm overcomes the problem of overflowing a limited computation range by using a partial product to adjust a partial remainder before a multiply-addition of the partial product. Furthermore, an approximate method is developed to reduce the comparator which determines the partial remainder. Consequently, the modular multiplier using this algorithm based on radix 4 can compute 512-bit modular exponentiation at a throughput of 80 Kbits/s at 30 MHz.

2 New Fast Compact Algorithm

If "n" is the bit length of the modulus N, then modular multiplication is represented as $A \times B$ *modulo* N where A, B, and N are n-bit binary integers related by A, B

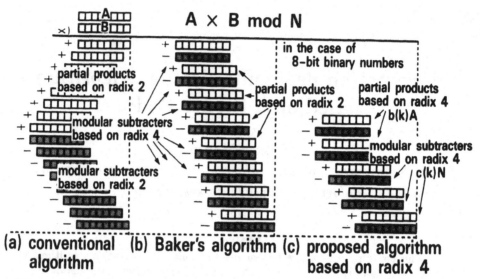

A × B mod N

(a) conventional algorithm

(b) Baker's algorithm

(c) proposed algorithm based on radix 4

Figure 1 Comparison of modular multiplication algorithms

$\in [0, N-1]$. A conventional modular-multiplication algorithm shown in *Figure 1(a)* multiplies first and then divides the $2n$-bit product by the modulus N. This algorithm cannot accomplish high-speed computation and needs a massive amount of hardware because data transmission between processors and memories occurs frequently.

Consequently, methods using specialized hardware have been developed [2,3,4]. These methods use compact n-bit-length operators in which each subtraction step in binary division is embedded in the repeated multiply-addition. Brickell [2] has particularly proposed a modular multiplier that can perform one step of addition and subtraction simultaneously in each clock pulse. The modular multiplier needs about n clock pulses.

This section describes a new algorithm based on a radix higher than two, which can reduce the amount of processing.

2.1 Approaches

A higher radix has been used to speed-up ordinary multiplication and division. For modular multiplication, Baker [5] has designed an algorithm which combines modular subtraction based on radix 4 and multiply-addition based on radix 2 to simplify operation as shown in *Figure 1(b)*. However, until now, no algorithm using a higher radix to speed-up modular multiplication has been developed because of the problem of overflowing a finite computation range.

The new algorithm presented here was designed to speed-up modular multiplication by using the same higher radix throughout. In practice, the addition and subtraction steps can be reduced to half or less those of the other algorithms as shown in *Figure 1 (c)*.

The proposed algorithm is carried out by using the following equation repeatedly.

$$R^{(k-1)} \leftarrow rR^{(k)} + b(k)A - c(k)N \tag{1}$$

where "k" is the step number of repeated processing, "r" is the radix number, $R^{(k)}$ and $R^{(k-1)}$ are partial remainders, $b(k)A$ is a partial product, and $c(k)N$ is a modulus subtracter. To overcome the problem of overflowing, this algorithm uses the following approaches:

(1) To prevent the absolute value of the next partial remainder $R^{(k-1)}$ from overflowing the upper limit dN (the variable d is derived in *Appendix A*), the modulus subtracter $c(k)N$ is determined by using the next partial product $b(k-1)A$ in advance.

(2) To reduce the absolute range of the partial product $b(k)A$, the multiplicand A is modified from the range $[0, N-1]$ into the range $[-N/2, N/2]$.

2.2 Procedure based on a Higher Radix

The main procedure of the algorithm is explained by using the modified Robertson's diagram. *Figure 2* shows the diagram for radix 4 in which the boundary variable d equals $7/12$. The horizontal axis shows the partial dividend $(rR^{(k)} + b(k)A)/N$ of the present remainder $R^{(k)}$ plus the present partial product $b(k)A$. The vertical axis shows the next remainder $R^{(k-1)}/N$. The graph c (where $c \in \{-2, -1, 0, 1, 2\}$ for radix 4) in the diagram represents Eq. (1). After the subtracter $c(k)N$ is determined by the graph to have the value of $(rR^{(k)} + b(k)A)/N$ in the horizontal axis, the remainder $R^{(k-1)}$ is calculated.

The graph c takes the form of several discrete lines, each with a fixed 45-degree slope. However, this modified Robertson's diagram is different from the ordinary Robertson's diagram [6]. For example, in *Figure 2*, the window enclosing the range $[-7/3, 7/3]$ and $[-7/12 - bA/(4N), +7/12 - bA/(4N)]$ moves up or down according to the value of the each coefficient $b(k-1)$. Then, the boundary indices, $\ell_2, \ell_1, \ell_{-1}$, and ℓ_{-2}, which show the boundaries between the discrete lines, move left or right.

The algorithm procedure is as follows:

Step 1 (initialize the numbers):

$$\text{If } N < 2A, \ A \leftarrow A - N. \tag{2}$$
$$n \leftarrow \lfloor log_2(N) \rfloor + 1$$
$$k \leftarrow \lfloor n/r' \rfloor + 1$$
$$R^{(k)} \leftarrow 0$$

where $r' = log_2(r)$.

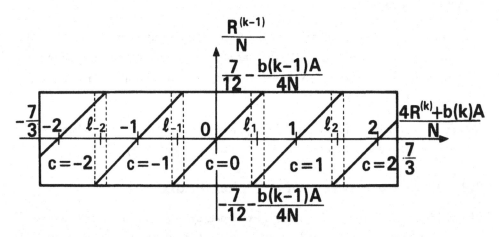

Figure 2 Modified Robertson's diagram for the new algorithm (in a case of radix 4)

Step 2 (repeat $\lfloor n/r' \rfloor + 1$ rounds):

$$c(k) \leftarrow f_c((rR^{(k)} + b(k)A), b(k-1)) \tag{3}$$

$$R^{(k-1)} \leftarrow rR^{(k)} + b(k)A - c(k)N \tag{4}$$

$$k \leftarrow k - 1$$

Step 3 (last routine):

$$A \leftarrow \begin{cases} R^{(0)} & \text{if } R^{(0)} \geq 0 \\ R^{(0)} + N & \text{otherwise} \end{cases}$$

In this procedure, we let variables R and A have sign bits, respectively.

Notes:

• function $f_c(R, b)$:

$$f_c \leftarrow \begin{cases} i & \text{if } \ell_i N < R \leq \ell_{i+1} N \\ 0 & \text{if } \ell_{-1} N \leq R \leq \ell_1 N \\ -i & \text{if } \ell_{-i-1} N \leq R < \ell_{-i} N \end{cases} \tag{5}$$

where

$\ell_i \equiv i - 1/2 - bA/(rN)$,

$\ell_{-i} \equiv -i + 1/2 - bA/(rN)$,

and the positive integer i is in $\{1, 2, \cdots, r/2\}$.

The boundary indices (ℓ_i, ℓ_{-i}) are prepared beforehand for all $b \in \{-r/2, \cdots, -1, 0, 1, \cdots, r/2\}$.

• function $b(k)$ for the multiplier B:

$$b(k) \leftarrow -rB[r'k] + \sum_{m=0}^{r'-1} rB[r'k - m]/2^{m+1} + B[r'k - r'] \tag{6}$$

where by choosing bit-level representation, the variable B is represented by the vectors $B[n]$, $B[n-1]$, $\cdots$, and $B[1]$, and $B[0] = 0$. Eq. (6) can satisfy $b(k) \in \{-r/2, \cdots, -1, 0, 1, \cdots, r/2\}$.

We can let R represent the usual binary remainder in a carry-save redundant form. R has two components: the sum R_s and the carry R_c, where $R \equiv R_s + 2R_c$. By using carry-save adders, we can reduce carry propagation until every addition and subtraction pair takes only one clock.

2.3 Approximate method

To simplify the n-bit-length comparison in Eq. (5) for determining the modulus subtracter cN, the comparison is replaced with a short-precision comparison of $\ell_i N$ and R. Consequently, the previous function $f_c(R, b)$ in *section 2.2* is replaced the following function.

- function $f_c(R, b)$:

$$
f_c \leftarrow \begin{cases} i & \text{if } L_i N_{top} < R_{top} \le L_{i+1} N_{top} \\ 0 & \text{if } L_{-1} N_{top} \le R_{top} \le L_1 N_{top} \\ -i & \text{if } L_{-i-1} N_{top} \le R_{top} < L_{-i} N_{top} \end{cases}
$$

(7)

where

$$L_i \equiv i - 1/2 - b A_{top}/(r N_{top}),$$
$$L_{-i} \equiv -i + 1/2 - b A_{top}/(r N_{top}),$$
$$R_{top} \equiv \{\text{top } (x + log_2(r)) \text{ bits of } R\},$$
$$N_{top} \equiv \{\text{top } x \text{ bits of } N\},$$
$$A_{top} \equiv \{\text{top } x \text{ bits of } A\}.$$

The number of top bits x ($x = 7$ for radix 4) is derived in *Appendix B*. L_i and L_{-i} which are approximate numbers corresponding to the boundary indices ℓ_i and ℓ_{-i} are prepared beforehand for $b \in \{-r/2, \cdots, -1, 0, 1, \cdots, r/2\}$.

2.4 Remarks

This algorithm is fast (as shown in *Table 1*) because steps for addition and subtraction are reduced, and it can use a compact operator with an n-bit word. Other features of the algorithm related to hardware are as follows:

(1) Small amount of hardware:

The partial product bA and the modular subtracter cN are produced by using only selectors and exclusive ORs. The coefficient $c(k)$ is determined by the short-precision comparator.

(2) Easy to speed-up:

The algorithm can use carry-save adders which have no carry propagation.

Table 1 Comparison of modular multiplication algorithms

	Steps of Addition and Subtraction		ratio
	proposed algorithm	Baker's algorithm	
average case	$2n(r-1)/(rr')$ (multiply: $n(r-1)/(rr')$) (modulo: $n(r-1)/(rr')$)	$5n/4$ (multiply: $n/2$) (modulo: $3n/4$)	$5rr'/8(r-1)$ (1.7 if $r=4$) (2.1 if $r=8$)
worst case	$2n/r'$ (multiply: n/r') (modulo: n/r')	$2n$ (multiply: n) (modulo: n)	r' (2 if $r=4$) (3 if $r=8$)

(3) Easy to expand:

The algorithm has a bit-slice structure.

3   Applications for Radix 4

A radix-4 modular multiplier is suitable for implementing the proposed algorithm in the latest C-MOS technology, so applications for radix 4 are described in this section.

3.1   Procedure for Radix 4

In the procedure in *section 2.2*, the new algorithm has to perform Eqs. (3) and (4) simultaneously. However, it is hard to speed-up this procedure, because the total delay time is the delay time of the function f_c of Eq. (3) plus the addition operation in Eq. (4).

Therefore, the procedure is modified to the following procedure:

Step 1 (initialize the numbers):

$$\text{If } N < 2A, \ A \leftarrow A - N.$$

$$n \leftarrow \lfloor log_2(N) \rfloor + 1$$
$$k \leftarrow \lfloor n/2 \rfloor + 1$$
$$R^{(k)} \leftarrow 0$$
$$c(k+1) \leftarrow 0 \qquad (8)$$

Step 2 (repeat $\lfloor n/2 \rfloor + 1$ rounds):

$$R^{(k-1)} \leftarrow 4(R^{(k)} - c(k+1)N) + b(k)A \qquad (9)$$
$$c(k) \leftarrow f_c(R^{(k-1)}, b(k-1)) \qquad (10)$$
$$k \leftarrow k - 1$$

Step 3 (last routine):

$$R^{(0)} \leftarrow R^{(0)} - c(1)N \qquad (11)$$
$$A \leftarrow \begin{cases} R^{(0)} & \text{if } R^{(0)} \geq 0 \\ R^{(0)} + N & \text{otherwise} \end{cases}$$

The modified procedure gives the function f_c a delay time of one clock pulse to produce the coefficient $c(k)$.

3.2 Generation of Partial Product Coefficient b related by Redundant Multiplier B

To speed-up modular exponentiation using the modular multiplier, the modular multiplier has to be able to deal directly with the multiplier B in a carry-save redundant form because the final remainder $R^{(0)}$ may be put in the place of the multiplier B. Brickell's algorithm can successfully deal with redundant numbers B_s and B_c of the multiplier B ($B = B_s + 2B_c$) by using the characteristic that

$$s \wedge \sigma = 0, \qquad (12)$$

where $s \leftarrow u \oplus v$, $\sigma \leftarrow u \wedge v$, and u and v are independently 0 or 1. However, our algorithm cannot use Brickell's technique which is based on radix 2. Therefore, we have extended Booth's multiplication [6] for the redundant multiplier B. Eq. (6) is modified to the following function $b(k)$. This new method produces a radix-4 partial product bA by using 4 neighborhood bits of B_s and B_c (shown in *Appendix C*).

• function $b(k)$ for the redundant multiplier B:

$$
\begin{aligned}
b(k) \quad \leftarrow \quad & -2(B_s[2k] \oplus B_c[2k-1]) + B_s[2k-1] + B_c[2k-2] \\
& -4\overline{(B_s[2k] \oplus B_c[2k-1])} \wedge B_s[2k-1] \wedge B_c[2k-2] \\
& +B_s[2k-2] \vee B_c[2k-3] \vee (B_s[2k-3] \wedge B_c[2k-4]) \quad\quad (13)
\end{aligned}
$$

where

$B_s[i] = B_s[n+1]$ and $B_c[i] = B_c[n+1]$ for $i \geq n+1$,

$B_s[i] = B_c[i] = 0$ for $i \leq 0$,

and $B_s[i] \wedge B_c[i] = 0$ for all $i \in [1, n]$.

Eq. (13) is derived in *Appendix C*. It satisfies $b(k) \in \{-2, -1, 0, 1, 2\}$.
If the multiplier B is a single number, then $B_c = 0$.

3.3 Hardware Implementation

The modular multiplier using this algorithm, which can perform one step of addition
and subtraction simultaneously in each clock pulse, is constructed by arranging n
cells into an array. Each cell, which has 5 registers, 3 full adders, and some logic
gates as shown in *Figure 3*, contains about 100 gates.

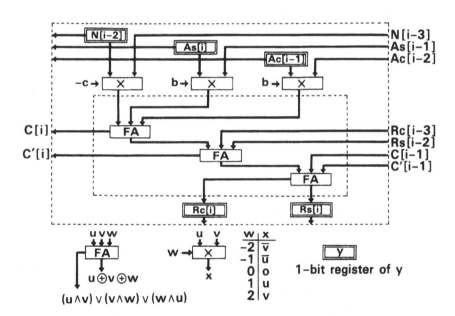

Figure 3 Cell of "$R^{(k-1)} \Leftarrow 4(R^{(k)} - c(k+1)N) + b(k)A$"

Using the latest C-MOS technology, the total delay time, most of which is the delay time of adders and the writing time for registers, is about 20 to 30 ns. Therefore, the 512-bit modular multiplier has about 50 Kgates and a delay time of about 8 μs. The delay time for 512-bit modular exponentiation using it is about 6 ms.

4   Conclusion

A new compact modular-multiplication algorithm has been developed based on a higher radix using an n-bit-length operator. The throughput of the algorithm is more than twice as fast as conventional ones. This algorithm allows a 512-bit modular multiplier based on radix 4 to be made with about 50 Kgates. The throughput of 512-bit modular exponentiation using it will be about 80 Kbits/s at 30 MHz.

Acknowledgment

The author wishes to express his thanks to Dr Kunio Murakami who provided him with the opportunity to pursue this research. He would also like to thank Tsutomu Ishikawa and the other members of NTT LABS who discussed the research.

References

[1] Rivest, R.L., Shamir, A., and Adleman, L., "A Method for Obtaining Digital Signatures and Public-Key Cryptosystems," Comm.ACM, Vol.21(2), pp.120-126, Feb.1978.

[2] Brickell, E.F., "A Fast Modular Multiplication Algorithm with Application to Two Key Cryptography," Advances in Cryptology- CRYPTO'82, pp.51-60, Plenum NY, 1983.

[3] Blakley, G.R., "A Computer Algorithm for Calculating the Product AB Modulo M," IEEE Trans.Comput., Vol.C-32, pp.497-500, May 1983.

[4] Hoornaert, F., Decroos, M., Vandewalle, J., and Govaerts, R., "Fast RSA-hardware: Dream or Reality ?," Advances in Cryptology- EUROCRYPT'88, pp.257-264, Springer-Verlag, 1988.

[5] Baker, P.W., "Fast Computation of A * B Modulo N," Electron.Lett., Vol.23, No.15, pp.794-795, July 1987.

[6] Hwang, K.,"Computer Arithmetic: Principles, Architecture, and Design," John Wiley & Sons, 1979.

Appendix A:
Derivation of the boundary variable d

(For radix 4)
The vertical boundary variable 7/12 in *Figure 2* is assumed to be the boundary variable d.
First, the following equation is the necessary condition for the graph to continue.

$$d > \frac{1}{2}. \tag{14}$$

The condition that $(4R + bA)/N$ exists in the horizontal range $[-4d, 4d]$ is

$$4d \le 2 + d - \frac{|bA|}{4N}. \tag{15}$$

The conditions of $|b| \le 2$ and $|A| \le N/2$ allow Eqs. (14) and (15) to be transformed into

$$\frac{1}{2} < d \le \frac{7}{12}. \tag{16}$$

Consequently,

$$d = \frac{7}{12} \tag{17}$$

is obtained.

(General case for radix r)
By using the same method as in the previous case and the conditions of $|b| \le r/2$, $|c| \le r/2$, and $|A| \le N/2$,

$$d = \frac{1}{2} + \frac{1}{4(r-1)} \tag{18}$$

is obtained.

Appendix B: Derivation of a top-bit number

(Definitions)

$$\hat{R} \equiv rR + bA \tag{19}$$

$$N_{top} \equiv \{ \text{ top } x \text{ bits of } N \} \tag{20}$$

$$A_{top} \equiv \{ \text{ top } x \text{ bits of } A \} \tag{21}$$

$$R_{top} \equiv \{ \text{ top } (x + log_2(r)) \text{ bits of } \hat{R} \} \tag{22}$$

where "x" is a positive integer, and $b \equiv b(k)$.

(*Case of radix 4*)
In *Figure 2*, the boundary index ℓ_1 between $c = 0$ and $c = +1$ is

$$\ell_1 \equiv \frac{1}{2} - \frac{\hat{b}A}{4N} \tag{23}$$

where $\hat{b} \equiv b(k-1)$.

Let L_1 be the approximate value of ℓ_1,

$$L_1 \equiv \frac{1}{2} - \frac{\hat{b}A_{top}}{4N_{top}}. \tag{24}$$

If the following equation is satisfied, then the n-bit-length comparison between ℓ_1 and $\hat{R}$ can be replaced by the short-precision comparison between L_1 and R_{top}.

$$\epsilon \le \delta - \delta' \tag{25}$$

where

$$\epsilon \equiv |\hat{R}/N - R_{top}/N_{top}| \tag{26}$$
$$\delta \equiv d - 1/2 = 1/12 \tag{27}$$
$$\delta' \equiv |L_1 - \ell_1| \tag{28}$$

By using $\hat{R}/N \le rd = 7/3$, Eq. (26) is transformed into

$$\epsilon \le |\frac{R_{top}+1}{N_{top}} - \frac{R_{top}}{N_{top}+1}| \le \frac{10}{3N_{top}}. \tag{29}$$

By using $|b| \le 2$,

$$\delta' < \frac{|b|}{4} \frac{2}{N_{top}} \le \frac{1}{N_{top}}. \tag{30}$$

From Eqs. (25), (27), (29), and (30),

$$N_{top} \ge 52. \tag{31}$$

Because the top bit of N_{top} is always 1,

$$N_{top} \ge 2^{x-1}. \tag{32}$$

Consequently, selecting the minimum value of x under the conditions of Eqs. (31) and (32) gives

$$x = 7. \tag{33}$$

In the other cases for the indices, ℓ_2, ℓ_{-1}, and ℓ_{-2}, Eq. (33) is also satisfied.

(*General case for radix r*)
By using the same method as in the previous case, we obtain

$$N_{top} \ge 4(r-1)(rd+2). \tag{34}$$

Therefore, the minimum value of x is

$$x = \lceil log_2\{(r-1)(rd+2)\}\rceil + 3. \tag{35}$$

Appendix C: Derivation of Eq. (13)

Let us modify the digits in the upper region "k" to radix-4-multiply coefficient $b(k)$ ($b(k) \in \{-2,-1,0,1,2\}$) by using the digits in the lower region "k-1" where the condition of Eq. (12) is satisfied (these regions are shown in *Figure C.1*).

First, assume the auxiliary variables (c_{k+1}, s_k) in the upper region "k" are the carry c_{k+1} and the sum s_k shown in *Table C.1*. These satisfy the conditions $c_{k+1} \in \{0,1\}$ and $s_k \in \{-2,-1,0,1\}$.

If the next equation is performed:

$$b(k) \leftarrow s_k + c_k, \tag{36}$$

then Eq. (36) satisfies $b(k) \in \{-2,-1,0,1,2\}$. Consequently, Eq. (13) is derived from Eq. (36) and the auxiliary variables shown in *Table C.1*.

	the upper region "k"		the lower region "k-1"		
B_S : $\cdots$	$B_S[2k]$	$B_S[2k-1]$	$B_S[2k-2]$	$B_S[2k-3]$	$\cdots$
B_C : $\cdots$	$B_C[2k-1]$	$B_C[2k-2]$	$B_C[2k-3]$	$B_C[2k-4]$	$\cdots$

Figure C.1 Alignment of B_S and B_C

Table C.1 Definition of (c_{k+1}, s_k)

$B_S[2k]\ B_C[2k-1]$	$B_S[2k-1]\ B_C[2k-2]$			
	00	01	11	10
00	0,0	0,1	1,-2	0,1
01	1,-2	1,-1	$\times$	$\times$
11	1,0	1,1	$\times$	$\times$
10	1,-2	1,-1	1,0	1,-1

Note: $\times$ means that (c_{k+1}, s_k) doesn't have any value.

Addition Chain Heuristics

Jurjen Bos
Matthijs Coster

Centrum voor Wiskunde en Informatica
Kruislaan 413
1098 SJ Amsterdam
The Netherlands

Introduction

Much current research focuses on fast evaluation of RSA, which consists of computing powers modulo a large number n. While some try to increase the speed of multiplications, here we consider reducing the number of multiplications. In particular, we present a precomputation method that reduces the number of multiplications for the computation of a given power.

Although we speak about RSA, our method is also applicable to computing elements in other large cyclic groups, such as elliptic curves [Len86], and the computation of elements of the Fibonacci and Lucas chains [Wil82].

Theoretical results and asymptotic bounds in this area are plentiful (see [Dow81], e.g.), but we are not aware of anyone applying heuristics, as we do, to make chains useable in practice.

Definitions and notation

An *addition chain* for a given number is a list of numbers having the following properties:
- the first number is one;
- every number is the sum of two earlier numbers;
- the given number occurs in the chain (at the end, that is).

In the case of an addition *sequence*, the last condition becomes:
- the given numbers occur in the sequence.

We view such a list as a series of exponents used to do an exponentiation. The *length* of an addition chain or sequence is the number of elements in the chain, apart from the initial one.

For example, the standard (binary) addition chain [Knu69] for the number 15 has length 6:

```
1 2 3 6 7 14 15
```

There is, however, a chain of length 5 that produces 15:

```
1 2 3 6 12 15
```

This means that one can compute x^{15} from x in 5 multiplications.

Naturally we are interested in addition chains with as small a length as possible. Our method is capable of producing an addition chain for a 512-bit number of length 605 on average. This is an improvement of 21% over the binary algorithm (which has length 768 on average) and an improvement of 5% over Knuth's 5-window algorithm (see below).

Finally, we define a *vector addition chain* of a given vector as the shortest list of *vectors* with the following properties:
- the first vectors are [1, 0, 0, ..., 0], [0, 1, 0, ..., 0], ..., [0, 0, 0, ..., 1];
- each vector is the sum of two earlier vectors;
- the last vector is equal to the given vector.

We define the length of a vector addition chain as the number of vectors after the initial vectors.

Example:

```
[1 0 0] [0 1 0] [0 0 1] [1 0 1] [0 1 1] [1 1 2] [1 2 3]

  [2 3 5] [4 6 10] [6 9 15] [8 12 20] [14 21 35] [15 21 35]
```

is a vector addition chain of [15 21 35] with length 10.

We use the following simple functions:

$L(a_1, a_2, ...)$	a shortest addition sequence containing $a_1, a_2, ...$
$l(a_1, a_2, ...)$	length of a shortest addition sequence containing $a_1, a_2, ...$
$v(n)$	the number of ones that occur in the binary representation of n
$\log n$	$^2\log n$

Brief review of the literature

Computing the shortest addition chain is an NP-complete problem [Dow81].
It is known that

$$\log n + \log v(n) - 2.13 \le l(n) \le \lfloor \log n \rfloor + v(n) - 1.$$

The lower bound is from [Sch75], and the upper bound is just the binary algorithm [Knu69]. [Bra39] gives an upper bound of

$$l(n) \le \log n + \log n / \log \log n + o(\log n / \log \log n).$$

Less is known about addition sequences. [Yao76] gives the bound:

$$l(a_1, a_2, ..., a_k) \leq \log a_k + cn\log a_k / \log \log a_k, \text{ where}$$

$$c \approx 2 + 4 / \sqrt{\log a_k}.$$

Here a_k is the largest number in the sequence.

There is a one-to-one correspondence between addition sequences and vector addition chains [Oli81]: An addition sequence of length l with k requested numbers can be converted to a vector addition chain of length $l + k - 1$ and dimension k, and vice versa. For example, the vector addition chain mentioned above can be mapped to the addition sequence 1 2 3 4 7 10 14 <u>15</u> <u>21</u> <u>35</u>.

The algorithm

The computation of an addition chain can of course be done every time the chain is needed. The algorithm must then be fast to be useful. In practice, though, it is often true that an RSA exponent is known a long time in advance and used very often.

For a given number n, the algorithm computes an addition chain. It consists of two parts. The first reduces the computation of an addition chain for n to the computation of an addition sequence that contains a given set of numbers which are much smaller than n. This is comparable to the algorithm mentioned in [Thu73b], but we use it for much bigger numbers. The second part produces a sequence for those numbers.

The Window method

The first method we demonstrate is derived from [Knu69]. The idea is to write the number in binary and split it in pieces (*windows*). With a window size of 1 it is the binary method.

As an example, we take 26235947428953663183191, and windows of width 5.

The window division then looks like this:

<u>1011</u>000<u>111</u>00<u>1</u>000000<u>11101</u>00<u>101</u>00<u>11101</u>0<u>1</u>00000<u>10111</u> <u>1</u>00000<u>11111</u>00<u>11001</u>0<u>10101</u> <u>11</u>

  11   7 1   29   5   29 1   23 1   31   25   21 3

The addition chain now consists of two parts:

- an addition sequence producing the needed window numbers
- a long part, consisting of doublings, with the addition of numbers from the first chain in the proper places.

The first part is:

1 2 <u>3</u> 4 <u>5</u> <u>7</u> <u>11</u> 16 <u>21</u> <u>23</u> <u>25</u> <u>29</u> <u>31</u>

We then take the first window and repeatedly square it. For each window, we do one extra multiplication to put it in place.

The resulting chain is as follows:

Length of sequence that computes intermediates:	12
Number of squarings needed:	71
Number of multiplies for the intermediates:	12 +
Total number of multiplies:	95

Knuth proposes to make a precomputed table containing all odd numbers up to, say, 5 bits. (Of course, it is more efficient to use an addition sequence producing only the needed numbers).

Because we use addition sequences instead of tables, we can also choose a much bigger window size. In this example, we will use 10. Note that the first window is bigger than 10 bits:

1011000111001000000011101001010011101010000001011110000011111001100101010111

| 5689 | 933 | 117 | 47 | 499 | 343 |

The addition sequence yielding the first part is:

1 2 4 8 10 11 18 36 <u>47</u> 55 91 109 <u>117</u> 226 <u>343</u> 434 489 <u>499</u> <u>933</u>

  1422 2844 5688 <u>5689</u>

We get this chain:

Length of sequence that computes intermediates:	22
Number of squarings needed:	62
Number of multiplies for the intermediates:	5 +
Total number of multiplies:	89

In general, it is the case that using addition sequences instead of tables allows one to use bigger window sizes, giving shorter addition chains for the original number. The graph on the next page shows an example of this effect.

The optimization of the window distribution generates a window distribution with the following properties:
- Each window is maximally the given size.
- There are as few windows as possible.
- The sum of the logarithms of the window values is minimal.

This can be done in linear time. (Actually, a trivial improvement can be done on the window division algorithm: instead of giving the window a maximal size, we give them a maximal *value*. This value can then be chosen as a prefix of the number. For example, the windows of a number that starts with 1101001... will all be at most equal to 11010 for a window size of 5.)

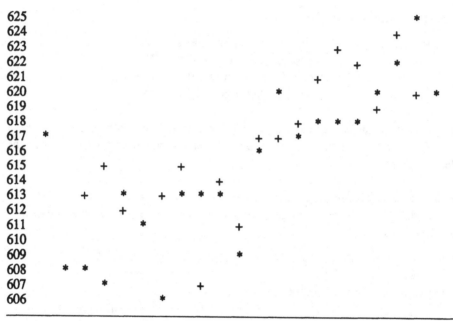

This is an example of a random 512-bit number whose binary representation has about two thirds ones. The number of bits in one window is shown horizontally, and the total number of multiplications is shown on the vertical axis. The + signs indicates the length of the chain using a crude left-to-right method for assigning the windows. The * signs are obtained using a method that optimizes the window distribution.

The Makesequence algorithm

Here we describe a routine that makes an addition sequence of a set of numbers. It starts with a *protosequence* consisting of 1, 2 and the requested numbers. It then transforms this to another one using a heuristic algorithm. In each step, we reduce the protosequence to a simpler one, having smaller numbers.

We write such a protosequence as 1, 2, ..., f_2, f_1, f. The algorithm inserts some numbers by one of four methods and leave f. The four methods for making an addition sequence are called Approximation, Division, Halving and Lucas. The motivation to choose these four methods is that with these four methods it is possible to find all $L(a,b)$ for pairs (a, b) with $a < b \leq 50$. It is not obvious to find good sequences for the protosequences $\{4, 23\}$ and $\{17, 48\}$. Good sequences can be found by Lucas and Division respectively. The question is which method has to bo chosen. This is a hard and at the moment unsolved question. We use a so called *weight function*, and we choose the method having the lowest related weight function.

The weight function will only be scetched. We found in all cases we tried that for protosequences $\{a_1, a_2, ..., a_n\}$ with $a_n \leq 1000$ the length of the sequence could be estimated by $l(a_1, a_2, ..., a_n) \leq \frac{3}{2} \log a_n + n + 1$. We use this bound in our weight function for the part of the protosequence which will remain after leaving f. In addition the number of inserted elements has to be added. Finally, in the function Δ we express the "hardness" of elements that have to be inserted.

Approximation
(There are two elements a and b in the sequence with a+b = f–ε, where ε is positive and small; insert a +ε.)

Condition:	$0 \leq f - (f_i + f_j) = \varepsilon$ (is "small"); $f_i \leq f_j$.
Insert:	$f_i + \varepsilon$.
Weight function:	$\frac{3}{2} \log(f_1) + k + 1 + \Delta(\varepsilon)$.
Example:	49 67 85 117
	$\varepsilon = 1$ (namely $117 - (49 + 67)$)
Insert:	50
Result:	49 <u>50</u> 67 85 (117)

Division
(f is divisible by a small prime p; put f/p, 2f/p, ..., f in the sequence.)

Condition:	p=3, 5, 9 or 17. f is divisible by p.
	$L(p) = \{1, \alpha_1 = 2, ... , \alpha_r = p\}$.
Insert:	$f/p, 2f/p, \alpha_2 f/p, ..., \alpha_{r-1} f/p$
Weight function:	$\frac{3}{2} \log(f_i) + k + l(p) + i + \Delta(\max \delta(j))$.
Example:	17 48
Insert:	16 32
Result:	<u>16</u> 17 <u>32</u> (48)

Halving
(Take a (small) number s that occurs earlier in the sequence, and put f–s, (f–s)/2, (f–s)/4, ... to a certain point in the sequence.)

Condition:	$f/f_1 \geq 2^u$; $[f/2^u] = k$.
Insert:	$d = f - k \cdot 2^u, f - d = k 2^u, k 2^{u-1}, ..., k/2, k$.
Weight function:	$\frac{3}{2} \log(f_i) + u + 1 + \Delta(f_i - k)$.
Example:	14 382

$$f/f_1 = 27.2; \; u = 4; \; k = 23; \; d = 14.$$

Insert: 23 46 92 184 368

Result: 14 <u>23</u> <u>46</u> <u>92</u> <u>184</u> <u>368</u> (382)

Lucas $(u_{n+1} = u_n + u_{n-1})$

(Put a Lucas sequence in the sequence that has f as last element.)

Condition: f and f_i are the elements of a Lucas series

(i.e. $f_i = u_0$ and $f = u_k$, $k \geq 3$).

Insert: $u_1, u_2, \ldots, u_{k-2}, u_{k-1}.$

Weight function: $\frac{3}{2} \log(f_i) + k + \lambda + i + \Delta(r).$

Example: 4 23

Insert: 5 9 14

Result: 4 <u>5</u> <u>9</u> <u>14</u> (23)

After applying one of those insertions, the process is repeated until the sequence contains only the numbers 1 and 2.

For the faster but less effective real-time version, we use only A and H to remove f. A simple rule decides which of these algorithms to take, and we do not use a weight function in this case.

Further work

We have considered using subtraction in a chain. In practice, this will not make the chain much shorter, while the cost of a subtraction in practice (eg., in RSA) is considerable.

We did not consider the effect of having a squaring operation that takes less time than a multiplication. Of course, if squaring is *very* cheap, we can use that

$$ab = [(a+b)^2 - (a-b)^2]/4$$

to reduce a multiplication to two squarings. However, from the example given earlier in this article one can see that our algorithm uses a lot of squarings. This makes our algorithm relatively more effective over the binary algorithm. It might be interesting to investigate this further.

The weight function we use does not give really satisfactory results. We have several ideas for improving the weight function.

Furthermore, we consider making a makesequence function that also tries steps that have an almost optimal weight, and tries out all possibilities, taking the shortest resulting chain. We tried using using simulated annealing (statistical cooling) [Laa87] methods, but until now we have not found a way to accomplish this. We expect that those improvements yield an algorithm that produces addition chain of length less than 600 for a 512-bit number.

References

[Bel63] R. Bellman: *Advanced problem 5125*, Amer. Math. Monthly **70** (1963), 765.

[BBBD] F. Bergeron, J. Berstel, S. Brlek, C. Duboc: *Addition Chains Using Continued Fractions*, Journal of Algorithms **10**, (1989), 403-412.

[Bra39] A. Brauer: *On addition chains*, Bull. Am. Math. Soc. **45** (1939), 736-739.

[Cot73] A. Cottrell: *A lower bound for the Scholz-Brauer problem*, Notices AMS, Abst. #73T-A200, **20** (1973), A-476.

[Dob80] D. Dobkin and R. J. Lipton: *Addition chain methods for the evaluation of specific polynomials*, Siam J. Comput. **9** (1980), 121-125.

[Dow81] P. Downey, B. Leony and R. Sethi: *Computing sequences with addition chains*, Siam Journ. Comput. **3** (1981), 638-696.

[Erd60] P. Erdős: *Remarks on number theory III, on addition chains*, Acta Arith. **6** (1960), 77-81.

[Fia89] A. Fiat: *Batch RSA*, Abstracts Crypto '89, to be published.

[Gio78] A. A. Gioia and M. V. Subbarao: *The Scholz-Brauer problem in addition chains II*, Proc. eighth Manitoba conference on numerical math. and computing, (1978),251-274.

[Knu69] D. E. Knuth: *The art of computer programming*, Vol. 2, Seminumerical algorithms, Addison-Wesley, Reading, Mass., (1969), pp. 398-419.

[Laa87] P. J. van Laarhoven and E. H. L. Aarts: *Simulated Annealing: Theory and Applications*, D. Reidel Publishing Company, Dordrecht, 1987.

[Lee77] J. van Leeuwen: *An extension of Hansen's theorem for star chains*, J. Reine Angew. Math. **295** (1977), 203-207.

[Len86] H. W. Lenstra, jr.: *Factoring integers with elliptic curves*, Report 86-18, Universiteit van Amsterdam, 1986.

[Oli81] J. Olivos: *On Vectorial Addition Chains*, J. of Algorithms **2** (1981), 13-21.

[Sch75] A. Schönhage: *A lower bound on the length of addition chains*, Theoret. Comput. Sci. **1** (1975), 1-12.

[Thu73a] E. G. Thurber: *The Scholz-Brauer problem on addition chains*, Pacific J. Math. **49** (1973), 229-242.

[Thu73b] E. G. Thurber: *On addition chains $l(mn) \leq l(n)-b$ and lower bounds for $c(r)$*, Duke Math. J. **40** (1973), 907-913.

[Thu76] E. G. Thurber: *Addition chains and solutions of $l(2n) = l(n)$ and $l(2^n-1) = n+l(n)-1$*, Discr. Math. **16** (1976), 279-289.

[Tsa87] Y. H. Tsai and Y. H. Chin: *A study of some addition chain problems*, Intern. J. Comp. Math. **22** (1987), 117-134.

[Veg75] E. Vegh: *A note on addition chains*, J. Comb. Th. (A) **19** (1975), 117-118.

[Vol85] H. Volger: *Some results on addition/subtraction chains*, Inf. Proc. Lett. **20** (1985), 155-160.

[Wil82] H. C. Williams, *A $p+1$ method of factoring*, Math. Comp. **39** (1982), 225-234

[Yao76] Andrew Yao, *On the evaluation of powers*, Siam J. Comput. **5**, (1976).

How easy is collision search.
New results and applications to DES
(abstract and results)

Jean-Jacques Quisquater & *Jean-Paul Delescaille*

Philips Research Laboratory Brussels
Avenue Van Becelaere, 2; Box 8
B–1 170 Brussels, Belgium
jjq@prlb.philips.be — jpdesca@prlb.philips.be

1 Update about collisions in DES

Given a cryptographic algorithm f (depending upon a fixed message m and a key k), a pair of keys with collision k_0 and k_1 (in short, a *collision*) are keys such that

$$f(m, k_0) = f(m, k_1).$$

The existence of collisions for a cryptographic algorithm means that this algorithm is not *faithful* in a precise technical sense (see [2]).

An efficient algorithm (called algorithm 1 in the tables) was used on a network of workstations (thirty SUN's and ten microVAXes) for finding pairs of keys with collision in the DES. The algorithm is based on the so-called theory of *distinguished points* (see [3], [4]) and is described in [4]. Table 1 gives the set of 26 collisions found with the same plaintext 0404040404040404.

The same algorithm was used to find a collision when using a double DES in encryption mode (with 2 distinct keys, k and k') with the same fixed plaintext. Table 2 gives one such a collision.

2 Meet-in-the-middle attack

The *meet-in-the-middle* attack is the finding of a pair of keys k, k' such that

$$f(f(m_0, k), k') = m_1$$

where f is again the DES in encryption mode and m_0 and m_1 are fixed messages.

The classical meet-in-the-middle attack is based on the computations of $f(m_0, k_0)$ for 2^{32} distinct keys and the same number of computations for $f^{-1}(m_1, k_1)$; then a common value is likely (the birthday paradox) found by sorting the two obtained sets. One problem is to store 2^{33} values of 8 bytes. Here instead of storing each computed value, we only store distinguished points (output values with 11 zeroes at the left) from the two sets: we need more output values (and thus more computations) for finding a common value but less memory. The output values were computed using the same strategy than for the algorithm 1: that is, we found new collisions during the process. Table 3 gives the 22 found collisions when the plaintext is "WELCOME ". Table 4 gives the 31 found collisions when the ciphertext is "CRYPTO89" and DES is used in decryption mode.

The common value was found a specific algorithm using hashing tables. The full paper will explain the strategy we use. Table 5 gives the value found during the first effective meet-in-the-middle attack. Let us notice that the common value has 11 *predetermined* bits set at 0.

3   Other results

We also used a variant of algorithm 1 (named algorithm 3 in the tables) both for finding collisions and for the meet-in-the-middle attack. This variant consists to replace in algorithm 1 (see [4]) the iteration $y \leftarrow f(m, y)$ by $y \leftarrow f_{bit_\ell}(m_\ell, y)$ where bit_ℓ is the ℓ-th bit of y, with ℓ fixed; the functions f_0 and f_1 are respectively the DES in encryption mode with the plaintext "WELCOME " and the DES in decryption mode with the ciphertext "CRYPTO89", for this application. This idea was independently found by Coppersmith ([1]). Table 6 gives 4 new collisions. Table 7 gives 2 new meet-in-the-middle attacks.

References

[1] Don Coppersmith, *Mathematical foundations of cryptography*, 1989, in preparation.

[2] Burton Kaliski, Ronald Rivest and Alan Sherman, *Is the Data Encryption Standard a group? (Results of cycling experiments on DES)?*, J. Cryptology, vol. 1, 198, pp. 3–36.

[3] Jean-Jacques Quisquater and Jean-Paul Delescaille, *Other cycling tests for DES*, Springer Verlag, Lecture notes in computer science **293**, Advances in cryptology, Proceedings of CRYPTO '87, pp. 255–256.

[4] Jean-Jacques Quisquater and Jean-Paul Delescaille, *How easy is collision search. Application to DES*, Proceedings of EUROCRYPT '89, To appear.

Table 1. Collisions (k_0, k_1) found in DES (mode encryption)
with fixed plaintext = 0404040404040404, using algorithm 1.

k0	k1	plain	cipher
46b2c8b62818f884	4a5aa8d0ba30585a	0404040404040404	f02d67223ceaf91c
1680b00c1c22c6b4	d296c2ca66be3c60	0404040404040404	e20332821871eb8f
22a64edc20e07032	6edaa03254d2a298	0404040404040404	7237f9e44466059f
620e08e886aa8c1c	cc3adc3616cc1c32	0404040404040404	345d8975676ffde0
b41ebe7a88c4a8c8	a2aa9adc56a60ad6	0404040404040404	301c9a64b903048d
8654a2b862a82486	5888c640ee3016d4	0404040404040404	8f4a67da0852722d
0ed86014328cf2da	1e620c46682e325c	0404040404040404	96f0faf4f80b6b29
92f69c5aa2c84ee8	780a76586c7c0ca4	0404040404040404	1d901196097a93f4
1680f2049484b4b2	46f422a832ac0c18	0404040404040404	85795a73b4af5d78
e4f06aaea2022e02	3eb8406c969c9c84	0404040404040404	46184d44b739a147
36a0f03afe48c226	28e8161878343ea0	0404040404040404	c5ed963b29a48bf6
5c4afa4ae0c62a84	060c0e048614bc42	0404040404040404	c931dab489f515a1
d8fc6cba3c0a946c	d0e4aa90baba681c	0404040404040404	a3c7d6d33eb1400d
2c2c5a243cd882fa	36da7e6010d6a07e	0404040404040404	6a5d431ed4863421
ac78ca74c6a0ea6e	7aac9c602e9854b6	0404040404040404	2edeaaa86e5141af
ae8838904874c606	ce806eee7cfcd2ec	0404040404040404	150e0b6ff35b4f0e
76f6527c54447ade	366cf4baa8cc6c80	0404040404040404	77964b1e86be688e
be827240c8bc3e6a	6ece1e20bef2b0f8	0404040404040404	f29fdbc8dc6c174a
5406c60cb4d6f0c8	5e301c2452d88476	0404040404040404	c6120f53b62eed0d
b45e08326ea40e10	0e5ebe562c961274	0404040404040404	ef5293f14f84fc4f
a862d2aef0c06c54	624e36aa48926a2e	0404040404040404	7dd3c3d34ea30c2f
02e6f2c46a40ba0e	125eb8b03c589c54	0404040404040404	3af6bac78416503d
1c3a0ed4f4cca240	bee020625838006a	0404040404040404	2b1331f0ae189c68
e0127ea26e0a9c80	6a3e00f268f0c4f6	0404040404040404	69e7467667b85945
f4c84030841492cc	72c6000236321cbe	0404040404040404	5db67a19b33fc3ab
4ceaf854e44a0a8e	a6367c24c0c8c258	0404040404040404	677277df7822abbf

Table 2. Collision (k_i, k_i'), $i = 0, 1$, found in *double* DES (mode encryption)
with fixed plaintext = 0404040404040404, using algorithm 1.

i	k$_i$	k'$_i$	plain	cipher
0.	a6daeac810281cfa	1068d04ed4acbc3c	0404040404040404	b8c78d848dcc1a64
1.	aaa2bcda8c40ca5e	d21476e4b69466be	0404040404040404	b8c78d848dcc1a64

Table 3. Collisions (k_0, k_1) found in DES (mode encryption)
with fixed plaintext "WELCOMEⅬ" (in hexadecimal) during use of algorithm 2.

k0	k1	plain	cipher
9ae23a0c4c8a226e	b68858b28a6eae32	20454d4f434c4557	8c94880b085330c7
3af8987236e69410	0cc8a6cc46c442be	20454d4f434c4557	bae455f4f9825466
e00a7ce87c56668a	d2fa5cb4461a7036	20454d4f434c4557	2ddee611bd255625
708ce29a6662443a	d032fc7e5cece010	20454d4f434c4557	9f989601e97eea08
ccb246c24ceec4c0	fac6b210a0a0e66e	20454d4f434c4557	9bdfd47aa8765800
8c42ec6ce2968230	669eaabcdabca6e4	20454d4f434c4557	f1b9c371cb484fbd
840ee66a505e00a6	3e1a36600a08925c	20454d4f434c4557	f4210871ad57427a
70bab4769a2c5254	fe866cac0c4a3248	20454d4f434c4557	684cb0a558dedea9
c4d63aec50745c16	e4949a3ab288d4f0	20454d4f434c4557	3886c01aad1ceb09
5ccc388c468e1c20	46c42a823c746836	20454d4f434c4557	d5944d3a27a8be52
76b65c8c84fabe32	9a86b298d880ec1a	20454d4f434c4557	56d73aa99035444b
c09020b4988c085e	464488de18746a24	20454d4f434c4557	e8a6d4d4b3d62ddf
f2f6da5256ec74a2	bae2e4da3890d416	20454d4f434c4557	8ae91121e209f9e8
fcbc7ee6cc3e9254	90b88a08041e969a	20454d4f434c4557	87057985fb756003
92908280a4e23a78	ce2492885e48f670	20454d4f434c4557	e43be5d1d51a4ac9
dab83c0c56108ae2	64207cb054da746a	20454d4f434c4557	f9c33b251a5ec47b
7894ee4a721a4482	6e6e1874e6daf018	20454d4f434c4557	85048af612532963
ca82c8fc1e54bed6	42202ed48c5c0aae	20454d4f434c4557	c9666f42a86b968e
e6f428e470ac2e7e	c8828266646a9e32	20454d4f434c4557	71f9208a9547a8b1
8658c486b81894c4	08641cfe966c4064	20454d4f434c4557	afe5c27ed0b2d778
52b6c8e46c32d0d2	e852448260688a8a	20454d4f434c4557	35c3c1252413d072
3c600e2cb6a404b6	8402b48c48882e36	20454d4f434c4557	b8c97f4ece12c6f2

Table 4. Collisions (k_0, k_1) found in DES (mode decryption)
with fixed cipher "CRYPTO89" (in hexadecimal) during use of algorithm 2.

k0	k1	plain	cipher
02800e14b49ee86e	1280448278408620	4c1ad155fbc14716	39384f5450595243
5e9476e0ea2e4ab0	96fe66dce89c3448	3af999c9e1058c54	39384f5450595243
04b2a4a2e21a40a2	e0680ad6fa58487c	de348d105fc37ab3	39384f5450595243
0884a0d264025496	928e6e5a6e1a604c	4a6d235062f7e190	39384f5450595243
1e302c1666d8c280	3622cadee6ea7e78	88985912677cdbc3	39384f5450595243
70e45cc4803eec28	560050de5ea6dcc6	6eefe5e81c0e4af9	39384f5450595243
100ce63c74d4a2cc	30c8c818429ce6fe	6ca608fd45504b76	39384f5450595243
06f24006105a80b4	0052b616145aca40	2c375311e776aa97	39384f5450595243
da5ce25a84707208	7038e67080107434	b465c16b7d3a5ef3	39384f5450595243
3c781edce2b428c8	26e6b44894aab866	8e185a3b82633e3c	39384f5450595243
b2b2c814ac1ea2b6	ca963a306ee86eda	27b00453e16dd132	39384f5450595243
3042d4f8e4185e80	de62d4120a94302e	aa9489ba55276236	39384f5450595243
24e86a486e28ae60	926894b89e5ae0fa	f308907f59a2f273	39384f5450595243
1c2e66da5a46523c	fe42884ab83622c8	76f268301f944e6e	39384f5450595243
5a6a3838662856e0	42cca4ccc4665846	2a5b57ec38d95b1a	39384f5450595243
dc604826a476042a	4ce62014a8cc141e	4da1409fe4f97098	39384f5450595243
c0b0520a200cf004	4e8a5442c092f6b2	a09ad87ef26962bf	39384f5450595243
5e88d0487aeac8b0	5c045c842a16c076	c513e925a73ce3ca	39384f5450595243
9ed6d874106c6a0e	9eeefeda7c30823a	a91e0ad2717c5165	39384f5450595243
a62458ec32186260	beb06aa4e69a9c0a	32e338ccc8f61304	39384f5450595243
eab474b62276060e	e6e862c42cfa08c8	da8469d3f789170f	39384f5450595243
900ed69cf8e2dafe	fe222e58c072aa7e	e5a9587ee976d768	39384f5450595243
aadc88468e466898	32588a922844f2d4	49f386509b43490c	39384f5450595243
78b61a009444de6a	8004349e4a90306a	392269f09bf3056c	39384f5450595243
8e86e8946cfad0a2	60d858b8b8da6ac8	5617f9c377565524	39384f5450595243
e2a6f6d492389646	06365e0c464a7a40	697451d10c2a52f5	39384f5450595243
2284841e347cd2e8	bea4f09c62604830	702241d5ebb242f9	39384f5450595243
9a6260c48068e68e	98488cf6d85accd8	4bf50ce58bce531e	39384f5450595243
a22ef8d4beb28460	1ee4683e687cba34	2089ef2739e30ace	39384f5450595243
e45ec2f294187830	54003c400c5a6cf8	e5076d5fb1c6c97f	39384f5450595243
c010844e4a3030ec	363ee0f0fe0c9aa0	108c44a64de03689	39384f5450595243

Table 5. Meet-in-middle "attack" (k, k') against *double* DES (mode encryption)
with fixed plaintext "WELCOME␣" (in hexadecimal) and
fixed ciphertext "CRYPTO89" (in hexadecimal), using algorithm 2.

k	k'	plain	cipher
9a86e458dce6c46a	f2dc6822b028069e	20454d4f434c4557	39384f5450595243

Table 6. Collisions (k_0, k_1) found in DES (mode encryption)
with fixed plaintext "WELCOMEⓊ" (in hexadecimal), using algorithm 3.

k0	k1	plain	cipher
e24a2ca412be62ec	ca225aa270ac4e36	20454d4f434c4557	c0ee4acf421d8c16
2868be64201c12de	42d4d460105adc8c	20454d4f434c4557	e3d78af2e104a331
86a41682ea02a43a	3a8c9856848696de	20454d4f434c4557	a567b1c48dd5f045
4260fed06c5090e4	e01a788492d2f46a	20454d4f434c4557	5cc665796edb52ad

Table 7. Two other meet-in-the-middle "attacks" and collision $(k_i, k_i'), i = 0, 1$,
found for *double* DES (mode encryption) with fixed plaintext "WELCOMEⓊ"
(in hexadecimal) and fixed ciphertext "CRYPTO89" (in hexadecimal)
using algorithm 3.

i	k_i	k_i'	plain	cipher
0.	4a445612aa58e264	ca7e4098dc243818	20454d4f434c4557	39384f5450595243
1.	f4a2ce847e08886a	f2e2288aeae2b6fa	20454d4f434c4557	39384f5450595243

Chair: BOB BLAKLEY [1]

---

[1] Replacing hospitalized James L. Massey on short notice — Thanks Bob!

A Design Principle for Hash Functions

Ivan Bjerre Damgård[1]

Abstract

We show that if there exists a computationally collision free function f from m bits to t bits where $m > t$, then there exists a computationally collision free function h mapping messages of *arbitrary* polynomial lengths to t-bit strings.

Let n be the length of the message. h can be constructed either such that it can be evaluated in time linear in n using 1 processor, or such that it takes time $O(log(n))$ using $O(n)$ processors, counting evaluations of f as one step. Finally, for any constant k and large n, a speedup by a factor of k over the first construction is available using k processors.

Apart from suggesting a generally sound design principle for hash functions, our results give a unified view of several apparently unrelated constructions of hash functions proposed earlier. It also suggests changes to other proposed constructions to make a proof of security potentially easier.

We give three concrete examples of constructions, based on modular squaring, on Wolfram's pseudoranddom bit generator [Wo], and on the knapsack problem.

1 Introduction and Related Work

A hash function h is called *collision free*, if it maps messages of any length to strings of some fixed length, but such that finding x, y with $h(x) = h(y)$ is a hard problem. Note that we are concentrating here on publicly computable hash functions, i.e. functions that are not controlled by a secret key.

The need for such functions to ensure data integrity, and for use with digital signature schemes is well known - see for example [Da], [De], [DP].

Several constructions of hash functions have been proposed, based for example on DES [Wi], [DP] or on RSA [DP], [Gir]. The construction in [Da] was the first for which collision freeness could be proved, assuming security of the atomic operation on which it was based - one-wayness of modular squaring in that case, and more generally, the existence of claw free pairs of permutations. A later example is [Gi]. Unfortunately, this pleasant theoretical property meant a decrease in efficiency compared to other proposals: the time needed for these functions is roughly equivalent to applying RSA to the whole message.

The problem of constructing provably collision free AND fast hash functions is therefore still open.

---

[1]The author is with Mathematical Institute, Aarhus University, Ny Munkegade, DK 8000 Aarhus C, Denmark.

Many of the difficulties with giving proofs for the known constructions arise from the fact that things seem to get more complex as the length of the messages hashed increases. On the other hand, a hash function is of no use, if we are not allowed to hash messages of arbitrary lengths.

In the present paper, we show that this difficulty can be removed, if the right construction is used: it turns out that ability to cut just 1 bit off the length of a message in a collision free way implies ability to hash messages of arbitrary lengths. The proof suggests a basically sound design principle which can be used as a guideline in designing new hash functions and in revising existing ones.

Our construction is very similar to Merkle's "meta-method", discovered independently [Me]; in comparison, the present construction contains several extra elements that make a formal proof possible without any extra assumptions on the parameters of the functions.

There are also similarities with the methods used in independent work by Naor and Yung [NaYu]. They also prove that fixed size hash functions can be composed to obtain compression of arbitrary polynomial length messages. This is done, both for our type of hash function, and for hash functions with a somewhat weaker property: an enemy is allowed to choose x, and is then given a randomly chosen instance from the hash function family. He can now not in polynomial time find another y such that $f(x) = f(y)$. Naor and Yung construct functions of this type from any one-way permutation, and use them to build digital signature schemes.

From a practical point of view, our construction is more efficient and direct. This is because [NaYu] in order to make their construction work for hash functions with the weaker property, must choose a new independent instance of the fixed length hash function for each message block to process.

Finally, some very recent independent work by Impagliazzo and Naor [ImNa] should be mentioned. They prove that a hash function constructed from the knapsack problem in the same way as in Section 4.3 of this paper is secure in the sense of [NaYu] if the knapsack used induces a one-way function.

2 Preliminaries

We first define the concept of a collision free function family:

Definition 2.1

A *fixed size collision free hash function family* $\mathcal{F}$ is an infinite family of finite sets $\{F_m\}_{m=1}^{\infty}$, and a function $t : \mathbf{N} \to \mathbf{N}$, such that $t(m) < m$ for all $m \in \mathbf{N}$.

A member of F_m is a function $f : \{0,1\}^m \to \{0,1\}^{t(m)}$, and is called *an instance of $\mathcal{F}$ of size m.*

$\mathcal{F}$ must satisfy the following:

1. There is a probabilistic polynomial (in m) time algorithm Θ which, given a value of m, selects an instance of $\mathcal{F}$ of size m at random.

2. For any instance $f \in F_m$ and $x \in \{0,1\}^m$, $f(x)$ can be computed in polynomial time.

3. Given an instance $f \in \mathcal{F}$ selected randomly as in 1), it hard to find $x, y \in \{0,1\}^m$, such that $f(x) = f(y)$ and $x \neq y$.

   More formally: For any probabilistic polynomial (in m) time algorithm Δ, and any polynomial P, consider the subset of instances f of size m for which Δ with probability at least $1/P(m)$ outputs $x \neq y$ such that $f(x) = f(y)$. Let $\epsilon(m)$ be the probability with which Θ selects one of these instances. Then as a function of m, $\epsilon(m)$ vanishes faster than any polynomial fraction□

Condition 1) and 2) say that $\mathcal{F}$ is useful in pratice: instances can be selected, and function values computed efficiently. 3) states the collision free property.

One basic implication of 3) is that functions in $\mathcal{F}$ have a sort of one-way property:

Lemma 2.1

Let $\mathcal{F}$ be a collision free function family, f an instance of size m. Let P_f be the probability distribution on $\{0,1\}^{t(m)}$ generated by selecting x randomly and uniformly in $\{0,1\}^m$ and and outputting $f(x)$.

Then no algorithm inverting f on images selected according to P_f succeeds with probability larger than $1/2 + 1/P(m)$ for any polynomial P

If P_f is the uniform distribution over the image of f or if $m - t$ is $O(m)$, then no inversion algorithm succeeds with probability larger than $1/P(m)$.

Proof

Assume the Lemma is false. Given an algorithm Δ that inverts f with probability at least $1/2 + 1/P(m)$, we select x uniformly and give $f(x)$ as input to Δ. If Δ is successful, we are given a y, such that $f(x) = f(y)$. Let A be the event that the preimage of $f(x)$ has size at least 2. $\{0,1\}^m$ is at least twice as large as the image of f, and therefore A occurs with probability larger than $1/2$. Hence, by assumption on Δ, it succeeds with probability at least $1/P(m)$ when A occurs. Clearly, Δ's choice of which element in the preimage of $f(x)$ to give us is uncorrelated to the choice of x (given $f(x)$). Hence $x \neq y$ with probability at least $1/2$, given that A occurs and that Δ is successful.

For the second statement, note that if P_f is the uniform distribution, then Δ's success is uncorrelated to occurrence of A. And if $m - t = O(m)$, then A occurs with overwhelming probability. In either case, Δ gives us a collision with probability essentially $1/P(m)$ □

Finally, we define the concept of a collision free hash function family:

Definition 2.2

A *collision free hash function family* $\mathcal{H}$ is an infinite family of finite sets $\{H_m\}_{m=1}^{\infty}$, and a polynomially bounded function $t : \mathbf{N} \to \mathbf{N}$.

A member of H_m is a function $h : \{0,1\}^* \to \{0,1\}^{t(m)}$, and is called *an instance of $\mathcal{H}$ of size m.*

$\mathcal{H}$ must satisfy the following:

1. Given a value of m, there is a probabilistic polynomial (in m) time algorithm Θ which on input m selects an instance of $\mathcal{H}$ of size m at random.

2. For any instance $h \in H_m$ and $x \in \{0,1\}^*$, $h(x)$ is easy to compute, i.e. computable in time polynomial both in m and $|x|$.

3. Given an instance $h \in \mathcal{H}$ selected randomly as in 1), it hard to find $x, y \in \{0,1\}^*$, such that $h(x) = h(y)$ and $x \neq y$.

   More formally: For any probabilistic polynomial time algorithm Δ, and any polynomial P, consider the subset of instances h of size m for which Δ with probability at least $1/P(m)$ outputs $x \neq y$ such that $h(x) = h(y)$. Let $\epsilon(m)$ be the probability with which Θ selects one of these instances. Then as a function of m, $\epsilon(m)$ vanishes faster than any polynomial fraction□

Note that the essential difference between Definition 2.1 and 2.2 is that in 2.2, we do not place any restrictions on the lengths of the inputs to the functions, other than what follows from the obvious fact that polynomial time algorithms cannot hash messages of superpolynomial length.

3 Basic Constructions

The main result in this section is that collision free hash function families can be constructed from fixed size collision free hash function families:

Theorem 3.1

Let $\mathcal{F}$ be a fixed size collision free hash function family mapping m bits to $t(m)$ bits. Then there exists a collision free hash function family $\mathcal{H}$ mapping strings of arbitrary length to $t(m)$-bit strings.

Let h be an instance in $\mathcal{H}$ of size m Then evaluating h on input of length n can be done in at most $n/(m - t(m) + 1) + 1$ steps using 1 processor (we count evaluation of functions in $\mathcal{F}$ as 1 step).

Proof

For each instance $f \in \mathcal{F}$ of size m, we will construct an instance $h \in \mathcal{H}$ of size m. Put $t = t(m)$. For bit strings a, b, we let $a||b$ denote the concatenation of a and b.

The construction will be divided into two cases: first we will discuss the case where $m - t > 1$, and take the $m - t = 1$ case later.

We describe how to compute the value of h on input $x \in \{0,1\}^*$:

Split x in blocks of size $m - t - 1$ bits. If the last block is incomplete, it is padded with 0's. Let d be the number of 0's needed. Let the blocks be denoted by $x_1, x_2, ..., x_{n/(m-t-1)}$, where $n = |x|$ (the length after padding).

We append to this sequence one extra $m - t - 1$-bit block $x_{n/(m-t-1)+1}$, which contains the binary representation of d, prefixed with an appropriate number of 0's.

Then define a sequence of t bit blocks $h_0, h_1, ...$ by:

$$h_1 = f(0^{t+1} \| x_1)$$

$$h_{i+1} = f(h_i \| 1 \| x_{i+1})$$

Finally, put $h(x) = h_{n/(m-t)+1}$.

Checking that $\mathcal{H}$ satisfies condition 1 and 2 in Definition 2.2 is easy. For condition 3, assume for contradiction that we are given an algorithm Δ which finds $x \neq x'$ such that $h(x) = h(x')$.

Let h_i, x_i (resp. h'_i, x'_i) be the intermediate results in the computation of $h(x)$ (resp. $h(x')$).

If $|x| \neq |x'| \mod (m - t)$, then certainly $x_{n/(m-t)+1} \neq x'_{n'/(m-t)+1}$, so that $h(x) = h(x')$ gives us immediately a collision for f. So we may now assume that $|x| = |x'| \mod (m - t)$ and without loss of generality that $|x'| \geq |x|$.

Consider now the equation

$$h(x) = f(h_{n/(m-t)} \| x_{n/(m-t)+1}) = f(h'_{n'/(m-t)} \| x'_{n'/(m-t)+1}) = h(x')$$

If $h_{n/(m-t)} \| x_{n/(m-t)+1} \neq h'_{n'/(m-t)} \| x'_{n'/(m-t)+1}$, we have a collision for f, and are done. If not, we may consider instead the equation

$$f(h_{n/(m-t)-1} \| x_{n/(m-t)}) = f(h'_{n'/(m-t)-1} \| x'_{n'/(m-t)})$$

and repeat the argument. Clearly this process must stop either by creating a collision for f, or (since $x \neq x'$) by establishing the equation

$$0^{t+1} \| x_1 = h'_i \| 1 \| x'_{i+1},$$

which is clearly impossible.

Summarizing, we have now a reduction that transforms Δ into an algorithm that finds a collision for f. Suppose Δ takes at most $T(m)$ bit operations. Then x and x' must be of length less than $T(m)$.

Therefore the whole reduction takes time $O(T(m)F(m))$, where $F(m)$ is the time needed to compute 1 f-value, in particular if T is a polynomial, then the whole reduction is in polynomial time. This finally establishes a contradiction with condition 3 in Definition 2.1

Finally, we discuss the case where $m - t = 1$. An easy, but not very efficient solution is prefix-free encode all messages before they are hashed, and then use a construction similar to the above, changing the definition of the h's to:

$$h_1 = f(0^t \| x_1)$$

$$h_{i+1} = f(h_i \| x_{i+1})$$

Here, of course the x_i's are 1-bit blocks. This can be proved secure in much the same way as above.

If f satisfies the second condition in Lemma 2.1, there is a more efficient solution: we choose a t bit string y_0 uniformly, and define

$$h_1 = f(y_0 \| x_1)$$

$$h_{i+1} = f(h_i \| x_{i+1})$$

this time without doing the prefix free encoding of x. The argument from above will now show that a collison for h will either give us a collision for f or a preimage of y_0. But then we are done by Lemma 2.1. □

Remarks

- The last version of the construction using Lemma 2.1 will not only work when $m - t = 1$, but will work whenever P_f is (close to) the uniform distribution, or $m - t = O(m)$. This should be noted because this version allows hashing of 1 bit more per application of f than the general construction, and is therefore slightly more efficient.

- The trick in the proof above of appending an extra block to the message is only necessary to ensure that we can recognize the difference between messages that need to be padded with d 0's, and messages that simply end with d 0's before padding. In many applications, it is perfectly acceptable that trailing 0's in the last block are ignored, in which case this part of the construction can be skipped.

Let us look at the connection between Theorem 3.1 and previously known hash functions. In [Da], hash functions are constructed based on claw-free pairs of permutations, i.e. pairs of permutations (f_0, f_1) with the same domain D, for which finding $x \neq y$ such that $f_0(x) = f_1(y)$ is a hard problem. We can construct an instance in a collision free function family from the pair (f_0, f_1) by defining a function $f : D \times \{0, 1\} \to D$ by:

$$f(x, b) = f_b(x)$$

for $x \in D$ and $b \in \{0, 1\}$. Using Theorem 3.1 on the function family thus defined will yield exactly the hashfunctions presented in [Da], except that we have removed the need for the prefix free encoding of messages used there (P_f is uniform in this case).

As a second example, consider one of the first ideas for constructing a hash function from a conventional cipher, due originally to Rabin: Let E be an encryption algorithm that encrypts messages of size t bits, using a key of size k bits. Put $m = t + k$. We split the message x in blocks of size k bits $x_1, x_2, ..., x_n$. We then choose a fixed t bit block h_0 at random and let $h_{i+1} = E_{x_{i+1}}(h_i)$. $h(x)$ is defined to be h_{n+1}.

This fits into the framework of Theorem 3.1 by letting $f(a, b) = E_a(b)$ for a t-bit block b and k-bit block a. Unfortunately, this f is NOT collision free: enciphering any message with an arbitrary key and deciphering with a *different* key will yield a collision for f with high probability. This does not necessarily mean that the function is weak. It does mean, however, that a proof of security cannot be based only on properties of f itself, but must depend on the global structure of the function.

For concrete examples of f, weaknesses have been found, however: if DES is used as E, such that t is only 64, it is well known that the function h constructed as above, permits an enemy which is given x and $h(x)$ to find a $y \neq x$ such that $h(x) = h(y)$, using the "birthday paradox". This is in fact a stronger statement than saying that the hash function is not collision free.

Within ISO, it is currently proposed to standardize a modification of this scheme, where f is defined as $f(a, b) = E_a(b) \oplus b$. For this version of f, there is in fact hope that we can use Theorem 3.1 to prove collision freeness of the entire function by looking only at f: Given c, it is not easy to solve $f(a, b) = c$ for a and b, if E is a strong encryption algorithm, and thus there good reason to believe that this version of f is collision free.

3.1 Parallellizing Hash Functions

Based on Theorem 3.1, we can give alternative constructions that allow computation in parallel of a hashvalue:

Theorem 3.2

Let $\mathcal{F}$ be a collision free function family mapping m bits to $t(m)$ bits. Then there exists a collision free hash function family $\mathcal{H}$ mapping arbitrary strings to $t(m)$-bit strings with the following property:

Let h be an instance in $\mathcal{H}$ of size m. Put $t = t(m)$. Then evaluating h on input of length n can be done in $O(log_2(n/t)t/(m - t))$ steps using $n/2t$ processors (we count evaluation of functions in $\mathcal{F}$ as 1 step).

Proof

We are given an instance $f \in \mathcal{F}$ of size m. By Theorem 3.1, we can construct a hash function h', which maps $2t$ bits to t bits in $t/(m - t)$ steps. Note, that since the length of the input is fixed, we do not need to append an extra input block in the construction of h'.

We then construct an instance $h \in \mathcal{H}$ as follows:

Let a message x of length n be given. We pad x with a number of 0's, such that the resulting bit string x_0 has length equal to $2^j t$ for some j. Now construct a sequence $x_0, x_1, ..., x_j$ by defining x_{i+1} in terms of x_i: split x_i in blocks of length $2t$, apply h' to each block and concatenate the results to obtain x_{i+1}.

The sequence stops at x_j, which has length t. We then hash the binary representation of the length n of x using Theorem 3.1 to obtain a t bit block len_x. Finally we put

$$h(x) = h'(x_j \| len_x).$$

The statements on the time and processors needed to compute h are trivial to verify.

As for collision freeness, suppose we could produce $x \neq x'$ with $h(x) = h(x')$ in expected polynomial time.

If $x'_{j'} \| len_{x'} \neq x_j \| len_x$, we have a collision for h', contradicting Theorem 3.1. Hence we may also assume that $n = n'$, since otherwise $len_{x'} = len_x$ would imply a collision.

Now, $x \neq x'$ implies that we may choose an i such that $x_i \neq x'_i$, but $x_{i+1} = x'_{i+1}$. This clearly implies a collision for $h' \square$

Finally, it is also easy to see how to make a construction that allows c processors to cooperate in computing a hashvalue, acheiving a speed up by a factor of c for long messages. Loosely speaking, we split the message in c parts of roughly the same size, hash each part in parallel using Theorem 3.1, and finally hash the c output blocks using Theorem 3.1 once again. Formalizing this and proving collision freeness is left to the reader.

4 Concrete Constructions

In the following we propose three concrete constructions of collision free functions with fixed inputsize. These functions can then be turned into hashfunctions by a straightforward application of Theorem 3.1.

4.1 Based on Modular Squaring

We give first a construction based on the hardness of extracting square roots modulo large numbers with two prime factors. The construction bears some similarities with the functions considered in [Gir], but is fundamentally different in that the functions from [Gir] do not allow for application of Theorem 3.1.

Let $n = pq$, where p and q are large primes. Let the length of n be s bits. For concreteness, one can think of $s = 512$. Next, choose I, a proper subset of the numbers $1, 2, ..., s$. For any s-bit string $y = y_1, y_2, ..., y_s$, let $f_I(y)$ be the concatenation of all y_j for which $j \in I$.

Finally, we can define our candidate collision free function f from m bits to t bits by setting $m = s - 8$, $t = |I|$, and defining

$$f(x) = f_I((3F|x)^2 \ mod \ n),$$

where $3F|x$ denotes the concatenation of the byte $3F$ (in hex) and x. This concatenation implies that all inputs to the modular squaring are less than $n/2$, but large enough to guarantee that modular reductions always take place. We therefore prevent trivial collisions implied by $x^2 = (-x)^2 \ mod \ n$, and also attempts to find collisions by choosing for example small 2-powers as input.

We also need to specify choices of I that will make f secure and efficient. The problem of finding a collision for f can be reformulated: find numbers $x \neq y$, such that their squares modulo n match at the positions designated by I. Girault [Gir] shows how to do this if I designates a reasonably small (less than 64) number of the least significant, or the most significant bits.

This suggests that we should choose the positions to be spread evenly over the s possible ones, since Girault's method and related ones [GTV] will then fail. On the other hand there are good practical reasons for not using completely random positions, but at least lumping them together in bytes. Moreover, $|I|$ should not be chosen too small, to prevent "birthday collisions".

To be concrete, if $s = 512$, the above suggests that good choices would be $|I| = 128$, and letting f_I extract every 4'th byte.

This function will hash up to 376 bits pr. modular squaring, which on for example an IBM P/S II model 80 will give a speed of about 100 Kbits/sec. Special purpose hardware will give speeds in the Mbit/sec area.

4.2 Based on Wolfram's Pseudorandom Bit Generator

The second suggestion bases itself on the pseudorandom bit generator proposed by Wolfram [Wo]. In general, a pseudorandom bit generator is an algorithm that takes as input a short, truely random seed, and stretches this into a long, seemingly random output string. It is intuitively clear that such a generator must in some sense implement a one-way function from its seed to its output: if the seed was easy to find given some part of the output, then the whole output could be predicted and hence be recognized as being non-random.

However, this one-way property does NOT in general imply collision freeness of a function constructed directly from the generator - an analysis of the concrete instance is therefore very much required.

Let us therefore have a look at the algorithm suggested by Wolfram: We define a function g from n bit strings to n bit strings: let $x = x_0, x_2, ..., x_{n-1}$, then the i'th bit of $g(x)$ is

$$g(x)_i = x_{i-1} \oplus (x_i \vee x_{i+1}),$$

where addition and subtraction of 1 are modulo n. One can think of this as a register R in which the bits are updated in parallel by setting $R := g(R)$. This is known as a one-dimensional cellular automat.

To use this for pseudorandom bit generation, one does the following:

1. Choose x at random.

2. $x := g(x)$.

3. Output x_0. Go to 2.

In [Wo], this pseudorandom bitgenerator is analyzed, and results of a large number of statistical tests are given. Its security is proved against enemies restricted to certain types of computations, but its ability to foil arbitrary polynomial time enemies remains a conjecture. All the known evidence, however, indicates that the generator is in fact very strong.

Let the bits produced by the algorithm on input x be denoted by $b_1(x), b_2(x), \dots$.

The natural way to use this to construct a collision free function is to choose two natural numbers $c < d$, and let a function f_0 be defined by

$$f_0(x) = b_c(x), b_{c+1}(x), \dots, b_d(x).$$

There are two possible flaws in this idea, which must be taken care of:

First, a natural demand to a function like this is that all output bits depend on all input bits. It is easy to see that changing 1 bit of x will eventually after many executions of $x := g(x)$ affect all of x - but the effect only propagates slowly through the register: 1 bit to the right, and about .25 bit to the left pr. application of g [Wo]. Hence choosing c too small will clearly be dangerous. A natural minimum value of c would therefore be one that guaranties that all output bits depend on all input bits.

The second problem is that g itself is not collision free: for example, $g(1^n) = g(0^n) = 0^n$. And clearly, $g(x) = g(y)$ implies $f_0(x) = f_0(y)$. More generally, if $g^v(x) = g^v(y)$ for small v, then there is at least a nonnegligible chance that $f_0(x) = f_0(y)$.

One natural way to get rid of this difficulty is to restrict f to a subset of the n-bit strings, thereby lowering the chance that pairs x, y of the above form exist, or at least making them harder to find. One concrete possibility is to restrict to strings of the form $x||z$, where z is a randomly chosen constant string in $\{0,1\}^r$, $r < n$.

Thus we will define our final candidate f so that it maps an $n - r$ bit string x to

$$f(x) = f_0(x||z).$$

The following lemma provides evidence in favor of this approach:

Lemma 5.1

If $g^v(x) = g^v(y) = z$, and $2v$ consecutive bits of x and y are equal, then $x = y$.

Proof

Let j be the index of the position immediately to the right of the $2v$ bits we know to be equal. Each bit of z depends on at most $2v+1$ bits of x(or y). Let l be chosen such that z_l is a function of bits $j, \dots, j + 2v$ of x(or y). Now, since inverting x_j will invert z_l, our assumptions imply that $x_j = y_j$. We can now "slide" the same argument one position to the right$\square$

This provides good evidence that choosing a relatively large r will make "trivial" collisions more sparse and harder to find.

As a concrete example, suppose we choose $n = 512$, $r = 256$, $c = 257$ and $d = 384$. The resulting f will map 256-bit strings to 128-bit strings, and thus the hash function constructed from f by Theorem 3.1 will hash messages in blocks of 128 bits, and produce 128 bit outputs.

This function will be extremely well suited for a hardware implementation: in VLSI, we can compute g by updating all bits in parallel, and thus one application of g would only take 1 or 2 clock cycles, *independently* of n. This will produce speeds in the Mbit/sec area even with quite modest clock speeds. Moreover such a hardware implementation would be extremely easy and cheap to build.

4.3 Based on the Knapsack Problem

Although the knapsack problem is NP-complete, and therefore probably very hard in the worst cases, making use of this hardness in cryptography is not easy, as shown by the fate of many public-key systems based on this problem.

The difficulty, however, is largely due to the fact that an encryption function must be invertible, and that the knapsacks used must therefore have some built-in structures, which in many cases turn out to be useful to a cryptanalyst. A hash function, on the other hand, never has to be inverted, and therefore completely randomly generated knapsacks can be used.

The naive way of doing this is to choose at random numbers $a_1, ..., a_s$ in the interval $1..M$, where s is the maximal length of a message to be expected. We can then hash the binary message $m_1, m_2, ..., m_s$ to

$$f(m_1, ..., m_s) = \sum_{i=1}^{s} m_i a_i$$

As shown in [GC], this is completely insecure for large s, more precisely when $M \leq s^{log(s)/4}$. To solve this, we propose to fix s to something reasonably small compared to M, and use Theorem 3.1 to construct the actual hash function. As an example, one could choose s to be about $2log(M)$, which implies that f compresses s bits blocks to $s/2$ bit blocks, and that the condition of [GC] is very far from being satisfied.

Concrete choices could be $s = 256$ and $M = 2^{120} - 1$. This would give an output from the final hash function of length 128 bits. On an IBM P/S II Model 80, this version will run at a speed of about 250 Kbits/sec.

To specify the function one needs to specify about 4 Kbytes of data. On e.g. a PC with 640K of RAM, this does not seem excessive. But in situations with a smaller memory, one can trade time for memory and generate the a's pseudorandomly in stead of remembering all of them.

The result of [ImNa] is a strong indication that this function is indeed collision free, although the security property proved is weaker than what we need here (see Section 1).

Another indication of the strength of the function is the fact that the problem of deciding in general whether a given knapsack induces an injective mapping is co-NP complete. A collision is of course a witness of non-injectiveness (the decision problem is clearly trivial if the knapsack compresses its input, but this does not imply that a witness is easy to find).

We remark that even knapsacks that expand their input slightly (and therefore cannot be used by [ImNa]) can be used to build hash functions secure in the sense of [NaYu], if one is willing to assume that they induce collision free mappings. This seems reasonable in view of the co-NP completeness of the problem involved and the fact that the decision problem is non trivial in this case. The construction and proof can be obtained by adapting the techniques of [NaYu].

References

[Da] Damgård: "Collision Free Hash Functions and Public Key Signature Schemes", Proceedings of EuroCrypt 87, Springer.

[De] D. Denning: "Digital Signatures with RSA and other Public Key Cryptosystems", CACM, vol.27, 1984, pp.441-448.

[DP] Davis and Price: "The Application of Digital Signatures Based on Public Key Crypto-Systems", Proc. of CompCon 1980, pp.525-530.

[GC] Godlewski and Camion: "Manipulation and Errors, Localization and Detection", Proceedings of EuroCrypt 88, Springer.

[Gi] Gibson: "A Collision Free Hash Function and the Discrete Logarithm Problem for a Composite Modulus", Manuscript, 1/10/88, London, England.

[Gir] Girault: "Hash Functions Using Modulo-n Operations", Proceedings of EuroCrypt 87, Springer.

[GTV] Girault, Toffin and Vallée: "Computation of Approximate L-th Roots Modulo n and Application to Cryptography", Proceedings of Crypto 88, Springer.

[ImNa] Impagliazzo and Naor: "Efficient Cryptographic Schemes Provably as Secure as Subset Sum", Proc. of FOCS 89.

[Me] Merkle: "One Way Hash Functions and DES", these proceedings.

[NaYu] Naor and Yung: "Universal One-Way Hash Functions", Proc. of STOC 89.

[Wi] Winternitz: "Producing a one-way Hash Function from DES", Proceedings of Crypto 83, Springer.

[Wo] Wolfram: "Random Sequence Generation by Cellular Automata", Adv. Appl. Math., vol 7, 123-169, 1986.

One Way Hash Functions and DES

Ralph C. Merkle

Xerox PARC

3333 Coyote Hill Rd.

Palo Alto, CA. 94304

merkle@xerox.com

ABSTRACT

One way hash functions are a major tool in cryptography. DES is the best known and most widely used encryption function in the commercial world today. Generating a one-way hash function which is secure if DES is a "good" block cipher would therefore be useful. We show three such functions which are secure if DES is a good random block cipher.

Introduction

DES can be used to build a one-way hash function which is secure if DES is a "good" block cipher. Previous efforts have not produced a satisfactory result[4,5,11,12] (although recent work at IBM[18, 19] appears very hopeful). We will use the meta-method discussed by Merkle[1,2] for the construction of one-way hash functions. Similar ideas have also been presented by Damgaard[20] and Naor and Yung[3].

One way hash functions (also called MDC's (Manipulation Detection Codes), fingerprints, cryptographically secure checksums, one way functions, and others) have been generally known for some time. The first definition was apparently given by Merkle [1,2] who also gave a method of constructing one-way hash functions from random block ciphers. More recent overviews have been given by Jueneman, Matyas, and Meyer[11], Jueneman[4], and Damgaard[20]. The method of construction used by Merkle was provably secure[2], provided that the block cipher was "random" (see below). Naor and Yung[3] also proved security results in the context of polynomial time reducibilities.

We will review the definitions and method of construction required to build a one-way hash function. We will then show how DES can be used to build a function that satisfies the desired properties, assuming that DES is "random." Because DES is in fact non-random in several known special cases, the constructions shown here would have to be modified to take this into account before being used in a real system.

Definitions

Broadly speaking, there are two definitions for one-way hash functions. The first definition is for a "weak" one-way hash function. A weak one-way hash function is a function F such that:

1.) F can be applied to any argument of any size. For notational convenience, F applied to more than one argument is equivalent to F applied to the bit-wise concatenation of all its arguments.

2.) F produces a fixed size output. (The output might be 56 bits).

3.) Given F and x, it is easy to compute F(x).

4.) Given F and a "suitably chosen" (e.g., random) x, it is computationally infeasible to find an x' ≠ x such that F(x) = F(x').

The phrase "computationally infeasible" used above can be replaced with any of several more precise definitions -- we defer a more detailed definition for purposes of this paper till later, but note in passing that each precise definition of computational infeasibility will in turn result in a somewhat different definition of a one way hash function.

In a weak one way hash function there is no guarantee that it is computationally infeasible to find pairs of inputs that map onto the same output. That is, it might be that F(z) = F(z') for some inputs z and z' that someone in fact found. However, if x ≠ z and x ≠ z', then this doesn't matter. Clearly, we must prevent someone from deliberately picking x so that it is equal to a value of z or z' which they know has this undesirable property. What's more, it must be difficult to generate too many z-z' pairs (and it clearly must be impossible to generate z-z' pairs in which we can effectively control the value of z or z') or even a randomly chosen x would not be safe. Thus, choosing x in a random fashion should make it unlikely that anyone can find an x' such that F(x)=F(x'). It is possible, however, to choose x in a non-random fashion and still be safe. If we assume that F is random (often a reasonable assumption in practice as discussed later), then any method of choosing x that does not depend on F is effectively random with respect to F and therefore suitable. This observation is sometimes important in practice, for it allows simpler (therefore faster and cheaper) methods of selecting x. Weak one-way hash functions have been described based on DES[12].

Various methods of randomizing x have been proposed. Merkle[2] proposed that x be encrypted with a good block cipher using a truly random key. The key would be pre-pended to the resulting ciphertext, and the new message would then be random. Damgaard[private communication] proposed selecting a short random pre-fix to x. When hashed in the manner suggested here and in [20], such a random pre-fix would effectively randomize the entire hash. Naor and Yung[3] do not randomize x, instead they randomly choose the function applied to x from a family of functions (also providing the advantages of parameterization discussed in the next paragraph). These various methods have different advantages and disadvantages, depending on the specific objectives being pursued.

Weak one-way hash functions also suffer from the problem that repeated use weakens them. That is, if a weak one-way hash function is used to hash 1,000 different random values for x (which might represent 1,000 different messages signed by a 1,000 different people) then the chances of finding an x' such that *one* of the thousand values of x satisfies $F(x) = F(x')$ might be 1,000 times higher. As more people sign more messages with the same weak one-way hash function, the overall security of the system is degraded. This undesirable state of affairs can be dealt with by parameterizing the family of one-way hash functions F. We simply define a family of one-way hash functions with the property that each member F^i of the family is different from all other members of the family, and so any information about how to break F^i will provide no help in breaking F^j for $i \neq j$. If the system is designed so that every use of a weak one-way hash function is parameterized by a different parameter, then overall system security can be kept high.

The less mnemonic term "property 2" was used in [2] -- the term "weak" seems preferable.

The alternative definition is of a "strong" one-way hash function. A strong one-way hash function is a function F such that:

1.) F can be applied to any argument of any size. For notational convenience, F applied to more than one argument is equivalent to F applied to the bit-wise concatenation of all its arguments.

2.) F produces a fixed size output. (The output might be 112 bits).

3.) Given F and x, it is easy to compute $F(x)$.

4.) Given F, it is computationally infeasible to find any pair x, x' such that $x \neq x'$ and $F(x) = F(x')$.

Strong one-way hash functions are easier to use in systems design than weak one-way hash functions because there are no pre-conditions on the selection of x, and they provide the full claimed level of security even when used repeatedly (or misused either because of error or sub-optimal system design). Many authors recomend the exclusive use of strong one-way hash functions[4,11] because of the practical difficulties of insuring that the pre-conditions on x imposed by a weak one-way hash function are met, and the increased problems in insuring that different parameters are selected for each use. In practice, the constraints imposed by use of a weak one-way hash function imply that x cannot be chosen by an agent who has a motive to break the system. If A signs a message which B provides, then A will have to "randomize" the message by some means before signing it. If A fails to randomize the message, then B can select a "rigged" message, and later surprise A by exhibiting a novel message and showing that A signed it.

We shall not consider weak one-way hash functions further, except to note they can be quite valuable in some system designs, although they must be used with caution. Parameterized weak one-way hash functions in particular appear to be under-rated. Although the design process is more complex, systems built in this fashion will require half as much storage for the "y" values. In essence, this is because the size of the output for a strong one-way hash function must be twice as large as one might expect to avoid "birthday" or "square root" attacks (see later). That is, a typical weak one-way hash function might have an output size of 56 bits, and might require 2^{56} operations to break. A typical strong one-way hash function might have an output size of 112 bits but still require only 2^{56} operations to break.

The phrases "it is computationally infeasible" and "it is easy to compute" can be replaced with many different definitions. A fully satisfactory definition for practical applications must consider both constant factors and average case complexity. DES has been criticized for having a key size that is "too small" (only 56 bits), while a slightly larger key size (64 bits) would eliminate most criticism. A satisfactory definition of "computationally infeasible" should be able to distinguish meaningfully between these two cases. For this reason, the definition we use here is stronger than the often-used definitions based on polynomial time reductions. This stronger definition allows us to prove stronger results (results of more practical cryptographic significance) but in exchange we must provide better informal reasons for believing that a function reasonably approximates our definition.

For purposes of this paper we will use the "random function", "demon in a box" or "oracle" model of complexity for DES. That is, we will assume that DES is actually random, in the sense that encryption and decryption are accomplished by looking up the correct value in a large table of random numbers. The table is secret and information about table entries can be learned only by requesting the value for some table entry -- which costs one "operation". More or less equivalently, we can view DES as a black box with a demon inside -- whenever we wish to encrypt or decrypt a value with some key, we must slip the input into the box and ask the demon to tell us the value. The demon will generate a truly random number and return it to us, again charging us one "operation" for his efforts. The demon promises to be consistent -- once he's given you the ciphertext for a given key and plaintext, he will always return the same ciphertext when given the same key and plaintext. He will also give you the correct plaintext if you happen to give him the ciphertext and key just mentioned.

Although we assume that DES is random, it is not immediately obvious how to apply DES to a large x and produce a small output in a secure manner. Several previous efforts have failed[4,5,11,13]. (A recent proposal by IBM[18, 19] looks very hopeful and has been carefully scrutinized within IBM. Although there is as yet no proof that it is correct, should such a proof be found the IBM proposal would then be preferable because of its superior performance). The successful attacks on these methods do not require any knowledge of the internal structure of DES and so would still work if DES were truly random. Therefore, it is useful to show a method of generating a one-way hash function by using repeated applications of DES which is immune from this class of attacks.

While there has been a lively debate about the actual security level provided by DES[14,15,16,17] the fact remains that no major deviations from random behavior have been found. The most significant deviation noted would effectively reduce the key size by one bit to 55 bits [9]. To circumvent the problem caused by this non-random behavior would require the redesign of the proposals made here to use a 55-bit block cipher, with a corresponding slight reduction in either performance or security. Other known cases of non-randomness in DES would require case-by-case analysis and possible redesign. Aside from the few known cases of non-random behavior, DES is generally viewed as a "random" function in the literature[17] and it seems almost certain that *some* block cipher exists with the desired properties, regardless of the eventual fate of DES. The existence of "random block ciphers" seems almost assured in some intuitive sense, and DES appears to be a reasonable approximation to one.

The primary use of one-way hash functions is authentication[1,11]. If $y = F(x)$, and we are already confident that we know y, then we can obtain x from any source (in particular, an untrustworthy, unreliable but cheap and convenient source) and verify that $y = F(x)$. Because it is computationally infeasible to find an x' such that $y = F(x')$, we now have confidence that we have the correct value of x.

The advantages of using one-way functions are clear if, for example, x is a one-megabyte document, while y is 112 bits. If we can design a system that provides good security for y, then we can always double-check x any time we wish -- thus, we can be much more casual (i.e., spend less money) in storing x. One-way hash functions are virtually a necessity in digitally signing large messages because most digital signature methods are rather inefficient. If we first reduce a one-megabyte x to a small y, then signing the small y is much easier. One-way hash functions are a universal building block in authentication systems, and have been used to define practical digital signatures[1,2,6] and to detect fraudulent changes in messages[4,11]. When used in a tree-structure, one-way hash functions can be used to conveniently authenticate any individual entry in the "public directory" (so often needed in public-key based systems)[1,7].

The meta-method

We first define a meta-method (given in [1,2]) for constructing F. In this meta-method, we build F (which accepts an arbitrarily large argument, x) from a simpler function F_0. The definition of F_0 is exactly the same as the definition of F, except that F_0 accepts only a fixed size argument. That is, F_0 might accept an input of 224 bits, while producing a smaller output of perhaps 112 bits. As we shall see, the larger the input that F_0 accepts the better, for this will mean we can more rapidly hash down the arbitrarily large input, x. We require, however, that F_0 have an input that is larger than its output.

We can now define F in terms of F_0 as follows:

Function F(x) returns FixedSizeOutputString; -- This might be 112 bits

x: ARRAY[1 .. n] OF convenientlySizedChunks; -- perhaps 112 bits

-- Note that SizeOf(input to F_0) =

-- SizeOf(convenientlySizedChunks) + SizeOf(FixedSizeOutputString).

result: FixedSizeOutputString; -- perhaps 112 bits

BEGIN

result = 0;

FOR i = 1 to n DO result = F_0(result,x[i]);

RETURN(result);

END;

As an aside, we note that x is padded with 0's until its size is an integral multiple of the size of the convenientlySizedChunks. Note that padding with 0's might introduce some ambiguity about the exact value of x that is being authenticated, as discussed by Jueneman[4]. The message "010110" padded to 8 bits would be "01011000" and it is now unclear how many trailing 0's were present in the original message. Several methods are available to resolve this ambiguity. We select a method that will also be useful in resolving a further problem: we append the length of x, in bits, at the end of x. To make this additional "length" field easy to find, we shall right justify it in the final block. If the length field won't fit, we add additional blocks to the end of x. For purposes of notation, we shall assume that the final few blocks of x hold this count; for example, if we desire a 64-bit count and the "convenientlySizedChunks" are 8 bits, then the count would occupy x[n-7], x[n-6], x[n-5], ... x[n-1], and x[n].

As a second aside, the linear pattern of computing F used above can be replaced with a tree pattern, as discussed in [1, 2, 7 page 170]. This tree structure is very useful when we wish to authenticate not the entire input, but only a single item (or leaf) from the input. This occurs in practice when, for example, we wish to authenticate the public key of a single user from the public directory. Certainly, if we know the correct hash value for the entire public directory, we could re-hash and re-verify the whole thing before believing that the single entry we were interested in was correct. This, however, is very inefficient. If the one-way hash function used a tree pattern, then we could authenticate a single leaf node (the one entry in the public directory that we"re interested in) if we knew only that entry, and the log n entries along the authentication path from the leaf to the root. This reduces $O(n)$ computations to verify the whole public directory to $O(\log n)$ computations to verify the single leaf entry we"re interested in.

In looking at the definition of F we note that the input, x, is treated as an array of "convenientlySizedChunks". These chunks will have a size which is the size of the input to F_0 less the size of the output from F_0. If the input is 224 bits, and the output is 112 bits, then each chunk will be 224-112 = 112 bits. Clearly, bigger chunks imply fewer applications of F_0, which will make the computation of F more efficient. On the other hand, the chunks can be as small as one bit[3,20], which is inefficient but still secure.

Using this construction, we can now prove that breaking F (finding an x and x' such that $F(x) = F(x')$ and $x \neq x'$) is at least as hard as breaking F_0. This is easily shown by induction. We first make the assumption that x and x' have the same length -- we shall relax this assumption later.

Basis:

for n = 1, $y = F(x) \equiv F_0(0, x[1])$ (where 0 is the all zero bit pattern).

Clearly, breaking F must be as hard as breaking F_0 in this case, for F and F_0 are the same. That is, if $x \neq x'$ and $F(x) = F(x')$ and n = 1, then $x[1] \neq x'[1]$ and $F_0(0, x[1]) = F_0(0, x'[1])$. Thus, by definition a "break" of F implies a "break" of F_0.

Induction:

We know the property holds for n, and we wish to show it holds for n + 1.

$y = F(x) \equiv F_0(F(x[1 .. n]), x[n + 1])$.

Neither $F(x[1 .. n])$ nor $x[n + 1]$ (i.e., neither of the arguments to F_0) can be modified successfully, for then we would have broken F_0 directly. But if $F(x[1 .. n])$ is correct then, by the induction hypothesis, x[1 .. n] cannot have been modified without breaking F_0. This means that no bit of x could have been modified without breaking F_0. Q.E.D.

In the more general case, it might be that the length of x is not the same as the length of x'. We can assume, without loss of generality, that x is shorter than x'. (If this is not the case, then simply swap the names of x and x'). If x is shorter than x', and $F(x) = F(x')$, then the proof given above shows that x is a postfix of x'. In particular, the length fields of both x and x' must be the same. It is now a simple matter to reject the string whose length is incorrect.

The particular method selected here to solve the problems caused when x is a pre-fix or postfix of x' is only one of many. Several other techniques are possible. Which method is actually used will vary depending on the precise circumstances and design objectives.

The ability to prove that a break of F implies a break of F_0 works for most definitions of complexity. This will be useful later in the paper when we construct an F_0' and an F_0'' that are not random, but such that breaking them is still "computationally infeasible".

As an aside, it should be noted that a random block cipher in which the size of the key was greater than the desired input size to F_0 could easily be used to generate a suitable F_0. We need only define $F_0(x)$ as ENCRYPT(x, 0) (where x is used as the key, and 0 is the plaintext input consisting of all 0's). If the key size were, say, 224 bits then our problem would be well solved. That was exactly the approach taken in [1,2]. Construction of random block ciphers with large keys seems well within current capabilities. DES, for example, uses 768 bits of key material internally (16*48 bits). Any problems in using DES as a one-way hash function stem almost exclusively from its limited key size. This paper primarily addresses the specific problems involved in using DES as currently defined as the basis for a one-way hash function -- if DES had a significantly larger key size then the problem solved here would be trivial.

With the construction of F from F_0 now in hand, it is clear what to do: define F_0 in terms of DES. This is simpler than trying to define F in terms of DES directly -- which has been tried and can lead to subtle problems[4,5,11]. Defining F_0 in terms of DES will involve a fixed number of applications of DES in some particular pattern. Analyzing the complexity of a fixed pattern of applications of DES can be tedious, but has proven easier than analyzing the indefinite number of applications of DES that are required when F is defined directly in terms of DES.

A Method

In our first method, we shall simply attempt to produce an F_0 such that its input is larger than its output; we won't worry about efficiency. In our second and third methods, we"ll see improvements in efficiency but at the cost of more complex analyses. The methods presented here are by no means unique, nor is there any reason to believe they are the most efficient. Further work should produce improved methods. The principle, however, should be clear -- try to combine a few applications of DES in such a way that we produce a satisfactory F_0 -- (and such that the analysis is tractable...).

For this first method we will adopt a fixed size output of 112 bits for both F and F_0 because we are building a strong one-way hash function which we wish to be as secure as DES, i.e., it must require at least 2^{56} operations to break. The output size must be at least 112 bits because we know that smaller values of the output will make the system vulnerable to "square root attacks"[4,5,8,11]. If the output size were 56 bits, then hashing 2^{28} arbitrarily chosen messages would result in a high probability that two of those messages produced the same 56-bit output. Because the probability of a collision goes up sharply as the number of messages exceeds the square root of the number of possible output values, such attacks are called "square root attacks" (also known as "birthday attacks"[5] because the probability that two people at a party were born on the same day goes up sharply when the number of people at the party exceeds the square root of 365, or about 19 people).

We turn now to some definitions. DES accepts 64 bits of input, 56 bits of key material, and produces a 64-bit output. We denote encryption by:

$$64\text{-bit-ciphertext} = ENCRYPT(56\text{-bit-key}, 64\text{-bit-plaintext})$$

We denote decryption by:

$$64\text{-bit-plaintext} = DECRYPT(56\text{-bit-key}, 64\text{-bit-ciphertext})$$

We can view ENCRYPT and DECRYPT as functions that map from 120 bits onto 64 bits. That is, ENCRYPT and DECRYPT can be viewed as very large tables which have random (or nearly random -- see below) entries. We do not initially know the random values in these tables, and can find out only by using one of the two functions ENCRYPT or DECRYPT. (The concept of random encryption functions was given by Shannon[10]). In some sense, our 2^{120} random 64-bit entries are just 2^{126} random bits. These 2^{126} random bits can be used in any way want -- if we desire a large number of random bits, we need only look up many different values in our giant table. We are fundamentally limited only by the total number of random bits, not the particular format they are packaged in. We can repackage the bits to best suit our needs -- which is exactly what we will be doing.

Unfortunately, ENCRYPT (and similarly DECRYPT) is non-random in the following sense: we can easily generate a legitimate input-output pair in which the output value is non-random. Even worse, we can easily generate an input-output pair in which the output value is anything that we want! Given a 64-bit value that we want produced as the output, we can easily find many 120-bit inputs that produce the desired output value. That is, we can easily find many keys and plaintexts such that ENCRYPT(key,plaintext) = ciphertext. We simply pick a random 56-bit key, and then decrypt the 64-bit ciphertext with that key. This is bad. To remedy this, we can XOR the 64-bit output with the 64-bit input, to produce a new 64-bit output. We will define this operation with a lower case f_0 (this definition has been used before[12]). By definition, if the 120-bit input to f_0 is arbitrarily divided into a 56-bit key and a 64-bit plaintext, then

f_0(key,plaintext) $\equiv$ ENCRYPT(key, plaintext) XOR plaintext

All our further use of DES will be through this new function, f_0. This function maps 120 bits onto 64 bits. It will be a good approximation to a random function if DES is a good approximation to a random function. In particular, f_0 has the interesting property that *the output value will be random no matter how it is computed.* If we compute n values of f_0 by computing DES n different times, then the n output values of f_0 will be randomly distributed. In contrast, the input values might be quite systematic -- we could simply compute $f_0(0)$, $f_0(1)$, $f_0(2)$, ... $f_0(n-1)$. The sequence of input values 0, 1, 2, ... n-1 certainly qualifies as non-random. However, no matter how hard we try, the output values will be random, as can be easily proven. First, we note that there are only two possible methods of computing an output value of f_0 -- either we encrypt some plaintext with DES, or we decrypt some ciphertext. If we encrypt some plaintext, then the ciphertext produced by the encryption is random (courtesy of our demon). When we exclusive-or this random ciphertext with the (possibly non-random) plaintext, the result is also random. Equivalently, if we decrypt a ciphertext, then the plaintext produced by the decryption is random (again courtesy of our demon). When we exclusive-or this random plaintext with the (possibly non-random) ciphertext, the result is also random. As a result, the output of f_0 is always random, no matter how it was computed.

In this paragraph we first discuss and then decide we can safely ignore a minor deviation from randomness caused by the fact that DES is a permutation. If we compute ENCRYPT(key, plain1)=cipher1, then we know that computing ENCRYPT(key, plain2)=cipher2 will *not* produce cipher1, i.e., that cipher1 $\neq$ cipher2. (We are simply observing that each plaintext has one and only one ciphertext, and each ciphertext has one and only one plaintext. For this reason, DES is not quite random). This, however, is a very minor deviation from randomness in the context in which we are using DES. Recall that we only wish to achieve a level of security equivalent to DES, which means that we only need to insure that f_0 behaves randomly for at most 2^{56} different values applied to the input. Now, if we have actually applied f_0 2^{56} times, then at worst there will not be 2^{64} possible output values left, but instead only $2^{64} - 2^{56}$. This corresponds to about 63.994 bits -- a loss which we can and will neglect. (Put another way, this means that our demon might compute a random 64-bit value and then occasionally reject the value because it's already been used for some other plaintext-ciphertext pair. The demon will reject a random value at most one time in 256. This slight deviation from randomness has almost no practical impact on the proofs that follow).

Because f_0 is such a good approximation to a random function, we will be unable to find two inputs which map onto a 64-bit output in significantly less than 2^{32} operations (as a consequence of the birthday problem). This, however, does not provide good enough security. We want to force cryptanalysis to take at least 2^{56} operations, which will require an output of 112 bits. To accomplish this, we will simply look up "x" twice, and concatenate the two outputs. This will produce 128 bits. This is more than we need, so we throw away the extra bits. However, we only have a single function f_0 -- how can we look up x twice? By reducing the size of x from 120 bits to 119 bits, and using the additional bit to effectively split f_0 into two different functions.

Formally, we declare that x is 119 bits. We define F_0 as:

$F_0(x) \equiv First112bitsOf(f_0("0", x), f_0("1", x))$

$F_0(x)$ is simply the concatenation of the two applications of f_0. We first prefixed x with a "0", and then with a "1" to distinguish the two applications of f_0. To produce the desired 112 bit output, we threw away the final 16 bits of the 128 bits produced.

Intuitively, f_0 is just a very large random table. The index into this table is a 120 bit number. By making x only 119 bits in size, we effectively produce two tables -- the first half of f_0 and the second half of f_0. By looking up x first in the first half, and then in the second half, we obtain two totally unrelated random numbers. This produces 128 random bits from a single value of x. Now, we need only throw away 16 bits. We are left with 112 random bits, which is what we desired.

As a result, we have a random function F_0 which accepts a 119 bit input and produces a 112 bit output. Therefore we can use F_0 to build a one-way hash function F that will accept 119-112 = 7 bits per iteration. Each iteration requires two computations of DES, so we require one application of DES for every 3.5 bits to be hashed. The performance is poor -- but we can prove rather easily that it's as secure as DES under the assumption that DES is a random function.

A Faster Method

We can show a faster method is also secure, though the analysis is somewhat more complex. The faster method will require that we divide x into two pieces: x_1 of 118 bits and x_2 of 54 (= 120-64-2) bits. In total, x will be 172 (118+54) bits. We will reduce these 172 bits to 128 bits using 4 applications of DES, which allows us to hash (172-128)/4 = 11 bits per application of DES. This is clearly better than 3.5, though better is still possible.

We will define F_0' as follows:

$F_0' \equiv$

a: $f_0("00"$, c: $f_0("10", x_1), x_2)$,

b: f_0("01", **d**: f_0("11", x_1), x_2)

Note that F_0' (and so F') produce a 128 bit output. We will use this additional output only to guarantee 56 bits of equivalent security -- we will not provide the full 64 bits of security that might seem possible, but will instead "waste" a few bits to make the construction go through. (The actual security is somewhat better than 56 bits, though we will not prove this).

Notationally, we have labeled the intermediate values in the computation with the letters **a**, **b**, **c**, and **d**.

The degradation in security in this computation occurs because different values of x_1 might produce the same intermediate values for **c** or **d**. That is, it might happen that **c** = f_0("10", x_1) = **c**" = f_0("10", x_1"). If such collisions did not occur, then we could guarantee that different values of x_1 would produce different values for both **c** and **d**. This in turn would let us guarantee that all pairs x, x' such that x ≠ x' would result in selection of the values for both **a** and **b** from different entries in our giant table. That is, if x ≠ x' then either x_2 ≠ x_2" or both (**c** ≠ **c**" and **d** ≠ **d**"). But then the two values used as input to f_0 to compute **a** and **a**" must be different, and the two values used as input to f_0 to compute **b** and **b**" must also be different. Thus, we have guaranteed that **a** and **b** were selected from different locations in our giant table, which lets us conclude that the probability of a collision in both **a** and **b** is a random event whose probability we can compute, and which is small (less than one in 2^{56}).

Of course, collisions involving **c** or **d** *will* occur, and so the foregoing logic is false. However, we can bound the number of collisions that are expected to occur, and use this bound to determine a bound on the deterioration in the security of F_0'.

We observe that **c** and **d** are always random, because they are produced as outputs from f_0 and we have already shown that outputs from f_0 are always random, no matter how computed. Therefore, no matter how cleverly x_1 is chosen, the probability that the same value of **c** (or of **d**) is produced by two different values of x_1 is random. Therefore, if we limit ourselves to 2^{56} applications of f_0, the expected maximum number of collisions will be $2^{56} * (2^{56}/2^{64})$ or 2^{48}. (This also holds for computations of values of **d**). Given that there are at most 2^{48} such collisions, the expected maximum number of 3 way collisions is $2^{56} * (2^{48}/2^{64}) = 2^{40}$. The expected maximum number of n-way collisions is 2^{64-n*8}, which implies there are probably no 8-way collisions. We can use a 7-way collision as an upper bound.

Now, if F_0'(x) = F_0'(x'), and x ≠ x', then either x_1 ≠ x_1" or x_2 ≠ x_2". If x_2 ≠ x_2", then the computations of **a** and **b** were random, and the probability of a random collision for both of them is negligible (if 2^{56} computations of **a** and **b** had already been done, the probability of a collision would be $2^{56}/2^{128}$ -- negligible as far as we"re concerned). If, on the other hand, x_1 ≠ x_1" and x_2 = x_2", we can further divide the situation into two cases: either (**c** = **c**" or **d** = **d**"), or (**c** ≠ **c**" and **d** ≠ **d**"). If (**c** ≠ **c**" and **d** ≠ **d**") then by the logic used before the computations of **a** and **b** were random, and the probability of a random collision for both of them is negligible. If, on the other hand, ($c = c''$ or $d = d''$) then we can use our upper bound on the number of collisions to limit the number of distinct values of x_1 for which this can occur. (We reject the case where $c = c''$ and $d = d''$ as being sufficiently improbable that we can ignore it). We can assume that $c = c''$ (symetrical considerations hold if, instead, $d = d''$). Obviously there are at most 7 different values for x_1 that map onto the same value for c. Therefore, instead of getting random values when we pick a and b, we might at worst get 7 non-random trials in which the 7 values computed for a were always the same (because c and x_2 were always the same, and hence $a = f_0("00", c, x_2$) would be the same). This would generate 7 different trials for b, but b is only 64 bits -- so these 7 trials have a higher probability of success than 7 trials that randomly selected a 128-bit value. Specifically, the probability of success in these 7 random trials for b is at most $7^2/2^{64}$ or $49/2^{64}$. This produces an equivalent security level of ($64 - \log_2 49$) or 58.3 bits. This is greater than 56, as desired. (This does not imply our security level is 58.3 bits -- remember that we have already assumed a limit of 2^{56} in a few places. It simply confirms that we can reach at least 56 bits of security. For various reasons, we could actually achieve more than 56 bits of security -- but this suffices to show the idea).

Although the foregoing discussion was relatively informal because of the relative simplicity of the problem, the techniques become harder to apply in more complex cases. In the following case, a more formal analysis was needed because of the sheer complexity of the situation.

A Complex And Yet Faster Method

It is again possible to improve the performance, though to do so requires a significantly more complex analysis. We will divide a 234 bit x into 2 pieces, each of 117 bits in size: x_1 and x_2. We will define F_0'' as:

$F_0'' \equiv$

$f_0("00", \text{First59bitsOf}(f_0("100", x_1)), \text{First59bitsOf}(f_0("101", x_2)))$,

$f_0("01", \text{First59bitsOf}(f_0("110", x_1)), \text{First59bitsOf}(f_0("111", x_2)))$

Essentially, we have built a small tree of f_0's. Because there are six applications of f_0, we have used the first two or three bits to divide f_0 into six distinct functions. Thus, $f_0("00", ...)$, $f_0("01", ...)$, $f_0("100", ...)$, $f_0("101", ...)$, $f_0("110", ...)$ and $f_0("111", ...)$ can be viewed as six unrelated random functions. The "leaf" functions in this tree map 117 bits onto 59 bits. The "root" functions map 118 bits onto 64 bits. Overall, F_0'' maps 234 bits onto 128 bits using six applications of DES, which means we can hash $234-128 = 106$ bits/iteration, or $106/6 =$ almost 18 bits/application of DES. This is an improvement over 11 bits/application of DES.

However, we are now left with the problem of showing that we have not significantly degraded security. Again, there *is* degradation in security caused by collisions during the intermediate computations. This is why we kept 128 bits of output -- F_0" is not perfectly random and we must retain additional output bits in order to reach our desired objective of 2^{56} operations to break it. Our proof will actually not be able to show that we have retained the full 56-bits of security that we desire, though we will come close. Tightening up the proof would make it even more complex, though probably (although not certainly) providing the 56-bit security level desired.

First, we shall label the various values produced by this computation.

F_0" $\equiv$

a: $f_0($"00", **c**: First59bitsOf($f_0($"100", x_1)), **e**: First59bitsOf($f_0($"101", x_2))),

b: $f_0($"01", **d**: First59bitsOf($f_0($"110", x_1)), **f**: First59bitsOf($f_0($"111", x_2)))

We first note that **c**, **e**, **d**, and **f** are random. No matter how cleverly we pick x_1 and x_2, these values are random and we can apply statistical methods to them. In particular, every value of x_1 and every value of x_2 will generate a tuple; that is, every value for x_1 will generate a tuple $\langle c,d \rangle$, and every value for x_2 will generate a tuple $\langle e,f \rangle$. Because f_0 is random, the actual values of x_1 and of x_2 are irrelevant -- the only thing that matters is that we have generated tuples $\langle c,d \rangle$ and $\langle e,f \rangle$.

This leads to our first **definition**: we define a *random linkage map* as two sets of tuples, each tuple having two chosen 59-bit elements, and each set of tuples containing 2^{56} elements. The two 59-bit elements in a tuple are "linked" because they are generated from a single value of x_1 or of x_2. Note that this is equivalent to saying that the two elements in a tuple are generated randomly, hence the name *random* linkage map.

Intuitively, a random linkage map is all the useful information that any algorithm can ever hope to obtain about the four possible intermediate values. A random linkage map actually requires 2^{58}th computations of f_0 to compute, so it actually is an upper bound on the information that can be obtained. Any actual algorithm that attempts to crack F_0" will in fact have less information than is present in a random linkage map. However, it can't hurt to give the algorithm additional information for free. Any optimal algorithm to crack F_0" should not slow down if it is given all the information in a random linkage map, instead of getting only the sub-set of information about a random linkage map that it actually computed. The major reason for providing all the information in a random linkage map is that, although an actual algorithm would use only part of the information, it is not clear which part it would select. By providing all the information, we avoid the problems involved in determining optimal strategies for dealing with the partial information that can actually be computed.

For any computation of F_0'' and any actual value of x, we will generate four intermediate values **c**, **e**, **d**, and **f**. By definition, both $\langle c,d \rangle$, and $\langle e,f \rangle$ will appear in the corresponding random linkage map. This motivates the following **definition**: a quadruple $\langle c,e,d,f \rangle$ is ***doubly linked*** with respect to a random linkage map if the tuple $\langle c,d \rangle$ appears in the first set and the tuple $\langle e,f \rangle$ appears in the second set.

Given a doubly linked quadruple $\langle c,e,d,f \rangle$, we can compute a valid output of F_0''. This output is valid because there exist an input x_1 concatenated with x_2, where x_1 links the tuple $\langle c,d \rangle$ and x_2 links the tuple $\langle e,f \rangle$, which generates the intermediate quadruple $\langle c,e,d,f \rangle$ from which the output is then computed. That is, a doubly linked quadruple is just as good as an actual input, x.

We now prove that the expected running time for an optimal algorithm to find two values x, x' such that $F_0''(x) = F_0''(x')$ (where F_0'' is based on DES in the manner described, and DES is assumed to be random), is at least as long as the expected running time for an algorithm to find a pair of doubly linked quadruples such that both quadruples generate the same output (the same values for **a** and **c**), given only a random linkage map and the ability to compute values for **a** and **c** using f_0. That is, the algorithm that uses the random linkage map cannot use f_0 to compute new values for **c**, **e**, **d**, and **f** (after all, it already has the random linkage map which is supposed to provide at least as much information as could ever be obtained by computing such intermediate values with f_0 -- so letting it compute more intermediate values would provide it with an unfair advantage). Instead, valid intermediate quadruples must be obtained from the linkage map. Both algorithms can apply f_0 to arguments that are prefixed with "0", for these are just the values used to compute either **a** or **c**. The random linkage map contains no information about computations of **a** or **c**.

The proof is relatively simple -- given the foregoing definitions. If we are given any algorithm for cracking F_0'' we can use it to define an algorithm that is just as good at solving an equivalent problem defined in terms of the random linkage map. Given a random linkage map and an F_0'' cracking algorithm, we run the F_0'' cracking algorithm, but now lie to it whenever it tries to compute f_0. Instead of giving it the "correct" truly random value, we instead give it a value selected at random from the random linkage map. Of course, we must be consistent. If the optimal algorithm gives us the same argument twice, we return the same value. In addition, if it gives us a value for which we"ve already returned a **c**, and now requests a **d**, we must return the proper linked value. This does not introduce any bias, though, because all the entries in a random linkage map are random. The truly random values generated by the DES "oracle" are just as good as the truly random values taken from the random linkage map, and so the expected running time of this "random linkage map" cracking algorithm must be less than or equal to the expected running time for the corresponding F_0'' cracking algorithm. Therefore, a lower bound on the expected running time of a "random linkage map" cracking algorithm is also a lower bound on the expected running time of any F_0'' cracking algorithm.

We can now concentrate on finding a lower bound for the running time of an algorithm to crack a random linkage map. We start by analyzing the intermediate values c, e, d, and f in a random linkage map.

We define a *collision* for c, e, d, or f with respect to a linkage map as a value of c, e, d, or f which appears in two different tuples in the same set and in the same position in the two tuples.

First, because c, e, d, and f are 59 bits, an upper bound on the expected number of collisions for each of them is $(2^{56}/2^{59}) * 2^{56}$ or 2^{53}. The number of triple collisions will be bounded by $(2^{53}/2^{59}) * 2^{56}$ or 2^{50}. In general, the expected number of n-tuple collisions is bounded by 2^{59-3*n}. There will probably not be any 20-tuple collisions, so we can safely use this as the expected maximum.

Our objective is to find a lower bound for the running time of the best algorithm that finds two doubly linked quadruples $\langle c,e,d,f \rangle$ and $\langle c'',e'',d'',f'' \rangle$ such that they produce the same output, i.e., such that $a \equiv f_0("00", c, e)$ is equal to $a'' \equiv f_0("00", c'', e'')$, and $b \equiv f_0("01", d, f)$ is equal to $b'' \equiv f_0("01", d'', f'')$. (Note that the two quadruples are each doubly linked internally, independently of the other -- the links do not extend from one quadruple to the other). To do this, we will consider what happens during an actual run of a linkage-map cracking algorithm. The only things that such a run can do are compute a value of a from some tuple $\langle c,e \rangle$, or compute a value b from some tuple $\langle d,f \rangle$ (note that these tuples are not the tuples that appear in the linkage map -- those were tuples $\langle c,d \rangle$ and $\langle e,f \rangle$). We can ask, each time such a computation is performed, what the probability is that that particular computation will result in finding a pair of quadruples with the desired property -- i.e., the probability that that particular computation of f_0 will terminate the run successfully. Clearly, if we can provide an upper bound on the probability of success for each such computation during the course of the run, then we can determine a lower bound on the expected running time.

Now, if we were to compute $a = f_0("00", c, e)$ then we could succeed if and only if there were already two doubly linked quadruples $\langle c,e,d,f \rangle$ and $\langle c'',e'',d'',f'' \rangle$, and further the case that $b = f_0("01", d, f) = f_0("01", d'', f'')$. We would then succeed if, after computing a, we found that it matched the value for a'', i.e., $a = f_0("00", c, e) = a'' = f_0("00", c'', e'')$. If there were only one other quadruple $\langle c'',e'',d'',f'' \rangle$ such that $b = b''$, then the probability of success would be one chance in 2^{64}. However, there might be several. In particular, it might be the case that $b = b''$ because $d = d''$ and $f = f''$. The only other alternative is that $b = b''$ and either $d \neq d''$ or $f \neq f''$. In the first case, because there are at most 20 collisions for either d or f, there could be at most $20^2 = 400$ quadruples matching this criteria. Obtaining a bound for the second case is more difficult, but is possible by noting that every distinct computation of a produces a random number.

There are at most 2^{56} computations of b. Therefore, the expected maximum number of collisions for b is 2^{48}. The number of triple collisions is 2^{40}, the number of quadruple collisions is 2^{32}, and the number of n-way collisions is 2^{64-8*n}. Clearly, the expected number of 8-way collisions is 0, and can be neglected. The maximum number of 7-way collisions is 2^8, which is rather small. We could use 7 as a simple bound on the number of collisions, or we could perform a more complex analysis to show that, on average, the number of collisions is more like 2 or 3. If we content ourselves with the easier bound of 7, we can then produce a bound on the probability of success following each computation of **a** or **b**.

For each quadruple $\langle c,e,d,f \rangle$ there are at most 400 quadruples $\langle c'',e'',d'',f'' \rangle$ such that $b = b''$ because $d = d''$ and $f = f''$. Further, there are at most 7 collisions such that $b = b''$ and either $d \neq d''$ or $f \neq f''$. Therefore, there are at most $7*400 = 2,800$ quadruples $\langle c'',e'',d'',f'' \rangle$ which might cause the computation of **a** to terminate the run. Therefore, the probability of success is upper bounded by $2,800/2^{64}$. This corresponds to $64 - \log_2 2,800$ bits of security, or $64 - 11.5$ or about 52.5 bits. This is somewhat lower than we desire (by 3.5 bits) but it seems likely that tightening the proof would recover most if not all of this loss.

The most obvious places where this lower bound could be tightened are the following. First, we always assumed 2^{56} operations could be performed for the computation of all intermediate values. Clearly, this is not possible. In fact, these 2^{56} operations need to be parcelled out among all computations of all values in some optimal way. Second, we gave away a great deal of information for free. This information would in fact have to be computed by some means. Third, we used simple bounds of 7 collisions for elements **a** or **b** and 20 collisions for elements **c**, **e**, **d**, or **f**. These upper bounds are achieved only infrequently. That is, if the upper bound of 20 were achieved for only a hundred elements, then it would only improve the overall probability of success modestly. The more frequently occuring values of 10 or 11 would have greater significance, for they would involve the bulk of the computations actually made.

Conclusion

We have shown three methods for building a strong one-way hash function from DES. All methods are provably secure if DES is a random function. All methods rely on producing a "building block" function which is of fixed and finite size, and using this "building block" to build the actual one-way hash function which can then accept an input of indefinite size. In the first method, a simple pattern of two applications of DES was used, and the proof was not complex. The resulting method, though, was not very efficient. The second method improved the efficiency, but a moderately complex analysis of a particular pattern of four applications of DES was used to prove the required security properties. The final method improved efficiency further, but a complex analysis of six applications of DES was used to prove that the security level was at least equivalent to 52.5 bits -- and areas where the proof could be "tightened up" (hopefully to the desired 56-bit level of security) were noted. There is no reason to believe that this particular pattern of six applications of DES is optimal -- indeed, it would be very surprising if it were. It seems probable, therefore, that more efficient patterns of application of DES exist, and can be derived using the general methods outlined here.

Acknowledgements

The author would like to thank many people for their interest and comments, and would particularly like to thank Don Coppersmith, Ivan Damgaard, Dan Greene, Mike Matyas, Carl Meyer, and Moti Yung.

Bibliography

1.) "Secrecy, Authentication, and Public Key Systems", Stanford Ph.D. thesis, 1979, by Ralph C. Merkle.

2.) "A Certified Digital Signature", unpublished paper, 1979. To appear in Crypto '89.

3.) "Universal One-Way Hash Functions and their Cryptographic Applications", Moni Naor and Moti Yung, Proceedings of the Twenty First Annual ACM Symposium on Theory of Computing, Seattle, Washington May 15-17, 1989, page 33-43.

4.) "A High Speed Manipulation Detection Code", by Robert R. Jueneman, Advances in Cryptology - CRYPTO '86, Springer Verlag, Lecture Notes on Computer Science, Vol. 263, page 327 to 346.

5.) "Another Birthday Attack" by Don Coppersmith, Advances in Cryptology - CRYPTO '85, Springer Verlag, Lecture Notes on Computer Science, Vol. 218, pages 14 to 17.

6.) "A digital signature based on a conventional encryption function", by Ralph C. Merkle, Advances in Cryptology CRYPTO 87, Springer Verlag, Lecture Notes on Computer Science, Vol. 293, page 369-378.

7.) "Cryptography and Data Security", by Dorothy E. R. Denning, Addison-Wesley 1982, page 170.

8.) "On the security of multiple encryption", by Ralph C. Merkle, CACM Vol. 24 No. 7, July 1981 pages 465 to 467.

9.) "Results of an initial attempt to cryptanalyze the NBS Data Encryption Standard", by Martin Hellman et. al., Information Systems lab. report SEL 76-042, Stanford University 1976.

10.) "Communication Theory of Secrecy Systems", by C. E. Shannon, Bell Sys. Tech. Jour. 28 (Oct. 1949) 656-715

11.) "Message Authentication" by R. R. Jueneman, S. M. Matyas, C. H. Meyer, IEEE Communications Magazine, Vol. 23, No. 9, September 1985 pages 29-40.

12.) "Generating strong one-way functions with cryptographic algorithm", by S. M. Matyas, C. H. Meyer, and J. Oseas, IBM Technical Disclosure Bulletin, Vol. 27, No. 10A, March 1985 pages 5658-5659

13.) "Analysis of Jueneman's MDC Scheme", by Don Coppersmith, preliminary version June 9, 1988. Analysis of the system presented in [4].

14.) "The Data Encryption Standard: Past and Future" by M.E. Smid and D.K. Branstad, Proc. of the IEEE, Vol 76 No. 5 pp 550-559, May 1988

15.) "Defending Secrets, Sharing Data: New Locks and Keys for Electronic Information", U.S. Congress, Office of Technology Assessment, OTA-CIT-310, U.S. Government Printing Office, October 1987

16.) "Exhaustive cryptanalysis of the NBS data encryption standard", Computer, June 1977, pages 74-78

17.) "Cryptograhy: a new dimension in data security", by Carl H. Meyer and Stephen M. Matyas , Wiley 1982.

18.) "Secure program code with modification detection code", by Carl H. Meyer and Michael Schilling; Proceedings of the 5th Worldwide Congress on Computers and Communication Security and Protection -- SECURICOM 88, pp. 111-130, SEDEP, 8, Rud de la Michodiese, 75002, Paris, France.

19.) "Cryptography -- A State of the Art Review," by Carl H. Meyer, COMEURO 89, Hamburg, May 8-12, 1989. Proceedings - VLSI and Computer Peripherals, 3rd Annual European Computer Conference, pp. 150-154.

20.) "Design Principles for Hash Functions" by Ivan Damgaard, Crypto '89.

Properties of Cryptosystem PGM

Spyros S. Magliveras[1]

Nasir D. Memon

University of Nebraska-Lincoln

Abstract

A cryptographic system, called PGM, was invented in the late 1970's by S. Magliveras. PGM is based on the prolific existence of certain kinds of factorization sets, called *logarithmic signatures*, for finite permutation groups. Logarithmic signatures were initially motivated by C. Sims' bases and strong generators. Statistical properties of random number generators based on PGM have been investigated in [7], [8] and show PGM to be statistically robust. In this paper we present recent results on the algebraic properties of PGM. PGM is an endomorphic cryptosystem in which the message space is $\mathcal{Z}_{|G|}$, for a given finite permutation group G. We show that the set of PGM transformations $\mathcal{T}_G$ is not closed under functional composition and hence not a group. This set is 2–transitive on $\mathcal{Z}_{|G|}$ if the underlying group G is not hamiltonian. Moreover, if $\mid G \mid \neq 2^a$, then the set of transformations contains an odd permutation. An important consequence of the above results is that the group generated by the set of transformations is nearly always the full symmetric group.

1 Introduction

A *Cryptosystem* Π is an ordered four–tuple $(\mathcal{M}, \mathcal{K}, \mathcal{C}, \mathcal{T})$, where $\mathcal{M}, \mathcal{K}$, and $\mathcal{C}$ are finite sets called the *message space, the key space, and the cipher space* respectively, and $\mathcal{T}$ is a family of transformations $\{E_k : \mathcal{M} \to \mathcal{C}, \ k \in \mathcal{K}\}$ such that for each $k \in \mathcal{K}$, E_k is invertible. We denote the inverse of E_k by D_k. Implicit in a cryptosystem $(\mathcal{M}, \mathcal{K}, \mathcal{C}, \mathcal{T})$ is the mapping $E : k \to E_k$ which associates to each key $k \in \mathcal{K}$ the

---

[1] Partially Supported by a US West Communications Grant

transformation E_k induced by k. The cryptosystem is said to be *faithful* if E is an injection.

If the message space and cipher space are the same, then the cryptosystem is called *endomorphic* and in this case for every key k, $E_k : \mathcal{M} \to \mathcal{C}$ is a permutation on $\mathcal{M}$. An endomorphic cryptosystem Π is said to be *closed* if and only if $\mathcal{T}$ is closed under functional composition. In other words, Π is *closed* if and only if for every two keys $i, j \in \mathcal{K}$ there exists a key $k \in \mathcal{K}$ such that $E_i E_j = E_k$. We wish to remark that the term *closed* had been used by Shannon [9] to mean something totally different. Our usage follows current terminology [4]. Since $\mathcal{T}$ is finite it follows that Π is closed if and only if $\mathcal{T}$ forms a group under composition. Let $\mathcal{G}_\Pi = \,<\mathcal{T}>$ be the group generated by $\mathcal{T}$ and $\mathcal{S}_\mathcal{M}$ the *symmetric group* on $\mathcal{M}$. Then, of course, $\mathcal{G}_\Pi$ is a subgroup of $\mathcal{S}_\mathcal{M}$.

Although the terminology that follows is not standard, it is natural and extends the terminology used in [4]. A Cryptosystem Π is said to be *t-transitive* if given any ordered t-tuple of distinct messages $(m_1, \ldots, m_t) \in \mathcal{M}^t$ and any ordered t-tuple of distinct ciphertexts $(c_1, \ldots, c_t) \in \mathcal{C}^t$, there is some $k \in \mathcal{K}$ such that $E_k(m_i) = c_i$ $(1 \leq i \leq t)$. Here we also write $E_k(m_1, \ldots, m_t) = (c_1, \ldots, c_t)$. Note that we speak of a t-transitive system whether or not $\mathcal{T}$ is a group. It is clear that a t-transitive system is $(t-1)$-transitive.

2 Logarithmic Signatures and PGM

If G is a finite permutation group of degree n we call an ordered collection $\alpha = \{B_i : i = 1, \ldots, s\}$ of ordered sets $B_i = \{u(i, j) : j = 1, \ldots, r(i)\}$, where $\mid B_i \mid$ and s are bounded by a polynomial in n, a *logarithmic signature* of G if each element g of G can be expressed uniquely as a product of the form

$$g = q_s \cdot q_{s-1} \cdots q_2 \cdot q_1 \tag{1}$$

with $q_i \in B_i$. The elements q_i are not necessarily elements of G, but could belong to a much larger group in which G is embedded. The B_i are called the *blocks* of α and the vector of block lengths $\mathbf{r} = (r(1), \ldots, r(s))$ is called the *type* of α. We also write $\mathbf{r} = (\alpha)$ for the type of α. The logarithmic signature is called *non-trivial* if $s \geq 2$ and $r(i) \geq 2$ for at least two indices i, where $(1 \leq i \leq s)$. Otherwise it is called *trivial*. A logarithmic signature is called *tame* if the factorization (1) can be achieved in time polynomial in the degree n of G, it is called *supertame* if (1) can be achieved in time $O(n^2)$. A logarithmic signature is called *wild* if it is not tame. We denote by Λ the collection of all logarithmic signatures of G.

Let $\gamma : G = G_0 > G_1 > \cdots > G_s = 1$ be a chain of subgroups of G, and $\{B_i : i = 1, \ldots, s\}$, an ordered collection of subsets of G, where each $B_i = \{u(i, j) :$

$j = 1, \ldots, r(i)\}$ is a complete set of right coset representatives of G_i in G_{i-1}. It is easily seen that $\{B_i\}$ forms a logarithmic signature for G. Such a logarithmic signature is called *transversal* with respect to γ. Here the type $\mathbf{r} = (r(1), \ldots, r(s))$ has $r(i) = [G_i : G_{i-1}]$. In view of the fact that membership in a permutation group can be tested in time polynomial in the degree [3], it is easily seen that a transversal logarithmic signature is tame. We denote the set of all transversal logarithmic signatures of G with respect to a chain γ by $\Lambda(\gamma)$. In section 4 we indicate how $\Lambda(\gamma)$ is a single regular orbit under the action of a certain monomial group. Existence of supertame logarithmic signatures is established in the following lemma :

Lemma 2.1 *If G is a permutation group then there exists a supertame logarithmic signature for G.*

Proof: Suppose G acts on the letters of $\Omega = \{1, 2, \ldots, n\}$. Let $G = G_0 > G_1 > \cdots > G_s = 1$ be a chain of nested stabilizers in G. Thus, $G_0 = G$ and for $i \geq 1$, G_i fixes pointwise the letters $1, 2, \ldots, i$ of Ω. Suppose now that the orbit of $i \in \Omega$ under G_{i-1} is $B = \{\delta_1 = i, \delta_2, \ldots, \delta_{r(i)}\}$ and that $u(i, j) \in G_{i-1}$ moves δ_1 to δ_j, then $G_{i-1} = G_i u(i, 1) + G_i u(i, 2) + \cdots + G_i u(i, r(i))$. Consider the logarithmic signature

$$\alpha = [u(1, 1), \ldots, u(1, r(1)); u(2, 1), \ldots, u(2, r(2)); \cdots; u(s, 1), \ldots, u(s, r(s))]$$

Now, note that an element h in G_{i-1} belongs to the coset $G_i u(i, j)$ if and only if h moves $\delta_1 = i$ to δ_j. Thus determining the right G_i coset in G_{i-1} to which h belongs requires $O(1)$ operations. The element $h \cdot u(i, j)^{-1}$ fixes $1, 2, \ldots, i-1, i$, and therefore belongs to G_i. Computing $h \cdot u(i, j)^{-1}$ requires $O(n)$ operations. Recursively, given any element $g \in G$, we descend in at most n steps and have $g \cdot u(1, j_1)^{-1} \cdot u(2, j_2)^{-1} \cdots u(s, j_s)^{-1} = 1$. Inverting yields the unique factorization $g = u(s, j_s) \cdots u(2, j_2) \cdot u(1, j_1)$. $\qquad \square$

For the remaining of this paper it is more convenient to write $\{u(i, j) : 0 \leq j < r(i); 1 \leq i \leq s\}$ rather than $\{u(i, j) : 1 \leq j \leq r(i); 1 \leq i \leq s\}$ for a logarithmic signature of a group. Before we describe PGM we introduce some notation. By $\alpha[i; j]$ we mean the j'th element of the i'th block of α. Also, if $\mathbf{r} = (\alpha) = (r(1), \ldots, r(s))$ and $(p_1, \ldots, p_s) \in \mathcal{Z}_{r(1)} \times \cdots \times \mathcal{Z}_{r(s)}$ then $\alpha(p_1, \ldots, p_s) := \alpha[s; p_s] \cdots \alpha[2; p_2] \cdot \alpha[1; p_1]$.

If $\mathbf{r} = (r(1), \ldots, r(s))$ is the type of a logarithmic signature α, define the integers $m_i, i = 1, 2, \ldots, s$ by :

$$m_1 = 1, \quad m_i = \prod_{j=1}^{i-1} r(j), \quad i = 2, \ldots, s.$$

Let λ be the bijection from $\mathcal{Z}_{r(1)} \times \cdots \times \mathcal{Z}_{r(s)}$ onto $\mathcal{Z}_{|G|}$, defined by

$$\lambda(p_1, \cdots, p_s) = \sum_{i=1}^{s} p_i m_i$$

then for $x \in \mathcal{Z}_{|G|}, \lambda^{-1}(x)$ is efficiently computable by successive subtractions [representation of x with respect to mixed base $(r(1), \ldots, r(s))$]. For a group G and a logarithmic signature $\alpha = \{\alpha[i; j] : j = 0, \ldots, r(i) - 1; i = 1, \ldots, s\}$ define the bijection $\Theta_\alpha : \mathcal{Z}_{r(1)} \times \cdots \times \mathcal{Z}_{r(s)} \to G$ by

$$\Theta_\alpha(p_1, \cdots, p_s) = \alpha(p_1, p_2, \cdots, p_s)$$

Next, define a map $\hat{\alpha} : \mathcal{Z}_{|G|} \to G$ by $\hat{\alpha} = \lambda^{-1}\Theta_\alpha$. The function $\hat{\alpha}$ is always efficiently computable, but $\hat{\alpha}^{-1}$ is not unless α is tame.

Having defined the mappings $\hat{\alpha}$, for $\alpha \in \Lambda$, the basic cryptographic system PGM is defined as follows : For a given pair of logarithmic signatures, α, β with β tame, the *encryption* transformation $E_{\alpha,\beta}$ is the mapping

$$E_{\alpha,\beta} = \hat{\alpha} \cdot \hat{\beta}^{-1} : \mathcal{Z}_{|G|} \to \mathcal{Z}_{|G|}$$

The corresponding *decryption* transformation is obtained by reversing the order of the pair of logarithmic signatures, that is

$$D_{\alpha,\beta} = E_{\alpha,\beta}^{-1} = E_{\beta,\alpha} = \hat{\beta} \cdot \hat{\alpha}^{-1}$$

3 An Example

To clarify the ideas presented in the previous section, we illustrate PGM by means of an example. The group used here is the alternating group on five points, $\mathcal{A}_5$, of order 60. This implies that the message space $\mathcal{M}$ and the ciphertext space $\mathcal{C}$ are the set $\{0, 1, \ldots, 59\}$. A supertame logarithmic signature α, with respect to a chain of stabilizer subgroups is obtained by Knuth's algorithm [5] using the generators (1 2 3 4 5) and (1 2 3)(4)(5). Another supertame logarithmic signature β is obtained by applying the procedure *shuffle* to α. The blocks of α consist of right coset representatives in a chain of subgroups in G. Procedure *shuffle* consists of changing the coset representatives and their relative order within each block. The number of blocks is $s = 3$, and the vector of block lengths is $\mathbf{r} = (5, 4, 3)$. The integers m_i are computed to be 1, 5, and 20 respectively. The two logarithmic signatures along with the appropriate knapsack $\mathbf{v}$ needed to compute λ and λ^{-1} efficiently, are shown in Figure (3).

Let us now demonstrate the operation of encipherng. If, for example, the message is 49, then it can be decomposed uniquely with respect to $\mathbf{v}$ as, $49 = (4 + 5 + 40)$. This process determines the vector of row-indices $\lambda^{-1}(49) = (4, 1, 2)$. We next compute $\pi = \Theta_\alpha(4, 1, 2) = \alpha[12;] \cdot \alpha[7;] \cdot \alpha[5;] = (1\ 5\ 4)(2)(3)$. We then compute $\Theta_\beta^{-1}(\pi)$, that is, the representation of π with respect to β. Since β is supertame and $\pi(1) = 5$, we locate the element in block 1 of β that sends 1 to 5. This element is $\beta[5;]$. So,

α	v	β
(1)(2)(3)(4)(5)	0	(1 4 2 3 5)
(1 2 3 4 5)	1	(1)(2)(3 5 4)
(1 3 5 2 4)	2	(1 2 5 4 3)
(1 4 2 5 3)	3	(1 3)(2 4)(5)
(1 5 4 3 2)	4	(1 5 3 4 2)
(1)(2)(3)(4)(5)	0	(1)(2 3)(4 5)
(1)(2 3)(4 5)	5	(1)(2 5 3)(4)
(1)(2 4 3)(5)	10	(1)(2 4 3)(5)
(1)(2 5 3)(4)	15	(1)(2)(3)(4)(5)
(1)(2)(3)(4)(5)	0	(1)(2)(3)(4)(5)
(1)(2)(3 4 5)	20	(1)(2)(3 5 4)
(1)(2)(3 5 4)	40	(1)(2)(3 4 5)

Figure 1: The two logarithmic signatures and the knapsack

$\pi = h_1 \cdot \beta[5;]$ for some $h_1 \in G_1$. Solving for h_1, yields $h_1 = \pi \cdot \beta[5;]^{-1} = (1)(2\ 4)(3\ 5)$. Now h_1 fixes 1 and sends 2 to 4. Now, we locate the element of the second block of β which sends 2 to 4, namely $\beta[8;]$. Hence, $h_1 = h_2 \cdot \beta[8;]$ which yields $h_2 = (1)(2)(3\ 5\ 4)$. Continuing in this manner we completely factor π with respect to β and get $\pi = \beta[11;] \cdot \beta[8;] \cdot \beta[5;]$. This determines the vector of row pointers for β to be $(4, 2, 1) \in \mathcal{Z}_5 \times \mathcal{Z}_4 \times \mathcal{Z}_3$ and $\lambda(4, 2, 1)$ is $4 + 10 + 20 = 34$. Thus, we have $E_{\alpha,\beta}(49) = 34$. The reader can easily verify that $D_{\alpha,\beta}(34) = E_{\beta,\alpha}(34) = 49$.

4 Transformations on logarithmic signatures

Suppose that $\beta = \{B_i : i = 1, \ldots, s\}$ is a transversal logarithmic signature of a group G with respect to the chain of subgroups $\gamma : G = G_0 > G_1 \cdots > G_s = 1$. Note that while $\beta = \{B_i : i = 1, \ldots, s\}$ is a logarithmic signature for $G = G_0$, the set of blocks $\beta(k) = \{B_{k+1}, \ldots, B_s\}$ is a logarithmic signature for G_k. If the element $u(i,j) \in B_i$ of $\beta(k)$ is replaced by $h \cdot u(i,j)$, where $h \in G_i$, the resulting collection $\beta(k)^*$ forms a new logarithmic signature for G_k. Moreover, any rearrangement of the elements of a block $B_i \in \beta(k)$ yields a new logarithmic signature for G_k. We call this procedure *shuffle*.

Procedure *shuffle* for generating new logarithmic signatures from a given one can be concisely described by considering a certain group action. If $\beta = \{B_i : i = 1, \ldots, s\}$, $B_i = \{u(i,j) : j = 0, \ldots, r(i) - 1\}$ is a transversal logarithmic signature of G with respect to the chain $\gamma : G = G_0 > G_1 > \cdots > G_s = 1$ of subgroups, let M be the group of all matrices of the form :

$$M = \begin{bmatrix} H_1 & 0 & \cdots & 0 \\ 0 & H_2 & \cdots & 0 \\ \vdots & \vdots & & \vdots \\ 0 & 0 & \cdots & H_s \end{bmatrix}$$

where H_i is an $r(i) \times r(i)$ monomial matrix with entries in G_i. This means that H_i can be thought of as an $r(i) \times r(i)$ permutation matrix whose unity entries have been replaced by arbitrary elements of G_i. The procedure described above for obtaining new logarithmic signatures of G corresponds to acting on

$$(u(1,0), \ldots, u(1, r(1) - 1); u(2,0), \ldots, u(2, r(2) - 1); \cdots; u(s,0), \ldots, u(s, r(s) - 1))$$

on the left by some $M \in \mathbf{M}$, that is,

$$(v(1,0) \ldots, v(s, r(s)))^T = M \cdot (u(1,0), \ldots, u(s, r(s)))^T$$

Thus, the totality $\Lambda(\gamma)$ of logarithmic signatures with respect to γ is an $\mathbf{M}$-orbit. We observe that since only the identity of $\mathbf{M}$ fixes a logarithmic signature in $\Lambda(\gamma)$, $\mathbf{M}$ acts regularly on $\Lambda(\gamma)$. This implies that

$$| \Lambda(\gamma) | = | \mathbf{M} | = \prod_{i=1}^{s} | G_i |^{r(i)} r(i)! = \prod_{i=1}^{s} (\prod_{j=i+1}^{s} r(j))^{r(i)} r(i)!$$

Now we define another group action on Λ. Let

$$\mathbf{T} = G \times S_n \times S_n \times \cdots \times S_n \times G$$

be a direct product, where n is the degree of G and the the symmetric group S_n occurs $s - 1$ times. For $q = (g_0, g_1, \ldots, g_s) \in \mathbf{T}$ and

$$\alpha = (\alpha[1;0], \ldots, \alpha[1; r(1) - 1]; \ldots; \alpha[s;0], \ldots, \alpha[s; r(s) - 1]) \in \Lambda$$

let q act on α by $(q, \alpha) \to \alpha^q$ where

$$\alpha^q = (g_1^{-1}, \ldots, g_1^{-1}; \ldots; g_s^{-1}, \ldots, g_s^{-1}) \cdot \alpha \cdot (g_0, \ldots, g_0; \ldots; g_{s-1}, \ldots, g_{s-1})$$

This means that all the elements of the first block are multiplied by g_1^{-1} on the left and by g_0 on the right, the elements of the second block are multiplied by g_2^{-1} on the left and g_1 on the right and so on. Finally the elements in block s are multiplied by g_s^{-1} on the left and g_{s-1} on the right. It is easily seen that $\alpha^1 = \alpha$ and $(\alpha^q)^t = \alpha^{qt}$, hence $\mathbf{T}$ acts on the collection of logarithmic signatures in Λ having s blocks. If $g_0 = g_s = 1$, we say that α^q is a *sandwich* of α. If $g_1 = g_2 = \cdots = g_s = 1$ then we effectively multiply only the elements of the first block on the right by g_0. We call this transformation a *right translation* of α. On the other hand if

$g_0 = g_1 = \cdots = g_{s-1} = 1$ then we call the transformed logarithmic signature a *left translate* of α. Let $\mathbf{S}$ be the subgroup of $\mathbf{T}$ which consists of the elements of the form $(1, g_1, \ldots, g_{s-1}, 1)$ of $\mathbf{T}$, and $\mathbf{H}$ the subgroup of $\mathbf{S}$ which consists of all elements $(1, g_1, \ldots, g_{s-1}, 1)$ with $g_i \in G_i$.

Suppose that α is a logarithmic signature for a group G of type $(\alpha) = (r(1), \ldots, r(i), r(i+1), \ldots, r(s))$. We can create a new logarithmic signature β by *fusing* two consecutive blocks of α , say B_i and B_{i+1} of lengths $r(i)$ and $r(i+1)$ to a single block of length $r(i) \cdot r(i+1)$. Thus, if $g = q_s \cdots q_{i+1} \cdot q_i \cdots q_2 \cdot q_1$ is the factorization of g with respect to α, then the factorization of g with respect to β will be $g = q_s \cdots q_{i+2} \cdot t \cdot q_{i-1} \cdots q_2 \cdot q_1$ where $t = q_{i+1} \cdot q_i$. In this case we say that α is a *refinement* of β. The refinement relation defines a partial order on Λ and we write $\alpha < \beta$ to denote that α is a refinement of β.

Finally, observe that if $g = q_s \cdot q_{s-1} \cdots q_2 \cdot q_1$ then we have $g^{-1} = q_1^{-1} \cdot q_2^{-1} \cdots q_s^{-1}$. This implies that if

$$\alpha = \{\alpha[i; j] \ : \ j = 0, \ldots, r(i) - 1; \ i = 1, \ldots, s\}$$

is a logarithmic signature then

$$\alpha' = \{\alpha[i; j]^{-1} \ : \ j = r(i) - 1, \ldots, 0; \ i = s, \ldots, 1\}$$

is also a logarithmic signature. We call α' the *inversion* of α. Inversion induces a duality on Λ_G. For example, a system of right coset representatives in a chain γ of subgroups (*right transversal* logarithmic signature), is transformed into a system of left coset representatives (*left transversal* logarithmic signature). In this paper we do not study properties of inversion.

Definition 4.1 *Two logarithmic signatures α, β are said to be* equivalent *if $\hat{\alpha} = \hat{\beta}$.*

We denote the equivalence of two logarithmic signatures α and β by $\alpha \sim \beta$. If α, β and γ are logarithmic signatures of a group G then it follows from the definition that $E_{\alpha, \gamma} = E_{\beta, \gamma}$ if and only if $\alpha \sim \beta$. Also, we see that if α is a refinement of β then $\alpha \sim \beta$. Hence if two logarithmic signatures are equivalent then they need not have the same type. The concept of equivalence is very important from a cryptanalytic point of view. For a cryptanalyst to break PGM, he only needs to construct logarithmic signatures which are equivalent to the ones specified by the key. The following result was shown by Magliveras and Kreher but its proof has not appeared in print.

Theorem 4.1 *Let α and β be two logarithmic signatures of a group G, which have the same type $\mathbf{r} = (r(1), \ldots, r(s))$. Then α and β are equivalent if and only if they are in the same sandwich $\mathbf{S}$-orbit.*

Proof : It is easy to see that if α and β are in the same sandwich S–orbit then they are equivalent. For the converse, let $\alpha = \{B_1, B_2, \ldots, B_s\}$ and $\beta = \{B'_1, B'_2, \ldots, B'_s\}$, where $B_i = \{u_{i,1}, u_{i,2}, \ldots, u_{i,r(i)}\}$ and $B_i' = \{u'_{i,1}, u'_{i,2}, \ldots, u'_{i,r(i)}\}$. Now since $\alpha \sim \beta$, we have

$$\alpha(j_1, \ldots, j_s) = \beta(j_1, \ldots, j_s), \quad 0 \le j_i < r(i). \tag{2}$$

Specifically, we have $\alpha(j, 0, \ldots, 0) = \beta(j, 0, \ldots, 0)$ for $0 \le j < r(s)$. That is, $u_{s,j} \cdot u_{s-1,0} \cdots u_{1,0} = u'_{s,j} \cdot u'_{s-1,0} \cdots u'_{1,0}$. Let $t_{s-1} = u'_{s-1,0} \cdots u'_{1,0} \cdot u_{1,0}^{-1} \cdots u_{s-1,0}^{-1}$, then, $u_{s,j} = u'_{s,j} \cdot t_{s-1}$, and consequently $B_s = B'_s \cdot t_{s-1}$. In particular note that

$$u'^{-1}_{s,0} \cdot u_{s,0} = t_{s-1}^{-1}. \tag{3}$$

Next, from (2) we have $\alpha(0, j, 0, \ldots, 0) = \beta(0, j, 0, \ldots, 0)$ for $0 \le j_i < r(i)$. This means that, $u_{s,0} \cdot u_{s-1,j} \cdot u_{s-2,0} \cdots u_{1,0} = u'_{s,0} \cdot u'_{s-1,j} \cdot u'_{s-2,0} \cdots u'_{1,0}$ therefore, $u_{s,0} \cdot u_{s-1,j} = u'_{s,0} \cdot u'_{s-1,j} \cdot (u'_{s-2,0} \cdots u'_{1,0} \cdot u_{1,0}^{-1} \cdots u_{s-2,0}^{-1})$. Letting $t_{s-2} = u'_{s-2,0} \cdots u'_{1,0} \cdot u_{1,0}^{-1} \cdots u_{s-2,0}^{-1}$ and using (3) we get $u_{s-1,j} = t_{s-1}^{-1} \cdot u'_{s-1,j} \cdot t_{s-2}$, hence $B_{s-1} = t_{s-1}^{-1} \cdot B'_{s-1} \cdot t_{s-2}$. Continuing in this manner we get $\alpha = (t_1^{-1}, \ldots, t_{s-1}^{-1}, 1) \cdot \beta \cdot (1, t_1 \ldots, t_{s-1})$. $\square$

It is easy to see that the monomial shuffle and inversion of a transversal logarithmic signature remain transversal. It is also clear that a subgroup involved in a transversal logarithmic signature can be refined in a 'non–transversal' way. Therefore refinement does not preserve the transversal property. In the cases of sandwiching and left and right translations, although the resulting logarithmic signature is not a transversal, we give a polynomial algorithm for constructing a transversal equivalent to the transformed logarithmic signature in Fig (2). In view of this fact we broaden the use of the term *transversal* to include logarithmic signatures for which there exists a polynomial time algorithm to compute an equivalent transversal. The algorithm starts with the last block B_s and *standardizes* it by multiplying on the right by the inverse of the first element $\alpha[s; 1]^{-1}$. The resulting block B'_s is the subgroup G_s with the identity as its first element. We then proceed upwards, standardizing the $j'th$ block by multiplying on the left by $\alpha[j-1; 1]$ and on the right by $\alpha[j; 1]^{-1}$. We proceed recursively, finally standardizing the first block by multiplyling on the left by $\alpha[2; 1]$. It is easily seen that the resulting logarithmic signature β is transversal. Since β is a sandwich of α, we have $\alpha \sim \beta$. Note that we could have used any element of a block for standardization, rather than the first one. An interesting question which arises is whether there exist new types of transformations which would map a tame logarithmic signature to an equivalent wild one. An answer in the affirmative would lead to a public key cryptosystem based on PGM.

The logarithmic signatures we have mentioned so far have all been transversal and hence tame. A conjecture has been made by the first author that wild logarithmic signatures will occur in profusion for arbitrary groups. The second author

Input : A logarithmic signature $\alpha = \{B_1, \ldots, B_s\}$
which is the sandwich of a transversal.

Output : A transversal β which is equivalent to α.

Begin

$x = \alpha[s; 0]^{-1}$;
$xinv = \alpha[s; 0]$;
For $j = 0$ to $r(s) - 1$ do
    $\beta[s; j] = \alpha[s; j] \cdot x$;
For $i = s - 1$ to 2 do
    begin
        $y = \alpha[i; 0]^{-1}$;
        For $j = 0$ to $r(i) - 1$ do
            $\beta[i; j] = xinv \cdot \alpha[i; j] \cdot y$;
        $xinv = y^{-1}$;
    end;
For $j = 0$ to $r(i) - 1$ do
    $\beta[1; j] = xinv \cdot \alpha[1; j]$;

End.

Figure 2: Algorithm to construct an equivalent transversal

G	$|\hat{\Lambda}_G|$	$|\mathcal{T}_G|$	$\mathcal{G}_G$	$\mu = |\mathcal{T}_G| / |G|$	comments
$\mathcal{Z}_4$	16	24	$\mathcal{S}_4$	1.00	all transversal
$\mathcal{V}_4$	24	24	$\mathcal{S}_4$	1.00	all transversal
$\mathcal{Z}_6$	132	500	$\mathcal{S}_6$	0.69	all transversal
$\mathcal{S}_3$	288	702	$\mathcal{S}_6$	0.98	all transversal
$\mathcal{Z}_8$	1152	5568	$\mathcal{S}_8$	0.14	not all transv.
$\mathcal{Z}_4 \times \mathcal{Z}_2$	2304	17088	$\mathcal{S}_8$	0.42	all transversal
$\mathcal{V}_8$	4032	10432	$\mathcal{S}_8$	0.26	all transversal
$\mathcal{Q}_8$	1344	5280	$\mathcal{S}_8$	0.13	all transversal
$\mathcal{D}_8$	3328	32640	$\mathcal{S}_8$	0.81	all transversal
$\mathcal{Z}_9$	648	1224	$\mathcal{S}_9$	0.01	all transversal
$\mathcal{V}_9$	2160	8208	$\mathcal{S}_9$	0.02	all transversal
$\mathcal{A}_4$	304128		$\mathcal{S}_{12}$		all transversal

Figure 3: Logarithmic Signatures of Small Groups

has recently constructed many non–transversal logarithmic signatures for the cyclic group $\mathcal{Z}_8$ and the alternating group $\mathcal{A}_5$. In fact the cyclic group $\mathcal{Z}_8$ turns out to be the smallest group for which there exist non–transversal logarithmic signatures.

Finally, we note that the algorithm in Fig (2) can be modified to yield an efficient algorithm to determine whether a given logarithmic signature is a transversal. At every stage, after standardizing the current block B_i, we check the order of the group generated by $< B_i, B_{i+1}, \ldots, B_s >$. This can be done in polynomial time from [3] and the fact that the number of generators is polynomial in n. If the order equals $r(i) \cdot r(i+1) \cdots r(s)$, we continue otherwise the logarithmic signature is not a transversal. In Figure (3) we tabulate some facts about logarithmic signatures of small groups.

5   Algebraic properties of PGM

In the case of PGM we see that the message space and the cipher space is $\mathcal{Z}_{|G|}$ where G is the underlying group, hence PGM is endomorphic. The key space is $\Lambda_G \times \Lambda_G$ the collection of all ordered pairs of logarithmic signatures of G. We denote by $\mathcal{T}_G$, the set of transformations defined by the key space and by $\mathcal{G}_G$ the group generated by $\mathcal{T}_G$ under functional composition. Since sandwiching produces equivalent logarithmic signatures we see that PGM is not faithful. We proceed to discuss some important algebraic properties of PGM.

Lemma 5.1 *Given a group G which is not cyclic of prime order, let $x \in \mathcal{Z}_{|G|}$ and $g \in G$. Then there exists a non–trivial logarithmic signature $\alpha \in \Lambda$ such that $\hat{\alpha}(x) = g$.*

Proof: Let $\mid G \mid = m \cdot p$ where p is a prime and $m \neq 1$, then there exists a subgroup $P \leq G$ with $\mid P \mid = p$. Let γ be a transversal logarithmic signature for G with respect to the chain $G = G_0 > G_1 = P > G_2 = 1$. Clearly, γ has two blocks B_1 and B_2, and is of type $\mathbf{r} = (m, p)$. Now, if $g \in G$, then $g \in Pu$ for some $u \in B_1$, hence $g = qu$ for some $q \in P$. On the other hand, given $x \in \mathcal{Z}_{|G|}$, we have $\lambda^{-1}(x) = (i, j)$ with respect to the type $\mathbf{r}$, where $0 \leq i < m$ and $0 \leq j < p$. Let α be a logarithmic signature which arises from γ by rearranging its elements so that u appears in the $i'th$ position of the first block and q in the $j'th$ position of the second block. Then we have $\hat{\alpha}(x) = g$. $\square$

Theorem 5.1 *Given a group G, $x, y \in \mathcal{Z}_{|G|}$, there exist $\alpha, \beta \in \Lambda$ such that $E_{\alpha,\beta}(x) = y$. In other words $\mathcal{T}_G$ is 1-transitive.*

Proof: Let g be an arbitrary element of G. From lemma 5.1 there exist $\alpha, \beta \in \Lambda$ such that $\hat{\alpha}(x) = g$ and $\hat{\beta}(y) = g$. This implies that $E_{\alpha,\beta}(x) = \hat{\alpha}\hat{\beta}^{-1}(x) = y$. $\quad\square$

Theorem 5.2 *If a group G has a proper subgroup H, which is not normal in G, then T_G is 2-transitive.*

Proof: Although T_G is not a group, without loss of generality, it will suffice to show that given $x, y \in \mathcal{Z}_{|G|} - \{0\}$, there exist $\alpha, \beta \in \Lambda$ such that $E_{\alpha,\beta}(0, x) = (0, y)$. Let α be a logarithmic signature for G with respect to the chain $G = G_0 > H = G_1 > 1$. Then α has two blocks B_1 and B_2, and type $\mathbf{r} = (k, h)$ where $h = |H|$ and $k = [G : H]$. Given $x, y \in \mathcal{Z}_{|G|} - \{0\}$, let $\lambda^{-1}(x) = (i_x, j_x)$ and $\lambda^{-1}(y) = (i_y, j_y)$ with respect to $\mathbf{r}$, where $0 \leq i_x, i_y < k$ and $0 \leq j_x, j_y < h$. Now we shall consider various cases for the values of i_x, i_y, j_x, j_y and in each case construct a logarithmic signature β with type $\mathbf{r}$ such that $E_{\alpha,\beta}(0, x) = (0, y)$.

Case 1 : $i_x, i_y, j_x, j_y > 0$

Let β be the same as α except that we exchange the elements in positions i_x and i_y of the first block and the elements in positions j_x and j_y in the second block. So we have $\beta[1; i_y] = \alpha[1; i_x]$ and $\beta[2; j_y] = \alpha[2; j_x]$. It follows that $E_{\alpha,\beta}(0, x) = (0, y)$.

Case 2 : $i_x = i_y = 0$ and $j_x, j_y > 0$

This can be dealt with in a similar manner as Case 1. Here we need exchange the elements in the second block only.

Case 3 : $i_x, i_y > 0$ and $j_x = j_y = 0$

Again this is similar to Cases 1 and 2. This time we only need to exchange the elements in position i_x and i_y of the first block.

Case 4 : $i_x = 0$ and $i_y, j_x, j_y > 0$

Since H is not normal there exist $u \in H$ and $t \in G$ such that $tut^{-1} \notin H$. Rearrange, if necessary, the second block of α so that $\alpha[2; j_x] = u$, and place the identity $1 \in G$ in position $\alpha[1; 0]$ as the coset representative of H and also in position $\alpha[2; 0]$. So we have $\hat{\alpha}(x) = \alpha[2; j_x] \cdot \alpha[1; 0] = u \cdot 1 = u \in H$. Now since $v = u^{-1}tut^{-1} \notin H$, v lies in some coset of H, the coset representative of which is $\alpha[1; i]$ for some $i \neq 0$. Let γ be a logarithmic signature which is obtained from α by (i) replacing $\alpha[1; i]$ by $u^{-1}tut^{-1}$; (ii) exchanging the elements in $\alpha[1; i]$ and $\alpha[1; i_y]$; (iii) exchanging $\alpha[2; j_x]$ and $\alpha[2; j_y]$. We then right-translate γ by t and left-translate it by t^{-1} to obtain a new logarithmic signature β. The resulting β has $\beta[1; 0] = t$, $\beta[1; i_y] = u^{-1}tu$ and $\beta[2; 0] = t^{-1}$, $\beta[2; j_y] = t^{-1}u$. It follows that $\hat{\beta}(0) = 1$ and $\hat{\beta}(y) = u$. Hence $E_{\alpha,\beta}(0, x) = (0, y)$.

Case 5 : $i_y = 0$ and $i_x, j_x, j_y > 0$

By Case 4, there exist two logarithmic signatures α and β such that $E_{\alpha,\beta}(0, y) = (0, x)$. But then we have $E_{\beta,\alpha}(0, x) = (0, y)$.

Case 6 : $i_x, j_y = 0$ and $i_y, j_x > 0$

Again as in case 4 we assume that $\alpha[1; 0] = \alpha[2; 0] = 1 \in G$ and $\alpha[2; j_x] = u$ where $t^{-1}ut \notin H$. Then we have $\hat{\alpha}(x) = \alpha[2; j_x] \cdot \alpha[1; 0] = u \cdot 1 = u$. Since $v = t^{-1}ut \notin H$, v belongs to some coset of H, with coset representative $\alpha[1; i]$ for some $i \neq 0$. Let γ be the same as α except that we replace $\alpha[1; i]$ by $t^{-1}ut$ and then exchange the elements $\alpha[1; i]$ and $\alpha[1; i_y]$. We now right–translate γ by t^{-1} and left–translate by t to get β. The resulting β has $\beta[1; 0] = t^{-1}, \beta[1; i_y] = t^{-1}u$ and $\beta[2; 0] = t$. It follows that $E_{\alpha,\beta}(0, x) = (0, y)$.

Case 7 : $i_y, j_x = 0$ and $i_x, j_y > 0$

This is symmetric to Case 6 and follows in the same way as case 5 was obtained from case 4.

Case 8 : $j_x = 0$ and $i_x, i_y, j_y > 0$

Again we begin with $\alpha[1; 0] = \alpha[2; 0] = 1 \in G$. Let $\hat{\alpha}(x) = \alpha[2; 0] \cdot \alpha[1; i_x] = v$ where $v \notin H$. We now construct β from α by (i) Exchanging the elements $\alpha[1; i_x]$ and $\alpha[1; i_y]$; (ii) For $\alpha[2; j_y] = u \in H$ replacing $\alpha[1; 0]$ by u^{-1}; this is possible because $u^{-1} \in H$ and $1, u^{-1}$ represent the same right H coset. (iii) And finally exchanging the elements $\alpha[2; 0]$ with $\alpha[2; j_y]$. We now have $\beta[1; 0] = u^{-1}, \beta[1; i_y] = a, \beta[2; 0] = u$ and $\beta[2; j_y] = 1$. It follows that $E_{\alpha,\beta}(0, x) = (0, y)$.

Case 9 : $j_y = 0$ and $i_x, i_y, j_x > 0$

This is symmetric to the previous case. $\qquad\qquad\qquad\qquad\qquad\qquad\qquad$ $\square$

Theorem 5.3 *Given a group G, $\mathcal{T}_G$ is not closed in general*

Proof : In Figure (3) we tabulate the size of $\mathcal{T}_G$ and $\mathcal{G}_G$ for several small groups. It is seen that, in general, $\mathcal{T}_G \neq \mathcal{G}_G$. $\qquad\qquad\qquad\qquad\qquad\qquad$ $\square$

Theorem 5.4 *If a group G has a proper subgroup H of odd order then $\mathcal{T}_G$ has a transformation which is an odd permutation in $S_{|G|}$.*

Proof : Consider a transversal logarithmic signature α with respect to the chain $G = G_0 > G_1 = H > G_2 = 1$. α has two blocks and type $\mathbf{r} = (k, h)$, where $h = \mid H \mid$

and $k = [G : H]$. Now let β be a second logarithmic signature which is identical to α, except that the first two elements in the first block are interchanged. It is clear that $\hat{\alpha}\hat{\beta}^{-1}$ will be an element of order two and have a factorization as a product of h transpositions. More precisely, we have :

$$\hat{\alpha}\hat{\beta}^{-1} = (0,1)(k,k+1)(2k,2k+1)\cdots((h-1)k\,,\,(h-1)k+1)$$

$$\square$$

In view of the fact that every finite 2–transitive group contains a unique minimal normal subgroup which is elementary abelian or simple [1], [10], the recent classification of finite simple groups yields a classification of finite 2–transitive groups. This in turn leads to the following interesting consequence :

Theorem 5.5 *If G is a finite non–hamiltonian group with $\mid G \mid$ different from q, $(1 + q^2)$, $(1 + q^3)$, $\frac{(q^n-1)}{(q-1)}$, $2^{n-1}(2^n \pm 1), 11, 12, 15, 22, 23, 24, 176, 276$, where q is the power of a prime and n is a positive integer, then $\mathcal{T}_G$ is 2–transitive and $\mathcal{G}_G \cong \mathcal{S}_{|G|}$.*

Proof : The finite doubly transitive groups of degree m are known and consist of the class of alternating groups $\mathcal{A}_m$, the class of symmetric groups $\mathcal{S}_m$, certain infinite classes of groups of degrees q, $(1 + q^2)$, $(1 + q^3)$, $\frac{(q^n-1)}{(q-1)}$, $2^{n-1}(2^n \pm 1)$, where q is a power of a prime and n a positive integer, and a finite set of certain sporadic groups of degrees $11, 12, 15, 22, 23, 24, 176, 276$. Since the degree of $\mathcal{G}_G$ is $\mid G \mid$, it follows from the hypothesis that $\mathcal{G}_G$ must be isomorphic to $\mathcal{A}_{|G|}$ or $\mathcal{S}_{|G|}$. However, since $\mid G \mid \neq 2^a$, by Theorem 5.4 there is an odd permutation in $\mathcal{G}_G$. Hence $\mathcal{G}_G \simeq \mathcal{S}_{|G|}$. $\square$

6 Closing Remarks

Many questions still remain unanswered. We have asked earlier whether there exist transformations which convert a tame logarithmic signature to a wild one. Such a transformation would lead to a public key cryptosystem. Besides, the question whether there exist non–transversal logarithmic signatures which are tame needs to be addressed.

Evidence from Figure (3) suggests that the condition that G possess a non–normal subgroup may not be necessary for the 2–transitivity of $\mathcal{T}_G$. It would be interesting to investigate whether this condition can be removed.

For encryption purposes being able to factor all of G is not a requirement. For example, for a given $\epsilon > 0$, it may be possible to find subsets $X_1, X_2, \ldots, X_s, Z \subset G$ with $\mid Z \mid / \mid G \mid < \epsilon$ such that each element $g \in G - Z$ has a unique factorization

$g = x_s \cdots x_2 \cdot x_1$, where $x_i \in X_i$. Such *near-factorizations* have been studied in [2] for $Z = \{1\}$, but not much is known for non-abelian G and $Z \neq \{1\}$.

Moreover, we wish to pose the following questions. Is it true that $\mathcal{T}_G^k$ covers S_G, for some fixed integer k independently of G, if so, is $k = 2$. Finally, is it true that $\mathcal{T}_G$ can be used as a source of random permutations of very large degree.

References

[1] P. Cameron, Finite permutation groups and finite simple groups, *Bull. London Math. Soc.*, **13**(1981), 1–22.

[2] D. de Caen, D. A. Gregory, I. G. Hughes and D. L. Kreher, Near–factors of finite groups, *Preprint*, (1989).

[3] M. Furst, J. E. Hopcroft, and E. Luks, Polynomial-time algorithms for permutation groups, In *Proceedings of the 21'st IEEE Symposium on Foundations of Computation of Computer Science*, (1980), 36–41.

[4] B. S. Kaliski. Jr., R. L. Rivest, and A. T. Sherman, Is the data encryption standard a group? *Journal of Cryptology*, 1(1988), 3–36.

[5] D. E. Knuth, Notes on efficient representation of permutation groups, *Correspondence with M. Furst*, (1981).

[6] S. S. Magliveras, A cryptosystem from logarithmic signatures of finite groups. In *Proceedings of the 29'th Midwest Symposium on Circuits and Systems*, North-Holland, (1986), 972–975.

[7] S. S. Magliveras and N. D. Memon, The Linear complexity analysis of the cryptosystem PGM, Submitted, (1989).

[8] S. S. Magliveras, B. A. Oberg, and A. J. Surkan, A new random number generator from permutation groups, *Red. del Sem Matemat. di Milano*, **54** (1985), 203–223.

[9] C. E. Shannon, The mathematical theory of communication, *Bell Systems Technical Journal*, **28**(1949), 379–423.

[10] E. Shult, Permutation groups with few fixed points, In P. Plaumann and K. Strambach, editors, *Geometry - Von Staudt's point of view*, (1981), 275–311.

On the Construction of Block Ciphers Provably Secure and Not Relying on Any Unproved Hypotheses

(Extended Abstract)

Yuliang Zheng
Tsutomu Matsumoto
Hideki Imai

Division of Electrical and Computer Engineering
Yokohama National University
156 Tokiwadai, Hodogaya, Yokohama, 240 Japan

Abstract   *One of the ultimate goals of cryptography researchers is to construct a (secrete-key) block cipher which has the following ideal properties: (1) The cipher is provably secure, (2) Security of the cipher does not depend on any unproved hypotheses, (3) The cipher can be easily implemented with current technology, and (4) All design criteria for the cipher are made public. It is currently unclear whether or not there really exists such an ideal block cipher. So to meet the requirements of practical applications, the best thing we can do is to construct a block cipher such that it approximates the ideal one as closely as possible. In this paper, we make a significant step in this direction. In particular, we construct several block ciphers each of which has the above mentioned properties (2), (3) and (4) as well as the following one: (1') Security of the cipher is supported by convincing evidence. Our construction builds upon profound mathematical bases for information security recently established in a series of excellent papers.*

1. Motivations and Summary of Results

Data Encryption Standard (DES) designed by IBM about *fifteen* years ago is the first modern (secrete-key) block cipher whose algorithm is publicly available [NBS]. It is a kind of product ciphers with Lucifer as its direct predecessor [FNS] [K]. A little more specifically, both DES and Lucifer consist of 16 rounds of *Feistel-type transformations (FTT's)* which are invented by and named (by us) after Feistel.

From the beginning of DES, however, there had a lot of controversy about its security, and especially, about its design criteria [K] which have been classified by NSA and its designer IBM. Many computer scientists and cryptography experts were concerned about the possibilities that DES may possess weaknesses only NSA and IBM are aware of, and that trap-doors may have been inserted into the S-boxes of DES which would give a cryptoanalytic advantage to a knowledgeable party. For these reasons, a great amount of effort has been invested in attempting to break the cipher, or to find its weaknesses. And many researchers have tried revealing the myths around the design criteria.

In their nice paper [LR], Luby and Rackoff showed that DES would be provably secure if its f-functions were secure pseudorandom ones. Unfortunately, the f-functions of DES cannot be secure in any reasonable sense. In the same paper, Luby and Rackoff proved also a result about FTT's: A function consisting of three rounds of randomly and independently chosen FTT's, which is in fact a permutation, cannot be efficiently distinguished from a truly random one. This result is very appealing, since it relies on no unproved hypotheses, and more importantly, it suggests that there is an extremely *simple* constructive method for designing a theoretically secure block cipher which does not rely on any unproved hypotheses. However, it is practically impossible to construct such a cipher, simply because it takes a huge amount of memory to implement the cipher.

Therefore both practical needs and theoretical interest encourage us to seek for an ideal block cipher having the following properties:

(1) The cipher is provably secure,

(2) Security of the cipher does not depend on any unproved hypotheses,

(3) The cipher can be easily implemented with current technology, and

(4) All design criteria for the cipher are made public.

It is still an open problem whether or not there really exists such a block cipher. The best thing we can do currently is to construct a block cipher such that it approximates the ideal one as closely as possible.

In this paper, we make a significant step in this direction. In particular, we propose a kind of transformations — *Generalized Type-2 transformations*, and show that it is an excellent building block for cryptosystems. Utilizing this type of transformations, we construct several concrete block ciphers which have the above mentioned properties (2), (3) and (4) as well as the following one:

(1') Security of the cipher is supported by convincing evidence.

Our results build upon profound mathematical bases for information security recently established in a series of excellent papers such as [BM],[Y],[L],[GGM],[S] [1] and especially [LR].

The remaining part of the paper is organized as follows: Section 2 defines terminology used later, reviews one of the main design rules for DES — FTT's, and introduces the result of Luby and Rackoff on the rule. Section 3 proposes various types of transformations and shows that all these transformations can be used to construct permutations not efficiently distinguishable from a truly random

---

[1] The main result of [S] had been found to be false [O] [R] [ZMI]. But here the correct version of the result is used.

one. Among the transformations, Generalized Type-2 ones are proved to be most preferable. Section 4 constructs a theoretically provably secure block cipher (PSBC) by the use of Generalized Type-2 transformations. Section 5 presents a variant of PSBC. Section 6 proposes four concrete block ciphers based on theoretical results of Sections 2 – 5. Finally in Appendices A, B and C, three issues — minimum rounds for security, optimal transformations and super-security are discussed. For the sake of space, most results are presented without proofs. We will enclose proofs necessary in the full paper.

2. Preliminaries

This section defines the notions of pseudorandom number/function generators, and introduces the result of Luby and Rackoff on FTT's. Readers who are not interested in the definitions can jump over Section 2.1.

2.1 Pseudorandom Number/Function Generators

For purposes which will become clear later, our notions introduced below are slight generalizations of those given in [Y], [GGM] and [LR], mainly in the following aspect: In contrast to those in [Y], [GGM] and [LR], we will not impose polynomial bound upon the running time of an algorithm realizing a pseudorandom number/function generator or on the size of a (local) statistical test for strings/functions.

2.1.1 Pseudorandom Number Generators

The set of positive integers is denoted by $\mathcal{N}$. By a string we mean a binary string over the alphabet $\{0,1\}$. For each $n \in \mathcal{N}$, denote by I_n the set of all 2^n strings of length n. For $s_1, s_2 \in I_n$, let $s_1 \oplus s_2$ denote the bit-wise XOR of the two strings. Denote by H_n the set of all 2^{n2^n} functions and by Sym_n the set of all $2^n!$ permutations on I_n. The *composition* of two functions f and g in H_n, denoted by $f \circ g$, is defined by $f \circ g(x) = f(g(x))$ for all $x \in I_n$. By $x \in_R X$ we mean that x is drawn randomly and uniformly from a finite set X, and by a function in n (or t etc.) we mean, unless otherwise specified, a function from $\mathcal{N}$ to $\mathcal{N}$.

Let P be a function in n with $P(n) > n$. A *pseudorandom number generator* (PNG) is a collection of functions $S = \{S_n \mid n \in \mathcal{N}\}$, where each function S_n maps an n-bit string *seed* into a $P(n)$-bit string $S_n(seed)$ and it can be computed by some deterministic algorithm. Security (or strength) of PNG's is defined in terms of local statistical tests for strings.

[**Definition 1**] Let Θ and $\mathcal{L}$ be sets of functions in n, and Υ a set of functions from $\mathcal{N}$ to $[0,1]$. Let P be a function in n with $P(n) > n$, and let $\theta \in \Theta$ and $L \in \mathcal{L}$ with $0 < L(n) \leq P(n)$. A family of circuits $T^s = \{T_n^s \mid n \in \mathcal{N}\}$ is called a *local* (θ, L) *statistical test for strings* if each T_n^s is of size $\theta(n)$, [2] and on input an $L(n)$-bit fixed portion of a $P(n)$-bit string x, outputs a single bit $T_n^s[x]$. Call θ the size of

---

[2] The size of a circuit is the total number of connections in the circuit.

T^s. Now let $S = \{S_n \mid n \in \mathcal{N}\}$ be a PNG where S_n maps an n-bit string into a $P(n)$-bit one. We say that

(1) S *locally ε-passes the test* T^s if for all sufficiently large n, $|Pr\{T^s_n[r] = 1\} - Pr\{T^s_n[S_n(t)] = 1\}| < \varepsilon(n)$, where $r \in_R I_{P(n)}$, $t \in_R I_n$ and $\varepsilon \in \Upsilon$;

(2) S is *locally (θ, L, ε)-secure* if it locally ε-passes all (θ, L) tests;

(3) S is *locally $(\Theta, \mathcal{L}, \Upsilon)$-secure* if it is locally (θ, L, ε)-secure for any $\varepsilon \in \Upsilon$ and any $(\theta, L) \in \Theta \times \mathcal{L}$ with $0 < L(n) \le P(n)$.

Especially, a locally $(\Theta, \mathcal{L}, \Upsilon)$-secure PNG S is said

(4) *locally $(\infty, \mathcal{L}, \Upsilon)$-secure* if Θ is the set of all functions in n, and

(5) *strong* if, furthermore, $\mathcal{L}$ is the infinite set of all polynomials in n and Υ that of all inverse polynomials in n. (An inverse polynomial in n is a function like $1/Q(n)$ where Q is a polynomial.)

Finally, assume that $S = \{S_n \mid n \in \mathcal{N}\}$ is a PNG where S_n can be computed in deterministic *polynomial* time in n. Then

(6) S is called *locally polynomially secure* if it is locally $(\Theta, \mathcal{L}, \Upsilon)$-secure where both Θ and $\mathcal{L}$ are the infinite set of all polynomials in n, and Υ that of all inverse polynomials in n.

Note that Yao's definition for *polynomial size statistical tests for strings* [Y] [GGM] is obtained from ours by letting P, θ and L be polynomials in n with $P = L$. Now assume, as at the end of Definition 1, that $S = \{S_n \mid n \in \mathcal{N}\}$ is a PNG where S_n can be computed in deterministic *polynomial* time in n. For such a PNG S, Yao defined that it *passes a polynomial size statistical test for strings* $T^s = \{T^s_n \mid n \in \mathcal{N}\}$ if for any polynomial P_1 and for all sufficiently large n, $|Pr\{T^s_n[r] = 1\} - Pr\{T^s_n[S_n(t)] = 1\}| < 1/P_1(n)$, where $r \in_R I_{P(n)}$ and $t \in_R I_n$, and that S is *polynomially secure* if it passes all polynomial size statistical tests for strings.

The following fact is an immediate consequence of Yao's famous theorem on statistical tests [Y] [GGM]: *Assume that $S = \{S_n \mid n \in \mathcal{N}\}$ is a PNG where S_n can be computed in deterministic polynomial time in n. Then S is polynomially secure iff it is locally polynomially secure.*

2.1.2 Pseudorandom Function Generators

Let P be an increasing function in n. A *pseudorandom function generator* (PFG) is a collection of functions $F = \{F_n \mid n \in \mathcal{N}\}$, where F_n specifies for each $P(n)$-bit string *key*, (the description of) a function $F_n(key) \in H_n$ that can be computed by some deterministic algorithm.

Security of a PFG is defined in terms of statistical tests for functions, and the latter uses the concept of oracle circuits which are counterparts of often used *oracle Turing machines*. An *oracle circuit* C_n is an acyclic circuit which contains, in addition to ordinary AND, OR, NOT and constant gates, also a particular kind of gates — *oracle gates*. Each oracle gate has an n-bit input and an n-bit output, and it is evaluated using some function from H_n. The output of C_n, a single bit, is denoted by $C_n[f]$ when a function $f \in H_n$ is used to evaluate the oracle gates.

[Definition 2] Let Θ and $\mathcal{Q}$ be sets of functions in n, and Υ a set of functions from $\mathcal{N}$ to $[0,1]$. Let $\theta \in \Theta$ and $Q \in \mathcal{Q}$ be two functions with $0 \le Q(n) < \theta(n)$. A family of circuits $T^f = \{T_n^f \mid n \in \mathcal{N}\}$ is called a (θ, Q) *statistical test for functions* where T_n^f is an oracle circuit which is of size $\theta(n)$ and has $Q(n)$ oracle gates. Let P be an increasing function in n, and $F = \{F_n \mid n \in \mathcal{N}\}$ a PFG where F_n specifies for each $P(n)$-bit string *key* a function $F_n(key) \in H_n$. We say that

(1) F *ε-passes the test* T^f if for all sufficiently large n, $|Pr\{T_n^f[r] = 1\} - Pr\{T_n^f[F_n(g)] = 1\}| < \varepsilon(n)$ where $r \in_R H_n$, $g \in_R I_{P(n)}$ and $\varepsilon \in \Upsilon$.

(2) F is (θ, Q, ε)-*secure* if it ε-passes *all* (θ, Q) tests.

(3) F is $(\Theta, \mathcal{Q}, \Upsilon)$-*secure* if it is (θ, Q, ε)-secure for any $\varepsilon \in \Upsilon$ and any $(\theta, Q) \in \Theta \times \mathcal{Q}$ with $0 \le Q(n) < \theta(n)$.

Especially,

(4) a $(\Theta, \mathcal{Q}, \Upsilon)$-secure PFG F is said $(\infty, \mathcal{Q}, \Upsilon)$-*secure* when Θ is the set of all functions in n.

Finally assume that for each n and for each $key \in I_{P(n)}$, the function $F_n(key)$ can be computed in deterministic *polynomial* time in n. (This implies that P is a polynomial in n.) Then

(5) F is called *polynomially secure* when it is $(\Theta, \mathcal{Q}, \Upsilon)$-secure for Θ and $\mathcal{Q}$ being the infinite set of all polynomials in n and Υ being the infinite set of all inverse polynomials in n.

We are mainly interested in a special kind of PFG's — pseudorandom permutation generators which are invertible. Let P be an increasing function in n. A *pseudorandom permutation generator* is a pseudorandom function generator $F = \{F_n \mid n \in \mathcal{N}\}$, where F_n specifies for each $P(n)$-bit string *key* a *permutation* $F_n(key) \in Sym_n$ that can be computed by some deterministic algorithm. A pseudorandom permutation generator $F = \{F_n \mid n \in \mathcal{N}\}$ is called *invertible* if there is a pseudorandom permutation generator $\widetilde{F} = \{\widetilde{F}_n \mid n \in \mathcal{N}\}$ such that for each $P(n)$-bit string *key*, $\widetilde{F}_n$ specifies the inverse of $F_n(key)$. Security of (invertible) pseudorandom permutation generators is defined in exactly the same way as for pseudorandom function generators.

2.2 Feistel-Type Transformation (FTT)

For a function $f_i \in H_n$, we associate with it a function $g_i \in H_{2n}$ defined by

$$g_i(B_1, B_2) = (B_2 \oplus f_i(B_1), B_1)$$

where $B_1, B_2 \in I_n$. Note that g_i is obtained from f_i by applying one of the main design rules for DES, and it corresponds roughly to a layer of DES (Figure 1). Since the design rule was due to Feistel, we call g_i a *Feistel-type transformation* (FTT).

For $f_1, f_2, \ldots, f_s \in H_n$, let $\psi(f_s, \ldots, f_2, f_1) = g_s \circ \cdots \circ g_2 \circ g_1$. We say that $\psi(f_s, \ldots, f_2, f_1)$ consists of *s rounds* of FTT's. Obviously, g_i is an invertible permutation, and hence so is $\psi(f_s, \ldots, f_2, f_1)$.

Luby and Rackoff proved the following result which was called *Main Lemma* in [LR] but is called *FTT Lemma* in this paper: For independent random functions

$f_1, f_2, f_3 \in H_n$, it is infeasible to distinguish $\psi(f_3, f_2, f_1)$ from a function drawn randomly and uniformly from H_{2n}. (See Figure 2.)

[FTT Lemma] (Version 1, [LR]) *Let Q be a polynomial in n and C_{2n} be an oracle circuit with $Q(n) < 2^n$ oracle gates. Then $|Pr\{C_{2n}[r] = 1\} - Pr\{C_{2n}[\psi(f_3, f_2, f_1)] = 1\}| \le \frac{Q(n)^2}{2^n}$, where $r \in_R H_{2n}$ and $f_1, f_2, f_3 \in_R H_n$.*

FTT Lemma is surprising in the sense that it does not depend on any unproved hypotheses. It implies that we can construct as follows a block cipher which does not relying on any assumption and is provably secure against chosen-plaintext attack: Let the length of a plaintext be $2n$. Choose randomly and uniformly from H_n three functions f_1, f_2 and f_3, and let the enciphering algorithm be $\psi(f_3, f_2, f_1)$ and the deciphering algorithm be the inverse of $\psi(f_3, f_2, f_1)$.

However one soon finds that such an approach is impractical: To make the cipher secure against some trivial attacks such as exhaustive search, $2n$ must be sufficiently large, say ≥ 64, i.e., $n \ge 32$. When $n = 32$, specifying $\psi(f_3, f_2, f_1)$ takes at least $3 \cdot 32 \cdot 2^{32} \approx 4 \cdot 10^{11}$ bits, which is infeasible currently and even in the foreseeable future. In other words, there is still a big gap between practically constructing a provably secure block cipher and the nice theory initiated by Luby and Rackoff. In the following sections we will examine various types of transformations, and fill the gap greatly.

3. Cryptographically Useful Transformations

This section introduces various types of transformations, and generalizes FTT Lemma in many directions. First we introduce two operations on strings in I_{kn} — the *ρ-position left rotation* and the *ρ-position right rotation*. These two operations are denoted by $\mathrm{L}_{rot}^{(\rho)}$ and $\mathrm{R}_{rot}^{(\rho)}$, and defined as

$$\mathrm{L}_{rot}^{(\rho)}(B_1, B_2, \ldots, B_k) = (B_{\rho+1}, \ldots, B_k, B_1, B_2, \ldots, B_\rho),$$
$$\mathrm{R}_{rot}^{(\rho)}(B_1, B_2, \cdots, B_k) = (B_{k-\rho+1}, \ldots, B_k, B_1, B_2, \ldots, B_{k-\rho})$$

respectively, where $1 \le \rho < k$ and $B_j \in I_n$. Note that both $\mathrm{L}_{rot}^{(\rho)}$ and $\mathrm{R}_{rot}^{(\rho)}$ are permutations on I_{kn}, and that $\mathrm{L}_{rot}^{(\rho)}$ is the inverse of $\mathrm{R}_{rot}^{(\rho)}$ and vice versa.

3.1 Various Transformations

3.1.1 Type-1 Transformations

Following [FNS, pp.1547-1549] and [S], we associate with an $f_i \in H_n$ a function $g_{1,i} \in H_{kn}$ defined by

$$g_{1,i}(B_1, B_2, \ldots, B_k) = (B_2 \oplus f_i(B_1), B_3, \ldots, B_k, B_1),$$

where $B_j \in I_n$. Functions obtained in such a way are called *Type-1 transformations*.

Note that $g_{1,i}$ can be decomposed into $g_{1,i} = \mathrm{L}_{rot}^{(1)} \circ \pi_{1,i}$ where $\pi_{1,i}$ is defined by $\pi_{1,i}(B_1, B_2, \ldots, B_k) = (B_1, B_2 \oplus f_i(B_1), B_3, \ldots, B_k)$. (See Figure 3.) It is easy to check that $\pi_{1,i} \circ \pi_{1,i}$ is the *identity transformation* on I_{kn}, i.e., $\pi_{1,i}$ is the inverse of itself. Such a function is usually called an *involution* [K]. Now we see that $g_{1,i}$ is an invertible permutation on I_{kn}, and its inverse, denoted by $\widetilde{g}_{1,i}$, is given by $\widetilde{g}_{1,i} = \pi_{1,i} \circ \mathrm{R}_{rot}^{(1)}$.

For $f_1, f_2, \ldots, f_s \in H_n$, define $\psi_1(f_s, \ldots, f_2, f_1) = g_{1,s} \circ \cdots \circ g_{1,2} \circ g_{1,1}$. $\psi_1(f_s, \ldots, f_2, f_1)$ is also an invertible permutation on I_{kn}, and by definition, its inverse is $\widetilde{\psi}_1(f_s, \ldots, f_2, f_1) = \pi_{1,1} \circ \mathrm{R}_{rot}^{(1)} \circ \cdots \pi_{1,s-1} \circ \mathrm{R}_{rot}^{(1)} \circ \pi_{1,s} \circ \mathrm{R}_{rot}^{(1)}$.

3.1.2 Type-2 Transformations

Let $k = 2\ell$, where $\ell \in \mathcal{N}$. Associate with a function-tuple $h_i = (f_{i,1}, f_{i,3}, \ldots, f_{i,2\ell-1})$, where $f_{i,j} \in H_n$, a function $g_{2,i} \in H_{kn}$ defined by

$$g_{2,i}(B_1, B_2, \ldots, B_k) = (B_2 \oplus f_{i,1}(B_1), B_3, B_4 \oplus f_{i,3}(B_3), \ldots,$$
$$B_{k-1}, B_k \oplus f_{i,k-1}(B_{k-1}), B_1).$$

$g_{2,i}$ is called a *Type-2 transformation*, and can be decomposed into $g_{2,i} = \mathrm{L}_{rot}^{(1)} \circ \pi_{2,i}$ where $\pi_{2,i}$ is defined by $\pi_{2,i}(B_1, B_2, \ldots, B_k) = (B_1, B_2 \oplus f_{i,1}(B_1), B_3, \ldots, B_{k-1}, B_k \oplus f_{i,k-1}(B_{k-1}))$. (See Figure 4.) Obviously, $\pi_{2,i}$ is an involution. For s function-tuples $h_1, h_2, \ldots, h_s$, define $\psi_2(h_s, \ldots, h_2, h_1) = g_{2,s} \circ \cdots \circ g_{2,2} \circ g_{2,1}$. The inverse of $\psi_2(h_s, \ldots, h_2, h_1)$ is $\widetilde{\psi}_1(h_s, \ldots, h_2, h_1) = \widetilde{g}_{2,1} \circ \cdots \circ \widetilde{g}_{2,s-1} \circ \widetilde{g}_{2,s}$, where $\widetilde{g}_{2,i} = \pi_{2,i} \circ \mathrm{R}_{rot}^{(\rho)}$.

3.1.3 Type-3 Transformations

Associate with a function-tuple $h_i = (f_{i,1}, f_{i,2}, \ldots, f_{i,k-1})$, where $f_{i,j} \in H_n$, a function $g_{3,i} \in H_{kn}$ defined by

$$g_{3,i}(B_1, B_2, \ldots, B_k) = (B_2 \oplus f_{i,1}(B_1), B_3 \oplus f_{i,2}(B_2), \ldots, B_k \oplus f_{i,k-1}(B_{k-1}), B_1).$$

Call $g_{3,i}$ a *Type-3 transformation*. We decompose $g_{3,i}$ into $g_{3,i} = \mathrm{L}_{rot}^{(1)} \circ \pi_{3,i}$ where $\pi_{3,i}$ is defined by $\pi_{3,i}(B_1, B_2, \ldots, B_k) = (B_1, B_2 \oplus f_{i,1}(B_1), B_3 \oplus f_{i,2}(B_2), \ldots, B_k \oplus f_{i,k-1}(B_{k-1}))$. See Figure 5. $\pi_{3,i}$ is a permutation and its inverse is given by $\widetilde{\pi}_{3,i}(C_1, C_2, \cdots, C_k) = (B_1, B_2, \cdots, B_k)$, where $B_1 = C_1$ and $B_j = C_j \oplus f_{i,j-1}(B_{j-1})$ for each $2 \leq j \leq k$. One can soon find that $\pi_{3,i}$ is *not* an involution (Figure 6).

For s function-tuples $h_1, h_2, \ldots, h_s$, define $\psi_3(h_s, \ldots, h_2, h_1) = g_{3,s} \circ \cdots \circ g_{3,2} \circ g_{3,1}$. Since both $\pi_{3,i}$ and $\mathrm{L}_{rot}^{(1)}$ are permutations, hence so are $g_{3,i}$ and $\psi_3(h_s, \ldots, h_2, h_1)$. The inverse of $\psi_3(h_s, \ldots, h_2, h_1)$ is $\widetilde{\psi}_3(h_s, \ldots, h_2, h_1) = \widetilde{\pi}_{3,1} \circ \mathrm{R}_{rot}^{(1)} \circ \cdots \circ \widetilde{\pi}_{3,s-1} \circ \mathrm{R}_{rot}^{(1)} \circ \widetilde{\pi}_{3,s} \circ \mathrm{R}_{rot}^{(1)}$.

3.1.4 Generalized Transformations

From its definition, we see that $\pi_{1,i}$ can be obtained from $\pi_{3,i}$ by dropping functions $f_{i,j}$ in $h_i = (f_{i,1}, f_{i,2}, \ldots, f_{i,k-1})$ for all $2 \leq j \leq k - 1$. Similarly, when k is even, $\pi_{2,i}$ can also be obtained from $\pi_{3,i}$ by dropping functions $f_{i,j}$ in $h_i = (f_{i,1}, f_{i,2}, \ldots, f_{i,k-1})$ for all *even* $1 < j < k - 1$.

Denote by $\pi_{\tau,i}$ a permutation obtained from $\pi_{3,i}$, by dropping certain functions $f_{i,j}$ in $h_i = (f_{i,1}, f_{i,2}, \ldots, f_{i,k-1})$. (Note: $\pi_{\tau,i} = \pi_{3,i}$ when dropping no function.) Define $g_{\tau,i}^{(\rho)} = L_{rot}^{(\rho)} \circ \pi_{\tau,i}$, where $1 \leq \rho \leq k - 1$. Call transformations so obtained *Generalized Type-τ transformations*. Likewise, for s functions/function-tuples $h_1, h_2, \ldots, h_s$, define $\psi_\tau^{(\rho)}(h_s, \ldots, h_2, h_1) = g_{\tau,s}^{(\rho)} \circ \cdots \circ g_{\tau,2}^{(\rho)} \circ g_{\tau,1}^{(\rho)}$.

3.2 Theorems on the Transformations

Let E be a permutation consisting of $2k - 1$ rounds of Type-1, or $k + 1$ rounds of Type-2, or $k + 1$ rounds of Type-3 transformations, each of which is chosen randomly and independently. The following Theorems 1-3 say that *no* oracle circuit with polynomially many oracle gates can distinguish between E and a truly random function.

[Theorem 1] *Let Q be a polynomial in n and C_{kn} be an oracle circuit with $Q(n) < 2^n$ oracle gates. Then $|Pr\{C_{kn}[r] = 1\} - Pr\{C_{kn}[\psi_1(f_{2k-1}, \ldots, f_2, f_1)] = 1\}| \leq \frac{(k-1)Q(n)^2}{2^n}$, where $r \in_R H_{kn}$ and $f_1, f_2, \ldots, f_{2k-1} \in_R H_n$.*

[Theorem 2] *Let Q be a polynomial in n and C_{kn} be an oracle circuit with $Q(n) < 2^n$ oracle gates where $k = 2\ell$. Then $|Pr\{C_{kn}[r] = 1\} - Pr\{C_{kn}[\psi_2(h_{k+1}, \ldots, h_2, h_1)] = 1\}| \leq \frac{\ell^2 Q(n)^2}{2^n}$, where $r \in_R H_{kn}$ and $h_i = (f_{i,1}, f_{i,3}, \ldots, f_{i,k-1})$ with $f_{i,j} \in_R H_n$.*

[Theorem 3] *Let Q be a polynomial in n and C_{kn} be an oracle circuit with $Q(n) < 2^n$ oracle gates. Then $|Pr\{C_{kn}[r] = 1\} - Pr\{C_{kn}[\psi_3(h_{k+1}, \ldots, h_2, h_1)] = 1\}| \leq \frac{k(k-1)Q(n)^2}{2^{n+1}}$, where $r \in_R H_{kn}$ and $h_i = (f_{i,1}, f_{i,2}, \ldots, f_{i,k-1})$ with $f_{i,j} \in_R H_n$.*

Theorem 2 can be proved by essentially the same technique developed in [LR] for proving FTT Lemma. Details will appear in the full paper. Proofs for Theorems 1 and 3 can be derived from the proof for Theorem 2.

For Generalized Type-2 transformations, we have the following theorem, which is crucial to our construction of block ciphers described in Sections 4-6, and can be proved by modifying the proof for Theorem 2. For the other types of generalized transformations we have no results similar to Theorem 2-G. For reasons see Appendix A where many other results are presented.

[Theorem 2-G] *(Version 1) Let $k = 2\ell$, where $\ell \in \mathcal{N}$, and let ρ be an odd integer in $[1, k]$. Let Q be a polynomial in n and C_{kn} be an oracle circuit with $Q(n) < 2^n$ oracle gates. Then $|Pr\{C_{kn}[r] = 1\} - Pr\{C_{kn}[\psi_2^{(\rho)}(h_{k+1}, \ldots, h_2, h_1)] = 1\}| \leq \frac{\ell^2 Q(n)^2}{2^n}$, where $r \in_R H_{kn}$ and $h_i = (f_{i,1}, f_{i,3}, \ldots, f_{i,k-1})$ with $f_{i,j} \in_R H_n$.*

3.3 Optimal Transformations

Let E be a permutation consisting of s rounds of randomly chosen Generalized Type-τ transformations. From Theorem A5 in Appendix A we see that $s \geq$

$k + 1$ is a necessary condition for E being indistinguishable from a truly random function by all oracle circuits with polynomially many oracle gates. Call a type of transformations *optimal* if

    (1) a permutation E consisting of $k + 1$ rounds of randomly chosen transformations is indistinguishable from a truly random function by all oracle circuits with polynomially many oracle gates, and

    (2) the inverse of E can be computed in the same parallel time as E.

For a rigorous definition of optimality, see Appendix B. The following theorem is proved in the same appendix.

[Theorem B1] *Among all types of transformations discussed in this paper, Generalized Type-2 transformations $g_{2,i}^{(\rho)} = L_{rot}^{(\rho)} \circ \pi_{2,i}^{(\rho)}$ with even k and odd ρ, are the only optimal ones.*

4. PSBC — A Provably Secure Block Cipher

Applying the only optimal Generalized Type-2 Transformations we construct a provably secure block cipher (PSBC) in this section.

4.1 A Few Observations

As pointed out in [S], FTT Lemma remains true even if the number of oracle gates is replaced by $Q(n) \leq 2^{o(n)}$ [S]. Here $Q(n) \leq 2^{o(n)}$ means that $Q(n) \leq 2^{f(n)}$ for some $f(n)$, which satisfies $\lim\limits_{n \to \infty} \frac{cf(n)}{n} = 0$ for every positive constant c, i.e., $f(n) = o(n)$.

[FTT Lemma] (Version 2, [S]) *Let C_{2n} be an oracle circuit with $Q(n) \leq 2^{o(n)}$ oracle gates. Then $|Pr\{C_{2n}[r] = 1\} - Pr\{C_{2n}[\psi(f_3, f_2, f_1)] = 1\}| \leq \frac{Q(n)^2}{2^n}$, where $r \in_R H_{2n}$ and $f_1, f_2, f_3 \in_R H_n$.*

Schnorr's observation also applies to our Theorem 2-G (Version 1) stated in Section 3.

[Theorem 2-G] (Version 2) *Let $k = 2\ell$, where $\ell \in \mathcal{N}$, and let ρ be an odd integer in $[1, k]$. Let C_{kn} be an oracle circuit with $Q(n) \leq 2^{o(n)}$ oracle gates. Then $|Pr\{C_{kn}[r] = 1\} - Pr\{C_{kn}[\psi_2^{(\rho)}(h_{k+1}, \ldots, h_2, h_1)] = 1\}| \leq \frac{\ell^2 Q(n)^2}{2^n}$, where $r \in_R H_{kn}$ and $h_i = (f_{i,1}, f_{i,3}, \ldots, f_{i,k-1})$ with $f_{i,j} \in_R H_n$.*

Next we make a few more observations. Let $t \in \mathcal{N}$ and $n = \lceil (\log t)^{1+\varepsilon} \rceil$ for some $\varepsilon \in (0, 1]$, where the logarithm is taken to the base 2. Then for any constants c and ε' with $c > 0$ and $0 \leq \varepsilon' < \varepsilon$, we have $c \log t \leq c(\log t)^{1+\varepsilon'} = o(\lceil (\log t)^{1+\varepsilon} \rceil) = o(n)$, and $t^c = 2^{c \log t} \leq 2^{c(\log t)^{1+\varepsilon'}} = 2^{o(n)}$. Thus we obtain from Theorem 2-G (Version 2) the following one.

[Theorem 2-G] (Version 3) *Let $k = 2\ell$, where $\ell \in \mathcal{N}$, and let ρ be an odd integer in $[1, k]$. Assume that $t \in \mathcal{N}$, $\varepsilon \in (0, 1]$, $n = \lceil (\log t)^{1+\varepsilon} \rceil$ and*

$Q(t) \leq 2^{o(n)}$ *is a polynomial in* t. *(Notice that* $2^n = 2^{\lceil (\log t)^{1+\epsilon} \rceil}$ *is quasi-polynomial in* t.) [3] *Let* C_{2n} *be an oracle circuit with* $Q(t)$ *oracle gates. Then* $|Pr\{C_{kn}[r] = 1\} - Pr\{C_{kn}[\psi_2^{(\rho)}(h_{k+1}, \ldots, h_2, h_1)] = 1\}| \leq \frac{\ell^2 Q(t)^2}{2^n}$, *where* $r \in_R H_{kn}$ *and* $h_i = (f_{i,1}, f_{i,3}, \ldots, f_{i,k-1})$ *with* $f_{i,j} \in_R H_n$.

4.2 Enciphering/Deciphering Algorithms for PSBC

Theorem 2-G (Version 3) says that theoretically, if one is quasi-polynomially powerful, then one can construct a block cipher secure against any polynomially powerful adversary.

Let $n = \lceil (\log t)^{1+\epsilon} \rceil$, where $t \in \mathcal{N}$ and $\epsilon \in (0, 1]$. Let $\ell \in \mathcal{N}$, $k = 2\ell$ and ρ be an odd integer in $[1, k]$. Assume that the plaintext and ciphertext spaces are I_{kn}. Denote by $B = (B_1, B_2, \ldots, B_k)$ a plaintext in I_{kn} and by $C = (C_1, C_2, \ldots, C_k)$ the ciphertext of B, where $B_i, C_i \in I_n$.

PSBC consists principally of s rounds of Generalized Type-2 transformations where $s \geq k+2$. The reason for choosing $s \geq k+2$ is as follows: When $s = k+1$, our block cipher PSBC is secure against chosen plaintext attack, but not secure against chosen plaintext/ciphertext attack. When $s \geq k+2$, PSBC is secure against chosen plaintext/ciphertext attack. See Appendix C and [LR].

The enciphering algorithm E for PSBC can be concisely expressed as

$$E = \pi_{2,s} \circ L_{rot}^{(\rho)} \circ \cdots \circ L_{rot}^{(\rho)} \circ \pi_{2,2} \circ L_{rot}^{(\rho)} \circ \pi_{2,1}.$$

See Figure 7. The inverse of E is $\pi_{2,1} \circ R_{rot}^{(\rho)} \circ \cdots \circ R_{rot}^{(\rho)} \circ \pi_{2,s-1} \circ R_{rot}^{(\rho)} \circ \pi_{2,s}$. So the deciphering algorithm D for PSBC is obtained from E by

(1) interchanging h_i with h_{s+1-i} for each $1 \leq i \leq \lfloor \frac{s}{2} \rfloor$, and

(2) changing the mapping (or wiring) representing $L_{rot}^{(\rho)}$ to the mapping (or wiring) representing $R_{rot}^{(\rho)}$.

Notice that when ℓ is odd and $\rho = \ell$, there is no need for changing the mapping (or wiring), since $L_{rot}^{(\rho)} = R_{rot}^{(\rho)}$ in this case.

5. A Variant of PSBC

The block cipher PSBC described in Section 4 requires quasi-polynomially many memory cells for both enciphering and deciphering procedures. Thus it is practically impossible to realize the cipher. This section presents a variant of PSBC, in order to pave the way to practically realizable ciphers. The variant is obtained by adding to PSBC a *key-expanding part*. The key-expanding part stretches a short string into a long one, i.e., is a PNG. The PNG we use is a *strong* one (see Definition 1), and it is essentially due to Ohnishi and Schnorr [O] [S].

5.1 A Strong Pseudorandom Number Generator

Ohnishi observed that FTT Lemma remains valid even when *two* independent random functions are available [O].

---

[3] We call a function f *quasi-polynomial* in t if for any polynomial P, for any constant $c > 0$ and for all sufficiently large t, we have $P(t) < f(t) < 2^{t^c}$.

[FTT Lemma] (Version 3, [O]) *Let Q be a polynomial in n, and let C_{2n} be an oracle circuit with $Q(n) \leq 2^{o(n)}$ oracle gates. Then $|Pr\{C_{2n}[r] = 1\} - Pr\{C_{2n}[\psi(f_2, f_1, f_1)] = 1\}| \leq \frac{2(Q(n)+1)^2}{2^n}$, and $|Pr\{C_{2n}[r] = 1\} - Pr\{C_{2n}[\psi(f_2, f_2, f_1)] = 1\}| \leq \frac{2(Q(n)+1)^2}{2^n}$, where $r \in_R H_{2n}$, $f_1, f_2 \in_R H_n$.*

Schnorr [S] showed that FTT Lemma implies that we can explicitly construct a PNG without any hypotheses. Putting together observations made in [O] and [S], we have the following PNG.

First we note that there is a natural one-one correspondence between functions in H_n and strings in I_{n2^n}, i.e., a bijection Φ_n from H_n to I_{n2^n}. The bijection maps a function $f \in H_n$ into the concatenation of $\coprod_{x \in I_n} f(x)$, where x ranges over all strings $x \in I_n$ in a predetermined (such as lexicographical) order, and $\coprod$ is the concatenation operation on more than two strings. By this bijection, $\psi(f_2, f_2, f_1)$ constructed from $f_1, f_2 \in H_n$ via FTT's yields a function $S_{2n2^n} : I_{2n2^n} \to I_{2n2^{2n}}$. S_{2n2^n} maps a string $x = x_1 x_2$ where $x_1, x_2 \in I_{n2^n}$, into a string $y \in I_{2n2^{2n}}$ in the following way: $S_{2n2^n}(x) = \Phi_{2n}(\psi(\Phi_n^{-1}(x_2), \Phi_n^{-1}(x_2), \Phi_n^{-1}(x_1)))$.

Now we describe concretely an algorithm G_n computing the function S_{2n2^n}. The algorithm follows a similar one in [S]. (See Figure 8.) We write a string $x \in I_{2n2^n}$ as the concatenation of two strings $x_1, x_2 \in I_{n2^n}$, each of which is written as the concatenation of 2^n strings in I_n, i.e., $x = x_1 x_2 = \coprod_{i \in I_n} x_{1,i} \coprod_{i \in I_n} x_{2,i}$, where $x_{1,i}, x_{2,i} \in I_n$. Likewise, we write a string $y \in I_{2n2^{2n}}$ as the concatenation of 2^{2n} strings in I_{2n}, i.e., $y = \coprod_{i \in I_{2n}} y_i$, where $y_i \in I_{2n}$. For a string $y \in I_{2n}$, let $B_1(y)$ and $B_2(y)$ be the left and right half strings in I_n.

Algorithm $G_n(x)$
/* This algorithm outputs a $2n2^{2n}$-bit string y
    on input a $2n2^n$-bit string $x = x_1 x_2 = \coprod_{i \in I_n} x_{1,i} \coprod_{i \in I_n} x_{2,i}$. */

(1) **For all** $i \in I_{2n}$, **let** $y_i^0 := i$;
(2) **For all** $i \in I_{2n}$ **do**
    $\{ w := y_i^0;\ u := x_{1, B_1(w)};$
    $y_i^1 := (B_2(w) \oplus u, B_1(w)) \}$;
(3) **For** $j = 1, 2$ **do**
    For all $i \in I_{2n}$ **do**
    $\{ w := y_i^j;\ u := x_{2, B_1(w)};$
    $y_i^{j+1} := (B_2(w) \oplus u, B_1(w)) \}$;
(4) **Output** $y = \coprod_{i \in I_{2n}} y_i^3$.

Let $S = \{S_{e(n)} | e(n) = 2n2^n, n \in \mathcal{N}\}$. From [S] we know that the PNG S passes all statistical tests for strings which receive at most $2^{o(n)}$ bits as input. In our terms, this can be formally stated as follows.

[Theorem 4] (Version 1) *The PNG $S = \{S_{e(n)} | e(n) = 2n2^n, n \in \mathcal{N}\}$ is locally $(\infty, \mathcal{L}, \Upsilon)$-secure where $\mathcal{L}$ is the infinite set of functions L in n with $L(n) \leq 2^{o(n)}$ and Υ that of all inverse polynomials in n.*

Proof: A local statistical test for strings $T^s = \{T^s_n \mid n \in \mathcal{N}\}$, where T^s_n has a $Q(n)(\leq 2^{o(n)})$-bit input, can be viewed as a statistical test for functions $T^f = \{T^f_n \mid n \in \mathcal{N}\}$, where T^f_n has at most $Q(n) \leq 2^{o(n)}$ oracle gates that are evaluated using a function from H_{2n}. Thus the theorem is true by FTT Lemma (Version 2) in Section 4.1. ∎

Applying our observation made in Section 4, this theorem can be translated into the following theorem.

[Theorem 4] (Version 2) *Let $n = \lceil (\log t)^{1+\epsilon} \rceil$, where $t \in \mathcal{N}$ and $\epsilon \in (0,1]$. Then the PNG $S = \{S_{\bar{e}(t)} | \bar{e}(t) = e(n) = 2n2^n, n = \lceil (\log t)^{1+\epsilon} \rceil, t \in \mathcal{N}\}$ where $S_{\bar{e}(t)}$ maps an $\bar{e}(t) = e(n) = 2n2^{2n}$-bit string into a $2n2^{2n}$-bit one, is locally $(\infty, \mathcal{L}, \Upsilon)$-secure where $\mathcal{L}$ is the infinite set of all polynomials in t, and Υ that of all inverse polynomials in t. That is to say, S is a strong PNG.*

5.2 PSBC with Key-Expanding

Let $n = \lceil (\log t)^{1+\epsilon} \rceil$, where $t \in \mathcal{N}$ and $\epsilon \in (0,1]$. Let I_{kn} be the plaintext/ciphertext spaces where $k = 2\ell$, $\ell \in \mathcal{N}$, and let ρ be an odd integer in $[1, k]$, s an integer with $s \geq k + 2$.

The enciphering algorithm consists of two parts: *the enciphering part* and *the key-expanding part* (Figure 9). The enciphering part, as PSBC, consists essentially of s rounds of Generalized Type-2 transformations. The key-expanding part is an algorithm G_m that computes a function $S_{\hat{e}(t)}$ from a strong PNG $S = \{S_{\hat{e}(t)} | \hat{e}(t) = 2m2^m, m = n\lceil \log n \rceil, n = \lceil (\log t)^{1+\epsilon} \rceil, t \in \mathcal{N}\}$, and it can expand a $2m2^m$-bit input string into a $2m2^{2m}$-bit output string.

The deciphering algorithm is obtained by

(1) reversing the portion, which is used by the enciphering part, of the output of the key-expanding part and

(2) changing the mapping (or wiring) representing $L_{rot}^{(\rho)}$ to the mapping (or wiring) representing $R_{rot}^{(\rho)}$.

The following theorem implies that the block cipher PSBC with key-expanding is secure against any polynomial size adversary. It can be proved by making some obvious modifications on the proof for Theorem 1 of [LR].

[Theorem 5] *Let $k = 2\ell$ where $\ell \in \mathcal{N}$, and ρ be an odd integer in $[1, k]$. Also let $t \in \mathcal{N}$, $\epsilon \in (0,1]$, $n = \lceil (\log t)^{1+\epsilon} \rceil$ and $S = \{S_{m(t)} | \hat{e}(t) = 2m2^m, m = n\lceil \log n \rceil, n = \lceil (\log t)^{1+\epsilon} \rceil, t \in \mathcal{N}\}$ be the above constructed strong PNG. Assume that P and Q are polynomials in t and that C_{2n} is an oracle circuit with $Q(t)$ oracle gates. Then for any $r \in_R H_{kn}$, for any $x \in_R I_{\hat{e}(t)}$, and for any $h_1, h_2, \ldots, h_{k+1}$ where $h_i = (f_{i,1}, f_{i,3}, \ldots, f_{i,k-1})$ and each $f_{i,j}$ corresponds to a distinct $n2^n (= 2^{o(m)})$-bit portion of the output of $S_{\hat{e}(t)}(x)$, we have $|Pr\{C_{kn}[r] = 1\} - Pr\{C_{kn}[\psi_2^{(\rho)}(h_{k+1}, \ldots, h_2, h_1)] = 1\}| < 1/P(t)$.*

6. Practical Block Ciphers

PSBC with key-expanding requires still quasi-polynomial amount of memory to specify an enciphering/deciphering algorithm. In addition, the enciphering/deciphering part uses only an extremely small portion of the output of the key-expanding part.

Experience tells us that concatenating a number of transformations, each of which may not be so cryptographically strong, can produce a very strong one [M]. This folklore has recently been proved to be correct by Luby and Rackoff. See Theorem 2 in the preliminary version of [LR].

Along this guideline, we consider how to modify PSBC with key-expanding so that it is practically secure and can be implemented with current technology. We focus on the following three aspects: the size of a key, the sizes of n and k, and the rounds of transformations.

1. A key should be relatively short to make the cipher easy to be implemented. However to beat back the exhaustive search attack, the key should not be too short.

2. n should not be too large since it takes $n2^n$ bits to specify a random function from H_n. However, kn and hence k should be sufficiently large, otherwise the cipher is insecure even against the trivial exhaustive search attack.

3. When a relatively short key and a small n are chosen, the strength of the cipher will be significantly reduced. An effective method of resolving the problem is increasing the number of rounds of transformations.

The remaining part of this section proposes four example ciphers which we hope are secure enough for practical applications. Main parameters of the ciphers are collected in Table 1. For completeness, the definitions of the parameters are summarized below the table.

These parameters are chosen according to the preceding three aspects. In addition, $n = 4$ and $n = 8$ are chosen for easier implementation by software and/or hardware. The key-expanding part of each example cipher is realized by the algorithm G_m expanding a key of length $2m2^m$ bits into a long string of length $2m2^{2m}$ bits. All output bits of G_m are used by the enciphering part.

Notice that in Examples 2 and 3, the output of G_m is only half of the bits required by the enciphering part. We take two $2m2^m$-bit strings, and use G_m to stretch them into $2m2^{2m}$-bit ones. Then we combine the $2m2^{2m}$-bit strings into a $4m2^{2m}$-bit one. A recommended method for combining strings is concatenating them in bit/bits unit.

7. Conclusion

We have investigated various types of transformations, and showed that among them Generalized Type-2 transformations are the most preferable. Two provably secure block ciphers, PSBC and PSBC with key-expanding, have been constructed by the use of Generalized Type-2 transformations. And finally, based on PSBC with key-expanding, practically implementable block ciphers have been presented.

Table 1 Four Example Ciphers

Parameters	Example 1	Example 2	Example 3	Example 4
Length of Plaintext/ Ciphertext (bits)	64	96	112	128
Length of Key (bits)	768	1536 $(= 2 \cdot 768)*$	3584 $(= 2 \cdot 1792)*$	4096
Size of Enciphering Part (kilo-bytes)	6	12	56	128
s (rounds)	96	128	32	64
n (bits)	4	4	8	8
k	16	24	14	16
m	6	6	7	8

* (G_m is used twice)

Definitions of Parameters

- Length of Plaintext/Ciphertext $= n \cdot k$ (bits).
- Length of Key $= t \cdot 2 \cdot m \cdot 2^m$ (bits), where t is the number of times G_m is applied.
- Size of Enciphering Part $= \ell \cdot s \cdot n \cdot 2^n$ (bits) $= \ell \cdot s \cdot n \cdot 2^n / 2^{13}$ (kilo-bytes).
- s — the number of rounds of Generalized Type-2 transformations applied in the enciphering/deciphering part.
- n — the length of a substring B_i (or C_i).
- k — ($= 2\ell$) the number of substrings B_i's (or C_i's).
- m — specifying the length, $2m2^m$, of an input to G_m.

References

[BM] M. Blum and S. Micali: "How to generate cryptographically strong sequences of pseudo-random bits," *SIAM Journal on Computing*, Vol. 13, No. 4, (1984), pp.850-864.

[FNS] H. Feistel, W.A. Notz and J.L. Smith: "Some cryptographic techniques for machine-to-machine data communications," *Proceedings of IEEE*, Vol. 63, No. 11, (1975), pp.1545-1554.

[GGM] O. Goldreich, S. Goldwasser and S. Micali: "How to construct random functions," *Journal of ACM*, Vol. 33, No. 4, (1986), pp.792-807.

[K] A.G. Konheim: *Cryptography : A Primer*, John Wiley & Sons, Inc. (1981).

[L] L.A. Levin: "One-way functions and pseudorandom generators," *Combinatorica*, Vol. 7, No. 4, (1987), pp.357-363.

[LR] M. Luby and C. Rackoff: "How to construct pseudorandom permutations from pseudorandom functions," *SIAM Journal on Computing*, Vol. 17, No. 2, (1988), pp.373-386.

[M] C.H. Meyer: "Ciphertext/plaintext and ciphertext/key dependence vs number of rounds for the data encryption standard," *AFIPS Conference Proceedings*, Vol. 47, (1978), pp.1119-1126.

[NBS] *Data Encryption Standard*, Federal Information Processing Standards (FIPS) Publication 46, National Bureau of Standards, U.S. Department of Commerce, (1977).

[O] Y. Ohnishi: "A study on data security," *Master Thesis* (in Japanese), Tohoku University, Japan, (1988).

[R] R.A. Rueppel: "On the security of Schnorr's pseudorandom generator," *Presented at EUROCRYPT'89*, Houthalen, (April 10-13, 1989).

[S] C.P. Schnorr: "On the construction of random number generators and random function generators," *Advances in Cryptology — EUROCRYPT'88*, LNCS Vol. 330, Springer-Verlag, (1988), pp.225-232.

[Y] A.C. Yao: "Theory and applications of trapdoor functions," *Proceedings of the 23rd IEEE Symposium on Foundations of Computer Science*, (1982), pp.80-91.

[ZMI] Y. Zheng, T. Matsumoto and H. Imai: "Impossibility and optimality results on constructing pseudorandom permutations," *Presented at EUROCRYPT'89*, Houthalen, (April 10-13, 1989).

Appendix A —Minimum Rounds for Security

This appendix discusses minimum rounds for achieving security when a permutation is constructed from some kind of transformations.

First we consider transformations related to Type-3 ones. For these transformations we have the following useful lemma.

[Lemma A1] *Let P be a subset of H_{kn}. If for any function $p \in P$ and for any input $s = (s_i, s_\ell, s_j) \in I_{kn}$, the output of p takes the form of $(\ldots, s_\ell \oplus (\cdots \widehat{s_\ell} \cdots), \ldots)$, where $0 \le i, \ell, j \le kn, \ell \ge 1, i + \ell + j = kn, s_i \in I_i, s_\ell \in I_\ell, s_j \in I_j$ and $(\cdots \widehat{s_\ell} \cdots)$ means that the string does not depend on s_ℓ, then there is a simple oracle circuit distinguishing between a function $p \in P$ and a function randomly and uniformly selected from H_{kn}.*

Recall that for a function-tuple $h_i = (f_{i,1}, f_{i,2}, \ldots, f_{i,k-1})$, where $f_{i,j} \in H_n$, a Type-3 transformation is defined as $g_{3,i} = L_{rot}^{(1)} \circ \pi_{3,i}$, where $\pi_{3,i}(B_1, B_2, \ldots, B_k) = (B_1, B_2 \oplus f_{i,1}(B_1), B_3 \oplus f_{i,2}(B_2), \ldots, B_k \oplus f_{i,k-1}(B_{k-1}))$, and that for s function-tuples $h_1, h_2, \ldots, h_s$, a permutation consisting of s rounds of Type-3 transformations is defined as $\psi_3(h_s, \ldots, h_2, h_1) = g_{3,s} \circ \cdots \circ g_{3,2} \circ g_{3,1}$.

Let $\pi_{\tau,i}$ be a permutation obtained from $\pi_{3,i}$ by dropping certain functions $f_{i,j}$ in $h_i = (f_{i,1}, f_{i,2}, \ldots, f_{i,k-1})$. ($\pi_{\tau,i} = \pi_{3,i}$ when dropping no function.) Define $g_{\tau,i} = L_{rot}^{(1)} \circ \pi_{\tau,i}$, and call it a Type-$\tau$ transformation. Also let $\psi_\tau(h_s, \ldots, h_2, h_1)$ be a permutation in H_{kn} consisting of s rounds of Type-τ transformations.

Let λ_τ denote the minimum number s at which $\psi_\tau(h_s, \ldots, h_2, h_1)$ is secure. Now we are in a position to prove that $\lambda_\tau \ge k + 1$, i.e., a necessary condition for

$\psi_\tau(h_s, \ldots, h_1, h_1)$ to be secure is that $s \geq k+1$. Formally, we have

[Theorem A2] *(1)* $\lambda_\tau \geq k+1$. *(2)* $\lambda_1 \geq 2k-1$.

A type of transformations is called *singular* if a transformation g of that type is defined as $g(B_1, \ldots, B_i, \ldots, B_k) = (C_1, \ldots, C_{j-1}, C_j, C_{j+1}, \ldots, C_k)$, where $C_j = B_i$ and neither $(C_1, \ldots, C_{j-1})$ nor $(C_{j+1}, \ldots, C_k)$ depends on B_i. For example, Type-1 transformations are singular, but Type-2 and Type-3 ones are non-singular.

[Theorem A3] *Let Q be a polynomial in n and C_{kn} be an oracle circuit with $Q(n) < 2^n$ oracle gates. Let $\psi_\tau(h_s, \ldots, h_2, h_1)$ be a permutation consisting of s rounds of singular Type-τ transformations, where $h_s, \ldots, h_2, h_1$ are independent random function tuples. Then (1) when $s \leq k+1$, $\psi_\tau(h_s, \ldots, h_2, h_1)$ is insecure, and (2) when $s = 2k-1$, $|Pr\{C_{kn}[r] = 1\} - Pr\{C_{kn}[\psi_\tau(h_s, \ldots, h_2, h_1)] = 1\}| \leq \frac{(k-1)^2 Q(n)^2}{2^n}$, where $r \in_R H_{kn}$.*

[Theorem A4] *Let Q be a polynomial in n and C_{kn} be an oracle circuit with $Q(n) < 2^n$ oracle gates, and let $\psi_\tau(h_s, \ldots, h_2, h_1)$ be a permutation consisting of s rounds of non-singular Type-τ transformations, where $h_s, \ldots, h_2, h_1$ are independent random function tuples. Then when $s = k+1$, $|Pr\{C_{kn}[r] = 1\} - Pr\{C_{kn}[\psi_\tau(h_s, \ldots, h_2, h_1)] = 1\}| \leq \frac{k(k-1)Q(n)^2}{2^{n+1}}$, where $r \in_R H_{kn}$.*

Now we consider Generalized Type-τ transformations $g_{\tau,i}^{(\rho)} = \mathrm{L}_{rot}^{(\rho)} \circ \pi_{\tau,i}$. Let $\psi_\tau^{(\rho)}(h_s, \ldots, h_2, h_1)$ be a permutation in H_{kn} consisting of s rounds of Generalized Type-τ transformations. Denote by $\lambda_\tau^{(\rho)}$ the minimum number s at which $\psi_\tau^{(\rho)}(h_s, \ldots, h_2, h_1)$ is secure, where h_i are independent random function tuples. In particular, $\lambda_\tau^{(\rho)}$ is defined to be $+\infty$ if $\psi_\tau^{(\rho)}(h_s, \ldots, h_2, h_1)$ is insecure no matter how large s is. We have the following theorem which is easy to prove.

[Theorem A5] *(1)* $\lambda_\tau^{(\rho)} \geq \lambda_\tau \geq k+1$. *(2)* $\lambda_2^{(\rho)} = \lambda_2$ *when ρ is an odd integer in* $[1, k]$, *and* $\lambda_2^{(\rho)} = +\infty$ *when ρ is an even integer in* $[1, k]$.

Appendix B — Optimal Transformations

The computing procedures for Generalized Type-τ transformations $g_{\tau,i}^{(\rho)}$, and hence for $\psi_\tau^{(\rho)}(h_s, \ldots, h_2, h_1)$, can be represented by acyclic *computation graphs*. There are three kinds of nodes in a computation graph: input nodes, output nodes and internal nodes. Each internal node in a computation graph represents a generic operation: computing a function $f_{i,j}$ or XORing two strings.

The length of a path between two nodes is defined as the number of arcs in the path. Now assume that the length of the longest path(s) from input nodes to output nodes in a computation graph is L. Then the *depth* of the graph is defined to be $L-1$. The *normal-delay* $D^+(\rho, \tau, s)$ of a permutation $\psi_\tau^{(\rho)}(h_s, \ldots, h_2, h_1) \in H_{kn}$ is defined as the depth of the computation graph for the permutation, the *inverse-delay* $D^-(\rho, \tau, s)$ is defined as that for the inverse of the permutation, and the *sum-delay* $D(\rho, \tau, s)$ is defined as $D(\rho, \tau, s) = D^+(\rho, \tau, s) + D^-(\rho, \tau, s)$.

Clearly, $D^+(\rho, \tau, s) = 2s$, and $D^-(\rho, \tau, s) \geq D^+(\rho, \tau, s) \geq 2s$. Thus $D(\rho, \tau, s) = D^+(\rho, \tau, s) + D^-(\rho, \tau, s) \geq 2D^+(\rho, \tau, s) \geq 4s$.

Recall that $\lambda_\tau^{(\rho)}$ denotes the minimum number of rounds s at which $\psi_\tau^{(\rho)}(h_s, \ldots, h_2, h_1)$ is secure. From Theorem A5, we have $\lambda_\tau^{(\rho)} \geq k + 1$. Hence, $D(\rho, \tau, \lambda_\tau^{(\rho)}) \geq 4(k + 1)$.

Call a Generalized Type-τ transformation *optimal* if $D(\rho, \tau, \lambda_\tau^{(\rho)}) = 4(k + 1)$.

Now we discuss the optimality of transformations. First we have two facts: (1) When $g_{\tau,i}^{(\rho)} = L_{rot}^{(\rho)} \circ \pi_{\tau,i}^{(\rho)}$ with $\pi_{\tau,i}^{(\rho)}$ being not an involution, we have $D^-(\rho, \tau, s) > 2s$. So, transformations like Type-3 cannot be optimal. (2) When $\pi_{\tau,i}^{(\rho)}$ is an involution but $g_{\tau,i}^{(\rho)}$ is singular, we have $\lambda_\tau^{(\rho)} > k + 1$, and hence $D(\rho, \tau, \lambda_\tau^{(\rho)}) > 4(k + 1)$. So transformations like Type-1 cannot be optimal.

Consider the following two cases: odd k and even k. In the former case, either $g_{\tau,i}^{(\rho)} = L_{rot}^{(\rho)} \circ \pi_{\tau,i}^{(\rho)}$ is singular or $\pi_{\tau,i}^{(\rho)}$ is not an involution. Thus by the above two facts, no optimal transformation can be obtained. In the latter case, it is not hard to verify that the only non-singular transformations $g_{\tau,i}^{(\rho)} = L_{rot}^{(\rho)} \circ \pi_{\tau,i}^{(\rho)}$ with $\pi_{\tau,i}^{(\rho)}$ being involutions are Generalized Type-2 ones with ρ odd. For such transformations we have $D(\rho, 2, \lambda_2^{(\rho)}) = 4(k + 1)$. Thus we have proved:

[**Theorem B1**] *Among all types of transformations discussed in this paper, Generalized Type-2 transformations $g_{2,i}^{(\rho)} = L_{rot}^{(\rho)} \circ \pi_{2,i}^{(\rho)}$ with even k and odd ρ, are the only optimal ones.*

Appendix C — Super-Security

Luby and Rackoff introduced also the notion of *super-secure pseudorandom permutation generators* in [LR]. Intuitively, a pseudorandom permutation generator is super-secure if no super-oracle circuit can tell a permutation randomly specified by the generator from a randomly and uniformly chosen one. A *super-oracle circuit* is an oracle circuit with two kinds of oracle gates. The first is called the *normal* oracle gates which are evaluated using some permutation, and the second the *inverse* oracle gates which are evaluated using the inverse of the permutation.

When a secure pseudorandom permutation generator is used to construct a block cipher, the cipher is secure against the chosen plaintext attack, but not necessarily secure against the chosen plaintext/ciphertext attack. When a super-secure pseudorandom permutation generator is used to construct a block cipher, the cipher is secure against the chosen plaintext/ciphertext attack [LR].

Luby and Rackoff showed that functions consisting of 4 rounds of FTT's are super-secure. We can generalize their result to the following one.

[**Theorem C1**] *Let $k = 2\ell$, where $\ell \in \mathcal{N}$, and let ρ be an odd integer in $[1, k]$. Assume that $\psi_2^{(\rho)}(h_s, \ldots, h_2, h_1)$ consists of s rounds of Generalized Type-2 transformations, where $h_i = (f_{i,1}, f_{i,3}, \ldots, f_{i,k-1})$ with $f_{i,j} \in_R H_n$. Then $\psi_2^{(\rho)}(h_s, \ldots, h_2, h_1)$ is super-secure iff $s \geq k + 2$.*

478

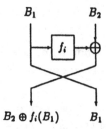

Figure 1: Feistel-Type Transformation (FTT)

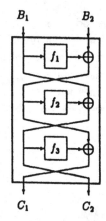

Figure 2: Feistel-Type Transformation (FTT) Lemma

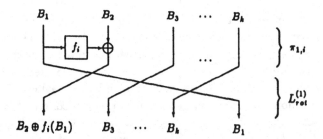

Figure 3: Type-1 Transformation

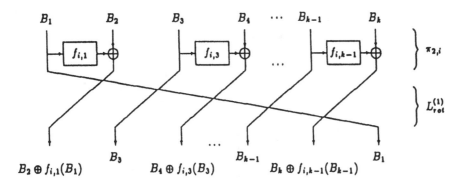

Figure 4: Type-2 Transformation

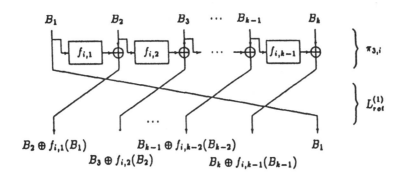

Figure 5: Type-3 Transformation

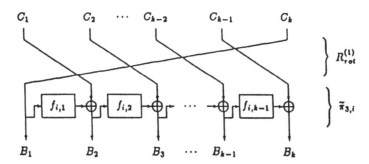

Figure 6: Inverse of Type-3 Transformation

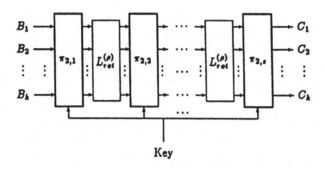

Figure 7: Enciphering Algorithm for PSBC

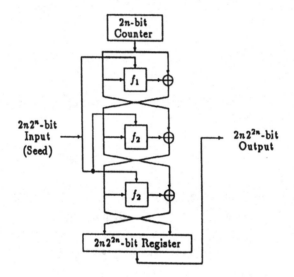

Figure 8: Algorithm G_n for Computing S_{2n2^n}

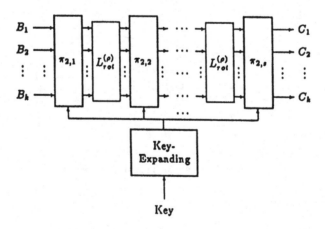

Figure 9: Enciphering Algorithm for PSBC with Key-Expanding

Disposable Zero-Knowledge Authentications and Their Applications to Untraceable Electronic Cash

Tatsuaki Okamoto   *Kazuo Ohta*

NTT Communications and Information Processing Laboratories
Nippon Telegraph and Telephone Corporation
1-2356, Take, Yokosuka-shi, Kanagawa-ken, 238-03, Japan

Abstract

In this paper, we propose a new type of authentication system, *disposable zero-knowledge authentication system*. Informally speaking, in this authentication system, double usage of the same authentication is prevented. Based on these disposable zero-knowledge authentication systems, we propose a new *untraceable electronic cash* scheme satisfying both *untraceability* and *unreusablity*. This scheme overcomes the problems of the previous scheme proposed by Chaum, Fiat and Naor through its greater efficiency and provable security under reasonable cryptographic assumptions. We also propose a scheme, *transferable untraceable electronic cash* scheme, satisfying *transferability* as well as the above two criteria, whose properties have not been previously proposed in any other scheme. Moreover, we also propose a new type of electronic cash, *untraceable electronic coupon ticket*, in which the value of one piece of the electronic cash can be subdivided into many pieces.

1. Introduction

"Zero-knowledge proofs" are useful for many application areas [B, BC, BCC, Cr, GMR, etc.]. A typical application area is authentication systems such as identifications and digital signatures [FFS, FS, GQ, MS, OhO]. For zero-knowledge proofs, coin flips of the prover are essential for zero-knowledgeness of the proof, while coin flips of the verifier are essential for the ability of the proof. Therefore, if the coin flips of the prover are restricted, the usage of the proof must be restricted under the zero-knowledge condition.

In this paper, by using this property of zero-knowledge proofs, we propose a new type of zero-knowledge authentication, *disposable zero-knowledge authentication*. Informally speaking, in this authentication double usage of the same authentication is prevented. This type of zero-knowledge authentication is considered to have many applications such as electronic cash, checks, and tickets, because in these applications a piece of information has value itself, and multiple invalid usage of this piece of information must be prevented.

To endow electronic cash with properties similar to those of real cash, electronic cash should satisfy the following conditions:

(1) *Untraceability*: The privacy of the user should be protected. That is, the relationship between the user and his purchases should be untraceable by anyone. Ideally, any partial information about the user's purchases should be untraceable by anyone (we call this property *perfect* untraceability).

(2) *Unreusability*: The ability to use the electronic cash more than once should be prevented.

(3) *Transferability*: The electronic cash can be transfered to other users.

Criterion (1) can be satisfied by using blind signatures [Ch, D, OkO]. To satisfy criteria (1) and (2), Chaum, Fiat and Naor [CFN] have developed an elegant electronic cash scheme (*untraceable electronic cash*) based on the cut-and-choose methodology and collision free functions. However, their scheme has two major problems from the viewpoint of efficiency and formal provability of security:

- (Efficiency) In their scheme, a customer must undergo a complex procedure including the cut-and-choose methodology to obtain each electronic coin.
- (Provability of security) The assumptions under which the scheme is provably secure are not clear.

Although the scheme [CFN] satisfies the first two criteria, so far no scheme has been proposed that satisfies all three criteria: (1) untraceability, (2) unreusability, and (3) *transferability*.

In this paper, we propose a new untraceable electronic cash scheme that satisfies the criteria (1) and (2) based on disposable zero-knowledge authentications as well as the cut-and-choose methodology. This scheme overcomes the problems of the previous scheme [CFN] in the following ways:

- (Efficiency) In our scheme, a customer undergoes a complex procedure including the cut-and-choose methodology *only once* when he opens his account at a bank. After that, only a minimal procedure is required to obtain each electronic coin. In this case, however, our scheme does not satisfy *perfect* untraceability, although it satisfies untraceability. That is, the relationship between a user and his purchases cannot be traced by anyone, but a purchase history of an anonymous user can be traced.

Note that, in our scheme, we can choose the degree of efficiency and the degree of untraceability, and they have a trade-off. If we choose the degree of untraceability as maximal (or perfect untraceability), the degree of efficiency is minimal (or comparable to that of the previous scheme [CFN]).

- (Provability of security) Our scheme is proven to be secure under the following assumptions:
  (i) (*Digital signature assumption*) There exists a secure digital signature scheme [GoMiRi] and secure multiple blind digital signature scheme. (If a secure multiple blind digital signature scheme exists, a secure digital signature scheme exits.)
  (ii) (*RSA assumption*) The RSA scheme is secure, and to break the RSA scheme in which the plaintext's redundancy is 0 is as hard to break as the RSA scheme in which the plaintext's redundancy is less than 1/2. (If the latter condition holds, the former condition holds.)

In this paper, we show a typical case where we construct our scheme based on the extended Fiat-Shamir scheme [GQ, OhO]. Note, however, that our scheme can be constructed based on other disposable zero-knowledge authentications with a unique solution S for I such that $(I, S) \in R$ (e.g., discrete logarithm problem).

In this case, the second assumption for the scheme's security is replaced by the following one (The first assumption is the same as above) :

> (ii) (*Invulnerable relation assumption*) A relation R is *invulnerable* (it is hard to compute S from I, where $(I, S) \in R$). And, to compute S from I in which S's redundancy is 0 is as hard to compute as S from I in which S's redundancy is less than $1/2$.

Next, we propose a new electronic cash scheme, *transferable untraceable electronic cash* scheme that, to our knowledge, has never been proposed, that satisfies criteria (1), (2) and (3). This scheme is constructed based on the above untraceable electronic cash scheme.

Moreover, we also propose another type of electronic cash (*untraceable electronic coupon ticket*) with the following property: The value of one piece of electronic cash can be subdivided into many pieces. For example, a user with a piece of electronic cash worth \$100 could subdivide it into 100 pieces of cash worth \$1. If we add the notion of transferability (criterion (3)), *transferable* untraceable electronic coupon ticket could be constructed in a way similar to the transferable untraceable electronic cash.

2. Notations

(P, V) is an interactive pair of Turing machines, where P is the prover, and V is the verifier [GMR, TM]. Let $T \in \{P, V\}$. $T(s)$ denotes T begun with s on its input work tape. $(P, V)(I)$ refers to the probability space that assigns to the string σ the probability that (P, V), on input I, outputs σ.

$(P(s), \underline{V(t)})(I)$, V's history, denotes (I, t, ρ', m'), where ρ' is the finite prefix of V's random tape that was read, and m' is the final content of the communication channel tape on which P writes. P^A means P with oracle A, where P^A's oracle tapes correspond to P's communucation channel tapes with A. $R \subseteq X \times Y$ is a relation, where X and Y are sets of finite strings. $\|$ denotes concatenation.

3. Disposable Zero Knowledge Authentication

There are two types of interactive proofs. One is the interactive proof *for membership in language L*, in which a membership of an instance in language L is demonstrated [GMR]. The other is the interactive proof *for possession of knowledge*, in which a prover's possession of information is demonstrated [FFS, TW]. In the latter proof, the prover's power is bounded in polynomial time, while, in the former proof, its power is not bounded.

In this section, first, we show the *revealability* of the zero-knowledge interactive proofs for possession of knowledge. Then, we define the *disposable zero-knowledge authentication* and show an implementation of this authentication.

Definition 1. Let R be a relation, and (P, V) be a zero-knowledge interactive proof for possession of some S satisfying $(I, S) \in R$. We say that (P, V) is *k-revealable* if there exists a polynomial-time probabilistic Turing machine M_V (with complete control over V) that computes S' such that $(I, S') \in R$ after k executions of the proof fixing the coin flips ρ of P with overwhelming probability, where ρ corresponds to one execution of the proof. (When $k = O(|I|^c)$ and c is a constant, k-revealable is called *poly-revealable*.)

Lemma 1.   Every zero-knowledge interactive proof for possession of knowledge is poly-revealable.

Proof Sketch: From the definition of the soundness of the zero-knowledge interactive proof for possession of knowledge [FFS], the existence of M_V can be shown.   **QED**

Lemma 2.   If there exist secure encryption schemes, any NP relation has a 2-revealable zero-knowledge interactive proof for possession of knowledge.

Proof Sketch: Under the assumption that NP reductions are one-to-one and efficiently invertible, it suffices to prove that Blum's zero-knowledge interactive proof for possession of knowledge of the graph Hamiltonicity ([FFS]'s Theorem 1.) is 2-revealable. The iterated number of rounds of this proof is $|I|$ (one round means steps 1-7 of [FFS]'s Theorem 1.). Suppose that Blum's proof (P, V) is executed twice fixing the coin flips ρ of P. Let ρ'_i $(i = 1, 2)$ be the verifier's coin flip in the i-th execution of the proof, where $|\rho'_i| = |I|$. If $\rho'_1 \neq \rho'_2$, a Hamiltonian cycle S can be computed in polynomial-time from the history of the two executions of this proof. The probablity that $\rho'_1 \neq \rho'_2$ is $1 - 1/2^{|I|}$.   **QED**

Definition 2.   Let A be the authority, P_i be a prover with a secret knowledge S such that $(I, S) \in R$, and V_i be a verifier with public knowledge I and R. Each party follows the below authentication procedure:

(Step 1) Prover P_i sends a message X to authority A.

(Step 2) A generates a digital signature C of X and sends it to P_i. (C, X) means A's permission to P_i's authentication. One permission corresponds to one execution of the prover's authentication procedure.

(Step 3) P_i shows A's permission (C, X) and proves his possession of S to a verifier V_i. V_i accepts P_i to be valid if he verifies the validity of both (C, X) and his proof of possession of S.

Let $\overline{P}_i$ and $\overline{V}_i$ be valid prover and verifier that follow their designated protocols, respectively. Let $\widetilde{P}_i$ and $\widetilde{V}_i$ be invalid polynomial-time prover and verifier that can deviate from their correct protocols in arbitrary ways, respectively. Let P_i be either $\overline{P}_i$ or $\widetilde{P}_i$, and V_i be either $\overline{V}_i$ or $\widetilde{V}_i$.

Let $(A, \{P_i, V_i\})$ $(i = 1, 2, \ldots)$ be an *authentication system*, if the following two conditions are satisfied.

- *Completeness*: $\overline{P}_i(S)$'s authentication is accepted to be valid by $\overline{V}_i$ with overwhelming probability.

- *Soundness*: There exists a polynomial-time probabilistic Turing machine M_{P_i} (with complete control over P_i) such that if P_i's authentication is accepted to be valid by $\overline{V}_i$ with non-negligible probability, then M_{P_i} breaks cryptographic assumptions on A's digital signatures with overwhelming probability and the output produced by M_{P_i} on input I satisfies the relation R with overwhelming probability.

Note: Informally, soundness means that invalid prover $\widetilde{P}_i$ is accepted by $\overline{V}_i$ with negligible probability.

Definition 3. Authentication system $(A, \{P_i, V_i\})$ is *disposable zero-knowledge* if the following conditions are satisfied.

- *Zero-knowledgeness*: For any V_i, I, and t, there exists a polynomial-time probabilistic Turing machine $M_{V_i}^A$ such that $((C, X), (\overline{P}_i(S), \underline{V_i(t)})(I))$ and $M_{V_i}^A(I, t)$ are polynomially indistinguishable.

- *Disposability*: There exists a polynomial-time probabilistic Turing machine $M_{\overline{V}_i, \overline{V}_j}$ (with complete control over $\overline{V}_i$ and $\overline{V}_j$) such that if $\overline{P}_i$'s authentication is executed successfully twice with the same (C, X) to $\overline{V}_i$ and $\overline{V}_j$ respectively, then the output produced by $M_{\overline{V}_i, \overline{V}_j}$ on input I satisfies the relation R with overwhelming probability.

Note: Informally, zero-knowledgeness means that when valid prover $\overline{P}_i$'s authentication is executed once with the same (C, X), then any knowledge about secret information S cannot be revealed by anyone. Disposability means that valid prover $\overline{P}_i$'s authentication is executed twice with the same (C, X), then secret information S can be revealed by the coalition of the authority and valid verifiers.

Theorem 1. If there exist secure encryption schemes [GM] and secure digital signature schemes [GoMiRi], then a disposable zero-knowledge authentication system can be constructed using any NP relation.

Proof Sketch: Under the assumption that NP reductions are one-to-one and efficiently invertible, it suffices to prove that a disposable zero-knowledge authentication system can be constructed using Blum's zero-knowledge interactive proof for graph Hamiltonicity.

Construction:

The public input I is a graph, and S such that $(I, S) \in R$ is a Hamiltonian cycle in I. H is a probabilistic encryption [GM, Y].

(Step 1) P_i randomly permutes the vertices of graph I (using permutation π_k, $k = 1, 2, \ldots, |I|$) to obtain

- Graph $\widehat{I}_k$,
- An $|I| \times |I|$ matrix $\alpha_k = \{\alpha_{kst} \mid s, t = 1, 2, \ldots, |I|\}$, where $\alpha_{kst} = H(v_{kst})$, and $v_{kst} = 1$ if edge st is present in the $\widehat{I}_k$, and 0 otherwise, and
- $\beta_k = H(\pi_k)$.

P_i sends $X = (\alpha_1, \ldots, \alpha_{|I|}, \beta_1, \ldots, \beta_{|I|})$ to authority A.

(Step 2) A generates a digital signature $\{C_k\}$ of $\{(\alpha_k, \beta_k)\}$ $(k = 1, 2, \ldots, |I|)$ and sends them to P_i.

(Step 3-1) $k \leftarrow 1$.

(Step 3-2) P_i sends (α_k, β_k) and C_k to V_i.

(Step 3-3) V_i verifies the validity of the digital signature of C_k. If it is invalid, V_i rejects. Otherwise, V_i chooses at random $\rho_k' \in \{0, 1\}$, and sends ρ_k' to P_i.

(Step 3-4) If $\rho_k' = 1$, P_i sets $\delta_k = ($ decryptions of α_{kst} and $\beta_k)$. Otherwise, $\delta_k = \{$decryption of $\alpha_{kst} \mid$ edge st is in a Hamiltonian path in $\widehat{I}_k\}$. P_i sends δ_k to V_i.

(Step 3-5) If P_i is unable to perform steps 3-4 correctly, V_i rejects. Otherwise, $k \leftarrow k + 1$ and go to step 3-2, if $k < |I|$. If $k = |I|$, V_i accepts.

Completeness: A valid prover can be accepted by a verifier with probability 1.

Soundness: If P_i's authentication is accepted to be valid by $\overline{V}_i$ with non-negligible probability, then P_i can generate A's digital signature for non-negligible fraction of the message space. Therefore, from the assumption of the existence of secure digital signature, there exists a polynomial-time probabilistic Turing machine M_{P_i} (with complete control over P_i) such that M_{P_i} breaks cryptographic assumptions of A's digital signature with overwhelming probability. On the other hand, if P_i's authentication is accepted to be valid by $\overline{V}_i$ with non-negligible probability, then, from the soundness of Blum's protocol, M_{P_i} on input I outputs S' such that $(I, S') \in R$ with overwhelming probability.

Zero-knowledgeness: In a manner similar to the proof of the zero-knowledgeness of Blum's protocol, it can be proven that $((C, X), (P_i(S), \underline{V_i(t)})(I))$ and $M_{V_i}^A(I, t)$ are polynomially indistinguishable.

Disposability: From Lemma 2., we can show that there exists a polynomial-time probabilistic Turing machine M_{V_i} that produces S' satisfying $(I, S') \in R$ with overwhelming probability. **QED**

An application to traceable electronic cash: Here, we show a straightforward application example of the disposable zero-knowledge authentication to traceable electronic cash sytems. Let authority A be a bank, prover P_i be a customer, and verifier V_i be a shop. The authority's permission (C, X) corresponds to an electronic coin worth $100 that the bank issues to the customer when he withdraws $100 from his account. When P_i purchases an article for $100 from shop V_i, he makes the disposable zero-knowledge authentication regarding (C, X) to the shop. The shop sends the history of this authentication with (C, X) to the bank to obtain $100 from the bank. If the customer uses (C, X) more than once, the bank will reveal S' satisfying $(I, S') \in R$, and withdraw more than the $100 from his account to penalize the customer. Otherwise, S' is never revealed by anyone. Here, S' witnesses the customer's abuse of the electronic cash, and we assume that the bank and the customer have signed a contract such that the customer must pay a penalty to the bank when the bank reveals S' satisfying $(I, S') \in R$. In other words, we can consider this situation as a game between the bank and the customer. In this game, the customer loses and pay some money to the bank when the bank reveals S' satisfying $(I, S') \in R$, where I is determined by the customer.

Discussion: The above-mentioned example is an application to a *traceable* electronic cash system, in which the customer's purchase history is traceable. Although the above-mentioned example is very simple and efficient, we can easily construct other implementations with almost the same functions by using digital signatures of the customer without using disposable zero-knowledge authentication.

In contrast to this application, a number of distinct advantages can be realized by applying disposable zero-knowledge authentication to *untraceable* electronic cash and tickets systems. We will describe these applications in some detail in sections 4, 5 and 6.

4. Untraceable Electronic Cash

In this section, we show an untraceable electronic cash scheme satisfying two criteria, *Untraceability* and *Unreusability*, based on disposable zero-knowledge authentications. This scheme has advantages over the previously proposed scheme [CFN] in the standpoints of efficiency and provability of its security, as described in Section 1. This scheme can be constructed based on some disposable zero-knowledge authentications with a unique solution S for I such that $(I, S) \in R$. In this section, however, we show a typical case based on the extended Fiat-Shamir scheme [GQ, OhO].

Before describing the untraceable electronic cash protocol, we will introduce a specific type of blind digital signature, *multiple* blind digital signature.

Definition 4. Let A, P, and e_A be a signer, requester, and the signer's public key, respectively. Let F be an algorithm for P, D be an algorithm for A, and $G_{e_A}(m_1, \ldots, m_k)$ be A's multiple digital signature of k messages, $m_1, \ldots, m_k$. Let (A, P, F, D, G) be a *multiple blind digital signature* system, if A and P follow the below procedure:

(Step 1) P generates k blind messages $\{F_{e_A}(m_i) \mid i = 1, 2, \ldots, k\}$ from k messages $\{m_i \mid i = 1, 2, \ldots, k\}$, and sends them to A. Here, each $F_{e_A}(m_i)$ is independently blinded.

(Step 2) A generates the multiple blind digital signature $D_{e_A}(F_{e_A}(m_1), \ldots, F_{e_A}(m_k))$ from the k blind messages, $F_{e_A}(m_1), \ldots, F_{e_A}(m_k)$, and sends it to P.

(Step 3) P extracts A's multiple digital signature $G_{e_A}(m_1, \ldots, m_k)$ of $m_1, \ldots, m_k$.

(A, P, F, D, G) is a *secure* multiple blind digital signature system, if (A, P, F, D, G) satisfies the criteria for blind digital signature [Ch, OkO] and P can generate $G_{e_A}(m_1, \ldots, m_k)$ from $D_{e_A}(m_1^{(1)}, \ldots, m_1^{(1)}), \ldots, D_{e_A}(m_1^{(l)}, \ldots, m_t^{(l)})$ with negligible probability, where k, t, l are positive integers, and for any subset $\{i_1, \ldots, i_j\} \subset \{1, \ldots, l\}$, $\{m_1, \ldots, m_k\} \neq \{m_1^{(i_1)}, \ldots, m_t^{(i_1)}, \ldots, m_1^{(i_j)}, \ldots, m_t^{(i_j)}\}$, and every m_i's and $m_i^{(j)}$'s are in a randomly determined negligible fraction $\mathcal{M}$ of the message space (e.g., $\mathcal{M} = \{m \mid |m|/c$-prefix of m is a (randomly) fixed sequence, where c is a constant $\})$.

Note: The secure multiple blind digital signature schemes seem to be implemented based on the previously proposed blind digital signature schemes [Ch, OkO]. Note that the multiple blind digital signature scheme contains the previous (single) blind digital signature scheme as a special case where $k = 1$. In the electronic cash scheme [CNF], the multiple blind digital signature scheme based on [Ch] has been used. We can also construct a multiple blind digital signature scheme based on a divertible zero-knowledge proof for *endomorphic* CRSR relation [OkO]. Here, note that, in this scheme based on [OkO], A must send a pre-message to P. However, for simplicity in this paper, we omit this pre-message sending phase when describing the multiple blind digital signature.

Protocol 1. (Untraceable electronic cash) Bank A has a secure multiple blind digital signature generation algorithm D. A has published his public keys, e_A, e'_A, of this blind digital signature scheme, where e_A corresponds to the *electronic license* that A issues, and e'_A corresponds to the value of the *electronic coin* that A issues. The bank A also sets the security parameter $K = O(|n|)$. Customer P has a bank account number ID_P and a secure digital signature generation algorithm G, and publishes his public-key e_P of the digital signature scheme.

Part I.

When a customer P opens an account at bank A, A issues an electronic license B to use electronic cash of bank A. (Precisely, an electronic license is $(B, \{I_i, N_i, L_i\})$. For simplicity, however, we call B an electronic license.) To get B, P conducts the following protocol with A. This procedure is executed *only once* when P opens the account, unless P reuses the electronic cash invalidly.

(Step 1) Customer P chooses random values a_i, and composite numbers N_i with two large prime factors P_i, Q_i ($N_i = P_i \cdot Q_i$), for $i = 1, \ldots, K$. P also fixes prime integer L_i such that $\gcd(L_i, \phi(N_i)) = 1$, where $\phi(N_i) = \mathrm{lcm}(P_i - 1, Q_i - 1)$. For simplicity, we assume that all $|N_i| = O(|e_A|)(i = 1, \ldots, K)$ are equivalent, and that $L_i = O(1)$.

(Step 2) P forms and sends K blind candidates $W_i (i = 1, \ldots, K)$ to bank A.

$$W_i = F_{e_A}(I_i \parallel N_i \parallel L_i) \quad \text{for } 1 \leq i \leq K,$$

where

$$I_i = S_i^{L_i} \bmod N_i,$$

$$S_i = ID_P \parallel a_i \parallel G_{e_P}(ID_P \parallel a_i).$$

(Step 3) A chooses a random subset of $K/2$ blind candidates indices $U = \{i_j\}, 1 \leq i_j \leq K$ for $1 \leq j \leq K/2$ and transmit it to P.

(Step 4) P displays the $a_i, P_i, Q_i, L_i, G_{e_P}(ID_P \parallel a_i), ID_P$ for all i in U, and random values that make messages W_i blinded, then A checks them. If they are not valid, A halts this protocol.

To simplify notations, we will assume that $U = \{K/2 + 1, K/2 + 2, \ldots, K\}$.

(Step 5) A gives P

$$D_{e_A}(W_1, \ldots, W_{K/2}).$$

(Step 6) P can then extract the electronic license B.

$$B = G_{e_A}(I_1 \parallel N_1 \parallel L_1, \quad \ldots \quad , I_{K/2} \parallel N_{K/2} \parallel L_{K/2}).$$

Notes:

(1) Every L_i's for every customers can be replaced by a unique prime integer L determined by the system (or a bank). Note that in this case P must select N_i such that $\gcd(L, \phi(N_i)) = 1$.

(2) For example, when we use the RSA multiple blind digital signature scheme [Ch, CFN], $B = \prod_{1 \le i \le K/2} g(I_i \parallel N_i \parallel L_i)^{1/e} \bmod n$, where (e, n) is A's RSA public key, and g is an appropriate one-way hash function.

Part II.

When customer P wants bank A to issue an electronic coin worth one dollar C which corresponds to e'_A, P conducts the following protocol with A (Precisely, an electronic coin is $(C, \{X_i\})$. For simplicity, however, we call C an electronic coin.):
(Step 1) P chooses random values R_i $(i = 1, \ldots, K/2)$, and forms and sends Z to A.

$$Z = F_{e'_A}(X_1 \parallel \ldots \parallel X_{K/2} \parallel B),$$

$$X_i = R_i^{L_i} \bmod N_i \quad \text{for } 1 \le i \le K/2.$$

(Step 2) A gives $D_{e'_A}(Z)$ to P and charges P's account one dollar.
(Step 3) P can then extract the electronic coin $C = G_{e'_A}(X_1 \parallel \ldots \parallel X_{K/2} \parallel B)$.

Note: We can reduce the amount of information that P posseses as follows:
In place of possessing $K/2$ pieces of information, $\{X_i \mid 1 \le i \le K/2\}$, P possesses only one piece of infromation X. In Part II, P obtains $C = G_{e'_A}(X \parallel B)$. In Part III, we regard X as X_i for all $1 \le i \le K/2$, and P computes $R_i = X^{1/L_i} \bmod N_i$ for $1 \le i \le K/2$.

Part III.

To pay a shop V one dollar, P and V proceed as follows:
For each $i = 1, 2, \ldots, K/2$, steps 1-4 are executed iteratively.

(Step 1) P sends I_i, N_i, L_i, X_i to V. When $i = K/2$, P also sends B and C to V.
(Step 2) V selects a random value $E_i \in Z_{L_i}$, and sends it to P. When $i = K/2$, V verifies the validity of the signatures B for $\{(I_i, N_i, L_i)\}$, and C for $(X_1, \ldots, X_{K/2}, B)$. If B and C are valid, V selects a random value $E_{K/2} \in Z_{L_{K/2}}$, and sends it to P. Otherwise V halts this protocol.
(Step 3) P computes $Y_i = R_i \cdot S_i^{E_i} \bmod N_i$ and sends it to V.
(Step 4) V verifies that $Y_i^{L_i} \equiv X_i \cdot I_i^{E_i} \pmod{N_i}$.

If P passes this protocol successfully for all $i = 1, 2, \ldots, K/2$, then V accepts the electronic coin C as one dollar.

Notes:

(1) This protocol can be modified in a manner similar to the parallel version of the extended Fiat-Shamir scheme.
(2) To prevent bank A from crediting an invalid shop's account in Part IV, in steps 2 and 3, we can enhance the protocol as follows:
   In step 2, V selects a random value d_i, and sends V's identity ID_V, time T, and d_i to P in place of sending E_i. V computes $E_i = f(ID_V \parallel T \parallel d_i)$, where f is a one-way function whose output is uniformly random. In step 3, P also computes E_i.

Part IV.

For bank A to credit V's account by one dollar, V sends the history of Part III of this protocol, H, to A, which credits V's account after verifying whether H is a correct history of Part III and whether H has not been stored already in A's database. If H is valid, bank A must store H in its database.

(End of Protocol 1)

In the rest of this paper, we adopt the following notations:

(1) $\overline{C}$ represents valid cash which is correctly issued by valid bank A through its designated protocol. $\overline{P}$ represents a valid customer with $\overline{C}$.

(2) $\widetilde{C}$ represents invalid cash generated through an arbitrary polynomial-time algorithm of an invalid customer $\widetilde{P}$.

(3) C represents either $\overline{C}$ or $\widetilde{C}$. P represents either $\overline{P}$ or $\widetilde{P}$.

(4) $\overline{H}$ represents the valid history of the protocol between a valid customer $\overline{P}$ and a valid shop $\overline{V}$.

(5) $\widetilde{H}$ represents an invalid history generated through an arbitrary polynomial-time algorithm of an invalid shop $\widetilde{V}$.

(6) H represents either $\overline{H}$ or $\widetilde{H}$. V represents either $\overline{V}$ or $\widetilde{V}$.

Definition 5. The untraceable electronic cash system (Protocol 1) is *secure* if the following conditions are satisfied:

- *Completeness*: Any valid cash $\overline{C}$ is accepted as valid by any shop $\overline{V}$ through part III of Protocol 1. Any valid history $\overline{H}$ is accepted as valid by bank $\overline{A}$.

- *Soundness*: Any invalid cash $\widetilde{C}$ is accepted by any shop $\overline{V}$ through part III of Protocol 1 with negligible probability. Any invalid history $\widetilde{H}$ is accepted by bank $\overline{A}$ with negligible probability.

- *Untraceability*: For any V, I_i, N_i, L_i, and t, there exists a polynomial-time probabilistic Turing machine M_V such that $(C, \{X_i\}, B), (\overline{P}(\{S_i\}), \underline{V(t)})(\{I_i, N_i, L_i\}))$ and $M_V^A(\{I_i, N_i, L_i\}, t)$ are polynomially indistinguishable.

- *Unreusability*: There exists a polynomial-time probabilistic Turing machine $M_{\overline{V}_1, \overline{V}_2}$ (with complete control over $\overline{V}_1$ and $\overline{V}_2$) such that if $\overline{P}$'s coin $\overline{C}$ is used twice through part III of Protocol 1 to $\overline{V}_1$ and $\overline{V}_2$ respectively, then $M_{\overline{V}_1, \overline{V}_2}$, on input these histories $\overline{H}_1$ and $\overline{H}_2$, outputs at least one piece of information $S_i = ID_P \parallel a_i \parallel G_{e_P}(ID_P \parallel a_i)$ $(i \in \{1, \dots, K/s\})$ with overwhelming probability.

Note: Informally, untraceability means that when a valid coin $\overline{C}$ is used only once, the identity of the customer who uses $\overline{C}$ cannot be revealed by anyone. Unreusability means that when a valid coin $\overline{C}$ is used twice, bank A can obtain the identity of the customer who uses $\overline{C}$ with overwhelming probability.

Theorem 2. Protocol 1 is secure if the following two assumptions are satisfied:

(*Digital signature assumption*) There exist a secure digital signature scheme [GoMi Ri] and a secure multiple blind digital signature scheme.

(*RSA assumption*) The RSA scheme is secure. And, to break the RSA scheme in which the plaintext's redundancy is 0 is as hard to break as the RSA scheme in which the plaintext's redundancy is less than $1/2$, where S's redundancy is r if S is randomly selected from a source with the entropy of $(1-r)|S|$ bits. (Here, "as hard as" is defined from the viewpoint of usual "polynomial-time reduction.")

Proof Sketch:

Completeness: $\overline{C}$ and $\overline{H}$ are accepted with probability 1.

Soundness: First, we prove the following (the soundness can be directly reduced from the folowing result if the digital signature assumption and RSA assumption are satisfied, because a polynomial-time algorithm can be constructed to break these assumptions using M_p if $\widetilde{C}$ is accepted):

There exists a polynomial-time probabilistic Turing machine M_P (with complete control over P) such that if C is accepted to be valid by $\overline{V}$ through part III of Protocol 1 with non-negligible probability, then M_P breaks cryptographic assumption on A's digital signatures with the public key e'_A, and, for any positive constant $b < 1$, M_P, on input $\{I_i\}$ and b, outputs a subset $S \subset \{S_i\}$ such that $\#S/(K/2) > b$ with overwhelming probability, where $\#$ denotes the cardinality of a subset.

If C is accepted by $\overline{V}$ with non-negligible probability, then P can generate A's digital signature for non-negligible fraction of the message space. Therefore, from the definition of secure blind digital signature [GoMiRi], there exists a polynomial-time probabilistic Turing machine M_P such that M_P breaks cryptographic assumptions of A's blind digital signature with overwhelming probability. Next we show that when C is accepted by $\overline{V}$ with non-negligible probability, then, for any positive constant $b < 1$, M_P can output a subset $S \subset \{S_i\}$ such that $\#S/(K/2) > b$ with overwhelming probability. Let T be the truncated execution tree of $(P, \overline{V})$. T has $(K/2)$ levels, and each vertex in T has at most L_i $(=O(1))$ sons, because $\overline{V}$ may ask L_i possible questions at each stage. A vertex is called heavy if it has at least two sons. If we can find a heavy vertex of the i-th level, we can compute S_i, since L_i is prime. Then, for a positive constant $b < 1$, we assume that at least $(1-b)(K/2)$ levels have at least one non-heavy vertex. Then, the total number of leaves in T is at most a negligible $(O(2^{-K}))$ fraction of the possible leaves. Therefore, for any positive constant $b < 1$, more than $b(K/2)$ levels have all heavy vertices. Hence, we can find at least one heavy vertex in each level with all heavy vertices in polynomial-time by blind exploration of T, since a non-negligible fraction of the leaves is assumed to survive the truncation.

Finally, we can conclude the proof of soundness by showing in a similar manner that there exists a polynomial-time probabilistic Turing machine M_V (with complete control V) such that if history H is accepted to be valid by $\overline{A}$ through part IV of Protocol 1 with non-negligible probability, then M_V breaks cryptographic assumption on A's digital signatures with the public key e'_A.

Untraceability: In a manner similar to the proof of the zero-knowledgeness of the extended Fiat-Shamir scheme [OhO], it can be proven that there exists M_V such that $(C, \{X_i\}, B)$, $(\overline{P}(\{S_i\}), \underline{V(t)}(\{I_i, N_i, L_i\}))$ and $M_V^A(\{I_i, N_i, L_i\}, t)$ are polynomially indistinguishable.

Disposability: We show that when $\overline{C}$ is used twice, any S_i cannot be revealed with negligible probability. Let $\mathcal{E}=\{E_i \mid E_i$ selected by V_1 and E_i selected by V_2 are different in part III, $1 \leq i \leq K/2$ $\}$. Then, for any positive constant $b < 1$, $\#\mathcal{E} > b(K/2)$ with overwhelming probability. Since L_i is prime, we can calculate $I_i^{1/L_i} \bmod N_i$ for i whose E_i is in $\mathcal{E}$. Therefore, to make all S_i's be concealed from anyone, at least $b(K/2)$ blind candidates W_i must be invalid in part I, and all these invalid candidates must not be selected in U. Hence, all S_i's can be concealed from anyone with probability $2^{-b(K/2)}$ (or negligible probability). In other words, if $\overline{C}$ is used twice, at least one piece of information S_i can be revealed with overwhelming probability.   **QED**

5. Transferable Untraceable Electronic Cash

In this section, we propose an electronic cash scheme satisfying the criterion of *tranferability* in addition to untraceability and unreusability.

Protocol 2. (Transferable untraceable electronic cash)
This protocol is constructed based on Protocol 1. Therefore, undefined notations and procedures follow the definitions in Protocol 1. To simplify the description of this protocol, we suppose a case where bank A issues one dollar electronic coin C to customer P_1, who transfers C to customer P_2, and P_2 uses C at shop V.

Part I.
When customers P_1 and P_2 open their accounts at bank A, A issues electronic licenses $B^{(j)}$ to a customer P_j $(j = 1, 2)$. Hereafter, in this protocol, $x^{(j)}$ means x of P_j, where variable x follows the definition in Protocol 1.

Part II.
Suppose that customer P_1 have bank A issue an electronic coin worth one dollar C.

Part III.
To transfer C to another customer P_2, P_1 and P_2 proceeds as follows:
(Step 1) P_1 and P_2 follow the same protocol as that for P_1 to pay shop P_2 one dollar (Part III of Protocol 1).
(Step 2) P_1 sends a certification T that denotes the transfer of C from P_1 to P_2. For example, P_1 sends a digital signature $G_{(N_1^{(1)}, L_1^{(1)})}(C \parallel B^{(2)})$ (e.g., $T = g(C \parallel B^{(2)})^{1/L_1^{(1)}} \bmod N_1^{(1)}$).
P_2 generates

$$R_i^{(2)} = (X_i^{(1)})^{1/L_i^{(2)}} \bmod N_i^{(2)} \quad \text{for } 1 \leq i \leq K/2.$$

If P_2 accepts P_1's electronic coin C through step 1 and verifies the validity of T, then P_2 pays one dollar to P_1.

Part IV.
To pay shop V one dollar, P_2 and V proceeds as follows:
(Step 1) P_2 sends the history of Part III of this protocol, $H^{(1)}$, to V. V checks the validity of $H^{(1)}$.

(Step 2) P_2 follows Part III of Protocol 1 with shop V to pay C.

Part V.
To have bank A credit V's account by one dollar, V sends the history of Part IV of this protocol, $H^{(2)}$, to A, which credits V's account after verifying whether $H^{(2)}$ is a correct history of Part IV and whether $H^{(2)}$ has not been stored already in A's database. If $H^{(2)}$ is valid, bank A must store $H^{(2)}$ in its database.

(End of Protocol 2)

Note: Informally, Protocol 2 is secure if the following conditions are satisfied. The formal definition and proof regarding the security of Protocol 2 will be shown in the final paper.

- *Completeness*: Any (original/transferred) valid cash $\overline{C}$ of $\overline{P}_1$ and $\overline{P}_2$ is accepted to be valid by $\overline{P}_2$ and any shop V, respectively. Any valid history $\overline{H}^{(2)}$ is accepted to be valid by bank $\overline{A}$.
- *Soundness*: Any (transfered) invalid cash $\widetilde{C}$ is accepted by P_2 and any shop $\overline{V}$ with negligible probability. Any invalid history $\widetilde{H}^{(2)}$ is accepted by any bank with negligible probability.
- *Untraceability*: When a valid coin $\overline{C}$ is used only once, any knowledge about the identity of the customer who uses $\overline{C}$ cannot be revealed by anyone.
- *Unreusability*: When coin $\overline{C}$ is used twice correctly by a customer, bank $\overline{A}$ can obtain the identity of the customer with overwhelming probability. When coin $\overline{C}$ is used twice correctly by two different customers $\overline{P}_1$ and $\overline{P}_2$, bank $\overline{A}$ can obtain the identity of $\overline{P}_1$ with overwhelming probability.

6. Untraceable Electronic Coupon Tickets

In this section, we also propose another type of untraceable electronic cash (*untraceable electronic coupon ticket*) with the following property in addition to those of the untraceable electronic cash: The value of one piece of electronic cash can be subdivided into several pieces. For example, a user with a piece of electronic cash worth $100 could subdivide it into 100 pieces of cash worth $1. Here, the data size of 100 coupon tickets is comparable to one piece of electronic cash.

If we add the notion of transferability (criterion (3)), *transferable* untraceable electronic coupon ticket could be constructed in a way similar to the transferable untraceable electronic cash.

Protocol 3. (Untraceable electronic coupon ticket) This protocol is constructed based on Protocol 1. Therefore, undefined notations and procedures follow the definitions in Protocol 1.

Part I.
To obtain license B from bank A, customer P follows the same protocol with A as Part I of Protocol 1.

Part II.
To obtain a piece of information (electronic coupon tickets), C, which is 100 tickets

each worth \$1, customer P conducts the same protocol with bank A as Part II of Protocol 1. Here, the value of e' indicates the value and type of electronic coupon tickets C (e.g., 100 tickets each worth \$1).

Part III.

To pay shop V the j-th one dollar ticket $(1 \leq j \leq 100)$, P and V proceeds as follows:

First, P generates $X_i^{<j>} = f_j(X_i)$ and $R_i^{<j>} = (X_i^{<j>})^{1/L_i} \bmod N_i$. Here, $f_j(x)$ means a one-way function with a parameter j. For example, we can construct f_j by a one-way function f such that

$$f_j(x) = f(x \parallel j), \quad \text{or} \quad f_j(x) = f(x \parallel 1^j).$$

For each $i = 1, 2, \ldots, K/2$, steps 1-4 are executed iteratedly.
(Step 1) and (Step 2) are the same as those of Protocol 1.
(Step 3) and (Step 4) are the same as those of Protocol 1 except replacing X_i and R_i by $X_i^{<j>}$ and $R_i^{<j>}$, respectively. Here, P also sends j, and V checks that $1 \leq j \leq 100$ and generates $X_i^{<j>} = f_j(X_i)$.
If P passes this protocol successfully for all $i = 1, 2, \ldots, K/2$, then V accepts the j-th one dollar ticket of the \$100 electronic coupon tickets C.

Part IV.

For bank A to credit V's account by one dollar, V sends the history of Part III of this protocol, $H^{<j>}$, to A, which credits V's account after verifying whether $H^{<j>}$ is a correct history of Part III and whether $H^{<j>}$ has not been stored already in A's database. If $H^{<j>}$ is valid, bank A must store $H^{<j>}$ in its database.

$$\text{(End of Protocol 3)}$$

7. Conclusion

In this paper, we have proposed a new type of authenticatication, *disposable zero-knowledge authentication*, and described its applications to untraceable electronic cash schemes. To find other applications of the disposable zero-knowledge authentication remains further work. We improved the efficiency of our scheme by reducing the degree of untraceability. We will concentrate on improving the efficiency of these schemes with perfect untraceability in further work. In the proof of the security of these protocols, we have supposed some assumptions. To reduce these assumptions to even more fundamental assumptions remains an open challenge.

Acknowledgements: We would like to thank Eugène van Heyst for many valuable comments and suggestions on the earlier version. We would also like to thank anonymous referees for their helpful comments.

References

[B] J.C.Benaloh, "Cryptographic capsules: A disjunctive promitive for interactive protocols," The Proc. of Crypto'86, pp.213-222 (1986)

[BC] G.Brassard and C.Crépeau, "Non-Transitive Transfer of Confidence: A perfect Zero-Knowledge Interactive Protocol for SAT and Beyond," The Proc. of FOCS'86, pp.188-195 (1986)

[BCC] G.Brassard, D.Chaum, and C.Crépeau, "Minimum Disclosure Proofs of Knowledge," Journal of Computer and System Sciences, Vol.37, pp.156-189 (1988)

[Ch] D.Chaum, "Security without Identification: Transaction Systems to Make Big Brother Obsolete," Comm. of the ACM, 28, 10, pp.1030-1044 (1985)

[Cr] C.Crépeau, "A zero-knowledge poker protocol that achieves confidentiality of the players' strategy or How to achieve an electronic poker face," The Proc. of Crypto'86, pp.239-247 (1986)

[CFN] D.Chaum, A.Fiat and M. Naor, "Untraceable Electronic Cash," to appear in the Proc. of Crypto'88 (1988)

[D] I.B.Damgård, "Payment Systems and Credential Mechanisms with Provable Security Against Abuse by Individuals," to appear in the Proc. of Crypto'88 (1988)

[FFS] U.Feige, A.Fiat and A.Shamir, "Zero Knowledge Proofs of Identity," The Proc. of STOC, pp.210-217 (1987)

[FS] A.Fiat and A.Shamir, "How to Prove Yourself," The Proc. of Crypto'86, pp.186-199 (1986)

[GM] S.Goldwasser, and S.Micali, "Probabilistic Encryption," Journal of Computer and System Science, Vol.28, No.2 (1984)

[GMR] S.Goldwasser, S.Micali, and C.Rackoff, "Knowledge Complexity of Interactive Proofs," The Proc. of STOC, pp291-304 (1985)

[GoMiRi] S.Goldwasser, S.Micali, and R.Rivest, "A Digital Signature Scheme Secure Against Adaptive Chosen-Message Attacks," SIAM J.Compt., 17, 2, pp.281-308 (1988)

[GMW] O.Goldreich, S.Micali, and A.Wigderson, "Proofs that Yield Nothing But their Validity and a Methodology of Cryptographic Protocol Design," The Proc. of FOCS, pp.174-187 (1986)

[GQ] L.C.Guillou, and J.J.Quisquater, "A Practical Zero-Knowledge Protocol Fitted to Security Microprocessors Minimizing Both Transmission and Memory," The Proc. of Eurocrypto'88, pp.123-128 (1988)

[MS] S.Micali, and A.Shamir, "An Improvement of The Fiat-Shamir Identification and Signature Scheme," The Proc. of Crypto'88 (1988)

[OhO] K.Ohta, and T.Okamoto "A Modification of the Fiat-Shamir Scheme," to appear in the Proc. of Crypto'88 (1988)

[OkO] T.Okamoto, and K.Ohta "Divertible Zero-Knowledge Interactive Proofs and Commutative Random Self-Reducible," to appear in the Proc. of Eurocrypt'89 (1989)

[TW] M.Tompa and H.Woll, "Random Self-Reducibility and Zero Knowledge Interactive Proofs of Possession of Information," The Proc. of FOCS, pp472-482 (1987)

[Y] A.C. Yao: Theory and Applications of Trapdoor Functions, The Proc. of FOCS, pp.80-91 (1982)

Session 11:

Zero-knowledge and Oblivious transfer

Chair: CLAUDE CRÉPEAU

Efficient Identification Schemes
Using Two Prover Interactive Proofs

Michael Ben-Or
Hebrew University

Shafi Goldwasser*
MIT

Joe Kilian[†]
MIT

Avi Wigderson
Hebrew Universoity

Abstract

We present two efficient identification schemes based on the difficulty of solving the subset sum problem and the circuit satisfiability problem. Both schemes use the two prover model introduced by [BGKW], where the verifier (e.g the Bank) interacts with two untrusted provers (e.g two bank identification cards) who have jointly agreed on a strategy to convince the verifier of their identity. To believe the validity of their identity proving procedure, the verifier must make sure that the two provers can not communicate with each other during the course of the proof process. In addition to the simplicity and efficiency of the schemes, the resulting two prover interactive proofs can be shown to be perfect zero knowledge, making no intractability assumptions.

1 Introduction

Ben Or, Goldwasser, Kilian and Wigderson [BGKW] introduced the idea of multi-prover interactive proofs, in order to show how to achieve perfect zero-knowledge interactive proofs for all of IP without using any intractability assumptions.

A multi-prover interactive proof is an extension of an interactive proof. Instead of one prover attempting to convince the verifier that x (the input string) is in a language, the prover consists of two separate agents (or rather two provers) who jointly agree on a strategy to convince the verifier that x is in the language. Although the provers can agree on a strategy before they talk to the verifier, once the interaction

* Supported in part by NSF grant CCR-86-57527, DARPA Contract N00014-89-J-1988, and by a US Israel binational grant

† Supported in part by NSF postdoctoral fellowship and NSF grant CCR-86-57527

with the verifier starts they can no longer send each other messages or see the messages exchanged between the verifier and the "other prover".

The main novelty of this model is that the verifier can check interactions with the provers against each other. This allowed [BGKW] to prove that anything provable in this model has a *statistical* zero-knowledge proof, without any intractability assumptions.[1] Of more practical significance, they give a direct, efficient proof that membership in any NP language can be done in *perfect* zero-knowledge. The zero-knowledge protocol for NP proposed in [BGKW] is an adaptation to the two-prover model of any of the known zero-knowledge proofs for NP-complete problems in the one-prover model.

Essentially, the cryptographic encryption schemes used by the protocols of [GMW], [Bl], and [Sh], are replaced by new commit and reveal protocols. In the commit protocol, the first (designated) prover commits to a bit value such that the verifier can not (information theoretically) distinguish between a commitment to a 0 and commitment to a 1. In a reveal protocol, the second prover reveals to the verifier the value committed to by the first prover. The probability that the provers can cheat and reveal a different bit to the verifier than the one committed to, can be made negligible. The commit and reveal protocols consist of a few addition operations which are of trivial complexity. No other operations such as large modular multiplications are necessary.

We note that the overall efficiency of our protocols can be increased by using efficient weaker commital protocol in which the the provers have a non-negligible probability of error.

The application of zero-knowledge interactive proofs to identification schemes has been demonstrated in [FS], [MS], [GQ] among others.

In this paper, we suggest applications of the two prover model to the area of identification schemes. We propose two identification schemes which are much more efficient than those known for the one prover model. The first is based on the intractability of the subset sum problem, and implements a variant of a protocol due to Shamir [Sh]. The second is based on the intractability of the circuit satisfiability problem, and implements a variant of protocols due to Brassard–Chaum–Crépeau [BCC] and Impagliazzo–Yung [IY]. The verifier, which in this case of the identification application is the central computer (or a local center such as an ATM machine), receives two cards (or one card with two physically separated CPU's) and interacts with them to receive a proof that the cards belong to a legal and valid user. It is up to the verifier to ensure the cards can not communicate with each other while interacting with him.

2 Definitions and Background

In this section we review the definitions of multi-prover interactive proofs and the theorem of [BGKW] that all NP languages have perfect zero-knowledge multi-prover

---

[1]Authors' note: More recently, this proof has been strengthened to achieve perfect zero-knowledge (to appear in the journal version of [BGKW].)

interactive proofs.

Let P_1, P_2 be computationally unbounded Turing machines and V be a probabilistic polynomial time Turing machine. Machines P_1, P_2, and V each have a read-only input tape, a work tape, communication tapes on which V and P_i can write messages for each other, and a random tape. In addition, P_1 and P_2 share the same random tape.

Definition: Let P_1, P_2, V have access to the same input tape. We call (P_1, P_2, V) a *two prover interactive protocol.*

Definition: Let $L \subset \{0,1\}^*$. We say that L has a *two prover interactive proof system* if there exists a probabilistic polynomial time Turing machine V such that:

1. There exists P_1, P_2 such that (P_1, P_2, V) is a two-prover interactive protocol and for all $x \in L$, $prob(V$ accepts $x) = 1$.

2. For all P_1, P_2 such that (P_1, P_2, V) is a two-prover interactive protocol, for all $x \notin L$,

$$prob(V \text{ accepts } x) \leq \frac{1}{|x|^t},$$

for all constant t, and for all sufficiently large x.

If the above conditions hold, we call (P_1, P_2, V) from Condition 1 a *multi-prover interactive proof* for L.

Definition: Let (P_1, P_2, V) be an interactive protocol. Let $View_{P_1, P_2, V}(x)$ denote the verifier's view during the protocol, i.e the sequence of messages exchanged between the verifier and the two provers and the verifier's coin tosses. We say that a two-prover interactive protocol (P_1, P_2, V) is *perfect zero knowledge* for a language L if for all V^* there exists a probabilistic Turing machine M such that for all $x \in L$, $M(x)$ is identically distributed to $View_{P_1, P_2, V^*}(x)$ and $M(x)$ terminates in expected polynomial time. We say that L has a *perfect zero knowledge interactive proof* if

there exists an interactive protocol (P_1, P_2, V) which is an interactive proof for L and perfect zero-knowledge for L.

The following theorem is instrumental to prove the correctness and security of our authentication schemes.

Theorem [BGKW] : For every $L \in NP$, L has a perfect zero knowledge two prover interactive proof.

3 Subset Sum Based Authentication Scheme

In [Sh] a zero-knowledge proof for 0/1 modular knapsack was presented for the one-prover model. We use of the ideas in [Sh] for our first two-prover identification scheme.

Throughout this section we refer to the verifier as V, and to the provers as P_1, P_2.

For concreteness sake we suggest the reader envisage the verifier V as an ATM machine, and the two provers P_1, P_2 as a pair of cards issued to every customer. The cards and the ATM have a common input, which the Bank gave the customer. When the customer logs in, this information is visible to the Bank. Ordinarily, the bank stores pairs (user-name, common input.)

We let P_1 and P_2 share a random string $R = r_1 r_2 ... r_k$ where $r_i \in \{0, 1, 2\}$ chosen at random and k is a polynomial in the number of identifications R will ever be used for. R can be thought of as either truly random (as we do for the sake of this abstract) in which case P_1, P_2 change it on their own after k authentications, or an outcome of a pseudo random number generator.

We first need to introduce two protocols called *commit* and *reveal*.

Let σ_0 be the identity function and $\sigma_1(0) = 0, \sigma_1(1) = 2, \sigma_1(2) = 1$.

Commit (b,j): (*b* denotes the bit being committed to, and *j* how many commits were performed thus far.)

1. V flips a coin $c \in \{0, 1\}$ and send c to P_1

2. P_1 computes $v_j = \sigma_c(r_j) + b \bmod 3$ and sends v_j to V.

3. V stores (j, c, v_j).

Reveal (j): (reveal the j-th bit which was committed to)

1. P_2 sends r_j to V

2. V looks up its stored values, (j, c, v_j), and computes

$$b = v_j - \sigma_c(r_j) \bmod 3.$$

Claim 1: Let $c, g \in \{0, 1\}$. If $prob(r = i) = \frac{1}{3}$ for $i = 0, 1, 2$, then

$$prob(b = g | v = \sigma_c(r) + b \bmod 3) = prob(b = g) = \frac{1}{2}.$$

proof: see [BGKW].

Claim 2: Let $prob(c = 0) = prob(c = 1) = \frac{1}{2}$. Then $\forall \epsilon \geq 0$:
if for $b \in \{0, 1\}$,

$$prob(P_2 \text{ successfully reveals } b) \geq 1 - \epsilon,$$

then,

$$prob(P_2 \text{ successfully reveals } \bar{b}) \leq \frac{1}{2} + \epsilon.$$

proof: see [BGKW].

Note then that the probability with which the prover can cheat is bounded by the,

$$\max\{\min\{1 - \epsilon, \frac{1}{2} + \epsilon\}\} \leq \frac{3}{4},$$

which is achieved at $\epsilon = \frac{1}{4}$.

We are now ready for the subset sum authentication protocol.

The input to (P_1, P_2, V) protocol is an instance of the subset sum problem denoted by the tuple $(w_i, 1 \le i \le n, T, t)$ where the weights w_i are picked from a range $[1, S_n]$, where n is the security parameter of the application and t denotes the number of w_i in the subset in question.

Prover P_1 has as a private input an index set $J \subset \{1, ..., n\}$ such that $\sum_{i \in J} w_i = T$ and $|J| = t$.

The Identification Protocol

The following protocol for the above variant of subset sum is similar to [Sh]. Let language L be the set of tuples of integers,

$$(w_1, \ldots, w_n, T, t),$$

such that there exists a set $J \subseteq [1, n]$ such that,

- $|J| = t$, and,

- $\displaystyle\sum_{i \in J} w_i = T$.

In the protocol below, let S_n denote a strict upper bound on $\sum w_i$.

1. P_1 permutes the w_i at random and accordingly the set J. Denote the permuted values as w_i', J' such that $\sum_{i \in J'} w_i' = T$. P_1 and V now run a commit protocol on secrets A, B, C, D, E (defined below) using the commit protocol (defined above).

   - $A = \{r_i | 1 \le i \le n\}$ where r_i's are picked at random from $[1, S_n]$.
   - $B = \{w_i' | 1 \le i \le n\}$.
   - $C = \{s_i = w_i' + r_i \bmod S_n | 1 \le i \le n\}$.
   - $D = J'$.
   - $E = \sum_{j \in J'} r_i \bmod S_n$.

2. V uniformly chooses $t \in \{1, 2, 3\}$ and sends t to P_2.

3. Using the reveal secrets protocol defined above between P_2 and V:

   - if $t = 1$, P_2 reveals to V committed secrets A, B and C.
   - if $t = 2$, P_2 reveals to V committed secrets C, D and E.
   - if $t = 3$, P_2 reveals to V committed secrets A, D and E.

4. V checks that indeed

- if $t = 1$, $s_i = r_i + w'_i \bmod S_n$ for all i
- if $t = 2$, $\sum_{i \in D} s_i = E + T \bmod S_n$
- if $t = 3$, $\sum_{i \in D} r_i = E \bmod S_n$.

Now to get a high chance of correctness, this protocol is repeated k times where k is the security parameter, chosen by the parties who are running the protocol.

Theorem 1: Let C be an illegal user pretending to be the legal provers P_1, P_2. Under the assumption that solving the subset-sum problem is hard, for all k, for all $t > 0$, for all sufficiently large n,

$$prob(C \text{ cheats successfully}) \leq \left(\frac{11}{12}\right)^k + \frac{1}{n^t}.$$

(the $\frac{1}{n^t}$ error accounts for the probability that C solves the subset sum instance.)

Theorem 2: The above protocol is a perfect-zero-knowledge multi-prover interactive proof for the subset sum language.

3.1 Efficiency

The new scheme is more efficient than any other identification scheme thus far proposed based on the theory of zero-knowledge. All other schemes can be classified into two classes: they are either based on the factoring intractability assumption(such as Fiat-Shamir) which we call Type 1, or they are based on zero-knowledge proofs for NP-complete problems which we call Type 2. The identification schemes of Type 1 all use as a basic operation large modular multiplications. The identification schemes of Type 2 all use evaluations of one-way functions, for which the only known suggested implementations use as primitive operations large modular multiplications. Thus, a bottle neck for efficiency is the ability to perform fast modular multiplications.

In our scheme, no such operations are necessary. The primitive operations in the commit and reveal protocols are simple additions modulo 3, which is of trivial complexity.

In terms of number of rounds, [BGKW] have already shown that the scheme remains perfect zero-knowledge even if many executions of the protocol are performed in parallel. An interesting open question is that of analyzing the confidence amplification afforded by running protocols in parallel.

3.2 How to Choose Subset Sum Instances

We choose the subset sum problem as suitable for our purpose, since it is easy to generate instances of it at random, and the complexity of checking that indeed a specific subset of the weights adds up to a target, given a description of the subset, is quite inexpensive.

However, one must be careful in choosing instances of the subset sum problem so that the instances are hard ones to solve. In the above protocol we did not address this issue. This of course is not sufficient. The verifier (Bank) should choose the subset-sum instance among the believed to be hard high density instances, as widely studied in the literature by Lagarias and Odlyzko [LO] and others.

We proceed to suggest one more implementation of an authentication scheme based on the multi-prover model, whose security is based on the circuit satisfiability problem.

4   A Circuit Satisfiability Authentication Scheme

As mentioned before, subset sum is an NP complete problem. In principle, any identification system based on possessing a witness to an arbitrary NP set may be reduced to this identification scheme. However, such reductions may be extremely inefficient, wiping out the efficiency gains obtained by using our system. This motivates the consideration of other NP complete problems for use in identification schemes.

In this section, we briefly describe a second protocol for identification, based on the circuit satisfiability problem. The circuit satisfiability problem is as follows: Given a boolean circuit C, with a single output, is there a setting of the input bits such that C will output a 1? This problem is eminently suitable for reductions from other NP languages, since the procedure for checking a witness is fairly easy to write down as a circuit.

The work of [BCC] and [IY] gives a protocol for the circuit satisfiability problem with the following properties.

1. Given a circuit C of size $s(n)$, each iteration of the protocol requires the prover to commit $\Theta(s(n))$ bits to the verifier. For cryptographic based implementations of this scheme, the prover must send $\Theta(s(n)k)$ bits to the verifier, where k is the security parameter being used.

2. If C is satisfiable, and the prover obeys the protocol, then the verifier will always accept. If C is not satisfiable, then the verifier will reject with probability at least $1/2$, for each iteration of the protocol.

A more recent protocol, given in [KMO], allows for an asymptotically more communication efficient zero-knowledge protocol for circuit satisfiability. Instead of sending $\Theta(s(n)k)$ bits per iteration of the protocol, the prover need only send $\Theta(s(n) + k^2)$ bits.

Using a two card system, we can in fact create a protocol which only requires a total of $\Theta(s(n))$ bits of communication per iteration. Furthermore, iterations can be executed in parallel.

We simply use the circuit construction of [BCC] or [IY] modified to use our commit and reveal schemes of section 4 whenever a commitment is called for.

We also note that as a by product of the type of simulation that is done in the two-prover model (no rewinding of the simulator tape is necessary), many interactions of the modified [BCC] and [IY] protocols can be run in parallel and remain perfect zero-knowledge.

The protocol we obtain has the the following specifications:

1. Given a circuit C of size $s(n)$, each iteration of our protocol requires the provers to commit $\Theta(s(n))$ bits to the verifier. This is accomplished by sending a total of only $\Theta(s(n))$ bits to the verifier.

2. If C is satisfiable, and the provers obey the protocol, then the verifier will always accept. If C is not satisfiable, then the verifier will reject with probability at least 1/8, for each iteration of the protocol. (by Section 4, Claim 2)

We note that the rejection probability for an iteration of a bad proof is now only 1/8, instead of the factor of 1/2 of the original scheme. This is because the verifier will reject only if the provers are forced to decommit a bit which would reveal their cheating if correctly decommitted (which occurs with probability $\frac{1}{2}$), and in this case the verifier detects them trying to decommit a value other than what they originally committed with probability at most $\frac{1}{4}$. Recall, whereas in the ideal abstraction for bit-commital, the provers cannot change the value of a decommitted bit, in our system they can do so with only a $\frac{1}{4}$ chance of detection.

Naively, one might suggest amplifying the security of the bit commital protocol by running it many times. This would allow us to realize a bit-commital protocol that is indistinguishable from an ideal protocol. However, such a strategy turns out to be inefficient, since even with an ideal scheme, the rejection probability will still only be 1/2. Thus, n (where $(\frac{7}{8})^n < \frac{1}{2}$) iterations of our protocol, using the simple commital scheme, will prove more efficacious than a single iteration of our protocol, with an arbitrarily amplified commital scheme. For efficiency, it makes sense to use a few very cheap iterations rather a single very expensive one. Metaphorically, we have a weakest link phenomenon: There is no point paying to make some links of a chain very strong if a single other link in this chain will still be weak.

5 References

[Bl] Blum, "How to Prove a Theorem So No One Else Can Claim It", Zero Knowledge Proofs, ICM 1986.

[BGKW] Ben-Or, Goldwasser, Kilian, and Wigderson, "Multi-Prover Interactive Proofs: How to Remove Intractability Assumptions," Proceedings of STOC 1988.

[BCC] Brassard, Gilles, David Chaum, and Claude Crépeau, "Minimum Disclosure Proofs of Knowledge," JCSS, Oct. 1988.

[FS] Fiat, and Shamir, " How to Prove Yourself: Practical Solutions to Identification and Signature Problems", CRYPTO 86.

[GQ] Guillou, and Quisquater, "A Paradoxical Identity Based Signature Scheme Resulting from Zero Knowledge", CRYPTO 88.

[GMR] Goldwasser, Micali, and Rackoff, "The Knowledge Complexity of Interactive Proofs", SIAM J. of Comp., Feb. 1989.

[GMW] Goldreich, Micali, and Wigderson, "Proofs that Yield Nothing But the Validity of the Assertion", Proceedings of FOCS 1986.

[IY] Impagliazzo, Russell and Moti Yung, "Direct Minimum Knowledge Computations," CRYPTO 87.

[KMO] Kilian, Micali, and Ostrovsky, "Efficient Zero Knowledge Proofs with Bounded Interaction," Proceedings of FOCS 89.

[LO] Lagarias, and Odlyzko, "Solving Low Density Subset Sum Problems", Proceedings of FOCS 1983.

[MS] Micali and Shamir, "An Improvement of the Fiat-Shamir Identification and Signature Scheme", CRYPTO 88.

[Sh] A. Shamir, "A Zero-Knowledge Proof for Knapsacks", presented at a workshop on Probabilistic Algorithms, Marseille (March 1986).

On the concrete complexity of zero-knowledge proofs

Joan Boyar[*]
Computer Science Department
University of Chicago

René Peralta[†]
Computer Science Department
University of Wisconsin - Milwaukee

Abstract

The fact that there are zero-knowledge proofs for all languages in NP has, potentially, enormous implications to cryptography. For cryptographers, the issue is no longer "which languages in NP have zero-knowledge proofs" but rather "which languages in NP have practical zero-knowledge proofs". Thus, the concrete complexity of zero-knowledge proofs for different languages must be established.

In this paper, we study the concrete complexity of the known general methods for constructing zero-knowledge proofs. We establish that circuit-based methods have the potential of producing proofs which can be used in practice. Then we introduce several techniques which greatly reduce the concrete complexity of circuit-based proofs. In order to show that our protocols yield proofs of knowledge, we show how to extend the Feige-Fiat-Shamir definition for proofs of knowledge to the model of Brassard-Chaum-Crépeau. Finally, we present techniques for improving the efficiency of protocols which involve arithmetic computations, such as modular addition, subtraction, and multiplication, and greatest common divisor.

1 Introduction

From a practical point of view, the bottleneck in the zero-knowledge interactive proof systems and in the "interactive arguments"[1] which are produced by the techniques of [1, 5, 7, 14] is the amount of interaction necessary. In this paper we provide powerful

---

[*]Supported in part by NSA Grant Number MDA904-88-H-2006.

[†]Supported in part by NSF Grant Number CCR-8909657.

[1]Protocols, which are proofs in the model of Brassard-Chaum-Crépeau [4], are not technically interactive proof systems, so we will refer to them as *interactive arguments*.

tools for reducing the number of bits communicated. We call the number of bits communicated the "communication cost" of the proof system.

2 The communication cost of the known general methods

Let L be a language which has a zero-knowledge interactive proof system or interactive argument. Fix a zero-knowledge proof for L. Let $CC_k(n)$ be the number of bits communicated in this zero-knowledge proof to achieve probability of error no more than $(1/2)^k$, for a security parameter k, when the input size is n.

The technique of GMW for producing a zero-knowledge interactive proof system for an arbitrary NP language proceeds by reduction of the language to the graph 3-colorability problem. A simple, zero-knowledge protocol is then used to prove that the resulting graph is 3-colorable. Thus we are interested in the communication cost of GMW's protocol for graph 3-colorability. Let n be the number of vertices of the graph and e be the number of edges. The GMW proof involves the encryptions of the colors of vertices. In this paper we will consider as constant the cost of encrypting one bit. Thus, in the graph 3-colorability problem, encrypting a color also has constant cost.[2] With this parameterization, the complexity turns out to be $CC_k^{3COL}(n) \in O(k \cdot e \cdot n)$.

If L is a language in NP, then a zero-knowledge proof system for L would be constructed as follows:

1. Transform L to a SAT instance S via Cook's theorem [10].

2. Transform S to a 3-SAT instance 3S via [10].

3. Transform 3S to a graph 3-colorability instance G via [13].

4. Prove, via GMW, that G is 3-colorable.

The size of the SAT instance S depends on the time complexity of the NDTM for L. Let us assume this time complexity to be linear in the size n of the problem instance. Then the transformation at step 1 will produce a SAT instance of size $O(n^2)$. With no further blowup at steps 2 and 3, the final graph will have $O(n^2)$ vertices and edges. This yields a complexity of the interactive proof $CC_k(n) \in O(k \cdot n^4)$. If the time complexity of the NDTM for L is $O(n^2)$, as it would be for many number theoretic languages, the complexity of the interactive proof would be $CC_k(n) \in O(k \cdot n^8)$. Thus we see that the technique of reduction to graph 3-colorability, elegant as it is, cannot reasonably be used in practice for arbitrary languages in NP.

An alternative technique for producing zero-knowledge proofs ([1, 4, 5, 6, 7]), proceeds by reduction to a verifying boolean circuit rather than to an NP-complete

---

[2]In fact, this cost should probably be k rather than constant, but we make this simplifying assumption to avoid multiplying all communication costs mentioned in this paper by the same factor, k.

language.[3] From now on we refer to this technique as "circuit-based proofs". In circuit-based proofs, the communication cost is $CC_k(S) \in O(k \cdot S)$, where S is the circuit size. The circuit size has been related to the time necessary for membership verification by a Turing Machine. If this time is $p(n)$ for a problem of size n, then there exists a verification circuit of size $O(p(n) \log p(n))$ ([20]). If the time complexity is linear, then the complexity of this protocol is $CC_k(n) \in O(k \cdot n \log n)$. If the time complexity is quadratic, then the complexity of this protocol is $CC_k(n) \in O(k \cdot n^2 \log n)$.

Thus the circuit-based methods have the potential of producing proofs which can be used in practice. However, if the known techniques are used, the hidden constants in the expressions for the asymptotic costs are quite large. In this paper, we introduce several techniques which greatly reduce the concrete complexity of circuit-based proofs.

3   Blobs

A blob encryption scheme is a technique for encrypting a single bit. Several implementations of blobs are described in [3, 4].

Formally, a blob encryption scheme is a function $\mathcal{E} : \{0,1\} \times D \to \Sigma^n$ for suitably large n and set D. Given $y \in \Sigma^n$ a blob decryption is a string $x \in D$ such that either $\mathcal{E}(0, x) = y$ (y is a 0-blob) or $\mathcal{E}(1, x) = y$ (y is a 1-blob).

The following properties of this bit encryption technique are relevant to this paper.

- **Security** - the blobs that encrypt zero have the same distribution as the blobs that encrypt one, so Peggy's[4] blobs contain no information, in the information-theoretic sense.

- **Authenticity and Independence** - after creating several blobs, Peggy can reveal the bit encrypted to produce one of those blobs, she can convince Vic that this was in fact the bit she encrypted to produce that blob, and she can do this without revealing any information about any of the other blobs.

- **Equality** - if Peggy produced two blobs from the same bit b, then she can convince Vic of this fact without revealing b or any other information. Similarly, she can convince Vic that two blobs are encryptions of different bits if that is the case.

Consider, for example, the following blob encryption scheme:

Definition 1 *(Brassard-Crépeau) - Let N be a fixed composite number and α be a fixed quadratic residue modulo N. We define "BC-blobs" by $\mathcal{E}(0, x) = x^2 \ (mod \ N)$ and $\mathcal{E}(1, x) = \alpha x^2 \ (mod \ N)$, for $x \in Z_N^*$.*

---

[3]Impagliazzo and Yung [17] also present a technique for giving direct proofs for the computation of a Turing machine.

[4]In this paper, it will at times be convenient to think of the verifier as being named Vic, and the prover being named Peggy. This has the advantage that personal pronouns such as "he" and "she" can be used to unambiguously identify one of the parties.

Thus, BC-blobs encrypt a 0 by the square of a random number in Z_N^* and a 1 by α times the square of a random number in Z_N^*. We note that protocols using BC-blobs begin with a zero-knowledge subprotocol whereby the verifier convinces the prover that α is a square modulo N and that he knows a square root of α. The fact that there is an exponentially small probability that the verifier can cheat during this subprotocol means that BC-blobs can only yield almost perfect (or statistical) zero-knowledge proofs.

The authenticity property of blob encryption functions (see [3]) implies that the prover can not produce $x_1, x_2 \in D$ such that $\mathcal{E}(0, x_1) = \mathcal{E}(1, x_2)$. BC-blobs rely on the assumption that it is impossible to compute a square root of α modulo N in probabilistic polynomial time. If the prover was to somehow produce x_1, x_2 such that $\mathcal{E}(0, x_1) = \mathcal{E}(1, x_2)$, then we have $x_1^2 = \alpha x_2^2$ which implies $\sqrt{\alpha} = (x_1/x_2) (mod\ N)$.

Definition 2 *We call the evidence that Peggy gives when convincing Vic that a blob is the encryption of a particular bit the "decryption" of the blob. We call the evidence Peggy gives to show that she produced two blobs from the same bit or from different bits the "XOR-certificate" of the two blobs. We assume that both blob decryptions and XOR-certificates are strings of bits (i.e. non-interactive proofs).*

Given BC-blobs u, v the prover convinces the verifier that u, v encrypt the same bit by displaying a square root of uv modulo N. The prover convinces the verifier that u, v encrypt different bits by displaying a square root of αuv modulo N. These square roots are the XOR-certificates of BC-blobs.

Let $t_1 = \mathcal{E}(b_1, x_1)$, $t_2 = \mathcal{E}(b_2, x_2)$, and $t_3 = \mathcal{E}(b_3, x_3)$. That is, t_i is a BC-blob encryption of b_i. The reader can easily verify that given XOR-certificates $C_{1,2}$ between t_1 and t_2 and $C_{2,3}$ between t_2 and t_3, an XOR-certificate for t_1 and t_3 is given by $C_{1,3} = (C_{1,2}C_{2,3}/(t_2\alpha))\ (mod\ N)$ if $b_1 \neq b_2$ and $b_2 \neq b_3$ or by $C_{1,3} = (C_{1,2}C_{2,3}/t_2)\ (mod\ N)$ otherwise. Thus, given a set of BC-blobs $\{t_i\}$ and XOR-certificates $\{C_{i,j}\}$ for some pairs of blobs, if the relationship between blobs t_r and t_s can be inferred from $\{C_{i,j}\}$ then the XOR-certificate $C_{r,s}$ is computable in polynomial time.

Definition 3 *When an XOR-certificate for blobs t_1, t_3 is computable in polynomial time from the XOR-certificates for blobs t_1, t_2 and t_2, t_3, we say that XOR-certificates are "transitive".*

We note that in BC-blobs, obtaining contradictory XOR-certificates constitutes breaking the system: if $C_{1,2}$ certifies that t_1 and t_2 encrypt the same value and $C'_{1,2}$ certifies that t_1 and t_2 encrypt different values, then $\sqrt{\alpha}$ is given by $\sqrt{\alpha} = (C_{1,2}C'_{1,2})/(t_1t_2)\ (mod\ N)$. This motivates the following definitions.

Definition 4 *We say that the prover "breaks" the blob encryption scheme $\mathcal{E}$ if it can compute x_1, x_2 such that $\mathcal{E}(0, x_1) = \mathcal{E}(1, x_2)$.*

Notice that our definition is very strong in the sense that the ability to decrypt a single blob into two different values constitutes breaking the blob encryption scheme.

Definition 5 *An implementation of blobs has the "strong equality property" if and only if (1) the XOR-certificates are transitive and (2) obtaining contradictory XOR-certificates constitutes breaking the system.*

Finally, we note that several implementations of blobs in the literature, including BC-blobs and those based on the discrete logarithm problem (see [3, 8]), are "normal" in the sense of the following definition.

Definition 6 *A blob encryption scheme $\mathcal{E}$ is "normal" if there is a BPP machine T, such that from any pair of blobs t_1 and t_2 created by $\mathcal{E}$, any decryption x_1 of t_1, and any XOR-certificate $C_{1,2}$ for t_1, t_2, T can compute a valid decryption x_2 of t_2.*

Normality will turn out to be an important property in proving that our protocols are proofs of knowledge.

4   The Brassard-Crépeau proof system

Let us recall the Brassard–Crépeau interactive arguments. The prover and verifier, Peggy and Vic, have agreed upon a circuit which has S gates, all of which have bounded (or at most $O(\log S)$) fan-in; they have agreed upon a security parameter k; Peggy knows a satisfying assignment for the circuit; and she wishes to convince Vic that she knows such an assignment. In order to do this, Peggy, who is assumed to have only BPP power, uses a blob encryption scheme. The protocol is as follows:

Peggy and Vic repeat the following steps k times.

1. For each gate in the circuit, Peggy produces a truth table for the boolean function computed by that gate. For each of the truth tables, she then, randomly and independently, chooses a permutation of the rows. For every wire in the circuit, she determines which value that wire would be carrying if the input wires carried the values corresponding to her satisfying assignment. Then, Peggy encrypts all of the bits on the wires and all of the bits in her permuted truth tables and sends the resulting blobs over to Vic.

2. Vic then flips a coin to get a random bit b and sends that bit over to Peggy.

3. If $b = 0$, Peggy shows Vic that all of the truth tables were formed correctly by decrypting them. She will also show that the blob for the output of the circuit is an encryption of a one. If $b = 1$, Peggy shows that the inputs and output of each gate correspond to some row in the truth table for that gate. She does this using the blob equality property, showing that the blobs, on the wires which are the inputs and output of the gate, are encryptions of the same bits as the blobs in some row of the truth table.

4. Vic checks everything that Peggy has sent him.

5   Eliminating truth tables

In this section, we will present techniques which can be useful in improving the efficiency of perfect and almost perfect zero-knowledge proofs which use the techniques of the original Brassard–Crépeau [5] proof system.[5]

In designing circuits for NP-problems, one would often want to use MAJORITY gates or AND or OR gates with large fan-in. It is, of course, relatively easy to replace these gates with AND, OR, and NOT gates with bounded fan-in so that one could directly apply the Brassard–Crépeau [5] proof system. It is more efficient, however, to skip this replacement and to use the techniques in the following sections to prove that these gates with large fan-in work correctly. These techniques can also be used to improve the efficiency of the protocols for circuits which only have gates with bounded fan-in.

5.1   MAJORITY gates

First, consider MAJORITY gates with fan-in n, where $n = 2k+1$. The output should be one if at least $k + 1$ of the inputs are one, and zero if at least $k + 1$ of the inputs are zero. Thus, we need only show that there are $k + 1$ inputs which are equal to the output. In order to hide which of the inputs are the same as the output, we will have Peggy produce n more blobs corresponding to the original input blobs for this gate. These additional n blobs will be encryptions of the same bits as the input blobs, but Peggy will send them to Vic in random order, so Vic will be unable to determine the correspondence. Then if the bit b Vic sends to Peggy is a zero, Peggy will show the correspondence between the input blobs and the n additional blobs, using the equality property. If the bit b is a one, Peggy will show that $k + 1$ of the additional blobs are encryptions of the same bit as the output bit, again using the equality property. If the number of inputs equal to the output is greater than $k + 1$, Peggy will randomly choose $k + 1$ additional blobs which have the same value as the output.

MAJORITY gates can be used to simulate AND and OR gates. Consider first an AND gate with n inputs. This can be simulated by a MAJORITY gate with $2n - 1$ inputs, n of which are the same inputs as to the AND gate and $n - 1$ of which carry the value zero. The output of this majority gate will be one if and only if all of the inputs to the AND gate were one, so the simulation is correct. OR gates with n inputs can be simulated similarly, but in this case the extra $n - 1$ inputs must all be ones. Thus, in order to simulate an AND or OR gate with n inputs, Peggy will create $2n - 1$ additional blobs, with n corresponding to the inputs to the AND or OR gate and $n - 1$ being encryptions of zeros for an AND gate or ones for an OR gate. Then, if the bit b Vic sends to Peggy is a zero, Peggy will show the correspondence between the inputs to the AND or OR gate and n of the additional blobs, and she will decode the remaining $n - 1$ blobs to show that they are all zeros or all ones, depending on

---

[5]Unfortunately the techniques presented here must be greatly modified for compatibility with the complementation of the bits on the wires, which occurs with the Brassard–Chaum–Crépeau system [4] .

whether the gate was an AND or OR gate. If the bit b is a one, Peggy will show that n of the additional blobs are encryptions of the same bit as the output bit.

NOT gates require no additional blobs. When Vic sends Peggy $b = 0$, Peggy will show that the NOT gates are working correctly by using the equality property to show that the blobs on the inputs and outputs of the NOT gates are encryptions of different bits. Peggy can ignore the NOT gates when $b = 1$.

Notice that the simulation of AND and OR gates with large fan-in never required that the fan-in be greater than two. If the original gates had only two inputs, Peggy would only need to create three additional blobs per gate, rather than the twelve needed to represent a truth table.[6] If the number of inputs is N and the number of gates is S, the total number of blobs on the circuit wires is $N + S$. If T of the S gates are NOT gates, then the original protocols which use truth tables use $N + 13(S - T) + 5T$ blobs per round, while the protocols described here use $N + 4(S - T) + T$ blobs per round, at most $(N + 4S)/(N + 13S)$ times as many. This is approximately three times more efficient than the Brassard-Crépeau system. Of course, the gain in efficiency is much greater when the circuit contains MAJORITY gates with large fan-in.

5.2   PARITY gates

Peggy can show that PARITY gates with n inputs are working correctly using $n + 1$ additional blobs. These blobs will correspond to the n inputs plus the output. When $b = 0$, Peggy will show the correspondence. When $b = 1$, Peggy can show that a PARITY gate is working correctly by exhibiting a pairing of the additional blobs for the gate (including the blob for the output bit), and using the equality property to show that the blobs within a pair are encryptions of the same bit. If n is even, there will be an unpaired additional blob, and Peggy must show that it was the encryption of a zero.

5.3   Proofs of security

For simplicity we assume, throughout this section, that no two NOT gates have the same input, that the output of one NOT gate is never the input to another NOT gate, and that the output of every gate (except for one) is an input to some other gate. We impose no further restrictions on fan-out.

We begin by showing that our interactive arguments are perfect or almost-perfect zero-knowledge proofs, depending on which implementation of blobs is used. Note that our interactive arguments are obviously zero-knowledge if the blob implementation used has the forgeability property (see [3]). The following theorem shows that the forgeability property is not necessary.

Theorem 1 *Our interactive arguments are perfect zero-knowledge if Peggy and Vic*

---

[6]Independently of this work, den Boer[11] has also decreased the number of blobs necessary for validating the computation of binary boolean functions.

use any implementation of blobs such as that in [3, 8], which leads to perfect zero-knowledge proofs in the original Brassard-Crépeau interactive arguments.

proof : We will construct a simulator for these interactive arguments. The simulator starts by setting the bits on the wires so that the output of the circuit is equal to one and so that the input of every NOT gate is different from the output of the same gate. To do this, the simulator assigns values to the wires, level by level, starting with the inputs. First, the input wires are all given the value one. The first level of gates is the set of gates which have as their inputs the inputs to the circuit. The kth level of gates is the set of gates which are not on any of the first $k-1$ levels and which have as their inputs only the inputs to the circuit and the outputs of gates at lower levels. As the simulator is assigning values to the wires corresponding to the outputs of the gates at level k, it will negate the value on the input wire for all NOT gates, and it will assign the value one otherwise. The simulator has completed its first step unless the final gate in the final level, level t, of the circuit is a NOT gate and its input is a one. If this is the case, the input to this final gate came from a unique gate on level $t-1$. The simulator will change the output of that gate from a one to a zero. Since we have assumed that this gate on level $t-1$ cannot be a NOT gate, the simulator has finished its first step.

Then, the simulator flips a coin in an attempt to guess which bit Vic will send. If the coin flip leads to a guess of $b = 0$, the simulator will set up the additional blobs for each gate so that they correctly correspond to the appropriate values on the input and output wires and so that those blobs which are supposed to have fixed values (for the AND and OR gates) have those values. The simulator then randomly permutes the additional blobs for each gate and sends everything over to Vic. If Vic sends $b = 0$, the simulator will have no problem responding correctly. Otherwise it will back up the tape for the transcript it is creating and will try again.

If the simulator's coin flip leads to a guess of $b = 1$, the simulator will set up the additional blobs for each gate so that it can respond correctly if $b = 1$. For a MAJORITY gate with $n = 2k+1$ inputs, it will set up all of the additional blobs with the same value as the output blob. For an n-input AND gate, it will set $n-1$ of the additional blobs to zero, and will make the remaining n blobs encryptions of the same bit which has been assigned to the output wire. An n-input OR would be similar except that the first $n-1$ additional blobs would be encryptions of one, rather than of zero. For a PARITY gate, all of the additional blobs can be encryptions of zero. Then, if Vic sends $b = 1$, the simulator will have no problem responding correctly. Otherwise, it will back up the tape for the transcript it is creating and will try again. With each coin flip, the simulator has a 50-50 chance of guessing the correct value of b, so the simulation will take expected polynomial time.

The simulator will produce transcripts which have exactly the same distribution as those which would be produced with the true prover because of the blob properties mentioned above. The key to this is that zero blobs and one blobs are drawn from exactly the same distributions .□

Theorem 2 *If a blob implementation is used which leads to almost perfect zero-knowledge proofs in the original Brassard–Crépeau interactive arguments, then our interactive arguments are almost perfect zero-knowledge.*

proof : Analogous to the proof of the previous theorem .□

Now we will show that our interactive arguments are proofs of knowledge. We will use the formalism developed in [12], which we will call the "FFS model". In the FFS model the prover and verifier are BPP in power and have an input tape, a random tape, and a "knowledge" tape. Paraphrasing FFS, such a proof system is a proof of knowledge system for the predicate $P(I, W)$ [7] if

> There exists a polynomial-time probabilistic Turing machine M such that for any prover A (honest or dishonest), for any initial contents of A's knowledge tape K and random tape R, and any sufficiently large input I, if the execution of the protocol on input I (assuming an honest verifier B) succeeds with nonnegligible probability, then the output produced by M at the end of the execution of $M(A, R, K)$ on input I satisfies the predicate P with overwhelming probability. [8]

Given that our interactive arguments rely on the security of blob encryption mechanisms (and that the above definition allows arbitrary initialization of the prover's knowledge tape), the possibility arises that the prover can convince the verifier that the circuit is satisfiable simply because it "knows" how to break the blob encryption scheme. Our theorem will state that after the successful execution of the protocol the verifier has obtained a proof that either the prover knows a satisfying assignment to the boolean circuit or the prover knows how to break the blob encryption scheme. But what does it mean to "know" how to break a blob encryption scheme? As pointed out by [12], the concept of Turing machine "knowledge" is a very subtle one. Lest we are forced to develop a new formalism to capture this notion, we must state our definition (of what it means to know how to break a blob encryption scheme) in terms of (a BPP observer M) being able to compute a satisfying assignment to a predicate.

Definition 7 *We say that the prover "knows" how to break the blob encryption scheme $\mathcal{E}$ if it knows (in the sense of [12]) a satisfying assignment to the predicate $\mathcal{E}(0, x_1) = \mathcal{E}(1, x_2)$ where the free variables are x_1 and x_2.*

In order to show that a BPP observer M can break the blob encryption scheme if the prover cheats, we need to assume that the encryption scheme is normal (see section 3, definition 6).

---

[7] $P(I, W)$ should be thought of as a family of circuits indexed by I and with input a binary string W.

[8] For a formal definition see [12]. Note that our interactive arguments are "restricted input", not "unrestricted input", zero-knowledge proofs of knowledge.

Theorem 3 *Suppose the circuit contains AND, OR, NOT, and MAJORITY gates. After a successful execution of our protocol using a normal blob encryption scheme $\mathcal{E}$, the verifier is convinced that the prover knows either a satisfying assignment to the circuit or how to break the scheme $\mathcal{E}$. This remains so even if gates have unbounded fan-in.*

proof : From the proof in [12] that every problem in NP has an interactive proof system of knowledge which is zero-knowledge, we see that to prove that our protocol is a proof of knowledge, we need only show that if an observer is able to see Peggy respond to receiving $b = 0$ and $b = 1$ for the same set of blobs, that observer can learn a satisfying assignment for the circuit or a satisfying assignment to the predicate $\mathcal{E}(0, x_1) = \mathcal{E}(1, x_2)$. If the observer sees any prover respond correctly to both possible challenges for a given set of blobs, the observer can learn one of these satisfying assignments by performing a breadth-first search of the circuit, starting with the output, determining the values on the wires it encounters. When processing a gate G in this breadth-first search, the observer already knows the value of the output. If G is a NOT gate, the input is the complement of the output. If G is an AND, OR, or MAJORITY gate, the answer to the challenge $b = 0$ will tell the observer the correspondence between the additional blobs and the blobs on the inputs to G. The answer to the challenge $b = 1$ will show that some of the additional blobs are equal to the output blob. From the correspondence between the additional blobs and input blobs, the observer will be able to determine the values of enough of the inputs to force that output value. After completing the breadth-first search, the observer will know values for enough of the circuit's inputs to force an output value of one. The other inputs can be assigned arbitrary values. This process can fail if, in processing a gate, the observer gets a contradictory assignment to an input wire. That is, a wire which has already been assigned a boolean value c is now assigned $\bar{c}$. In this case, using the fact that the encryption scheme is normal, the observer can decrypt a blob both to a 1 and to a 0, and therefore can satisfy the predicate $\mathcal{E}(0, x_1) = \mathcal{E}(1, x_2)$. $\Box$

Now let us suppose the circuits also have PARITY gates which are treated as described in section 5.2. We will prove that if an implementation of blobs is used which has the strong equality property (see section 3, definition 5), then our protocols are still proofs of knowledge. Unfortunately, the blob implementation described in [3, 8], which leads to perfect zero-knowledge proofs does not have the strong equality property. The problem with this implementation is that it is possible for Peggy to create two blobs t_1 and t_2 which she is unable to decrypt as either a zero or a one but which she can "prove" are both encryptions of the same bit and encryptions of different bits.[9]

Suppose we attempt the breadth-first search technique used in the proof of the previous theorem in a circuit which contains PARITY gates. When the observer

---

[9]She can do this by setting $t_1 = g^{r_1}\sqrt{g^c a} \ (mod \ p)$ and $t_2 = g^{r_2}\sqrt{g^c a} \ (mod \ p)$, where c is 0 or 1 depending on whether a is a quadratic residue or nonresidue, respectively.

encounters a PARITY gate, he may not learn enough of the gate's input values to force the correct output. If the PARITY gate has an even number of inputs, the observer will learn that the value on some wire is a zero and it will learn which wire, though that wire might be the gate's output. If the output of the PARITY gate is paired with one of the inputs, the observer will learn that that particular input wire carries the same value as the output. For the other wires, the observer will only learn that some wires carry the same value as some other wires. We will show, however, that this is enough information for the observer to efficiently compute a satisfying assignment.

Theorem 4 *Suppose the circuit contains AND, OR, NOT, MAJORITY, and PARITY gates. Suppose that the blob implementation used has the strong equality property. Then, after a successful execution of our protocol the verifier is convinced that the prover knows either a satisfying assignment to the circuit or how to break the blob encryption scheme. This remains so even if gates have unbounded fan-in.*

proof : As in the proof of the previous theorem, we assume that the observer has seen the prover respond to both a $b = 0$ challenge and a $b = 1$ challenge from the verifier and we perform a breadth-first search of the circuit.

Before beginning the breadth-first search, the observer should assign distinct symbolic variables to the wires of the circuit. The symbolic variable on a wire which is the output of a NOT gate can be pushed through the gate by assigning the negation of that symbolic variable to the input. Thus the wires may be assigned a symbolic variable, the negation of a symbolic variable, or a Boolean value. In the breadth-first search, whenever the observer learns that two wires carry the same value, either because of a PARITY gate or because one is the input wire to an AND, OR, or MA-JORITY gate and one is the output wire, both wires should be given the same value, according to the following rules:

- If both wires have a Boolean value, they should have the same value, so no updating is necessary. If they have different values, the prover has cheated; the observer should terminate the breadth-first search and break the system as described below.

- If one wire has a Boolean value and the other has a symbolic variable, all wires in the circuit labeled with that symbolic variable should be given the Boolean value and all wires labeled with the negation of that symbolic variable should be given the complement of that Boolean value.

- Similarly, if one wire is labeled with a Boolean value and the other has the negation of a symbolic variable, all wires in the circuit labeled with that symbolic variable or its negation should be labeled with the appropriate Boolean value.

- If both wires are labeled with symbolic variables or both are labeled with the negations of symbolic variables, all wires currently labeled with one of them or with the negation of that one should be labeled with the other or the negation of the other.

- If one wire is labeled with a symbolic variable and the other with the negation of a second symbolic variable, those wires labeled with the second symbolic variable should be relabeled with the negation of the first symbolic variable, and those wires labeled with the negation of the second symbolic variable should be relabeled with the first symbolic variable.

After the breadth-first search has been completed, some input wires will have been assigned Boolean values, but some may still be labeled with symbolic variables or the complements of symbolic variables. The observer can then assign arbitrary Boolean values to the symbolic variables and let these assignments determine values for those input wires which have not yet been assigned Boolean values. The resulting assignment will force the output of the entire circuit to be a one.

To see this, consider numbering the gates according to the order in which they are processed during the breadth-first search, with the output gate being given the number one. Look at the subcircuit C_k defined by the first $k-1$ gates. The inputs to this subcircuit are all encountered before we begin processing the kth gate. We claim that if these inputs to C_k are given any Boolean values consistent with the labels on the corresponding wires immediately before the processing of gate k, then the output of the circuit will be a one. This can be proved by induction on k. The base case, $k = 1$, is easy because before the first gate is processed, the output is given the value one. Suppose this is true for k and let us look at the kth gate. The processing described above ensures that the inputs to this gate will get appropriate values to force the output value. This processing may affect the labeling of previously encountered wires, but only to be more restrictive in the values allowed. If the labeling becomes so restrictive that no Boolean values are consistent with the labeling, then the prover must have cheated either in decrypting some blobs or in showing that two blobs are equal or not equal to each other. In this case, the observer can break the encryption scheme as described below. Thus, if the output for the subcircuit C_k is one for any consistent (according to the labeling immediately before gate k is processed) set of Boolean values assigned to the inputs, the output for the subcircuit C_{k+1} will be one if the inputs to C_{k+1} are given any Boolean values consistent with the labels on the corresponding wires after the processing of gate k. Since C_S is the entire circuit, the method described above will enable the observer to find a satisfying assignment, unless the observer found a contradiction.

If such a contradiction occurs, the observer can break the blob encryption scheme. Any contradiction which arises results from two strings of blob equalities and blob inequalities, with both strings starting and ending at the same blobs. Since each blob equality or inequality is proven with an XOR-certificate, and since these certificates are transitive, the observer has a certificate that the first blob on these strings is the encryption of the same bit as the last blob and also a certificate showing that they are encryptions of different bits. Since the blob implementation has the strong equality property, the observer can use these contradictory certificates to break the blob encryption scheme . $\square$

6 Integer operations

Convincing an adversary that a circuit is satisfied by an input with a given blob encryption is a special case of the following problem:

> Suppose that a given circuit computes a function $F(I)$. Then, given the blob encryption of an input I, and a blob encryption of an output O, convince an adversary that $F(I) = O$.

There are several alternatives to the straightforward verification of the circuit's computation. The protocol for verifying $F(I) = O$ could be, for example, probabilistic in the sense that, even if the prover is honest, the protocol only shows that $F(I) = O$ with probability exponentially close to one. Another technique is to express the function F as a composition of two functions $F = G \circ H$. In this case, the verifier could produce a blob encryption I' of $H(I)$ and convince the verifier that $H(I) = I'$ and $G(I') = O$. If the H and G are chosen appropriately then the communication cost of proving the latter two statements may be smaller than the communication cost of the direct proof (and, of course, it would still be a zero-knowledge proof).

A third technique is to add to the input I whatever additional information I' (where I' will also be encrypted using blobs) might help establish $F(I) = O$. More precisely, we seek a relation $R(I', I, O)$ such that $F(I) = O$ if and only if there exists an I' such that $R(I', I, O)$ holds. For example, if $F(I)$ is the GCD function of two integers A and B, then we let $R(X, Y, A, B, F(A, B)) = [(X * A + Y * B) = F(A, B)]\&[F(A, B) \ divides \ A]\&[F(A, B) \ divides \ B]$ (here $I = (A, B)$ and $I' = (X, Y)$). Then $F(A, B) = O$ if and only if there exists $I' = (X, Y)$ such that $R(X, Y, A, B, O)$ holds. This technique is useful when the communication cost of proving $R(I', I, O)$ is smaller than the communication cost of directly proving that $F(I) = O$. We note that this technique is closely related to the concept of program "checking", as developed by Blum and Kannan [2] and therefore their methods may prove useful in lowering the communication complexity of zero-knowledge proofs.

It is outside the scope of this paper to classify and explore all the different techniques that might prove useful in lowering the communication cost of zero-knowledge proofs. We focus on integer multiplication/division and GCD computation, which are common operations requiring circuits which are super-linear in size. We make use of the techniques discussed above to design protocols for these operations which have almost-linear communication cost.

For integer operations, we formulate the problem as follows : Let $OP(X, Y)$ be a binary operation on integers. Let X, Y, Z be integers such that $OP(X, Y) = Z$. Let $F(X), F(Y), F(Z)$ be blob-based encryptions of X, Y and Z respectively. Then we want a zero-knowledge protocol by which the prover can convince the verifier that $OP(X, Y) = Z$.

We start by noting that the techniques of section 3 reduce the communication cost of proofs for integer addition by a factor of seven. To see this, note that a circuit for adding two n-bit numbers requires 5 gates per bit (2 XOR gates, 2 AND gates, and 1 OR gate). Therefore the BC protocol requires the prover to produce $65 \cdot n$ additional blobs. By using PARITY and MAJORITY gates instead, it is not hard to see that only $9 \cdot n$ additional blobs are needed. This is an important optimization since integer addition is a basic step in circuits for most arithmetic operations. Subtraction, for instance, can be done using addition because convincing the verifier that $X - Y = Z$ is equivalent to convincing the verifier that $Z + Y = X$.

6.1 Multiplication

Let $F(A)$, $F(B)$, and $F(C)$ be given, where F is a blob-based encryption function. We will show a zero-knowledge protocol through which the prover can convince the verifier that $C = A \cdot B$ with $O(n \log n)$ communication cost when C is n bits long. This is much faster than the BCC and BC protocols would be if implemented in the obvious manner.

Note that the bit-length n of C is public, since blob-based encryption reveals length. Let p_i be the ith prime and let m be the smallest integer such that $\prod_{i=1}^{m} p_i > 2^n > C$. Let $T_n = \{p_i : i = 1, \dots, \lambda \cdot m\}$ where λ is a constant greater than 1. Note that the product of any m primes in T_n exceeds C. If $A \cdot B$ does not equal C, then $A \cdot B \equiv C \pmod{p_i}$ for at most $m - 1$ primes p_i. Thus $A \cdot B \not\equiv C \pmod{p_i}$ for at least $\lambda m - m + 1 > (\lambda - 1) \cdot m$ primes p_i. Thus, if a random $p_i \in T_n$ is chosen by the verifier then, with probability at least $1 - (1/\lambda)$, the prover will not be able to show that $A \cdot B \equiv C \bmod p_i$. This is the basis for our protocol.

Protocol for multiplication

1. The prover commits to $F(A)$, $F(B)$ and $F(C)$, where C is n bits long.

2. The verifier chooses a random prime $p \in T_n$.

3. The prover produces $(F(K_A), F(K_B), F(K_C), F(R_A), F(R_B), F(R_C))$ such that $0 \leq R_A, R_B, R_C < p$ and proves, using the BCC general protocol, that

   - $K_A \cdot p + R_A = A$
   - $K_B \cdot p + R_B = B$
   - $K_C \cdot p + R_C = C$
   - $R_A \cdot R_B = R_C \bmod p$.

Note that the 4 equations imply $A \cdot B \equiv C \bmod p$.

To show that $R_A \cdot R_B = R_C \bmod p$, the prover can commit to $F(k)$ and prove that $R_A \cdot R_B = R_C + k \cdot p$. The equalities can be shown using the equality property of blobs.

The communication cost of this protocol depends on the size of $p_{\lambda \cdot m}$, the largest prime in T_n. In order to obtain a concrete upper bound on $p_{\lambda \cdot m}$ we will need the following lemma:

Lemma 1 *For $x > 29$, the product of primes less than x is greater than 2^x.*

proof : We will use the following inequality (due to Chebyshev [9])

$$.92(x/\ln x) < \pi(x) < 1.11(x/\ln x).$$

Consider the sum

$$S(x) = \sum_{p<x} \ln p = \sum_{p\leq x} \ln p - \tau(x)\ln x$$

where p denotes a prime number and $\tau(x)$ is 1 if x is prime and 0 otherwise. Using Theorem 6.15, page 145 of [19], it is not hard to show that

$$S(x) = \pi(x) \ln x - \int_2^x \pi(t)/t \, dt - \tau(x)\ln x.$$

Thus $S(x) > f(x)$ where

$$f(x) = .92x - 1.11 \int_2^x \frac{dt}{\ln t} - \ln x.$$

Notice that $f'(x) = .92 - 1.11 \cdot \ln^{-1}(x) - x^{-1}$. Thus, for $x > 600$ we have $f'(x) > f'(600) > \ln 2$. Therefore $f(x)$ increases faster than the line $(\ln 2)\cdot x$ for $x > 600$. On the other hand, numerical integration reveals that $f(600) > 416 > (\ln 2)\cdot 600$. Thus we have, for $x > 600$,

$$\prod_{p<x} p = e^{S(x)} > e^{f(x)} > e^{(\ln 2)x} = 2^x.$$

Thus we have reduced the problem to that of verifying that $\prod_{p<x} p > 2^x$ for $29 < x \leq 600$. This verification was performed by computer .□

Corollary 1 *If $p_m > 29$, then $\log_2 C > p_m$.*

proof : Note that $C > \prod_{p<p_m} p$.

Corollary 2 *If $p_m > 29$, then $m < 2 \cdot (\log_2 C)/(\log_2 \log_2 C)$.*

proof : Since $\log_2 C > p_m$, we have $m < \pi(\log_2 C)$ and, using Chebyshev's inequalities, $\pi(\log_2 C) < 2 \cdot (\log_2 C)/(\log_2 \log_2 C)$.□

Corollary 3 *If $\lambda < (1/2)log_2 log_2 C$, then $p_{\lambda m} < 2\lambda \log_2 C$.*

proof : For $p_r > 5$ we have $p_r < r \log_2 r$ (this can be derived from theorem 3 of [21]). Therefore

$$\begin{aligned}
p_{\lambda \cdot m} &< \lambda \cdot m \log_2(\lambda \cdot m) \\
&< \frac{2\lambda \log_2 C}{\log_2 \log_2 C}(\log_2 \lambda + 1 + \log_2 \log_2 C - \log_2 \log_2 \log_2 C) \\
&< 2\lambda \log_2 C
\end{aligned}$$

where the second inequality follows from the previous corollary and the third inequality from the assumption that $\lambda < (1/2)log_2 log_2 C$. $\square$

Thus, $p_{\lambda \cdot m}$ is no more than $\log_2(2\lambda n)$ bits long, where n is the size of C. Noting that the general BCC protocol has $O(r \cdot s)$ communication cost per round to multiply an r-bit number by an s-bit number, using the "classic" multiplication algorithm, we conclude that the communication cost of each round of our protocol is $O(n \cdot \log_2 n)$.

6.2   Integer GCD

Given blob-based encryptions $F(A), F(B), F(\delta)$ of integers A, B, δ, the prover wants to convince the verifier that $GCD(A, B) = \delta$. The communication cost of the BC and BCC proofs for this problem is $O(n^2)$ when A, B are n-bit integers. A much cheaper protocol is the following:

Protocol for integer GCD

1. The prover commits to $F(u), F(v), F(w)$ and $F(x)$ where $A \cdot u + B \cdot v = \delta$.

2. The prover proves

   - $\delta \cdot w = A$
   - $\delta \cdot x = B$
   - $A \cdot u + B \cdot v = \delta$.

Note that the 3 equations imply that $GCD(A, B) = \delta$.

The proofs at step 2 are done using the techniques of the previous section. Thus, the per-round communication cost of this protocol is $O(n \log n)$ for A and B of size n.

7   Combining logical gates and arithmetic gates

The techniques of sections 5 and 6 can be used to prove the satisfiability of circuits containing both logical and arithmetic gates. We first note that GCD, DIV, and MOD gates can be replaced by multiplication and addition gates (plus additional, prover supplied, inputs) in the manner of section 6.2. Since addition gates are implemented using standard (linear size) logical circuits, we need only consider a circuit containing logical gates and multiplication gates. Such a circuit can be proven satisfiable through the following protocol:

Protocol for circuits containing multiplication gates

1. The prover commits to blobs for each wire of the circuit (including the inputs and outputs of the multiplication gates) and to the additional blobs required by logical gates as described in section 5.

2. For each multiplication gate with inputs A, B and output C, the verifier sends a random prime p of size $2\lambda \log n$ where n is the size of the output to the gate.

3. The prover commits to blobs for the wires and to the additional blobs required by the logical gates in the circuit induced by step 3 in our protocol for multiplication (section 6.1). i.e. the boolean circuit induced by the statements

$$K_A \cdot p + R_A = A$$

$$K_B \cdot p + R_B = B$$

$$K_C \cdot p + R_C = C$$

$$R_A \cdot R_B = R_C + k \cdot p.$$

4. The verifier challenges the prover for either a proof that all of the blobs were constructed according to protocol (type 0 challenge) or for a proof that the output blob for each logical gate is correct (type 1 challenge).

5. The prover responds to the challenge.

If the circuit is not satisfiable then the commitment to the output blob for at least one gate is not the correct computation for that gate. If that gate is a logical gate the prover will be caught with probability $(1/2)$. If the gate is a multiplication gate with inputs A, B and (incorrect) output C, then the prover will get caught if $A * B \neq C \bmod p$ (this happens with probability at least $1 - \frac{1}{\lambda}$) and the verifier sends the correct challenge. Thus the probability of cheating on each iteration is no more than $(1/2) + \frac{1}{2\lambda}$.

8 Remarks

The results in this paper have been significantly improved recently. Gilles Brassard has succeeded in reducing the communication cost of integer multiplication to $O(nc^{\log^* n})$, for a constant c. In addition, if BC-blobs are used, then the blobs for the outputs of NOT and PARITY gates can be computed by the verifier without help from the prover (and hence without communication) [5]. Carsten Lund has shown that the resulting protocol is still a restricted input zero-knowledge proof of knowledge.

The techniques described in this paper can also be used in circuit-based proofs which are interactive proof systems according to the GMR [16] definition. If one substitutes probabilistic encryption with the quadratic residuosity assumption [15] for the BC-blobs, everything still works (except that of course the proofs will now be only computational, rather than almost perfect, zero-knowledge).

At this conference, a paper by Kilian, Micali, and Ostrovsky [18] was presented which introduces a different technique for reducing the communication cost of zero-knowledge proofs. The techniques they use to reduce the number of envelopes necessary in "subset-revealing" protocols can easily be extended to protocols such as ours which also reveal the XOR of pairs of bits. We believe combining their techniques and ours carries us a long way towards the goal of being able to produce zero-knowledge proofs which are practical for any NP problem.

References

[1] J. C. Benaloh. Cryptographic capsules: A disjunctive primitive for interactive protocols. In *Advances in Cryptology - proceedings of CRYPTO 86*, Lecture Notes in Computer Science, pages 213–222. Springer-Verlag, 1987.

[2] M. Blum and S. Kannan. Designing programs that check their work. *Proceedings of the 21th Annual ACM Symposium on the Theory of Computing*, pages 86–97, 1989.

[3] J. Boyar, M. Krentel, and S. Kurtz. A discrete logarithm implementation of zero-knowledge blobs. Technical Report 87-002, University of Chicago, 1987. To appear in Journal of Cryptology.

[4] G. Brassard, D. Chaum, and C. Crépeau. Minimum disclosure proofs of knowledge. *Journal of Computer and System Sciences*, 37:156–189, 1988.

[5] G. Brassard and C. Crépeau. Nontransitive transfer of confidence: a perfect zero-knowledge interactive protocol for SAT and beyond. In *Proceedings of the 27th IEEE Symposium on the Foundations of Computer Science*, pages 188–195, 1986.

[6] G. Brassard and C. Crépeau. Zero-knowledge simulation of boolean circuits. In *Advances in Cryptology - proceedings of CRYPTO 86*, Lecture Notes in Computer Science, pages 223–233. Springer-Verlag, 1987.

[7] D. Chaum. Demonstrating that a public predicate can be satisfied without revealing any information about how. In *Advances in Cryptology - proceedings of CRYPTO 86*, Lecture Notes in Computer Science, pages 195–199. Springer-Verlag, 1987.

[8] D. Chaum, I. Damgård, and J. van de Graaf. Multiparty computations ensuring privacy of each party's input and correctness of the result. In *Advances in Cryptology - proceedings of CRYPTO 87*, Lecture Notes in Computer Science, pages 87–119. Springer-Verlag, 1988.

[9] P.L. Chebyshev. Mémoire sur les nombres premiers. *J. Math. Pures et Appl*, (I)(17):366–390, 1852.

[10] S. A. Cook. The complexity of theorem-proving procedures. In *Proceedings of the 3rd Annual ACM Symposium on the Theory of Computing*, pages 151–158, 1971.

[11] B. den Boer. An efficiency improvement to prove satisfiability with zero knowledge with public key. In *Advances in Cryptology - proceedings of EUROCRYPT 89*, Lecture Notes in Computer Science, 1989. To appear.

[12] U. Feige, A. Fiat, and A. Shamir. Zero-knowledge proofs of identity. *Journal of Cryptology*, 1(2):77-94, 1988.

[13] M.R. Garey, D.S. Johnson, and L. Stockmeyer. Some simplified np-complete graph problems. *Theoretical Computer Science*, 1:237-267, 1976.

[14] O. Goldreich, S. Micali, and A. Wigderson. Proofs that yield nothing but their validity and a methodology of cryptographic protocol design. In *27th. IEEE Symposium on Foundations of Computer Science*, pages 174-187, 1986.

[15] S. Goldwasser and S. Micali. Probabilistic encryption. *Journal of Computer and System Sciences*, 28:270-299, 1984.

[16] S. Goldwasser, S. Micali, and C. Rackoff. The knowledge complexity of interactive proof-systems. *SIAM Journal of Computation*, 18(1):186-208, 1989.

[17] R. Impagliazzo and M. Yung. Direct minimum-knowledge computations. In *Advances in Cryptology - proceedings of CRYPTO 87*, Lecture Notes in Computer Science, pages 40-51. Springer-Verlag, 1988.

[18] J. Kilian, S. Micali, and R. Ostrovsky. Efficient zero-knowledge proofs with bounded interaction. In *Advances in Cryptology - proceedings of CRYPTO 89*, Lecture Notes in Computer Science. Springer-Verlag, 1990. To appear.

[19] W. LeVeque. *Fundamentals of Number Theory*. Addison-Wesley, 1977.

[20] N. Pippenger and M. Fischer. Relations among complexity measures. *Journal of the Association for Computing Machinery*, 23:361-381, 1979.

[21] J. Rosser and L. Schoenfeld. Approximate formulas for some functions of prime numbers. *Illinois Journal of Mathematics*, 6:64-94, 1962.

Zero Knowledge Proofs of Knowledge in Two Rounds

U. Feige, A. Shamir

Department of Applied Mathematics

The Weizmann Institute of Science

Rehovot 76100, Israel

Abstract

We construct constant round ZKIPs for any NP language, under the sole assumption that oneway functions exist. Under the stronger Certified Discrete Log assumption, our construction yields perfect zero knowledge protocols. Our protocols rely on two novel ideas: One for constructing commitment schemes, the other for constructing subprotocols which are not known to be zero knowledge, yet can be proven not to reveal useful information.

1 Introduction

The concept of zero knowledge interactive proofs (ZKIPs) was introduced by Goldwasser, Micali and Rackoff (see [18] for definitions). Goldreich, Micali and Wigderson [17] show that under the assumption that secure bit commitment schemes exist, any NP language has a ZKIP system. In a remark they hint how to modify their protocols and obtain a 4-move ZKIP (a move is a message from verifier V to prover P, or from P to V, and a round is two consecutive moves). Alas, proving the correctness of the construction implied by this hint met unexpected technical difficulties, and was recently characterized by Goldreich (in a private communication) as an open problem.

In this paper we study the model where both P and V are polynomial time with auxiliary input (as studied in [5], [12] and others). We present a construction of constant round ZKIPs for any NP language, which relies on the polynomiality of P, and differs from the suggested construction in [17] (such ZKIPs are termed "computationally sound" by Goldreich, and "arguments" by Brassard and Crépeau). The protocol is a proof of knowledge, and not just a proof of assertion. Its success is evidence that P "knows" a witness to the given NP statement. (See [12] or [23] for definitions and discussion of the importance of proofs of knowledge). Our protocol offers different levels of security, depending on the strength of the cryptographic assumption we make:

1. By relying only on the assumption that oneway functions exist, our protocol takes 5 moves and is computational zero knowledge. This assumption is used in two ways: As a special case of the more general *Invulnerable Generator Assumption* (IGA), which in essence means that it is possible to generate hard, certified elements of some NP sets, and in order to construct secure commitment schemes. The construction of commitment schemes from any oneway function follows from recent results in [20] and [21], and requires a preliminary move).

2. By relying on the assumption that one-to-one oneway functions exist, our protocol takes only 4 moves, and is still computational zero knowledge. The fact that the oneway functions are one-to-one enables the construction of commitment schemes without the preliminary move, thus saving one move in the protocol.

3. By relying on the *certified discrete log assumption*, our protocol takes 4 moves, and is *perfect* zero knowledge.

The 4 moves protocols are optimal among all the zero knowledge protocols in which the zero knowledge property is proved by resettable blackbox simulation. This follows from [15], where it is proved that only languages in BPP have 3 move interactive proofs which can be proven zero knowledge by such a simulation.

Other general schemes for constant round ZKIPs (though not 2-rounds) have been independently discovered. Brassard, Crépeau and Yung [6] construct a 6-move protocol which is perfect zero knowledge (in the model where the prover is polynomial time). Their protocol relies on the Certified Discrete Log Assumption (or alternatively, on a generalization of this assumption). Our construction achieves 4-move perfect zero knowledge protocols, in the same model and under the same assumption, and reduces the number of bits communicated by a factor of $O(n)$. Goldreich and Kahn [14] announced a 5-move bounded round ZKIP based on claw-free pairs of functions. The cryptographic assumptions made in order to prove the correctness of their protocols are stronger than the assumption we make.

The reader should not confuse the issue of constant round ZKIPs with that of noninteractive (one move) zero knowledge protocols [4], as noninteractive zero knowledge assumes the existence of a random string agreed upon by P and V. Our protocols start from scratch. Likewise, the reader should not confuse our perfect zero knowledge protocols with Fortnow's [13] "impossibility" result, as Fortnow proves his result in a model where the provers are not limited to polynomial time.

We want to highlight two aspects of our protocol:

1. One of the subprotocols we use is not known to be zero knowledge, yet provably does not reveal any useful information. This is an application of a new concept of *witness hiding* [11], which can replace the standard concept of zero knowledge in many cryptographic applications.

2. We show a general technique for constructing commitment schemes out of ZKIPs. This is a dual to the well known technique of constructing ZKIPs out of commitment schemes. (This result was discovered independently by Damgard [9]).

2 Notation and Definitions

For a discussion on the following definitions, see [18] (interactive proofs and zero knowledge),[12] and [23] (proofs of knowledge).

Our model of computation is the probabilistic polynomial time interactive Turing machine (both for provers P and for verifiers V). The common input is denoted by x, and its length is denoted by $|x| = n$. Each machine has an auxiliary input tape. P's auxiliary input is denoted by w. V's auxiliary input is denoted by y, and for truthful V y is empty. $\nu(n)$ denotes a function vanishing faster than the inverse of any polynomial. Formally:

$$\forall k \; \exists N \; s.t. \; \forall n > N \;\; \nu(n) < \frac{1}{n^k}$$

Negligible probability is probability behaving as $\nu(n)$. *Overwhelming* probability is probability behaving as $1 - \nu(n)$.

$A(x)$ denotes the output of algorithm A on input x. This may be a random variable, if A is allowed to toss coins. $V_P(x)$ denotes V's output on input x, after participating in an interactive proof (P, V). $M(x, A)$ (where A may be either P or V) denotes algorithm M's output on input x, where M may use algorithm A as a subroutine (blackbox). Each call M makes to A counts as one computation step for M.

Definition 2.1: Let L be an NP language accepted by the polynomial time nondeterministic Turing machine M_L. A *computation path* is a sequence of nondeterministic choices that M_L makes. The set of M_L's accepting computation paths on input $x \in L$ is called the *witness set* of x, and is denoted by $w(x)$. ⋄

Definition 2.2: An *interactive proof of knowledge* system for NP language L is a pair of algorithms (P, V) satisfying:

1. Completeness: For any $x \in L$, for any $w \in w(x)$, $V_{P(x,w)}(x)$ accepts with overwhelming probability. Formally:

$$\forall x \in L \; \forall w \in w(x) \; Prob(V_{P(x,w)}(x) \, accepts) > 1 - \nu(n)$$

The probability is taken over the coin tosses of P and V.

2. Soundness: For any x, for any P', P' can convince V to accept only if he actually "knows" a witness for $x \in L$. Expected polynomial time knowledge extractor M is used in order to demonstrate P's ability to compute a witness. Formally:

$$\exists M \; \forall P' \; \forall x \; \forall w'$$

$$(Prob(V_{P'(x,w')}(x) \, accepts) - Prob(M(x, P'(x, w')) \in w(x))) < \nu(n)$$

The probability is taken over the coin tosses of V and M. P' is assumed not to toss coins, since his favorable coin tosses can be incorporated into the auxiliary input w'. The knowledge extractor M is allowed to use P' as a subroutine.

◇

Remark: For $x \notin L$, the probability that V accepts is negligible, since the witness set of such inputs is empty. ◇

We recall the definition for indistinguishability of ensembles which is needed for the subsequent definition of zero knowledge (and later will be used in the definition of witness indistinguishability).

Definition 2.3: Let I be an infinite set of strings, and let E_1 and E_2 be two probability ensembles. (For any $x \in I$, $E_1(x)$ and $E_2(x)$ are random variables). For any algorithm D denote by $P_1^D(x)$ ($P_2^D(x)$ respectively) the probability that D outputs 1 on input x and an element chosen according to probability distribution $E_1(x)$ ($E_2(x)$). The ensembles E_1 and E_2 are *polynomially indistinguishable* if for any nonuniform polynomial time distinguisher D,

$$|P_1^D(x) - P_2^D(x)| < \nu(n)$$

◇

Instead of using the term "polynomial indistinguishability" we shall just use "indistinguishability". Two variants on the definition are the following: If D is not restricted to polynomial time, the ensembles are termed *statistically* indistinguishable. If furthermore, the condition required is $P_1^D(x) = P_2^D(x)$, the ensembles are termed *perfectly* indistinguishable.

Definition 2.4: Proof system (P, V) is *zero knowledge* over L if there exists a simulator M which runs in expected polynomial time, such that for any probabilistic polynomial time V', for any input $x \in L$, associated witness w and auxiliary input to V' y, the two ensembles $V'_{P(x,w)}(x, y)$ and $M(x, V'(x, y))$ are polynomially indistinguishable. M is allowed to use V' as a subroutine. ◇

The concept defined above is also termed *computational* zero knowledge. *Statistical* (*perfect* respectively) zero knowledge is defined with *polynomial* indistinguishability replaced by *statistical* (*perfect*) indistinguishability.

Definition 2.5: A *move* of an interactive proof is a messages sent by one of the participants. Two moves (a message sent by V followed by a message sent by P) are called a *round*. ◇

In our protocols we make use of two cryptographic assumptions. Before stating the assumptions, we borrow (and modify) terminology from [1], which discusses the generation of hard, certified elements of NP sets.

Definition 2.6: Let G be a random polynomial time generating algorithm producing on input 1^n instances $(x, w) \in S$ of length n, where $S = \{(x, w)\}$ is a set recognizable in polynomial time. G is an *almost everywhere $\nu(n)$-invulnerable generator* (or just *invulnerable generator*) if for any polynomial time nonuniform adversary algorithm A, $Prob((x, A(x)) \in S) < \nu(n)$. The probability is taken over the coin tosses of G (A is assumed not to toss coins, as the most advantageous coin tosses can be incorporated into his nonuniform description). $\diamond$.

We stress that G must be invulnerable to *nonuniform* adversaries, unlike the case in [1]. Our first assumption, which is used for constructing computational zero knowledge protocols, relates to the existence of invulnerable generators.

Invulnerable Generator Assumption (IGA): There exists an invulnerable generator.

IGA is a very weak assumption, and follows from the more widely used assumption: The existence of oneway functions secure w.r.t. nonuniform algorithms.

Definition 2.7: Let G be a random polynomial time generating algorithm producing on input 1^n instances x of length n, and let f be a length preserving function whose domain is the range of G. f is *oneway* if it can be computed in polynomial time, but there is no nonuniform polynomial time algorithm which inverts f with nonnegligible probability, where the probability is taken over the distribution generated by G. $\diamond$

The next assumption is used only for our perfect zero knowledge protocols. The same assumption is used in [6] in the construction of their perfect zero knowledge protocols.

Certified Discrete Log Assumption (CDLA): There exists an invulnerable generator for the set $\{((p, g, c, x), y)\}$, where p is a prime, g is a generator for Z_p^*, c a certificate for the first two facts (e.g. a recursively certified complete factorization of $p - 1$ [22]), and $g^y = x \pmod{p}$. $\diamond$

We assume that the invulnerable generator for CDL chooses y (and x) with uniform probability from $[1, p-1]$ (any other invulnerable generator can be modified to achieve this using the self randomizing properties of the discrete log problem [2]).

3   Overview of the protocol

In suffices to present a constant round zero knowledge proof of knowledge for one NP complete language. Any other NP statement can be proved in zero knowledge by first reducing the statement to an instance of the NP complete language. This reduction must satisfy three properties:

1. It must be computable in polynomial time.

2. It must be *witness preserving*. This property is necessary for the completeness property of the protocol. It enables P, which has a witness to the original NP statement, to construct a witness to the generated instance of the NP complete language.

3. Witnesses must be *efficiently invertible*. This property is necessary for the knowledge soundness property of the protocol. It allows V to conclude that P knows a witness to the original NP statement, even though P only demonstrates knowledge of a witness to the syntactically different NP complete statement.

The particular NP complete language we choose is DHC (directed Hamiltonian cycle). We specify a polynomial reduction procedure from any NP language L to DHC, to be used whenever such a reduction is called for. This ensures that the reduction process itself conveys no information (and thus the zero knowledge property is preserved). We assume L is initially given as a nondeterministic Turing machine which accepts L. The reduction proceeds in two stages: Reducing the computation of this nondeterministic Turing machine to an instance of SAT (see [8]), and reducing SAT to DHC (see [19]). The reader may check for himself that this chain of reductions is witness preserving and efficiently invertible.

Our starting point is the basic step of Blum's [3] ZKIP for the Directed Hamiltonian cycle (DHC) problem. In the rest of this presentation, we assume that all the graphs are directed, and that all the cycles are directed Hamiltonian cycles.

Protocol 1: Common input: A Hamiltonian graph G with n nodes. P has H, a cycle in G, on his knowledge tape. The basic step of Blum's protocol is composed of three moves:

1. P secretly chooses a random permutation π and permutes the nodes of G. P secretly constructs the adjacency matrix of $\pi(G)$ and commits himself to each entry ('1' if an edge exists, '0' otherwise) independently.

2. V randomly selects a bit '0' or '1' as a challenge and sends it to P.

3. If P receives '0', P reveals π and all the committed bits. V can check that the edges revealed indeed correspond to the graph $\pi(G)$. If P receives '1', P reveals only n edges, comprising a cycle in G. V can easily check that this is the case from the structure of the adjacency matrix.

Blum's full protocol is constructed by sequentially iterating this basic step n independent times (sequential composition). It is complete (truthful P and V can successfully execute the protocol), sound (assuming the commitment scheme is sound, P's ability to complete the protocol implies his knowledge of a cycle in G), and zero knowledge (proven by resettable simulation, assuming the commitment scheme is secure). If the basic step is carried out n times in parallel (parallel composition), the protocol remains complete and sound, but it is conjectured not to be zero knowledge (unless DHC $\in$ BPP [15]).

We did not specify the exact commitment scheme to be used in Protocol 1. GMW [17] suggested using probabilistic encryption functions, where P commits to a bit by encrypting it. A different approach, which relies on P being polynomial time, was suggested in [5]. P commits to a bit by his internal state of knowledge. For $b \in \{0, 1\}$ and commitment c, if P knows a string $w_b(c)$, he can open c as b. P cannot know both $w_0(c)$ and $w_1(c)$, as this implies the knowledge of a certain value which cannot be computed in polynomial time. If furthermore, V has secret "trapdoor" information which allows V (unlike P) to compute matching pairs $(w_0(c), w_1(c))$, the scheme is termed *trapdoor commitment scheme* (or *chameleon* in [5]). Our intention is to use a trapdoor commitment scheme in Protocol 1. In this case, the protocol remains zero knowledge even under parallel composition (which needs only 3 moves). The simulator M, simulating the protocol, would be allowed to open each bit either as 1 or 0 (because V can), and M could imitate P's role without ever resetting P.

The approach described in the previous paragraph is not new, and it serves as the starting point of [6]'s protocol as well. This approach has two problematic aspects:

1. The trapdoor commitment schemes described in [5], rely on very specific cryptographic assumptions (typically number theoretic). We want our protocols to rely on assumptions which are as weak as possible.

2. How do we know that the commitment scheme P uses is really trapdoor? In other words: How do we know that V can open committed bits both as 0 and as 1? V must somehow prove his knowledge of trapdoor information, without revealing the trapdoor information itself. The obvious way of doing this is by V giving a zero knowledge proof that he knows the trapdoor. As our goal is to construct 4-move ZKIPs, it seems unattainable: V's proof must take less than 4 moves, and thus, as noted earlier for 3-move protocols, it cannot be zero knowledge!

In [6] the authors do not set it as a goal to solve the first of the two problems, and the second problem is ingeniously avoided (at the expense of increasing the number of moves to 6). Our new construction solves both problems.

4 A Novel Trapdoor Commitment Scheme

Definition 4.1: A *trapdoor bit commitment scheme* consists of a *commit* stage and a *reveal* stage. The scheme must satisfy the following properties:

- Completeness: Party A can commit to any bit b (either 0 or 1).

- Soundness: A has negligible probability of constructing a commitment which he can later reveal in two possible ways: both as 0 and as 1.

- Security: Party B has negligible probability of predicting the value of a committed bit.

- Trapdoor: B (through some trapdoor information) can construct commitments, indistinguishable from A's commitments, which he can later reveal in two possible ways: both as 0 and as 1.

Our construction of trapdoor commitment schemes is based on the following observation: The basic step of zero knowledge proofs of knowledge can be used as a commitment scheme, provided the prover does not have the knowledge he "claims" to have. Recall the 3-move basic step protocol we presented earlier (Protocol 1). If P could complete the third move in a satisfactory way no matter what V sends in the second move, this would imply P's knowledge of a cycle in G. Conversely, if P does not know a cycle in G, P cannot answer both a '0' challenge and a '1' challenge of V. This leads to the following commitment scheme:

- Preliminary phase: V sends P a Hamiltonian graph G, in which the polynomial time P presumably cannot find a cycle.

- P commits to 0 by choosing a random permutation π, permuting the nodes of G, and committing to the entries of the resulting adjacency matrix (but this time using a commitment scheme which need not be trapdoor!). P may reveal the committed bit '0' by revealing π and the entries of the matrix.

- P commits to 1 by choosing the n node clique and committing to its adjacency matrix (which is all 1). P may reveal the committed bit '1' by opening a random cycle in this matrix.

The above trapdoor commitment scheme has all the desired properties:

- Completeness: P can commit to any bit.

- Soundness: Even a cheating P cannot open the same committed value both as '0' and as '1', for this would imply his knowledge of a cycle in G, and this we assume he does not know.

- Security: V's ability to predict P's bit from the commitment phase implies V breaking the nontrapdoor commitment scheme.

- Trapdoor: If V knows a cycle in G, he can open bits he originally committed to as '0', both as '0' and as '1'.

It remains to fill in a few technical details.

- Our trapdoor commitment scheme is based on a nontrapdoor commitment scheme. Nontrapdoor commitment schemes can be constructed from any one-to-one oneway function (e.g. see [16]). At the price of one preliminary move, they can be constructed from any oneway function (see [20] and [21]).

- To make the trapdoor commitment scheme sound, we have to assume that P does not know a cycle in G, and thus V must choose a difficult instance of DHC. This can be done easily under IGA (see definition 2.6). Using the invulnerable generator, V chooses a random instance $(x, w) \in S$, where S is the corresponding invulnerable set, and reduces the problem "there exists w such that $(x, w) \in S$" to an instance G of the NP complete problem DHC. Since the reductions are efficiently invertible, finding a cycle in G implies associating a witness to the original x, and this problem is assumed to be hard.

The commitment scheme we constructed is trapdoor. This is necessary for the zero knowledge property of our 2-round protocol. But zero knowledge is a property which protects honest provers P against dishonest verifiers V. If V is dishonest, how can P trust him to send a graph which indeed contains a cycle? And even if the graph does contain a cycle, how do we know that V can find such a cycle? The answer is that a preliminary step is missing: V must prove beforehand that he knows a cycle in G. This must be done under the following constraints:

- V's proof must convince P.

- P must not be able to use this proof to learn a cycle in G.

- A simulator M (which is allowed to use V as a subroutine) should be able to extract the cycle from V.

This can be done easily. The commitment scheme is the basic step of some zero knowledge proof of knowledge. Thus V can just execute the complete zero knowledge proof of knowledge to show that he himself knows a cycle, without revealing any useful information about this cycle to P.

There is one problem left. V's proof takes too many moves, as in order to guarantee the zero knowledge property, V must employ sequential composition of the basic step. However, the zero knowledge property is not really necessary in V's proof. In order to guarantee the soundness property of the trapdoor commitment scheme it suffices that P does not learn any cycle in G from V's proof, and we do not care if other "irrelevant" information is revealed to P. This extra flexibility in the security demands of V's protocol can be exploited by employing parallel composition instead of sequential composition in the construction of V's proof of knowledge from Protocol 1. In the next section we show that under suitable conditions (which are easy to meet) the parallel composition, though not zero knowledge, does not reveal any cycle in G.

5 Introduction to Witness Hiding Protocols

The concept of witness hiding protocols is a development of the concept of "transferable information", used in proving that the parallel version of the Fiat-Shamir protocol is secure [12]. For a full treatment of witness hiding protocols see [11]. This section only offers an introduction sufficient for the purposes of this paper.

The concept of Witness Hiding (WH - to be defined shortly) is a possible alternative to zero knowledge. It is a weaker requirement than zero knowledge, but in many cases, it still satisfies the security demands of cryptographic protocols. It comes together with a technical tool (witness indistinguishability), which replaces the technique of resettable simulation. The advantage WH has over zero knowledge is that (under well defined conditions) it is preserved under general composition of protocols. As a special case of general composition, it is preserved under parallel composition.

Informally, a protocol (P, V) is WH if participating in the protocol does not help the verifier (which can be either the original V or a cheating V') to compute appropriate witnesses to the input. This is a natural security requirement of many cryptographic protocols. In order to prove the WH property, one must show that if V' can compute a witness to the input after participating in the interactive proof, then he had this capability in him even before the protocol began. To this end we introduce the witness extractor M. We give the technical definition of this concept, and refer the reader to [11] for a discussion on this definition and a comparison between WH and zero knowledge.

Definition 5.1: Let (P, V) be a proof of knowledge system for language L. Let $\pi = \pi(n)$ be a probability distribution on the inputs $x \in L$ of size n, and on their corresponding witnesses $w(x)$. (P, V) is *witness hiding* (WH) on (L, π) if there exists a witness extractor M which runs in expected polynomial time, such that for any nonuniform polynomial time V'

$$Prob(V'_{P(x,w)}(x) \in w(x)) - Prob(M(x, V') \in w(x)) < \nu(n)$$

The probability is taken over the distribution of the inputs and witnesses, as well as the random tosses of P and M. The witness extractor is allowed to use V' (but not P) as a subroutine. ◇

In order to make use of the notion of WH, we need a technical tool for proving that protocols are WH. For this end we define *witness indistinguishability* (WI).

Definition 5.2: Proof system (P, V) is *witness indistinguishable* (WI) if for any V', for any large enough input x, for any $w_1 \in w(x)$ and $w_2 \in w(x)$, and for any auxiliary input y for V', the ensembles, $V'_{P(x,w_1)}(x, y)$ and $V'_{P(x,w_2)}(x, y)$, generated as V''s view of the protocol are indistinguishable.◇

WI involves no simulator M, and is suggested as an alternative to the resettable simulation technique. The next Theorem shows that WI is implied by zero knowledge.

Theorem 5.1: Let (P, V) be any zero knowledge protocol. Then the protocol is WI.

Proof (sketch): The proof follows from the transitivity of the indistinguishability relation. For input x, assume distinguisher D has probability p of outputting 1 on V's view of P's proof, when P is using w_1. By the zero knowledge property,

D has the same probability p (up to negligible additive terms) of outputting 1 on the simulated view created by M. But the view M creates is independent of the witness P is using. Thus D has probability p of outputting 1 on V's view even if P is using w_2. ◇

Theorem 5.2: WI is preserved under parallel composition of protocols.

Proof (sketch): Consider polynomially many parallel executions of a WI protocol (P, V). Assume that there exists a verifier V' for which this parallel composition is not WI. That is, there exist infinitely many n, inputs $x(n)$, auxiliary inputs $y(n)$ to V', and witnesses $w_1(n)$ and $w_2(n)$, such that the two ensembles $V'_{P(x,w_1)}(x, y)$ and $V'_{P(x,w_2)}(x, y)$ are polynomially distinguishable. Then somewhere there must be a "polynomial jump": For any n, there exists $k(n)$, such that if P uses witness $w_1(n)$ for executions of index less than $k(n)$, and P uses witness $w_2(n)$ for executions of index greater than $k(n)$, the ensembles (which differ only in the witness used in iteration $k(n)$) are distinguishable. We construct a modified cheating V^* for the original protocol (P, V). V^* has as auxiliary input $y^*(n) = (y(n), k(n), w_1(n), w_2(n))$. This random polynomial time V^*, when interacting with truthful P, simulates by himself all the other parallel iterations which are taking place with V'. We use here the fact that both V' and P are polynomial time, and so V^* can simulate both these protocols. Now V^* can distinguish between truthful P using $w_1(n)$ and $w_2(n)$, which is a contradiction to our assumption that the original protocol was WI. ◇

The above two Theorems establish a methodology for constructing WI protocols. Take the basic step of a ZKIP. By Theorem 5.1 it is also WI. Iterate the basic step n times in parallel. This is not zero knowledge, but by Theorem 5.2, it is WI. What we need now is to establish a connection between WI and WH. We cannot prove that any WI protocol is also WH, but we can specify conditions under which WI implies WH. These conditions involve the particular method by which input instances are generated. A protocol may be trivially WI because every input has only one possible witness. In this case WI cannot imply anything. But if any input has at least two "independent" witnesses, than the WI property is nontrivial, and it may be possible to infer WH from WI. We demonstrate this point by the following protocol, which will subsequently be used in our *perfect* zero knowledge 2-rounds proofs of knowledge.

Protocol 2 is based of the discrete log problem. We modify this problem so that each instance of the new modified problem has two independent witnesses.

Protocol 2: The common input is generated by a slight twist to the invulnerable generator of the certified discrete log assumption, which forces the input to have two witnesses. The input is (p, g, c, x_1, x_2), where p, g, and c are as described in CDLA, and x_1 and x_2 are integers in Z_p^* chosen randomly and independently. This instance is defined to have two possible witnesses: w_1 satisfying $g^{w_1} = x_1 \bmod p$, and w_2 satisfying $g^{w_2} = x_2 \bmod p$. (w_i is the *discrete logarithm* of x_i). P receives as witness $w \in \{w_1, w_2\}$. P proves that he knows the discrete log of either x_1 or x_2. The basic step of the protocol is:

1. P chooses secretly, randomly and independently r_1, r_2, and computes $y_1 = x_1 g^{r_1} \bmod p$, $y_2 = x_2 g^{r_2} \bmod p$. P sends these two values in a random order to V.

2. V replies by a random challenge: 0 or 1.

3. If P receives 0, P reveals r_1 and r_2, and V checks that y_1 and y_2 were constructed correctly (satisfy $y = xg^r \bmod p$). If P receives 1, P reveals the discrete log of *only one of* the y's (which equals $w + r \pmod{p-1}$).

This basic step is executed $\log p$ independent times *in parallel*.

Theorem 5.3: The above protocol is a complete and sound witness hiding proof that P knows the discrete log of one of two inputs, under the distribution of inputs specified in CDLA (see section 2).

Proof (sketch): The proof of the completeness and soundness properties of the protocol is standard. We prove only the WH property.

The basic step of the protocol is zero knowledge (and even perfect zero knowledge). The parallel composition of the basic step gives a protocol which is presumably not zero knowledge, but still (by Theorems 5.1 and 5.2) this protocol is WI. Assume that for some V' Protocol 2 is not WH. Then V' learns with nonnegligible probability one of the discrete logs (w.l.o.g., assume it is w_1). But because of WI, V' has the same probability of learning w_1 whether P is really using w_1 or the other witness w_2. This gives a random polynomial time algorithm for computing the discrete log, contradicting CDLA: On input (p, g, c, x), M has to compute w satisfying $x = g^w \bmod p$. M chooses randomly and uniformly w_2 and creates $x_2 = g^{w_2} \bmod p$. M sets $x_1 = x$ and uses (p, g, c, x_1, x_2) as input to Protocol 2. In this protocol M simulates P and uses his control over V' to obtain V's replies. By our assumption, V' has nonnegligible probability of extracting w_1 from this protocol. Thus M has nonnegligible probability of computing the discrete log of x, violating CDLA. ⋄

The basic step of protocol 2 can be used as a trapdoor commitment scheme, provided P knows neither w_1 nor w_2. P commits to 0 by constructing y_1 and y_2 as in move 1 of protocol 2. P commits to 1 by choosing random r, and constructing one of the y's as g^r.

In order to construct the 3-move WH protocol (protocol 2), we composed two random instances of the discrete log problem. This procedure of composing two random instances can be followed with any NP language. Protocol 2 uses self randomizing [2] properties of the discrete log. For other NP languages, we may not have direct protocols for proving knowledge of one of two witnesses, and in this case, P and V may reduce the composed input instance to an instance of the NP-complete set DHC, and use protocol 1. If the instances of the original NP language are generated by an invulnerable generator, then the proof that the resulting protocol is WH is similar to the proof of Theorem 5.3. In [11] we prove a stronger and more general Theorem, stated here without proof.

Theorem 5.4: Let G be any generator for a set $S = \{(x, w)\}$ recognizable in BPP (which need not be invulnerable). Let π be the distribution obtained by two independent applications of G, taking (x_1, x_2) as common input, and one of w_1 or w_2 at random as a corresponding witness. Let (P, V) be any WI system for proving knowledge of a witness w s.t. $((x_1, w) \in S$ or $(x_2, w) \in S)$. Then (P, V) is WH. ◇

6   The Full Protocols

We first present a 3-round *perfect* zero knowledge proof of knowledge for DHC, based on CDLA. Then we show how this protocol can be modified to two rounds. Finally we show how the cryptographic assumption can be weakened, from CDLA to the existence of any one-to-one oneway function, at the price of obtaining a protocol which is only computationally zero knowledge. The construction of 5-move protocols from any oneway function (using Naor's [21] bit commitment scheme) is an easy consequence of our techniques.

Protocol 3a: Perfect zero knowledge proof of knowledge for DHC. Cryptographic assumption: CDLA. Protocol 3a is a sequential composition of Protocol 2 and Protocol 1, described in sections 5 and 3 respectively.

Common input: G, a Hamiltonian graph. P's witness is H, a cycle in G.

Move 1: V uses the modified invulnerable generator based on CDLA to generate an input $I = (p, g, c, x_1, x_2)$ for protocol 2. V is to act as prover in protocol 2, and so he discards randomly either w_1 or w_2, and keeps the other (denoted as w) as his auxiliary input. V sends I to P.

Null Move: P uses the certificate c to check that p is prime and g a generator. If this check fails, P stops.

Moves 1-3: V and P now perform Protocol 2 with I as input. Note that in this subprotocol, the roles are reversed: V is the prover (with w as auxiliary input) and P is the verifier.

Null Move: If Protocol 2 is completed successfully, than P is convinced that V knows a witness to I. Otherwise P stops.

Moves 4-6: P and V execute the parallel composition of Protocol 1, with common input G, and P's auxiliary input is H. As a bit commitment scheme, P uses the basic step of Protocol 2 with I as input. This commitment scheme is trapdoor, because V already proved (in the previous subprotocol) that he knows a witness for I.

Null Move: If Protocol 1 is completed successfully, V accepts.

◇

Protocol 3a consists of 6 moves. In order to reduce the number of moves to 4 (i.e. the number of rounds to 2), we modify this protocol:

Protocol 3: 2-Round perfect zero knowledge proof of knowledge for DHC. The protocol proceeds exactly as protocol 3a, but executes subprotocols 2 and 1 almost in parallel by regrouping the six moves into four super-moves: (1); (2,4); (3,5); (6). (The reader should work out this regrouping by himself, from the explicit description of protocols 1 and 2). ◇

Protocol 3 assumes CDLA, which is a strong assumption. The modified discrete log problem was used as a trapdoor commitment scheme. In order to use a weaker cryptographic assumption, we base the trapdoor commitment scheme on DHC (as explained in section 4). The protocol we obtain this way is only computational zero knowledge.

Protocol 4a: Computational zero knowledge proof of knowledge for DHC. Cryptographic assumptions: IGA and the existence of bit commitment schemes. Both assumptions follow from the single assumption that one-to-one oneway functions exist.

Common input: G, a Hamiltonian graph. P's witness is H, a cycle in G.

Move 1: V uses the invulnerable generator to create two hard certified instances $(x_1, w_1) \in S$ and $(x_2, w_2) \in S$. V reduces the NP statement "there exists w such that either $(x_1, w) \in S$ or $(x_2, w) \in S$" to an instance I of the NP complete problem DHC. The witnesses w_1 and w_2 are transformed into two cycles in I, of which V randomly discards one and keeps the other (denoted as w). V sends (I, x_1, x_2) to P.

Null Move: P checks that I is indeed obtained from (x_1, x_2) by the publicly known polynomial reduction. If this check fails, P stops.

Moves 1-3: V and P now perform the parallel composition of Protocol 1 on input I. Note that in this subprotocol, the roles are reversed: V is the prover (with auxiliary input w) and P is the verifier. In order to execute the prover's part in Protocol 1, V must randomly choose a bit commitment scheme. We denote this commitment scheme by C_V.

Null Move: If Protocol 1 is completed successfully, then P is convinced that V knows a witness to I. Otherwise P stops.

Moves 4-6: P and V again execute the parallel composition of Protocol 1, this time with P as the prover, V as the verifier, G as the common input, and H as P's auxiliary input. As a trapdoor bit commitment scheme, P uses the basic step of the same Protocol 1, but with I as input. For this basic step, P needs to use another (nontrapdoor) bit commitment scheme (see Protocol 1), and we denote this commitment scheme by C_P.

Null Move: If Protocol 1 is completed successfully, V accepts.

⋄

Protocol 4a takes 6 moves. As before, we can reduce the number of moves to 4 by parallelizing some of the steps:

Protocol 4: 2-Round computational zero knowledge proof of knowledge for DHC. Transform protocol 4a into protocol 4 in exactly the same way as protocol 3a is transformed to protocol 3. ⋄

7 Correctness

Theorem 7.1: Under the certified discrete log assumption, Protocol 3 is a complete, sound and perfect zero knowledge proof of knowledge of a Hamiltonian cycle in a directed graph.

Proof (sketch): We sketch the proof for Protocol 3a. The proof for Protocol 3 is similar. We need to prove three properties: Completeness, soundness, zero knowledge.

Completeness: Trivial.

Soundness: We describe a knowledge extractor M, which stops in expected polynomial time, and the probability it outputs a cycle in G is the same (up to negligible additive terms) as the probability that P' convinces a truthful V.

Given (a possibly cheating) P', M first executes the whole protocol (P', V), by faithfully simulating V's part. If V rejects, M stops and outputs nothing. Otherwise, M repeatedly resets P' to step 5 of the protocol, chooses new random challenges (in step 2 of Protocol 1), until P' again meets these challenges successfully. When this happens, or if P' failed to answer 2^n successive challenges, M stops. Now there are three possible events:

1. P' failed to answer 2^n successive challenges.

2. The second set of challenges was met by P' by opening some committed bit differently than in his original success.

3. The soundness of the trapdoor commitment scheme was not violated, and from the two successful executions, M can derive a cycle in G. (This is because P' opened the committed matrix and showed its isomorphism to G, and showed a cycle in the same matrix).

We have to show two things: That M's expected running time is polynomial, and that the first two events have negligible probability. In order to analyze M's running time, we specify by p P''s conditional probability of completing the protocol, given that move 4 was completed. Then M's expected running time is proportional to $(1 - p) \cdot 1 + p \cdot \frac{1}{p} < 2$ times the running time of V (which is polynomial). This also shows that the probability of the first event is negligible ($O(2^{-n})$). As to the probability of the second event: Consider its a-priori probability at the beginning of the protocol. If it is negligible, we ignore it. If it is not negligible, this violates the CDLA, as described in the proof of Theorem 5.3 (the WH property of Protocol 2).

Zero-knowledge: We describe a simulator M, which for any (possibly cheating) V', creates in expected polynomial time a view of the protocol indistinguishable from the view of V'. The simulator first performs P's part in moves 1-3. If V' does not complete this subprotocol successfully, M stops. Otherwise, M repeats move 2, each time with different randomly chosen challenges, until V' again successfully meets M's challenges. From the two successful executions M can find a discrete log w. To guard against an infinite execution in case there is only one set of challenges that V answers correctly, M tries in parallel to find w_1 by himself (using exhaustive search).

Once M finds a w, he can create instances of the trapdoor commitment scheme which he can open both as 0 and as 1. This allows him to carry out P's part in moves 4-6, without knowing a Hamiltonian cycle and without using resettable simulation.

The analysis of M's running time is similar to the analysis of knowledge soundness. The view created is perfectly indistinguishable from V's view of the protocol when executed with a real P. ◇

Theorem 7.2: Under the invulnerable generator assumption, and under the assumption that secure (nontrapdoor) bit commitment schemes exist, Protocol 4 is a complete, sound and computational zero knowledge proof of knowledge of a Hamiltonian cycle in a directed graph.

Proof (sketch): We sketch the proof for Protocol 4a (the proof for Protocol 4 is similar). The main new complication is the use of the two nontrapdoor commitment schemes: C_V and C_P. We concentrate only on aspects that do not appear in the proof of Theorem 7.1.

Completeness: Proving this property involves only one subtle point: The derivation of I, which serves as the basis of the trapdoor commitment scheme, is done by a polynomial reduction to DHC which preserves witnesses. This ensures that V can complete his part of the protocol in moves 1-3, where he has to know a cycle in I.

Soundness: The knowledge extractor M works in a way analogous to the proof of Theorem 7.1. The proof that its expected running time is polynomial is similar. Complications arise from two sources:

1. In addition to the three events we had earlier, we now have a fourth possible event: P' met two challenges, by violating the soundness property of his nontrapdoor commitment scheme C_P.

2. P' may learn a cycle in I in moves 1-3, by violating the security of V's nontrapdoor commitment scheme C_V.

Thus in proving the knowledge soundness property, we must exclude the above two events as having negligible probability. This follows from the assumption that there exist sound and secure bit commitment schemes.

Zero knowledge: Again, the nontrapdoor commitment schemes cause complications.

1. The simulator M, in trying to extract a witness for I from moves 1-3, may not succeed, and instead discover a violation of the soundness of C_V (a bit commitment V once opened as 0 and once as 1).

2. The protocol is not perfect zero knowledge. The view generated by M differs from the view generated in real executions of the protocol in the value of the unopened commitments to bits by C_P.

In proving that the protocol is zero knowledge, we must prove that the first event has negligible probability. This follows from the assumption that C_V is a sound commitment scheme. We must also prove that no nonuniform polynomial time distinguisher can take advantage of the differences between the two ensembles. This follows from the assumption that C_P is a secure commitment scheme. ◇

8 Concluding Remarks

Witness hiding is an attractive alternative to zero knowledge not only in interactive proofs. Its use offers advantages also in noninteractive proofs. Noninteractive zero knowledge proofs, as introduced in [4] and [10], postulate the existence of a publicly known random string (such as tables of random numbers prepared by the RAND corporation). [4] and [10] show how a prover may use this random string to write down a noninteractive zero knowledge proof of any NP statement. However, the prover may not use the same common random string in order to prove many (more than $\log n$) statements, since the zero knowledge property breaks down. In [11] we show that WH does not suffer from the same drawback, and noninteractive witness hiding protocols may use the same common random string repeatedly, without jeopardizing the WH property. This property is valuable in using noninteractive WH protocols as a basic primitive in the construction of more complicated cryptographic primitives (such as signature schemes [7]). More details appear in [11].

Acknowledgements

We thank Gilles Brassard, Joan Feigenbaum, Oded Goldreich, Shafi Goldwasser, Joe Kilian and Mike Luby for helpful discussions.

References

[1] M. Abadi, E. Allender, A. Broder, J. Feigenbaum, L. Hemachandra, *On Generating Solved Instances of Computational Problems* Proc. of CRYPTO88.

[2] D. Angluin, D. Lichtenstein, *Provable Security of Cryptosystems: a Survey* TR-288, Yale University, 1983.

[3] M. Blum, *How to Prove a Theorem So No One Else Can Claim It* Proc. of the International Congress of Mathematicians, Berkeley, California, USA, 1986, pp. 1444-1451.

[4] M. Blum, P. Feldman, S. Micali, *Non-Interactive Zero-Knowledge and its Applications* Proc. of 20th STOC 1988, pp. 103-112.

[5] G. Brassard, D. Chaum, C. Crépeau, *Minimum Disclosure Proofs of Knowledge* JCSS, Vol. 37, 1988, pp. 156-189.

[6] G. Brassard, C. Crépeau, M. Yung, *Everything in NP can be argued in perfect zero-knowledge in a bounded number of rounds* Proc. of 16th ICALP, Stresa, Italy, 1989.

[7] M. Bellare, S.Goldwasser, *New Paradigms for Digital Signatures and Message Authentication Based on Non-Interactive Zero Knowledge Proofs* these proceedings.

[8] S. Cook, *The Complexity of Theorem Proving Procedures* Proc. of 3rd STOC 1971, pp. 151-158.

[9] I. Damgård, *On the Existence of Bit Commitment Schemes and Zero Knowledge Proofs* these proceedings.

[10] A. De Santis, S. Micali, G. Persiano, *Non-Interactive Zero-Knowledge Proof Systems* Proc of CRYPTO-87, pp. 52-72.

[11] U. Feige, A. Shamir, *Witness Hiding Protocols and Their Applications* In preparation.

[12] U. Feige, A. Fiat, A. Shamir, *Zero Knowledge Proofs of Identity* Journal of Cryptology, Vol 1, 1988, pp. 77-94. (Preliminary version in Proc. of 19th STOC 1987, pp. 210-217.)

[13] L. Fortnow, *The Complexity of Perfect Zero-Knowledge* Proc. of 19th STOC, 1987, pp. 204-209.

[14] O. Goldreich, private communication.

[15] O. Goldreich, H. Krawczyk, *On the Composition of Zero-Knowledge Proof Systems* manuscript, May 1989.

[16] O. Goldreich, L. Levin, *A Hard-Core Predicate for all Oneway Functions* Proc. 21st STOC 1989, pp. 25-32.

[17] O. Goldreich, S. Micali, A. Wigderson, *Proofs that Yield Nothing But Their Validity and a Methodology of Cryptographic Protocol Design* Proc. 27th FOCS, 1986, pp. 174-187.

[18] S. Goldwasser, S. Micali, C. Rackoff, *The Knowledge Complexity of Interactive Proof Systems* SIAM J. Comput. Vol. 18, No. 1, pp. 186-208, February 1989.

[19] E. Horowitz, S. Sahni, *Fundamentals of Computer Algorithms* Computer Science Press, Computer Software Engineering Series, (pp. 526-529).

[20] R. Impagliazzo, L. Levin, M. Luby, *Pseudo-Random Generation From Oneway Functions* Proc. 21st STOC, 1989, pp. 12-24.

[21] M. Naor, *Bit Commitment using Pseudo-Randomness* these proceedings.

[22] V. Pratt, *Every Prime Has a Succinct Certificate* SIAM J. Computing 4 (1975), pp. 214-220.

[23] M. Tompa, H. Woll, *Random Self-Reducibility and Zero Knowledge Interactive Proofs of Possession of Information* Proc. 28th FOCS, 1987, pp. 472-482.

Minimum Resource
Zero-Knowledge Proofs

(Extended Abstract)

Joe Kilian[*]   Silvio Micali[†]   Rafail Ostrovsky[‡]

Abstract

What are the resources of a zero-knowledge Proof? *Interaction, communication, and envelops.* That interaction, that is the number of rounds of a protocol, is a resource is clear. Actually, it is not a very available one: having someone on the line to answer your questions all the time is quite a luxury. Thus, minimizing the number of rounds in zero-knowledge proofs will make these proofs much more attractive from a practical standpoint. That communication, that is the number of bits exchanged in a protocol, is a resource is also immediately clear. Perhaps, what is less clear is why envelopes are a resource. Let us explain why this is the case.

Zero-knowledge proofs work by hiding data from a verifier. Only some of this data will be later revealed, at the verifier's request: enough to convince him that the statement at end is true, but not enough to give him any knowledge beyond that. Data can be hidden in two ways: physically – e.g. by putting it into an envelope – or digitally – by encrypting it. But why is it important to minimize the number of envelopes? Physically, because a GOOD envelope is expensive – it actually must be a led box or a safe. Digitally, because minimizing the number of envelopes corresponds to reducing the transmitted bits. In fact, to transmit an encrypted message, one needs to send more bits than in the message itself. For instance, to send an encrypted bit, one needs to send at least 60 bits in some probabilistic encryption scheme. Also, to decrypt each ciphertext, one has to send the decryption key. However, many bits may be encrypted and decrypted with the same overhead of a few bits. Thus if one manages to package the data that should be hidden in as few envelopes as possible, while maintaining zero-knowledge, the protocol will require transmitting much less bits.

[*]MIT, partially supported by NSF 865727-CCR and ARO DALL03-86-K-017.

[†]MIT, supported in part by NSF grant DCR-84-13577.

[‡]Boston University, supported in part by NSF grant DCR-86-07492.

MINIMIZING ENVELOPES AND COMMUNICATION

How many envelops are sufficient for any (not a specific) zero-knowledge proof? Certainly 0 is not enough. And 1 alone does not seem to help. Shamir [oral communication] a few years ago presented a zero-knowledge proof for Knapsack problems which required only 3 envelopes. Recently, Levin [oral communication] a few months ago presented a 3-envelope ZK proof for Graph Coloring. Why was this not satisfactory? Because their solution only works for the mentioned specific problems. That is, it is not a technique that applies to any NP problem. Assume that you want to prove in zero-knowledge that a graph is Hamiltonian. You wish to use few envelopes. First you would transform your input to an instance of Knapsack. Then you would prove, using only 3 envelopes, that the resulting Knapsack problem is solvable. However, this transformation DOES NOT PRESERVE THE SIZE OF THE PROBLEM. In fact, if your original problem consisted of n bits, the resulting Knapsack may easily consist of n^2 bits. That is, you may use only 3 envelopes, but these envelopes are enormous, as they have to contain n^2 bits. This defeats the motivation of using few envelopes in the first place.

We present a scheme for proving statements in zero-knowledge that

1. uses only 2 envelopes and

2. works for any NP statement.

That is, you can apply our method to your problem directly, without blowing up its size.

MINIMIZING INTERACTION

Blum, Feldman and Micali, and De Santis, Micali and Persiano have shown that if two parties agree on a common random string, then they can perform zero-knowledge proofs. Their result requires some interaction at the beginning for choosing the common random string. After that, however, the prover, for each theorem that he discovers, may send to the verifier a single message (to which the verifier needs not to respond) that constitutes a zero-knowledge proof of the discovered theorem. Their result, however, assumes that a specific, number theoretic permutation is trap-door. Usually cryptography starts with very specific assumptions and later manages to find solutions that work given any general assumption. This is also the case here.

We succeeded in achieving non-interactive zero-knowledge proofs by using ANY general trap-door permutation (algebraic or not). More specifically, we prove that after a pre-processing stage consisting of $O(k)$ executions of Oblivious Transfer, *any* polynomial number of NP-theorems of any poly-size can be proved non-interactively and in zero-knowledge, based on the existence of *any* one-way function, so that the probability of accepting a false theorem is less then $\frac{1}{2^k}$. The Oblivious transfer may be easily implemented given a trap-door permutation.

AN EXTENDED VERSION OF THIS PAPER APPEARS IN THE PROCEEDINGS OF 30TH ANNUAL SYMPOSIUM ON FOUNDATIONS OF COMPUTER SCIENCE

Non-Interactive Oblivious Transfer
and Applications

Mihir Bellare[*]   Silvio Micali[†]

MIT Laboratory for Computer Science
545 Technology Square
Cambridge, MA 02139

Abstract

We show how to implement oblivious transfer without interaction, through the medium of a public file. As an application we can get non-interactive zero knowledge proofs via the same public file.

1 Introduction

1.1 Non-Interactive Oblivious Transfer

The intriguing concept of an *oblivious transfer* was introduced by Rabin, and has since then proven to be a powerful tool in the design of cryptographic protocols. Interaction, however, has seemed so far to be crucial to any implementation of it. Could one design a non-interactive version of this important primitive? We propose here several ways in which to do this.

The setting we consider is a public key one. Each user B is equipped with a public key P_B and a secret key S_B. A non-interactive oblivious transfer is a means whereby any A can obliviously transfer something to such a B, without the recipient's having to take any action at all. A little more formally,

Non-Interactive Oblivious Transfer : A has two strings s_0 and s_1. As a function of these and B's public key P_B she computes a message m and sends it to B. Using his secret key S_B, B can extract from m exactly one of the strings s_0 or s_1. A will not know which of the two B got.

---

[*] Supported in part by NSF grant CCR-87-19689 and DARPA Contract N00014-89-J-1988.

[†] Supported in part by NSF grant DCR-84-13577, ARO grant DAALO3-86-K-0171, and DARPA Contract N00014-89-J-1988.

A related concept is that of an *oblivious transfer channel*. This is a means of obliviously transferring a lot of information.

Oblivious Transfer Channel (OT channel): An oblivious transfer channel from A to B is a pair $C = (C^0, C^1)$ of channels such that

- A can send any number of bits on either C^0 or C^1

- One of the channels is clear to B (in the sense that he will see any bit that is sent on it) while the other is opaque

- A does not know which channel is clear to B.

OT channels are usually easier to think about and we will see that a single non-interactive oblivious transfer of a pair of short strings can be used to establish these channels.

It should be noted that although an OT channel allows lots of bits to be obliviously transmitted, the obliviousness in not independent. That is, suppose A sends b_0 on C^0 and b_1 on C^1, and suppose B gets b_0. Then, if A now sends c_0 on C^0 and c_1 on C^1, it is c_0 that B will get. Although A does not know which bit of each pair B got, he does know that it is either both b_0 and c_0 or both b_1 and c_1. This can be both an advantage and a drawback. For many applications, though, it is good enough. One such application, which we will describe here, is a construction of multi-user non-interactive zero knowledge systems.

In any case, in a science concerned with secret transmission, a primitive like non-interactive OT remains of fundamental importance and independent interest, over and above the applications visible at this stage.

1.2 Non-Interactive Zero Knowledge

We apply the non-interactive OT to obtain public key non-interactive zero knowledge systems. This is a setup in which there are many users, each with a public key, who can prove theorems to each other in zero knowledge and without interaction. A little more precisely,

Public Key Non-Interactive Zero Knowledge Systems: Consider a community of users, where each user B has a public key P_B and a secret key S_B. We call this a *public key non-interactive zero knowledge system* if for each pair of users A and B, and for each theorem T, it is possible for A to give B a *non-interactive zero knowledge proof* of T. This is a message m which A computes as a function of her theorem and B's public key and which she then sends to B. B's secret key enables him to decode m to the extent that he is satisfied of the correctness of the theorem, but he learns nothing more than that the theorem is true. Note that the communication is in one direction only: in order to receive the proof B need send nothing to A. Moreover, not only can any other user C also send proofs to B, but the number of theorems that can be proved to B is not limited.

Ours are the first implementations of non-interactive zero knowledge proofs which permit many provers and verifiers who do not have to interact individually with one another before proving theorems (non-interactively) in zero knowledge.

Non-interactive zero-knowledge was introduced by Blum, Feldman, and Micali [BFM][1]. They showed how a prover could prove a theorem to a verifier when both parties share a common random string. The drawback of their system, however, was that it was restricted to two parties: if many users wished to prove theorems to each other, each pair of them would have to share a separate random string. This becomes quickly prohibitive as the number of users grows. Their implementation was also somewhat impractical.

Kilian [K1] showed how a theorem could be encoded and then transmitted using oblivious transfer in such a way as to achieve zero knowledge. Kilian, Micali and Ostrovsky [KMO] have a scheme which moves the oblivious transfer to a short pre-processing stage. That is, the prover and verifier first exchange some information via oblivious transfer. This enables the prover, in a later stage, to send the verifier zero knowledge proofs without interaction. The initial interactive phase scheme again means, however, that this scheme is restricted to two parties. On the other hand the encoding of proofs used is quite efficient and the system does not restrict the sizes of theorems.

Our public key zero knowledge systems evolve from the [KMO] work. We replace the initial interactive phase with public keys. To prove theorems we use the same encoding of theorems as [KMO] and accomplish the proofs via non-interactive OT. Since each user either creates his public key himself or gets it from some center (*without* interaction with the person proving theorems to him), anyone can prove theorems to him.

Given that some of our implementations of non-interactive OT are quite efficient, and we use the [KMO] proof encodings, we get some quite efficient implementations of zero knowledge.

Public Key non-interactive knowledge proofs themselves have cryptographic applications; for example, Bellare and Goldwasser [BG] have shown how they can be used for message authentication.

Remark: As pointed out by Crépeau, proofs in [BFM] are transitive·(that is, if B received a proof of a theorem from A she could show it to C, and C too would be convinced of the proof). Our proofs are *not* transitive, as is desirable in a zero knowledge proof.

1.3   Results and Organization of this Paper

We begin (§2) with a simple, concrete, and easily implementable scheme for non-interactive oblivious transfer.

The next set of schemes we present (§3) are more theoretical, and involve having a key distribution center. These centers are *not* trusted, and we show appropriate protocols whereby a user can get a key from them and the center gains no information which could compromise the key. These schemes have the advantage of being based on the general assumption of trapdoor permutations.

---

[1] The implementation described in the original [BFM] paper is not known to have a proof; a correct scheme has been announced by S. Micali [M].

We have relegated to an appendix the description of our principal application: how non-interactive OT can be used to get non-interactive zero knowledge proof systems.

2 Implementing Non-Interactive OT

We describe a simple, concrete implementation of non-interactive oblivious transfer based on the Diffie-Hellman assumption, and then suggest generalizations of this approach to get alternative implementations.

2.1 A Simple Scheme

Fix some prime p and generator g of Z_p^*. Suppose that these, as well as some element C of Z_p^*, are known to all the users in the system, but suppose that nobody knows the discrete log of C (ways of arriving at such situations are discussed later).

The arithmetic in this section will be understood to be mod p; we will write simply g^x rather than g^x mod p, etc.

How to Get Keys : B picks $i \in \{0,1\}$ at random, $x_i \in \{0,\ldots,p-2\}$ at random, and sets

- $\beta_i = g^{x_i}$
- $\beta_{1-i} = C \cdot (g^{x_i})^{-1}$.

His public key is (β_0, β_1) and his secret key is (i, x_i).

Anyone can check that B's public key (β_0, β_1) is correctly formed by checking that $\beta_0 \beta_1 = C$, and before sending him any proofs they will do so. Granted that the discrete log of C is unknown, B cannot know the discrete logs of both β_0 and β_1. Moreover, the public key does not reveal which of the two discrete logs B knows: the pair (β_0, β_1) is randomly distributed over the set of all pairs of elements of Z_p^* whose product is C. This will be crucial to the non-interactive OT we describe below.

The mechanism we use for non-interactive OT is similar to the Diffie-Hellman secret key exchange protocol, and is based on the same complexity assumption:

Diffie-Hellman Assumption : Given g^x and g^y, but neither x nor y, it is hard to compute g^{xy}.

The Diffie-Hellman assumption is one of the oldest and most tried in cryptography.

We can now describe how the non-interactive oblivious transfer of a pair of strings (s_0, s_1) is accomplished:

Non-Interactive OT(s_0, s_1):

In the above notation, let B's public key be (β_0, β_1) and his secret key (i, x_i).

- A picks at random $y_0, y_1 \in \{0,\ldots,p-2\}$ and sends $\alpha_0 = g^{y_0}, \alpha_1 = g^{y_1}$ to B. A then computes $\gamma_0 = \beta_0^{y_0}$ and $\gamma_1 = \beta_1^{y_1}$, and sends $r_0 = s_0 \oplus \gamma_0$ and $r_1 = s_1 \oplus \gamma_1$ to B.

- On receiving α_0 and α_1, B uses his secret key to compute $\alpha_i^{x_i} = \gamma_i$. He then computes $\gamma_i \oplus r_i = s_i$.

B thus receives s_i. The Diffie-Hellman assumption implies that he cannot compute γ_{1-i} (say $\beta_{1-i} = g^{x_{1-i}}$; then $\gamma_{1-i} = g^{x_{1-i}y_{1-i}}$ and B knows $g^{x_{1-i}}$ and $g^{y_{1-i}}$ but neither x_{1-i} nor y_{1-i}). Thus he cannot compute s_{1-i}. A has thus succeeded in obliviously transferring the pair of strings s_0 and s_1. Note that the transfer is indeed non-interactive: B sends nothing to A.

2.2 A More Secure Scheme

The above scheme is simplified as much as possible. In particular, it is not clear exactly how secure s_{1-i} is: the Diffie-Hellman assumption does not say anything about the bit security. This can be fixed by the standard method of using a hard-core bit. The theorem of Goldreich and Levin [GL] implies that predicting the bit $\langle g^{xy}, r \rangle$ given g^x, g^y and random r is as hard as computing g^{xy} given g^x, g^y (where $\langle g^{xy}, r \rangle$ denotes the inner product mod 2 of the strings g^{xy} and r). For a pair of bits (b_0, b_1) we then have

Non-Interactive OT(b_0, b_1):

In the above notation, let B's public key be (β_0, β_1) and his secret key (i, x_i).

- A picks at random $y_0, y_1 \in \{0, \dots, p-2\}$ and computes $\gamma_0 = \beta_0^{y_0}$ and $\gamma_1 = \beta_1^{y_1}$. She then picks random $r_0, r_1 \in \{0, 1\}^k$ (where $k = |p|$) subject to the restriction that $\langle \gamma_0, r_0 \rangle = b_0$ and $\langle \gamma_1, r_1 \rangle = b_1$. She sends $\alpha_0 = g^{y_0}, \alpha_1 = g^{y_1}$ and r_0, r_1 to B.

- On receiving α_0, α_1 and r_0, r_1, B uses his secret key to compute $\alpha_i^{x_i} = \gamma_i$. He then computes $b_i = \langle \gamma_i, r_i \rangle$.

The Goldreich-Levin theorem together with the Diffie-Hellman assumption imply that b_{1-i} is unpredictable to B.

As an aside, let us also point out that it is easy to modify our implementation of non-interactive OT to obtain a protocol for an *interactive* 1 out of 2 oblivious transfer based on the Diffie-Hellman assumption. Although it was known [GHY],[K2] that oblivious transfer in the interactive framework was possible under this assumption, the implementation arising out of the modification of our non-interactive scheme is simpler and more efficient.

2.3 Non-Interactive OT of More Bits: OT Channels

Suppose that A wishes in fact to oblivious transfer many pairs of strings to B, as would be required, for example, in the applications to non-interactive zero knowledge proofs that we present in Appendix A. She could, of course, just repeat the above as often as is necessary. More efficient, however, might be the following.

A begins by non-interactive oblivious transferring to B a pair of random k bit strings (s_0, s_1). This is done by non-interactively oblivious transferring $((s_0)_j, (s_1)_j)$ for each $j = 1, \ldots, k$ (where $(s_i)_j$ denotes the j-th bit of s_i) via the scheme of §2.2. Using a pseudo-random bit generator G (the hardness of discrete log, which is implied by the Diffie-Hellman assumption, implies the existence of pseudo-random bit generators [BlMi]) she then expands these seeds into the pair of long pseudo-random sequences $G(s_0)$ and $G(s_1)$. To oblivious transfer a pair of strings (r_0, r_1), A sends to B the bitwise X-OR of r_0 with the next unused bits of $G(s_0)$ and the bitwise X-OR of r_1 with the next unused bits of $G(s_1)$. B gets r_i since he knows the seed s_i, but gets no information about r_{1-i} since without the knowledge of s_{1-i} the sequence $G(s_{1-i})$ looks random to him.

More formally, the above establishes an OT channel. The method used is a general one.

Once OT channels are available, we can implement non-interactive zero knowledge proof systems via the methods outlined in Appendix A.

2.4   2 Out of 3 Non-Interactive OT

A particularly interesting variant of OT is the 2 out of 3 OT. Here A has three bits (b_0, b_1, b_2). B selects two of them and A does not know which pair of bits B got. The above scheme for 1 out of 2 non-interactive OT can easily be modified to directly implement a non-interactive 2 out of 3 OT. B will make his public keys as follows:

B picks at random a pair of distinct values $i, j \in \{0, 1, 2\}$, and then picks at random $x_i, x_j \in \{0, \ldots, p-2\}$. He sets

- $\beta_i = g^{x_i}, \beta_j = g^{x_j}$
- $\beta_l = C \cdot (g^{x_i})^{-1}(g^{x_j})^{-1}$, where $l \in \{0, 1, 2\}$ is the value not equal to i or j.

His public key is $(\beta_0, \beta_1, \beta_2)$ and his secret key is (i, j, x_i, x_j).

It is then easy to see how to generalize the scheme of §2.2 to define a **Non-Interactive 2 Out of 3 OT**(b_0, b_1, b_2), and we omit the details.

The interest of this variant of OT lies in its application to zero knowledge proofs via the results of [KMO]. They show a simple, efficient, general, and *non-cryptographic*[2] method of "zero knowledge proofs for NP in three envelopes" which can be used to directly implement non-interactive zero knowledge proofs via our non-interactive 2 out of 3 OT.

We note that the scheme described here is easily generalized to achieve a $t - 1$ out of t non-interactive OT for any t.

2.5   The Central Public Key

The above schemes requires the presence of some short string, common to all parties and satisfying some constraints, which can be used by any user to create his public

---

[2] The two envelope scheme described in Appendix A is cryptographic in the sense that creating the envelopes requires using encryption functions.

and secret keys. We might call this a *central public key*. Specifically, the central public key in the above consists of a random string C whose discrete log nobody know, together with a prime p and a generator g of Z_p^* for which the discrete log problem is hard.

How can a central public key with the desired properties be obtained? The simplest and most direct way would be to have a center create it. Its job done, the center could disappear. This would probably work well enough in practice.

If one does not want a center then multi-party protocols as in [GMW],[BGW], or [CCD] could be used by the users themselves to agree on a central public key. These protocols have the necessary feature of not allowing any user (or any small subset of users) to influence the choice of the key to their advantage.

2.6 A Proof of Security

In order to formally prove that the oblivious transfer has the right properties, we will have to add one more step. When B makes his public key, we have him publish a zero knowledge proof that he really did it correctly (formally, that he knows i, x_i such that $\beta_i = g^{x_i}$). In the simulation the simulator will use this proof to extract the value of i.

Such a proof could be implemented via [BFM]. Unfortunately the scheme of [BFM] is based on quadratic residuosity. In the final paper we will show how to get some kind of proof based on discrete log, at the expense of a small interaction with the center.

2.7 Other Implementations

In the final paper we will consider a general framework which encompasses schemes of the above sort. The idea is that a user should be able to create his public key on his own, using some central public key. Moreover, there is a pair of secrets associated with his public key of which he only knows one. This is guaranteed by the fact of some relation between his public key and the central key being true, and this relation can be checked by anyone. Given this, there is a way to establish two encryption algorithms only one of which the key holder can decrypt. These are used for the non-interactive OT.

3 Schemes with Centers

The simplest and most direct way in which to establish public and secret keys which permit non-interactive OT would be through the use of a key distribution center. For example, consider a center who gives B two numbers N_0 and N_1, only one of which is given in factored form. B makes (N_0, N_1) his public key. To non-interactively oblivious transfer things to B, A can use these numbers to establish encryption algorithms which are used to send the bits in encrypted form. B can only decrypt those bits sent using the number whose factorization he knows.

A closer examination of this idea shows that some care must be exercised. There are a variety of drawbacks to the naive use of centers:

- The center knows which channel is clear to B (he knows which number B has the factorization of). If he reveals this to A the latter can cheat.

- B might disregard what the center gives him and simply create, on his own, a key in which he places a pair of numbers *both* of whose factorizations he knows. He now extracts knowledge from the proofs he receives.

We propose here a way in which a key distribution center can be used to get appropriate keys while avoiding drawbacks of the above form. We will guarantee that after B gets a key from the center,

(1) The center does not know which channel is clear to B

(2) B cannot change his key, or use another key which he builds to suit himself.

We will do this using oblivious circuit evaluation, trapdoor permutations, and digital signatures.

Oblivious Circuit Evaluation : K has some input x and B has some input y. Both know a function F. At the end of the protocol the following holds:

- B learns the value of $F(x, y)$

- B learns no more information about x than that conveyed by the knowledge of $F(x, y)$

- K learns nothing about y or $F(x, y)$.

Oblivious circuit evaluation is a well known protocol of which numerous implementations exist. In particular it can certainly be done given the existence of trapdoor permutations.

Let G be a trapdoor permutation generator (that is, G is a probabilistic polynomial time algorithm which can be used to produce a random trapdoor permutation together with its inverse). Suppose that the center K has a public key P_K with respect to which it can provide signatures; secure digital signatures with trapdoor permutations are possible via [BeMi]. In order to compute the signatures K also has a secret key S_K.

The circuit F we consider takes as input a secret key S and a public key P for signatures, a bit i, and two strings r and s. The output is

$$F(S, P, r, s, i) = ((f_0, f_1), \sigma, f_i^{-1}) ,$$

where f_0 and f_1 are trapdoor permutations, f_i^{-1} is the inverse to f_i, and σ is a signature, with respect to the public key P, of the pair (f_0, f_1). To create these trapdoor permutations, F runs G twice, using as coin tosses the string $r \oplus s$. From the two pairs $(f_0, f_0^{-1}), (f_1, f_1^{-1})$ so obtained, F outputs (f_0, f_1) and a signature σ, with respect to P, of the string (f_0, f_1). The latter is created using P and S. F then also outputs f_i^{-1}.

When user B wishes to get keys, he engages in an oblivious circuit evaluation protocol for F with the center K. B provides the inputs s and i which he chooses at random. K provides r, which he chooses at random, and his own keys $P = P_K$

and $S = S_K$ for signatures. The output goes to B. He makes $((f_0, f_1), \sigma)$ his public key and f_i^{-1} his secret key. The two properties listed above do hold: (1) K does not learn i and hence does not know which channel will be clear to B (2) B cannot make a key to suit himself because he would not be able to produce a signature of it with respect to K's public key (the strong properties of the digital signatures of [BeMi] insure that this latter remains true even after B has seen many signatures from the center).

We note that we cannot, of course, protect against a totally corrupted center: for example, one who is willing to conspire with B and sign for him a bogus public key not obtained through the oblivious circuit evaluation.

To implement non-interactive OT with keys of the form B obtains here is easy: the trapdoor permutations can be used by A to send B encrypted bits. B can decode only one of these streams of bits since he knows only one of the trapdoors. The distribution according to which B's public key is chosen is such that A cannot tell which trapdoor permutation it is that B knows the inverse of.

4   The Non-Interactive OT Primitive

One of the features of the usual interactive OT which makes it a tool of such universal application in the design of interactive protocols is that many stronger versions of OT can be reduced to the simplest kind. Such reductions appear in the work of Brassard, Crépeau, and Robert [BCR]. The same holds true for non-interactive OT. In several cases the reductions of [BCR] apply since they do not involve interaction over and above that of the original protocol. It is interesting to note, however, the case of the most interesting reduction: how a 1 out of n bit transfer yields a 1 out of n string transfer. For the non-interactive case, the reduction is actually much *simpler* than the one for the interactive case.

A Appendix: Non-Interactive Zero Knowledge Proofs

This appendix describes how non-interactive zero knowledge proofs are accomplished via OT channels. For a definition of OT channels see §1.1.

Kilian, Micali and Ostrovsky [KMO] presented a method via which theorems could be proved, non-interactively and in zero-knowledge, based on obliviously transferred pseudo-random sequences; two seeds would be known to the prover, and only one of them (with the prover unaware of which one) to the verifier. Their scheme will work in the more general framework of oblivious transfer channels, and we describe it in that form here.

Suppose A wishes to prove some NP statement T of which she knows a witness. She transforms this to a graph $G = (V, E)$ of which she knows a Hamiltonian cycle, where $V = \{1, \ldots, n\}$. Let A_G be the adjacency matrix of G and let the edges of the Hamiltonian cycle be $(u_1, v_1), \ldots, (u_n, v_n) \in E$. Let k be a security parameter. We assume that k OT channels $C_1 = (C_1^0, C_1^1), \ldots, C_k = (C_k^0, C_k^1)$ from A to B are available (k being some security parameter).

A picks a random permutation π of the vertices of G and computes $G' = \pi(G) = (V, \pi(E))$, the isomorphic image of G under π. Let $A_{G'} = [a']_{ij}$ be the adjacency matrix of G'. She then picks some encryption function $\mathcal{E}(\cdot, \cdot)^3$, and does the following:

- Choosing r at random she encrypts π as $y = \mathcal{E}(\pi, r)$.

- She encrypts the adjacency matrix of the permuted graph by choosing r_{ij} at random and computing $y_{ij} = \mathcal{E}(a'_{ij}, r_{ij})$ for each $i, j = 1, \ldots, n$.

She now sends y and y_{ij} ($1 \leq i, j \leq n$) to B in the clear.

Finally, we arrive at the point where A uses an OT channel. She flips a coin. If it is heads, she sends r, r_{ij} ($1 \leq i, j \leq n$) along C_1^0 and $r_{\pi(u_1)\pi(v_1)}, \ldots, r_{\pi(u_n)\pi(v_n)}$ along C_1^1. If the coin is tails she reverses the roles of C_1^0 and C_1^1 in the above.

Actually, A repeats this entire procedure k times. That is, she obtains k encodings as described, and she uses C_i to transfer the i-th encoding to B.

To prove a further theorem, A does the same thing. She uses the same set of k channels (recall that they can take an unlimited number of bits).

At the receiving end, B sees either the permutation and the permuted graph, or a Hamiltonian cycle in a permuted version of the graph. This is a well known zero-knowledge proof of Hamiltonian cycle. A full proof of correctness, however, would require showing a simulator and a reduction via which the ability to distinguish the simulator's output from the prover's would compromise either the encryption function or the channels. Details of this sort are left to the final paper.

---

[3] This is [GM] style probabilistic encryption: to encrypt a string x, choose a random r and compute $\mathcal{E}(x, r)$; to decrypt, reveal r.

References

[BG]   Bellare, M., and S. Goldwasser, "A New Paradigm for Digital Signataures and Message Authentication based on Non-Interactive Zero Knowledge Proofs," CRYPTO 89.

[BeMi]   Bellare, M., and S. Micali, "How to Sign Given Any Trapdoor Function," STOC 88.

[BGW]   Ben-Or, M., S. Goldwasser, and A. Wigderson, "Completeness Theorem for Non-Cryptographic Fault Tolerant Distributed Computing," STOC 88.

[BlMi]   Blum, M., and S. Micali, "How to Generate Cryptographically Strong Sequences of Pseudo-Random Bits," *SIAM Journal on Computing*, Vol. 13, No. 4 (November 1984), 850-864.

[BCR]   Brassard, G., C. Crépeau, and J.-M. Robert, "Information Theoretic Reductions among Disclosure Problems," FOCS 86.

[BFM]   Blum, M., P. Feldman and S. Micali, "Non-Interactive Zero Knowledge and its Applications," STOC 88.

[CCD]   Chaum, D., C. Crépeau and I. Damgård, "Multiparty Unconditionally Secure Protocols," STOC 88.

[GHY]   Galil, Z., S. Haber and M. Yung, "Cryptographic Computation: Secure Fault-Tolerant Protocols and the Public Key Model," CRYPTO 87.

[GM]   Goldwasser, S., and S. Micali, "Probabilistic Encryption," *Journal of Computer and System Sciences* 28 (April 1984), 270-299.

[GL]   Goldreich, O. and L. Levin, "A Hard-Core Predicate for any One-Way Function," STOC 89.

[GMW]   Goldreich, O., S. Micali and A. Wigderson, "A Completeness Theorem for Protocols with Honest Majority," STOC 87.

[K1]   Kilian, J., "Founding Cryptography on Oblivious Transfer," STOC 88.

[K2]   Kilian, J., personal communication.

[KMO]   Kilian, J., S. Micali and R. Ostrovsky, "Efficient Zero Knowledge Proofs with Bounded Interaction," CRYPTO 89.

[M]   Micali, S., personal communication, March 1989.

Session 12:

Multiparty computation

Chair: KEVIN McCURLEY

Multiparty Protocols Tolerating Half Faulty Processors

Donald Beaver[*]
Aiken Computation Laboratory
Harvard University

Abstract

We show that a complete broadcast network of n processors can evaluate any function $f(x_1, \ldots, x_n)$ at private inputs supplied by each processor, revealing no information other than the result of the function, while tolerating up to t maliciously faulty parties for $2t < n$. This improves the previous bound of $3t < n$ on the tolerable number of faults [BGW88, CCD88]. We demonstrate a resilient method to multiply secretly shared values without using unproven cryptographic assumptions. The crux of our method is a new, non-cryptographic zero-knowledge technique which extends verifiable secret sharing to allow proofs based on secretly shared values. Under this method, a single party can secretly share values $v_1, \ldots, v_m$ along with another secret $w = P(v_1, \ldots, v_m)$, where P is any polynomial size circuit; and she can prove to all other parties that $w = P(v_1, \ldots, v_m)$, without revealing w or any other information. Our protocols allow an exponentially small chance of error, but are provably optimal in their resilience against Byzantine faults. Furthermore, our solutions use operations over exponentially large fields, greatly reducing the amount of interaction necessary for computing natural functions.

1 Introduction

For fault tolerance and security in a distributed system, it is desirable to be able to execute secure multiparty protocols. Such protocols allow a system to evaluate a function f at private inputs $x_1, \ldots, x_n$, each supplied by a member of the system, and to reveal the result to a designated recipient. Nothing about the private information held by each participant is revealed, other than what could otherwise be computed solely from the value of the function.

A secret ballot, for example, requires a tally of private votes, each of which must be restricted to a 0-1 value. The system must produce the tally without revealing any individual votes, and without allowing any misbehavior to affect the result.

---

[*]This research was supported in part under NSF grant CCR-870-4513.

In the case of a unanimous vote, for example, information about the inputs might inevitably be revealed by the value of the output; but no additional information is gained during the run of a protocol.

In [BGW88,CCD88] methods for secure, multiparty computations without using any unproven cryptographic assumptions were given. Those methods allowed for up to t Byzantine faults, where $3t < n$. It can be shown that, for information-theoretic, errorless security, those results were optimal. It was not clear, however, whether $2t < n$ could be achieved at the cost of allowing a negligible chance of error. For larger numbers of faults, of course, the faulty players constitute a majority and it becomes impossible merely to share a secret.

A natural question to ask, then, is whether multiparty computations can be achieved when $2t < n \leq 3t$. Recently [Rab88] made initial progress in this direction by demonstrating a method for verifiable secret sharing for $2t < n$, using a broadcast network, and having a small probability of error. Earlier methods for verifiable secret sharing with a faulty minority required cryptographic assumptions [CGMA85]. The extension to performing computations for $2t < n$, however, has remained open until now.

We present new and efficient methods for performing multiparty computations that tolerate $2t < n$. Our techniques utilize verifiable secret sharing for $2t < n$, and allow the field used for secret sharing to be of exponential size. Because we can simulate large-field arithmetic operations quickly and directly while alternative methods use bit-simulations or small-field arithmetic, our protocols have the practical advantage of using fewer rounds of communication for many natural functions.

Note that our methods are secure against adversaries with unbounded resources, while at the same time requiring only polynomial time to execute.

Methods for multiparty protocols tolerating a faulty minority were independently discovered by Ben-Or [BR89] and Kilian [Kil]. Whereas [BR89] use boolean circuit simulation (and implicitly require that the field used for secret sharing be polynomial size), our methods use a different and broader technique which allows direct computations in fields of exponential size, and are superior in terms of efficiency and flexibility.

In addition to proving that multiparty computations are possible when the honest players hold the majority, we show how zero-knowledge proofs can be implemented using a distributed system. Our new method for zero-knowledge proofs requires no cryptographic assumptions and allows up to half the participants to be faulty.

1.1 Secret Sharing and Computation

In Shamir's method for secret sharing [Sha79], a player Alice distributes a secret value s as follows. Let $p > n$ be prime and consider the field Z_p. Alice chooses t numbers $a_1, \ldots, a_t$ at random mod p, and sets $g(x) = a_t x^t + \cdots a_1 x + s$. Then she tells the "piece" $g(i)$ to player i, where i is a nonzero identifier. (In its most general form, secret sharing uses a unique evaluation point $\alpha_i \neq 0$ for each player, but for clarity and simplicity we take $\alpha_i = i$.) Clearly, $t + 1$ pieces are required to reconstruct a secret, and t or fewer pieces provide no information about the secret.

The design of noncryptographic multiparty protocols is greatly facilitated by dividing the goal into three stages. First, all private inputs to the protocol are secretly shared. The second stage produces a new secretly shared value w which is equal to $f(x_1, \ldots, x_n)$. This stage is known as *oblivious circuit evaluation* or *secret computation*. Finally, w is reconstructed and revealed to the proper recipients.

This modularization ensures independence of the inputs (faulty players choose their inputs independently of the inputs of nonfaulty players) and makes analysis of privacy and correctness easier. It also provides a means to link various multiparty protocols, using the secret outputs created by one protocol as inputs to the next protocol.

Thus, given methods to share secrets and to verify that they have been shared correctly, we can focus our attention on creating new secretly shared values based on old ones.

1.2 Results

Two basic protocols form the basis for building protocols to evaluate arbitrary arithmetic circuits. Secret addition provides each player with a piece of a new secret whose value is the sum of earlier secrets. Similarly, secret multiplication creates a new secret whose value is the product of earlier secrets. These two fundamental tools provide the means to construct a protocol to perform any secure and fault-tolerant multiparty computation.

In the sequel, let E be a finite field of size $2^{O(n)}$, and consider a complete, broadcast network with private channels.

Our main result is based on the following theorem, which reduces the problem of secret multiplication to that of secret addition, even when $2t < n$. By *t-resilient* we mean a protocol that preserves correctness and privacy, in the face of up to t Byzantine faults coordinated by a dynamic adversary.

Theorem 1 *For $2t < n$, if there exists a t-resilient protocol to add secrets, then there exists a t-resilient protocol to multiply secrets.*

The verifiable secret sharing methods of [Rab88,BR89] are not directly suitable for secret addition unless the original secrets are shared by a single party. We extend those methods, however, with some additional techniques that make it possible to add secrets regardless of their origin.

Thus, the supposition of Theorem 1 is satisfied, showing that multiplication is indeed possible for $2t < n$. As a direct consequence we have our primary result:

Theorem 2 *(Main Result.) Let $\{ C_n \}$ be a uniform polynomial size circuit family where each C_n computes a function f_n over a field E. For $2t < n$, there exists a t-resilient protocol to evaluate $f_n(x_1, \ldots, x_n)$, preserving the privacy of the inputs.*

Theorem 1 and Theorem 2 are based on a new and powerful technique whereby a single player shares secrets u, v, and w and can prove to the network that the value of w is indeed the product of the values of u and v, without revealing any other information. This non-cryptographic zero-knowledge technique generalizes to allow a player to prove that a secret w holds the value $P(v_1, \ldots, v_m)$, for any function P computed by a polynomial size circuit C_P, without revealing any additional information about w or about any of the v_i. In particular, any player in the network can give a zero-knowledge proof to any other player; the network simply reconstructs w for the verifier. This result has value of its own right.

Theorem 3 *(Zero-Knowledge.) Suppose that Alice knows the values $v_1, \ldots, v_m$, which have been secretly shared. Let P be a publicly known function of m arguments which is described by a polynomial size circuit C_P. For $2t < n$, there exists a t-resilient protocol by which Alice can share a secret w whose value is $P(v_1, \ldots, v_m)$, and by which she can prove to all other players that $w = P(v_1, \ldots, v_m)$, without revealing w or any other information.*

Lemma 4 *Any language in IP is provable in zero-knowledge in the presence of a network as described above, without using unproven cryptographic assumptions.*

Our protocols are time and communication efficient. All of the protocols in this paper require message sizes that are polynomial in the number n of players, the size of the arithmetic circuit C_f to be simulated, and a unary security parameter k ensuring correctness and privacy with probability at least $1 - \frac{1}{2^k}$. Let T be the number of rounds needed for Verifiable Secret Sharing (see section 2.2). The number of rounds of interaction is proportional to dT, where d is the depth of an algebraic circuit C_f with polynomial fanin $+$-gates and bounded fanin $\times$-gates over a field of size up to $2^{O(n)}$. The methods of [BB88] can be applied to reduce the number of rounds to $O(dT/\log n)$, or even to $O(T)$, the latter at a possible increase in message size.

Furthermore, we use no unproven cryptographic assumptions.

In section 2 we introduce some definitions and discuss protocol properties. Section 3 describes the overall design for multiparty protocols. In section 4 we discuss how secrets can be added, and in section 5 we give the novel result that if secrets can be added then secrets can be multiplied (Theorem 1). Using our methods for secret addition, secret multiplication, and zero-knowledge proofs, we show the main theorem in section 6. Finally, non-cryptographic zero-knowledge proofs of properties of secrets (Theorem 3) are discussed in section 7.

An earlier version of this paper appeared as [Bea88b].

2   Preliminaries

In this section we list some definitions, including desired properties of verifiable secret sharing and of protocols to compute functions. For purposes of this extended abstract, however, proofs of the formal properties listed here will not be given in detail.

564

2.1 Protocol Properties

Definition 1 *A protocol is a set of n interactive Turing machines $\{\,M_i\,\}$ with inputs $\{\,(x_i,1^k)\,\}$, communication tapes $\{\,t_{ij}\,\}$, broadcast tapes $\{\,b_i\,\}$, and outputs $\{\,y_i\,\}$, where k is a security parameter expressed in unary.*

Our protocols will be resilient against Byzantine faults coordated by a dynamic adversary. That is, we allow an adversary to choose to substitute $M_{i'}$ for an arbitrary M_i at any time, based on information held by processors whose programs have already been corrupted. The adversary is restricted to t corruptions, where $2t < n$.

In order to consider the correctness and other properties of the protocol, we let P_i denote the probability distribution according to which x_i is selected. Let $f : P_1 \times P_2 \times ... \times P_n \to \{0,1\}$ be the function we want to compute. If T is a coalition of at most t processors, $w = f_T(x_1,...,x_n)$ denotes the correct value of the function, where f_T is the function obtained from f by substituting default inputs for the processors in T who are disqualified during the Input stage.

Let VIEW_i be a random variable describing a transcript of everything written on the input, output, and communication tapes that are readable or writable by processor i. For a coalition T, let VIEW_T be the set of views of all processors in T.

1. (Independence of Inputs) During the Input stage, faulty processors share an input value x_j which is independent of those shared by the good processors.

2. (Privacy) For any coalition T of at most t faulty processors, no additional information is obtained from the protocol. More formally, for any input values $\vec{x}_T$ held by the coalition and for any output w, there is a machine which (probabilistically) generates a string V, whose distribution is nearly identical with that on VIEW_T :

$$\sum_{\text{VIEW}_T} |\Pr[M(\vec{x}_T,w) = \text{VIEW}_T] - \Pr[\text{VIEW}_T \mid \vec{x}_T]| < \frac{1}{2^k}.$$

3. (Fairness) All good players can compute the correct output whenever the faulty players can:

$$\Pr[\,y_j = w \mid j \text{ is faulty}\,] \le \Pr[\,y_i = w \mid i \text{ is non-faulty}\,].$$

4. (Correctness) All good players compute the correct output with high probability:

$$\Pr[\,y_i = w \mid i \text{ is non-faulty}\,] \ge 1 - \frac{1}{2^k}.$$

2.2 VSS

Verifiable secret sharing (cf. [CGMA85]) is a fundamental tool for our protocols. In *secret sharing,* one player holds a secret value, which he distributes among the other players, giving each player a quantum of information called a "piece." Two properties must be satisfied:

1. (Privacy) The pieces held by any coalition of fewer than $t + 1$ players are independent of the secret.

2. (Reconstructability) Any coalition containing $n - t$ honest players can reconstruct the secret in full from their information.

In this paper we shall explicitly require the following property as well:

3. (Verifiability)

   - If the secret is not shared correctly and uniquely reconstructible, all honest players output CHEATING, with probability at least $1 - \frac{1}{2^t}$.

   - If the secret is uniquely reconstructible, all honest players agree on its validity.

We shall utilize the solution to VSS for $2t < n$ given by [Rab88]. Briefly, it uses Shamir's method for sharing a secret, and requires that each piece be reshared using a weak form of sharing. The weaker form of sharing includes information called "check vectors," which allow verification of the pieces. We refer the reader to [Rab88, BR89] for details.

2.3 Disqualification

We consider a processor *disqualified* if $t + 1$ or more players have broadcast impeachments of it. When player i is disqualified, the remaining players run a recovery protocol to reshare all the secrets using polynomials of smaller degree (since there are fewer faulty players left to participate). This protocol involves synthesizing and broadcasting one new piece of each secret, in order to reduce the degree of the secret polynomial by one; we omit it from this abstract. (During the Input stage, however, a faulty player's information is replaced by a default value.) Thereafter the good players ignore player i and continue to evaluate the circuit C_f, using a new $t\prime = t - 1$ as the resiliency parameter.

3 Compiling Multiparty Protocols

Given a function $f(x_1, \ldots, x_n)$ and a polynomial size circuit for it, C_f, we wish to construct a protocol to compute f.

The three-stage paradigm [GMW87,BGW88,CCD88] will serve as our model for protocols. In the Input stage, the inputs x_i are verifiably shared. In the Evaluation stage, the circuit C_f is evaluated, producing a new secret $w = f(x_1, \ldots, x_n)$. In the Output stage, the secret w is reconstructed and revealed.

The Input and Output stages are easy to describe. During the Input stage, each player i uses VSS to share his input x_i. Any honest player who detects misbehavior impeaches the misbehaving player by broadcasting a vote against him. If a player is disqualified, substitute a default value. (As an aside, we may require that the default value be secret and selected according to some samplable distribution. In that case, use a circuit C'_f which has additional, random inputs supplied by each player, which are used to compute the desired default value.)

The Output stage operates exactly like the reconstruction stage of a VSS protocol; following the Evaluation stage, the players hold a set of information about w exactly as though it were shared using VSS. The reconstruction of w involves a broadcast of pieces and "check vectors" to verify the pieces before interpolating.

The Evaluation stage forms the crux of our protocols, and contains our new methods for multiparty computations. We follow the outline of [BGW88, CCD88], in which we simulate the computation of a circuit gate by gate using algebraic operations over the field used for secret sharing. Our protocols work for larger numbers of faults, however.

4 Addition of Secrets

It is possible though not trivial to extend [Rab88] to a method for linearly combining secrets.

Lemma 5 *Let u and v be secretly shared values, and let a, b and c be publicly known field elements. Then for $2t < n$, there exists a t-resilient protocol $w \leftarrow au + bv + c$ to provide each player with a piece of a new secret w whose value is $au + bv + c$, without revealing any information about $u, v,$ or w.*

Each player i uses $af(i) + bg(i) + c$ as his piece of $h(x) = af(x) + bg(x) + c$, the desired new polynomial which represents the secret w.

In order that w be a verifiable secret according to the VSS protocol, each $h(i)$ must be reshared in a weak fashion. This involves the use of check vectors for the pieces of $h(i)$. In the full paper we describe in detail how to generate new check vectors for $h(i)$; because the method involves examining in detail the methods used by [Rab88], in this abstract we only sketch the idea. If $f(x)$ and $g(x)$ were generated by different sources, the check vectors associated with them will not be compatible for checking that $h(i) = af(i) + bg(i) + c$. On the other hand, player i can create new check vectors for $f(i)$ and $g(i)$ that will be compatible for checking linear combinations; and there is a protocol revealing nothing about $f(i)$ and $g(i)$ that ensures that player i creates new check vectors which are consistent with the previous check vectors.

5 Multiplication of Secrets

We come now to one of two important results.

Theorem 6 *Let u and v be secretly shared values. Then for $2t < n$, there exists a t-resilient protocol to provide each player with a piece of a new secret w whose value is uv, without revealing any information about u, v, or uv.*

By Lemma 5 it suffices to show Theorem 1. We prove Theorem 1 by describing the protocol.

Our solution follows a few brief steps (cf. [BGW88]). Let u be shared using $f(x)$ and v be shared using $g(x)$.

Step 1.

Each player i secretly shares the value $f(i)g(i)$ and "proves" that he has in fact shared this value (see section 5.1). If his proof fails, he is disqualified (see section 2.3).

Step 2.

From the collection of secret products, the polynomial $f(x)g(x)$, of degree $2t$ and free term uv, is determined. Using a protocol to truncate the polynomial to degree t (see section 5.2), and then to add a random polynomial of degree t and free term 0, each player i is supplied with the value $h(i)$ for the resulting polynomial $h(x)$ of degree t and free term uv.

□.

In section 5.1 we describe the method by which player i can share $f(i)g(i)$ and prove with respect to the secrets $f(i)$ and $g(i)$ that he has in fact shared the correct secret product. The protocol for reducing the degree of the polynomial is based on linear combinations of secrets, and is presented in section 5.2.

5.1 Verifiable Multiplication

In order to accomplish Step 1, the verifiable sharing of $f(i)g(i)$ and zero-knowledge proof of its correctness, let us first define and solve a more general problem, which forms the basis for the results of this paper.

The ABC problem. Let Alice know the values of secrets a and b. Alice must share a new secret c and prove to the other players that the secret value of c is indeed ab. No other information about a, b, or c must be revealed (unless Alice is faulty).

Given a protocol for the ABC problem, Alice will be able to prove to the network that a new secret which she shares is indeed $f(i)g(i)$.

Lemma 7 *(ABC Lemma.) If there exists a t-resilient protocol for linear combinations of secrets, then there exists a t-resilient protocol to solve the ABC problem.*

We prove the ABC lemma by exhibiting the protocol. First, an overview: In the first phase, Alice shares several triples of secrets (R, S, D) satisfying a simple equation (of the form $D = (a + R)(b + S)$), which will be used to ensure that Alice does not misbehave. In the second phase, the players select and reveal combinations of some of these triples in order to confirm that every triple satisfies the simple equation. Finally, each unrevealed triple of secrets gives rise to a simple linear combination of secrets that should equal the desired product ab. The third phase checks that the linear combinations are consistent.

Protocol ABC.

Phase 1.

Let a and b be verifiably secret shared. Alice verifiably shares a third value $c = ab$. Then Alice chooses and shares several random secrets $r_1, \ldots, r_{2k}$ and $s_1, \ldots, s_{2k}$ chosen uniformly from the field used for sharing. (The chance of incorrectness will be bounded by $\frac{1}{2^k}$.) For simplicity we take $k > n$ and k a power of two. Alice also shares secrets $d_1, \ldots, d_{2k}$ having (secret) values $d_j = (a + r_j)(b + s_j)$.

Phase 2.

Next, the system confirms that in fact each $d_j = (a + r_j)(b + s_j)$. The system selects and announces a set $Y = \{j_1, \ldots, j_k\}$ of k random indices. (Selecting indices at random can be achieved by the following method: each player selects a random secret in the field $GF(k)$ and shares it over $GF(k)$; together, they secretly compute the sum; and finally, the sum is revealed.) For each $j \in Y$, the system secretly computes the sums $(a + r_j)$ and $(b + s_j)$, then reconstructs each of them, along with the value of d_j. Every processor checks that the product of the sums matches the value of d_j; if not, Alice is disqualified.

Phase 3.

If Alice passes the test in Phase 2, then the system reconstructs and reveals the values of r_j and s_j for every index $j \notin Y$. For each index $j \notin Y$, the system then secretly computes (but does not reveal) the linear combination $c_j = d_j - r_j b - s_j a - r_j s_j$. (This is a linear combination since r_j and s_j are now public.) If Alice has behaved properly, then in fact each secret c_j will contain the value ab.

The system now computes and reveals the differences $(c - c_j)$ for every $j \notin Y$. If any difference is nonzero, Alice is disqualified. Otherwise, if Alice has passed all the tests, then the system accepts Alice's sharing. $\square$.

In Phase 2, the sums $(a + r_j)$ and $(b + s_j)$ are independent of a and b, respectively, since r_j and s_j are uniformly random field elements. Their product d_j is also independent of a and b. Therefore, revealing the sums and d_j values for $j \in Y$ reveals nothing about a and b. If Alice has behaved, then regardless of the values of a and b, the secrets $(c - c_j)$ computed in Phase 3 will all be zero, so that revealing them will give no information about a or b.

How may Alice cheat without being detected? We shall show that she must behave properly on exactly those indices chosen in Phase 2 and she must misbehave on all the others. Let X be the set of indices j for which Alice shares d_j correctly, that is, for which Alice shares d_j having the value $(a + r_j)(b + s_j)$. In Phase 2, the set Y of indices chosen by the system must be a subset of X, or else Alice's misbehavior is detected. In Phase 3, the remaining indices $j \notin Y$ must all satisfy $c = d_j - r_j b - s_j a - r_j s_j$ or else Alice is caught. If $c \neq ab$ (Alice is cheating), no index $j \notin Y$ is in X. Hence $X = Y$, and since Y is chosen randomly after Alice has shared all her secrets, the probability that Alice can cheat without being detected is no more than $\frac{1}{2^t}$.

5.2 Degree Reduction

Lemma 8 *Let $p(x)$ be a polynomial of degree $2t$ with hidden coefficients, having $c = p(0)$ as its free term, and suppose each player i knows the secret value $p(i)$. Let each value $p(i)$ itself be verifiably shared among the players. Assuming a protocol for linear combinations of secrets, there is a protocol to verifiably share $c = p(0)$ using a random polynomial $q(x)$ of degree t.*

One method for interpolating polynomials, given a list of n values $p(1), \ldots, p(n)$, is to use LaGrange polynomials:

$$L_i(x) = \prod_{j \neq i} \frac{x - i}{j - i}$$

$$p(x) = \sum_{i=1}^{n} L_i(x) p(i).$$

If we denote by $\overline{f}(x)$ the truncated polynomial $f(x) \bmod x^{t+1}$, then

$$\overline{p}(x) = \sum_{i=1}^{n} \overline{L_i}(x) p(i).$$

The polynomials $L_i(x)$, and hence $\overline{L_i}(x)$, are publicly known; they depend only on the fixed, known interpolation points (which we have taken to be $1, \ldots, n$ for simplicity.)

We shall provide each player m with the value $\overline{p}(m) + r(m)$, where $r(x)$ is a random polynomial of degree t and free term 0. The reason for including $r(x)$ is to ensure that coefficients of the new polynomial $q(x)$ are indeed random. (The generation of $r(x)$, along with the providing of $r(m)$ to player m, is left as an exercise to the reader.)

Define $q(x) = \overline{p}(x) + r(x)$. Recall that each value $p(i)$ is a secret known only to player i, and can itself be shared. For each m, the value $q(m)$ can be written as a linear combination of *secrets* $p(1), \ldots, p(n)$:

$$q(m) = (\overline{p} + r)(m) = r(m) + \sum_i \overline{L_i}(m) p(i).$$

(Recall that each $\overline{L_i}(m)$ is publicly known, and serves as a weight for the secrets.) By performing this linear combination of secrets and revealing the result to player m, it is possible to provide each player m with the value $q(m)$, solving the problem at hand.

5.3 Proving the Multiplication Theorem

As in [BGW88,CCD88], given the power to reduce the degree of the product polynomial $f(x)g(x)$ and to prove (in zero-knowledge) that the new pieces are correct, we have completed the proof of Theorem 6, that there exists a t-resilient multiplication protocol.

6 Multiparty Protocols

Addition and multiplication protocols (Lemmas 5, 7, and 8) make the Evaluation stage possible. In order to evaluate C_f, the protocol simulates the circuit layer by layer, producing a new set of secrets each time.

The overall protocol consists of verifiably secret-sharing the input values $x_1,\ldots,x_n$, evaluating a circuit C_f on those values to produce a new secret w, and finally reconstructing w. This completes the proof of our main result, Theorem 2.

7 Zero-Knowledge Proofs

For definitions and background concerning interactive proof systems and zero-knowledge proofs, we refer the reader to [GMR89]. In the full paper we formally define and extend these concepts to the network setting.

The method of section 5.1 for proving that a secret contains the product of two others extends immediately to proving that a secret w contains the value of some polynomial size arithmetic circuit C_P applied to secrets $v_1,\ldots,v_m$. Alice secretly shares the output of each gate g_l when C_P is applied to $v_1,\ldots,v_m$. The network must verify that the output of each g_l is correct with respect to its two inputs. Let w_l be the output of gate g_l, and u_l and v_l represent its inputs. If g_l is a linear combination gate, the network secretly computes the linear combination $w_l - (au_l + bv_l + c)$ and reveals it to verify that it is zero. If g_l is a multiplication gate, Alice uses the ABC protocol to prove that $w_l = u_lv_l$.

Theorem 3, which states that zero-knowledge proofs are possible in the presence of a partly-corrupt network, follows from these observations. Notice that this technique for zero-knowledge proofs of predicates on secretly shared values uses only a *constant* number of rounds and a message complexity proportional to the size of the circuit C_P.

In order to show Lemma 4, stating that any language which has an interactive proof system is also provable in zero-knowledge in the presence of a network, we must demonstrate how such a zero-knowledge proof runs. Let $L \in$ IP and let $<P,V>$ be a proof system for L. Without loss of generality assume V runs for exactly $p(n)$ steps on all inputs of length n, where $p()$ is a polynomial. The verifier is a deterministic machine, given its random tape. The trick to showing the Lemma is to note that the network can generate secret random bits for V, and then simulate the operation of V, ensuring not only that the state of V and its tapes is never revealed, but also that the final output of the simulation is a correct assessment of what a true verifer would answer. Alice takes the position of the prover, sharing her messages to V among the network, while the network simulates a message from V to P by reconstructing it only for Alice.

8   Conclusion

We have shown the new and powerful result that multiparty computations can be performed securely and secretly despite Byzantine faults by up to half the parties. No unproven assumptions are needed. Furthermore, our techniques require only a small polynomial number of message bits and a small constant number of rounds of interaction per basic operation (multiplication, addition, logical "and," logical "or").

We have also shown how a member of a network can share two secrets along with their product, proving to the network that the secret product is correct. More generally, we have demonstrated that a player can prove anything "provable" (in the sense of interactive proofs) about a set of *secrets* which she knows, without revealing anything else about the values of the secrets. She can also prove any IP-statement about *known* values without revealing anything other than that the statement holds. This new method for zero-knowledge proofs in the presence of a network of processors requires no unproven assumptions and is correct with exponentially small chance of error.

In comparison to other solutions, the methods in this paper are more practical and efficient. They allow field operations over an exponentially large field, which permits direct secret computations of many naturally occurring operations, such as arithmetic. This is a great advantage over the requirements and inefficiencies of bit-simulations, on which all other methods rely.

Each of our results allows an exponentially small chance of error, but it is easily proven that for $3t \geq n$ no protocol can tolerate t Byzantine faults without error. Since it is impossible even to *share* a secret when more than half the parties are faulty, our results are optimal.

References

[BB88]   D. Beaver, J. Bar-Ilan. "Non-Cryptographic Fault-Tolerant Computing in a Constant Expected Number of Rounds of Interaction." Proc. of 21st STOC (1989), 201-209.

[Bea88b] D. Beaver. "Secure Multiparty Protocols Tolerating Half Faulty Processors." Technical Report TR-19-88 (September, 1988), Harvard University.

[BGW88] M. Ben-Or, S. Goldwasser, A. Wigderson. "Completeness Theorems for Non-Cryptographic Fault-Tolerant Distributed Computation." Proc. of 20th STOC (1988), 1-10.

[Bla81]   G. R. Blakley, "Security Proofs for Information Protection Systems." Proceedings of the 1980 Symposium on Security and Privacy, IEEE Computer Society Press, NY (1981), 79-88.

[BR89]   M. Ben-Or, T. Rabin. "Verifiable Secret Sharing and Multiparty Protocols with Honest Majority ." 21st STOC (1989), 73-85.

[CCD88]   D. Chaum, C. Crépeau, I. Damgård. "Multiparty Unconditionally Secure Protocols." Proc. of 20th STOC (1988), 11-19.

[CGMA85]   B. Chor, S. Goldwasser, S. Micali, B. Awerbuch. "Verifiable Secret Sharing and Achieving Simultaneity in the Presence of Faults." Proc. of 17th STOC (1985), 383-395.

[GMR89]   S. Goldwasser, S. Micali, C. Rackoff. "The Knowledge Complexity of Interactive Proof Systems." SIAM Journal on Computing 18, no. 1 (1989), 186-208.

[GMW87]   Goldreich, O., Micali, S., A. Wigderson. "How to Play Any Mental Game, or A Completeness Theorem for Protocols with Honest Majority." Proc. of 19th STOC (1987), 218-229.

[Kil]   J. Kilian, personal communication.

[Kil88]   J. Kilian. "Founding Cryptography on Oblivious Transfer." Proc. of 20th STOC (1988), 20-29.

[Rab88]   T. Rabin. "Robust Sharing of Secrets When the Dealer is Honest or Cheating." Masters Thesis, Hebrew University, 1988.

[Sha79]   A. Shamir. "How to Share a Secret." CACM 22 (1979), 612-613.

[Yao86]   A. Yao. "How to Generate and Exchange Secrets." Proc. of 27th FOCS (1986), 162-167.

Controlled Gradual Disclosure Schemes for Random Bits and Their Applications

Richard Cleve[*]

International Computer Science Institute
1947 Center St., Suite 600
Berkeley, CA 94704-1105, U.S.A.

Abstract

We construct a protocol that enables a secret bit to be revealed gradually in a very controlled manner. In particular, if Alice possesses a bit S that was generated randomly according to the uniform distribution and $\frac{1}{2} < p_1 < \cdots < p_m = 1$ then, using our protocol with Bob, Alice can achieve the following. The protocol consists of m stages and, after the i-th stage, Bob's best prediction of S, based on all his interactions with Alice, is correct with probability exactly p_i (and a reasonable condition is satisfied in the case where S is not initially uniform). Furthermore, under an intractability assumption, our protocol can be made "oblivious" to Alice and "secure" against an Alice or Bob that might try to cheat in various ways. Previously proposed gradual disclosure schemes for single bits release information in a less controlled manner: the probabilities that represent Bob's confidence of his knowledge of S follow a random walk that eventually drifts towards 1, rather than a predetermined sequence of values.

Using controlled gradual disclosure schemes, we show how to construct an improved version of the protocol proposed by Luby, Micali and Rackoff for two-party secret bit exchanging ("How to Simultaneously Exchange a Secret Bit by Flipping a Symmetrically-Biased Coin", *Proc. 22nd Ann. IEEE Symp. on Foundations of Computer Science*, 1983, pp. 11–21) that is secure against additional kinds of attacks that the previous protocol is not secure against. Also, our protocol is more efficient in the number of rounds that it requires to attain a given level of security, and is proven to be asymptotically optimal in this respect.

[*]Research partially conducted while the author was at the University of Toronto, partially supported by an NSERC postgraduate scholarship.

We also show how to use controlled gradual disclosure schemes to improve existing protocols for other cryptographic problems, such as multi-party function evaluation.

1 Introduction

Suppose that $S \in \{0,1\}$ and Alice knows the value of S, but Bob has no idea about what the value of S is in the sense that Bob's best guess of S is correct with probability $\frac{1}{2}$ (such a state of knowledge could be obtained by having Alice flip a fair coin and look at the outcome but not show it to Bob). We are concerned with multistage protocols, called *disclosure schemes*, that, informally, enable Alice to provide Bob with partial information about S at each stage. We say that, at a particular stage, Bob's *confidence* about the value of S is the probability that Bob's best guess of S is correct (initially, Bob's confidence is $\frac{1}{2}$). A *gradual* disclosure scheme is, informally, a disclosure scheme in which Bob's confidence changes in small increments from $\frac{1}{2}$ to 1.

An example of a gradual disclosure scheme (considered by Luby, Micali and Rackoff [10], and Vazirani and Vazirani [12]), which we shall refer to as the *biased coin scheme*, operates as follows. Alice constructs a coin C that is biased towards S by ε, so that each time it is flipped its value is S with probability $\frac{1}{2}+\varepsilon$. Then, at each stage of the protocol, Alice flips C and sends the outcome to Bob. At each stage, Bob's best estimate of S is the majority value of the outcomes of C that he has received so far, and Bob's confidence depends on the "strength" of this majority (i.e. the difference between the number of 1s and 0s). Bob's confidence does not necessarily increase as the stages progress, but the *expected* value of Bob's confidence does increase. Also, at each stage, Bob's confidence changes by at most ε (and, thus, "gradually" if ε is small). It can be shown that if $\varepsilon = \frac{1}{m}$ then, after $\omega(m^2 \log^2 m)$ stages, the expected value of Bob's confidence is very high: $1 - (\frac{1}{m})^{\omega(1)}$.

A gradual disclosure scheme is *oblivious* if Alice learns nothing about Bob's current best estimate of S or confidence that she could not determine independently of the particular execution of the protocol. The biased coin scheme described above is not oblivious since Alice can completely determine Bob's state of knowledge about S from the values of the coin flips. If a third party, Ted, is allowed to participate, the biased coin scheme can be made oblivious by having Ted flip the coin C and reveal the outcomes to Bob but not to Alice.

Under a reasonable intractability assumption, the biased coin scheme can be made modified to be oblivious without the presence of Ted. It can also be modified to be secure against an Alice or Bob that may try to cheat in several possible ways. Alice could attempt to not send the coin flips according to the appropriate distribution (for instance Alice might try to convince Bob that S is 0 when S is really 1). In order to be able to deal with this possibility, it is assumed that Alice initially sends Bob a cryptographic commitment of S. It is then possible for Bob to determine if Alice is behaving "consistently" with respect to the value of this committed bit. Bob could attempt to learn more about S than he is supposed to at a particular stage. The above possibilities can all be prevented.

Informally, a *controlled* gradual disclosure scheme is a gradual disclosure scheme with the additional property that, at each stage of the protocol, Bob's confidence level is a predetermined value, independent of the particular execution of the protocol. That is, there is a sequence of probabilities $p_1, ..., p_m$ (which are parameters of the protocol) such that, after stage i, Bob's confidence is p_i. Note that the biased coin scheme described above is *not* controlled.

One obvious advantage of a controlled gradual disclosure scheme over the biased coin scheme is in the number or stages required to attain a given bound on the incremental changes in Bob's confidence level during the disclosure. By setting $p_i = \frac{1}{2} + \frac{i}{2m}$, the change in Bob's confidence between successive stages is bounded by $\frac{1}{2m}$ and the secret is revealed within m rounds, whereas, to attain this bound and reveal the secret with high probability with the biased coin scheme, $\omega(m^2 \log^2 m)$ stages are required. (In all protocols considered here, a stage consists of a constant number of rounds. Therefore, these bounds also translate into similar bounds in terms of rounds.)

Another important advantage of a controlled gradual disclosure scheme arises from the property that the sequence of probabilities representing Bob's confidence level follows predetermined values. In particular, we can use this property to construct an improved version of the protocol proposed by Luby, Micali and Rackoff [10] (also considered by Yao [15]) for two-party secret bit exchanging. More specifically, the improved secret bit exchanging protocol has (in addition to the desirable properties of the previous protocol) the following property. Even if one party, say Alice, obtains information (possibly from some events in the outside world) about what Bob's current knowledge of her secret is, then she still cannot infer more information about Bob's secret from this than otherwise. (Circumstances similar to this and their affect on protocols are considered by Halpern and Rabin [9].) The previous two-party secret bit exchanging protocol is very vulnerable to these circumstances, whereas our protocol is very secure against such circumstances.

In Section 2, we present more formal definitions about our assumptions and our model. In Section 3, we show how to construct a controlled gradual disclosure scheme that is oblivious as well secure against an Alice or Bob that might try to cheat. In Section 4, we informally explain how our controlled gradual disclosure scheme can be used to construct an improved version of the secret bit exchanging protocols proposed by Luby, Micali and Rackoff [10]. Also, we sketch the proof of a lower bound on the number of rounds required to attain a particular level of security that implies that our protocol is asymptotically optimal in the number of rounds that it requires. In Section 5, we informally explain how our controlled gradual disclosure scheme can be used to improve previous protocols for multi-party function evaluation (considered by Yao [15], and Beaver and Goldwasser [1]).

2 Definitions

2.1 Protocols

We represent a *two-party protocol* as an interacting pair of Turing machines (A, B) with the following tapes and properties. A and B have individual (read-only) *input* tapes, (read/write) *work* tapes, (read-only) *random* tapes, and (write-only) *output* tapes. Also, there are two *communication* tapes, one which is write-only to A and read-only to B, and one which is write-only to B and read-only to A. The input tapes are initialized with the input to the protocol, and the random tapes are initialized with independent random sequences of bits; all other tapes are initialized with the null string.

Both A and B have *sleep* states as well as *final* states. When the protocol is executed, beginning with A, the parties take turns running, each one running until it enters its sleep state or final state and then the other one starts running. This process continues until both parties are in their final states.

We also require that the running time of the protocol be polynomial in the following sense. For any B' and $x, y \in \{0,1\}^*$, when (A, B') is executed with x and y on the respective input tapes, the total running time of A is bounded by a polynomial in $|x|$ and $|y|$. Also, a similar condition holds if A is replaced by A'.

Each turn of A running until entering a sleep state, followed by B running until entering a sleep state is called a *round*. For convenience, we may partition the rounds into *stages*, (which each consist of a number of consecutive rounds).

In the special case of a trusted third party (considered in Section 3.1), the scheme is an interacting *triple* of Turing machines (A, B, T), defined similarly as above, where (A, T) and (B, T) have private communication tapes.

2.2 Controlled Gradual Disclosure Schemes

A *controlled gradual disclosure scheme* is a protocol that has the following properties. The protocol is run with A's input tape initialized with a random bit S followed by a string of n 1s, and B's input tape also initialized by a string of n 1s. The protocol first runs for a *commitment* stage which consists of a constant number of rounds (with respect to n). Informally, in this stage, Alice is committing her value of S to Bob. Alice cannot be prevented from choosing a different secret bit S' and revealing this to Bob. What a protocol *can* guarantee is that Alice behaves consistently relative to *some* fixed secret bit S' which she must determine during the commitment stage (otherwise, Bob detects that Alice is inconsistent). Following the commitment stage, are a series of stages numbered $1, ..., m$. On completion of the i-th stage, B outputs b_i. Loosely speaking, b_i represents Bob's knowledge about S (or S') after stage i. Alice may deviate from the protocol at any time (represented by replacing A by another Turing machine A') and, similarly, Bob may deviate from the protocol at any time.

We adopt the following terminology in order to simplify our presentation. We write $\delta(n) \preceq \gamma(n)$, if $\delta(n) \leq \gamma(n) + (\frac{1}{n})^{\omega(1)}$, and $\delta(n) \simeq \gamma(n)$ if $\delta(n) \preceq \gamma(n)$ and $\gamma(n) \preceq \delta(n)$.

There are four conditions that we require a controlled gradual scheme to satisfy:

Correctness: If A and B follow the protocol correctly then, for all i, $b_i \in \{0, 1\}$ and $\Pr[b_i = S] \simeq p_i$.

Informally, this means that if Alice and Bob both follow the protocol correctly then, on completion of the i-th stage, Bob learns the equivalent of the outcome of one coin that is biased towards S with probability p_i.

Consistency of Secret: If B correctly follows the protocol then, for all i, either $b_i \in \{0, 1\}$ and $\Pr[b_i = S'] \succeq p_i$, or $b_i = \text{CHEAT}$.

Informally, this means that, after the commitment stage, there is no strategy for Alice to modify the information that she discloses to Bob without this being detected by him.

Security of Secret (from B): If A correctly follows the protocol then, for all i, $\Pr[b_i = S] \preceq p_i$.

Informally, this means that there is no strategy for Bob that increases the amount of information that he learns about S.

Obliviousness of Disclosure (to A): If B correctly follows the protocol and $i_{\max} = \max\{i : b_i \neq \text{CHEAT}\}$ then $\Pr[b_{i_{\max}} = S'] \succeq p_{i_{\max}}$.

The significance of this condition is more subtle than the previous conditions. Suppose that, at some stage i of the protocol, $p_i = \frac{3}{4}$. Then, with probability $\frac{1}{4}$, Bob's best estimate of S at this stage is wrong. If Alice were to know that this has occurred then, by quitting the protocol at this stage, she would leave Bob having significant confidence in something that she knows is false. If the disclosure is oblivious then, whenever Alice quits at this stage, from her point of view, Bob's final estimate of her secret is correct with probability $\frac{3}{4}$.

The above definition of a controlled gradual disclosure scheme assumes that, before executing the protocol, from Bob's point of view, the prior distribution of S is uniformly random. The situation is more complicated if this is not the case. In particular, if Alice does not know what Bob's prior information about S is then no protocol can have the property that Bob's confidence level follows a predetermined sequence of values. On the other hand, any controlled gradual disclosure scheme in the above sense (i.e. that satisfies the above properties when S is uniformly random) will satisfy a reasonable property when it is executed with with S chosen according to an arbitrary distribution. Intuitively, the property is that the information that Bob learns about S from the protocol after stage i is equivalent to Bob learning the outcome of a single coin that is biased towards S with probability p_i. Although this information may combine with Bob's prior information about S in different possible ways, yielding different possible confidence levels for Bob's knowledge about S, the amount of *new* information that Bob obtains is, in a reasonable sense, the same. This property is best expressed in terms of *likelihoods*, where the likelihood of an event is $l(p) = \log(\frac{p}{1-p})$ where p is the probability of the event. Then, after stage i, Bob's likelihood that $b_i = S$ satisfies $l(\Pr[b_i = S | \text{Bob's prior information}]) \simeq l(p_i) + l(q)$, where q is Bob's prior probability that $S = b_i$.

2.3 Complexity Theoretic Assumptions

For concreteness, let us base our scheme on the difficulty of determining certain quadratic residues.

We assume the **Quadratic Residuosity Conjecture**, which is that there is no probabilistic polynomial-time (in n) algorithm that achieves the following. The input to the algorithm is n, $p \cdot q$, where p and q are randomly chosen n-bit primes (and p and q are not explicitly given to the algorithm), and x, a random element of $\mathbf{Z}'_{p \cdot q}$. The goal of the algorithm is to determine with probability $\frac{1}{2} + (\frac{1}{n})^{O(1)}$ whether or not x is a quadratic residue (i.e. whether $x = y^2$, for some $y \in \mathbf{Z}'_{p \cdot q}$).

3 A Controlled Gradual Disclosure Scheme for a Random Bit

In this section, we construct a controlled gradual disclosure scheme that is oblivious as well secure against an Alice or Bob that try to cheat. Intuitively, the main idea behind our protocol is to simulate the flips of a special coin that adjusts its bias each time it is flipped. The new bias of the coin depends on the outcome the previous time it was flipped.

Let $\frac{1}{2} < p_1 < \cdots < p_m = 1$. Our protocol operates in m stages and, after the i-th stage is completed, achieves the following conditions. Bob's best guess of S (based on the information that Bob has seen so far) is correct with probability p_i. Moreover, Alice's best guess of what Bob's best guess of S is (based on the information that Alice has seen so far) is correct with probability p_i.

In Section 3.1, we describe how to adjust the biases of the coin so as to obtain the desired behavior, and, to simplify the presentation of this, we make the assumption that a trusted third party is present. In Section 3.2, we describe how to implement the protocol without a trusted third party.

3.1   First Implementation (with Trusted Third Party)

Assume that there is an honest third party, Ted, trusted by both Alice and Bob (in Section 3.2, the protocol will be modified to work without the presence of Ted). Initially, Alice sends Ted a copy of S, and Ted sends Bob a sequence of bits $C_1, ..., C_m$, which can intuitively be viewed as outcomes of a coin whose bias "evolves" each time it is flipped. We would like the biases of the coin to be such that, for all $i \in \{1, ..., m\}$, after seeing the outcomes of $C_1, ... C_i$, no matter what they are, Bob's best guess of S is the outcome of C_i, and for this guess to be correct with probability exactly p_i. That is, for all $x_1...x_i \in \{0,1\}^i$ and $x \in \{0,1\}$,

$$\Pr[S = x | C_1...C_i = x_1...x_i] = \begin{cases} p_i & \text{if } x = x_i \\ 1 - p_i & \text{if } x \neq x_i. \end{cases}$$

It can be shown that, unless $n \leq 2$, this condition cannot be satisfied if the distributions of $C_1, ..., C_n$ are independent.

Ted generates the outcomes of coins $C_1, ..., C_m$ inductively as follows (where the quantities $s_1, ..., s_m, t_1, ..., t_m \in [0,1]$ will be defined later). C_1 is a biased coin generated such that $\Pr[C_1 = S] = s_1$ and $\Pr[C_1 \neq S] = t_1$. Once $C_1, ..., C_i$ have been generated, C_{i+1} is generated according to the following distribution. For all $x_1...x_i \in \{0,1\}^i$,

$$\Pr[C_{i+1} = x_i | S = x_i \wedge C_1...C_i = x_1...x_i] = s_{i+1}$$

$$\Pr[C_{i+1} = x_i | S \neq x_i \wedge C_1...C_i = x_1...x_i] = t_{i+1}.$$

It can be verified that, if $C_1, ..., C_m$ are generated in this manner then, for all $x_1...x_{i+1} \in \{0,1\}^{i+1}$,

$$\Pr[S = x_1 | C_1 = x_1] = s_1 = 1 - t_1,$$

and, by applying Bayes' rule, for all $i \in \{1, ..., m-1\}$,

$$\Pr[S = x_{i+1} | C_1...C_{i+1} = x_1...x_{i+1}] = \begin{cases} \frac{p_i s_{i+1}}{p_i s_{i+1} + (1-p_i)t_{i+1}} & \text{if } x_{i+1} = x_i \\ \frac{(1-p_i)(1-t_{i+1})}{(1-p_i)(1-t_{i+1}) + p_i(1-s_{i+1})} & \text{if } x_{i+1} \neq x_i. \end{cases}$$

Therefore, in order to satisfy

$$\Pr[S = x_i | C_1...C_i = x_1...x_i] = p_i,$$

for all $i \in \{1,...,m\}$ and for all $x_1...x_i \in \{0,1\}^i$, it is necessary and sufficient for $s_1,...,s_m,t_1,...,t_m$ to satisfy $s_1 = p_1$, $t_1 = 1 - p_1$, and, for all $i \in \{1,...,m-1\}$,

$$\frac{p_i s_{i+1}}{p_i s_{i+1} + (1 - p_i)t_{i+1}} = p_{i+1} = \frac{(1 - p_i)(1 - t_{i+1})}{(1 - p_i)(1 - t_{i+1}) + p_i(1 - s_{i+1})}.$$

These equations yield a unique solution of $s_1 = p_1$, $t_1 = 1 - p_1$, and for all $i \in \{1,...,m-1\}$,

$$s_{i+1} = \left(\frac{p_{i+1}}{p_i}\right)\left(\frac{p_i + p_{i+1} - 1}{2p_{i+1} - 1}\right)$$

$$t_{i+1} = \left(\frac{1 - p_{i+1}}{1 - p_i}\right)\left(\frac{p_i + p_{i+1} - 1}{2p_{i+1} - 1}\right)$$

and, since $\frac{1}{2} < p_1 < \cdots < p_m = 1$, it can be verified that $s_1,...,s_m,t_1,...,t_m$ are all valid probabilities (i.e. they are all in the range $[0,1]$).

Intuitively, the values of $C_1,...,C_m$ can be viewed as the states of the execution of a Markov chain. If Alice's secret is 0 then Ted selects an initial state to be 0 with probability s_1 and 1 with probability t_1, and shows Bob the states of an execution of the following Markov chain.

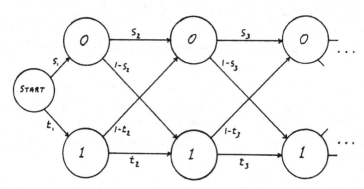

If, on the other hand, Alice's secret is 1 then Ted selects an initial state to be 1 with probability s_1 and 0 with probability t_1, and shows Bob the states of an execution of the following Markov chain.

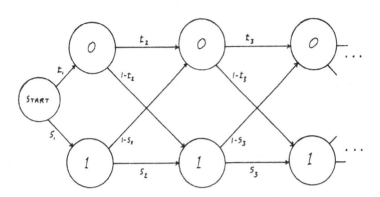

Bob does not know which Markov chain is being executed but Bob does know that it is one of two (depending on what S is). Bob observes the sequence of states of the Markov chain that is executed and, from this and Bob's knowledge of probability theory, at stage i, infers that S is the current state of the Markov chain with probability p_i.

3.2   Second Implementation (without Trusted Third Party)

In this section, we give an overview of how Alice and Bob can cryptographically simulate the role that Ted plays in the protocol of Section 3.1. Essentially, what Alice and Bob are able to do is simulate the execution of the appropriate Markov chain for Alice's secret S with the following conditions holding: (1) (To protect the consistency of the secret) the Markov chain is certified to Bob to be the one that corresponds to S (explained in Section 3.1); (2) (To protect the security of the secret) Bob learns nothing about the Markov chain except what he can infer from the execution that he sees; (3) (To protect the obliviousness of the execution) Alice learns nothing about the particular execution of the Markov chain that Bob sees.

First, we design our protocol to satisfy conditions (2) and (3) under the assumption that Alice and Bob both correctly follow the protocol (but are then allowed to make inferences based on the messages that were exchanged during the protocol). (We later explain how to modify the protocol to satisfy (1), (2), and (3) when Alice and Bob are allowed to deviate from the protocol in an arbitrary manner.)

Our protocol relies on an implementation of a "one-out-of-k" oblivious transfer protocol (explained by Brassard, Crépeau and Robert [4]). This protocol enables Alice to set up k bits and Bob to read a bit of his choosing such that: Alice has no idea which bit Bob read; and Bob learns nothing about the other $k-1$ bits. Under the Quadratic Residuosity Conjecture, a one-out-of-k oblivious transfer protocol can be constructed as follows. Suppose the k bits are $b_1, ..., b_k$. Alice first generates two distinct random n-bit primes, p and q, and then generates $d \in \mathbf{Z}'_{p \cdot q}$ such that d is a quadratic nonresidue. Then Alice independently generates random $x_1, ..., x_k \in \mathbf{Z}'_{p \cdot q}$ subject to x_i being a quadratic residue iff $b_i = 1$ ($i \in \{1, ..., k\}$) and Alice sends $p \cdot q, d, x_1, ..., x_k$ to Bob. (Note that, at this point, under the Quadratic Residuosity Conjecture, Bob cannot deduce anything about the value of any of the bits $b_1, ..., b_k$ from the information that he has.) Now, for Bob to learn bit b_{i_0}, he generates a random $y \in \mathbf{Z}'_{p \cdot q}$ and a random $t \in \{0, 1\}$ and sends $d^t \cdot y^2 \cdot x_{i_0}$ to Alice, who determines whether this quantity is a quadratic residue or not, and informs Bob of the result. From Alice's point of view, $d^t \cdot y^2 \cdot x_{i_0}$ is a random element of $\mathbf{Z}'_{p \cdot q}$, so she cannot deduce anything about the value of i_0 from this transaction. By the algebraic properties of $\mathbf{Z}'_{p \cdot q}$, Bob can infer whether x_{i_0} is a quadratic residue or not from the knowledge of whether $d^t \cdot y^2 \cdot x_{i_0}$ is a quadratic residue or not, and, thus, he can infer b_{i_0}. Also, it is straightforward to show that, under the Quadratic Residuosity Conjecture, Bob does not learn any information from this transaction about the value of the other b_is, ($i \neq i_0$).

Using a one-out-of-k oblivious transfer protocol, Alice can simulate a coin with a bias of her choosing and Bob can obtain an outcome of this coin so that: Alice does not see the outcome; and Bob learns nothing about the bias of the coin (except what he can infer from the outcome). To achieve this, Alice randomly chooses k bits subject to the condition that the proportion of 1s to 0s corresponds to the bias of the coin. To obtain an outcome, Bob randomly chooses $i \in \{1, ..., k\}$ and, using a one-out-of-k oblivious transfer protocol, determines the value of the i-th bit.

Using several of the above simulations of biased coins, Alice and Bob can appropriately simulate the execution of any Markov chain in which each state has at most two possible successors. To do this, Alice simulates a biased coin for each state in the Markov chain, where each of these simulations are in terms of elements of the same set $\mathbf{Z}'_{p \cdot q}$ (i.e. the p and q are the same for each coin). At each step, Bob obtains an outcome of the appropriate coin for the current state of the Markov chain to determine the next state (that is, he selects a random x_i from those that Alice sent him that correspond to the current state, and determines, through Alice, whether it is a quadratic residue or not). Since, at each stage, Alice only receives a random element of $\mathbf{Z}'_{p \cdot q}$ (and she determines its residue/nonresidue status and reveals this to Bob), Alice learns nothing about the states traversed in the specific execution of the Markov chain. Also, by the Quadratic Residuosity Conjecture, it can be shown that Bob learns nothing about the specific transition probabilities of the Markov chain (except what he can infer from the states traversed in its execution). Thus, under the assumption that Alice and Bob both correctly follow the protocol, conditions (2) and (3) are satisfied.

We now consider the general case where Alice and Bob may deviate from the protocol. For condition (1), Alice can initially send $p \cdot q$, d and several elements of $Z'_{p \cdot q}$ that represent the Markov chain to Bob and certify that they are valid for some S' by a zero-knowledge proof (explained by Goldreich, Micali, and Wigderson [6]). Also, during the further execution of the protocol, both Alice and Bob can certify that they are faithfully executing the protocol by zero-knowledge proofs. Since both Alice and Bob are constrained to probabilistic polynomial-time computations, all these zero-knowledge proofs can be implemented in a constant number of rounds.

4   Two-Party Secret Bit Exchanging Protocols

Suppose that parties Alice and Bob possess secret bits S_a and S_b (respectively) and that they would like to know each other's secrets and are willing to make an exchange of one secret for another. Suppose further that Alice and Bob do not trust each other in the following two senses. First, neither party is willing to believe that the other party is telling the truth about its secret—unless the other party *proves* the validity of the information that it sends. Also, each party is reluctant to reveal its secret first, for fear that the other party will not reveal its secret in return. This problem was investigated by Yao [13,14,15], Halpern and Rabin [9], Luby, Micali and Rackoff [10], and Tedrick [11]. Similar secret exchanging problems (except that they involve secrets that are multi-bit "keys") were investigated by Blum [2], Brickell, Chaum, Damgård, and van de Graaf [5], and Tedrick [11].

In this section, we give an informal sketch of how a controlled gradual disclosure scheme can be used to strengthen the security of the secret bit exchanging protocols proposed by Luby, Micali and Rackoff [10], and Yao in [15]. In all these protocols (as well as ours) it is assumed that, initially, each party presents a correct commitment of its secret to the other party.

4.1   Overview of Previous Results

In this section, we briefly review previous work on protocols for fair secret bit exchanges.

Halpern and Rabin [9] overcome the main difficulties of the problem by making the assumption in their model that, as soon as one party, say Alice, learns Bob's secret, Alice performs some action that Bob can observe. From this and what Bob has learned during the execution of the protocol, Bob is then able to infer what Alice's secret is.

In [14], Yao claims that in some contexts, a "fair" secret bit exchanging protocol does not exist. In [15], Yao claims that there exists a protocol for a generalized form of secret exchanging in which the protocol of Luby, Micali and Rackoff [10], explained below, arises as a special case.

The protocol of Luby, Micali and Rackoff [10] is a secret exchanging scheme that satisfies the following properties. If both parties follow the protocol faithfully then, with very high probability, they successfully exchange secrets. If one party cheats then (under the quadratic residuosity conjecture) the amount of information that it obtains about the other party's secret is "fairly close" to the amount of information that the other party obtains about its secret. More precisely, if the total number of rounds in the protocol is $\omega(m^2 \log^2 m)$ then, after the execution of the protocol, the following holds. If both parties are honest then they can both guess each other's secrets with probability $1 - (\frac{1}{m})^{\omega(1)}$. If one party, say Alice, is honest and she can guess Bob's secret with probability p then Bob (even if he has cheated) can guess Alice's secret with probability bounded by $p + \frac{1}{m}$. (Note that, in this protocol, the discrepancy of $\frac{1}{m}$ between Alice's and Bob's knowledge cannot be made super-polynomially small (i.e. $(\frac{1}{n})^{\omega(1)}$) unless it runs for a super-polynomial number of rounds (i.e. $n^{\omega(1)}$). The lower bound that we show in Section 4.3 implies that no other protocol can achieve a super-polynomial discrepancy in a polynomial number of rounds.)

The protocol of Luby, Micali and Rackoff simulates a "symmetrically biased coin" that enables Alice and Bob to both gain a little knowledge (in a probabilistic sense) about each others secrets at each stage. Informally, if the secrets of Alice and Bob are S_a and S_b (respectively) then the symmetrically biased coin, C, is biased towards $S_a \oplus S_b$ by $\frac{1}{m}$. The protocol repeatedly "flips" C, each time enabling Alice and Bob, in turn, to see the outcome. Neither Alice nor Bob knows what the exact bias of C is (if one of them did, it would know $S_a \oplus S_b$ and could deduce the other party's secret). But seeing the outcome of a flip of C gives each party a little probabilistic information about the bias of C and, thus, the value of $S_a \oplus S_b$. Since each party also knows its own secret, each party as a result learns a little probabilistic information about the secret of the other party. As the coin C is flipped repeatedly, each party's expected knowledge of the other party's secret increases. After $\omega(m^2 \log^2 m)$ rounds, the expected confidences of the two parties about each others secrets are both $1 - (\frac{1}{m})^{\omega(1)}$. If one party cheats by quitting the protocol early, it only learns the outcome of at most one more coin flip of C than the other party learns. Thus, since C is only biased towards $S_a \oplus S_b$ by $\frac{1}{m}$, the discrepancies between the two parties confidence of their knowledge of each other's secrets is bounded by $\frac{1}{m}$.

During the execution of the above protocol, the pieces of knowledge that the two parties have about each other's secrets are highly correlated with each other. In fact, Alice and Bob's best guesses of each other's secrets after each stage are either both right or both wrong. Suppose that at some time before the execution of the protocol terminates, one party, say Alice, is confident about her knowledge of Bob's secret and performs some "action in the outside world" based on what she thinks Bob's secret is, and Bob observes this action. Then Bob can infer Alice's secret in the following way. Bob knows his own secret and what Alice thinks Bob's secret is. If Alice is right then Bob knows that his current estimate of Alice's secret is right, otherwise Bob knows that his current estimate of Alice's secret is wrong. It is desirable for secret exchanging protocols to be secure against any such inferences. If Alice and Bob's knowledge about each other's secrets are independent of each other then no such inferences can be made. In the next section, we present a secret bit exchanging protocol, based on our controlled gradual disclosure scheme, that has this property and is thus secure against the aforementioned kinds of inferences.

It is important to note that the independent interleaving of two biased coin schemes (as described in Section 1) will yield a very insecure secret bit exchanging scheme. This observation (due to Luby, Micali and Rackoff [10]) is based on the fact that two sequences of probabilities that follow independent random walks will be very likely to, at some point, drift apart significantly. Thus, during the execution of such a protocol, there will likely be some point where there is a significant gap between Alice and Bob's respective knowledge about each other's secrets.

4.2 A Secret Bit Exchanging Protocol Based on a Controlled Gradual Disclosure Scheme

An m-round secret exchanging protocol can by constructed by interleaving two controlled gradual disclosure schemes, one in which Alice discloses her secret to Bob, and one in which Bob discloses his secret to Alice. The two executions of the controlled gradual disclosure scheme can be run independently in the sense that the honest parties use different random bits for the two protocols. If one party quits a protocol or does not send a valid message at some stage then the other party immediately quits both protocols and retains its current best estimate of the other party's secret.

This protocol has the property that if one of the players is honest then, during the execution of the protocol, the information that the parties have about each other's secrets are independent and, therefore the protocol is secure against the kinds of attacks discussed in Section 4.1.

Also, by setting $p_i = \frac{1}{2} + \frac{i}{2m}$ ($i \in \{1, ..., m\}$) in the controlled gradual disclosure schemes, we obtain the following property if one party cheats. After the execution of the protocol, if the honest party can guess the secret of the cheating party with probability p then the cheating party can guess the secret of the honest party with probability bounded by $p + \frac{1}{m}$ (thus, the discrepancy is $\frac{1}{m}$). The total number of rounds in the protocol is $O(m)$ (whereas the protocol of Luby, Micali and Rackoff [10] requires $\omega(m^2 \log^2 m)$ rounds to obtain the same discrepancy). In Section 4.3, we prove that this relationship between discrepancy of information and number of rounds is asymptotically the best possible.

4.3 A Lower Bound on the Number of Rounds Required for a Secret Exchanging Protocol With a Given Level of Security

Theorem: *For any m-round secret exchanging scheme, one party can learn $\Omega(\frac{1}{m})$ more (in terms of its confidence level) about the other party's secret than it reveals about its own secret by quitting at an opportune time.*

Sketch of Proof: To understand the intuition behind this proof, consider the confidence of each party at intermediate stages during the execution of the protocol. Initially, these quantities are both close to $\frac{1}{2}$ and eventually they must approach 1 so the average "gap" between these confidence levels during the execution of the protocol is $\Omega(\frac{1}{m})$. A party that cheats by quitting where one of these gaps arises will have an advantage of $\Omega(\frac{1}{m})$. $\square$

5 Multi-Party Function Evaluation Protocols

Suppose that Alice possesses bits $x_1, ..., x_k$ and Bob possesses bits $y_1, ..., y_k$ and that they are interested in learning the value of some function $f(x_1, ..., x_k, y_1, ..., y_k)$ through the execution of some protocol. Supposing that Alice and Bob do not trust each other, there are several notions of security that are of interest. One of these notions, called "fairness", is the property that one party, even by cheating during the execution of the protocol, cannot learn more about the value of $f(x_1, ..., x_k, y_1, ..., y_k)$ than the other party learns. A two-party version of this problem was considered by Yao [15], and a multi-party version is considered by Beaver and Goldwasser [1].

In this section, we very briefly review how the previous protocols handle the issue of fairness, and how a controlled gradual disclosure scheme can be used to make the protocols more efficient in the number of rounds that they require (and asymptotically optimal in this respect).

For simplicity, let us only consider the case where $f(x, y) = x \oplus y$ (so $k = 1$), and the prior distributions of x and y are independent and uniformly random (the results that we discuss here extend to more general functions, and more general prior distributions of x and y).

Along the lines of the theorem in Section 4.3, it can be shown that any m-round protocol for this problem has the property that one party, by quitting an an opportune time, can obtain an "advantage" of $\Omega(\frac{1}{m})$ in the following sense. That party's confidence level about the value of $f(x, y)$ exceeds the confidence level of the other party by $\Omega(\frac{1}{m})$.

The protocols proposed by Yao [15], and Beaver and Goldwasser [1] (in the two-party case), operate as follows. Alice and Bob jointly construct a coin C that is biased towards $f(x, y)$ by $\frac{1}{m}$, and, at successive stages, learn the outcome of independent flips of C. After $\omega(m^2 \log^2 m)$ stages, the expected value of Alice and Bob's confidence levels (about the value of $f(x, y)$) are $1 - (\frac{1}{m})^{\omega(1)}$. If one party cheats by quitting the protocol early then the advantage of that party is at most the result of one more coin flip of C and is thus bounded by $\frac{1}{m}$. Note the gap between this result and the lower bound above: to bound the possible advantage of one party by $\frac{1}{m}$, $\Omega(m)$ rounds are necessary, while these protocols show that $\omega(m^2 \log^2 m)$ rounds are sufficient.

Using a controlled gradual scheme, an (asymptotically optimal) $O(m)$ round version of the above protocols is possible. This is achieved by (independently) interleaving the execution two controlled gradual schemes, one disclosing $f(x, y)$ to Alice, the other disclosing $f(x, y)$ to Bob.

6   Acknowledgments

Michael Luby and Charles Rackoff made many helpful remarks concerning this research.

References

[1] D. Beaver, and S. Goldwasser, "Multiparty Computation with Faulty Majority", *Advances in Cryptology — CRYPTO '89 Proc.*, these proceedings.

[2] M. Blum., "How to Exchange (Secret) Keys", *Proc. 15th Ann. ACM Symp. on Theory of Computing*, 1983, pp. 440–447.

[3] M. Blum, and S. Micali, "How to Generate Cryptographically Strong Sequences of Pseudo-Random Bits", *Proc. 23th Ann. IEEE Symp. on Foundations of Computer Science*, 1982, pp. 112–117.

[4] G. Brassard, C. Crépeau, and J.-M. Robert, "Information Theoretic Reductions Among Disclosure Problems", *Proc. 27th Ann. IEEE Symp. on Foundations of Computer Science*, 1986, pp. 168–173.

[5] E. F. Brickell, D. Chaum, I. B. Damgård, and J. van de Graaf, "Gradual and Verifiable Release of a Secret", *Advances in Cryptology — CRYPTO '87 Proc.*, C. Pomerance (ed.), Lecture Notes in Computer Science **293**, Springer, 1988, pp. 156–166.

[6] O. Goldreich, S. Micali, and A. Wigderson, "Proofs That Yield Nothing But Their Validity and a Methodology for Cryptographic Protocol Design", *Proc. 27th Ann. IEEE Symp. on Foundations of Computer Science*, 1986, pp. 174–187.

[7] O. Goldreich, S. Micali, and A. Wigderson, "How to Play Any Mental Game", *Proc. 19th Ann. ACM Symp. on Theory of Computing*, 1987, pp. 218–229.

[8] S. Goldwasser, S. Micali, "Probabilistic Encryption & How to Play Mental Poker, Keeping Secret All Partial Information", *Proc. 14th Ann. ACM Symp. on Theory of Computing*, 1982, pp. 365–377.

[9] J. Y. Halpern, and M. O. Rabin, "A Logic to Reason About Likelihood", *Proc. 15th Ann. ACM Symp. on Theory of Computing*, 1983, pp. 310–319.

[10] M. Luby, S. Micali, and C. Rackoff, C., "How to Simultaneously Exchange a Secret Bit by Flipping a Symmetrically-Biased Coin", *Proc. 22nd Ann. IEEE Symp. on Foundations of Computer Science*, 1983, pp. 11–21.

[11] T. Tedrick, "How to Exchange Half a Bit", *Advances in Cryptology: Proc. of CRYPTO '83*, D. Chaum (ed.), Plenum, 1984, pp. 147–151.

[12] U. Vazirani, and V. Vazirani, V., "Trapdoor Pseudo-Random Number Generators, With Applications to Protocol Design", *Proc. 22nd Ann. IEEE Symp. on Foundations of Computer Science*, 1983, pp. 23–30.

[13] A. Yao, "Theory and Applications of Trapdoor Functions", *Proc. 21st Ann. IEEE Symp. on Foundations of Computer Science*, 1982, pp. 80–91.

[14] A. Yao, "Protocols for Secure Computations", *Proc. 21st Ann. IEEE Symp. on Foundations of Computer Science*, 1982, pp.160–169.

[15] A. Yao, "How to Generate and Exchange Secrets", *Proc. 25th Ann. IEEE Symp. on Foundations of Computer Science*, 1986, pp. 162–167.

Multiparty Computation with Faulty Majority*

Donald Beaver   Shafi Goldwasser
Harvard University   MIT

Abstract. We address the problem of performing a multiparty computation when more than half of the processors are cooperating Byzantine faults. We show how to compute any boolean function of n inputs distributively, preserving the privacy of inputs held by nonfaulty processors, and ensuring that faulty processors obtain the function value "if and only if" the nonfaulty processors do. If the nonfaulty processors do not obtain the correct function value, they detect cheating with high probability. Our solution is based on a new type of verifiable secret sharing in which the secret is revealed not all at once but in small increments. This slow-revealing process ensures that all processors discover the secret at roughly the same time. Our solution assumes the existence of an oblivious transfer protocol and uses broadcast channels. We do not require that the processors have equal computing power.

1 Introduction

Consider a network of n processors, each holding a private input x_i. Given a function $f(x_1, \ldots, x_n)$, the processors must compute f while maintaining the privacy of the local inputs. The problem of achieving correct and private computation of f in the presence of malicious processor faults has recently received much attention in [10], [5], [6]. [1], [3], [2] , [7], [4] among others.

In this paper we consider the case that *more than half* the network consists of cooperating Byzantine faults. The faulty processors are allowed probabilistic polynomial time. We assume broadcast channels are available. Our main result is a completeness theorem for multiparty boolean protocols tolerating any number of faults.

Let n be the total number of players in the network and $t \leq n$ be the number of faulty players. Let $f : D_1 \times \cdots \times D_n \rightarrow GF(2)$ be any polynomial-time boolean function. Our solution satisfies four essential properties (formal definitions can be found in the full version of the paper in the proceedings of FOCS89.):

- **Independence of Inputs:** The faulty players choose and commit to their inputs x_i independently of the honest players inputs.

- **Privacy:** At the the end of the execution of the protocol, t Byzantine faults cannot to compute any more information about honest players inputs than already implied by the faulty players' private inputs and outputs.

---
[1]The first author was supported in part under NSF grant CCR-870-4513. The second author was supported in part by NSF grant CCR-8657527 with IBM matching funds, and US-Israel binational grant. A full version of the paper appears in the proceeding of the FOCS89 conference.

- **Validity:** The honest players will either output the value CHEATING (if the number of active Byzantine faults is greater than $n - t$), or output v such that $v = f(x_1, ..., x_n)$.
- **Fairness:** The speed in which the faulty players and the non-faulty players learn the result of the computation is the same (at any time duing the of the computation.)

Theorem 1 *Let f be a boolean function of n variables represented by a polynomial size arithmetic circuit family. Let the number of faults t satisfy $t < n$. Assume that a protocol for two party oblivious transfer exists. Then there exists a protocol to compute f which achieves independence of inputs, privacy, validity and fairness.*

The assumption of an oblivious transfer protocol is necessary.

Acknowledgements Many friends helped us, especially in discussions on the nature of fairness. We are particularly grateful to Richard Cleve, Oded Goldreich and Yishai Mansour. The observations about the necessity of an oblivious transfer protocol were obtained with Yishai. Thanks also to Benny Chor (via Otto), Phil Klein, Nati Linial, and Ron Rivest.

References

[1] M. Ben-Or, S. Goldwasser, A. Wigderson. "Completeness Theorems for Non-Cryptographic Fault-Tolerant Distributed Computation." Proc. of 20th STOC (1988), 1-10.

[2] M. Ben-Or, T. Rabin. "Verifiable Secret Sharing and Multiparty Protocols with Honest Majority." Proc. of 21st STOC (1989).

[3] D. Chaum, C. Crépeau , I. Damgård . "Multiparty Unconditionally Secure Protocols." Proc. of 20th STOC (1988), 11-19.

[4] D. Chaum. "Multi Party Protocols with Disruptors and Colluders." CRYPTO88 Rump Session.

[5] Goldreich, O., Micali, S., A. Wigderson. "How to Play Any Mental Game, or A Completeness Theorem for Protocols with Honest Majority." Proc. of 19th STOC (1987), 218-229.

[6] Z. Galil, S. Haber, M. Yung. "Cryptographic Computation: Secure Faulty-Tolerant Protocols and the Public Key Model." Proc. of CRYPTO 1989.

[7] J. Kilian. "Founding Cryptography on Oblivious Transfer." Proc. of 20th STOC (1988), 20-29.

[8] M. Luby, S. Micali, C. Rackoff. "How to Simultaneously Exchange a Secret Bit by Flipping a Symmetrically Biased Coin." Proc. of 24th FOCS (1983).

[9] A. Shamir. "How to Share a Secret." CACM 22 (1979), 612-613.

[10] A. Yao. "How to Generate and Exchange Secrets." Proc. of 27th FOCS (1986), 162-167.

The Spymasters Double-Agent Problem
Multiparty Computation Secure Unconditionally from Minorities and Cryptographically from Majorities

David Chaum

Centre for Mathematics and Computer Science
Kruislaan 413   1098 SJ   Amsterdam

SUMMARY

A multiparty-computation protocol allows each of a set of participants to provide secret input to a mutually agreed computation. Such protocols enforce two security properties: (1) secrecy of the inputs, apart from what is revealed by the output; and (2) correctness of the output, as defined by the agreed computation. All solutions, including those presented here, are based on two kinds of assumptions: (a) public-key cryptography; and (b) limited collusion in a setting where pairs of participants can exchange messages with secret and authenticated content. Some of the previous solutions relied totally on assumption (a), the others totally on (b).

The main result presented here is a protocol that also provides both security properties, (1) and (2), but that does not rely on either assumption (a) or assumption (b) alone—security can be violated only by violating *both* assumptions.

The second construction improves the previously published multiparty computation results based on assumption (b). Let the number of participants be n, the largest tolerable number of disrupters be d, and the largest tolerable number of participants in any collusion be c. (Note that many collusions may exist, even to the extent that all participants are involved, but c is the maximum number of participants in any single collusion.) The construction requires $n > 2d + c$ and $n > 2c$. The first inequality gives a trade-off between the number of disrupters and the largest collusion size, which includes the previously achieved case of both less than a third. The second inequality, which means that all collusions of minorities can be tolerated, is argued to be optimal and makes the main result also optimal.

A third construction, on which the second is based but which is interesting in its own right, is that of an "all-honest world." This is a setting, relying only on assumption (b), in which any participant who has revealed secrets to any other can prove publicly that the secrets revealed are correct and receivable by the second participant—even if the second participant denies receipt or correctness.

1 INFORMAL INTRODUCTION

A spymaster's deepest fear, it might be said, is that of a "double agent." If the spymasters of major countries would be willing to pool all the information they have on their agents, then they could discover—to their mutual benefit— all double agents who play one side off against the other. But for a spymaster, revealing this sensitive data to "the other side" is, of course, unthinkable.

A solution to the spymasters' problem illustrates the main result achieved here: optimal security for general multiparty computations, given only cryptography and diplomatic pouches. And since these are the means available to spymasters, this is the kind of security they require.

If only the spymasters could use a physical computer that they all trust. Then they could simply supply their ultra-secret dossiers on each agent as input to a mutually agreed program that would derive and output the identities of all double agents. It is assumed that a suitable program can be agreed on. The only difficulty is the computer: How could such a device be physically built and operated securely? (But see [C].)

Spymasters know, from the literature, that the effect of such a mutually trusted computer can be achieved merely by exchanging messages. They know also that two quite different kinds of protocols have been proposed for this. The most recent type [CCD & BGW] requires only that each pair of participants exchange messages in a way that ensures authenticity and secrecy of message content. This the spymasters can readily achieve by diplomatic pouch and courier. The problem they have with this kind of approach, however, is that if a sufficient number of countries collude, these countries can learn all the secret-agent profiles of the other countries.

The earlier kind of protocol in the literature [GMW2 & CDG] does not have this problem; with it, collusion yields no advantage. Its drawback, though, is that secrecy relies on public-key cryptography. Thus, if some country were able to break the agreed public-key system, its intelligence service could clandestinely learn all the other countries' secrets.

Neither approach alone is optimal and hence acceptable to the spymasters. And simply conducting both kinds of protocol in parallel would be ridiculous, since it would give the disadvantages of both—a country breaking the cryptosystem could discover all other countries' secrets, and any sufficient collusion could also learn the secrets.

The new techniques presented here allow the best of both approaches in a single protocol. No collusion of countries is sufficient to obtain secrets of non-colluders; nor does breaking the cryptosystem yield any information whatsoever. The only way some countries can learn the secrets of others is for a collusion of a majority of countries to break the cryptosystem.

1.1 EXAMPLE OF THE CONSTRUCTION

The figure shows a setting with three countries a, b, c. In addition to national headquarters buildings, the countries have embassies located near one another in a neutral zone N. The embassies' mutual proximity is convenient, since couriers will transfer pouches containing secret messages between them. Headquarters use only another means of communication, which is also used by the embassies: staff members who write messages on rooftop blackboards. All countries are ensured of obtaining the identical message "broadcast" in this way, via their spy satellites.

The spymaster of each country a, b, c has secret input for the computation S_a, S_b, S_c, respectively. A spymaster (not shown) does not provide these most sensitive secrets to the embassy or headquarters staff (shown on the rooftops). Instead, spymaster i "Feistels" S_i into two parts [F], a random string R_i and the bit-wise exclusive-or sum $R_i \oplus S_i$, and personally delivers the first part to the embassy and the second to headquarters. Notice that this arrangement means, for example, that what is known to the headquarters of country b alone, $S_b \oplus R_b$, reveals nothing about S_b; similarly, what is known to b's embassy, R_b, also gives no clue about S_b.

1.2 THE PROTOCOL

To uncover double-agents, both types of protocols for multiparty computations are used—but in a special way. The cryptographic type is performed as a four-party protocol. Each headquarters is a party to the protocol, and the fourth party is played by the embassies outputting in unison. This means that the embassies, whenever they are required to do so by the four-party protocol, must all write the same thing on their blackboards.

To decide what to write, the embassies together perform a three-party protocol. They do this every time they must write something for the four-party protocol; thus, they perform one complete three-party protocol each time the four-party protocol requires a contribution from them. (Consistency across three-party protocols is ensured by "bit commitments.") These three-party protocols use pouches to provide security that does not depend on cryptography. (To achieve optimal security, as detailed later, they also use the blackboards, but only while the four-party protocol awaits their decision.)

The embassies provide outputs to the four-party protocol that are the same as would be provided by a single party knowing all of the R_i's—but the three-party protocols prevent any embassy from learning more than its R_i. The function

f computed by the four-party protocol is $f(R_a\|R_b\|R_c, R_a{\oplus}S_a, R_b{\oplus}S_b, R_c{\oplus}S_c) = e(S_a, S_b, S_c)$, where e is the agreed double-agent outputing function and "$\|$" denotes concatenation. Thus, the computation of f by the four-party protocol first X-ORs out the R_i's (that it gets as inputs from the embassies) from the headquarters inputs, and then computes e on the S_i.

1.3 WHY IS IT SECURE?

The cryptographic protocols of [CDG] offer optimal security, in the sense that they allow a single designated participant whose secret input is protected without any reliance on cryptographic assumptions. This participant is played by consensus of the embassies, which is itself a protocol that also does not require cryptographic assumptions. Thus, the $S_b{\oplus}R_b$, which reveal nothing about the S_i, are the only inputs exposed to cryptanalysis. On the other hand, the only protocol vulnerable to collusion is the embassy consensus protocol; but its only inputs are the R_i, which also reveal nothing about the S_i.

2. COMBINING CRYPTOGRAPHY AND POUCHES

This section treats the protocol introduced in the previous section more precisely. First it makes the model explicit. Then it describes the protocol, relying on the introduction of the previous section. Finally, the main result is contained in two theorems: one for secrecy of the inputs; the other for a topic ignored in the previous section, correctness of the output.

2.1 MODEL

The construction is based on two assumptions:

(a) Trap-door one-way bijections and "claw-free" functions exist. (Such assumptions underlie the cryptographic protocol [CDG] and are satisfied by the well-known quadratic residuosity assumption [GM].)

(b) Less than the specified number of participants collude and each pair of participants can communicate with secrecy and authentication. (This assumption underlies the protocols of [CCD] and [BGW]. The channel required can be achieved in practice in various ways: by exchanging long keys in person and then using a one-time pad and corresponding authentication coding; by exchanging short keys in person and then using a conventional cryptosystem; or perhaps even by realizing quantum cryptography [BB].)

2.2 PROTOCOL

The participants in the protocol correspond to the spymasters, of whom there are n. This means that the i'th participant, $1 \le i \le n$, knows both S_i and R_i. Thus, the participant is involved in one $n+1$-party [CDG] protocol and also in a number of n-party protocols of the type presented in [CCD] or [BGW] or section 3.

The computations performed by the protocols are as described in section 1. A technical point only hinted at there, though, is the source of randomness used by the n-party protocols. The X-OR of unconditionally-privacy-protecting bit commitments issued initially by all participants can be used as the "random tape" of the computation playing the role of the $n+1$'th participant. Participants then show, by "blob equality" [BCC], that their input to each protocol round is consistent with their contributions to the random tape.

2.3 PROPERTIES

The protocol has the following two security properties:

Theorem 2.1: The secrecy of each participant's input is protected unless both assumptions (a) and (b) are violated.

Proof: (Sketch) The inputs to either individual protocol by a participant following protocol are statistically independent of that participant's secrets. The output of the protocol that relies on assumption (b) only enters the other protocol through a predetermined participant, whose privacy also depends only on (b). Thus, it is necessary (and sufficient) to violate both (a) and (b) in order to gain information about a participant's secrets. Q.E.D.

Theorem 2.2: The correctness of the output is ensured with probability exponentially high in a security parameter unless both (a) and (b) are violated.

Proof: (Sketch) The [CDG] protocol gives exponential certainty that the first n participants cannot cause incorrect output. The $n+1$'th participant can falsify output, but only by violating assumption (a). For the pouch-based protocols playing this $n+1$'th participant, the correctness of their contribution is guaranteed with exponential certainty unless assumption (b) is violated ([BGW] achieve a stronger result of not allow even an exponentially small chance of cheating). Thus, violation of both (a) and (b) is necessary to give a non-negligible probability of false output. Q.E.D.

3 IMPROVED POUCH CONSTRUCTION

The model underlying this section is stated in §3.1. Next, §3.2 describes a "cut-and-choose" originally proposed by [Be] for other purposes, and used by [CCD] and [BGW]. Then §3.3 presents the "all-honest world" construction. Finally, §3.4 shows how circuits are simulated, using the essence of the "double-degree polynomial" trick proposed in both [CCD] and [BGW].

3.1 MODEL

As already mentioned, the number of participants is denoted n, the largest tolerable number of disrupters d, and the largest tolerable number of participants in any single collusion c.

Disrupters are defined as participants whose outputs do not follow protocol. Once a participant is agreed to be a disrupter, the protocol can (if necessary) be restarted without that participant (but see §4); this is why disrupters may try to falsely blame others for sending them improper messages. Violation of property (2), correctness of the result, requires active cheating, and hence disrupters.

A collusion, on the other hand, is a set of participants who merely share their information in efforts to learn the secret input of others. Because a collusion could even be a secretly conducted instance of the type of protocol described here, each participant could be a member of multiple collusions. It will be sufficient, however, simply to ensure that no collusion has access to information from more than c participants.

The construction requires $n > 2d+c$ and $n > 2c$. If $n = 3$, for instance, then $d = 0$, which means that even a single disrupter can falsify the output; but, since even this small n allows $c = 1$, secrecy of the inputs can be protected unconditionally against any participant acting alone. When $n = 4$, a single disrupter can be tolerated. More generally, $c = 1$ allows almost half the participants to be disrupters. At the other end of the trade-off, with d at about a quarter n, any c less than half n is possible. This last is optimal; otherwise, disjoint sets of participants could conduct an arbitrary two-party protocol with both parties protected unconditionally—and this, as argued in [CDG], is impossible.

3.2 SET-UP BLOBS

Included in the mutually agreed and public protocol definition are: an integer k such that $2^k > n$; an assignment of a distinct point in $GF(2^k)$ to each participant; and a security parameter s.

A participant issues a *blob* by first choosing a polynomial of degree at most c, uniformly over $GF(2^k)$, with a value at 0 of 1 or 0. Then the issuing participant uses the corresponding pouch to supply every other participant with a *share*—the value of the polynomial at that other participant's point. When a blob must be *opened*, every participant broadcasts the share it holds for the blob and the issuer separately broadcasts what each other participant should output.

Every blob used in the remaining protocol is subjected to s challenges by each participant. Consider a single challenge of a particular participant. First, the issuer creates a new blob, and then the challenger broadcasts a random bit. If this challenge bit is 0, the new blob is opened (as defined above); if it is 1, each participant computes the sum of the share it held of the original blob with the share of the new blob, and the resulting sum blob is opened.

If the challenger and issuer disagree on the value of the polynomial at the challenger's point, the challenger is said to *object*; further objections can result if and when the original blob is opened. If more than d participants ever object for any single issuer, then that issuer is clearly indicated as a disrupter (under the assumption of at most d disrupters) and the protocol terminates.

Theorem 3.1: If the number of objections for a blob does not exceed d, then it can be opened both as 1 and 0 with probability at most 2^{-s}.

Proof: (Sketch) With probability $1-2^{-s}$, all non-objecting non-disrupters, of whom there are at least $c+1$, will broadcast shares consistent with a single polynomial p. This is a simple consequence of the challenge and response technique. Because each polynomial has degree at most c, it is always completely determined by $c+1$ shares. Since $d+c+1$ consistent shares are broadcast during opening, at least d shares may be called redundant because they are consistent with p but are not necessary to determine p. For the blob to be opened as both 1 and 0, shares would have to be consistent with two distinct polynomials, p and q. If $d+c+1$ shares are consistent with p, then $d+1$ must be changed to be consistent with q, since the redundancy means that changing any d or fewer shares leaves sufficient shares to determine p. Thus at least $d+1$ shares must be changed, so $d+1$ disrupters are implied. Q.E.D.

3.3 THE ALL-HONEST WORLD

During the protocol proper, pouches will not be used (except possibly for Byzantine agreement [LPS] of broadcasts when $n \leq 3d$). Instead, by setting up an "all-honest world," the participants arrange in advance for every bit of message that will be sent between them. For each such message bit to be sent in the all-honest world, the parity of the bits in two blobs—one blob issued by each communicant—is made public in advance. There are two cases.

In the first case, the cardinality of the union of the objector sets for the two communicants does not exceed d. The intersection of the non-objecting sets for the two communicants thus contains at least $d+c+1$ participants. Two blobs are issued, one by each of the two communicants, and the sum of the two blob is opened. Such "opening" differs from that for an ordinary blob, since the issuers will not broadcast the shares they issued. If the shares broadcast by the participants in the intersecting set are consistent with a single polynomial having a binary value at zero, then this value at zero is the public parity bit. If no such bit is recognizable, both blobs are opened separately (which adds at least one member to one of the two objector sets) and the process is repeated for a new pair of blobs.

In the second case, that cardinality of the union of objector sets exceeds d, there will be $c+1$ participants, called a *common* set, who will successfully satisfy the first case with each of the pair of communicants. (To see this, notice that the second case implies that one of the two communicants is a disrupter—thus, a participant involved in such situations with d other participants is recognizable as a disrupter.) Consider, without loss of generality, a particular pair of communicants with a common set and a particular participant in that common set. This common participant will use two blobs satisfying the first case, one with each of the two communicants. The common participant asks everyone to add their shares corresponding to the two blobs, and opens this sum blob to reveal the parity of the contents of the two original blobs. The channel parity bit is then easily computed as an X-OR of all such bits made public by the common set.

To send a bit in the all-honest world once all the parity bits have been established, the sender simply makes public the actual message bit X-ORed with the sender's contribution to the parity bit. Then the sender can prove the correctness of the bit sent by using the sender's other blobs in a general satisfiability protocol, like that of [BCC] or [GMW1]. The secrecy of the transmission is ensured because at least $c+1$ other participants must collude to recover the secret contents of all blobs used in establishing the parity bit. The receiver can also use the bits received in proofs related to subsequent outputs, since these bits can be expressed as sums involving only public bits and the content of the recipient's own blobs.

3.4 THE PROTOCOL PROPER

The actual secret input of participants to the computation itself will be committed to by blobs issued in the all-honest world. When a share is sent in such a blob-issuing, the sender proves that the correct value of the share has been sent, and that it is receivable, based on the public parity bits. The blobs used in this proof are all from the initial set-up phase and include blobs committing to the "random tape" that determines the choice of polynomials.

When two bits in the circuit simulated by the computation (either actual secret inputs or intermediate values) are to be X-ORed, each participant adds the share they hold for each of the bits, which yields their share for the new bit.

When two bits are to be ANDed, each participant first multiplies the two shares held, yielding a share of a "double degree" blob having maximal degree $2c$. Then the resulting share is added to a share from n new "double-degree" blobs, one issued in the all-honest world by each participant. This sum double-degree blob is then "opened" in the all-honest world; each participant opens its part of the parity bits involved. A second blob is also issued in the all-honest world by each participant; it is shown to be properly formed and to contain the same bit as the corresponding double-degree blob issued by that participant. The result of the AND-gate is then formed by each participant as the X-OR of all second blobs, or the inverse of this, depending on whether the double-degree blob opened contains 0 or 1, respectively.

4 RELEASE OF RESULTS

Issuing an actual secret input as a blob in the all-honest world costs the issuer by creating exposure to collusion. To spread such exposure evenly, participants can reciprocally commit to more and more information about their secret inputs in a "gradual commit," which is essentially the inverse of the "release of secrets" notion surveyed in [BCDG].

After the gradual commit, participants could still be robbed of the benefit of their new exposure if the computation were not completed. Any participant can stop the all-honest-world computation, but not without being recognized by the others as having done so. Even if $2d$ participants stop, however, the $c+1$ remaining ones can input all the shares they received in the all-honest world to a new protocol with a reduced n (and, consequently, possibly a reduced c). This new protocol—which has information already proven correct and sufficient to determine all the original secret inputs—computes the same result as the original computation would have.

CONCLUSION

Some earlier results are extended, improved, and generalized here; and two previously unlinked but fundamental sets of results are unified.

ACKNOWLEDGEMENTS

It is a pleasure to acknowledge all the discussion with my coauthors Claude Crépeau and Ivan Damgård on our joint work [CCD] that laid a foundation for section 3. It is also a pleasure to thank Jurjen Bos for his help in simplifying and improving the presentation.

REFERENCES

[BB]   Bennett and Brassard: An update on quantum cryptography. Proc Crypto 84, pp. 474–480.

[BCC]   Brassard, Chaum and Crépeau: Minimum disclosure proofs of knowledge. JCSS October 1988, pp. 156–189.

[BCDG]   Brickel, Chaum, Damgård and van de Graaf: Gradual and verifiable release of a secret. Proc. Crypto 87, pp. 156–166.

[Be]   Benaloh: Secret sharing homomorphisms: keeping shares of a secret secret. Proc. Crypto 86, pp. 251–260.

[BGW]   Ben-Or, Goldwasser and Wigderson: Completeness theorems for non-cryptographic fault-tolerant distributed computation. Proc. STOC 88.

[C]   Chaum: Computer systems established, maintained, and trusted by mutually suspicious groups. Memorandum UCB/ERL M79/10, U.C. Berkeley, February 22, 1979

[CCD]   Chaum, Crépeau and Damgård: Multiparty unconditionally secure protocols. Proc. STOC 88. (To appear in JCSS.)

[CDG]   Chaum, Damgård and van de Graaf: Multiparty computations ensuring privacy of each party's input and correctness of the result. Proc. Crypto 87, pp. 87–119.

[F]   Feistel: Cryptographic coding for data-bank privacy. RC 2827, IBM Research, Yorktown Heights, March 1970.

[GM]   Goldwasser and Micali: Probabilistic encryption. JCSS, April 1984, pp. 270–299.

[GMW1]   Goldreich, Micali and Wigderson: Proofs that yield nothing but their validity and a methodology of cryptographic protocol design. Proc. of FOCS 86, pp. 174–187.

[GMW2]   Goldreich, Micali and Wigderson: How to play any mental game, Proc. of STOC 87.

[GV]   Goldreich and Vainish: How to play any mental game: an efficiency improvement. Proc. Crypto 87, pp. 73–86.

[LPS]   Lamport, Shostak and Pease: The Byzantine generals problem. ACM trans. Prog. Languages and Systems, 1982, pp. 382–401.

Chair: WHITFIELD DIFFIE

On the Structure of Secret Key Exchange Protocols

Mihir Bellare[*]   Lenore Cowen[†]   Shafi Goldwasser[†]

MIT Laboratory for Computer Science
545 Technology Square
Cambridge, MA 02139

1 Introduction

Modern cryptography is fundamentally concerned with the problem of secure private communication. Suppose two parties, Alice and Bob, wish to communicate privately over a public channel (for instance, a telephone line with an eavesdropper). If Alice and Bob are able to meet, privately, beforehand, and agree on some common secret key, then it becomes easy for them to achieve such private communication. But Alice and Bob might not be able to first meet in private and agree on a key. In this case, we ask under what assumptions they can still agree on a common secret key, where their conversation is conducted entirely in public.

A Secret Key Exchange is a protocol where Alice and Bob, having no secret information in common to start, are able to agree on a common secret key, conversing over a public channel. Secret Key Exchange is of course trivial if trapdoor permutations exist. However, there is no known implementation based on a weaker general assumption.

Recently [Impaggliazo, Rudich STOC 89] showed that any "natural" proof that secret key exchange was possible with one way permutations would imply a proof that $P \neq NP$. In this paper we look at the other side of the coin. We ask, what are the conditions necessary for Secret Key Exchange and what is its power to yield other important primitives? We define the *Matrix of Conversations* for any Secret Key Exchange protocol and show it must have strong structural properties. The results we obtain follow directly from our anaylsis of monochromatic blocks of this matrix.

In particular, we show that the existence of a Secret Key Exchange protocol implies that a one-way function exists, (as a corollary, we immediately get that Oblivious transfer implies the existence of one-way functions), and that Secret Key Exchange implies the existence of a bit commitment scheme where the prover has probability 0 of cheating.

Copies of the paper are available from the authors; the paper will also appear in the proceedings of the 1989 DIMACS workshop.

2 Definitions and Summary of Results

Let A and B be two probabalistic polynomial time interactive Turing Machines. Let $conv(R_A, R_B)$ denote the converstion between them, where R_A and R_B denote their respective random tapes. Each of A and B has a *key obtaining algorithm*, K_A or K_B; these are polynomial time functions which each party can compute on the conversation and his own coin tosses to yield his estimate of the key. For any instance (i.e. fixed choice of R_A, R_B)

[*] Supported in part by NSF grant CCR-87-19689 and DARPA Contract N00014-89-J-1988.
[†] Supported in part by NSF grant CCR-86-57527 and DARPA Contract N00014-89-J-1988.

of the protocol we say that A and B have *agreed* on a key if $K_A(R_A, conv(R_A, R_B)) = K_B(R_B, conv(R_A, R_B))$; this common value is the key they have agreed on. There is a security parameter k, and for convenience we assume that $|R_A| = |R_B| = k$.

Definition 2.1 A protocol constitutes a *secret key exchange (SKE)* if there is an $\alpha > 0$ such that we have

- **Agreement:** $P_{agree} \geq \alpha$, and on each instance, A and B *know* whether or not they agreed
- **Secrecy:** For all probabilistic polynomial time algorithms E, for all $d > 0$ and all sufficiently large k,

$$P(E(C) = K_A(R_A, C) = K_B(R_B, C) : R_A, R_B \leftarrow \{0,1\}^k; C \leftarrow conv(R_A, R_B)) \leq k^{-d} .$$

Definition 2.2 A protocol constitutes a *Weak Secret Key Exchange (weak SKE)* if there is an $\alpha > 0$ such that we have

- **Agreement:** $P_{agree} \geq \alpha$
- **Secrecy:** same as in Definition 2.1

It is easy to see that for any conversation C the set of pairs of tapes

$$\{(R_A, R_B) : conv(R_A, R_B) = C\}$$

is of the form $X \times Y$ (i.e. forms a rectangle). We define the *matrix of the conversation C* over $X \times Y$ as having as its row R_A column R_B entry $((R_A, R_B) \in X \times Y)$

- $K_A(R_A, R_B) = K_B(R_A, R_B)$ if these are equal
- some special symbol $*$ otherwise,

Call this matrix $M(C)$. The heart of our results concern properties of this matrix. For example, we show that

Theorem 2.1 For SKE all entries of this matrix are equal (i.e. if A and B agree on κ for some pair of random tapes that leads to the conversation C, then they agree (and moreover on this same key κ) for *all* such pairs of random tapes).

Theorem 2.2 For weak SKE, for any conversation C with a "large" area of the matrix not equal to $*$, there is a *single* key κ which covers a corrsponding large area (i.e. most of the time that A and B agree with conversation C, they agree on a particular key κ).

These structural properties imply

Corollary 2.1 SKE implies the existence of a one-way function.

Corollary 2.2 Oblivious transfer implies the existence of a one-way function.

Corollary 2.3 (non-uniform) Weak SKE implies the existence of a one-way function.

Theorems 2.1, 2.2 and the first two corollaries all hold in both the uniform and the non-uniform models. Independently, [Impaliazzo, Luby, (private comunication)], are able to obtain our results for the non-uniform case (corollary 2.3) by viewing Secret Key Exchange as an "identification scheme". Also in a non-uniform model of security, a result of [Naor, Crypto 89] coupled with [Impagliazzo, Levin, Luby STOC 89] implies that one-way functions are enough for bit committment. We prove a stronger result for bit commitment in that: (1) it does not use non-uniform assumptions (2) the scheme is non-interactive (3) the probability of the committer cheating is 0 rather than just very small.

Corollary 2.4 SKE implies bit commitment.

An Efficient Identification Scheme Based on Permuted Kernels (extended abstract)

Adi Shamir
Applied Mathematics Department
The Weizmann Institute of Science

Abstract. *In 1985 Goldwasser Micali and Rackoff proposed a new type of interactive proof system which reveals no knowledge whatsoever about the assertion except its validity. The practical significance of these proofs was demonstrated in 1986 by Fiat and Shamir, who showed how to use efficient zero knowledge proofs of quadratic residuosity to establish user identities and to digitally sign messages. In this paper we propose a new zero knowledge identification scheme, which is even faster than the Fiat-Shamir scheme, using a small number of communicated bits, simple 8-bit arithmetic operations, and compact public and private keys. The security of the new scheme depends on an NP-complete algebraic problem rather than on factoring, and thus it widens the basis of public key cryptography, which has become dangerously dependent on the difficulty of a single problem.*

1. The Basic Scheme

Notation:

Throughout this paper, we use upper case letters to denote vectors and matrices, and lower case letters to denote values. Greek letters denote permutations over $\{1, \ldots, n\}$, and their effect V_π on n-vectors V is defined as the vector W such that $w_j = v_{\pi(j)}$ for $1 \leq j \leq n$. The effect of permutations on matrices is defined as the column permutation $A_\pi = [a_{i\pi(j)}]$ so that for any matrix A and vector V, $A_\pi V_\pi = [\sum_{j=1}^n a_{i\pi(j)} v_{\pi(j)}] = [\sum_{j=1}^n a_{ij} v_j] = AV$. Permutations are composed as functions, and thus $V_{\pi\sigma}$ is defined as the vector W such that $w_j = v_{\pi(\sigma(j))}$ for $1 \leq j \leq n$. All the arithmetic operations in this paper are carried out modulo p, where p is a (small) prime. We define the kernel $K(A)$ of a rectangular $m \times n$ matrix A as the set of n-vectors W such that $AW = 0 \pmod{p}$, where 0 is the m-vector of zeroes. It is easy to see that $K(A)$ is a linear subspace of Z_p^n and that $K(A_\sigma) = (K(A))_\sigma$.

The Permuted Kernel Problem (PKP) is:

Given: a $m \times n$ matrix A, a n-vector V, and a prime p;
Find: a permutation π such that $V_\pi \in K(A)$.

The related problems of finding some, all, or randomly chosen vectors in $K(A)$ can be solved by straightforward techniques in linear algebra. The problem of finding good approximations in $K(A)$ to a given vector V (and in particular small non-zero vectors in $K(A)$) can be solved by more complicated (but polynomial) lattice reduction techniques. What makes the Permuted Kernel Problem difficult is that it forces us to choose a kernel vector with a particular set of entries. In fact, it is easy to see that the problem is NP-complete even for $m = 1$ and $V = (+1, +1, \ldots, +1, -1, -1, \ldots, -1)$ since this is just the partition problem for the weights in A. A slightly more complicated reduction from the problem of 3-partition (Garey and Johnson [1979], pp 224) shows that the PKP is NP-complete in the strong sense (i.e., its difficulty grows exponentially in p rather than in $\log(p)$, under appropriate assumptions). This makes it possible to use small numbers in the proposed identification scheme, which greatly enhances its simplicity and speed.

To use the permuted kernel problem as an identification scheme, the users agree on a universal matrix A and prime p, and then each user chooses a random permutation π (which serves as his secret key) and a random vector V such that $V_\pi \in K(A)$ (which serves as his public key). Users can now establish their identity by proving their knowledge of the secret permutation π. By using zero knowledge proofs, provers can guarantee that eavesdroppers and dishonest verifiers will not learn anything about π which will later enable them to misrepresent themselves as the prover to others.

The following protocol uses a hash function which commits the prover to his chosen values without revealing them prematurely to the verifier. Since the function is applied to highly redundant inputs with a large compression ratio in a non-invertible way, we believe that efficient DES-like functions will be sufficiently secure in practice.

Zero knowledge proofs for the Permuted Kernel Problem:

1. The prover chooses a random vector R and a random permutation σ, and sends the cryptographically hashed values of the pairs (σ, AR) and $(\pi\sigma, R_\sigma)$ to the verifier.

2. The verifier chooses a random value $0 \leq c < p$ and asks the prover to send $W = R_\sigma + cV_{\pi\sigma}$.

3. After receiving W, the verifier asks the prover to reveal either σ or $\pi\sigma$. In the first case the verifier checks that $(\sigma, A_\sigma W)$ hashes to the first given value, and in the second case the verifier checks that $(\pi\sigma, W - cV_{\pi\sigma})$ hashes to the second given value.

An honest prover who knows π will always pass this test, since $A_\sigma W = A_\sigma(R_\sigma + cV_{\pi\sigma}) = A(R + cV_\pi) = AR + cAV_\pi = AR$ and $W - cV_{\pi\sigma} = R_\sigma$ by definition. When a dishonest prover tries to choose the commited values in step 1, he should be prepared to answer $2p$ possible questions. If he can answer correctly $p + 2$ questions, then for the same committed (σ, X) and (τ, Y), there are at least two distinct values c' c'' whose response vectors W' W'' satisfy both conditions.

This leads to the following system of equations:

$$A_\sigma W' = X \qquad A_\sigma W'' = X \qquad W' - c'V_\tau = Y \qquad W'' - c''V_\tau = Y$$

This implies that $(W' - W'') \in K(A_\sigma)$ and $(W' - W'') = (c' - c'')V_\tau$. Since $c' - c'' \neq 0$, $V_{\tau\sigma^{-1}} \in K(A)$ and thus the secret permutation $\pi = \tau\sigma^{-1}$ can be extracted from any $p+2$ correct answers. Consequently, the probability of success when such an π is not known is at most $(p+1)/2p$. Since this value is essentially $1/2$, only 20 iterations are required to reduce the probability of cheating bellow the practical security threshold of $1/1,000,000$ for each misrepresentation attempt.

The technical proof that this protocol is zero knowledge will be given in the full version of the paper, but the intuition behind it is very simple: The randomness of R makes the vectors W, AR and R_σ completely random, and the randomness of σ makes the permutation $\pi\sigma$ completely random. The individual messages sent by the prover convey no knowledge, and it is only the prover's willingness to answer both questions for all the possible c's which convinces the verifier that the prover is genuine.

2. Implementation details

The minimum recommended size of n has not been determined so far, but we believe that it should be between 32 and 64. For these n the number of permutations π ranges between $32! = 2^{120}$ and $64! = 2^{296}$, while the fastest attacks we are aware of require between 2^{76} and 2^{184} steps. The prime p should not be too small (since multiple occurrences of values in V (mod p) reduce its number of distinct permutations), and should not be too large (since multiprecision arithmetic is slow). The best choice of p for 8 bit microprocessors seems to be $p = 251$. The choice of m should be based on the approximation $p^m \approx n!$, which describes the combination of parameters at which a randomly chosen instance of PKP is likely to have a unique solution ($p^m > n!$ implies that some of the m rows of A can be discarded without adding spurious PKP solutions, while $p^m < n!$ implies that some of the entries in π can be arbitrarily fixed without losing all the PKP solutions). For $p = 251$ and $n = 32$, m should be about 16, and for $p = 251$ and $n = 64$, m should be about 37.

The matrix A should be randomly chosen. Without loss of generality we can assume that A is given in the block form $A = [A' \mid I]$ where A' is a random $m \times (n - m)$ matrix and I is the $m \times m$ identity matrix, since both users and opponents can apply Gauss elimination to the published A without changing its kernel. Calculating AR (or $A_\sigma W$) is particularly easy in this representation. To demonstrate the actual time complexity of the new zero knowledge proofs, we consider the concrete case of a 16×32 matrix $A = [A' \mid I]$ and $p = 251$. The application of permutations and the addition of vectors of size 32 require negligible amounts of time. In addition, the prover performs one matrix-vector multiplication per iteration, and the verifier performs one matrix-vector multiplication every two iterations (on the average). The simplified 16×16 matrix-vector multiplications require 256 single-byte multiplications, which can be carried out in a few milliseconds on today's microprocessors. This compares very favorably with number-theoretic schemes, in which the calculation of the product of two 512 bit numbers requires 4096 single-byte multiplications (in addition to the overhead caused by the carry propagation and the modular reduction in multiprecision arithmetic). Since two hashed values (64 bits each) one vector (256 bits) and one permutation (120 bits) are sent in each iteration, the total communication is about 500 bits per round.

Another advantage of the new scheme (which is particularly important in smart card applications) is that it needs very little memory: The public key V of each user can be stored in 256 bits, and the secret key π can be stored in 120 bits. The universal matrix A' can be stored as a pseudo random function of i and j, rather than as an explicit matrix. Since we believe that most A' are usable, fairly simple pseudo random functions can suffice in practice. The elements of A' can be generated upon demand (in the original or permuted order) by invoking this function with appropriate arguments, and thus the calculation of the matrix-vector product needs only a few bytes of working space.

3. Extensions

The basic scheme can be extended in a variety of obvious ways. The underlying field Z_p can be replaced by other ring structures, the homogeneous equations can be replaced by non-homogeneous equations, and the matrix-vector products can be replaced by higher order tensor products. By adding the message m to the list of hashed arguments the prover can authenticate the contents of the message in addition to proving his identity, and by using the general technique introduced in Fiat and Shamir [1986] this authentication scheme can be turned into a signature scheme. However, PKP-based signatures are much longer than Fiat-Shamir signatures, and their practical significance is unclear.

A detailed analysis of the security of the new identification scheme for various choices of the parameters is underway, and its results will be published in the full version of this paper. In the meantime, we encourage readers to attack the scheme and warn potential users not to adopt it prematurely.

An Efficient Software Protection Scheme
(Abstract)

Rafail Ostrovsky, MIT

In 1979 Pippenger and Fischer [PF] showed how a two-tape Turing Machine whose head positions (as a function of time) are independent of the input, can simulate, on-line, a one-tape Turing Machine with a logarithmic slowdown in the running time. We show a similar result for random-access machine (RAM) model of computation. In particular, we show how to do an on-line simulation of arbitrary RAM program by probabilistic RAM whose memory access pattern is independent of the program which is being executed with a poly-logarithmic slowdown in the running time.

A main application of our result concerns *software protection*, one of the most important issues in computer practice. A theoretical formulation of the problem for a generic one-processor, random-access machine (RAM) model of computation was given by Goldreich [G]. In this paper, we present a simple and an efficient software protection scheme for this model. In particular, we show how to protect any program at the cost of a poly-logarithmic slowdown in the running time of the protected program, previously conjectured to be impossible.

Software is very expensive to create and very easy to steal. "Software piracy" is a major concern (and a major loss of revenue) to all software-related companies. Software pirates borrow/rent software they need, copy it to their computer and use it without paying anything for it. The question of how one prevents a pirate from illegal copying of software is a question of "software protection". Ad-hoc methods have been used for decades, but only recently, a precise formulation of the problem and a solution to it was given by Goldreich [G]. Current work builds on work started in [G], making the software protection scheme more efficient and using weaker assumptions.

Let us examine various options which any software company has when considering how to protect its software. On one hand, it can sell a *physically shielded* computer with all the software installed, which self-destructs if ever opened. Clearly, such a "solution" eliminates the problem of software piracy at the price of forcing customer to purchase a new computer for each new task. We consider such a "solution" infeasible and contradictory to a general-purpose machine paradigm. One would want to sell just the software, which runs on any general-purpose computer, but which is impossible to copy. This, however, is unachievable: if one sells software which runs on any general-purpose computer, the software can always be duplicated. Thus, we always need some physically-shielded hardware to prevent the duplication. What is the minimal amount of protected hardware one needs?

We require only a constant number of registers to be physically protected. That is, only a single *chip* with a fixed number of registers is protected while the entire memory is open to the pirate, who can inspect it and alter it, in order to learn something about the protected program. Thus, we assume that a physically shielded chip is connected to a random access memory (RAM) to which the pirate has a complete read/write access.

The next question we turn to is the interpretation of "software protection". Let us consider the following hypothetical situation: suppose you are a software producer selling a protected program which took you an enormous effort to write. Your competitor purchases your program, experiments with it widely and learns some partial information about your implementation. Intuitively, if the information he gained through experimentation with your protected program simplifies his task of writing a software package, then we consider the protection scheme to be insecure. Thus, the software protection must hide *all* the information about the implementation.

Software protection is secure if, intuitively, whatever any poly-time adversary can do when having access to an (encrypted) program running on a protected chip, he can also do when having access to a "specification oracle" (such an oracle on any input "magically" gives the output and the running time). Essentially, the protected program must behave like a black box which, on any input, hums for a while and gives an output and such that no information except its I/O behavior and running time can be extracted. Thus, not only the values stored in the general-purpose memory must be hidden (using encryption) but also the *sequence* in which memory locations are accessed during program execution must be hidden. Notice that if this is not the case, the program "loop structure" is revealed to the adversary, even if all the memory locations are securely encrypted. Surely, the information about the "loop structure" does provide some information about the structure of the code. To prevent this, the memory *access pattern* should be *independent* of the program which is being executed.

Nothing in this world comes for free. What is the price one has to pay for protecting the software? The answer is "speed". The protected program will run slower then the unprotected one. What is the minimal slowdown we can achieve without sacrificing the security of the protection? *Software protection overhead* is defined as the number of steps the protected program must make for each step of the source-code program.

The key problem of efficient software protection is to be able to hide the access pattern efficiently. Goldreich shows how to achieve $O((\log m)^c \cdot 2^{\sqrt{2 \log m \cdot \log \log m}})$ overhead for hiding the access pattern, where m is the total (RAM) memory size and c is some small constant. He conjectures that a poly-logarithmic (in m) overhead is impossible to achieve.

The main contribution of this paper is to show how to achieve a poly-logarithmic overhead of hiding the access pattern. (Actually, our result is even stronger: we show how to achieve a poly-logarithmic overhead *as a function of the program running time* for hiding the access pattern, instead of poly-logarithmic overhead of *total RAM memory size*, which could be much bigger then the program running time.)

Moreover, in addition to considerable efficiency speedup, the scheme presented in this paper gives a simple and explicit construction of the protection scheme, while the scheme shown in [G], gives a non-trivial recursive solution. It should also be noticed that in [G] one-way permutations are used, while here, we reduce the assumption to the existence of one-way functions only.

References

[G]   Goldreich, O. "Towards a Theory of Software Protection and simulation by Oblivious RAMs" *STOC 87*.

[PF]   Pippenger , N., and M.J. Fischer, "Relations Among Complexity Measures" *JACM*, Vol 26, No. 2, 1979, pp. 361-381.

Good S-Boxes Are Easy To Find

Carlisle Adams and Stafford Tavares

Department of Electrical Engineering
Queen's University, Kingston, Ontario, Canada, K7L 3N6

Abstract. *We describe an efficient design methodology for the s-boxes of DES-like cryptosystems. Our design guarantees that the resulting s-boxes will be bijective and nonlinear and will exhibit the strict avalanche criterion and the output bit independence criterion.*

1.   Introduction

In this work we describe the structured design of substitution boxes (s-boxes) for cryptosystems built as substitution-permutation networks (DES-like systems). There are several motivations for research in this area:

- s-boxes are a critical element of any S-P network since the remainder of the network is linear;
- some design and evaluation criteria in DES s-boxes remain classified; study in this area may help to shed some light on how the DES s-boxes were chosen;
- a *structured* approach to s-box design may help to speed up the process of finding new s-boxes for any desired application;
- the design of pseudorandom mappings is itself an active research area, independent of any possible applications.

Because we design s-boxes to satisfy several criteria simultaneously, our approach overcomes the deficiencies in the s-boxes designed by Pieprzyk and Finkelstein [8]. This results in s-boxes which appear to be cryptographically "good" and which can be designed extremely efficiently.

2.   Background

Pieprzyk and Finkelstein [8] have described a method for $n \times n$ bit s-box design which relies on finding n appropriate Boolean functions of n bits and setting these as the output bits. These Boolean functions can be found very easily: they give an algorithm for constructing one function and the rest are simple variations of this one. They focus on the nonlinearity property of an s-box (a necessary property since the remainder of the algorithm in an S-P network is linear) and state that an s-box will be as highly nonlinear as possible if its component Boolean functions are each as highly nonlinear as possible (this definition of s-box nonlinearity is similar to that proposed by Rueppel [10], who did some work on finding the closest linear approximation to any given s-box). The algorithm in [8], therefore, constructs a Boolean function of highest possible nonlinearity (subject to the restriction that it is 0-1 balanced) and gives $n-1$ simple variations which preserve nonlinearity. These n functions are then set as the output bits of the s-box.

S-boxes created by the method in [8] have several limitations, however. Firstly, the inverse s-box is almost completely linear (it has only one nonlinear function), which may be of some help to a cryptanalyst. Secondly, there is no guarantee that the s-boxes will have good avalanche (or "diffusion") [11, 5]. Thirdly, it is easy to show that *every* pair of output bits will have a correlation of ±1 with respect to the inversion of a single input bit. Finally, their algorithm is useful for constructing $n \times n$ bit s-boxes only when n is odd.

3. Criteria for a "good" $n \times n$ bit s-box

We have chosen four properties which we feel are necessary for general, cryptographically "good" s-boxes. They are:

1. bijection;
2. nonlinearity;
3. strict avalanche;
4. independence of output bits.

For some applications it is important that the inverse s-box also possess these properties, so we may add "bidirectionality" as an optional fifth property. Note that all but one of the evaluation criteria released about the DES s-boxes [3, 4] are covered by the above properties; the one criterion not covered deals with combining four 4×4 bit s-boxes into one 6×4 bit s-box. This criterion deals not with an *internal* property of $n \times n$ bit s-boxes but rather with the relationship *between* $n \times n$ bit s-boxes, and so is not addressed in this paper.

We now describe a procedure for efficiently producing s-boxes which are guaranteed to possess the above four properties.

4. Methodology for s-box construction

In our $n \times n$ bit s-box design we choose n Boolean functions (each of n input variables) that satisfy the following properties and set these as the output bits. Let these functions be $f_1, f_2, ..., f_n$.

Bijection: Choose the f_i such that $wt \left(\sum_{i=1}^{n} a_i f_i \right) = 2^{n-1} \pmod 2$, where $a_i \in \{0, 1\}$ and $wt()$ is the Hamming weight. This will guarantee that s-box S is bijective.

Nonlinearity: Choose the f_i to be as highly nonlinear as possible (see [8, 7, 10], and others). This will guarantee that S is nonlinear and that Rueppel's "closest linear approximation" to S is of no help to a cryptanalyst.

Strict Avalanche: Choose f_i which satisfy the Strict Avalanche Criterion [11]; this can be done using Forré's method [6] or some other. This will guarantee that S satisfies the SAC.

Output Bit Independence: Choose the f_i such that $(f_j \oplus f_k)$ is highly nonlinear and comes as close as possible to satisfying the SAC for all $j, k \in \{1, 2, \ldots, n\}$, $j \neq k$. This will guarantee that every pair of output bits will have a correlation as close as possible to zero when any single input bit is inverted (this is known as the output bit independence criterion [11]).

The proofs for the above statements are fairly straightforward and will appear in the full version of this paper [2].

5. Results

It turns out that there are no conflicting requirements in our design methodology so that all criteria can be met simultaneously. For 4×4 bit s-boxes there are only 2^{16} possible Boolean functions, so even an exhaustive search for functions which meet all our criteria is quite feasible. However, the search space is quickly reduced by relatively simple checks (weight, nonlinearity) so that more computationally intensive checks (SAC, for example) are only performed on a subset of the space. Furthermore, other methods (in particular, "bent" functions [9, 7, 1]) can be used to reduce the initial search space so that it may be possible to relatively quickly design 6×6 or 8×8 bit s-boxes.

We find that "good" s-boxes can be generated by our procedure in a few seconds of CPU time on a SUN workstation. Therefore, one can easily generate and store lists of "good" s-boxes so that new cryptosystem design may reduce to simply plugging new s-boxes into a general S-P framework (DES or an extended DES, for example). Furthermore, many "good" s-boxes exist, but not so many that they are easily found by random permutations of the numbers 1, 2, . . . , 2^n-1. We have generated and stored an exhaustive list of all 16-bit vectors which are 0-1 balanced, are highly nonlinear, and satisfy the SAC. From this list we can then choose vectors at random until we find four which combine in such a way as to guarantee bijection and output bit independence (as described above). A brief preliminary search for these 4×4 bit s-boxes has found:

- approximately 60 s-boxes which satisfy all our requirements in both forward and inverse direction;
- approximately 170 s-boxes which satisfy all our requirements if we consider the forward direction only;
- that if we relax the requirements slightly, the numbers quickly grow to 100's or 1000's of "fairly good" s-boxes — note that all of the DES s-boxes fall into this class.

Some example s-boxes generated by our procedure are:

$$S_1 = [9 \quad 13 \quad 10 \quad 15 \quad 11 \quad 14 \quad 7 \quad 3 \quad 12 \quad 8 \quad 6 \quad 2 \quad 4 \quad 1 \quad 0 \quad 5]^t$$
$$S_2 = [6 \quad 10 \quad 14 \quad 2 \quad 11 \quad 3 \quad 13 \quad 5 \quad 12 \quad 4 \quad 9 \quad 1 \quad 7 \quad 8 \quad 15 \quad 0]^t$$
$$S_3 = [11 \quad 10 \quad 9 \quad 8 \quad 13 \quad 15 \quad 6 \quad 7 \quad 5 \quad 3 \quad 2 \quad 14 \quad 4 \quad 1 \quad 12 \quad 0]^t$$

6. Suggestion

A simple way to extend DES in the short term might be to standardize a list of good s-boxes and have as part of the key the choice of s-boxes to use. In this way the algorithm itself would remain identical but the keysize would be made larger since the s-boxes would be replaced with other equally or more secure s-boxes in a key-dependent way. Whit Diffie has suggested (in the rump session of these proceedings) that it may be worthwhile to examine this "improved" DES using Shamir's algorithm for round-by-round cryptanalysis of the original DES.

Bibliography

[1] C. M. Adams and S. E. Tavares, *A Note on the Generation and Counting of Bent Sequences*, tech. rep., Department of Electrical Engineering, Queens's University, July 1989 (submitted to IEEE Transactions on Information Theory).

[2] ——, *The Structured Design of Cryptographically Good S-Boxes*, tech. rep., Department of Electrical Engineering, Queens's University, Mar. 1989 (submitted to the Journal of Cryptology).

[3] D. K. Branstad, J. Gait, and S. Katzke, *Report of the workshop on cryptography in support of computer security*, Tech. Rep. NBSIR 77-1291, National Bureau of Standards, Sept. 1976.

[4] E. F. Brickell, J. H. Moore, and M. R. Purtill, *Structure in the S-boxes of the DES (extended abstract)*, in Advances in Cryptology: Proc. of CRYPTO '86, Springer-Verlag, Berlin, 1987, pp. 3–8.

[5] H. Feistel, W. Notz, and J. L. Smith, *Some Cryptographic Techniques for Machine-to-Machine Data Communications*, Proceedings of the IEEE, 63 (1975), pp. 1545–1554.

[6] R. Forre, *The Strict Avalanche Criterion: Spectral Properties of Boolean Functions and an Extended Definition*, in Advances in Cryptology: Proc. of CRYPTO '88, Springer-Verlag, Berlin, 1989.

[7] W. Meier and O. Staffelbach, *Nonlinearity Criteria for Cryptographic Functions*, in Advances in Cryptology: Proc. of EUROCRYPT '89, to appear.

[8] J. Pieprzyk and G. Finkelstein, *Towards effective nonlinear cryptosystem design*, IEE Proceedings, Part E: Computers and Digital Techniques, 135 (1988), pp. 325–335.

[9] O. S. Rothaus, *On 'Bent' Functions*, Journal of Combinatorial Theory, 20(A) (1976), pp. 300–305.

[10] R. A. Rueppel, *Analysis and Design of Stream Ciphers*, Springer-Verlag, Heidelberg and New York, 1986.

[11] A. F. Webster and S. E. Tavares, *On the Design of S-Boxes*, in Advances in Cryptology: Proc. of CRYPTO '85, Springer-Verlag, Berlin, 1986, pp. 523–534.

Covert Distributed Processing with Computer Viruses

Steve R. White

IBM Thomas J. Watson Research Center

P.O. Box 704

Yorktown Heights, NY 10598

Abstract. *Computer viruses can be used by their authors to harness the resources of infected machines for the author's computation. By doing so without the permission or knowledge of the machine owners, viruses can be used to perform covert distributed processing. We outline the class of problems for which covert distributed processing can be used. A brute-force attack on cryptosystems is one such problem, and we give estimates of the time required to complete such an attack covertly.*

1. Introduction

Given the large aggregate computing power in the world, harnessing it to work on a single problem is an attractive idea. Systems which use the idle processing power of a collection of machines have been built, and shown to work well [1]. Previously, these have operated under the assumption that the owners of machines must give explicit permission for this use of their computing power. Computer viruses [2] can be inherently covert programs, which perform their actions without any explicit permission or awareness on the part of the owners of the machines that they use. This raises the possibility that viruses can be used for distributed processing tasks, perhaps in spite of the desires of the owners of the machines being used.

2. Covert Distributed Processing

Computer viruses can carry virtually any kind of task with them [3], [4]. In particular, they can use their ability to hide within innocuous programs to spread a distributed computing task among many users and many computers. Processes and information can be distributed unwittingly by users in the normal process of sharing other information. This paper gives an example of how a large number of computers can be harnessed as a distributed processor. This can be done covertly, without the explicit cooperation of those involved.

Our distributed processing virus is written to work on a part of the problem to be solved, and to create offspring viruses that also work on the problem. Depending upon the communication topology of the distributed system, and on the virus' knowledge of it, they could cooperate in any number of ways to solve the problem.

Here, though, we make the fewest possible assumptions about the virus' knowledge of the system's connectivity. We assume that a virus v can create a virus v', and that v can give information to v' about the progress that v has made on the solution of the problem. We do not assume that v and v' can communicate thereafter. The computational work is spread only as the viruses themselves spread.

With these communication assumptions, our distributed processing virus lends itself to working on tree-structured algorithms, in which offspring processes are initialized by parent processes, and work independently thereafter. This style of computation resembles the Unix[1] "fork" operation, with the restriction that the forked tasks have no intertask communication. Markov chain calculations are an example of a problem that fits this paradigm.

One of the goals of the virus is to obtain as much resource as possible to work on its problem (CPU time, disk space, etc.), while avoiding detection. The proper strategy will depend upon the details of the operating system used. In the type of single-tasking operating system used in most personal computers, for instance, the best strategy may be to "wake up" periodically and examine the state of the processor. If no active application task is running (i.e. the machine is idle), the virus task can be started. It would give up the processor as soon as any other system action began, to avoid detection due to slow system response. In a typical multi-tasking operating system, the virus task may run as a low-priority background task, and let the operating system handle this kind of resource allocation.

3. Covert Information Distribution

All viruses carry information with them, so designing a virus to distribute information covertly is straightforward. The information could simply be contained in the body of the virus, and each user whose system becomes infected could recover the information by peeking at the object code of the virus. Alternatively, the virus could respond to a particular keyboard sequence by displaying the information, so it is available more readily.

This technique can be used to retrieve results obtained by the various offspring viruses. Once a particular virus arrives at a result, it can spawn an "information carrying" virus that propagates through the distributed system. Eventually, it will reach the author of the covert task. It is possible to hide the result from owners of intermediate machines as well. This is done by having the virus that arrives at the result encrypt it with a public key before spawning the "information

---

[1]   Unix is a trademark of AT&T.

carrying" virus. Since the author of the covert task can keep the private key secret, only the author can decrypt the result.

4. Example: Brute-Force Attack on a Cryptosystem

Brute-force attacks on cryptosystems are attacks that require very large computational resources to mount. One such attack involves work by seeing if random keys can decrypt known ciphertext to known plaintext [4]. Another involves factoring large numbers [5], [6]. Several such attacks on cryptosystems have been proposed. They generally involve a substantial cost and/or a substantial engineering effort to build special-purpose hardware.

The idea of using computer viruses for such an attack was first proposed by Quisquater and Desmedt [7]. They suggested that a virus could both guess keys at random, and spawn other viruses that do the same thing. From the preceding discussion, it is clear that such a calculation is within the paradigm of covert distributed processing.

We consider implementing this attack by writing a virus that spreads between small computers which are not under any central control. Unlike previous methods of implementing such an attack, this one can be done (a) at virtually no cost (other than the cost of developing the appropriate virus); and (b) with a strong expectation of anonymity, since it is very difficult to trace a virus back to its author in this environment.

We can get a (very rough) idea of a lower bound on the time required for such an attack by making some estimates. We assume that we are attacking DES, which has a key space of size 2^{56}, and that the typical machine is a fairly fast personal computer.

$$\text{(Typical software DES rate)} \simeq 6.3 \times 10^4 \text{ Bytes/sec}$$

$$\therefore \text{(Typical rate of keys tried on one machines)} \simeq 2.5 \times 10^{10} \text{ keys/year}$$

$$\text{(Number of machines)} \simeq 10^7$$

$$\therefore \text{(Average rate of keys tried on all machines)} \simeq 2.5 \times 10^{17} \text{ keys/year}$$

$$\text{(Average number of guesses required)} = 2^{56} \text{ keys} \simeq 6.4 \times 10^{16} \text{ keys}$$

$$\therefore \text{(Time required)} \simeq 0.26 \text{ years}$$

This is a rather severe underestimate. We have assumed that the virus will infect every machine, that the virus will have exclusive use of the machine all the time, that the time required for the virus to propagate is negligible, and that this is the only such virus in circulation. These assumption are likely to be off by at least four orders of magnitude.

Nonetheless, it is instructive to have come this close! And, these estimates are based on comparatively simple 1989 technology. As the aggregate computing power in the world increases dramatically over the next decade, this covert use of it may become more of a threat.

Acknowledgements

The author thanks Yvo Desmedt, William Arnold, Steve Weingart, Frederica Darema, and Kevin McAuliffe for useful conversations.

Bibliography

[1] J.F. Shoch, J.A. Hupp, "The 'Worm' Programs - Early Experience with a Distributed Computation," CACM 25 (March 1982) pp. 172-180

[2] F. Cohen, "Computer Viruses: Theory and Experiment," Computers & Security 6 (1987) pp. 22-35

[3] F. Cohen, "On the Implications of Computer Viruses and Methods of Defense," Computers & Security 7 (1988) pp. 167-184

[4] W. Diffie, M.E. Hellman, "Exhaustive Cryptanalysis of the NBS Data Encryption Standard," Computer, Vol. 10, No. 6 (June 1977) pp. 74-84

[5] T.R. Caron, R.D. Silberman, "Parallel Implementation of the Quadratic Sieve," J. Supercomputing 1 (April 1988) pp. 273-290

[6] A.K. Lenstra, M.S. Manasse, "Factoring By Electronic Mail," Proc. Eurocrypt '89, Houthalen, Belgium (April 10-12, 1989) In press

[7] J.-J. Quisquater, Y. Desmedt, "Watch for the Chinese Loto and the Chinese Dragon," informal paper, Crypto '87 (To be published)

Progress in Data Security Standardisation

Wyn L Price

NPL, Teddington, UK

1 Introduction

This short paper is intended to provide a statement of current activities in the preparation of data security standards and is directed at the community active in research and development in cryptology, some of whom may not be aware of this aspect of the application of their work; it concentrates on the period since August 1987 when a previous statement was made on this subject in the same context.

2 Reorganisation

During the period since August 1987 the data security standards work within ISO has seen considerable reorganisation. In 1987, the committee with overall responsibility for information processing standardisation within ISO was Technical Committee 97 (TC97). The work of TC97 has now been allocated to the new body, Joint Technical Committee 1 (JTC1), which is joint between ISO and the International Electrotechnical Commission (IEC). The remit of JTC1 is very similar to that of TC97, though the title of the committee changes from "Information Processing" to "Information Technology".

Within JTC1 there has been significant dissatisfaction with the organisation of the
work in preparing data security standards. There have been signs of substantial over-
lap of interest between the various constituent bodies of JTC1. The former structure
of the work involved Sub-Committee 20 (SC20), with the remit of producing standards for data cryptographic techniques, and other sub-committees, such as SC6
(Data Communication), SC18 (Office Systems) and SC21 (Open Systems Interconnection (OSI)) and others, having responsibility for standards for the application
of cryptography in achieving secure services within particular areas. The boundary between these activities was never very precise, with the result that overlapping
work took place in some areas, particularly those involving communication protocols.
Existing liaison channels were not found to be particularly effective.

During 1988 and the early part of 1989 meetings took place between the various
interested parties in efforts to create a more viable structure for the work. It is not
necessary here to rehearse all the different arguments that arose at various stages of
the consultation, suffice it to say what has been decided by JTC1 and must now be
acted upon.

Perhaps the most striking change is the abolition of SC20 and its replacement by SC27
with an extended remit which will include the cryptographic techniques work of SC20
(but not that part of the work which addressed the enhancement of communication
protocols with security capability), with the addition of general security techniques
which do not involve cryptography. The formal title of the new sub-committee is "Information Technology Security Techniques". The change of title and of remit is meant
to take account of the numerous security-relevant techniques in which cryptographic
methods do not figure. Obvious examples are those involving access control, where
identity tokens and biometric methods will be relevant. Management of passwords
for access control is another area where SC27 can be expected to have an interest.

So much for the field of activity of the new sub-committee SC27. The other interested
sub-committees are expected to use and apply the techniques and mechanisms developed and standardised by SC27 in creating security services relevant to the standards
they are preparing.

The accounts that follow of published standards and of work in progress take note
only of activities within the orbit of JTC1. It is relevant to say that another area of
ISO, TC68 on banking procedures, also has work proceeding on security standards
particularly intended for financial systems, with several standards already published.
The latter include procedures for message authentication and for key management.

3 Published Standards

In the field of SC20 two data security standards achieved published status during the period 1987–1989. These related to modes of operation for a 64–bit block cipher (ISO 8372–1988) and to the interoperability requirements for data encipherment at the physical layer of OSI (ISO 9160–1987). Note that the latter came from SC20 and not from SC6, which has general responsibility for that part of the OSI structure which includes the physical layer; in the future, as a result of the reorganisation, we may expect that standards of this type will be published by the parent technical sub-committee.

Without doubt the security relevant standard of greatest significance published within the period is ISO 7498/2–1988. ISO 7498/1–1984 provides the basic open systems interconnection reference model. ISO 7498/2 describes the security architecture that may be adopted for providing security services within the OSI context. Note particularly that ISO 7498/2 describes an architecture; thus advice is given on where within OSI particular security services should be located, together with suggestions as to the individual security mechanisms that may be invoked in order to provide these services. Nowhere in ISO 7498/2 is there any attempt to define details of these services or mechanisms. An important section of the standard discusses aspects of security management.

4 Work in Progress

We begin this part of the review with algorithms; in 1986 ISO decided not to standardise algorithms, but rather to establish a register where users can refer for information on what is available. The rules under which this register will run have been embodied in a draft proposal (ISO DP 9979), which has already had one round of voting, but has not yet received approval. (Note: the progression of texts within ISO is from working draft, to draft proposal (DP), to draft international standard (DIS), to international standard.) This specifies the kind of information that may be expected to be found in a register entry, such as name, supplier, external characteristics, speed of operation of implementations, etc. It must be stressed that appearance of an algorithm on the register implies no guarantee of level of security. Optional information may include a description of how an algorithm works.

Another algorithm-related text is ISO DP 10116, which concerns modes of operation for n–bit block cipher algorithms. This is directly related to ISO 8372 and is a generalisation from that standard.

Significant effort has been devoted within SC20 to developing techniques for peer entity authentication. Three texts exist, and will be carried forward by SC27, forming eventually a single standard. These are ISO DP 9798, on peer entity authentication mechanisms using an n–bit secret key algorithm, ISO DP 9799, on a peer entity authentication mechanism using a public-key algorithm with two-way handshake, and ISO DP 10117, on a peer entity authentication mechanism using a public-key algorithm with a three-way handshake. Eventually we may have a fourth peer entity authentication text, based on zero knowledge techniques.

Considerable work has also been devoted to preparing texts for digital signature. It is recognised that two kinds of digital signature are required. One will sign a message after first inserting redundancy information according to specified rules. Recovery of a message is a direct result of verification and removal of the redundancy information. This technique is described in ISO DP 9796. The second technique will first calculate a hash function on the message and will then sign the hash result. Verification proceeds by recalculating the hash function from the received message and comparing it with that obtained in the verification process. No text has yet been prepared describing this signature mechanism, but ISO DP 10118 describes various ways of calculating hash functions.

Work is also in progress in preparing working drafts for the subject of key management, which is critical in successful data security operation. This work will be divided between key management using secret key techniques and that using public key techniques. There will also be a section on the operation of a public key register (not to be confused with the register of algorithms).

A recent development of great significance to SC27 and the other groups working on data security standards is the preparation of "frameworks" or "models" for security techniques and services. These are strongly oriented to applications and seek to proceed by analysing the need for a security function, with the management structure needed to support it, and then identifying the general category of service, technique or mechanism required to fulfill this need. The result of working in this way is that user requirements are given greater prominence than has been the case hitherto. In the past there has been a tendency to think of interesting mechanisms and to seek to develop these into services which users may wish to use. Now the process is being turned on its head, with likely benefit for all concerned.

The FEAL-8 Cryptosystem
and a Call for Attack

Shoji Miyaguchi

NTT Communications and Information Processing Laboratories
Y-509A, 1-2356, Take, Yokosuka-shi, 238-03, Japan

1 Introduction

With the aim of providing a highly <u>programming efficient</u> cipher system, NTT has developed the open cipher algorithm, FEAL-8 (Fast Data Encipherment Algorithm) [1][2][3], which is a type of secret key cryptosystem.

In general, the cryptanalysis of a secret key cipher can be classified as:

(1) Only ciphertext attack

(2) Known plaintext attack (Not chosen plaintexts are used.)

(3) Chosen plaintext attack

Dr. Shamir demonstrated an attack method for FEAL-8 (eight round FEAL) and eight round DES at Securicom '89, this past March. Some technical Journals have reported that the attack method he demonstrated was type (1), but we feel that the attack was actually type (3). It appears to us that Shamir's method estimates the key using only the ciphertexts that are obtained by enciphering the chosen plaintexts, where the plaintexts are generated by modifying ordinary messages according to Shamir's special rules (In this case, the ordinary messages are used as a source of pseudo-random numbers). For FEAL–8, the possibility of finding the chosen plaintexts from among the ordinary plaintexts is less than 2^{-64} for this attack method, because pairs of special plaintexts are necessary (We hosted him in June 1988, discussed a possible attack to FEAL–8, and got some information through correspondences). Therefore, we can state that his attack will only pose a threat to the practical use of FEAL–8, only if the following three requirements are <u>simultaneously</u> satisfied:

(a) An attacker provides special plaintexts or a program that generates special plaintexts.

(b) Mode of operation is ECB.

(c) The key remains unchanged after the encipherment process, i.e., the same key is used all the time.

As any one of these requirements can be easily avoided, we think that Shamir's attack will not pose a threat to the practical use of FEAL–8. In order to evaluate the security of FEAL–8 in practical usage, we would like to call throughout the world for possible methods to attack FEAL–8. This call will also contribute to further research in cryptology, especially regarding cryptanalysis of secret key cipher algorithms.

2 Outline of the call

2.1 General

2.1.1 Two confirmation stages

Confirmation is divided into two stages: preliminary and final confirmation. Only candidates who pass the preliminary can advance to the final confirmation stage.

2.1.2 Reward

The first attacker who successfully passes the final confirmation stage will be paid the equivalent of one million yen in his or her country's currency.

2.1.3 Effective application period

The call starts from 20th of August 1989, and ends on the 31st of August 1991.

2.1.4 Expenses

All applicants must personally pay all costs.

2.2 Problem of preliminary confirmation

8192 bytes of plaintexts and 8192 bytes of ciphertexts are given. The ciphertexts were made by the FEAL−8 encipherment procedure using a secret fixed key in the ECB mode. The problem is to determine the secret key. Applicant is not required to explain his attack method.

2.3 Final confirmation

2.3.1 Qualification for the final confirmation

Each candidate, who passes the preliminary confirmation and expresses his will to continue, can advance to the final confirmation stage.

2.3.2 The final confirmation problems

The applicant selects one of the two options below.

Option−1: This includes five problems of the following type.
   Problem: The secretariat of this call decides 8192 bytes of plaintexts, and enciphers them in the ECB mode using a secret key. The applicant can use both plaintexts and ciphertexts to determine the key used. Note that different keys will be used for each problem.

Option−2: This includes five problems of the following type.
   Problem: The applicant decides 8192 bytes of plaintexts, and the secretariat enciphers them in the CBC mode using a secret key. The applicant can use

both plaintexts and ciphertexts to determine the key used. Note that different keys will be used for each problem.

2.3.3 Time limits

Each candidate is permitted a processing time of five hundred hours to solve all five problems which includes the time requested for computer handling etc. Another two weeks are added for mailing.

3 Reference

(1) Application details are being published. One document will be an international call in English, other is the call in Japanese. However, the document entitled "The FEAL-8 Cryptosystem and a Call for Attack" delivered by Miyaguchi at CRYPTO '89 is effective, i.e., not cancelled.

(2) Because no successful attack is anticipated, NTT will continue to use FEAL-8 as we have in the past.

(3) FEAL-8 specifications have been expanded to FEAL-N (N round FEAL), where N is the number of main internal processings. N is even and equal to or larger than 4, but recommended values of N are 4, 8, 16, 32, ... When N=8 or N=4, FEAL-N is the same as FEAL-8 or FEAL-4 which are already published. Users of FEAL-N may select the number N by their own choice. For example, N=4 is suitable for generating Message Authentication Code, MAC, because of high program efficiency (i.e., 1,000 kbps using a 80286 (10MHz) assembler program (450 bytes)).

Reference

[1] S. Miyaguchi, A. Shiraishi, A. Shimizu, "Fast Data Encipherment Algorithm FEAL-8", *Review of the ECL*, Vol. 36, No. 4, 1988.

[2] A. Shimizu, S. Miyaguchi, "Fast Data Encipherment Algorithm FEAL", *Proceedings of EUROCRYPT 87*, April 1987.

[3] A. Shimizu and S. Miyaguchi, "FEAL — Fast Data Encipherment Algorithm", pp. 20-34 and pp. 104-106, *Systems and Computers in Japan*, Vol. 19., No. 7., 1988, SCRIPTA TECHNICA INC, A Wiley Company.

How to Explain Zero-Knowledge Protocols to Your Children

QUISQUATER Jean-Jacques[1], Myriam, Muriel, Michaël
GUILLOU Louis[2], Marie Annick, Gaïd, Anna, Gwenolé, Soazig

in collaboration with Tom BERSON[3] for the English version

[1] Philips Research Laboratory, Avenue Van Becelaere, 2, B–1170 Brussels, Belgium.
[2] CCETT/EPT, BP 59, F–35512 Cesson Sévigné, France.
[3] Anagram Laboratories, P.O. Box 791, Palo Alto CA 94301, USA.

The Strange Cave of Ali Baba

◇ Know, oh my children, that very long ago, in the Eastern city of Baghdad, there lived an old man named Ali Baba. Every day Ali Baba would go to the bazaar to buy or sell things. This is a story which is partly about Ali Baba, and partly also about a cave, a strange cave whose secret and wonder exist to this day. But I get ahead of myself ...

One day in the Baghdad bazaar a thief grabbed a purse from Ali Baba who right away started to run after him. The thief fled into a cave whose entryway forked into two dark winding passages: one to the left and the other to the right (The Entry of the Cave).

Ali Baba did not see which passage the thief ran into. Ali Baba had to choose which way to go, and he decided to go to the left. The left-hand passage ended in a dead end. Ali Baba searched all the way from the fork to the dead end, but he did not find the thief. Ali Baba said to himself that the thief was perhaps in the other passage. So he searched the right-hand passage, which also came to a dead end. But again he did not find the thief. "This cave is pretty strange," said Ali Baba to himself, "Where has my thief gone?"

The following day another thief grabbed Ali Baba's basket and fled, as the first thief had fled, into the strange cave. Ali Baba pursued him, and again did not see which way the thief went. This time Ali Baba decided to search to the right. He went all the way to the end of the right-hand passage, but he did not find the thief. He said to himself that, like the first thief, the second thief had also been lucky in taking the passage Ali Baba did not choose to search. This had undoubtedly let the thief leave again and to blend quietly into the crowded bazaar.

The days went by, and every day brought its thief. Ali Baba always ran after the thief, but he never caught any of them. On the fortieth day a fortieth thief grabbed Ali Baba's turban and fled, as thirty-nine thieves had done before him, into the strange cave. Ali Baba yet again did not see which way the thief went. This time Ali Baba decided to search the left-hand passage, but again he did not find the thief at the end of the passage. Ali Baba was very puzzled.

He could have said to himself, as he had done before, that the fortieth thief had been as lucky as each of the other thirty-nine thieves. But this explanation was so far-fetched that even Ali Baba did not believe it. The luck of the forty thieves was just too good to be a matter of chance. There was only one chance in a million million that all of the forty would escape! So Ali Baba said to himself that there must be another more likely explanation. He began to suspect that the strange cave guarded a secret!

And Ali Baba set out to discover the secret of the strange cave. He decided to hide under some sacks at the end of the right-hand passage. After a very uncomfortable wait he saw a thief arrive who, sensing he was pursued by his victim, whispered the magic words, "Open sesame." Ali Baba was amazed to see the wall of the cave slide open. The thief ran through the opening. Then the wall slid closed again. The pursuer arrived, and was all upset to find only Ali Baba under the sacks at the dead end of the passage. The thief had escaped. But Ali Baba was all happy, for he was finding out the Secret of the Strange Cave.

Ali Baba experimented with the magic words. He discovered to his amazement that when the wall slid open the right-hand passage was connected with the left-hand passage. Now Ali Baba knew how all of the forty thieves had escaped from him.

Ali Baba worked and worked with the magic words, and he finally managed to replace them with new magic words, a little like you change the combination for some padlocks. The very next day a thief was caught. Ali Baba recorded this story and his discovery in a lovely illuminated manuscript. He did not write down the new magic words, but he included some subtle clues about them.

The Fate of the Manuscript

Ali Baba's lovely illuminated manuscript arrived in Italy in the Middle Ages. Today it is in the United States, near Boston. There it has recently held the full attention of several curious researchers. Through decryption of the subtle clues, these researchers have even recovered the new magic words!

After several archaeological excavations in the ruins of the old Baghdad bazaar, the strange cave was located. It was not a myth! And, despite the centuries, the magic words still worked. All agog, the curious researchers went through the end wall between the two passages.

The television networks were quickly made aware of the unusual events taking place in Baghdad. A big American network even got an exclusive on the story. One of the researchers, a certain Mick Ali, a descendent perhaps of Ali Baba, wanted to demonstrate that he knew the secret. But he did not want to reveal the secret. Here is what he did.

First, a television crew filmed a detailed tour of the cave with the two dead-end passages. Then everybody went out of the cave. Mick Ali went back in alone and went down one of the passages. Then the reporter, accompanied by the camera, went inside only as far as the fork. There he flipped a coin to choose between right and left. If the coin come up heads he would tell Mick to come out on the right. If the coin came up tails he would tell Mick to come out on the left. It was heads, so the reporter called out loud, "Mick, come out on the right." And Mick did just that.

In memory of the forty thieves this demonstration scene was played forty times. Each of the times everybody went back out of the cave and Mick entered alone all the way in to one of the passages. Then the reporter and the camera went as far as the fork where he chose by flipping a coin which order to give to Mick. Mick succeeded in all forty scenes.

Anybody who did not know the secret of the cave would have been exposed on the first failure. Each new test divided by two the chances of success for someone without the secret. On the other hand, the secret allowed Mick to come out each time by the required exit.

The Jealous Reporter

Employed by another television network, a jealous reporter wanted to also film a story on the strange cave. Mick refused to participate because he had given exclusive rights to the story to the first network.

But Mick mischievously suggested to the jealous reporter that the story could be filmed without possessing the secret. The jealous reporter thought and thought, and finally he understood. He said to himself, "I even know a stage actor who looks like Mick Ali and who could be mistaken for him."

And the second story was filmed. In the course of the filming half of the scenes were spoiled because Mick's double did not know how to get from one passage to the other! The jealous reporter edited the tape and only kept the successful scenes until he had forty of them.

The two stories were broadcast at the same hour on the same evening by the two competing American networks. The matter was taken to court. Both videotapes were placed into evidence. But the judges and the experts could not tell the tapes apart. Which tape was simulated? Which tape was genuine? The tapes alone were not enough to judge by.

The simulation surely conveyed no knowledge of the secret. But the simulation and the genuine tape were indistinguishable. So the genuine tape did not convey knowledge of the secret either. The reporter who had gotten the exclusive story had been convinced at the time that Mick Ali knew the secret, but the reporter could not pass his conviction on to the judges in court or to the television audience either.

Mick Ali had achieved his real objective. He wanted, in fact, to show that it is possible to convince without revealing, and so without unveiling his secret.

The Tests in Parallel

Meanwhile, other researchers in Israel observed that by using several secrets and making tests in parallel, one could reduce the number of scenes in the films. In other words, the length of the authentication.

They imagined an apartment building with one cave per floor, each having its own magic words. They needed was one extra actor per cave. All the floors could be filmed at once to see where the actor came out on each floor.

They even proposed an arithmetic solution where a reply with a single number as proof could replaced many actors.

Still, a compromise between the number of secrets and the number of scenes to film may not always be optimal. It would be much better to have a single secret and a single scene.

Besides that, simulation by successive attempts becomes less and less practical as the number of secrets increases. Do we have no conveyance of knowledge when you cannot simulate with successive attempts?

The Prior Agreement

All of this really intrigued some European researchers. They made an observation that applies equally to the serial version and to the parallel version. To save time filming, the jealous reporter and Mick Ali's double would have been pretty clever to think of agreeing in advance on a list of forty random selections between right and left. During the filming, the jealous reporter would have then pretended to choose the questions at random in his head, and the double, who knew in advance the questions he would be asked, would not need to know the secret and could still pass all of the tests one after the other.

Therefore to the simulation technique of successive attempts where only the successful scenes are kept was added a simulation technique of prior agreement between prover and verifier.

A Single Test, A Single Secret

In response to this observation a new cave was set up with more passages ending at a fork (The Revised Cave). Certainly the physical construction of the cave becomes problematic when the number of passages increases. It is impossible to build a cave with a million million passages. But whatever the number of passages, you could simulate by prior agreement. A more arithmetic scheme would allow a verifier to choose a question from a set of a million million questions. With a single test you could directly reach the level of security obtained with forty successive tests in the cave with two passages.

The court is completely unable to tell the videotapes apart: one depicting a demonstration, the other a simulation by prior agreement. Therefore, even when the size of the question is large the demonstration does not show knowledge of the secret's value.

Epilogue

And so, my children, you have heard how Ali Baba learned the secret of the strange cave, and how his descendent, the clever researcher Mick Ali, was able to convince a television reporter that he knew the secret without having to tell him what the secret was. Countless people saw Mick Ali on the television, and he became famous and had adventures around the world. He still has not revealed the secret of the strange cave, but has convinced many others, including me, that he does know it. The keeping of secrets reminds me of the story of the Merkle Hellman and his super-increasing knapsack. But the hour grows late. That is another story for another time. □ □ □

Acknowledgment

Thanks to Gilles Brassard for his continous interest and support.

Author Index